# NICK COLLINS

# FIFTY

## CUP FINALS

### MY LIFE IN FOOTBALL

First published by Pitch Publishing, 2018

Pitch Publishing
A2 Yeoman Gate
Yeoman Way
Worthing
Sussex
BN13 3QZ
www.pitchpublishing.co.uk
info@pitchpublishing.co.uk

A CIP catalogue record is available for this book
from the British Library.


ISBN 978-1-78531-390-5

Typesetting and origination by Pitch Publishing

Printed in India by Replika Press

# Contents

## DEDICATION

To my three children, Ollie, Poppy and Louis, for putting up with me being away so often.

And to my dad Ken (1929–2017), who did not quite live long enough to see my book published.

# Foreword
# by Steven Gerrard

**D**URING my career with Liverpool I was lucky enough to win eight cup finals, many of which are featured in this book – so it is a pleasure to be asked to write a short foreword. I did lose a couple of finals to Chelsea (the least said about them the better!) and one to AC Milan in 2007, but for me personally a cup final tended to be a happy experience, none more so than in 2005 when we lifted the Champions League trophy thanks to the Miracle of Istanbul.

The last FA Cup Final in Cardiff in 2006 was another unforgettable experience – another three-all draw after extra time, another amazing win on penalties – scoring twice in that game is a very special memory for me.

Nick Collins became an increasingly familiar figure during my time with England. He was the man with the microphone (and moustache!) in the front row of the press conferences on the day before the game. He interviewed me many times, especially when I was captain, and I found his questions were usually pretty fair. I got the impression he was an England fan and was willing to give the players the benefit of the doubt. Like us, he would look for the positives.

Three times with England I lost in the quarter-finals of a major tournament after a penalty shoot-out. Being interviewed afterwards is never easy, but I did feel Nick managed to keep a sense of perspective. In the mixed zones around the world he was often the first person we would see as we left the dressing rooms to face the massed ranks of the media.

I was very happy to win 114 England caps, so I can imagine Nick is proud of his achievement of reporting on nearly 300 England games.

Talking of honours, Nick says he's named me third on his list of all-time favourite England players. Thank you – though I am gutted to lose out to Becks and Lamps!

So I wish him luck with *Fifty Cup Finals* – the last 25 years have been a hugely exciting time for our game and I hope we will be able to say the same about the next 25 as well.

# 1

# Live on Air When the Axe Fell

W ELL, almost! I was live on air at the Sky Sports News studios as a guest on the *Premier League Daily* morning show. Tom White was hosting with 'Galey' – my good friend Tony Gale – and George Boateng, when I felt the vibration of the mobile in my back pocket. We were discussing Gareth Southgate's imminent appointment as the permanent England manager and his potential backroom staff.

It was a good discussion and George provided some valuable insight about Southgate's early management career at Middlesbrough. Galey, as usual, brought a naturally witty sense of perspective about recent events. At the time I remember thinking, 'I'm really enjoying this, the concept is working well.'

It seems a little daft now, but I also thought this could be my future at SSN – going on set to reflect on recent events and to put into context exactly what it all meant. My area of expertise was mainly England and the Premier League, but I could cover European stories as well.

When I finished my piece and left the set I checked my phone. There were two missed calls from my line manager Brendan Henry, at 10.23am and four minutes later. Then the phone buzzed again. It was 10.39am and it was Brendan Henry once more.

'I need to speak to you, Nick. I've been calling you – where are you?'

'I've just come off air,' I said. 'Couldn't you see that from your desk?' He did, after all, sit just a few feet away from where our studio chat had taken place.

'No, I'm over in Sky Central,' he replied. 'We need to have a chat. Come across and up to the second floor. I'm in Area 3.' He hung up.

Sky Central? Area 3? Now I was puzzled, and I was also more than a little concerned. Sky Sports had seemed to be awash with redundancies in recent months, and we knew the cuts would be coming to Sky Sports News soon.

The changes were called 'Transformations' and mapped out Sky Sports' path forward in this digital age. The reality was that the company was struggling to cope with the absolutely vast sum it had paid out for the latest Premier League rights (for 2016 to 2019) – 11 million pounds a game! The perceived wisdom (certainly among many of the Sky Sports staff) was that Sky could have paid a billion pounds less than it bid and still won the rights. That could have safeguarded an awful lot of jobs.

But back to Sky Central. It was a vast building and I had never been inside it before – it was almost like a new world. Looking back, I suppose it is a reflection of the fact that Sky Sports and Sky Sports News are no longer the 'Be All And End All Of Sky'.

The company these days seems to be much more about operating on a lot of different fronts, so that it is no longer as dependent on sports rights (and the Premier League football broadcast rights in particular).

On the way up in the lift I was thinking that, if Brendan was with Sports News boss Andy Cairns, then I was definitely on my way out. Sure enough, when I reached Area 3, there was Brendan and Andy.

I said something like, 'This looks ominous!' Andy replied, 'Yes it is, Nick, it's all bad news I'm afraid.'

For the next two minutes Andy read from a prepared printed sheet and that was it. After a quarter of a century I was being discarded. Redundant at the age of 59. Not a good feeling. I was being put on gardening leave – effective immediately – and my final day was just a month away; 31 December 2016.

Andy and Brendan suggested I go straight home, but I wanted to see out the week. And like all good reporters I needed to go back into the office to do my expenses!

It had not come as a complete shock. I remember having a chat with some of the reporters in the August after I had got back from covering EURO 2016 and we all felt that our numbers would be reduced. We simply were not filming as many edited reports (or 'packages') as we used to, and knew that somewhere down the line there would be cutbacks.

Many of us believed that would happen at the end of the 2016/17 season. We imagined that the 18 London-based reporters would all be interviewed for about 12 available jobs, so we were expecting half a dozen or so redundancies. We just did not expect it to be as ruthless as it turned out.

The walk back over towards the newsroom felt totally strange. My head was full of a thousand thoughts, but priority number one was to appoint a good employment lawyer. I stopped off at the car park and climbed inside my company BMW (while I still had it!), so that I could study the redundancy package in detail – and in private.

On the surface it appeared reasonably generous. My one concern was that it did not take into account the fact that I had been employed by Sky since 1991, but had only been on the staff since 2002.

Back in the newsroom the first person I told was David Miles. 'Milo' was also under threat of redundancy and had been appointed the spokesperson for those facing the process. He was a senior producer and a top bloke, with nearly 20 years of service at Sky. His reaction was one of utter astonishment, but then he stunned me by explaining that Tim Abraham (our England cricket reporter), Phil Edwards (our England rugby reporter) and Pete Colley (Sky's 'Mr Midlands') had also all just been made redundant. We learned later that the experienced Peter Staunton and Fraser Robertson had gone as well.

'This is a crazy day,' he said, sadly, 'and I just don't know what to say.'

'Nothing to say,' I shrugged. 'I reckon the bullet-to-the-back-of-the-head technique they used today is better than the slow drip-drip Chinese water torture treatment you guys are facing.'

Milo and some of his colleagues – including my England producer Gemma Davies – had been under threat of redundancy since early September. Nine jobs were going, with only three replacing them – so that meant another six facing the scrapheap, and it would be several months before their fate was finally decided.

Perhaps not surprisingly, Milo and Gemma chose redundancy once their tortuous process had finally played out. I think by then they had just had enough – and I don't blame them.

Sat at a desktop doing my expenses helped to take my mind off what had happened, but word was spreading fast. Many colleagues came over to express their sympathy, surprise and anger. Around 6pm I called it a day, telling the news editor Nick Seymour that I was perfectly willing to come in the following day and talk live with the presenters about Gareth Southgate. His appointment was due to be ratified that next afternoon.

'I'll get back to you on that one,' he said, uncertainly. 'If it was up to me I would say definitely yes, come in.'

'But I'll have to run it past the powers that be, so leave it with me.'

The journey home round the M25 back to Kent was a long and difficult one – in keeping with the day. An accident near junction ten led to huge delays so I had plenty of time to work out how to tell my family that, after 37 years in journalism, I was about to be out of work.

Next morning I found myself pacing up and down, waiting to see if Sky would let me back in to go on set when the Southgate story was due to break.

Complicating the issue slightly was the fact that the papers had got wind of our redundancies. Charles Sale ran a story in his Sports Agenda column in the *Daily Mail*, entitled 'COST-CUTTING AXE FALLS ON SKY FOUR'.

Reproduced below is part of the article – for legal reasons it's perhaps best I make no comment, other than to thank Charlie for what he wrote about me:

'SKY SPORTS' brutal cost-cutting following their £11million-a-match spend on Premier League rights has claimed four more casualties including chief football reporter Nick Collins.

'The moustachioed Collins was best known as Sky Sports News's indefatigable England reporter. Such was his standing, he was given the opportunity to ask the England manager five or six questions before anyone else was allowed a turn at TV broadcast interviews. Gareth Southgate's first TV media conference as the newly appointed England boss tomorrow will be a strange affair without the ever-present Collins behind the mic.'

It seemed that no one really wanted to make the decision about my presence one way or the other, but full credit to Nick Seymour. My news editor forced the issue and just after midday he rang to say it was okay for me to come in to the Sky Sports studios.

I arrived at two o'clock and was told I would be able to go live on air that afternoon, once I had spoken with Brendan Henry. I was also informed that I would lead the Southgate news conference at Wembley the next morning. I think Brendan just wanted to make sure I was in the right frame of mind, and in a funny kind of way I almost felt sorry for him.

He was not comfortable with the turn of events, though he had given me a foretaste of what might be to come when I had reported back to Sky after those European Championships. He had informed me that I would not be getting a pay rise for the following year as there was a slight issue with the 'consistency' of my performance. After busting a gut at EURO 2016 I felt office politics might be at play here, so I bit my tongue and said nothing at the time.

Despite all this I felt elated that common sense was allowed to prevail. No way after 25 years at Sky was I going to 'go rogue' live on air and say something inappropriate. There is absolutely no point in feeling bitter, I told myself, because I had been lucky enough to have an amazing career at Sky that spanned three decades – many didn't even last five years!

Once the Southgate appointment was ratified I joined David Garrido and Hayley McQueen on the SSN set to discuss the issues and implications. It turned into a 15-minute interview as (unknown to me) there were a couple of technical issues behind the scenes which forced the running order to be scrapped. We discussed England past, present, and future until the ad break at the top of the hour came to our rescue.

It was quite an emotional afternoon, because many more colleagues came over to commiserate with me over losing my job – after a while I just did not know what to say to them, other than to offer the hope that there would be no more redundancies – unlikely.

I also went over to Sky Central to do a piece for our counterparts at Sky News about Gareth Southgate. It involved appearing in 'The Cube', a futuristic suspended glass studio where Kay Burley was presenting the early-evening news bulletins. It was a slightly strange experience but I must admit I did enjoy it – and I also got a sense of why Kay has remained at the top for so long. As an interviewer she is very sharp and slightly mischievous, but also sympathetic.

My final day of live broadcasting for Sky began early. We were live from outside the Bobby Moore statue at Wembley from 9am, to tee up the day and explain what would happen. It seemed very appropriate that Wembley would be my last on-location job for Sky as I had been there so many times over the previous three decades.

There is always a real sense of anticipation when a new England manager is unveiled. True, Gareth had been caretaker boss for four matches, but now he had a four-year contract with the mandate to take England to the 2018 World Cup and EURO 2020.

We screened the news conference live and I opened proceedings by asking Gareth about his hopes for England, Wayne Rooney's future and a host of other topics.

To my surprise, when the conference was about to end, Gareth took the mic and said some very kind words about my years covering England. It was a proud and humbling moment, but we had no time to rest on our laurels because there was still a lot of work to do. More filming, several live stand-ups and an edited piece to reflect the day.

My last piece to camera for Sky was filmed beside one of the goals as I explained how Wembley had provided Gareth with the worst moment of his playing career (when he missed a penalty in the semi-final shoot-out with Germany at EURO '96), but that if everything went according to plan Wembley could also provide him with his best moment as a manager – because this was where the final of EURO 2020 would take place.

I admit it's a long shot, but when you cover England you have to try and look on the bright side.

After that it was off to the Wembley Hilton for a quick glass of Prosecco and a final goodbye to some of my favourite colleagues. I won't deny this is when it really started to hit home what had happened over the last 24 hours or so.

When you cover England you form great bonds with your colleagues – it is the peak of your profession in my opinion, because it gives you the biggest highs, the biggest lows and the biggest challenges. Those people I have shared tournaments with are, inevitably, the ones I like and respect the most among my Sky Sports workmates.

I kept my emotions hidden but it did feel really sad knowing this might have been the last time I worked with a lot of them. Gemma Davies was a particular case in point. We started working together on England in 2012 and Gem was undoubtedly one of the rising stars of Sky Sports News.

She was an incredibly bright and bubbly girl who just implicitly understood the pressures and rewards of doing the England job. We formed a great bond (some would say an unlikely one), but I think what we both appreciated was that each one could help the other to become better at our respective jobs.

The fact that she also chose to take redundancy in March 2017 was also a bit of an indictment about what had happened. She was precisely the kind of person Sky should have been trying to keep.

The next day the *Daily Mail* again showed an interest in my story. This time a piece appeared with the headline 'BOSS HAILS SKY'S AXED REPORTER'.

'New England manager Gareth Southgate ended his first broadcast media conference at Wembley yesterday with a tribute to Sky Sports News' lead football reporter Nick Collins. Collins has been a familiar figure reporting on England but as Sportsmail was first to reveal on Wednesday, he is being made redundant as part of Sky's cost-cutting. To the applause of the media corps, Southgate said, "On behalf of the FA, I just wanted to acknowledge Nick Collins and the way you've covered the England team. We're grateful for how you've dealt with us – it's been a pleasure personally working with you and we all wish you well."'

As a footnote on a different page in the paper, Charlie Sale also wrote, 'Nick Collins, the Sky Sports News lead football reporter made redundant this week, was given rather more respect by his TV colleagues at Gareth Southgate's first broadcast conference as England manager. Collins, who came off gardening leave, asked the opening 14 questions. No one was going to interrupt his England swansong!'

Actually it wasn't quite my England swansong. A few days later I was back at Sky to record a one-to-one interview with former manager Roy Hodgson – it was the first one he had given to TV since he'd stepped down after EURO 2016. Roy is one of my favourite people in football so it was a great way for me to bow out. He may not have been the most successful of bosses, especially when it came to tournaments, but I can't think of another who helped me more during his time in the hot seat.

We discussed what went wrong at EURO 2016 and the game against Iceland in Nice. I genuinely hope his England career is not defined by that match, but I fear it might be. We should not forget that he is also responsible for England's 'Perfect Ten', when they won all ten qualifiers (a feat they had never achieved before) on the way to qualifying for the tournament in the first place.

Roy is one of football's gentlemen. He never forgot how Sky Sports helped him out when he lost his job at Blackburn Rovers and as a result was always very co-operative. There are plenty of others who have been down the same route and aren't, so I will always have massive respect for him.

On 19 December I attended the Football Association's Christmas drinks reception at the St Pancras Renaissance Hotel in London and was blown away to receive a framed England shirt, signed by all the players. The inscription at the bottom read:

272 England matches
11 England managers
1 Nick Collins
Thank you

It was the perfect early Christmas present and it hangs in pride of place on my study wall.

Two days before the new year I dropped off my security pass, company mobile and laptop, as I bade farewell to Sky for the last time. I really did not want to make a big deal of it but it was nice to say goodbye to a couple of the backroom staff – like my boss Andy Cairns's secretary Dawn Ellis, who had always been very helpful over the years.

Driving away I realised I had plenty to reflect upon: some amazing memories, a whole host of extraordinary events and countless matches from my 25 years at Sky Sports.

# 2

# Bristol Days

PEOPLE often ask me how I got to work for Sky and it's not always an easy question to answer. Luck, obviously, can play a part in these things – being in the right place at the right time might sound like a bit of a cliché – yet there is an element of truth to it.

I had wanted to be a journalist since about the age of 14. In those days there were two routes into the business: leave school at 16 or 18 and land a job on the local paper, learning from the bottom up; or go to university and read a relevant subject like English, history or politics. I chose the latter and went to Bristol University, where I studied history from 1975 to 1978, with an emphasis on socialising.

Also I probably spent too much time following the fortunes of the city's two professional football clubs. I saw Rovers first at their rather ramshackle old Eastville ground just by the M32, and was rewarded with a thrilling 4-2 win over Brian Clough's (pre-European Cup) Nottingham Forest.

I caught the last few months of one of football's most celebrated partnerships in the lower leagues in the shape of 'Smash and Grab', aka Bannister and Warboys, who were both from Yorkshire. 'Smash' was Alan Warboys, a tall and physical forward. 'Grab' was Bruce Bannister, shorter, quicker and with an eye for goal. The theory was Warboys would smash his way through a defence and set up Bannister to grab the goal.

They both actually were very talented strikers and both were prolific – with Bannister just shading it over the course of their careers. 'Grab' grabbed 167 league goals from just over 500 career appearances while 'Smash' smashed in 137 from just under 500. In five seasons they netted more than 130 goals between them for Rovers. A great double act in every sense of the word.

On that October day Bannister did manage to get on the scoresheet against a Forest side containing Frank Clark, John McGovern, Ian Bowyer (who scored) and John Robertson (who also netted). I went with my new American room-mate Dave, who was from Cleveland, Ohio. I think it is fair to say I was more enamoured with what I saw than him. This was his first taste of English football and sadly he never came back.

Two other Bristol Rovers games stand out – both in the FA Cup in 1978. Second Division Rovers entertained Southampton in round four. The Saints were flying high in the league and would go on to win promotion to the top flight a few months later. They brought around 5,000 fans and had memorably lifted the cup by beating Manchester United 1-0 in the final just a couple of years earlier.

In the Rovers team that January day was another hugely popular Eastville striker, Paul Randall. Born in Liverpool, 'Punky' (because of his love for punk rock music) was in his first season with the club and what a prodigious season it was: 22 goals in 35 games, including two in this particular tie. The first just before half-time was a glorious, instinctive chip. The second shortly before full time was an assured finish from an in-form forward. It triggered a pitch invasion from hundreds of Southampton supporters, who seemed to be hell-bent on getting the game abandoned. It was a not completely uncommon tactic of the time. Mercifully order was eventually restored, but when the final whistle blew they came back on to the pitch in their droves and headed for the home end!

Now Eastville, as I have suggested, was an old ground and – although it was fantastically atmospheric – it did leave a bit to be desired on the health and safety front. To exit the home terrace there was a narrow entrance at the back, which one person at a time could use. A huge crush was building up and I was starting to feel claustrophobic. There was a rising sense of alarm at the progress the Southampton followers were making as they came towards us.

To the rescue came one loud voice who bellowed, 'Come on lads, we're not having these bastards take our end! Let's go and get them!'

At this point the more adventurous of the Rovers fans turned and ran on to the playing surface to confront the visiting hordes, while we were all able to make good our escape. In the pub that night my fellow students all thought it sounded like a good laugh, but just for a while it was getting distinctly hairy – and those two words sum up football in that decade as well as the 1970s themselves.

Three weeks later I was back at Eastville for round five. This time I managed to persuade a couple of friends to come along – tempted, no doubt, by the prospect of seeing Bobby Robson's attractive Ipswich Town in action.

What followed was bizarre and dramatic. It had snowed heavily in Bristol and the club had performed a minor miracle in getting the game on at all. A good two inches of snow lay across the entire pitch, with the lines only just about visible. We had arrived early, so as to get a good spot on the Rovers terrace: behind and just above the goal, with a metal bar to lean against.

On that afternoon Rovers showed no fear in facing supposed First Division superiority and tore into the visitors with gusto. The orange ball was inevitable; the orange colour of the Ipswich shirts, though, was a bit more of a puzzle – it was an exact match and must have made the task of the officials even harder.

The weather conditions and the style of football at the time meant defenders dare not dally on the ball – not even for a moment. It cost Rovers, as young Robin Turner scored his first goal for the club after seizing on an opening.

In those days the playing surfaces were incomparable to the ones now. Trying to control the ball in the ice, snow and slush was virtually impossible, let alone dealing with a bumpy pitch as well. When your team was defending you held your breath and feared the worst, but when they were on the attack it was hugely exciting, because you just did not know what might happen next.

In the event Rovers staged a great fightback as two Bobby Gould corners led to two David Williams headers and the underdogs, having trailed, led 2-1 and they had their tails up. Gould intercepted a bad back-pass and stuck the ball in the net with a really cool finish from a tight angle. Eastville was in raptures at the prospect of a 3-1 lead, but the celebrations died as soon as they had started. The linesman on the far side had his flag up for offside (wrongly as it happens), and on such decisions games – and even entire competitions – can turn.

Into the closing stages, England international Paul Mariner drove at the very heart of the Rovers defence, who backed off, allowing Turner to score his and Ipswich's second. Moments later the final whistle blew. A 2-2 draw was a decent effort against a team from the division above, but the sense of disappointment among the players and fans alike was palpable.

The replay at Portman Road proved a little one-sided with Ipswich winning 3-0 and going through to the quarter-finals. West Country FA Cup dreams were over for another year, but for Ipswich they were only just beginning. A 6-1 thumping of Millwall was followed by a 3-1 success over West Bromwich Albion in the semi-final at Highbury. A stunning victory against Arsenal in the final catapulted Ipswich into the big time just a year after winning promotion. By a quirk of fate both Ipswich and Bristol Rovers finished 18th in their respective divisions, although they would reflect on their seasons very differently.

* * * * *

Bristol City was a different experience altogether. For my second year at university I had moved from the halls of residence at Stoke Bishop to affluent Clifton. Six of us rented a house near the famous suspension bridge. Ashton Gate was within walking distance – albeit two miles and 40 minutes away – and there was the lure of First Division football.

Up until then I had preferred catching the bus from the far north-west of the city down to Eastville in the east – a journey of well over an hour. To my 18-year-old mind Rovers was edgier, more working-class, and a bit more of an adventure.

As it happened, Bristol City's first season back in the top flight in 65 years was the adventure to end all adventures.

It began well, with a victory at Arsenal on the opening day, and after a handful of games City were lying second. Then a slump set in and by the time I had returned to Bristol for the academic year they were already in free-fall. I went to the Leicester City game: total domination, but no one was able to stick the ball in the net. Leicester won 1-0, scoring from one of their very few attacks.

And that's how the season looked to be going. The odd good result, but in the main the side was too inconsistent and there was a worrying lack of goals. The return of old favourite Chris Garland lifted the spirits briefly, but the goals were still proving hard to come by.

With ten games to go City were rock bottom and the tension at Ashton gate among the fans was almost unbearable. A vital win to complete the double over struggling Spurs was a bonus. Peter Cormack scored the only goal, and the walk back up to Clifton afterwards was much less of a slog than usual. Cormack had won the league title with Liverpool and was hugely experienced. He was to play a key role in the closing weeks of the season.

But City were still bottom, with nine games left, and the next four were all away. There was a priceless win at Queens Park Rangers but a draw and two defeats in the others meant the Robins were still propping up the table.

With five matches to go they were three points from safety (and remember in those days it was only two points for a win).

Thinking back, the run-in was pretty extraordinary. It certainly dominated most of my waking thoughts. Five games took place in 13 days, starting at home to Manchester United. A big crowd packed into Ashton Gate and we saw Garland put City ahead. I remember Stewart Houston being stretchered off with a broken leg, while Gerry Gow and Sammy McIlroy were both sent off for fighting.

In the second half Jimmy Greenhoff (one of my favourite players) scored an equaliser. It was a tough, feisty game, laden with anxiety at times and every bit as exciting as anything I had experienced at Eastville. It ended 1-1, a pretty good point all things considered, and now it was a case of bring on Leeds.

Tuesday, 10 May 1977 and just three days after holding Manchester United, City were taking on another of the really big clubs in English football, Leeds United. League champions, FA Cup winners and European Cup runners-up in recent years, Leeds were certainly successful but not universally popular. They had beaten

City at Elland Road just a couple of weeks earlier and the home fans were desperate for revenge.

It was another enthralling game with Bristol City again holding their own. Eventually the breakthrough came and again it was Garland. Could City hang on this time? In the defence that night and up against his former team was Norman 'Bites Yer Legs' Hunter. Now 33, Hunter may have been past his prime, but his organisation, determination and sheer desire to beat his old Leeds mates was a big factor.

The final whistle was greeted with a huge roar. Three points from two games and finally City were off the bottom with three games to go. More significantly it had fired the team and the fans with the belief that maybe they could, after all, survive.

By now I had a big emotional stake in Bristol City, even though I had been following their fortunes for less than two years, and on the Saturday afternoon I listened on the radio as they battled to a goalless draw up at Middlesbrough.

Then on Monday it was back down to Ashton Gate for another one of those magical nights that live long in the memory. Liverpool were the newly crowned champions of England (again) and were going for a league, FA Cup and European Cup treble. They oozed class, knocked the ball about with assurance and it was no surprise when David Johnson put them ahead after half an hour.

A season's best crowd of over 38,000 had squeezed into the stadium. We were surrounded by Liverpool fans and they just wanted to party, to celebrate their title. The result was almost irrelevant to them.

City gradually got a toe-hold and that man Garland grabbed the equaliser just before half-time. The atmosphere cranked up a level or two and the second half saw Liverpool having to defend for long periods. Perhaps the exertions of the last few weeks began to get to them because their intensity faded. That was quite understandable in a way as they had an FA Cup Final against Manchester United coming up five days later.

With 15 minutes to go Garland guaranteed his permanent place among the hearts of the City faithful with a second goal. It was his fifth in six games and would turn out to be the winner.

As we streamed out of the ground we heard that Stoke City had lost and been relegated. Tottenham had already gone down, so now there was only one other place to be decided. Moreover, City had now climbed out of the bottom three on goal difference from Coventry City.

And guess who the final opponents of that season would be? Yes, Coventry, away on Thursday, just three days after the Liverpool match.

You really could not have scripted it any better. Sunderland were also level on 34 points with the Robins and Coventry. A superior goal difference for them was offset by the fact their last match of the season would be the same night away to Everton.

Thousands of City fans made their way to the Midlands for that game. Sadly I was not one of them. Student finances and an important tutorial the next morning meant I would be unable to travel to Highfield Road.

Listening to the radio in the minutes leading up to the start, it became clear there was a good deal of congestion outside the ground so perhaps it was no surprise that the kick-off was delayed. Now, this is where the conspiracy theorists come in: some (especially Sunderland fans) were convinced it was a deliberate ruse by Coventry chairman Jimmy Hill to ensure that his team would be playing several minutes behind Sunderland's match at Goodison Park, so they would in effect be in control; others believed it was the local police who ordered the delayed kick-off on the grounds of safety (and also to give Coventry a better chance, which would make their life easier!).

Either way the drama started to unfold pretty quickly. Sunderland went a goal down at Everton (hooray), then Bristol City went a goal down at Coventry (boo).

The second half at Goodison got under way a good six or seven minutes before the game resumed at Coventry, and more goals started going in. City fell two behind and looked in deep trouble. Sunderland were still losing, but would survive on goal difference if things stayed the same.

Enter Gerry Gow, a curly-haired, pugnacious Scottish midfielder. He made his debut for the club in 1970 as a teenager and was idolised on the Ashton Gate terraces. Just moments after Tommy Hutchison

26

had made it 2-0, Gow volleyed City right back into the match with his first and only goal of the season on his 30th appearance.

Now it was all City, and before long Chris Garland nodded the ball down to right-back Don Gillies, who powered the ball into the net for 2-2. There was jubilation and pandemonium among the visiting throng, who by now were learning that Everton had scored a second goal against Sunderland.

News of the final whistle at Goodison was relayed round Highfield Road and as I listened on the radio it was obvious both sides had pretty much stopped trying. The final minutes seemed to be played out on the understanding that 2-2 would keep both teams up, and this is where that delayed kick-off undoubtedly played into Coventry and Bristol's hands. By all accounts, according to the commentary, it all descended into a bit of a farce, with both sets of forwards barely venturing into their opponents' halves!

It is something which would not happen today if it could possibly be avoided, and I did feel sympathy for Sunderland and their fans, who had also travelled in their thousands to Merseyside.

It was certainly a controversial ending to the gripping First Division relegation fight, all decided on a Thursday night so that no other games would need to be played on Saturday when Liverpool met Manchester United in the FA Cup Final.

Just listening on the radio I felt drained – exhausted even – but ultimately absolutely ecstatic. I never did get to meet or interview the manager Alan Dicks, although he had my eternal gratitude for providing an inspiring backdrop to my three-year Bristol University career.

Needless to say, I still went to Ashton Gate on a pretty regular basis in the 1977/78 season, but – not surprisingly – it lacked a bit of the passion and exhilaration of the previous campaign. City survived relegation by three points this time and doing the double over West Ham was probably the key. Oddly, they finished with an identical playing record from the previous season: played 42, won 11, drew 13, lost 18, points 35. I'm not sure what it all proved – except that they were somehow consistent in their inconsistency.

The season opener in August was against newly promoted Wolves, and having stayed down in Bristol to work at a bottling factory in the summer, we all piled along to Ashton Gate to witness what we thought would be more of the same from the previous campaign.

There was certainly drama but most of it occurred before kick-off. As we neared the ground we could see that Greville Smyth Park just behind the stadium was starting to resemble a bit of a battleground. Mounted police were trying to keep the scuffling fans apart, it seemed there was a gigantic rolling maul taking place, and we had to be fairly light-footed to escape the mayhem. Not exactly the ideal introduction to First Division football for my girlfriend at the time, Alison. Needless to say – like my American mate Dave – she never came back either.

To compound it all, it was quite spicy leaving afterwards as Wolves celebrated a 3-2 victory. A sobering experience all round.

I left Bristol in the summer of 1978, and though I still retain a real affection for both City and Rovers, my footballing allegiance, as will be revealed, lies elsewhere.

# 3

# The Aldershot News

ALMOST 12 months elapsed between me leaving Bristol University and finally landing my first job in journalism. I spent that time working as a warehouseman, an insurance clerk and a hospital porter. I was also appointed first XI captain at my local cricket club, Merrow, in the Three Counties League (Surrey, Hampshire and Berkshire, in case you were wondering).

The big break, as it were, came via a tiny classified advertisement in the *Daily Telegraph*, 'Sports Reporter required for busy bi-weekly paper in North-East Hampshire. Apply to Deputy Editor John Elliott at The Aldershot News.'

I wasted no time getting my application in and enclosed a copy of an interview I had done in the last month or so with David Howell, Guildford MP and a Cabinet minister.

He had kindly granted me some time to question him about his role during his weekly Friday night surgery in the constituency. He had been a journalist himself once and was happy to try and help another aspiring press man. It wasn't relevant to sport, but I suppose it showed if I had an aptitude for writing.

John soon got back to me, but what he had to say took the wind out of my sails somewhat.

'Thanks for your application, Nick,' he said, 'but I am afraid we have already appointed our new sports reporter.'

However, John did go on to say that he had been quite impressed with the piece I had submitted about David Howell and wanted to offer me a week's work experience (no guarantees) in the newsroom.

This was music to my ears, a chance to experience the working environment of a busy newspaper in the heart of its community. In my eagerness I set off that first Monday at around 6.30am. I wanted to be in Aldershot by eight, so I could have a good look around the town, before reporting for duty at nine sharp.

The Aldershot and District Bus Company had other ideas. They cancelled three consecutive services so it was nearly 9.45am before I arrived, breathless, at the newspaper's offices in The Grove.

News editor Ian Barron was not impressed and dispatched me immediately to Aldershot Magistrates' Court to meet up with the chief news reporter Steve Peacock.

Steve didn't normally have too much time for juniors, but for some reason he took me under his wing, patiently explaining how the court worked and how to fashion copy from the various cases. In exchange for buying him a couple of pints at lunchtime he also promised to run the rule over what I would write in the afternoon.

And that's how it started, on an early June day back in 1979: my first real taste of journalism.

By the end of the week I had even managed to win Ian over (again a couple of lunchtime pints probably helped) and on the Friday afternoon I was called into editor Phillip Green's office, where John offered me a job as the most junior reporter in the newsroom on the princely salary of £49.50 a week.

It was a fantastic feeling, and after shaking me by the hand he gently suggested that in future if I was to travel from Guildford to Aldershot each day, then I should go by train as it took just 17 minutes and the station was opposite the newspaper offices.

'Better still,' he added, 'pass your sodding driving test!'

For two and a half years I worked as a general news reporter, getting to know the patch, the people, the local personalities. Aldershot was an interesting town, a little rough round the edges – especially when the Paras (the Parachute Regiment) returned home from a tour of duty to Northern Ireland.

Going on an operational night out with Aldershot CID certainly proved an eye-opener. Sometimes, keeping the peace between the locals and the 'squaddies' was a difficult and delicate exercise, which called for some unique skills and insight. It was a useful lesson to absorb, and helped me in the news coverage of my 'patch'.

I did also learn to drive and took proud ownership of an old gold Hillman Imp, just after passing my test. Sadly it did not last long. A few months later I got cleaned out by an off-duty detective sergeant (not from Aldershot), who pulled out of a side road in his Ford Capri and sent me and my Hillman spinning and somersaulting through a fence across a garden until it came to rest on its side against a house.

The passenger door above me was pretty badly smashed in and would not open, so I was trapped. Worse still, the petrol tank was in the front of Hillman Imps, and I was watching the fuel spilling out through the hole where the petrol cap should have been. I was thinking that the car would spectacularly ignite and then blow up, just like in the movies.

Those negative thoughts did not really have too much time to take hold because moments later a fireman peered down into the car, asked if I was okay and broke into a big smile when I told him I was in one piece, albeit with an injured knee and ripped clothing. I think he was fearing the worst.

I was levered out of the car in no time. The Hillman was badly damaged – in fact to no one's surprise it was declared a complete write-off.

The fire engine, it turned out, had been travelling back from a shout and was just four vehicles behind the accident. They saw everything and were prepared to act as independent witnesses.

The other driver – the police officer – was very relieved I was okay, but he looked distinctly worried, and with good reason. He was prosecuted at Winchester Crown Court for careless driving and suspended from driving for the police for some time. Originally, he chose to plead not guilty – hence the Crown Court scheduling – but changed his mind the morning of the trial when he realised a local reporter who used to cover courts on a regular basis would not be intimidated when giving evidence.

My solicitor Ian Pearson did a fine job in ensuring I was adequately compensated for the loss of my car and the delays in paying up, so when I finally got back on the road I was able to afford a smart little Ford Escort. Ian went on to stand for the Labour party at the Aldershot constituency in the 1982 General Election. He got my vote, for the help and advice he gave me, but Maggie Thatcher was starting to reach the peak of her powers and the Conservatives – as they did through most of the south – swept away the Labour vote in this part of north-east Hampshire.

Going back to the accident itself: because the car had overturned the firemen insisted I went to hospital for a check-up and half an hour or so later, I was in the A & E at the Royal Surrey County hospital. I assured them I hadn't bumped my head, but they told me to take it easy for the next couple of days in case delayed shock set in.

However, just 24 hours later, I was due to make my broadcasting debut so I was never going to let delayed shock get in the way. It was a fairly humble beginning – half a dozen live reports by telephone into BBC Radio Sheffield to update their listeners on the progress of the all-conquering Blades. Sheffield United had been relegated into the bottom tier for the first time in their history at the end of the previous season. But they stormed back in style, dominating the Fourth Division and earning 96 points along the way.

That mid-April afternoon in 1982 they had brought a sizeable support down from South Yorkshire, which made for a great atmosphere. It was a really competitive game with Aldershot giving as good as they got in a 1-1 draw.

In the crowd that day, having travelled down from Sheffield, was a young Keith James. It was only 20 years later that we discovered we had actually both been at that game. Keith joined Sky in the late 1990s and was a top-class news editor as well as being a good friend over the years. He acted as my producer/fixer at EURO 2004 and the 2006 World Cup. We have often had a laugh about it ever since.

Keith maintained that Sheffield United battered Aldershot and were desperately unlucky not to win! The story I told Radio Sheffield was a slightly different one:

'One-all the final score here at the Recreation Ground, as Sheffield United move ever closer to promotion. A point won, rather than two points lost for the visitors, who had to withstand some heavy pressure in the second half.'

Those early days on the *Aldershot News* were a lot of fun. It was a massive learning curve for me but there were some good people willing to help you along the way.

Sat opposite me in the newsroom when I started was Ian Barron, the news editor. I've mentioned that I made a bad start with him but he soon forgave me and taught me a lot about how to write good, crisp copy, and the importance of an accurate, eye-catching intro. On the surface he was a tough-talking abrasive Scotsman with an uncanny ability to produce acerbic one-liners, which kept you in your place. However, he was a really decent guy, who enjoyed watching young reporters improve under his keen eye – even if he didn't always tell them. He was also a creature of habit: two lunchtimes a week without fail he played squash against sports editor Peter Hutchinson; the other three days he would be holding court at the Sportsman, a members' club and popular bar just opposite the Recreation Ground.

Ian certainly had the talent to go further in the business than a bi-weekly local newspaper but in those days there were not the opportunities that are around now, and I guess in the end he settled for what he knew best.

At the desk to Ian's right was chief reporter Steve Peacock – again, a good writer who could churn out terrific copy at speed under pressure. His slightly bedraggled look belied a sharp intelligence and at times he was the scourge of the local councils. The more they tried to bury or deny a story, the more tenacious he became. As I recall, he led a slightly entangled personal life and eventually moved down to work in Devon.

Next to me was the second newest reporter in the room – Martin Creasey. His outward extrovert personality (he was always cracking jokes – usually bad ones!) masked a slightly nervous character underneath. But he was good company, a very gifted singer, and a fanatical Brighton & Hove Albion fan. He genuinely loved his football. I remember he tried to get to Brighton's first away game in the top flight – a midweek match at Aston Villa – but he left work a bit late, became stuck on the M1 and had to admit defeat. Instead of seeing his own team make a piece of history, he pulled over and settled instead for a Fourth Division match between Northampton Town and Bradford City.

Completing the newsroom line-up were the two girls. They sat across the far side of the room to me by the big bay window. Lauretta Murphy was a flame-haired Irish girl who, like me, had a university degree. We were considered the brains of the outfit, but I have to admit she was far brighter.

Last, but by no means least, was Debbie Comfort. Debbie was a chatty, bubbly bundle of energy, who had absolutely brilliant people skills. As a result she landed many human interest stories for the paper – both in Aldershot, where her family lived, and Farnborough, when she moved on to become the deputy chief news reporter in that office.

She also became my first wife.

We had been friends and colleagues for nearly two years before our first date – in the Horse and Groom pub just outside Guildford. Eleven weeks later we were married.

The service took place at the parish church of St Michael's in Aldershot and was conducted by the splendidly named Stanley Zeal. I think a fair few among the congregation that day thought this might be a shotgun wedding, given how quickly events had moved that summer of 1981 – but it wasn't.

We had eight largely happy years. Debbie was tremendously ambitious for me and constantly urged me on to bigger and better things like applying for jobs and forcing me out of my comfort zone (no pun intended).

Eventually that ambition helped drive us apart. We were both working journalists, committed to our jobs and putting in long, unsociable hours.

The last straw, I suppose, was our move from north-east Hampshire to Kent (where I was working for Television South). It took Debbie away from her family and made her commute into London a really arduous one. The marriage was buckling under the pressure and we parted in June 1989. Our last weekend together was spent near Belfast at her brother's wedding.

Alan Comfort was a professional footballer and had the double satisfaction of winning promotion on the day he got married. To make it even more spectacular the two events took place in two different countries and involved a sports car, a helicopter, two aeroplanes, and a motorbike taxi!

A flying winger with a great turn of pace, Alan was one of the stars of Leyton Orient's 1988/89 promotion push. He and on-loan teenager Kevin Campbell (later of Arsenal, Everton and England B among others) formed a great partnership towards the end of that season, scoring 25 goals between them.

Orient finished the regular campaign with six wins and two draws from their last nine games, forcing themselves into sixth place and the play-offs. The semi-final was against Neil Warnock's Scarborough and a 2-0 first leg win at home put them in charge.

I was working in south London (interviewing Brough Scott at the *Racing Post* offices) on the day of the second leg, but made a late decision to charge north for the game. Alan had put a ticket on the players' entrance for me, but a hold-up near Leeds meant I would miss kick-off. I listened to the first-half commentary on the radio as I sped (not too fast) across the North Yorkshire moors towards the seaside town of Scarborough.

It was 0-0 at half-time when I arrived, but it wasn't too long into the second half before Scarborough scored. It was all hands to the pump after that for the O's as they clung on to their aggregate lead, despite a 1-0 defeat on the night.

There was no Wembley final in those early play-off days so Orient faced Wrexham over two legs with the first encounter in North Wales. Another long car journey, another sterling defensive performance and a 0-0 draw set up the second leg to perfection.

There was just one problem: Saturday, June 3 was also Alan's wedding day. Kick-off at Brisbane Road in east London was 3pm – exactly the time Alan was due to marry Jill in Bangor, County Down.

Now, you might wonder why Alan arranged to get married on this day of all days? To be fair he actually contacted the Football League months and months in advance and was assured that the domestic season would be over before the first weekend in June.

And so it would have been, but for the Hillsborough tragedy in April 1989, which led to the season being extended by a week. The team itself had looked anything but play-off contenders for much of the campaign anyway then that storming finish changed everything.

To the rescue came manager Frank Clark and the *Sunday Express*. Clark successfully managed to persuade the police and relevant authorities that this high-profile match needed an early kick-off. Then, in exchange for the exclusive story, the national newspaper supplied the transport, while over in Northern Ireland the wedding was put back to 5.30pm.

It was a strange experience as we gathered round the radio for updates and snatches of commentary from the game. Alan teed up Lee Harvey to put Orient in front, which was a great start. Wrexham fought back to equalise and the final was heading into extra time (which would have provided another logistical difficulty) when ex-Gillingham player Mark Cooper came up with a spectacular winner. Cue wild celebrations in a Northern Ireland hotel and among the vast majority of the 13,355 crowd at Brisbane Road.

Alan, by his own admission, raced straight from the ground (with his wedding suit and a bottle of champagne) in a chauffeur-driven fast car to a nearby helipad, which took him to Heathrow Airport. After landing in Belfast he transferred straight on to a flight to Newtonards, near Bangor – and then by motorbike taxi to the wedding service.

It was the ultimate happy ending that day for Alan, but sadly the same could not be said of his future football career.

A dream move to Second Division Middlesbrough was completed that same summer, which was followed by an electrifying start to life on Teesside in the second tier. But 17 games and three goals later it was all over. In the north-east derby against Newcastle he took a heavy tackle and sustained a really bad cruciate knee ligament injury. It ended his professional career a month short of his 25th birthday.

The Alan Comfort story did not end there. He went on to become a vicar, he wrote a book with fellow Christian Gavin Peacock (titled *You'll Never Walk Alone*) and was for many years the club chaplain at Leyton Orient.

As for Debbie, she always kept tabs on my career and though our paths did not really cross again (professionally or personally), I always knew she was pleased I had done pretty well.

Tragically Debbie died from breast cancer in October 2016, leaving husband Paul and two daughters, Francesca and Daisy.

However, I am getting ahead of myself, so back to the 1980s and the *Aldershot News*. Two court cases stand out for me during my time on the paper – and both are slightly disturbing.

One Tuesday I was in Aldershot County Court. It didn't always provide good copy as the cases often revolved around debt and repossession. On this particular morning a young couple were being evicted from their rental property but the evidence we heard suggested their landlord had behaved very badly towards them, harassed them, and threatened violence – basically he wanted them out at all costs. There was also a racial undertone to his behaviour.

It was no surprise when the court found in favour of the young couple – they were given generous repayment terms and the landlord received a public admonishment.

In the car park afterwards I was approached by the 'rogue' landlord. He wanted me to keep the details of the case out of the paper. Before I could explain that was not possible, he started stuffing £5 and £10 notes into my pockets, saying he was sure I would be able to take care of it all. I pulled the money back out and it just drifted around the floor of the car park as I shook my head before driving away. When I got back to the newsroom, I explained everything to Ian, the news editor. I still had two of the landlord's £5 notes, which were kept as evidence if required. Ian ensured that the story would DEFINITELY appear in the next edition and on the Friday it was our off-side lead.

At ten o'clock that morning the landlord rang the editor to complain. He claimed I had done a deal with him to keep the story out of the paper and then had kept the money for myself!

Because I had reported it immediately, the newspaper massively took my side. The landlord was given very short shrift and we never heard from him again. Cheeky sod.

Drink-drive cases were an all too familiar feature of proceedings at Aldershot Magistrates' Court. A guilty verdict meant an inevitable ban and fine – the only issue being the level of punishment.

Then one day this rich guy appeared in court. He was in his late 50s and wore a hugely expensive suit. He had even brought his own barrister (complete with silk wig) down from London.

The barrister told the court that his client was pleading not guilty to the charge of drink-driving, because the only reason he had been stopped in the first place was because the police were jealous of the car he was driving – a Rolls-Royce.

Good luck with that defence, I thought to myself. I had certainly never heard that excuse before.

The prosecution solicitor outlined the case, telling the court that the defendant had been stopped because he was driving erratically. He was given a breath-test at the roadside, which he had failed, and was then arrested. Back at the police station he failed another breathalyser, not by a substantial amount but enough for a regulation prosecution.

Nevertheless, his barrister persisted with the notion that his client should never have been apprehended. He went on to explain how important having a licence was for his business, and how he had raised thousands of pounds for charity.

This particular magistrates' bench consisted of three JPs; a lady chairwoman, who sat in the middle, and two male colleagues on either side.

The barrister concluded his case by addressing the two men on the bench, looking them both squarely in the eye, and telling them his client was also 'The Worshipful Master' of a well-known Freemasons' lodge in the capital.

The magistrates then retired to consider their verdict.

Half an hour later they returned. The lady chairwoman looked flustered and annoyed. The drink-driving conviction was upheld, and a fine meted out, but she then went on to say that because of the exceptional circumstances of the case they were not going to ban the defendant from driving.

This caused some consternation in the court. The chairwoman said it had been a 'majority' decision and she then got up and left without saying another word.

I caught up with her in the underground car park next to the courtroom.

'Did your two colleagues say he shouldn't be banned because he was such a senior mason?' I asked.

She looked at me and said, 'I can't discuss the details of this case with the press.'

'But was that the reason?' I persisted.

'Off the record, and I mean off the record?' she replied.

'Yes of course,' I said.

She nodded her head, got into her car and drove away.

Obviously we could not publish the details of that conversation. The rules around court reporting were pretty strict, and I always felt that what appeared in the next edition of the newspaper was a pretty watered-down version of the real story. It's not what you know, I reflected afterwards, it's WHO you know.

I'm now going to tell you about a murder case which convinced me once and for all that my future lay in sport and not news.

Marion Crofts was a 14-year-old schoolgirl who loved playing the clarinet. On Saturday, 6 June 1981 she was cycling along the Fleet Canal on her way to morning band practice when she was raped and murdered.

I was on weekend duty and got the call to cover the press conference the next day. The police sketched out what they knew about the killing and asked for the media NOT to contact the family, who were in a state of severe shock.

I respected what was said and filed my story for the paper on the Sunday. I was quite pleased with what I had written and showed it to my wife-to-be Debbie. She was a better news journalist than me, so when she said my copy was good, I was really encouraged.

The next morning *The Sun* was carrying an exclusive front-page lead with the father of the murdered girl. The news desk wanted to know why I had not approached the family. How do you respond? Human decency says give the bereaved time to come to terms with what has happened.

Under enormous pressure I found myself knocking on the door of the Crofts' family house early on the Monday morning, less than 48 hours after their only daughter had been savagely murdered.

Her father Trevor answered and when I saw him I was utterly shocked. He was a physio for the local non-league football team, Farnborough Town, and when I had last seen him at a sporting dinner a few weeks earlier he had a full head of black hair.

The man standing in front of me looked ten years older and his hair was WHITE. I just could not believe it, and that is when you start to realise the full impact a murder like this can have.

Trevor was amazing and put up with my questioning about what had happened and the effect it had on his family. He demonstrated a calm dignity that shone through his grief.

The headline on our front page said 'Vicious Killing Of A Quiet Girl' and was followed by my story of the murder and my interview with Trevor. I took no pleasure from it. People were coming up and congratulating me on what I had written. All I could think about was the dark-haired guy I had once met and how he looked now.

It was more than 20 years later before anyone was convicted of her killing – what must that have been like for her family? Former army chef Tony Jasinskyj was jailed for life thanks to advances in DNA forensic technology.

Over the years I have done other hard news stories. It goes with the territory but it never gets any easier. At TVS in the late 1980s I once had to cover a Crown Court case where this monster killed his 18-month-old child with salt poisoning. It was a totally gruesome story, and not one that I want to go into here, but it was another reason why I preferred covering sport rather than news.

In early 1982 the paper's deputy sports editor left and to my great satisfaction I was appointed as his successor. It was the job I had wanted originally, and I finally got my chance to report on sport.

I also won an important early battle. Up until then the newspaper had refused Aldershot Football Club's annual request to allow the sports reporter to travel on the team bus to away games. You would think it would be the other way round, but the editor reasoned it would lead to too cosy an arrangement and that editorial freedom would be compromised.

However, sports editor Peter Hutchinson and deputy editor John Elliott eventually relented (no doubt fed up with my constant pestering of them) at the start of the 1982/83 season. My first away match travelling with the players was at Layer Road, the then home of Colchester United, for a League Cup first round tie.

The pre-match meal was late afternoon at a hotel in the town and consisted of large portions of eggs on toast. Not terribly sophisticated fare by today's standards, but the idea was that the carbohydrate and protein would help give the players extra energy.

It didn't work. If anything the team ran out of steam in the closing stages and lost 2-0. The journey home was a pretty quiet one.

In those days the M25 did not exist, so our route took us down the A12, and all the way into London via the North Circular. One of the players, striker Dale Banton, used to jump out near Wembley. He lived nearby and would meet the coach for away matches up north at Toddington services on the M1. It seemed like we were forever detouring to drop players off, but then not many of them actually lived in Aldershot.

They were a good bunch of lads, though, and were led by the captain Joe Jopling – a tall central defender with distinctive long, dark, curly hair. He had joined Aldershot back in 1969 before leaving and then returning in 1974. He racked up around 400 appearances for the club and stayed on in the town after his retirement to run the Golden Lion pub. Joe would give you a pretty honest assessment of the team's performances – even if sometimes it had to be 'off the record'.

My particular favourite was Ian McDonald, a stylish midfielder who bagged almost 100 career goals and had once been on Liverpool's books. He never made a first-team appearance at Anfield and arrived at Aldershot after around 250 games for Colchester United, Mansfield Town and York City.

He was my best contact among the players, especially when he took over the captain's armband. Ian knew the value of keeping on good terms with the local media and occasionally would invite me down to the back of the bus to have a beer or two with the rest of the team – especially if the result had gone their way.

Ian played around 350 times for the Shots and led them to promotion in 1987 under manager Len Walker. He was also the man in charge when Aldershot went out of the league in 1992, playing a heroic role in trying to keep the club alive in those difficult final days.

Years later he told me how the players trained at the local park because the club could not afford their own facilities by that stage, often being chased off by irate council groundsmen. He would sign young amateur players just to make up the numbers for their closing games. The regular team had not been paid for months, so several understandably went elsewhere.

I was very pleased that Ian stayed in the game after what must have been a pretty harrowing experience at Aldershot. I used to bump into him at Millwall, then Portsmouth, before he returned to his native far north-west in later life.

That Aldershot team of the early 1980s didn't exactly pull up any trees but they did have one or two notable successes.

Saturday, 11 December 1982 was a case in point. In the second round of the FA Cup the Fourth Division strugglers were drawn away to Third Division high-flyers Portsmouth in a Hampshire 'derby'. It should have been a foregone conclusion. Pompey were certainly on the up, with Neil Webb in their side that afternoon and they were in good form.

But this was Aldershot's day. Midfielder Les Briley (way too good for the Fourth Division) started it all off with the first goal, then Dale Banton grabbed two in a spectacular 3-1 win against the odds.

Unfancied Aldershot were into the third round of the FA Cup and the newspaper had a great story. A small article on page one of the following Tuesday's edition (sport in those days very rarely made the front page!) was followed by massive coverage in the sports section at the back. It was a broadsheet newspaper and my banner headline across the entire page screamed, 'HOW ABOUT THAT!' We went to town on the photographic coverage as well and were pretty pleased with our efforts.

The only downside was that the third-round draw was made that evening after the game. I stood on the pitch with the team as we waited for the pairings to be made live on BBC Radio. Even player-coach Ian Gillard seemed excited. Ian had joined that season from Queens Park Rangers. He played three times for England at left-back and had reached the final of the 1982 FA Cup before losing the replay to Tottenham.

The side were in high spirits and deservedly so. Then they learned their 'reward' was an away tie to either Brentford (from the Third Division) or Swindon Town from their own division. That dampened the mood. The following month Aldershot travelled to the replay winners Swindon and got thrashed 7-0. Needless to say there were no beers for me with the players on that journey home.

The longest trip was to Hartlepool United. It was one of only four away games where the players were allowed to go up the day before (Darlington, Hull and York City were the other three), so there was an extra sense of anticipation as we gathered at the Recreation Ground on the Friday lunchtime after training.

On most of the journeys I used to sit with manager Len Walker and his genial Scottish assistant Johnny Anderson. We would invariably play a card game called 'Hearts' – it would keep them amused for hours, and the pair were brilliant at it. I don't think I ever won a single rubber against them all the way to Hartlepool and back (or on any other away trip for that matter).

It was late afternoon when our coach pulled up at the Darlington hotel where we were staying. After supper the players drifted off to their rooms, but I stayed and shared a couple of pints with Len and Johnny.

Then an old colleague arrived: Irishman Eoghan Mortell. He joined the *Aldershot News* about a year after me – a thoroughly decent guy, who was working for the *Northern Echo* at the time in its Darlington office. I'm afraid we climbed into the optics a bit that night and were drinking Pernod when the clock struck three and the bar closed.

At four, I was woken by room service. A bottle of champagne had apparently been 'ordered' by the occupant. It was obviously a player having a laugh at my expense and I never did discover the practical joker. And yes, I did have to pay for it.

Hartlepool's Victoria Park practically backs on to the North Sea and is one of lower-league football's real outposts. When I stepped off the team bus with the players it caused a bit of a stir. I was the first reporter from Aldershot who had ever come up to cover the game – the man on the spot had always filed the copy to us in the past.

The local paper arranged for a photograph with me and my Hartlepool counterpart to mark the occasion. As it happened he had a very memorable name, sharing it with Ian Fleming's masterful secret agent: 007 himself.

They sent me a copy of the picture and I captioned it 'Me and James Bond at Hartlepool v Aldershot'. Classic.

Unwittingly, I also provided the locals with a memorable moment. The press box was a bit of a shack with the fans pressed up hard against it. The journalists were all sharing a wooden bench inside, when just after half-time Hartlepool took the lead at the very moment Radio 210 (from Reading) crossed to me for a live telephone update. The noise of the goal forced me to lean away from the bench, I lost my balance, toppled backwards and did the report lying on the floor staring up at the ceiling with the phone in my lap.

My new friends were looking at me in total disbelief. Let's just say it was unorthodox, but effective.

Another long away trip was Boothferry Park, home of Hull City. On this occasion I agreed to travel up with the hardy bunch of fans who used to go to every away game, come rain or shine. The word dedicated does not even come close to describing these guys.

We met at Aldershot train station at 6.15am, travelled up to London, then on the tube to Kings Cross, where we had some good-natured banter with the London branch of the Middlesbrough supporters' club, who were on their way up to a 'home' game at Ayresome Park.

On the journey north the Shots fans told me about their passion for the club; some of these guys hadn't missed a game in two decades. I'm not quite sure how their other halves put up with it, especially when they would tell you stories of how they had been trying to redecorate their front room for the last seven years, but somehow had never quite managed to find the time to finish it!

We arrived early enough before kick-off to have a pint or two at a pub right by the ground. It was actually a decent boozer, though it had a big sign outside saying 'NO AWAY FANS!' The home supporters clocked us early on, but left us in peace – I think they secretly admired the fact we had travelled so far and then came and drank in their local.

The game itself was an exciting one. It finished 2-2, Aldershot played really well, and the fans were in good heart as they filed out ready for the long journey home.

And it was a long journey home – we got back to Aldershot station around 10.45pm, where I bade farewell to travel organiser Ian Read and his amazing bunch of superfans.

Covering Aldershot taught me a lot about lower-league football and I am very grateful. It is a world away from today's Premier League but I am proud to say that I have been to the likes of Rochdale, Bury, Hereford, Tranmere, Stockport, Torquay and Halifax.

As things stand I just need Carlisle United, Grimsby Town, Morecambe, Newport County, and now Forest Green Rovers to complete the current 92.

There were two games up north where I took my wife Debbie along in the car for a weekend away instead of going on the team bus. These were trips to Blackpool and York.

At Bloomfield Road I met Jimmy Armfield in the press box – a true footballing gent, who showed me round his club and its wonderful history (with pictures in the tea room of Stanley Matthews and the 1953 FA Cup Final). I think I amused him by explaining how Aldershot's chairman was a guy called Reg Driver, who was a fishmonger by trade. As a result he was known as 'The Codfather'.

The beautiful walled city of York was a real experience. For Aldershot it was a nightmare. They lost 4-0 and had two players – Ian Gillard and Howard Goddard – sent off. Gillard was so disgusted by the decision that he threw his shirt into the dugout and strode bare-chested down the tunnel back to the dressing room.

The club were upset at the report I filed, but the one board member who went to the game backed up my story 100 per cent. Yes, it was brilliant fun travelling with the players of Aldershot FC – and thank you so much for giving me the opportunity – but no, it did not affect my editorial judgement.

They were not the only football team in our patch as there was also Farnborough Town. The Isthmian League club gave me great access and I enjoyed my trips down to their ground at Cherrywood Road, although trips is probably not quite the right word as I lived less than a mile away in nearby Cove.

Manager Ted Pearce was a great football enthusiast and would talk about the matches with real passion and knowledge. I wasn't at all surprised that he went on to become a senior scout at West Ham United. It was a friendly club and many of the players would be happy to talk to me about the games afterwards, usually in the bar over a beer or two.

They enjoyed a measure of success, too. It seemed they were always fighting it out near the top of the table and they enjoyed some good cup runs in the minor non-league competitions.

I saw them lose 1-0 after a replay in the 1982 London Senior Cup Final to Leytonstone and Ilford at Dulwich Hamlet's ground. Leytonstone were managed in those days by John Still. Back then he had a bit more hair, and he did a nice – if slightly odd – interview with me after the game where he praised the efforts of the beaten Farnborough team. I use the word odd, because he conducted the entire interview sitting in the bath, surrounded by his victorious players. I thought then that he was a good bloke and I would come across him several times in his later career – with Maidstone (when I was at TVS) and at Dagenham, Peterborough, Barnet and Luton Town (when I was at Sky).

At The Dell in 1982 I saw Farnborough lift the Hampshire Senior Cup for only the second time after a 2-0 win over Basingstoke Town. The players and staff certainly partied hard afterwards and they would go on to win that competition three times in the space of five seasons.

No disrespect to the Farnborough lads, but I don't include those finals in my list of 'Fifty Cup Finals' because they were not major ones. I once spoke at their end-of-season dinner and re-visited Cherrywood Road when I was with Sky because we covered an FA Cup first round replay against Brentford. There was no giant-killing that night – Brentford won 4-0 – but the club were still very hospitable and were delighted that I took Andy Gray into their bar afterwards for a drink or two.

# 4

# County Sound and TVS

INDEPENDENT local radio came to Surrey and north-east Hampshire in 1983, and I was determined to be a part of it.

County Sound won the local franchise and I went along to Guildford to cover their victory press conference. Although it was not a sports story I sensed that the newspaper knew, even then, where my heart lay and they were happy enough to let me go.

Ever since I had started doing radio reports alongside my work for the *Aldershot News*, I had always been fascinated by live broadcasting. So when the station started recruiting, I was quick to apply and was lucky enough to be appointed sports editor, with some news reporting responsibilities as well.

Our top news reporter was Hugh Kirby, who quickly became a close friend. Like me, he was from a local newspaper background and we had come across each other before. We massively hit it off and were often to be found playing lunchtime games of snooker, or going to the Friary pub underneath the radio station in the shopping centre.

The glamour in the newsroom was provided by Kerry Swain. Although she was only in her early 20s she already had presenting experience at Television South West (TSW). That had not gone well, and she was determined to prove herself in broadcasting, which she did in style. Her success was all the more remarkable, given that she nearly died one morning on the way to work.

I remember driving in one day listening to our station on the radio when the news editor Malcolm Deacon announced, 'The top story this morning: County Sound reporter critically injured in a road accident.'

I was stunned to learn it was Kerry, who had been hit by a car as she turned on to the main road on her way to do her early shift. Her injuries were pretty extensive. By all accounts the impact had been severe, and it was almost a year before she seemed 100 per cent recovered.

Kerry, Hugh and I all ended up working together again at Television South later on in the 1980s, and I owe her big time – because she helped give me my big break to get into television.

In 1985 Kerry married Keith Malone, a charming guy who worked at TVS as a news reporter. My wife Debbie and I were invited to their wedding and met some of Keith's TVS colleagues. One of them was Guy Pelham, who I had known briefly during my *Aldershot News* days.

He invited me down to the TVS studios in Southampton to watch the lunchtime news bulletin. He also introduced me to programme controller Mark Sharman and the man who was to become the most influential person in my career: Vic Wakeling, the sports editor.

Again, I'm getting ahead of myself. More about TVS and Vic later.

Those early months at County Sound were all about learning the arts and techniques of broadcasting. It was six long days a week, and I think it is fair to say we worked hard and played hard.

There was a great dynamism about our young team – these were exciting and fulfilling days – culminating for me personally in being able to present the four-hour Saturday show, *Sportsound*.

It was a mix of music, live sport and recorded features. I made plenty of mistakes, but learned very quickly too. I also had to produce the programme as well. It was typical of local radio at the time – you were pretty much a one-man band, but that is how we all improved.

Broadcasting (and indeed journalism as a whole) is a vast industry, yet it is also a village. Friendships and contacts made early on can so often come back to help you and others along the way.

At County Sound I gave two young aspiring broadcasters their first opportunity.

One was Phil Edwards, who used to cover Wimbledon's games on a Saturday for me. He was a real enthusiast and a natural talent who went on to work for Independent Radio News (IRN) and ITN, before joining up with me again at Sky Sports News. By a strange quirk of fate, more than 30 years later, we were also both made redundant by Sky Sports News on the same day.

The other was Guy Havord, who again demonstrated a natural aptitude for broadcasting. From an early stage it was clear he knew his football, and he progressed well through BBC Radio Lancashire (covering Kenny Dalglish and Blackburn Rovers) to Sky News and on to Sky Sports, where years later we again worked together.

He also nagged me to write a book about my time at Sky and in journalism.

County Sound's patch wasn't exactly a hotbed of sport – yet the station also produced two other gifted broadcasters.

John Anderson bludgeoned his way into County Sound with huge enthusiasm and determination – and carved out a successful career in national radio and football commentary. He also wrote a very entertaining book called *A Great Face For Radio*.

Guy Phillips ended up concentrating on news broadcasting, but he was one of the most talented young journalists with whom I worked. It was hugely satisfying giving these people opportunities early on in their careers.

Whether it is a village or a vast industry, it is often said in journalism that 'what goes round, comes round' and that is fine by me.

Switching from newspapers to local radio did not mean the end of my association with Aldershot Football Club. I could not cover the weekend games because of my Saturday radio show but I still reported on the midweek home matches.

Most of the action seemed to be taking place off the pitch, where new owners took over and replaced manager Len Walker with the Chelsea legend Ron 'Chopper' Harris.

I felt sorry for Len as he had given everything to the club. His 12-year playing career which saw him make almost 500 appearances in all competitions was then followed by three more years as manager. In a sense though he had the last laugh, because the new regime failed and he was reinstated a year later. He carried on as manager until 1991 (winning promotion in 1987 – incredibly beating both Bolton Wanderers and Wolves over two legs).

When he lost his job originally in 1984 he agreed to record an exclusive interview with me, and he did not hold back about how betrayed he felt. It was great stuff, and on the drive back to the studios I remember thinking that it would make a really strong lead story for our Friday night sports and current affairs show which I co-hosted with Hugh.

Six miles outside of Guildford I came across some roadworks with temporary traffic lights and brought my car to a halt. Unfortunately the vehicle behind me didn't.

He slammed into the rear of my new Fiat Strada at almost 30 miles per hour, totally trashing the back of it, as well as inflicting some painful whiplash injuries on me.

Under normal circumstances I would have called the police, but I knew if I did the delay would mean I wouldn't get this story to air on time. Big mistake.

There was something a little suspicious about the driver – he was a bit of a wide boy, and less than convincing in his apologies. He exchanged details with me and couldn't wait to get going again.

Surprise, surprise, it turned out the car was stolen. He had no insurance and had given me a false address. Muggins had to foot a lot of the bill and my no-claims bonus was shot to bits. It was a valuable lesson learned. The job demands massive commitment, but it is not the be-all and end-all.

As for 'Chopper' Harris, he only lasted a year as Aldershot manager. My abiding memory of that time was playing in a charity cricket match with him at Tilford cricket green opposite the famous Barley Mow pub. It was an idyllic setting, we put on about 40 for the opening wicket and he hit a massive six out of the ground. He was a good guy, though, and we went on to work together quite a lot in the late 1990s when I was at Sky.

The most memorable achievement by Aldershot on the pitch during my County Sound days was their run in the 1984/85 League Cup. They beat Bournemouth 5-0 on aggregate over two legs in round one, then came back to win 4-3 over Brighton after losing the first game 3-1.

Round three was away to First Division Norwich City at Carrow Road. The ground had been damaged by a fire with the dressing rooms out of action, so Aldershot changed at their hotel beforehand. Gary Peters was one of many heroes that night as somehow the team hung on for a gallant 0-0 draw.

I went back to the hotel afterwards to do all the interviews as the lads were getting ready to go for a night out on the town. They did not have to return until the next day and invited me along, but sadly I needed to get the interviews to air in time for the early morning show.

I arrived back at the studios around 3am, edited up all the material and left just as the day shift started to arrive.

A few hours later, Aldershot or Norwich were drawn away to Second Division Notts County. Not exactly a glamour tie.

For the replay I took the radio car down to the Recreation Ground so that we could present live beforehand. We gave the game a big build-up but Aldershot got lost in the fog that night. Mike Channon was a class apart and Norwich triumphed 4-0.

The Canaries would go on to win the League Cup, beating Sunderland at Wembley, but they ended the season by being relegated. Aldershot finished 13th in the Fourth Division.

One other memory was a pre-season friendly game against Watford, when I was invited into the boardroom afterwards to interview their chairman Elton John. I wanted to talk music, he wanted to talk football – so we compromised and did a bit of both. He was very gracious, while I did my best not to be too star-struck.

Elton was not the only music legend I came across at County Sound. Rick Wakeman was chairman of non-league Camberley Town at the time and he had just married the former *Sun* Page Three model Nina Carter. Nina was keen to do some shifts at the radio station as a guest presenter, so Rick was more than happy to agree to my request for an in-depth interview with him.

I turned up, as arranged, at their house early one Saturday morning and walked nervously up their garden path. The reason for my trepidation was not the prospect of meeting two local celebrities, but the two large dogs who were patrolling the grounds and barking loudly at me. Luckily, the front door was swiftly opened and I was ushered into their enormous lounge. Rick came in shortly afterwards dressed in a brightly coloured and expensive-looking dressing gown. He organised some tea, but put his hand up when I went to introduce myself.

'First things first,' he said, and sat down at his piano. He then smashed away on the keyboards for a few minutes playing a spectacular piece of classical music, before shutting the lid.

'Right, I'm now all yours,' he said, shaking my hand. He went on to explain that was how he liked to start his day – especially if Camberley Town had a home game. He was an engaging, larger-than-life character, but he knew his football and was an excellent host. I spent a very entertaining 45 minutes with him before going off to present my afternoon sports show.

Despite those two huge names from the world of showbusiness, I suppose my biggest scoop while I was at County Sound was finding and interviewing Zola Budd.

The waif-like South African runner had been spirited out of her homeland by the *Daily Mail* and handed the chance to run for Britain as her grandmother was English. At the time South Africa was banned from international sport because of its apartheid regime so this was a controversial move.

The *Mail* kept her whereabouts a close secret, enabling them to enjoy exclusive access. But we got word that she had been spotted training in Stoke Park on the edge of Guildford and I managed to track her down.

Her coach was initially reluctant to let me near her, but eventually agreed I could interview Zola a few days later. I think he wanted to show the local people how much she was enjoying her new life in Surrey.

She was very quietly spoken, but it was a decent interview and got national radio coverage. The *Mail* went mental and banned me from talking to her, but once their exclusive deal ran out, she was happy to speak to the local radio station again.

What happened at the 1984 Los Angeles Olympics, when she tripped the American favourite Mary Decker, in a sense defined her. On the biggest stage she never quite achieved her potential, but she was very polite and I always followed her career from a distance.

By mid-1985 I had my eyes firmly set on joining TVS. Having been invited down to see their lunchtime operation, I ended up being 'interviewed' for a potential vacancy. Events seemed to be moving at a pace. Sports editor Vic Wakeling wanted me to join their operation at the Maidstone Studios immediately, but the unions insisted the position had to be properly advertised.

Vic and programme controller Mark Sharman had promised me that the job was mine, but until the formal interview process was completed I was told not to hand in my notice and carry on as normal.

In an ironic twist Keith Malone, whose wedding I had attended which had led to this opportunity, was then parachuted into Maidstone as the stand-in sports reporter. He did really well in the role, so much so that Mark Andrews (the man in overall charge of the Maidstone setup) was insisting Keith be given the job on a permanent basis.

In the end I had to return to Southampton to attend an interview board in October – four months after I had originally been offered the position. It was a close-run thing, but I just pipped Keith to the job and he was very generous in congratulating me afterwards. I never forgot his kindness (he could have been forgiven for wishing he had never invited me to his wedding in the first place!).

My first fortnight at TVS was spent at the Southampton studios getting to know the ropes under the eye of Vic and his deputy Gary Lovejoy. The two main sports presenters/reporters were David Bobin and Gareth Evans. To me they seemed to make the job look incredibly easy, but I was grateful how much they both taught me in that short period – particularly Gareth, who had a brilliant touch when it came to filming and scripting sports stories.

The first time I presented on *Coast To Coast* (Television South's nightly news and current affairs show) was, I don't mind admitting, a nerve-wracking affair. I got through it, but I definitely realised there was room for improvement.

With that particular hurdle out of the way, Vic told me it was time to join up with sports presenter Andy Steggall and the rest of the staff at the Maidstone studios.

I think it is fair to say the welcome I got was as chilly as the weather that December morning when I arrived in Kent.

Editor Mark Andrews made no secret of the fact he had wanted Keith Malone as his sports reporter – not this new boy with barely any TV experience. He and news editor John Flatt made my life pretty difficult in those early months, and quite a few times I found myself wondering whether I had made the right decision.

The 145-mile daily commute from our home near Farnborough to Maidstone was only possible because the final section of the M25 motorway had been completed a few months earlier. But it still took some getting used to.

Fortunately, Andy Steggall, deputy news editor Andy Cooper, and senior producer Jim Raven were much more supportive. Gradually I began to come to terms with working in television, as opposed to radio or newspapers – and there was a significant difference.

For a start there were eight league clubs in our patch, including First Division Southampton (the others, incidentally, were Portsmouth, Brighton, Reading, Bournemouth, Aldershot, Gillingham and Southend).

Add to that Hampshire, Sussex, Essex and Kent county cricket clubs, a good smattering of leading athletes and professional golfers, plus the Brands Hatch motor racing circuit, and there was plenty to keep us busy.

The hardest thing was often convincing the news desk that a sports story was worth covering. You have to remember that it was only a 30-minute show, and sport was often considered as the 'and finally' part of the running order. So, often we had to come up with the best picture story – preferably with some kind of gimmick (for example the husband and wife team who raced their 1930s vintage Bentleys round the lanes of Sussex with their dogs sitting in the passenger seats).

A case in point was trying to get a camera to cover the lower-league football teams. Back in the 1980s the game did not have anything like the hold over the population that it does now.

So, when Gillingham smashed eight goals past Southend one Saturday in late August 1987, Andy and I were determined to follow up the story. Our pleas for a camera fell on deaf ears.

Mark Andrews and John Flatt also turned down our request for a camera the following Saturday for Gillingham's home match with Chesterfield.

History records that on 5 September 1987 Gillingham beat Chesterfield 10-0.

It was a club record and unlikely to be beaten anytime soon. Eighteen goals scored over two consecutive Saturdays certainly won't.

Against Southend Steve Lovell had netted four, but this time it was more evenly spread out: Howard Pritchard, Dave Shearer, George Shipley and Karl Elsey all bagged two apiece. We managed to obtain some grainy, home-movie-style footage of a couple of the goals for Monday night's show, but it was scant consolation.

For the next match, the news desk finally relented and agreed to send a camera. It inevitably finished Gillingham 0 Blackpool 0.

My first contact with Gillingham came two days before my arrival at the TVS Maidstone studios. By contrast, the welcome I got at Priestfield could not have been warmer. Admittedly, the Gills won 6-1 that day (against Bognor Regis in the second round of the FA Cup), but manager Keith Peacock granted me some time for an introductory chat afterwards and we got along well.

I always found Keith to be very helpful throughout my career – whether he was with Gillingham, Maidstone United, Charlton Athletic or West Ham. Keith is one of football's good guys and someone who will always hold a place in the record books as the first substitute ever to be used in a Football League match, playing for Charlton at Bolton in the Second Division on the opening day of the 1965/66 season.

When I first started at TVS, Tony Cascarino was the main man at Gillingham (he scored twice that day against Bognor); a big and bustling centre-forward, who used his physicality well. He went on to play for Millwall, Aston Villa, Celtic, Chelsea and Marseille among others, as well as winning nearly 90 caps for the Republic of Ireland.

His last game as a Gillingham player was the 1987 Second Division play-off final replay. Gillingham had muscled their way into fifth place in the Third Division and grabbed the last of the play-off spots. Their two-legged semi-final pitched them against Sunderland, who had finished third from bottom in the Second Division (that's how they did it in those days).

At Priestfield, the visitors and favourites Sunderland went ahead, but a spectacular overhead kick from Cascarino levelled things up. 'Cas' then headed Gillingham into the lead and completed his hat-trick to make it 3-1. Before the end Sunderland clawed one back, so Gillingham took a slender 3-2 lead up to the north-east for the second leg at Roker Park.

Sunderland led 1-0 and then 2-1 to make the scores level on aggregate at 4-4.

Enter Cascarino again. His header made it 2-2 on the day, Sunderland went back in front, but then he got another: 3-3, with Sunderland now needing to score twice, because away goals would count. They managed one more, it finished 4-3 to Sunderland and 6-6 on aggregate, with Gillingham going through to the final against Swindon Town.

Some 18,000 people packed into Priestfield for the first leg as Gillingham snatched it 1-0 with a late free kick. These days a capacity crowd there is only around 11,000.

At the County Ground it got even better to start with, as Karl Elsey smashed in a spectacular volley to make it 2-0 on aggregate. It was a goal fit to win promotion, but sadly it didn't.

Lou Macari's Swindon responded well, eventually equalising inside the last half hour and then scoring a second with less than ten minutes to go.

Controversially, away goals DID NOT count in the final (as they had in the semi) or Gillingham would have been celebrating promotion to the second tier for the first time in their history. No champagne in Wiltshire that night – only the prospect of a third game on neutral territory at Selhurst Park, home of Crystal Palace.

This would be Cascarino's farewell match for Gillingham, and there was to be no happy ending. Swindon went ahead after only two minutes before easing to a 2-0 win. Cascarino had scored five goals in the play-off matches but he finished on the losing side.

It was to be 13 long years before Gillingham finally laid the play-off bogey to rest, winning promotion to that second tier under Peter Taylor after a thrilling fightback in extra time against Wigan. And all that after losing the previous year in the play-off final to Manchester City on penalties in controversial circumstances as referee Mark Halsey found SIX minutes of stoppage time from somewhere. Gillingham had gone into the added time leading 2-0. These were the days before a board was put up to tell everyone what the minimum added time would be. The norm was about two minutes – but six?

If you didn't know already, you probably would have guessed from that last paragraph that I am a Gillingham fan.

Starting with that first game in 1985, my allegiance steadily grew as Paul Scally came in to save the club from administration and possible extinction in the 1990s.

Tony Pulis then won promotion and established the side back in the third tier, before that heart-breaking play-off final defeat against Manchester City.

Taylor carried on the good work, won promotion, and moved on to Leicester City and the Premier League.

For five glorious seasons at the start of the millennium Gillingham competed (and competed well) in the second tier, before a 2-2 draw on the final day in 2005 at Nottingham Forest sent us down on goal difference with 50 points.

Despite a dramatic last-gasp play-off final win against Shrewsbury Town in 2009 (a team who had beaten us 7-0 in the regular season) and a title-winning League 2 campaign in 2013 under the great Martin 'Mad Dog' Allen, it was never quite the same as those heady days in the early 2000s.

But it did not stop me and my three children becoming season ticket holders, and I am proud to say we still are.

Despite Gillingham's play-off defeat, 1987 was something of a vintage year for the TVS clubs. Portsmouth won promotion to the top flight, Bournemouth were crowned Third Division champions and Southend also went up from the Fourth Division by finishing third. Not forgetting Aldershot who (as I mentioned previously) claimed play-off glory after beating two much bigger clubs to move into the third tier. The only team to buck the trend was Brighton, who finished bottom of the Second Division and were relegated. Dull it wasn't.

In the First Division Southampton finished comfortably mid-table, but embarked on a run to the semi-finals of the League Cup and after a goal-less draw in the first leg at The Dell against Liverpool, I was dispatched to Anfield for part two. It was the first time I had been to the famous ground and I found the atmosphere compelling. Mind you, the locals had plenty to cheer about that night as a 3-0 win sent them to Wembley, though they were to lose to Arsenal in the final.

The Southampton lads were naturally disappointed, but conducted themselves well afterwards. My post-match interview with a particularly recalcitrant Chris Nicholl did not exactly flow smoothly. The Southampton manager certainly did not do me any favours that evening, but he did (unwittingly) teach me a valuable lesson in taking extra care when talking to beaten managers.

My first visit to Old Trafford also occurred during my time at TVS. We took Dean White, a player who had been forced to retire early though injury, up north to be re-united with his best pal from their Gillingham days together.

That man was Steve Bruce. While Dean's career had suffered setbacks, Bruce had gone on from Gillingham (via Norwich City) to become a star in the Manchester United team in the First Division.

Nevertheless the pair remained firm friends (and so did their wives), and Bruce was happy to show his old mate round Old Trafford. He took us behind the scenes into the dressing rooms, out on to the pitch and gave us a guided tour of the museum.

Steve displayed endless patience and good humour as we filmed that afternoon. He gave an old mate who was down on his luck a day to remember. He gave us a good human-interest story to cover, but more than anything he showed me that he is an absolute class act. My impression of him never changed in all the years which followed. Whenever I had dealings with Steve – be it as player or manager – he was always top-drawer.

One other football memory I have from TVS came back at an old stomping ground. Again it was 1987, this time the FA Cup third round and Fourth Division Aldershot took on First Division Oxford United at the Recreation Ground.

Less than a year earlier Oxford had won the League Cup Final at Wembley, beating Queens Park Rangers 3-0. Amazingly that was also the score in this game. The underdogs well and truly had their day and Oxford had no answer, despite having John Aldridge in their line-up.

The second goal, by a guy called Glen Burvill, was a stunner and featured in ITN's headline sequence that night. It was a real pleasure to return to Aldershot with the TV cameras and film possibly their greatest-ever FA Cup performance.

It wasn't all football at TVS. We covered a wide variety of sports. I remember sitting having breakfast at Terry Marsh's house in Basildon on the morning of his world light-welterweight title fight with Joe Manley of the United States. That night was my first experience of sitting ringside (in the very front row) and I could not believe, even in this weight division, how hard they hit each other.

Marsh went on to win by a technical knockout in round ten. He was known as 'The Fighting Fireman' and next morning he took his world championship belt to show his colleagues on Blue Watch – it made great TV, because the banter with his fellow firefighters was memorable.

He certainly wasn't your average boxer. Marsh had been a schoolboy chess champion, a Royal Marine, and had also overcome epilepsy. He defended the title again and retired undefeated.

Later he was also implicated in an extraordinary plot to shoot his promoter Frank Warren and was charged with attempted murder, before being acquitted.

Gary Mason was another larger-than-life boxing character. Born in Jamaica, he based himself in the Medway towns in the 1980s, and opened up his own jewellery business in Gillingham High Street.

He was always game for a laugh and we used to film some terrific sequences with him as he prepared for his fights. He gave us great access and would always make sure his buddies on the local TV station had tickets left on the door. When he won the British heavyweight title in 1989 I almost lost my voice I was shouting so loud. It was his misfortune to be around at the same time as Lennox Lewis, though he gave him a tough contest when they battled it out for the European heavyweight title. Sadly he died in January 2011 after being involved in an accident with a van while out cycling. He was 48.

Liz Hobbs wasn't a boxer, but she was another of our region's top sports personalities. I first met her in 1986 at Tankerton, just outside Whitstable, as she practised for the world waterski racing championships. She had won the title five years earlier at the age of 21 and was fiercely determined to hang on to her crown.

After filming her from the shore, Liz asked me if I fancied a spin round the bay in her father Peter's speedboat. Problem was, I had come dressed in a suit and tie, while her dad could not bring his boat in beyond the shallows. So Liz waded ashore, told me to jump on her and promptly gave me a piggy-back out to Peter's boat.

They thought it was hysterical. I was just grateful my cameraman had gone home by then – and it was definitely worth it. For sheer exhilaration being in a speedboat at full throttle takes some beating. And I must admit that after that I always had a bit of a crush on her.

We covered Liz's progress until her retirement in 1987 and though we lost contact a few years later, I know she went on to become a highly successful businesswoman. I am not surprised.

As the years went by, our sports coverage at TVS became more ambitious. Vic Wakeling was now in charge of *Coast To Coast* as a whole, but still keeping an eye on my progress.

Sport was given a bigger profile and there was a more sympathetic regime in charge – Jim Raven and Andy Cooper had become the senior figures. From a professional and personal perspective by summer 1989 I had a greater reason to enjoy going to work than ever.

After my first marriage to Debbie ended, I began to see Sara Bassett, who worked on our assignments desk and was responsible for making sure all the crews got to their locations.

Later Sara would go on to work for Meridian TV as a production assistant. Later still, in 1994, we got married on the Greek island of Paxos.

It was another case of working hard and playing hard. Andy Steggall, myself and producer Simon Moore (son of legendary football commentator Brian) were responsible for a half-hour Friday night sports show, so were busier than ever.

In the evenings upstairs in the TVS bar it was also pretty hectic, a place where all the different programme-makers came together, and it helped create a great overall working environment.

We also had a lot of fun playing cricket for TVS. I remember one game down in the New Forest where I scored 90, but I blotted my copybook by denting my boss Gary Lovejoy's car with a six.

We also won a national media competition in 1988, playing in front of several thousand spectators at a Test match ground.

The star of our team was Andy Steggall. He had captained the British Universities side, played for Essex Young Cricketers and was good enough to open for The Mote first XI in the top division of the Kent League (I used to open for the second XI). In the semi-final at Kent's St Lawrence Ground in Canterbury, Andy finished unbeaten just short of a hundred as we chased down a pretty formidable total.

I scratched about for 13 that day, and have an old photograph of me playing a typically defensive shot. Still it was nice to play at the first-class ground with the famous lime tree.

The final was at an even grander setting – Birmingham's Test match venue, Edgbaston. Our game was the warm-up for an all-star charity match, raising funds for a major Amazon rainforest project.

Despite a long night in the local hotel bar the night before, we fielded like demons – it was a real buzz to be a boundary rider with the hum and chatter of hundreds of people just behind me watching on. Our bowlers hustled out the opposition for just over 100 and it all looked pretty straightforward.

It was then that the occasion started to get to us. The normally reliable Steggall fell cheaply and so did Mark Reeve, the brother of England Test all-rounder Dermot.

I made a positive start with a couple of boundaries to settle me down, but then I got stuck in a rut. I just could not seem to score to save my life. Truth was, the opposition had worked me out, blocked off my usual scoring areas and waited for the inevitable mistake.

Only it never came. The wickets continued to tumble, the scoring rate kept climbing and I had nightmare visions of being cast as the villain of the piece who selfishly refused to give up his wicket.

When all seemed lost big Joe Wilmington came striding to the crease. He was a fast bowler first and foremost, but he fancied himself as a bit of a hitter and on that day he was inspired. A couple of big sixes, followed by three fours and suddenly it was a different game – he finished with 30 not out and we scrambled home with a couple of balls to spare.

My contribution was 32 off 60 balls. Enough said.

We partied hard in our dressing room afterwards. The team was drawn from all kinds of different departments and offices at TVS, so it was a great morale-booster for the company as a whole.

But nothing lasts forever. Vic Wakeling left to help set up the sports news arm of the newly formed British Satellite Broadcasting organisation, and a few weeks later I was sitting in his office being interviewed for a reporting role – with the chance to cover sport on a national level. This prospect proved irresistible, I said yes, and ended my four-year association with TVS.

As it happened, I was to return to work again with my old colleagues for a few months in 1991, but more of that later. Now a new chapter was about to start.

# 5

# BSB 1990:
# 'It's Smart to be Square'

W HEN County Sound had gone on air for the first time
in 1983, we stood in the studios with champagne glasses
in our hands at 5.45am, listening to broadcaster and
comedian Frank Muir giving a witty opening speech.

With British Satellite Broadcasting I don't remember anything
like that.

Day one for us was 27 March 1990, and I was at Bisham Abbey
National Sports Centre near Marlow in Buckinghamshire. This was
where Bobby Robson's England were training ahead of their friendly
against Brazil the next night.

It was the first time I had covered the national team professionally,
and it was to be the start of a 26-year association (some would say
obsession!). I make no secret of the fact that I regarded working and
reporting on England as the peak of my career.

Back then England were preparing for Italia '90 and they were in
pretty good shape – unbeaten in 14 matches stretching back to 1988.

Robson's future was the big talking point. He was not being
offered a new contract after eight years in charge and had agreed to
manage PSV Eindhoven in Holland the following season. Graham
Taylor would be taking charge after the World Cup, so was Robson
a dead man walking?

Far from it, as it turned out. England's best performance at a World Cup abroad was about to unfold that summer and when Robson did leave, it may not have been as a national hero but it was certainly with the thanks of a grateful country.

Watching England beat Brazil 1-0 at Wembley, I did not realise I would have to wait nine games and 23 years before it would happen again.

Gary Lineker was the match-winner that night and duly obliged with a good post-match interview. He was always the go-to England player in those early years; happy to face the media win, lose or draw, and we all respected him for that. When he became hugely successful as a broadcaster in his own right, I certainly did not begrudge him – he had earned that opportunity by the way he worked with the media during his playing career. There were (and still are) some high-profile players working in TV that you would not have said that about.

Interviewing the manager after an England game at Wembley back then wasn't always straightforward. As live rights holders BSB were entitled to the first interview, but where to do it was always a bit of a tricky problem. The stewards at Wembley (and they were massively strict in the early 1990s) would not allow it to happen in sight of the fans, so we would shuffle across the pitch with Robson at the end, and 'pounce' on him at the mouth of the old tunnel.

But space here was also at a premium as both the team coaches were driven in before the final whistle and parked end to end, allowing the players the chance to make a quick getaway afterwards.

Finding a suitable spot acceptable to all could be difficult, but to be fair to Robson he was very patient with this fledgling TV company and England reporter. Like most managers he had his foibles and mannerisms, but I always enjoyed working with him and once the dust settled after Italia '90 I went out to Holland for an exclusive interview with him on his first day in charge of PSV.

Champion Television was the company which employed me when I worked for BSB. They had the live broadcasting rights for home England games and the FA Cup. Their headquarters were just off the A4 Great West Road near the Fuller's brewery in Chiswick.

When BSB first went on air in March 1990 they had five channels at their disposal – for movies, pop music, general entertainment, living/current affairs, and sport. Their slogan was 'It's Smart To Be Square', a reference to the unique technology they were using: the square aerial or 'squarial', to make it distinct from Sky's circular-shaped satellite dish.

On the sports channel we were responsible for four 30-minute sports news bulletins a day. It was pioneering stuff, and the precursor to Sky Sports and Sky Sports News.

Vic Wakeling was in charge of the news operation, while the main presenters were Jeff Stelling, Gary Richardson, Anna Walker and Graham Simmons. I occasionally filled in as well and used to particularly enjoy being on air with Jeff. It was clear he was a great broadcaster, an absolute natural with a razor-sharp wit and destined for success.

Graham went on to report on the rugby for Sky Sports for more than two decades. We were golfing partners, both ex-TVS, and for a while both lived in Kent. 'Simmo' was a better golfer than me, he could be quite highly-strung, but he always seemed to keep his cool on the course.

He was also an expert skier. When a group of us went to Zermatt in Switzerland on a skiing holiday, I soon found I was out of my depth and took a fairly spectacular fall towards the end of the first day. Simmo was first on the scene, but luckily there were no broken bones – just massively bruised pride.

Among the reporters was a young Gabriel Clarke, a big Everton fan and named after the Scotland and Everton forward Jimmy Gabriel. He joined the station from Radio Trent in Nottingham and was another who took to TV broadcasting like a duck to water.

After BSB he joined the *Saint And Greavsie* football show on ITV and has been with ITV Sport for more than a quarter of a century, going on to become an award-winning reporter and documentary maker. I hope I was able to play a small part in his early development.

In addition to my reporting duties for the sports news bulletins, I was also the touchline reporter for the live England and FA Cup games. We were a bit late to the party as far as the 1990 FA Cup was concerned. By the time we finally got on air the competition had reached the semi-final stage, though I remember going up to Boundary Park to see Second Division Oldham Athletic knock out Everton on their artificial pitch in a fifth round second replay (whatever happened to second replays?).

We covered the game for the BBC, but used it as a dry run for when we would officially be broadcasting. Presenting that day was Richard Keys, with Martin Tyler commentating and Andy Gray as co-commentator. It was a pretty impressive line-up for a programme which never really saw the light of day.

In round six Oldham overcame more top-flight opposition when they crushed Aston Villa 3-0 to reach the last four.

For the first time the two semi-finals were both screened live (by the BBC) and what amazing action-packed drama they produced. The early kick-off was Crystal Palace versus the holders Liverpool. After 90 minutes it was 3-3, then Alan Pardew scored the winner in extra time. The second semi had a lot to live up to but it delivered another memorable game as underdogs Oldham led Manchester United, before having to settle for a thrilling 3-3 draw after extra time.

The replay was at Maine Road and at BSB we were very excited because this time we had the broadcasting rights. Early on Oldham thought they had scored, but the officials believed (probably wrongly) that the whole ball had not crossed the line and the effort was disallowed. United went on to win 2-1 after extra time with Mark Robins scoring the decisive goal six minutes from the end.

So it was Crystal Palace against Manchester United on 12 May and I was about to cover my first FA Cup Final.

We sat on the grass behind the advertising hoarding at the players' tunnel end of the old Wembley. It was a fantastic view, in among the 'snappers' (photographers) and just a few feet from the pitch itself.

What a game it turned out to be. An early goal always helps and it was Palace who took the lead on 17 minutes with a deflected Gary O'Reilly header that just defeated United goalkeeper Jim Leighton. I was really pleased for Gary, because he must have done more interviews than anyone in the build-up to the final. Always patient, always polite – a true professional.

Back came United and it was no surprise when ten minutes before half-time Brian McClair crossed for skipper Bryan Robson to equalise. 'Robbo' was a legend and he was another who helped me in the early stages of my career reporting on England.

In the second half Mark Hughes fired United in front just after the hour and you sensed that might be it: that the favourites would now see the game out.

Palace manager Steve Coppell had other ideas. His response was to send on substitute Ian Wright, who promptly turned the game on its head. Wright had missed the semi-final as he recovered from a broken leg and he was determined to make up for lost time. Within three minutes of coming on he scored to level it at 2-2, jinking past two defenders before shooting beyond Leighton.

His very presence on the pitch galvanised Palace. They seemed to really believe they could cause an upset, although it was actually United and Mike Phelan who came closest to winning it in normal time when his chip struck the crossbar.

In extra time, John Salako crossed and Leighton hesitated but Wright didn't – and volleyed the ball into the net, causing pandemonium at the Palace end. The club had never won the FA Cup and south London was getting ready for a special party. Wright was undoubtedly the star of the show, and what a great story it made – battling back from serious injury just in time to be the super-sub hero.

Except that United had not read that particular script. Seven minutes from the end Mark Hughes raced on to a through ball and beat Nigel Martyn to make it 3-3, forcing a replay.

Understandably, the Palace players were gutted – I remember interviewing the normally talkative John Pemberton afterwards. He could barely speak.

Yet you could not begrudge United another chance. They had been drawn away in every single round and their league form may not have been the greatest, but in the cup they just seemed to be able to do enough (1-0 at Nottingham Forest, 1-0 at Hereford United, 3-2 at Newcastle United, 1-0 at Sheffield United, then 3-3 and 2-1 against Oldham Athletic).

Five days later the two teams met again under the Wembley floodlights – with one big difference. Alex Ferguson gambled by dropping his regular keeper Leighton and replacing him with Les Sealey. It was an inspired choice as Sealey made three crucial saves before Lee Martin scored a spectacular winner in the second half.

So Alex Ferguson had his first trophy with Manchester United and Robson lifted the cup for a third time. We did not know it that night, but we had just witnessed the start of what was to be more than two decades of utter dominance by one club and one manager. 'The Fergie Years' were under way.

This was the first all-seater FA Cup Final, hence the crowd being down to 80,000 for both games. The last Wembley standing areas had been removed as football continued to respond to the 1989 Hillsborough tragedy.

Crystal Palace were (and still are) the last all-English starting XI to contest the FA Cup Final.

A few weeks earlier I had covered a UEFA news conference in Switzerland, where the five-year ban on English clubs competing in Europe (following the 1985 Heysel tragedy) was finally ended. Manchester United would be free to compete in the following season's European Cup Winners' Cup competition, which they duly won. The juggernaut was gaining momentum.

The next major occasion for me was to be a visit to the 1990 World Cup in Italy.

When Vic Wakeling interviewed me for the BSB reporting job, he had intimated that we might be going to Italia '90. In the event the station opted not to send anyone but as England progressed through the knockout stages, that decision was revisited.

I watched the quarter-final in – of all places – the Cameroon Embassy in Holland Park, west London. Various dignitaries and representatives from the African nation turned up in full tribal dress to make it a truly unique occasion. For 20 minutes or so in the second half as England trailed 2-1 it looked like they would all be celebrating a famous victory. Two Gary Lineker penalties spared England's blushes that night and for the supporters of the Indomitable Lions, instead of tears of joy we ended up filming their tears of sadness. It was quite moving.

I was packed off to Turin for England's first World Cup semi-final in 24 years, with the vague promise that if England won I was to stay out in Italy, hook up with a local crew and film the preparations for the final. The venue itself was controversial. Turin was the home of Juventus, whose fans had suffered greatly at the Heysel Stadium disaster ahead of the 1985 European Cup Final against Liverpool. Thirty-nine supporters – the vast majority of whom were Italian – died that night, with 600 injured.

Five years on thousands of England fans were in the city, providing a stark reminder to the locals of what happened in Belgium on 29 May 1985.

From the moment we landed in Turin the security was the tightest I can ever remember for a game – and that is saying something. We had to leave the plane by the rear exit only, where armed Carabinieri (Italy's national police) frisked and searched us. The buses were pulled up right by the plane's steps, so that there was no chance of any contact in the terminal with the locals, and we were dropped on the edge of the city with strict instructions to keep out of trouble and not to miss the return journey that night.

I had met up on the flight with some fans from Northampton and we caught a tram into the city centre. Once aboard, as soon as it was apparent we were English football supporters, the locals all scurried down to the far end of the tram, leaving as much space between them and us as possible.

No amount of gentle and friendly communication could persuade them that we were not here to cause mischief. The good people of Turin were clearly fearing the worst, but the England supporters had come in peace – they just wanted to see their team reach the World Cup Final again.

Throughout the city there was a strictly enforced alcohol ban in operation – and yet just a couple of hundred yards from the stadium our group found a bar owner willing to serve the English a beer or two. We could not believe our luck and settled down for the afternoon.

After an hour we saw a German camper van pull in to the car park opposite and we beckoned them over. They were delighted to share a couple of pints with us. They had driven from Munich, and we had a great laugh with them.

Ninety minutes before kick-off, the police stormed in and immediately shut the bar down. The old lady who owned it got a fearful telling-off and we felt guilty. As we left we did manage to secretly hand over a sizeable tip for her troubles (which I suspect were only just starting).

On the short route to the ground we were hurried along by the police, who were keen not to let the large English contingent catch sight of their German counterparts. At one stage they appeared round a corner less than 50 yards away from us, but the mood was not threatening and we ended up pretty much queuing all together at the turnstiles, with no segregation.

When we got inside the Stadio delle Alpi we found we were behind the goal in the middle section with the Germans above and below us. It could have been a volatile mix, but both sets of fans were there for the football, nothing else.

The game itself may have taken place more than a quarter of a century ago, but it is still emblazoned on my memory.

England had stumbled a bit along the way to the last four but when it really mattered they produced a top performance.

West Germany were past masters at winning knock-out ties at World Cups, but that night England more than matched them. A breathless first half finished goalless with 23-year-old Paul Gascoigne again impressive in midfield.

In the second half West Germany were attacking towards us, so we got a good view of the goal that put them ahead on the hour.

A free kick just outside the area was touched to Andreas Brehme. The defender's shot struck Paul Parker and somehow ballooned up and over the defensive wall at a vicious angle, coming down just over Peter Shilton's head and into the net off the crossbar.

It was a freakish effort and we were stunned. Above and below us the Germans were going mad, while we silently prayed we would get an opportunity to score at the far end.

It came with ten minutes to go. Parker, so unlucky at that free kick, shrugged off the disappointment and hoisted a long high ball which caused chaos in the West Germany penalty area. Gary Lineker seized on it and scored with his left foot from an angle. A calm-as-you-like finish from a master striker.

Now it was our turn to celebrate – and we did!

The team and the fans were starting to believe something special could be about to happen. Shilton made a terrific reaction save in extra time from Jurgen Klinsmann, then Chris Waddle struck the post with a great shot. Before the end we all endured the agony of seeing Gazza booked. It meant he would be suspended from the final and England would not have their talisman.

First, though, they had to get there and with the score tied at one-all after 120 minutes, we now had to face a penalty shoot-out:

*Lineker went first and scored…1-0*
*Breheme stepped up for the West Germans…1-1*
*Next to go Peter Beardsley….2-1*
*Then it was Lothar Matthaus (who else?)…2-2*

The penalties were taking place in front of us and it was an incredibly bitter-sweet experience. The England spot-kicks were going in easily, while Shilton was getting desperately close to saving one, but without success. Still, so far so good.

*David Platt with the third England penalty…3-2 (huge cheers, we're getting close now)*
*Karl-Heinz Riedle just squeezed his penalty home…3-3*
*Amid unbelievable tension Stuart Pearce sent the keeper the wrong way, but Bodo Illgner managed to save it with his legs…still 3-3*
*Penalty number eight: Shilton goes the right way, but Olaf Thon scores in the corner…3-4*
*Last-chance saloon now. Chris Waddle can level it at 4-4 and at least force them to take their final penalty. If he misses, we're out… and he does, firing the ball high and wide, as West Germany go though 4-3 on penalties to face Argentina in a repeat of the 1986 final.*

I was numb with disappointment, so much so that I paid little attention on the way out, became separated from the group, and soon got lost in one of the streets around the stadium.

I was more than a little nervous, because I had emptied out my bank account before flying over and was carrying more than £1,000 in cash. The reason?

Well, because Italy had been eliminated the night before we reckoned the touts might be out in force afterwards to sell their unwanted tickets to the winning semi-finalists. We had it all figured out. Mark Southgate, a friend from TVS days, had a sister with a flat in Rome, so our accommodation was sorted. We just needed an England victory and a friendly tout to sell me four tickets. Happy days.

Except that the three Italian youths facing me in this dark street did not look particularly friendly – in fact they seemed quite hostile. I was starting to think this may end badly.

'Nick, what are you doing? You're going the wrong way, we're all over here!'

The voice that cut through the night belonged to our travel courier, and I was mightily relieved as I joined up with the main group a few moments later.

At the airport the police went ahead to explain to those inside the terminal that the England fans would be given a part of the building to wait for their flights. They took one look at the buses all lining up outside and scattered, leaving us with more room, but again with the uncomfortable thought that they were over-reacting.

The journey home was very subdued I eventually got to my bed shortly after seven o'clock, and went to sleep with a huge feeling inside of 'if only'.

\* \* \* \* \*

In January 1991 I was made redundant after BSB finally lost their battle with Sky for the right to be this country's satellite TV provider, and the news side of the sports channel shut down before the end of the month.

I was luckier than most. The FA Cup and live England games were still being screened so I was able to keep working on those specified days. Also, my old boss at TVS, Gary Lovejoy, kindly re-employed me on a freelance basis.

So, while everyone else gathered for the redundancy party at the Black Lion pub near Hammersmith, I was on my way up to Nottingham for Forest's FA Cup third round second replay with Crystal Palace.

The Forest boss was Brian Clough, who by this stage of his career was becoming quite reluctant to do TV interviews – but he was still such a huge name that we were very keen to get him on camera. We were struggling to convince him (even though Forest had won 3-0), but then our commentator Martin Tyler told him that I had been made redundant that very day. His tone softened, he changed his mind and granted me an interview after all.

Doing a live one-to-one interview with the great Brian Clough was a daunting prospect but it was another thing ticked off the bucket list. He was forthright, as you would expect, but also considerate, and I finished the interview with a sense of satisfaction and relief.

Later on that season I found myself back at the City Ground for a fifth round replay with Southampton. Forest won 3-1, but when I approached Clough to see if he would do another post-match chat he declined, saying, 'Anyway, I thought you'd been sacked!'

In essence the story of the 1991 FA Cup was about one man: Paul Gascoigne.

His performances in the early rounds had been brilliant, almost single-handedly dragging Tottenham through each time, none more so than against Oxford United.

Blackpool, Portsmouth and Notts County were also beaten along the way, as Tottenham reached the semi-final and a showdown at Wembley with arch-rivals Arsenal.

The decision to stage the semi under the Twin Towers was a bit of an issue, with fellow semi-finalists West Ham and Nottingham Forest claiming it would give the winners the advantage of already having played at Wembley.

The reality was that it was the safest and most practical place for this showpiece game. Over 77,000 were there – and they were rewarded with a sensational start.

After just five minutes Gascoigne scored a wonder goal, a free kick from fully 35 yards out that blasted past David Seaman into the net. It remains one of the best goals I have ever seen live and to this day I still shake my head in disbelief when I think of it.

Arsenal were the favourites and on their way to a second league title in three years, but any dreams of doing the double were shattered as Gary Lineker added a second soon after. Alan Smith did manage to pull one back right on half-time but a Seaman error 12 minutes from time let Lineker in for Tottenham's third.

So the 110th FA Cup Final would be Tottenham Hotspur versus Nottingham Forest, Terry Venables against Brian Clough.

By now we were operating as BSKYB (British Sky Broadcasting) and as rights holders we made a significant contribution to the traditional cup final players' pool. It does not exist now in these days of mega wages, but back then the theory was that it gave the players some extra money in return for increased access before and at the cup final.

I was allocated Tottenham with Gabriel Clarke given Nottingham Forest. We both had to produce a 15-minute preview piece on each club on the eve of the final.

As well as action from how they had got there, we were allowed to film some special sequences with the players. I took Norwegian goalkeeper Erik Thorstvedt swimming with his family at the local baths, and we also had half a dozen of the players sat round at the training ground playing a board game which Terry Venables had dreamed up ('Terry Venables Invites You To Be The Manager'). It was hilarious. And of course we had a big sit-down interview with English football's man-of-the-moment Paul Gascoigne.

Saturday 18 May was a beautiful sunny day and the stage was set for a classic FA Cup Final. In my opinion this was one of the best I ever saw – and I have covered 25.

My long-term girlfriend Sara had a sister called Pip, and her partner was Danny Matthews. We were very close, and he was desperate to see the game. He was actually a Charlton Athletic supporter but he was also a huge fan of Gary Lineker.

Armed with a cameraman's bib which I had kept from the semi-final (I know you shouldn't, but this was a different and much more carefree era) and a battery supplied by my cameraman Paul Quinn, Danny marched straight through the media entrance and out on to the pitch.

Again, we took up our positions behind the goal and watched as the eccentric Clough tried to hold Venables's hand when the two teams came out.

From the very early stages it was clear that Paul Gascoigne was a man possessed. In fact he was out of control. He got away with one outrageous tackle then charged into Forest full-back Gary Charles, catching him virtually chest high and in so doing seriously injuring himself. Referee Roger Milford should probably have sent him off, but soon realised that Gazza would be playing no further part in the final anyway, as he was stretchered away.

For Tottenham supporters and the neutrals this was a massive blow. Gascoigne was box-office, and one of the major reasons why the sport in England was enjoying a big revival. It was starting to become cool to be a football fan again, thanks to Gazza's tears at Italia '90 and the exploits of the national team.

Nottingham Forest punished the foul to the full. When the game resumed Stuart Pearce scored from the free kick to give his team the lead. After four League Cups, two European Cups and one league championship with Forest, would Clough finally get his hands on the FA Cup?

When Mark Crossley saved Lineker's penalty the answer looked to be yes.

Tottenham then staged a courageous fightback in the second half and equalised through Paul Stewart. Either team could have won it in normal time, but for my second cup final in a row I witnessed extra time.

The winner came from a corner. Forest's England defender Des Walker tried to clear but succeeded only in heading the ball into his own net. As he hit the ground he cried out in anguish and I found myself staring at him eye-to-eye from just a few feet away. I'll never forget the expression on his face.

Meanwhile, next to me, Danny was stood up with his arms aloft celebrating the goal. In *The Independent* on the Monday there was a picture across all ten columns captioned 'The Moment The Cup Was Won'. There was poor Des Walker lying on the ground, you could see the Tottenham players in a huddle, and behind the goal my mate Danny as clear as day.

I managed to get a copy of the photograph, Paul Stewart kindly signed it and we got it framed. It still hangs in pride of place in Danny's study all these years later.

In the tunnel afterwards the Tottenham players were rightly euphoric. To lose your star player injured, go a goal down, miss a penalty and still come back to win was an incredible achievement.

As part of the players' pool agreement, we were allowed on the Tottenham bus as it left Wembley. It was an amazing sight, watching it edge through all the celebrating fans on its way out of the famous stadium.

I was sat at a table with the FA Cup in the middle. Next to me was Gary Lineker and opposite was the captain Gary Mabbutt and fearsome defender Pat Van Den Hauwe. Interviewing Lineker and the ever-affable Mabbutt was a joy. Van Den Hauwe didn't want to know and glared at me throughout.

It was an unforgettable experience, made more memorable by the bus stopping at the hospital where Paul Gascoigne had been taken. We were not allowed in and had to wait on board, but then the Spurs players got back on and told us what it had meant to them to be able to visit their stricken team-mate.

The final stop was the celebration dinner and party. With wives, friends and supporters cheering wildly the Tottenham players brought the FA Cup into the room with 'Glory Glory Tottenham Hotspur' ringing out. An amazing end to an extraordinary day.

In August Vic Wakeling phoned me up and explained that a new show was starting on Sky called *Soccer Weekend*. It was a one-hour preview of the upcoming action and he wanted me to be the main reporter.

'I reckon it'll give you three days a week work,' he reasoned, and I accepted gratefully. From then on at Sky it was at least five days a week and I loved it.

Because TVS had been so good to me at the start of the year when I had been made redundant, I agreed to carry on doing their Saturday sports shift. One weekend, I found myself in Leicester Square at 8.30am to cover the weigh-in ahead of the Chris Eubank v Michael Watson WBO super-middleweight title fight.

Once that was over, it was back to Kent for Gillingham versus Barnet (the Gills won 2-1), before driving on to the TVS studios to edit a piece for the evening bulletin. Then I drove home, picked up Sara, her sister Pip and partner Danny, and we all headed for White Hart Lane.

Promoter Barry Hearn had left me four tickets on the door, but as soon as we got to the ground the atmosphere seemed really tense. Watson was a well-known Arsenal fan, this was the home of their greatest rivals and Eubank was unpopular in parts of London.

Above all there was a feeling of violence in the air. Pip was six months pregnant and we sent the girls straight back home in my car.

It was a good decision.

What followed was the most dramatic title fight I have ever attended. Watson and Eubank fought toe-to-toe over 11 epic rounds. When Watson knocked Eubank down it looked all over, but somehow Eubank got back up and then stunned everyone – Watson included – with a vicious and desperate uppercut. This time Watson went down and he didn't get back up.

As Watson was treated on the floor, fights started breaking out in the crowd just beyond the ring. One group tried to surge through the ropes to get at Eubank. He was based in Brighton, and was therefore our fighter, so we were delighted that he had won, but at the same time the story was patently all about Watson.

In the mayhem I managed to force my way into the tunnel in the hope of catching a few words with Eubank. Minutes later Watson came by on a stretcher. He was just inches away from me and I must admit I thought he was dead. Eubank also went to hospital that night and needless to say we did not get to speak to him.

We did talk to Barry Hearn upstairs in the hospitality area afterwards, but this was before the extent of Watson's injuries were known – and in the end we chose quite rightly not to run the interview. It is not because of what happened, but that fight remains the last boxing bout I ever attended.

One other memory from 1991 was the day I played at Wembley. Not football…but cricket!

It was a charity occasion – a Showbiz XI against a team of former players. I'm not sure how I qualified for the Showbiz side, but I found myself opening the batting with actor Glen Murphy (who played firefighter George Green in the hugely popular series *London's Burning*).

Up against me – with a new ball in his giant hand – was 'Big Bird' himself, the 6ft 8in West Indian fast bowler Joel Garner. He had only retired from Test cricket a couple of years earlier so this was a fantastic (and terrifying) challenge.

Somehow I flicked his third ball off my hips to the boundary for four. The crowd cheered, but Garner walked up the pitch towards me and said, 'Whatever you do, man, don't move when I bowl this next ball.'

I didn't – and I watched it fizz past my nose at something approaching 90 miles an hour. He chuckled to himself, while I breathed a huge sigh of relief.

My innings did not last too much longer: caught by Chris Broad (father of Stuart), who made a difficult catch on the boundary look ridiculously easy. And yes, the bowler was Joel Garner.

Replacing me at number three was Dennis Waterman, who called out cheerily, 'Hard luck son!' as he wandered out to bat. As it happened that was Garner's final delivery, because it was the end of his over and shortly afterwards the heavens opened.

Murphy had also just been dismissed so Rolling Stone Bill Wyman was on his way out to the crease, but never got to face a ball. Instead he shrugged his shoulders, lit up a cigarette and walked back through the pouring rain puffing on a fag.

In the bar afterwards my girlfriend Sara turned to the man next to her and asked, 'So, do you like cricket?'

'Well, yes, as I matter of fact I do,' he replied. That individual was once the world's number one batsman, Javed Miandad.

# 6

# 'A Whole New Ball Game'

'TWENTY times, 20 times Man United, 20 times, 20 times I say.' It's a familiar enough chant these days but it would have seemed almost inconceivable back in 1992, at the birth of the Premier League, that Liverpool's record of 18 titles would be overhauled by the men from Old Trafford (who had just seven at the time) within two decades.

Manchester United were undoubtedly English football's glamour club, but when the Premier League started it was Leeds United who were the defending Football League champions, with Liverpool the FA Cup holders.

These two got the season up and running with a dramatic and high-scoring Charity Shield encounter at Wembley. Leeds won 4-3 with Eric Cantona scoring a hat-trick. Twice Leeds led, twice Liverpool equalised – but in the end there was just no stopping the Frenchman, whose last two goals took the game out of the reach of the Merseysiders.

A week later the inaugural Premier League season got under way. I was at The Dell on that opening Saturday to see Southampton and Tottenham fight out the only goalless draw of that first weekend.

Sky had proudly trumpeted their coverage as 'A Whole New Ball Game', and the way the two teams came out together side by side was certainly novel for league matches.

Darren Anderton was making his debut for Tottenham. He was Southampton-born and a Saints fan, but because he had played for Portsmouth (where he had been the star of their epic run to the FA Cup semi-finals a few months earlier) he was mercilessly booed whenever he touched the ball. It seemed a cruel irony.

Kerry Dixon also made his debut for Southampton and after I had interviewed him in the tunnel he invited me in to the players' bar. We had just sat down with a pint when Glenn Cockerill wandered over and informed me that I would have to leave because the press were not allowed in there. I did as I was told.

The honour of scoring the first Premier League goal fell to Sheffield United's Brian Deane, who netted after just five minutes in a 2-1 win over Manchester United.

Teddy Sheringham scored the first live televised goal the next day in front of our cameras at the City Ground. Nottingham Forest beat Liverpool 1-0, but Sheringham moved on to Tottenham later that month and Forest ended up finishing bottom.

I had to wait until the Tuesday for my first live Premier League goal. In those first few months David Livingstone was the Premier League touchline reporter for the outside broadcast games, while I did that role for England matches. In December David moved to a new position presenting golf and I took over his role.

That night at Blackburn Rovers it was record signing Alan Shearer's home debut. He had already scored twice on his club debut in the 3-3 draw at Crystal Palace on Saturday and at Ewood Park they could not wait to see him in action.

There were just six minutes left when Shearer dispossessed Arsenal's Jimmy Carter on the halfway line. He had only one thought on his mind: go for goal. And he did.

The famous Arsenal back four of Dixon, Bould, Adams and Winterburn could not get near him as he thrashed a fierce shot past David Seaman before running straight over to our camera behind the goal to celebrate in earnest. My cameraman Paul Quinn had captured the goal beautifully from the moment Shearer won the ball until he finished up shouting into the lens.

The next night Paul and I were at Old Trafford to witness the Peter Beardsley show. The England man ran United ragged, scoring the first in a 3-0 win in the pouring rain. This new Premier League was already proving difficult to predict.

On Saturday Paul and I went back up north to watch Manchester United face Ipswich Town. The newly promoted visitors scored first, but Denis Irwin equalised with his first goal since moving from Oldham Athletic and United had their first point of the season.

Alex Ferguson told me afterwards he felt that the team had turned a corner that day after two defeats, and how right he was. United reeled off five straight Premier League wins after that, beating champions Leeds 2-0 as well as defeating Everton in the return game at Goodison Park.

Norwich City were settling well and I saw a David Phillips wonder-goal clinch a 2-1 victory over Crystal Palace.

The new league was full of big signings and the football, while it might not always have been 'A Whole New Ball Game', was certainly exciting.

Monday night live games meant dancing girls – the 'Sky Strikers' – and fireworks, although they eventually both fizzled out. The pyrotechnics were good fun but there were one or two hairy moments along the way. Stories of rockets coming down on petrol station forecourts and various other near misses started to circulate.

Sky were determined to get value for their five-year, £304m rights deal, and the emphasis was on trying to deliver a fresh approach to the way football was televised and analysed.

Andy Gray played a key role in this. He raised the bar in terms of co-commentating and post-match punditry, taking it to new levels. Those that have followed since (especially Gary Neville) have built on what he achieved.

He was also a larger-than-life personality, a brash Glaswegian who was up for a laugh. He was great for morale in those early days and he taught me a lot.

So did Richard Keys. Yes, he was a controversial character, but in terms of presenting live football without an autocue and controlling a studio with famous guests, well I never saw anyone do it better.

My 'partner-in-crime' in those first few Premier League seasons was Geoff Shreeves. Geoff would go on to become – in my opinion – the king of the touchline reporters, with an uncanny ability to keep cool in heated situations and to get the most out of his interviewees. He was also a genuinely funny man and that often helped defuse tense moments in the tunnel. Back in 1992/93 he was my floor manager and was responsible for bringing the players or managers to the interview points. But he was also much more than that – a sounding board, another pair of eyes and ears, and a good mate.

We learned a lot together in those pioneering seasons and I think it helped us greatly as our careers developed.

At Christmas, when I took over the live reporting duties from David Livingstone, Norwich City were top with Aston Villa, Blackburn Rovers and Manchester United not far behind. January would see Norwich, Villa and United all leading the table at various times.

Blackburn fell away after Shearer was injured, but they still finished fourth in their first season back up in the top flight for more than three decades. Over the next few seasons they would emerge as Manchester United's biggest rivals.

One significant transfer took place in the November. Eric Cantona, the inspiration behind Leeds United's title win, switched from Elland Road to Old Trafford. It would have a big impact on how the second half of the season panned out.

Meanwhile, just a couple of weeks into my new role, we ran into a major problem. Alex Ferguson banned his players from talking to Sky Sports and refused to do any interviews for us as well.

It all followed a tense *Monday Night Football* encounter at Loftus Road against Queens Park Rangers. It was a pretty feisty affair and at one point in the first half our cameras captured a shot of Ferguson and QPR boss Gerry Francis having a big disagreement on the touchline. We did not linger on the clash – it evaporated in seconds anyway – and afterwards we concentrated on United's performance. They had won 3-1 and were definite title contenders.

The next day, *The Sun* published a picture of the spat. Crucially they had lifted it from our coverage and Ferguson went ballistic. Not with *The Sun* – it was Sky Sports wholly to blame in his book, for showing the shot in the first place.

The first day of the ban was 19 January 1992 and it was to last for some time. As United stayed in the hunt for their first league title in 26 years, so our nervousness gradually increased. What if Fergie didn't relent? How could we do justice to the first season of

Premier League football without the co-operation of the potential champions?

It became a game of cat and mouse. Our senior producer Andy Melvin knew Ferguson from his Aberdeen days and was preparing for the worst-case scenario. He also predicted the ban would end when Ferguson felt he had made his point. And to be fair to Andy he was proved right – eventually.

January gave way to February and still there was deadlock. March came and went, and again there was no resolution.

Then on Monday, 5 April Manchester United travelled to Carrow Road for a key game with Norwich City. This was the night when they threw down the gauntlet to the chasing pack and played like true champions.

Inside 25 minutes they had raced into a 3-0 lead and buried Norwich's fading title challenge. Ryan Giggs, Andrei Kanchelskis and of course Eric Cantona were all on target, and you could see Ferguson practically purring with satisfaction on the touchline at the way his team were playing.

Afterwards, all was sweetness and light. Ferguson readily agreed to an interview, as if there had never been any ban imposed. He even let us talk to Ryan Giggs, who had been brilliant that night.

And that was it. Punishment meted out. The past forgotten. Move on. Much like football itself in many ways.

A few days later – in the famous 'Fergie Time' match – United took another massive step towards the title. Opponents Sheffield Wednesday struck first midway through the second half at Old Trafford and were still ahead with just four minutes of the 90 left.

Up popped Steve Bruce with a priceless equaliser as the game went into time added on. There were no electronic boards back then, just the discretion of the referee (with maybe a tiny little bit of influence from the sidelines?). In the 97th minute Bruce did it again, United led 2-1 and three precious points were secured. The momentum was completely with Ferguson's men. Whereas in the past they had faltered when in sight of the finish line (the previous season being a prime example), this time they looked rock solid.

On to Coventry for the next game – again live on *Monday Night Football*.

The lunchtime of the game, Ferguson had agreed to do a sit-down interview in the garden of the team hotel. Andy Melvin mentioned to me that Fergie had a soft spot for old Hollywood western movies like *High Noon* starring Gary Cooper, *The Man Who Shot Liberty Valance* (with Jimmy Stewart) and *The Searchers* (John Wayne). So, after the football stuff was out of the way, I brought up the subject of westerns.

While he didn't exactly go all misty-eyed, Ferguson did wax lyrical about those old films and the lessons that could be learned from them – in life and in football. It was a real insight into the man and I enjoyed it immensely.

That night the Manchester United bandwagon rolled on with another victory, thanks to a Denis Irwin goal on 40 minutes. The team were now unbeaten in 12 league games with just four to go and the holy grail of winning that elusive league title was moving within touching distance.

The race was now on to interview the players who had last brought the league championship to Old Trafford, way back in 1967.

Foremost of those was George Best, who had become our regular studio guest in recent weeks as his former club inched ever closer. It was fascinating to hear his tales of those days – what a different game it was back then. I never saw him play live for Manchester United but I had watched his heroics on TV as he helped deliver the 1968 European Cup. His six goals against Northampton Town in an FA Cup tie were the stuff of legend, as was his rock and roll lifestyle. For all his fame and talent, George came across as a really humble guy – and his presence definitely enhanced our coverage.

In the closing weeks of the season we also spoke to Alex Stepney, Pat Crerand, David Sadler, Denis Law and of course Bobby Charlton.

The abiding memory of talking to that generation was the genuine excitement they felt at the possibility of their club reaching the pinnacle of the English game once again.

So yes, we were hugely excited by the prospect of Manchester United ending their barren title years in our first season of live football, but we were equally impressed with the way Aston Villa had performed all season.

They were still in the title race and showing no real signs of weakening. Ron Atkinson was the manager, and while we had encountered those well-documented issues with Ferguson, 'Big Ron' could not have been more helpful.

Of course it helped that Andy Gray had been Ron's assistant at Villa and the two were still very close.

One Saturday morning in April I arrived at Ron's house just outside Birmingham to do a pre-arranged interview at 9am. I rang the bell and waited.

Eventually, Ron appeared a little bleary-eyed and in his dressing gown.

'You're early!' he bellowed at me.

At which point the clock in his hall struck exactly nine o'clock.

Ron looked at me and burst out laughing. He knew he had been caught out – and he thought it was a genuinely funny moment.

'Try and put the other person on the back foot,' he told me as we sat in his bar after the interview. 'That is what I was attempting to do with you. Until that bloody clock chimed!'

Ron's Villa team, with Dean Saunders and Dalian Atkinson to the fore, had been great entertainers all season. The fact that Ron used to be manager of Manchester United just added to the pathos.

Norwich, under Mike Walker, had also been a breath of fresh air. They made a lightning start, with ten wins in their first 16 games, and although they could not quite sustain it, they were nevertheless one of the stories of the season and worthy of their UEFA Cup qualification spot.

As the season entered its final phase, the title was United's to lose – except this time they were determined not to let it slip. And they underlined that with two more wins, over Chelsea and Crystal Palace.

Instead it was Villa who blinked first. They succumbed to the pressure, losing 1-0 at home to struggling Oldham Athletic and handing the title to United.

We had all been at Villa Park, George Best included – and he had become quite emotional as more than a quarter of a century of hurt finally ended for his old club in this season of all seasons.

We drove north to Manchester that evening, not knowing quite what to expect. In a way it seemed like a bit of an anti-climax as we hadn't actually seen the title won on the pitch. But what we witnessed was a city in utter jubilation.

Lee Sharpe actually went down to Old Trafford and joined in the celebrations with the fans. Steve Bruce had a party at his house and we did a phone interview with him live into *Super Sunday*, to get the players' reaction to their success. By all accounts, after he put the phone down to Sky, the party carried on well into the small hours and beyond.

As for George, he could not move anywhere without someone wanting to shake him by the hand – it was a joyous, emotional night for him and it was great to see.

Twenty-four hours later United were back in action, only this time there was nothing at stake and they could continue the party.

Blackburn briefly threatened to be killjoys by taking the lead. Truth be told, some of the United players were probably still suffering from hangovers – but the adrenaline kicked in and they took control. Ryan Giggs and Paul Ince scored to make it 2-1, and then in the final minute United won a free kick.

Gary Pallister was the only United regular who had not scored during the season and, with the title safely in the bag, he was persuaded to take the set-piece. To the delight of almost everyone at Old Trafford the popular defender scored with a rasping shot, and that really was the icing on the cake.

United went on to become champions by ten clear points, finishing the season unbeaten in their last 16 games – with 12 wins and four draws.

No one could begrudge them this moment of triumph.

Alex Ferguson had been under huge pressure earlier in his United career yet the board stuck by him – and how that decision paid off! This was just the start as 12 more titles followed over the next 20 years and English football's most successful club would no longer be Liverpool. United took over that mantle with Ferguson achieving his ultimate dream.

Little did a young Ryan Giggs know that the winning feeling would be repeated over and over and over again. Thirteen English league titles for one player is just insane, but that is what he achieved.

Cantona was in many ways the catalyst. Only after he joined in November did United really start to emerge as genuine title contenders. Winning back-to-back league championships with two different clubs is an incredible achievement – and he did it in his own unique, Gallic style.

But the two players I felt most pleased for were Bryan Robson and Steve Bruce. Neither of them were getting any younger and this was a fitting reward for their amazing careers.

Robson was known as 'Captain Marvel' with England, but he was also a brilliant leader and inspiration for his club; Bruce never got to play for his country, but the former Gillingham defender 'done good' and it was absolutely right that the two of them should go up together to lift the first Premier League title.

They were also two of the players most willing to do interviews afterwards, so from a media point of view we all enjoyed their success.

Five days later the top flight season drew to a close, with Oldham staying up on the last day courtesy of three consecutive victories to pip Crystal Palace on goal difference. After that heroic win at Villa they beat Liverpool 3-2 and then Southampton 4-3. It established a precedent. Almost unfailingly, the bottom of the table would provide fantastic drama, and this was no exception.

The top three were Manchester United, Aston Villa and Norwich, with Nottingham Forest finishing bottom and being joined by Middlesbrough and Crystal Palace in being relegated to what was now known as the First Division.

When it came to the cups, one team had a monopoly: Arsenal.

George Graham's team challenged for the title early on, before falling away, but in the the knockout competitions they were in a league of their own as they became the first team to land the domestic cup double.

They did it the hard way too, playing a total of 17 ties to secure the two trophies. Bizarrely both finals were against Sheffield Wednesday, managed by Trevor Francis.

Their most satisfying encounter of all was probably the Wembley victory over rivals Tottenham in the FA Cup semi-final (thanks to Tony Adams's late goal) to avenge their 1991 defeat at the same stage.

Steve Morrow scored the winning goal in the League Cup Final and was then injured quite seriously in the post-match pitch celebrations. In trying to lift him up, Adams inadvertently lost his grip and his team-mate's arm ended up broken. Morrow was taken to hospital and missed not only the chance to go up and get his medal but also the FA Cup Final the following month.

In the FA Cup, a replay was needed. Ian Wright scored in both games, putting Arsenal ahead each time, but Wednesday equalised through David Hirst in the initial game and Chris Waddle in the second attempt.

Deep into extra time in the replay, with literally seconds remaining, Andy Linighan headed home from a corner to give Arsenal a place in history as double cup winners.

There were great scenes of celebration at the end but I could not help but feel sorry for the Owls, who had contributed hugely to both occasions.

In the build-up to the first all-Sheffield semi-final, which also took place at Wembley, I had been despatched to the Steel City to get some colour. Tales of divided families abounded, and I came across one lady who had seven sons. They were all Sheffield United fans, and she worked at Bramall Lane as well – yet she supported Wednesday!

And that was the 1992/93 season. A Whole New Ball Game? I'll let others be the judge of that one.

# 7

# Blackburn's Turn

BEFORE the 1993/94 season got under way Sky covered the European Under-18 Championships, with England as hosts. It was to be the first time I would meet Robbie Fowler and the abiding memory of that tournament was what a prodigious talent he was. It was a case of when, not if, he would break into the Liverpool first team.

The answer to that particular query was a few weeks. He scored on his debut in a League Cup tie against Fulham. Then back at Anfield in the second leg the 18-year-old scored FIVE goals, a truly astonishing start. In his fifth league game he bagged a hat-trick against Southampton and managed 13 from his first 12 matches, which earned him a place in the England under-21 side. He scored on that debut too.

When England began their under-18 campaign Fowler was on the bench – Jamie Forrester of Leeds and Julian Joachim were the main strikers. Joachim went on to become one of the stars of this tournament but it was Fowler who would be the leading scorer.

With less than ten minutes to go against France in the opening game it was still 0-0, but then super-subs Kevin Gallen and Fowler scored to give England a 2-0 win. Fowler's goal was a gem, a 25-yard chip into the top corner.

He cheekily told me in his interview afterwards that he could just see a gap of about an inch and went for it. He had also decided that – because I had quite long curly hair in those days – I looked like the

Lion from *The Wizard Of Oz*! It was probably just as well that I got my hair cut soon after.

In the second game against Holland, Fowler and Gallen both started – and both scored, with Joachim grabbing two as well. The final score was England 4-1 Holland, a good three years before the senior team managed to emulate that feat in a European Championship group game.

Spain were reduced to ten men in the final group match against England, and Fowler took full advantage by scoring a hat-trick to propel his side into the final against the holders Turkey.

The England side that took the field for that game included Gary Neville and Sol Campbell in defence, Paul Scholes in midfield, and Fowler up front. Nicky Butt was only a substitute and David Beckham could not even get in the squad.

It was a tense and tight game in front of more than 23,000 at the City Ground, home of Nottingham Forest. Twelve minutes from time Joachim was fouled in the area and England's captain Darren Caskey put the penalty away to win the match and the tournament.

He played a holding midfield role and looked to be a real star in the making. But although he made over 30 appearances for Tottenham and more than 200 for Reading his career never really took off in the way we had all expected it to back then.

It was no surprise that Messrs Neville, Butt, Scholes, Campbell and Fowler would go on to have stellar careers – likewise Joachim. It was fascinating over the years to watch how they developed and for those of us at Sky who had covered the tournament it was great to see England lift the trophy at the end, and for us to be able to film the post-match celebrations.

Meanwhile, Manchester United began the 1993/94 season like they meant business. With the shackles off having secured their first Premier League title, they came flying out of the blocks – winning five and drawing one of their opening six games as they looked to retain their championship.

They lost 1-0 at Chelsea to a Gavin Peacock goal, but then responded by reeling off eight straight victories. After 15 games they had accumulated 40 points and were almost halfway to defending their crown.

The seventh game in that sequence was at Maine Road against rivals Manchester City. Two Niall Quinn goals put the hosts in charge, then Manchester United stormed back to win 3-2 with Eric Cantona netting twice and Roy Keane also on target. It sent out a powerful message to the rest.

In fact they did not lose another Premier League match until March, when Chelsea completed an unlikely double over the champions.

Ferguson, perfectionist that he was, still wanted more. Leading into the New Year a run of six draws in ten games left him a little frustrated, but the title was still United's to lose.

Meanwhile, Blackburn Rovers under Kenny Dalglish were building on their fine return to the top flight. A fourth-place finish the previous campaign was now being followed by an even better performance.

Blackburn took four points off United and very nearly did the double over them. It needed an 88th-minute Paul Ince equaliser to deny Rovers at Old Trafford on Boxing Day.

However, little did I know it, but I was about to get a harsh lesson in the realities of being a live TV tunnel reporter.

Blackburn were seething about the Ince goal and after the final whistle Dalglish strode straight up to me at the top of the tunnel, demanding to do his interview immediately.

'Ask me about that decision,' he said. 'It was a f****ing disgrace!'

We radioed the producer in the gallery and I said, 'Kenny wants to do his interview live right now, and he's got something to say about their goal.'

They pretty much cut straight to us and I began:

'Hard luck Kenny, I gather you're not happy with that late equaliser, then?'

His response went something like this:

'I have no problems with the decisions made by the referee, and it is very wrong for you to suggest otherwise. You are just trying to stir things up, and unless you stick to questions about the game, then this interview ends now.' I was flabbergasted. We carried on the interview for another couple of questions, but Dalglish was being quite difficult and I admit I struggled.

Afterwards I realised that Dalglish knew he would be in hot water if he told me what he really thought about the decision on the equaliser. He did a massive about-turn in the few seconds it took to put the interview live to air, and proceeded to make me into the villain of the piece.

It was a smart move on his part but it did nothing for the slightly rocky relationship I appeared to have with him.

Interviewing Kenny over the next few seasons became a tricky (and at times even toe-curling) experience. He would always want to contradict the reporter if he could, so staying sharp was absolutely vital.

The return at Ewood Park was to give us a glimpse of the future. Blackburn absolutely overran United, winning 2-0 with two Alan Shearer goals, but it could have been a few more. They dominated the reigning champions, and no one else did that in a league game in 1993/94.

It was a particularly sweet moment for Shearer, who had turned down a move to Old Trafford, choosing the less-fancied Blackburn instead.

That result delayed United's coronation as champions but nothing was going to stop their surge towards back-to-back titles.

In the end they amassed 92 points, with 27 wins, 11 draws and just four defeats from their 42 games.

One amazing match from that season which sticks in the memory came at Anfield in early January. My floor manager Geoff Shreeves and I used to like to have a bet occasionally, just to keep things interesting. On this particular evening we went for a draw overall with Manchester United to be leading at half-time. I think the odds were 14/1.

Denis Irwin, Steve Bruce, and Ryan Giggs all scored early on to give United what looked like an unassailable lead, and we toyed with throwing away our betting slip there and then.

Liverpool then stormed back. Nigel Clough scored, so did Neil 'Razor' Ruddock, and at half-time it was 3-2. Clough completed the comeback to make it 3-3 and we watched on in amazement as both sides somehow failed to find a winner. The bet paid out and we collected £75 each.

In the FA Cup, United were also looking in ominous form as they won away at three Premier League clubs in the early rounds (Sheffield United, Norwich City and Wimbledon) before cruising into the semi-finals with a 2-0 win over Charlton Athletic.

Oldham Athletic were again their opponents and again they gave United problems in the first game. In fact it took a stoppage-time equaliser from Mark Hughes to keep the Double dream alive. The replay was far more one-sided, with United winning 4-1 to set up a final against Glenn Hoddle's Chelsea.

In the pouring rain, I always felt the 4-0 scoreline flattered United that May day. After an hour it was still goalless but referee David Elleray awarded two penalties in six minutes, both of which were converted by Eric Cantona – and it was game over. Hoddle himself came on for the last 20 minutes or so, but could not prevent Hughes and Brian McClair also scoring.

It was a deserved Double for the men from Old Trafford – they really were a formidable outfit, but it could so easily have been a Treble.

United had beaten Aston Villa twice in the league and were firm favourites when they lined up for the League Cup Final against them on 27 March. Former United player Paul McGrath marshalled the Villa defence superbly that afternoon and his side took their chances.

Dalian Atkinson put them ahead, Dean Saunders pounced in the second half to make it 2-0, and although Mark Hughes pulled one back Villa would not be denied. Andrei Kanchelskis was later sent off for handball and Saunders scored from the spot as Villa won 3-1.

Because United had won both the Premier League and the FA Cup, the following season's Charity Shield featured league runners-up Blackburn against them.

Anyone looking for clues as to how the dramatic 1994/95 season would unfold was probably slightly wrong-footed by the traditional curtain-raiser. A Cantona penalty and a late goal from Paul Ince secured what was pretty much a regulation 2-0 victory for United.

Crucially, Blackburn were missing their twin strike force of Alan Shearer and new record signing Chris Sutton.

Both teams made good starts to their league programme. United won three and drew one of their four opening games, while Blackburn went unbeaten through their first seven and collected 17 points.

United then suffered an uncharacteristic blip as they lost three of their next five matches – at Leeds United, Ipswich Town (against whom they would exact spectacular revenge later in the season) and Sheffield Wednesday.

When the two rivals met at Ewood Park on *Super Sunday*, 23 October, it was a key game near the top: Blackburn had 21 points from ten games, United were on 19 from their ten.

But it was in fact third against fifth because other teams had got absolute flyers. Newcastle had beaten Sheffield Wednesday on the previous day to reach 29 points from 11 unbeaten games. Newly promoted Nottingham Forest were also undefeated with 27 points from eight wins and three draws. Liverpool, on 20 points, were lying fourth.

Clearly defeat for either would be a serious blow to their title aspirations but by the end of the afternoon it was Ferguson's men who had moved into the top three with a 4-2 victory in a dramatic match.

Frustratingly, I was forced to miss the game because of severe stomach cramps and diarrhoea and had to settle for watching it at home on TV.

Paul Warhurst put Blackburn ahead with a fantastic 30-yard effort. Then right on half-time Lee Sharpe broke away and Henning Berg looked to have made a great saving tackle – but controversially a penalty was awarded and Berg was sent off. Cantona scored the spot-kick to make it 1-1.

Ten-man Blackburn regained the lead through Colin Hendry's header, but United responded immediately though Andrei Kanchelskis. Mark Hughes put United ahead for the first time, then a superb counter-attack from Kanchelskis made it 4-2. That's how it stayed.

The next evening I had recovered sufficiently to travel to Elland Road for Leeds's *Monday Night Football* encounter with Leicester City.

When I bumped into Leeds manager Howard Wilkinson he said, 'So how come you didn't do the Blackburn – United game yesterday?'

I explained that I had been suffering from a touch of gastroenteritis.

Quick as a flash, Wilko responded with, 'More like a dose of Kenny-itis!'

He was well aware of the reputation Kenny Dalglish had, of sometimes being difficult to deal with, and he hugely enjoyed my stuttering denial.

Blackburn's reaction to the setback was impressive. They went to previously unbeaten Forest and won 2-0, Sutton scoring both the goals. The SAS combination (Shearer and Sutton) was gathering momentum and between them they scored 49 league goals (Shearer 34, Sutton 15) – a monumental achievement.

After that Rovers just got on a roll. By the end of the year they had won nine and drawn one of their last ten games, taking 28 points out of a possible 30.

By contrast, Forest went six league games without a win, while Newcastle plunged into freefall: two wins and four draws from ten games – ten points out of 30 and their title challenge was virtually over.

As for United, three days after that Ewood Park victory they travelled to Newcastle in the League Cup and lost 2-0.

But then they bounced back by beating the same opposition by the same score just three days later in the league – that was their priority.

A 5-0 thumping of local rivals Manchester City (with Kanchelskis netting a hat-trick) merely underlined how strong the desire at Old Trafford was to make it three consecutive Premier League title wins.

In January Andy Cole moved from Newcastle to United in a British-record £7m move – and made his debut at home to Blackburn!

This time it was second against first with Blackburn having won 17 of their 23 fixtures, drawn four and lost two for a tally of 55 points. United had played a game more but were five points adrift prior to the titanic clash. Cole had a great chance early on to score on his debut – and missed. But, in the second half, Ryan Giggs broke away, lost the ball, but somehow managed to win it back and sent an inch-perfect cross over to Cantona, who headed home the winner from close range.

In stoppage time Blackburn, agonisingly, had what would have been the equaliser disallowed as in the build-up Shearer was ruled to have fouled Roy Keane.

Dalglish was raging as he left the pitch, but this time I gave him a wide berth – once bitten, twice shy!

Cantona's flying header was a spectacular way to win the game but it was also the last goal he would score that season.

A few days later, at Selhurst Park, Cantona was sent off for lashing out at Richard Shaw. As he walked along the touchline towards the tunnel he reacted to the taunts from the Crystal Palace supporters in dramatic fashion.

The Frenchman leapt into the crowd and kung-fu kicked Matthew Simmons – stunning the football world as he did so. It was 25 January 1995 and within 48 hours the club suspended Cantona for the rest of the season. That ban was later increased by the Football Association and Cantona would not play again until the following October.

United had lost their talisman – the player who had won the league championship three times in three seasons, once with Leeds and twice with the Red Devils.

Cole's arrival helped offset Cantona's absence and he scored 12 goals in the second half of the season, including FIVE in the record 9-0 hammering of Ipswich Town – revenge indeed for that defeat at Portman Road back in September.

A couple of damaging defeats on Merseyside would slow down United's title challenge, but they never gave up and battled on until the very end. However, the real drama had not even started.

Two weeks after their defeat at Old Trafford, Blackburn were beaten by Tottenham, having been held at home by Leeds four days earlier. In all competitions their most recent five games had produced three defeats, a draw and only one win.

Were Blackburn starting to wobble? Not a bit of it. They went on another long unbeaten run, winning seven out of ten and drawing the other three games. Now they were on the brink of the title with just five matches left to play.

When the Easter programme began they had led United by eight points. That soon became six as United won 4-0 at Leicester while Blackburn were held at Leeds. On Easter Monday, United could only draw 0-0 at home to Chelsea but then Blackburn lost 3-2 at home to Manchester City, having led 2-1 at half-time.

Now there were five points between the two sides and United suddenly had the bit between their teeth. Don't forget, this was familiar territory for the men from Old Trafford – chasing down the title was becoming a habit. There were four games each left to go and Blackburn would play twice before United were next in action.

Thursday, 20 April saw another test of Blackburn's nerve as they entertained Crystal Palace. After a goalless first half, the home team exploded into life by scoring twice in three minutes through Jeff Kenna and Kevin Gallacher. With just under 20 minutes remaining Ray Houghton pulled one back for Palace and suddenly it was game on. Blackburn dug in and saw the 90 minutes out without conceding again, so they had three games left to United's four – but they led by eight points.

Upton Park was to play a pivotal role in the destination of the title even though West Ham had spent most of the season fighting relegation. A storming end to the season put those fears to rest, and when Blackburn arrived on Sunday, 30 April the Hammers were in confident mood. And with good reason, as it turned out. Harry Redknapp's team had gone six matches unbeaten before they faced the league leaders and on an atmosphere-charged Sunday afternoon in east London they made a mockery of their lowly position.

Don Hutchison and Danish international Marc Rieper scored the goals, Blackburn were second-best, and they had just two games to go, albeit with an eight-point lead.

United had had to wait 14 days to play again and they made up for lost time with a 3-2 win at Coventry City. It was a terrific game with Coventry twice hitting back to equalise. Cole scored two, including the 79th-minute winner, so United were five points behind with a game in hand.

It was Blackburn's turn to kick their heels as United played again – and won again. The 1-0 victory over Sheffield Wednesday on 7 May cut the deficit to two points with two each left to play.

Monday, 8 May produced the ultimate test of Blackburn's resolve. This was their final home game and opponents Newcastle had already won at Ewood in an FA Cup replay earlier in the season.

Alan Shearer powered home a close-range header to give Blackburn a priceless lead but after that it was the Tim Flowers show.

The popular keeper was in brilliant form that night, twice making magnificent saves to keep out Peter Beardsley and then producing an unbelievable stop to deny John Beresford.

In the tunnel afterwards a wide-eyed and clearly pumped-up Flowers told me, 'People said we don't have the bottle, but we showed plenty of bottle tonight and that's an absolutely massive win!'

It was. Blackburn led the table again by five points, and United had to win their next match or it was all over.

Forty-eight hours on from Blackburn's victory, United produced one of their own. A nerve-shredding 2-1 win at Old Trafford over Southampton ensured the title race would go down to the last day of the season. Southampton scored first early on, but Cole equalised on 21 minutes and United spent most of the next hour camped in the visitors' half.

The crucial second just would not come, until United were awarded a penalty and Denis Irwin scored to leave them just two points behind Blackburn going in to the final-day showdown.

This was the equation: If Blackburn won the Premier League was theirs; if Blackburn drew then United could still win it on goal difference, provided they were victorious; the bottom line was that anything less than a United victory and Blackburn would be celebrating their first championship in 81 years.

So on Sunday, 14 May 1995 it was Liverpool v Blackburn Rovers at Anfield and West Ham v Manchester United at Upton Park.

I went to Liverpool to see if history could be made and was rewarded with an unforgettable day.

Early on, everything seemed to be going to plan. Blackburn were bright, confident and looked dangerous. When Shearer put them ahead it was no less than they deserved.

Meanwhile, at Upton Park, Michael Hughes scored for West Ham, and at half-time Blackburn were winning the Premier League by five points. United had not won at Upton Park since 1989 and a defeat there in 1992 had handed the title to Leeds, so it was not exactly a lucky ground.

But gradually fortunes started to shift.

Brian McClair equalised early in the second half and it was United who carried the greater threat. Creating chances wasn't the problem but beating keeper Ludo Miklosko was a different proposition. The Czech was inspired that day, pulling off a string of saves to keep United at bay.

And up at Anfield things were starting to get a little more interesting. On 64 minutes John Barnes made it 1-1 and Blackburn's earlier confidence was starting to evaporate.

In the dugout Kenny Dalglish was being kept in touch with events at Upton Park and knew one more Manchester United goal would mean that the Blackburn dream was over. The fact that this was all taking place at Anfield, where he had been an absolute hero, just added to all the drama.

Back in east London, Miklosko denied United once again as both matches went into stoppage time. United's second half had started after the Rovers game but in the sunshine at Anfield referee David Elleray carried on playing.

In the fourth added minute Jamie Redknapp lashed home from 20 yards to put Liverpool ahead 2-1. Blackburn and their supporters were stunned, but it changed nothing. Provided United did not score, Blackburn would still be champions.

And seconds later they were.

News came through that Alan Wilkie had blown the final whistle at West Ham, where it had finished 1-1, and the Blackburn celebrations began. The players could see Dalglish and his backroom staff embracing each other and although Shearer nearly snatched an improbable equaliser, it wouldn't have mattered.

For the first time since 1914 Blackburn Rovers were champions of England.

Shearer's goals had played a huge part. His total of 34 equalled Cole's Premier League record set for Newcastle the previous year. Chris Sutton underlined what a talent he was too. Stuart Ripley's trickery down the flanks gave Blackburn an extra dimension. In midfield Tim Sherwood and Mark Atkins were immense. Central defender Colin Hendry led by example all season while left-back Graeme Le Saux continued to reproduce the exciting form which helped make him an England regular. And goalkeeper Tim Flowers, quite simply, proved he was one of the very best in the country.

And there were others too. My own personal favourite: at the age of 35 years and six months, and after making 15 appearances, the veteran Tony Gale landed himself a Premier League winner's medal – thanks in no small part to the heroics of his old team West Ham.

Owner Jack Walker had put his money where his mouth was and realised a life-long dream. His money helped bankroll Blackburn, enabling them to compete with the likes of Manchester United.

My interview with Kenny Dalglish just outside the Anfield dressing rooms was one of the easier ones I had conducted with him that season – and afterwards he allowed our cameras inside to capture the joyous scenes.

I sat down next to Alan Shearer and our live TV chat began well enough. Then all manner of objects started getting hurled at us. Shearer was ducking and weaving to try and avoid them while still managing to make sense. Then the beer and champagne arrived. We both got absolutely soaked but it was a great laugh.

I stank of alcohol as I drove all the way back down the M6, but I could not care less – it had been an amazing day.

Before I left there was one more slightly surreal experience. Kenny decided he wanted to interview me! The camera and microphone were rapidly produced and in the gallery they started recording.

I really was not sure how to play this. He had not exactly been Mr Friendly during this title-winning season, so I tried to mimic him by offering my 'interviewer' very little. Kenny still found it quite amusing and we ended with a handshake as Sky immediately put it to air.

In his subsequent autobiography he mentioned the interviews he did with me during that season and the jousts we had. I suppose it was quite flattering, so I am grateful to him for that – but he did put me through the wringer quite a few times!

I should say that away from the cameras and in the years that followed, he was always a very decent guy with me. Perhaps he mellowed, perhaps I learned how to deal with those situations better.

As a player I always thought of him as a total legend, particularly in his Liverpool days – and I was quite pleased when my eldest son Oliver started following the Reds (alongside Gillingham of course).

Later his daughter Kelly was to join us at Sky Sports. She was a delight, a really lovely lady, and it was great fun to work with her at the World Cup in Germany in 2006.

Blackburn was a truly great story in 1995 but you still had to feel sorry for Manchester United – they gave it their all in those closing weeks and turned the title race into a compelling drama.

Their dream of a hat-trick of consecutive titles was denied on this occasion – but not for long, as they would make it three in a row from 1999 to 2001. Seven times in the first nine years of the Premier League they emerged as champions – an awesome achievement.

I have written about my difficulties in the tunnel post-match with Kenny Dalglish, but that was nothing compared to the fall-out I once had with Alex Ferguson.

What a way to start a New Year. On 1 January 1997 I was at Old Trafford covering Manchester United against Aston Villa.

We had an agreement with Ferguson on the live games that we would ask him first as he came up the tunnel if it was okay for us to interview the man of the match when it was one of his players. He would always be ahead of the team, as invariably they would be milking the applause from the fans, but he liked them to meet him in the dressing room – even if it was for literally 30 seconds – before sending the player back out.

The system usually worked well enough. Only on this occasion Ferguson stopped to talk to the referee. He was unhappy at some of the decisions and unhappy at the goalless draw. As a result the man of the match Roy Keane was walking up the tunnel towards our cameras well ahead of his manager.

Aware of the protocol, I said to Keane, 'Roy, you are the man of the match, so if the gaffer is okay with it, will you come back out in a minute to do the chat with Sky?'

'Yes, no problem,' he replied.

Ferguson, meanwhile, had seen our exchange from further down the tunnel and when he reached me he went absolutely mental.

'What are you doing?' he said. 'You are a f***ing horrible c**t, trying to interview one of my players without my permission. You can f**k off!' I tried to explain, but he was having none of it and pushed straight past me into the dressing room. Now I am no shrinking violet and I know the language in the tunnel at the end of a game can become quite industrial as emotions run high, but I really did feel he was out of order.

A minute later, much to our surprise, Keane came out – with his manager's permission – to do the interview.

Not long after that, Ferguson emerged and we did a post-match interview live.

When it was over and Ferguson went to leave, I asked him for a quiet word.

'Alex,' I said, 'I don't care who you are, you had no right to speak to me like that in the tunnel. I had done nothing wrong, I was merely asking Roy if he would do an interview once you had given permission. I think you owe me an apology – that language was totally unacceptable'.

Ferguson stopped dead in his tracks and looked at me with a mixture of shock and incredulity. He opened his mouth, but no words came out. Then he turned on his heels and left.

The immediate reaction from my colleagues was positive. My producer Andy Melvin had told me before to stand up to the strong characters like Ferguson and Dalglish, and this time I had.

The BBC were due to interview Ferguson after me, but couldn't because he had disappeared. They reckoned it was worth missing out on the interview just to see him get his comeuppance.

I tried to explain to them that I was not trying to belittle him in any way, but that I wanted to put my point of view across. Then the whispers started that Nick Collins had pissed off Alex Ferguson in the tunnel and that Sky might have a problem.

And to a degree it appeared we did have.

For some time afterwards Ferguson was wary of me, and I felt that it was making our post-match interviews a bit stilted. I got the impression he thought I was looking to cause more trouble.

Nothing could have been further from the truth. As it happened, I left the live outside broadcast team at the end of the season to join Sky Sports Centre and then Sky Sports News, so our one-to-one interviews became very few and far between.

The last time we did a sit-down together was at the UEFA headquarters in Nyon, Switzerland. He had just become an ambassador for them, and we did a relaxed and wide-ranging interview. The hot topic at the time was David Moyes's struggles at Old Trafford after his fellow Scot succeeded him. His eyes made it clear that subject was strictly off limits, so I did not press him too hard and we parted with a warm handshake.

# 8

# England and the Road to EURO '96

EXACTLY ten weeks and 70 days after that crushing penalty shoot-out defeat to West Germany in Turin at Italia '90, the Graham Taylor era got under way with a win.

England's exploits at the World Cup had captivated the nation. There was a real feel-good factor about the national team, and Taylor was undoubtedly one of our most popular and talented young managers.

His task was to build on what Bobby Robson had achieved. True, heroes like Peter Shilton and Terry Butcher had retired, but he still had Paul Gascoigne and he still had Gary Lineker.

It was Lineker who gave Taylor his first win, in that opening game against Hungary at Wembley, and although there were no qualifying points at stake it was still important in helping to banish the heartbreak of the previous summer.

Lineker wore the armband in those early games as England lined up in a EURO '92 qualifying group with Poland, the Republic of Ireland, and Turkey.

All were teams that England had faced in the recent past, and Wembley rocked as Lineker and Peter Beardsley saw off the Poles 2-0 in the opening encounter.

Next up it was Ireland in Dublin, a midweek fixture with an afternoon kick off at Lansdowne Road. I was working for BSB back then and they did not have the rights for this game, so getting access to the players afterwards was tricky. Yet again Lineker came up trumps and so did Ireland manager Jack Charlton, who gave me a great interview while hanging out of the door of the team bus as it inched its way out of the ground. David Platt scored England's goal in a 1-1 draw.

Four months later in the return at Wembley it finished 1-1 again. Lee Dixon scored his first international goal and the by-now familiar chants of 'You'll Never Beat The Irish!' rang round. To be fair, they had a point. England had lost 1-0 in Stuttgart in their opening game of the disastrous EURO '88 tournament. It was 1-1 in Cagliari at Italia '90, then 1-1 both times in these qualifiers. To date in the three games since then we still haven't won and still they sing 'You'll Never Beat The Irish!'

Back-to-back 1-0 wins over Turkey put England in control of their group, and a 1-1 draw in Poznan saw England safely qualified for the finals in Sweden. Taylor was unbeaten in his first 12 games as England manager with nine wins and three draws, so the signs looked pretty good. The first defeat came in match 13, 1-0 against the newly-unified Germany.

His training sessions were lively and original – here was a manager at ease with his players – and as the son of a journalist he was media-friendly. The team came first, but he was very patient and spent a lot of time with the reporters who covered England.

Having scored in Taylor's first game, Lineker contributed another 11 goals in his next 13 appearances to leave him on 48 international goals and just one behind Sir Bobby Charlton's all-time record.

In the final Wembley warm-up game before EURO '92, Lineker had a chance to equal that milestone when England were awarded a penalty against Brazil.

We all groaned when his weak spot-kick was easily saved as it would have been the perfect send-off for him and the team. The game finished 1-1 so England went into the tournament unbeaten in eight.

What came next was a total anti-climax. A 0-0 draw with late entrants Denmark was not exactly the best of starts. Another goalless draw followed against France, and England found themselves needing a result against the hosts to progress to the semi-finals. They did manage to score first through Platt, but lost 2-1 and crashed out after their first defeat in 11 games.

This was the point Graham Taylor found that his honeymoon period was well and truly over.

The next day one newspaper ran the headline 'Swedes 2 Turnips 1'. The same paper later depicted Taylor's head as that root vegetable with the front-page headline 'That's Yer Allotment'.

The big story surrounded Gary Lineker. He had announced that he would be retiring after EURO '92, and with England trailing to Sweden in the second half Taylor hauled him off.

Even sub Alan Smith looked a little surprised to be replacing Lineker – it was a sad end to a fine international career, especially as it still left him tantalisingly one goal short of Charlton's scoring record.

Taylor explained afterwards that it was an attempt to help him equal the tally in the next game, by changing things round and hopefully fighting back to win. I don't think anyone really believed him – least of all Lineker, though magnanimously he said afterwards that Charlton was a far better player than him and deserved to keep the record.

The following season the World Cup qualifiers got under way – and for many England fans the prospect of the finals being staged in the United States was mouth-watering.

With two teams qualifying automatically, England appeared to be in a decent group. Holland looked the main threat, Turkey and Poland were familiar opponents who England usually got the better of, San Marino were complete outsiders, so that just left Norway.

Under manager Egil Olsen, Norway were definitely an improving side, but England would still expect to take at least three, if not four, points off them. How wrong we were. Incidentally, it is worth noting that for these qualifiers it was still two points for a win, not three.

The opener at Wembley was going well enough as Platt had put England ahead from Gascoigne's free kick just after half-time and Taylor's men looked in control. The Norwegian team did have a few familiar faces like Erik Thorstvedt (Tottenham), Roger Nilsen (Sheffield Wednesday), Stig Bjornebye (Liverpool) and Gunnar Halle (Oldham Athletic), but it was midfielder Kjetil Rekdal who stunned England with a spectacular 25-yard equaliser into the roof of the net.

Afterwards Taylor tried to look for positives and Gascoigne's performance had certainly been a plus, but whichever way you looked at it this was still a setback.

A month later Gascoigne scored twice against Turkey in a 4-0 win. Alan Shearer and Stuart Pearce were also on target. The Turks were pretty weak, but England felt that they were up and running.

The next game was three months later in February 1993 and England thrashed hapless San Marino 6-0, with Platt scoring four goals from midfield. He had the captain's armband and it seemed to inspire him. He was on target again in Izmir, a potentially difficult trip, but with Gascoigne also scoring England ran out fairly comfortable 2-0 winners to complete a double over Turkey.

Three wins and a draw seemed a pretty good start but then England hit problems, starting on 28 April 1993, and a pivotal qualifier at Wembley against Holland. After only drawing at home to Norway, this was almost must-win, and for most of the first half that's just what England looked like they were going to do.

John Barnes smashed in a wonderful left-footed free kick in the second minute for 1-0, prompting Martin Tyler on commentary to exclaim, 'Quite simply a sensational start!'

Platt's lightning reactions helped put England two up, Gascoigne was calling the tune for England and Holland were on the rack.

Later, Taylor was to describe that first half as, 'One of the best displays of my reign.'

But then right on half-time Holland got back into the game when Dennis Bergkamp scored with a sumptuous over-the-shoulder volley. In the second half, England still continued to carry the greater threat and Les Ferdinand hit the post when he should have made it 3-1. That was to prove critical.

There were two big talking points in this game: in the first half Jan Wouters appeared to blatantly elbow Gascoigne in the head, forcing England's star midfielder to go off injured at half-time. The referee missed it, or Holland would almost certainly have been down to ten men.

Five minutes from full time, with England leading 2-1, Marc Overmars broke away. Des Walker pulled him back, the initial foul taking place a yard outside the area, but Overmars's momentum carried him inside when he fell, and a penalty was awarded.

It was desperate luck for England, the spot kick was dispatched and the game ended 2-2. *The Sun*'s back-page headline screamed 'BLOODY DES-ASTER'. Yet again Taylor's side had failed to win a home qualifier, and things were to get worse as the season drew to a close.

The scheduling of two key away games in four days, on 29 May in Poland then on 2 June in Norway after a long and hard domestic campaign, massively rebounded on England.

In Katowice the team looked jaded, but Ian Wright's first international goal just minutes from the end earned a 1-1 draw.

There was no such luck in Oslo. Norway tore into England, Taylor's tactics of playing 3-4-1-2 with Gary Pallister as a third centre-back were roundly criticised, and the home side deservedly won 2-0. Towards the end England faded badly and were a little fortunate the margin wasn't even greater.

But the damage was done and after seven qualifiers England's record was three wins, three draws, and one defeat. Nothing less than three victories in the final three games would satisfy the nation and ensure qualification.

The first hurdle was cleared easily enough. England swept Poland aside at Wembley, winning 3-0 with Gascoigne on the scoresheet again.

Then came Rotterdam, where it all unravelled. Taylor's anguish was graphically captured by a TV documentary crew and unfairly led to him being ridiculed for his phrases such as 'Do I not like that.'

Yet England had every reason to feel aggrieved by the turn of events on that October night.

They were missing Stuart Pearce, Des Walker and Paul Gascoigne, Tony Dorigo's 25-yard free kick hit the post with the keeper nowhere, then Tony Adams had a shot cleared off the line.

To be fair England did have a moment of good fortune themselves as a Frank Rijkaard effort was wrongly disallowed for offside, and at half-time it was 0-0.

The big talking point came shortly before the hour as Platt accelerated past defender Ronald Koeman. The Dutchman pulled him back, it looked as if it was inside the area, and the referee awarded a penalty.

But the drama was only just starting as German official Karl-Josef Assenmacher then changed his mind after the linesman interceded and instead gave a free kick right on the 18-yard line. Worse still, he did not apply the 'professional foul' rule. FIFA was encouraging referees to issue red cards for the offence if a player was denied a clear goalscoring chance. Koeman somehow escaped a dismissal, getting away with just a yellow card – and that was to prove hugely significant just a few minutes later. To compound the error, Dorigo's free kick was charged down by the encroaching Dutch players, but again the official chose not to react.

At the other end of the pitch Paul Ince committed a foul just outside the area and Koeman stepped up to take the kick. His powerful shot crashed into the wall, but this time Assenmacher did take action – booking Ince for encroachment and ordering the free kick to be taken again.

As the England wall lined up, Koeman cleverly changed his tactics and chipped the ball over it, past David Seaman and into the net. So the man who really should not have still been on the pitch had given Holland the vital breakthrough.

That lead doubled a few minutes later as Bergkamp made it 2-0. In the press box we shook our heads as this was effectively the end of England's World Cup hopes.

It was cruel luck on Taylor – in this game it is sometimes not enough to be a good manager, you have to be a fortunate one too.

No wonder he was moved to say to the linesman that night, 'The referee's got me the sack, thank him ever so much for that won't you?'

Assenmacher never refereed an international match again.

The final act of that qualifying campaign was in Bologna, where England faced San Marino – their own tiny ground was not considered safe enough for this match. It was the first time I had been back in Italy since the 1990 World Cup, and for me personally it was to prove an oddly bitter-sweet experience.

Less than ten seconds into the game, Pearce's error allowed the no-hopers of San Marino to take the lead with the quickest goal in international history.

England's task was already pretty desperate: they needed Poland (with nothing to play for) to beat Holland, and then they also had to win by seven clear goals.

The Dutch never allowed the Poles a sniff, though once England had recovered from that early shock they did start piling on the goals. Wright scored four that night, but it was to no avail. England had finished third in their group and would not be going to the World Cup.

An emotional Pearce spoke to me on the pitch just after the final whistle and reflected that England had just not been good enough when it really counted. Yes, they had been desperately unlucky in big games, but five wins out of ten qualifiers tells its own story.

It always pained Taylor that he had failed in that qualifying campaign. Years later he remarked that he would probably be the only one who would go to his grave still regretting that England did not make it to the 1994 World Cup. Those words would have an extra poignancy when he died suddenly in January 2017. *The Times*'s headline said simply, 'We have lost a great and dignified man.'

There was a sombre mood on the plane as we flew back with the players to Luton, but England's failure to qualify had at least saved me from a bit of a dilemma.

My wedding to Sara in a few months' time on the little Greek island of Paxos could now be confirmed. With England out, I would not be going to USA '94 – so the ceremony on 2 July could take place as planned. Phew!

\* \* \* \* \*

Terry Venables succeeded Graham Taylor in late January 1994. In his time, Venables had been a really decent midfielder and won two England caps, while as a manager he enjoyed profitable spells at Crystal Palace, Queens Park Rangers, Barcelona and Tottenham.

He also found himself in the pretty unique situation of not having to qualify for a major tournament as the next one was EURO '96 and England were hosts. That meant the priority was to prepare the team for playing at Wembley, so 21 of his 24 games would be at home. That was good news for us, as Sky had the live rights for England home matches.

Denmark were Venables's first opponents, and he gave full debuts to two in-form Premier League players, Graham Le Saux and Darren Anderton, who would both go on to become regulars.

Platt scored the only goal that night and followed it up with two more in May as England gave Greece a 5-0 drubbing.

It wasn't until the fifth game of the Venables era that England even conceded a goal (to Romania in a 1-1 draw), while their first away game was match number seven against Ireland in Dublin on 15 February 1995.

It was like a trip back in time to the bad old hooligan-riddled days of the 1970s and '80s.

Even before kick-off we felt the atmosphere was confrontational, with England fans aggressively chanting 'Sieg Heil' and 'No surrender to the IRA'. We found out later that their numbers had been infiltrated by members of Combat 18, a violent neo-Nazi party formed just a few years earlier.

The Irish fans jeered the national anthem, which in turn infuriated the extremists.

The trigger point was a goal by David Kelly which put Ireland ahead after 21 minutes. England 'supporters' in the upper tier of the West Stand at Lansdowne Road began hurling missiles down on to the pitch and at the home fans below. At one stage a huge bench came cascading down into the crowd. In total 20 people were injured and around 40 were arrested.

The game – which we were televising live – was immediately halted, but the missile-throwing continued for several minutes and a lot of Irish fans spilled on to the pitch for their own safety.

Shortly afterwards, the Dutch referee Dick Jol abandoned the match and the Irish were allowed to leave, but the English contingent were kept in the ground and surrounded by a huge security presence.

Once the trouble started Geoff Shreeves and I had to rush round and establish what had happened – it was a frantic, slightly frightening, but ultimately rewarding experience.

In the *Dublin Evening Herald* the next day Cliona Foley wrote:

'Sky Sports' Nick Collins played a blinder on the sideline – up first with every story; first to mention the trouble; first to interview Graham Kelly, Terry Venables, the Chief Super and, most bizarrely, to tell us the game was abandoned a full four minutes before RTE.'

Kind words, but the reality was that Geoff also played a blinder on the sideline that night. He helped set up the interviews and kept me briefed with the latest information.

Once everything had finally calmed down and we had gone off air, we started to make our way out of the ground towards the coach for the airport. We were advised to remove our Sky coats so that we could not be identified as English. The locals, apparently, were looking for a spot of revenge.

For England the knock-on effects of the riot could have been serious. In just over one year they were due to host EURO '96 and this called into question our ability as a nation to host the tournament safely and satisfactorily. The images that were flashed around the continent of the trouble were far from flattering from an English perspective.

Happily, EURO '96 did go ahead in England and was a resounding success.

It was to be more than two decades before England and Ireland would meet again. Both occasions passed off peacefully, ending in draws (1-1 at Wembley in 2013 and 0-0 at the Aviva Stadium in Dublin in 2015).

The 1995 season ended for England with the Umbro Cup. It was a sort of dress rehearsal for the following year's European Championships, though it also featured teams from South America (Brazil) and Asia (Japan).

England squeezed past Japan 2-1 with a late Platt goal, fought back well in a thrilling 3-3 draw with Sweden at Elland Road, and were well-beaten 3-1 by tournament winners Brazil – despite taking the lead.

Not counting the abandoned game with Ireland, this was Venables's first defeat in his ten matches in charge.

Each time we would interview him afterwards and ask him what he had learned and how the preparations for the Euros were going. Each time he would play a straight bat and give us precious little information. It was understandable in a way, but frustrating for us as we contemplated the fact that we would televise every single England game (and there would be 19 of them) right up to the start of EURO '96, but would then have to step aside.

The 1995/96 season began with two goalless draws for England. The first against Colombia featured the now famous 'scorpion' kick clearance from keeper Rene Higuita. It was a fantastic piece of athleticism as the ball had passed over his head virtually on the line, before he brought his legs up behind his back to clear. Stunning! Had he missed it he would have looked extremely foolish, but I don't think that thought entered his head even for a moment.

The second game was away in Oslo – a truly turgid affair between two teams who knew each other well and were determined not to lose.

Victories over Switzerland, Bulgaria and Hungary followed, together with two more draws against Portugal and Croatia.

By May 1996, England had just one more game to get ready for the tournament and they chose to play it over 5,000 miles away in Beijing.

It was an historic first meeting between England and China, and for Venables it was a chance for the team to bond away from the spotlight in England.

You could understand the logic of that – football fever would grip the country during the summer and there would be no escaping from the iconic lines of 'Three Lions'. Football was indeed coming home.

Yet the trip did not quite go according to plan.

We greeted the England players as they arrived at Beijing Airport and if I appeared smug it was perhaps because mine was the only luggage that had arrived to that point. The rest of our party would have to wait a day or two to be re-united with their cases.

That first morning, as England relaxed and recovered from the effects of their long-haul flight, Geoff Shreeves, my cameraman Paul Quinn and I went into the centre of Beijing to film and sightsee. First stop was Tiananmen Square, scene of the notorious massacre of pro-democracy supporters in 1989, just seven years earlier. You were only allowed to film in certain directions and the police kept a close eye on us. The Forbidden City was another memorable experience and here cameras were forbidden!

After a couple of days, the jet-lag started to kick in. I awoke one day at 3.30am, just as it was getting light, and went out on to the fifth floor balcony of my room because I couldn't sleep.

A minute or so later a lone cyclist pedalled by on his way to work. A few minutes after that came another, and then another. By 6.30am the trickle had turned into a torrent – as far as the eye could see there were cyclists on the move everywhere and it was an amazing spectacle.

Katie Melua got it absolutely right when she sang, 'There are nine million bicycles in Beijing.'

The highlight, though, was definitely the Great Wall of China. The England team were making an official visit the day before the game and we were invited along to film the end of their great trek.

There was only one problem: our cable car got stuck near the top of the Great Wall and we were left hanging a little precariously over an enormous drop. To make matters worse, far below we could start to see the England players making their way along the wall towards our rendezvous point.

I was beginning to think we were going to miss the photo opportunity of the whole trip, but mercifully the cable car clanked into action again and we reached our drop-off point.

A quick sprint and we were in position to film and interview the England team in one of the most iconic places on earth. It was a real treat to sign off my piece to camera with the words, 'Nick Collins, Sky Sports, on the Great Wall of China.'

The match itself was always going to be a bit of an anti-climax after that but England won 3-0. Nick Barmby scored twice and Paul Gascoigne once.

The main interest centred around the Neville brothers. Phil's England debut (at left-back with Gary on the right) meant that they became the first footballing brothers to represent England since the Charltons. History in the making and it was good to interview them together afterwards.

The second leg of our Far East odyssey took us to Hong Kong, where England would play a Select XI in a gentle final warm-up game, with no caps being awarded.

It was also a chance for the players to let their hair down one last time before the serious business of EURO '96 got under way.

The pictures that appeared in the national newspapers over the following days made it clear that some players had had a really good time!

The Gazza 'Dentist's Chair' image, showing an extreme drinking game, was a prime example. It generated a lot of publicity – not much of it favourable – and Terry Venables was forced to defend the team in the strongest manner.

He was so angry with the way it was all being depicted that he called some of the media 'traitors'.

I think that was going a bit too far, but it was clear the Hong Kong incidents overshadowed the build-up to EURO '96 and maybe England might have been better off staying at home after all.

The three away games of the Venables era all generated headlines that were not favourable; the riot in Dublin, a desperately dull draw in Oslo, and now the drinking antics in Hong Kong, following the match in Beijing.

The tournament itself was probably a welcome relief to Venables and the players when finally it did get under way.

Because Sky did not have the broadcast rights, our roles were greatly reduced. From doing the live interviews in the tunnel after every England game we found ourselves on the outside.

Having said that, it meant we could watch and enjoy the tournament as fans.

Switzerland in the opener was frustrating, especially after Alan Shearer had broken his scoring drought in giving England the lead. The same opposition had been comfortably beaten 3-1 seven months earlier but at least England had a point on the board.

The Scotland game was extraordinary, though I must confess I could not get a ticket – so I was forced to watch it on TV at my local cricket club in Kent.

My innings (for Addington against Sevenoaks third XI) lasted all of two balls so I was back in my seat in front of the telly comfortably in time for kick-off.

This was when England really produced a performance under pressure. Shearer's second goal in two games finally put his critics to bed once and for all, David Seaman saved a penalty in the second half from Gary McAllister, and then a minute after that Gascoigne's sensational goal made it 2-0.

The technique he showed in flicking the ball up and over Colin Hendry before running round and volleying it into the net is the stuff of legend. So was the celebration afterwards as he fell on the ground and recreated the 'Dentist's Chair'.

The final group game, against Holland, was one of the best displays England have given against top opposition at a major tournament.

Shearer started it all off with his third goal in as many games – a coolly taken penalty after Paul Ince was fouled.

In the second half, Teddy Sheringham made it 2-0 with a header. The third goal was the best of the night – a brilliant combination between Gascoigne and Sheringham to set up Shearer again. Sheringham also scored again and at 4-0 Holland were going home, but they pulled one back to qualify – at the expense of Scotland. Shame.

The quarter-final against Spain was a case of conquering demons. Stuart Pearce had waited six years for another chance at a penalty shoot-out in a major tournament. He was so unlucky in Turin, but this time he was bang on target and his shriek of joy and determination was one of the abiding images of the tournament. It made the spot-kick score 3-1, and when Seaman produced another save England were on their way to the semis after triumphing 4-2 on penalties. The match itself had finished 0-0 after extra time.

For the second time in six years England would face Germany in the semi-finals of a major tournament and for the second time in six years they would lose on penalties after a 1-1 draw.

They made a great start with Shearer scoring early – his fifth goal in five games at EURO '96, which was enough to win him the Golden Boot as the leading scorer. But Stefan Kuntz soon equalised and it was still 1-1 after 90 minutes, so the game headed into extra time.

Twice England came within a whisker of scoring the Golden Goal which would have settled the game immediately. Darren Anderton hit the post and Gascoigne was just inches away from sliding the ball into the net.

Penalties. That dreaded nine-letter word as far as England were concerned.

But the confidence of coming through on spot-kicks against Spain seemed to have had a positive effect.

Shearer 1-0…top corner, sending keeper Andreas Kopke the wrong way.

Hassler 1-1…Seaman dives the right way, the ball beats him into the corner.

Platt 2-1…into the top corner just past Kopke's outstretched hand.

Strunz 2-2…sending Seaman the wrong way.

Pearce 3-2…trusty left foot sends Kopke the wrong way.

Reuter 3-3…this was the one. Seaman gets his hand to it, but can't quite keep it out.

Gascoigne 4-3…into the top-right corner, with the keeper nowhere.

Ziege 4-4…side-foots it into the corner.

Sheringham 5-4…keeper takes two steps off his line, but Teddy sends him the wrong way.

England and Seaman now one penalty save away from a major final.

Kuntz 5-5…never in doubt, now it's sudden death.

First up is Gareth Southgate and full marks for volunteering, but we couldn't help wondering, isn't there someone else? Like Paul Ince? Like Steve McManaman? Like Darren Anderton? Or like Tony Adams?

Southgate had only taken one penalty before. That was four years earlier and he hit the post. Hindsight says the body language wasn't quite right on the night. He struck the penalty low, but too near Kopke, who got a hand to it and became a German national hero.

But it was still 5-5 so could Seaman save England with a third penalty stop of the tournament?

No.

Borussia Dortmund's Andreas Moller smashed his spot-kick straight down the middle as Seaman dived left. The Germans won 6-5 and went on to beat the Czech Republic in the final – with a Golden Goal.

That was it for Terry Venables. He suffered only one defeat in 90 minutes in his 24 matches, against the reigning world champions, but he already knew he would not be getting a new contract and Glenn Hoddle, appointed in May just before the tournament, was to be the next man in the England hot seat.

# 9

# Glenn Hoddle's England

THE plane banked steeply before coming in to land. Touch-down would have woken any passengers still sleeping, as we hit the ground with quite a bang then bounced alarmingly along the bumpiest, most pothole-ridden runway I have ever experienced.

Late August 1996. Welcome to Moldova, one of Europe's newest – and poorest – countries. Wedged between Romania to the west and Ukraine to the north, east and south, this really did feel like a step into the unknown.

We were the advance party and had travelled via Frankfurt to reach the Moldovan capital Chisinau – or Kishinev as it used to be referred to in the Soviet era.

In three days' time, on Sunday, 1 September, England would kick off their World Cup Group Two qualifying campaign in eastern Europe, 1,300 miles from London – yet somehow it seemed further.

England were ranked seventh in the world after their EURO '96 exploits while Moldova were in 109th. The two things we did know about them was that they beat Wales 3-2 in a EURO '96 qualifier and that back then – according to one national newspaper – there were 'gangs of armed bandits roaming the streets'.

Happily we found no evidence of armed bandits, though the local mafia did appear to be running the casino at our hotel. Chisinau was a pleasant enough place, still coming to terms with its newly-won inde-pendence and hugely excited to be hosting the England football team. Gazza-mania had certainly spread to this European football outpost.

Our greatest sightseeing find while we were there was undoubtedly the 'Underground Wine Kingdom', 15 miles outside the capital. Wine was to prove a vital part of the fledgling Moldovan economy and it really was very good – especially the red. The Wine Kingdom stretched for miles – and I mean miles – underground, so a car was absolutely essential. Our guide told us the subterranean plot measured some 60 square kilometres. We took several bottles home with us.

Ordering food was interesting. No one in the restaurants spoke English and the menus were in Romanian or Moldovan – so we would walk around the tables of diners, until we found a dish we liked the look of, whereupon we would point excitedly at it and eventually that choice would be served up to us. By the end of our trip the system seemed to be working pretty well.

When we returned to Moldova 16 years later for a World Cup 2014 qualifier, much had changed – for a start nearly all the restaurants employed staff who could speak English. Still, we enjoyed those pioneering days.

The match in the Republican Stadium was one of many firsts: Glenn Hoddle's first game in charge of England; Alan Shearer's first game as England captain; Andy Hinchcliffe's international debut; and most significantly David Beckham's first game for England.

Yes, Beckham's bow took place in humble surroundings and in front of less than 10,000 fans, but it was a promising beginning and Hoddle definitely liked what he saw.

A couple of weeks earlier Beckham had scored a wonder goal against Wimbledon at Selhurst Park. He beat goalkeeper Neil Sullivan from the halfway line to seal a 3-0 win for Manchester United on the opening day of the Premier League season, so it was no wonder he was in Hoddle's plans.

This was England's first outing since the penalty shoot-out defeat to Germany in the semi-final of EURO '96 and they were keen to finally get that out of their system.

Nick Barmby was to have the honour of scoring the first goal of the Hoddle regime (a feat he repeated five years later when Sven-Goran Eriksson took over), and a minute later Gascoigne followed it up with a second.

That effectively killed the game as a contest, but just to make sure, new captain Shearer added a third to round off a satisfying victory and thereby avoid the proverbial banana skin.

Mind you, England did get an early shock in their next qualifier – they fell behind against Poland at Wembley after just seven minutes.

By half-time, though, they had recovered to lead 2-1 and that's how it stayed. Beckham started the fightback with a surging run and wonderfully flighted cross which Shearer headed home. Then Shearer smashed in a second after his first shot was charged down.

Played two, won two became played three, won three, after England journeyed to eastern Europe again. The venue this time was Tbilisi, the capital of Georgia. More sophisticated than Chisinau, but a lot less friendly.

The atmosphere inside the ground was a bit hostile, but goals from Teddy Sheringham and Les Ferdinand quietened things down and by the end the locals were resorting to scrapping with each other.

The Georgia star was Manchester City's Giorgi Kinkladze, but England's defence shackled him well throughout the 90 minutes, except for one breathtaking dribble in the second half. Tony Adams captained England, because Shearer was injured, while Sheringham contributed a goal and an assist on his first appearance since EURO '96.

On a personal level it was a difficult trip for me because just a few days before we flew to Tbilisi my wife Sara gave birth to our first child, Oliver. Leaving them was really tough but it had to be done. Over the years it did become a little less painful, waving goodbye to the family – basically it is the price you pay for having such a great job. It never did get easy, though.

The key games in this five-team group would be against the 1994 World Cup finalists Italy, who had beaten England when the two nations last met – in the third/fourth play-off game at Italia '90.

Unlike in England's last qualifying group, for USA '94, there were three points for a win, but crucially only the group winners would qualify. The runner-up would have to endure a two-legged play-off.

Three months after the victory in Tbilisi, England lined up at Wembley against the Italians, having made eight changes – Paul Ince,

David Batty and David Beckham the only three to remain. David Seaman, Tony Adams, Paul Gascoigne and Teddy Sheringham were all injured.

The two contentious selections were Tottenham goalkeeper Ian Walker, who was making his first – and last – start, and the mercurial Southampton playmaker Matthew Le Tissier.

I know Le Tissier can divide opinions but I was always a huge fan and felt he should have won far more than eight England caps.

His previous England start had been two years earlier, the ill-fated abandoned game in Dublin. He never played again for the senior team after the Italy match, and despite a barnstorming hat-trick for England B in 1998 he was somewhat controversially left out of Glenn Hoddle's World Cup squad that year.

To me, he was 'Le God' – an outrageously talented player and an absolute master at taking penalties, as his success rate of 47 from 48 attempts underlined.

I covered Southampton's final game at The Dell in May 2001 when fittingly Le Tissier snatched a last-gasp winner against Arsenal. It was an emotional day as the Saints said farewell to their old ground and I was grateful he let me interview him on the pitch at the final whistle. Little did we know then that we had just witnessed his last goal for Southampton as well. He never scored at St Mary's.

At Wembley that night he did miss a couple of chances, but the truth was Italy were technically superior to England and I thought it was a shame when he was replaced after 60 minutes.

Walker did not do too much wrong either, though maybe he could have done better when Chelsea's Gianfranco Zola beat him at his near post for the winning goal in the 19th minute. He had to wait more than seven years for his next England cap (as a substitute against Iceland in 2004) and that one would be his last.

So Italy were in the driving seat in terms of qualifying as England had nine points from four games, while Italy had nine from three. Hoddle had tasted his first defeat in his fourth match in charge.

England won their next four in a row before facing the Italians again in Nantes at Le Tournoi, a curtain-raiser for France '98. Two of those victories were in friendlies, but the other two were qualifiers: against Georgia at home and Poland away.

Both games finished 2-0 and the England SAS (Shearer and Sheringham) were responsible for all four goals. The victory over Poland in Chorzow was particularly impressive and meant England had 15 points from six games with just two to go. Italy still led the group by a point but they had failed to win in Poland and that had opened the door a little.

Le Tournoi was great fun to cover. England beat Italy 2-0 in Nantes in the opening round while hosts France drew 1-1 with Brazil, the game being memorable for an incredible 35-yard free kick from Brazilian defender Roberto Carlos which swerved viciously at the last minute to go in off the post and leave keeper Fabien Barthez stranded.

The two England goals against Italy had also been superb but were not quite on the same level as that free kick. Paul Scholes produced an inch-perfect ball over the top for Ian Wright to run on to and volley into the net, then just before half-time Scholes lashed home the second.

In round two England nicked a 1-0 win over France in Montpellier with Shearer scoring very late on. Italy and Brazil drew, which meant England had won the tournament with a game to spare. As I recall we went out in Montpellier and celebrated well into the early hours.

The final match in Paris against the world champions was a useful learning curve for Hoddle's team. Brazil won 1-0 but England returned home full of heart for the final two qualifiers and with a growing belief that they could win their group and then do well at France '98. I travelled home on the Eurostar, the first time I had been on the train, and really enjoyed it.

Thursday, September 1997 was a pivotal date in the qualifying group. On that night England crushed Moldova 4-0, but more significantly Italy dropped two points after only managing a 0-0 draw away to Georgia. So England were on 18 points from seven games with Italy a point behind. A draw in Rome would be enough to win the group and qualify automatically.

That was easier said than done, as England discovered. Paul Ince made history after he became England's first black captain. The decision by Hoddle to give him the armband proved inspired as Ince was England's man of the match, a bloodied hero who needed stitches in a head wound but returned to lead the rearguard action.

Italy dominated with home advantage and they needed to win to qualify automatically. England just dug in, weathered the storm and almost scored in the first half through Ince.

But off the pitch events at the Stadio Olimpico were definitely taking a turn for the worse. Italian riot police waded into the England supporters, some fierce fighting ensued, and several people were injured. It looked like a total over-reaction by the police and this was backed up by stories we heard of fans being set upon by the Carabinieri as they queued to get in – women and children were caught up in the violence.

In the second half the crowd problems calmed down, though England still found themselves in the eye of a storm. They had a lot more defending to do but gradually the clock ticked down and their task was made a little easier when Italy were reduced to ten men after Angelo di Livio was sent off for a reckless challenge on Sol Campbell.

It was nerve-wracking for the media as well as the fans. England had given everything to hold off the Italians, but stoppage time produced more drama.

Ian Wright wriggled free on the left, cut inside and shot against the post – agonisingly close for the Arsenal man. Seconds later at the other end Christian Vieri had the best chance of the whole match, but somehow he directed his header just wide – and England survived.

Hoddle and his coaching staff had a group hug on the edge of the pitch, the players went over to the fans and celebrated in front of them – perhaps an acknowledgement that they had seen the way some of the supporters had been treated.

The World Cup itself was still eight months away but Hoddle's players came of age in Rome that night and suggested that France '98 could be another exciting chapter for the national team.

England would play seven friendlies before they opened their first World Cup finals campaign in eight years, and ominously they only managed to win three of them.

A defeat at Wembley against Chile looked to be a real setback, but it was the match in which 18-year-old Michael Owen made his debut so it wasn't all bad. The final game on home soil before the World Cup was a tedious 0-0 draw against Saudi Arabia, not exactly the send-off England would have planned.

The next stop was the La Manga sports and leisure club in Spain, where England set up a warm-weather training camp. The first open session ended up being slightly delayed as players and journalists alike were enthralled by the amazing First Division play-off final between Charlton Athletic and Sunderland. It finished 4-4 with Clive Mendonca scoring a hat-trick for Charlton as they eventually made it to the Premier League thanks to a 7-6 win on penalties.

Two days later England played Morocco in Casablanca. It was the first time the two countries had met since a goalless draw in a group match at the 1986 World Cup. This time they were playing in the King Hassan II Cup, a three-team tournament which also involved Belgium. It was Paul Gascoigne's first start in six months and there was no doubting his talent as ever, but Hoddle mentally put a question mark against his fitness.

Secondly, Wright got injured. It was wretched luck for the Arsenal striker and the following evening we broke the story that he had been ruled out of the World Cup. Despite a wonderful career he was destined never to play in a major tournament.

The one real plus point for England was Michael Owen. He scored the only goal that night and clinched a place in the squad as a result. It was the first of his 40 England strikes.

Immediately after the match, England flew back to Spain before returning to Morocco 36 hours later for their final match against Belgium. The media stayed in North Africa while my cameraman David Caine and I were based all week in La Manga, filming for Sky Sports Centre – the daily news show.

Me and 'Cainey' had first met the previous August at the Stadium of Light as Sunderland officially opened their new ground with a friendly against Benfica.

We hit it off immediately and would go on to cover two World Cups and one European Championship together. He's my best mate from my time at Sky and is godfather to my youngest son Louis.

It was a bit frustrating to be left behind while the others travelled to Morocco, but it did mean we could try out La Manga's famous golf courses and use their fabulous swimming pool.

I remember Cainey saying to me, 'Enjoy this while you can, mate, because when Sky Sports News starts in four months, you'll never have the time to do this on foreign trips again.' How right he was.

England drew their second match 0-0 and lost 4-3 on penalties, so Belgium won the tournament outright and England had been beaten in yet another shoot-out. I suppose you could argue it was good practice given England's record when it came to taking penalties.

A couple of days later – on the eve of Hoddle's official squad announcement – we got word that Gascoigne had been left out and gone berserk when he realised his World Cup dream was over.

I must admit I thought he would be picked for the 22, because of the form he had shown at his two major tournaments. He was also the only member of the Italia '90 squad still involved with England. Maybe he would have had to accept a more minor role this time, but I was convinced he would go – and still believe now he should have done.

Hoddle thought otherwise. Originally he had selected a squad of 30 for the Saudi Arabia game and the two matches in Africa. Wright and Jamie Redknapp were ruled out by injury, so that meant he still had to axe six more players. He told them one by one on that Sunday afternoon. As well as Gascoigne the other players to miss out were Ian Walker, Phil Neville, Andy Hinchcliffe, Nicky Butt and Dion Dublin.

Gascoigne left La Manga in disgust, evading the media who had been dispatched to Murcia and Alicante airports in the hope of trying to catch him. He would never play for England again. When he was taken off after 50 minutes against Belgium and replaced by David Beckham that was the end of his international career.

For my money Paul Gascoigne was the best player I saw playing for England in my 26 years of covering the national team; 57 caps, ten goals, and countless moments of brilliance.

I flew to France on the opening day of the World Cup and reached my hotel room just in time to watch the second half of the opening game. Scotland put up a great fight before losing 2-1 to the defending champions Brazil.

Our base was the resort of La Baule on the west coast of France in southern Brittany. It was familiar territory – this was where we had all stayed when we covered Le Tournoi the year before.

The seven-mile-long beach was spectacular and the town itself had a good mixture of bars and restaurants.

Exactly two weeks after Hoddle's squad announcement, England opened their campaign on a Monday afternoon in the heat of Marseille.

By then the game had been completely overshadowed by the trouble and violence which had occurred around the Old Port (Vieux-Port de Marseille). We had just watched England's final training session inside the Stade Velodrome when reports started to emerge of fighting between English fans and North Africans.

My Sky News colleagues Ian Woods and Chris Skudder were dispatched straight to the scene. At one stage of the evening I remember 'Skudds' doing a live phone report into Sky News, while he was being chased through the streets!

Despite the problems, the England fans were out in force for the Tunisia game. After missing out on USA '94 they were determined to enjoy this tournament to the full and around 30,000 must have been in the stadium that afternoon.

In nine previous World Cups England had only managed to win their opening game twice, so there was real pressure on the team to get off to a good start.

Alan Shearer – who else – put England in front at the end of the first half, the captain heading in Graeme Le Saux's free kick. Paul Scholes was the star of the show and capped a fine display with a terrific shot to make it 2-0 late on. We also saw Michael Owen's first World Cup appearance, a little cameo after he replaced Teddy Sheringham, and it whetted our appetites for more. The teenager became the third-youngest player to appear at a World Cup.

A week later England faced Romania in Toulouse. Hoddle made one change to his starting line-up with Gary Neville coming in for Gareth Southgate. Romania had also won their opening game (1-0 against Colombia in Lyon) so this was very much seen as the match which would decide who finished top of Group G. There was another huge turnout from the England fans who formed the vast majority of the 33,500 crowd.

It was to be a frustrating evening. Romania had already clipped the bar before they took the lead through Viorel Moldovan just after half-time. England had their moments and Darren Anderton went desperately close from a really tight angle.

With time starting to run out Hoddle sent on Owen and with nine minutes to go he pounced to score the equaliser. That appeared to have earned England a point, but in the 90th minute Dan Petrescu out-thought and out-fought his Chelsea team-mate Le Saux to snatch a dramatic late winner. In stoppage time Owen burst through again, but his shot struck the post.

England went to Lens for their last group game knowing that a point would be enough to take them through to the last 16. Equally, Romania only had to draw with Tunisia in Paris to clinch the group (and they did with a 1-1 scoreline).

There were two changes for England with Owen coming in for his first start and Beckham replacing David Batty. It was tense early on because a defeat would mean England were out, but the team responded well and when Anderton lashed a fierce drive into the roof of the net England were on their way.

Nine minutes later Beckham scored a magnificent free kick – his first goal for England – and with less than half an hour gone they were cruising. It finished 2-0 so England were runners-up and that meant a knockout game in St Etienne against Argentina.

There was the chance of revenge after Diego Maradona's infamous 'Hand Of God' goal helped Argentina to a highly controversial quarter-final win against Bobby Robson's side at the 1986 World Cup.

The second-round tie started badly with David Seaman's legitimate challenge on Diego Simeone resulting in a penalty, and England found themselves a goal down after just six minutes.

But ten minutes later they were leading 2-1. First Owen won a penalty which Shearer converted, then Owen scored a goal which would be flashed around the world. The 18-year-old picked up the ball just inside Argentina's half, held off one challenge, danced round another and fired the ball high into the net in sensational style.

In first half stoppage time a clever free kick routine led to Javier Zanetti equalising, so it was 2-2 at the break.

Two minutes into the second half England were dealt a savage blow. The Argentine captain Simeone barged into the back of Beckham and was booked. Beckham flicked a kick at Simeone in retaliation and Danish referee Kim Milton Nielsen produced a red card. Despite the disadvantage England regrouped and battled on courageously,

Hoddle underlining what a fine tactician he had become with the way he organised the side. For one glorious moment just before the end of the 90 minutes we thought England had won it – but Sol Campbell's header was ruled out after Shearer had fouled the keeper.

England's ten men held out in extra time and no Golden Goal was scored so for the second major tournament in a row their fate would be decided by penalties.

By now our nerves were shredded in the press box – for the players it must have been torture. Argentina went first and this is how it all unfolded:

Sergio Berti scored to David Seaman's left…1-0

Shearer high into the net for his second successful penalty of the game…1-1

Hernan Crespo's penalty was brilliantly saved by Seaman diving to his left…still 1-1

Paul Ince took England's next penalty – it would have been Beckham had he not been sent off. Goalkeeper Carlos Roa went to his left just like Seaman and, just like Seaman, saved it…still 1-1

Juan Sebastian Veron scored cool as you like…2-1

Paul Merson hit a rising shot into the net…2-2

Marcello Gallardo scored easily…3-2

Michael Owen sent Roa the wrong way…and it was 3-3

No mistake from Roberto Ayala…4-3

Substitute David Batty had the chance to take it to sudden death but Roa guessed correctly, diving to his right, and making the save… Argentina win 4-3 on penalties. So England's World Cup was over after heartbreak again in a penalty shoot-out, and David Beckham was to find himself cast in the role of the villain of the piece.

When England were knocked out of the World Cup in 2006 after having to play for an hour with ten men because of Wayne Rooney's red card, manager Sven-Goran Eriksson made an impassioned plea on Rooney's behalf.

'Don't kill him,' he told the assembled media. 'He is the future.' It worked. Rooney never had to face anything like the backlash which was awaiting Beckham.

And maybe Hoddle should have taken a similar approach to the one adopted by Eriksson eight years later. While not condemning

Beckham, Hoddle spoke of the need to curb his temperamental side and made it pretty clear he held the player responsible for England's World Cup exit.

For the next few months Beckham was subjected to vile chanting every time he played away from Old Trafford. They say that what doesn't kill you makes you stronger, and that certainly applied to Beckham. He emerged from that difficult period with huge credit, became an even better player, and helped Manchester United win the Treble less than a year later.

We arrived back in La Baule at around 7am, exhausted and totally deflated. Having witnessed England now lose THREE times in penalty shoot-outs at major tournaments, I found myself briefly wanting the system scrapped – but excruciating though it is when you lose, it is still the best means of deciding drawn knockout games.

A visit to the Danish camp to film a preview of their upcoming quarter-final against Brazil in nearby Nantes was the best way to get the Argentina game out of our systems. They were very media friendly and in Peter Schmeichel they had one of the world's best goalkeepers, so they stood a chance. In the end Brazil squeezed through 3-2 while Argentina lost to a Dennis Bergkamp-inspired Holland.

That was it for us, too. Cainey and I were called home after the quarter-finals. We both had young families and could not wait to get back to see them, so we set off from La Baule at three o'clock in the morning – just as some members of the press corps were coming in from their night out!

For England there was to be no gentle introduction when it came to trying to qualify for EURO 2000 – their first match was arguably the hardest of the lot, away to Sweden in Stockholm.

Having said that, they got off to the perfect start as with just over a minute gone Alan Shearer curled a free kick into the corner to give England the lead.

Over the course of the next half hour they were to be hustled out of their stride by a Swedish team who grabbed the game by the scruff of the neck.

Under pressure, England made defensive mistakes. Seaman failed to hold a free kick and the rebound was bundled in via a deflection off Tony Adams then, two minutes later, a cross caused panic in the three-man defence and another deflection – this time off Paul Scholes – led to Jan Mjalby nipping in to make it 2-1 to Sweden.

That's how it stayed, Paul Ince was sent off in the second half (Beckham missed out through suspension because of his red card against Argentina) and for the second time in six years against Sweden in a competitive match England squandered an early lead before losing.

A minority of England fans high up in the stand behind one of the goals then gave vent to their feelings. A hot dog stand was pushed through a plate glass window and fell 60 feet into the car park housing the TV outside broadcast compound. The roof of one of the trucks was pierced by a shard of glass and there could have been fatalities if anyone had been unlucky enough to be in its way.

It was a disappointing and troubling way for the match to end. Sky News's Ian Woods was like a one-man media army as he pursued the story. At France '98 'Woodsie' taught me a lot about the skills and demands of working for a rolling news channel and it was to prove invaluable because Sky Sports News was about to launch.

As for England, they followed up the defeat to Sweden with an unimpressive 0-0 draw at home to Bulgaria, and for the first time Hoddle was starting to come under pressure.

I did not realise it at the time but that goalless draw would be the last competitive England game I saw with Hoddle in charge.

Four days later England played in Luxembourg and won 3-0 to get their first victory in this qualifying campaign. I was forced to pull out of the trip because of the impending birth of our daughter Poppy. As it happened, Poppy arrived a little later so I could have gone – but I don't think I would have been much use as my mind would very definitely have been elsewhere. Guy Havord went instead of me and did a fine job.

In November the Czech Republic visited Wembley for a friendly. Sol Campbell captained England for the first time, and without the pressure of qualifying points at stake the team produced a far more fluent display. Darren Anderton and Paul Merson scored in a 2-0 victory so England closed 1998 on a positive note. That was to be Merson's 21st and final England cap.

A hugely talented player, Merson had made his debut under Graham Taylor seven years earlier. His England career was a bit stop-start and Terry Venables never picked him because of his lifestyle issues (he loved a drink, as he detailed in his entertaining autobiography *How Not To Be A Professional Footballer*), but Hoddle restored him to the international line-up only for his successor to leave him out again.

Hoddle appeared to have weathered the storm on the pitch – but his problems were just beginning.

His relationship with some sections of the media was not all that it might have been. Certain newspapers were far from happy at a stunt he had pulled in Rome on the eve of the match with Italy in 1997.

At the final training session in the stadium Hoddle made Gareth Southgate and David Beckham sit out the part of the session to which the media had been invited, suggesting they were both injured and would not play the next night. This was reported in the national newspapers, but lo and behold both subsequently started the game. Now Hoddle claimed he was trying to outmanoeuvre the Italians, but the papers were not amused at being wrong-footed like that.

He had also been criticised in some quarters for trying to belittle Beckham at an open training session when he was showing him how to take free kicks.

Then there was faith healer Eileen Drewery. Controversially, Hoddle took her to France as part of his backroom staff. Some found that decision comical, others thought it was weird, but Hoddle liked to do things his own way.

His faith as a born-again Christian was well known, but some of his religious beliefs became a real issue after he gave an interview to Matt Dickenson of *The Times* which appeared on Saturday, 30 January 1999.

In it he suggested people with disabilities were being punished for their sins in a former life.

Several politicians were quick to condemn the comments, while Hoddle claimed he had been misinterpreted, but a media firestorm was under way and its momentum grew and grew.

By the Tuesday I was among a couple of dozen film crews camped outside the Football Association's headquarters at Lancaster Gate. We had been live with updates since six o'clock in the morning, and clearly this was going to be a long day as the FA deliberated what to do about their manager. Hoddle had already stated he was not resigning over the remarks.

His cause suffered a massive – and almost certainly fatal – blow when Prime Minister Tony Blair told *This Morning* on ITV that he should go because of what he had said. Then we heard reports that he had cleared his desk at his Wembley office and that some of the staff there were in tears as he went round saying his goodbyes.

Still we waited for official news of his resignation and eventually in the early evening the FA called a news conference at a nearby hotel.

As it started, one protestor tried to disrupt proceedings and had to be wrestled away by security staff.

FA executive director David Davies confirmed that Hoddle's contract had been terminated and said, 'The position had become increasingly untenable for both the FA and Glenn Hoddle, who accepts he made a serious error of judgement and of course he has apologised.'

Hoddle said sorry too in his brief statement and finished by wishing the new caretaker manager Howard Wilkinson good luck for the friendly against the world champions France in eight days' time.

Then he got up, walked out and climbed into the back of a chauffeur-driven FA vehicle to be taken home. His time as England manager was over.

It was a great shame in my opinion. Whatever the rights and wrongs of the affair – and you can certainly take issue over some of the things he said in that newspaper article – it somehow did not feel right that he was being dismissed for non-footballing reasons.

In a country where free speech is an absolute foundation of our society, here was a man losing his job for articulating his beliefs. Moreover, just as he used to before, he continues to donate towards charities for the disabled.

Opinion was divided because Glenn Hoddle as an international football manager had much to offer and would have continued to improve. He showed in Rome and St Etienne how tactically astute he could be, but others would argue that England were starting to go backwards in this latest qualifying campaign.

He was a great international coach but maybe not the greatest man-manager. The search was on for his replacement.

# 10

# Kevin Keegan: For Club and Country

THE Metropole Hotel in London is situated right by the A40 and is a ten-minute walk from Lord's cricket ground. This is where Kevin Keegan gave his first news conference after agreeing to take the England manager's position on a trial basis.

He was still in charge of Fulham and had four matches until the end of the season to see if he could make the dual roles work. It was 16 February 1999, just two weeks after the dramatic sacking of Glenn Hoddle, and yet another new era was about to begin.

Keegan was typically ebullient at the press conference – he was witty and charismatic in equal measure and the media lapped it up. I remember thinking that whatever was to happen, with Kevin Keegan as England manager it certainly wouldn't be dull.

I had loved watching him as a player – a quicksilver forward, with natural gifts and a real handful for opposing defences, despite being only 5ft 8in tall. He was a crowd favourite at Liverpool, Hamburg, Southampton and Newcastle after starting out at Scunthorpe United.

It was his misfortune to play for his country in an era when the national team consistently failed to qualify for the World Cup. He did finally make it in 1982, but was suffering from a back injury and appeared as a substitute in England's final game against the hosts Spain in the second group phase. He played for less than half an hour, missed a great scoring chance, and never played international football again. I was gutted.

He managed clubs the way he played: passionately with a capital P. Having taken over at Newcastle the previous year, he led them into the Premier League as First Division champions in 1993 and they took the top flight by storm.

They finished third in their first season, qualifying for Europe and scoring 82 goals – more than even champions Manchester United.

The following year they won their opening six games, scoring 22 goals, and stormed into the lead in the title race. Once they suffered their first defeat (at Manchester United on 29 October) they seemed to lose their momentum and eventually drifted out to sixth place – their cause not helped by the controversial decision to sell Andy Cole to Manchester United in that record £7m deal in January.

The Geordie fans were furious and I recall watching Keegan having to defend the board's position in front of hundreds of supporters who practically besieged St James' Park when they heard what had happened.

The following summer, Keegan made sure the club spent the Cole money on reinforcements. He brought in, among others, David Ginola, Les Ferdinand and Warren Barton – three great players and three top blokes.

Ginola was a particular favourite as he oozed French class and style, the fans adored him and he lapped it up.

A couple of years after he left Newcastle and was playing for Tottenham, I was at their training base at Chigwell when he came out into the car park and noticed my camera. Without being prompted he did the following little cameo:

'Hello, Sky, welcome to the players' car park. On my left is an Aston Martin belonging to David Howell. On my right is a Porsche belonging to Les Ferdinand. In the middle is my car, a Renault Megane. Do you know which of these three is the best? It is mine, because it is French.' Brilliant stuff.

Newcastle was our longest journey – from my home in Kent it was a round trip of over 600 miles. But we didn't mind, and in fact Sky Sports loved going up there – it was our favourite ground. The team was thrilling, the fans were amazing and we were nearly always rewarded with a real spectacle. They became known as 'The Great Entertainers' and had a period as the nation's second favourite team (outside of Sunderland). Keegan and his assistant Terry McDermott were funny as hell and quite a double act. Their favourite catchphrase was 'Wish You Well!' and they used it whenever they saw you.

Behind the jokey facade they did have a serious side and were fiercely determined to bring the Premier League title to Tyneside for the 'Toon Army', Newcastle's fanatical fans.

And, truth be told, they should have done. The 1995/96 season was the year that Newcastle United finished second, four points behind Manchester United. But it could and should have been so different.

They opened with ten wins in their first 11 games for a tally of 30 points out of 33, scoring 30 goals and conceding just seven. It was sensational stuff, their only blip coming in a 1-0 defeat at Southampton (one of Keegan's old clubs) in September.

When they went to Old Trafford on 27 December they led Manchester United by ten points. By the end of the game the cushion was just seven after former favourite Andy Cole scored early on and then Roy Keane added another in the second half.

This was the Christmas I spent in the north, in a little rented cottage in Huby, Yorkshire. It was cheaper to rent out a holiday cottage for a week than to keep coming up and down the motorways, and staying several nights in hotels.

It also meant my wife Sara and I could spend some time together over the holiday period as I had games at Leeds on Christmas Eve (they beat Manchester United 3-1), Blackburn on Boxing Day (Rovers won 2-0 against Manchester City) and then at Old Trafford a day later.

Despite that defeat, Newcastle continued to set the pace. Victories over Arsenal, Coventry and Bolton saw them extend their lead at the top to a massive 12 points in January. Surely this would be the year that they would become champions of England again, for the first time since 1927?

Keegan then produced what he hoped would be a masterstroke, the final piece of the jigsaw. In February he signed the Colombian striker Faustino Asprilla from Parma for £6.7m. Not that goals were in short supply, but Keegan loved exciting players and 'Tino' could certainly be that, with his trademark cartwheel goal celebration.

He began well, setting up the equaliser at Middlesbrough on his debut as Newcastle went on to win 2-1. His third game produced his first goal, making it 2-2 at Manchester City in a match which eventually finished 3-3.

They loved him on Tyneside but there was also a feeling among some sections of the fans that he was a bit of a disruptive influence. They believed the old mantra of 'if it ain't broke, don't fix it' and wondered why Keegan had tinkered with his winning formula.

Manchester United, meanwhile, had lost 4-1 at Tottenham on New Year's Day, but then their juggernaut started rolling.

They put together a run of five consecutive victories, the fifth one being a 6-0 win at Bolton Wanderers on an especially memorable afternoon for me, as I took a call from Sara shortly before kick-off to say her pregnancy test had confirmed that she was expecting our first child!

Monday, 4 March was the night Manchester United made it six in a row by winning at Newcastle to cut the gap down to just one point.

Goalkeeper Peter Schmeichel was magnificent, making several important saves including two from Les Ferdinand in the first five minutes. Philippe Albert then struck the bar with a great shot as Newcastle continued to dominate, but gradually United got a toe-hold in the game and six minutes into the second half Eric Cantona grabbed the winner as he converted Phil Neville's cross.

The momentum had definitely switched to Alex Ferguson's side and Newcastle soon surrendered top spot.

When Newcastle went to Anfield on Wednesday, 3 April they had lost two of their previous three games and were up against the team which would go on to finish third.

It was to be the game of the season, some would even say the game of the decade.

Because it was Newcastle the quality and entertainment was a given, but the drama turned it into a classic.

Inside two minutes and from Liverpool's first attack they found themselves trailing after Stan Collymore's cross left Robbie Fowler with an easy header.

The response was awesome. Asprilla produced some audacious skill inside the area to completely wrong-foot Neil Ruddock and set up an explosive turn and finish from Les Ferdinand. Ten minutes in and it was 1-1.

Then, from Ferdinand's pass, David Ginola surged away and struck a fierce left-footer past David James. Less than a quarter of an hour gone and the visitors led 2-1.

It was a game of 'you attack, we attack', played at breakneck pace. The crowd loved it and so did all those watching it on live TV. Keegan looked resplendent in his red jacket in the dugout at the club where he had become a star.

In the second half Keegan's jacket disappeared (replaced by a tracksuit top) and Newcastle's defence went missing too. Jason McAteer fed Steve McManaman and his cross was turned in by Fowler for the equaliser, Fowler diving headlong into the net to celebrate.

It didn't stay 2-2 for long as Asprilla beat the offside trap and curled a superb first-time shot round James to restore Newcastle's lead. The 'Great Entertainers' were at it again.

Liverpool, though, were far from finished. McAteer produced an inch-perfect cross from the right and Collymore levelled it up again at 3-3, with still more than 20 minutes to go.

The pace finally slackened but as the clock ticked down the nerves seemed to increase for Newcastle and their fans. They had taken four points from a possible 15 going into this game and were determined to prove they had what it took to maintain a title challenge.

But with seconds remaining they just could not clear the ball out of their area and it fell to the unmarked Collymore, who crashed it home to shatter the Geordies.

Keegan was famously pictured slumped in the dugout, while on commentary Martin Tyler said, 'Liverpool lead in stoppage time! Kevin Keegan hangs his head – he's devastated.' He also observed later, 'They've played like champions, but they go off beaten.'

That was not the end of Newcastle's bid to be the top team in England. In their next game they bravely came from behind to beat Queens Park Rangers, with Peter Beardsley scoring twice in the last 15 minutes.

But at Blackburn on Monday, 8 April – their third game in six days – they suffered arguably the most damaging defeat of their season.

They defended well that night and when David Batty put them ahead against his former club in the 77th minute, a priceless away win looked on the cards. With Manchester United having beaten Coventry City the day before, Newcastle were six points behind the leaders so it was absolutely vital to stay in touch.

With four minutes left they still led 1-0, but in a cruel twist of fate they conceded two late goals that were created and scored by two Newcastle-born players. Alan Shearer set them both up and 21-year-old Graham Fenton had the game of his life to put both chances away. Up until then he had only scored one goal for Blackburn.

From a psychological point of view this was a major, major blow. Keegan didn't quite concede the title that night but he talked about how pleased he would still be if his team could finish as runners-up.

So United were the red-hot favourites and closing in on a third Premier League crown in four seasons. Their form in recent weeks had been outstanding. Since beating Newcastle they had won four and drawn one, extending their unbeaten record to 12 games and taking 32 points out of a possible 36.

By contrast Newcastle's wretched run had seen them lose five times in eight games with seven points from a possible 24.

On the south coast, United were about to suffer a grey day. They trailed 3-0 at half-time to Southampton and Alex Ferguson claimed it was because his players could not pick out their team-mates in their grey away strips! It was a novel explanation and United were allowed to change to blue shirts, but they still lost 3-1; a case of 13th time unlucky after 12 without defeat.

Newcastle beat Aston Villa with a Ferdinand goal and followed that up with another 1-0 win at home to Southampton. On the same night, United laboured to a 1-0 home win over Leeds, who played for over 70 minutes with only ten men after goalkeeper Mark Beeney was sent off. Defender Lucas Radebe took over between the sticks, though it was Peter Schmeichel who was by far the busier keeper.

When the final week of the Premier League began, Manchester United topped the table with 79 points from their 37 games and a goal difference of +35. Newcastle were six points behind them with a goal difference of +28 – but, importantly, with two games in hand.

They were away to Leeds United and Nottingham Forest but that meant they would have to play three times between Tuesday and Sunday, while United had only the one fixture left – at Middlesbrough. With a superior goal difference (thanks to having just won their final home game against Forest 5-0) they really were in the driving seat.

And it was at this point that Ferguson introduced a little bit of psychological warfare into the title race. He suggested that Leeds, who were old rivals of his club, would not try as hard against Newcastle – and nor would Forest two days later. It was classic Fergie mind games and it had the desired effect.

Keegan was incensed by the remarks, and the implication that Newcastle would have an easier time of it than United. We were all about to discover just how livid he was after the final whistle at Elland Road.

Ironically, Newcastle did make it look easier against the 11 men of Leeds than United had managed against their ten earlier in the month. Keith Gillespie scored the only goal of the game and the gap at the top was back to three points.

Over the years a lot of people have come up to me and asked what it was like to be on the other end of the famous Keegan rant, and I have to tell them that it wasn't me! Keegan was wearing headphones and was doing his post-match reaction directly with the studio and presenter Richard Keys.

Richard suggested to Keegan that Ferguson's comments were all part and parcel of the inevitable war-of-words that accompanies major sport now, the 'psychological battle'.

In a voice charged with emotion, Keegan shook his head and with much jabbing of his finger, he said:

'No that's…when you do that with footballers, like he said about Leeds, and when you do things like that about a man like Stuart Pearce, I've kept really quiet, but I'll tell you something, he went down in my estimation when he said that. We've not resorted to that, but I'll tell you, you can tell him now if you're watching it, we're still fighting for this title, and he's got to go to Middlesbrough and get something and…and…I'll tell you, honestly, I WILL LOVE IT IF WE BEAT THEM. LOVE IT!'

It was an extraordinary outburst, all the more dramatic because it was live on TV. Keegan always wore his heart on his sleeve – this was the ultimate demonstration of that – and it has gone down in folklore as one of the great moments in the history of the Premier League. Forty-eight hours on from that victory at Elland Road, Newcastle were back in action at the City Ground. They led 1-0 at half-time with a Peter Beardsley goal and, if it had stayed that way, they would have pulled back six points on Manchester United in just a couple of days. Moreover, they would have been level with them at the top going into the final game.

Perhaps the exertions of the last few weeks finally caught up with them. Maybe their manager's meltdown on live TV had some sort of impact. Whatever it was, in the second half Newcastle could not consolidate their lead and with 15 minutes to go Forest hit back to equalise through Ian Woan. It finished 1-1, so after 37 games each they were two points behind United and with a significantly inferior goal difference.

This was the first season after the Premier League had been reduced from 22 clubs to 20 so there were only 38 games each – instead of 42. Yet Newcastle still found themselves playing Tuesday, Thursday, Sunday as their campaign ended. That sort of schedule would be frowned upon a lot more these days.

I went to the Riverside Stadium on that final day and had no doubts that I would see the new champions crowned. It duly happened. David May scored after 15 minutes, with Andy Cole and Ryan Giggs adding second half goals in a regulation 3-0 win.

As I sat interviewing some of the United players in the dressing room afterwards it became clear that this was a team which still believed it had plenty more to achieve. It struck me then that their appetite for success was insatiable; Ferguson had three Premier League titles and he believed there was still plenty more to come. There was huge satisfaction that – having lost the title on the final day of the previous season – they had won it back on the final day of this one.

Don't forget they were 12 points behind Newcastle in January, so it was a phenomenal comeback. Just one defeat in their last 16 games, with 13 wins and two draws, saw them take an incredible 41 points out of 48 and they were worthy champions.

Having said that, it was almost impossible not to feel sorry for Kevin Keegan and Newcastle United. They played some fabulous and exhilarating football but faltered just as Ferguson's men found their wings, which made for some compelling drama.

Realistically, on that last day their only hope was for United to lose. Even a draw meant that Newcastle would have to beat Tottenham by seven clear goals.

Almost inevitably it was an anti-climax. Ferdinand scored his 25th league goal of the season to salvage a 1-1 draw as Newcastle failed to win at home for only the second time all season (that defeat to United was the other one).

Keegan licked his wounds and came back the following season a stronger and wiser man, but also a sadder one.

He had one glorious moment when he kind of got even with Ferguson, but he would have swapped the 5-0 victory that October day for the title the previous season in a heartbeat.

Nevertheless, it was gripping stuff as the champions and league leaders were humbled. It was Manchester United's heaviest league defeat in 12 years, their first of the season, and it saw Newcastle replace them on top.

Alan Shearer was the architect of the victory. In the summer he had signed for his hometown club in a world record £15m deal and needed no extra motivation to put one over United. He scored one, made one, hit the post from nearly 30 yards out and generally ran the defence ragged.

David Ginola also scored a stunner but my favourite goal was the fifth – an absolutely glorious chip from Belgian defender Philippe Albert. Three months later Keegan was gone, having resigned on 8 January 1997 with the following statement:

'It was my decision and my decision alone to resign. I feel I have taken the club as far as I can, and that it would be in the best interests of all concerned if I resigned now. I wish the club and everyone concerned with it all the best for the future.'

Was it because he would not give the chairman Sir John Hall a long-term commitment? He had told the board he wished to resign at the end of the season. Or was he still upset at having to sell Andy Cole to title rivals Manchester United in 1995? Perhaps the pressure of the previous season's failed title campaign finally proved all too much.

Whatever the reason, 'King Kev' was off. Gone, but never forgotten, and he was back in football again before too long.

He joined Second Division Fulham as chief operating officer in September 1997 and became head coach the following May after Ray Wilkins was sacked just ahead of the play-off semi-final against Grimsby Town.

Fulham lost on that occasion, but – backed by the money of owner Mohamed Al-Fayed – Keegan did help deliver promotion to the First Division the following season.

He took part in the on-pitch celebrations at Craven Cottage at the end as the trophy was presented, but by now he was concentrating on England full-time. He had soon realised it would be practically impossible to do both jobs and his heart was set on trying to re-ignite England's faltering qualifying campaign for EURO 2000.

Sweden had stormed clear at the top after beating England in their opening qualifier and Keegan inherited a team with a win, a draw, and a defeat from their three games.

On a sunny Saturday afternoon in March, Keegan's England breathed new life into the qualifying group with a convincing 3-1 victory over Poland. The star of the show was Manchester United's Paul Scholes, who hit his first international hat-trick.

Wearing red, England stormed ahead after just ten minutes when Scholes nipped in to lift the ball over the goalkeeper. It was 2-0 on 21 minutes, albeit with a touch of fortune as Scholes appeared to turn in David Beckham's cross with his arm. Poland pulled one back soon afterwards but England would not be denied – 18 efforts at goal during the match underlined their dominance – and Scholes made it 3-1 inside the final 20 minutes with a header.

Keegan had paired together two of his favourite strikers, Andy Cole and Alan Shearer, had given midfielder Tim Sherwood a debut at the age of 30, and also introduced substitute Ray Parlour for his first England cap.

Above all he was positive. Beforehand he had pledged that his England team would not be afraid to attack and his arrival did appear to have given the national team a real shot in the arm. A month later we were all in Budapest, watching on with great amusement as Keegan wowed the locals at the end of the training session by scoring a stunning goal. He then wheeled away in a comical over-the-top celebration which had everyone laughing. His enthusiasm was infectious and we all looked forward to how his new-look side might perform against Hungary.

The night before the game, our interpreter took us up to the Royal Palace which overlooked the city – it was a stunning sight, with the River Danube running right through the middle. Buda on one side and Pest on the other, I still don't know which was which.

Wes Brown and Kevin Phillips were given their debuts from the start, with Michael Gray, Jamie Carragher and Emile Heskey all winning their first caps when they came on as substitutes. Keegan was determined to get a good look at the depth (or otherwise) of the talent at his disposal, but the game itself was a bit of a let-down.

After a promising start from England it finished 1-1 as Hungary cancelled out Shearer's penalty with an equaliser inside the last 15 minutes.

Still, I suppose we shouldn't complain. The Nep (People's) Stadium, where the game was played, was also the scene of England's biggest ever defeat, a 7-1 rout back in May 1954. The legendary Ferenc Puskas opened the scoring on ten minutes and after just over an hour England were trailing 7-0, before scoring a consolation goal.

In June England faced two qualifiers in the space of four days, which would give us a much clearer idea of whether the team was making progress. By now Keegan had fully committed himself to the national cause, signing a permanent deal.

Sweden came to Wembley and showed why they were clear at the top of the group, frustrating England at every opportunity in a 0-0 draw. Scholes was sent off so he missed the trip to Sofia.

More disappointment followed in the Bulgarian capital. Shearer gave England the lead but they conceded an equaliser soon after and in the second half were forced to hang on. Nineteen-year-old debutant Jonathan Woodgate made one last-ditch tackle, and despite being reduced to ten men by a red card, the hosts were pushing hard at the end.

After six games England had only two victories, with three draws and a defeat. Worryingly, they trailed Poland by three points with only two matches to go – and one of them was away to the Poles in Warsaw. Just making the play-offs was going to be tough.

In early September at Wembley, Keegan was smiling again after watching England thrash Luxembourg 6-0. Kieron Dyer made a sparkling debut at full-back while Shearer grabbed his first and only international hat-trick.

England were 5-0 up at half-time with Steve McManaman scoring his first two goals for his country to go with Shearer's three. Perhaps even more pleasing was that Michael Owen returned from injury to play his first game of the Keegan era – and he rounded off the scoring with the best goal of the afternoon, a sumptuous 20-yard curling shot into the top corner.

Now there was just one game to go – away to group rivals Poland. Both teams had 12 points, but Poland had a game in hand (away to Sweden), so England knew that a defeat would mean it was all over.

It was never a pretty game and England failed to find their rhythm – their cause not helped by an early injury to Gary Neville, who was stretchered off in the opening 15 minutes.

For their fans it wasn't a pleasant evening either as Polish supporters threw lighted flares into the visitors' section – and some suffered burns.

On the pitch England felt they should have had a penalty, chances continued to go begging and inside the last ten minutes David Batty was sent off. This was the third red card of the qualifying campaign (Paul Ince and Paul Scholes had collected the others) and it pretty much meant England would have to settle for a draw.

In the closing stages Poland's Andrzej Juskowiak had a great chance from four yards out, but his effort was straight at goalkeeper Nigel Martyn – otherwise England would have failed to qualify for Euro 2000.

As it was, their hopes were still dependent on Poland losing their last group game the following month away to Sweden. England had the better goal difference and head-to-head record, so they had a chance, but it would still be nerve-wracking.

The match took place in Stockholm on 9 October, the day before England were due to face Belgium in a friendly at Sunderland's Stadium of Light.

Keegan took training at the ground and planned to watch the Poland game there. Not surprisingly, he turned down our request to let us film him as he did so.

But from behind the locked door we heard a whoop of joy as Kennet Anderson put the Swedes in front on 64 minutes, then a roar of delight when Henrik Larsson made it 2-0 in the final minute. England had squeezed into the play-offs and Keegan was elated.

Although he hadn't let us film him watching (and I don't blame him), he was a really good guy to work with and gave us lots of – often exclusive – filming opportunities, whether it was playing basketball or pool with disadvantaged kids in inner London, or clowning around with pop group Atomic Kitten.

Four days after Sweden's victory the draw for the play-offs took place in Aachen, just over the Dutch border in Germany. There was no seeding, which meant England could face – among others – Ireland or Scotland. After the events of Dublin 1995 there was huge nervousness within the Football Association about the prospect of a two-legged game against the Irish.

In the end the first match drawn out was Scotland versus England, international football's oldest rivalry, with England having home advantage in the second leg.

So just over three years on from Paul Gascoigne's exploits at Wembley in EURO '96, the two would do it all over again. The prize at stake this time was a place in the main draw at EURO 2000.

My cameraman David Caine and I drove up to Glasgow with a mixture of excitement and trepidation. How would England cope in the cauldron of Hampden Park, a ground they had not visited in more than a decade?

Not surprisingly, Keegan opted for an experienced line-up: Seaman in goal; a back four of Campbell, Keown, Adams and Phil Neville; Beckham, Ince, Scholes and Redknapp in midfield; Shearer and Owen up front.

Keegan loved the idea of this being a local derby, the 'Battle Of Britain', and a winner-takes-all contest over two legs. It was just the sort of occasion that would bring the best out of him as a player – and luckily for him it also brought the best out of Scholes.

Before the start I had never heard the national anthem booed to the extent it was that day – it was totally drowned out. 'Cainey' and I didn't react, but inside both of us hoped England's team would be raging at what had happened and respond accordingly.

They did. After an early flurry from Scotland, England began to get on top. Sol Campbell swung a long ball in, Scholes took it on his chest and then lashed it past Neil Sullivan for the opener.

Moments later Kevin Gallacher raced through one-on-one with David Seaman for what looked like a certain equaliser, but Seaman saved superbly with his legs to keep the English lead intact. The Scots must have been fed up with the sight of him after that save and his penalty heroics against them at EURO '96.

Four minutes before half-time, Beckham's free kick was met by Scholes who out-jumped taller men to plant a fierce header into the back of the net for 2-0. Dreamland.

In the second half England sat back and defended their lead. Truth be told there weren't too many alarms and that two-goal advantage from the away leg looked to be decisive.

Keegan said afterwards, 'We've started under my reign to play the way I want to play.' Scotland manager Craig Brown, meanwhile, refused to give up and nor did his team.

Gareth Southgate for Martin Keown was the only change England made for the second leg at Wembley four days later. One goal would surely finish it, but the longer the game went on without England scoring the more tense it became.

Scotland outfought and outplayed England that night. From my pitchside position behind the goal it was excruciating to watch, and it was no surprise when Don Hutchison headed in Neil McCann's cross to give Scotland the lead six minutes before half-time.

Now it was game on again and England were no better in the second half – they failed to have a single shot on target in the entire 90 minutes. Hutchison had another chance, but could not take it, and yet again it was Seaman to England's rescue as a point-blank save ten minutes from time denied Christian Dailly and Scotland their moment of glory.

England were through 2-1 on aggregate and were going to Holland and Belgium for EURO 2000 – but they had limped into the finals and the feeling among the media was that it would be a bit of a struggle when it all got under way the following summer.

Before then the draw for the tournament took place in Brussels in December 1999. England were in the bottom pot of countries, because of their poor qualifying record. No team reached EURO 2000 with fewer points than England – their total of 13 was nine fewer than group winners Sweden.

So the pairings were never going to be particularly favourable, but it could have been worse. England were drawn in Group A along with top seeds Germany (winners of qualifying Group 3), Romania (winners of Group 7) and Portugal (as best runners-up, also in Group 7). But they did avoid the fancied co-hosts Holland and the world champions France.

England's opening match of 2000 came on 23 February against Argentina at Wembley. It was the first of four preparation games ahead of the championships in the summer.

It was billed as a repeat of the dramatic 1998 St Etienne encounter at the World Cup, David Beckham up against his nemesis Diego Simeone. The occasion could not hope to live up to that kind of comparison and the match ended 0-0, although it was a good test for England against the side ranked sixth in the world.

Before kick-off both teams observed a minute's silence after the death of Sir Stanley Matthews was announced earlier in the day. I never saw him play live, but I did interview him a couple of times and was never in any doubt just how important a figure he was in English football history.

To keep playing in the top flight to the age of 50 was extraordinary – his club career with Stoke City and Blackpool spanned 33 years, while he played for England from 1934 to 1957. He won 54 caps for his country and played a further 29 wartime internationals.

He'll forever be remembered for the 'Matthews Final' of 1953, when he inspired Blackpool's famous comeback from 3-1 down to beat Bolton Wanderers 4-3 in the FA Cup Final. At the time 'The Wizard of Dribble' was 38 and he carried on playing for England until he was 42, his final appearance for his country coming in a World

Cup qualifier away to Denmark in Copenhagen on 15 May 1957. Fittingly, England won 4-1.

World Cup runners-up Brazil were the next visitors to Wembley, less than three weeks before the start of EURO 2000. Michael Owen was in top form and thoroughly deserved his well-taken goal to put England into the lead. It did not last long as within minutes Brazil equalised from a corner, and this was to be a worrying trait for Keegan's England in the upcoming tournament: their failure to protect a lead.

Their final home game was against Ukraine, a last chance for the players to force their way into Keegan's plans before he announced his EURO 2000 squad.

And Steven Gerrard did just that. A mature and assured debut from the Liverpool youngster – just one day after his 20th birthday – meant he was on his way to the European Championships.

Teenager Gareth Barry came on as a second-half substitute for his debut and he too would win an 11th-hour place in Keegan's squad.

Both England goals that night came from Beckham corners. The first was just before half-time, when the goalkeeper could not hold Alan Shearer's header and Robbie Fowler poked the ball home from two yards out.

The second was a moment of history – although we did not know it at the time. Tony Adams scored his first in an England shirt since November 1988, a record gap between goals of 11 and a half years. It was also the last goal scored by an England player under the Twin Towers before the old stadium was closed for seven years and redeveloped.

Afterwards, Keegan announced his 22-man squad and there was no place for Andy Cole. This raised more than a few eyebrows, before Keegan explained that Cole had picked up a foot injury.

'If he had been fit I definitely would have taken him,' he insisted.

David James lost out to Richard Wright as third-choice goalkeeper, while Rio Ferdinand and Kieron Dyer were also omitted.

The last warm-up game was in Valletta on the sunny island of Malta, nine days before England opened their EURO 2000 campaign, so this was an ideal opportunity for fine-tuning on and off the pitch. The media worked hard and played hard on that trip, aware of how busy they would be once the tournament got under way.

Wright made his debut in goal and it was to be an incident-packed first appearance.

After Martin Keown had headed England in front on 22 minutes, Wright soon gave away a penalty, when he brought down David Carabott. The player got up and stuck the spot kick away with a confident shot but the Italian referee then ordered it to be re-taken because of encroachment. This time Carabott hit the post, but the rebound went in off Wright's head and Malta were level – the first time they had ever scored against England, even if it was an own goal.

On 50 minutes Shearer landed awkwardly and injured his knee, and after treatment he sat on the touchline with a large bag of ice around the injured joint. The next few days would be a race against time to see whether the England captain would recover quickly enough to play in the opening game against Portugal.

Emile Heskey replaced Shearer and scored his first England goal on 75 minutes with a tap-in, but two minutes from the end Wright gave away another penalty. Carabott sent him the wrong way, but fortunately the Ipswich Town man saved it with his legs. He then made a similar stop in added time to preserve England's 2-1 lead.

Victorious but unconvincing was the media reaction in a nutshell.

The next stop was Spa, a beautiful little town in eastern Belgium, where England had chosen to base themselves during the tournament. World-famous for the treatments which gave the place its name, this was also home to the Belgian Grand Prix. The circuit was in the next village of Francorchamps.

Intriguingly, Spa was also the 'birthplace' for Agatha Christie's renowned fictional detective Hercule Poirot.

For England it was all about settling in and preparing for Portugal in Eindhoven on 12 June. Shearer's knee gradually began to heal and the skipper did make it for the tournament opener.

Two minutes and 40 seconds into that game David Beckham crossed from the right and his Manchester United team-mate Paul Scholes headed the ball in off the bar to give England a flying start.

It got even better as inside 20 minutes Beckham produced another high-quality centre and Steve McManaman volleyed England into a 2-0 lead. This was the kind of football Keegan had been dreaming that his side would play: high-tempo and with plenty of width.

Unfortunately the defence had no real answer to Portugal's attacking flair and this game would soon be turned on its head.

Within four minutes of England's second goal, Portugal had the ball in the net twice – one that didn't count and one that did. Luis Figo scored a superb goal on the break with the help of a deflection and England's early confidence drained away.

Before half-time Portugal were level, Joao Pinto somehow squeezing a diving header past both Sol Campbell and David Seaman. He had scored eight goals in the qualifiers, so perhaps it was no surprise.

The winner came on the hour when Nuno Gomes completed a fine move with a deadly finish and from 2-0 down Portugal had come back to win 3-2. England contributed hugely to a fantastic spectacle but that was scant consolation. With Germany and Romania drawing their match 1-1 it meant England were already bottom of the group.

Cue the time-honoured siege mentality syndrome. Keegan was not quite so forthcoming in his news conferences, as England sought to turn things round, but who could blame him? Next up was Germany and defeat was not an option.

Tony Adams and Steve McManaman had picked up injuries, so were unavailable. In came Martin Keown and Chelsea's Dennis Wise – England would be combative, if nothing else.

The Stade du Pays in Charleroi was one of the smallest venues at EURO 2000, which was a great shame, because this meeting of two of Europe's keenest rivals deserved a bigger stage. A lot has been written about the crowd problems in the town beforehand – images of the water cannons being deployed were flashed around the world, but I wasn't there and will just stick to the football.

England had not beaten the unified German team in three attempts, and their last victory over West Germany had come in Mexico City back in 1985. Since then Germany had inflicted two major tournament semi-final penalty shoot-out defeats on England. Say no more.

While Germany had cruised their qualifying group with six wins and a draw from their eight games, they had come off second-best against a vibrant Romania side in the drawn game in Liege.

So the stage was set in Charleroi for what we hoped would be another memorable encounter, and earlier in the evening Portugal had defeated Romania 1-0 in Arnhem with a goal in the fifth minute of stoppage time to completely seize control of the group.

It was a tight, evenly-fought game. England kept their nerve and their composure. Those who say that Keegan's tactics were too naïve for international football should remember the discipline they showed in this fixture.

Germany shaded it early on, but then Oliver Kahn was forced to produce a magnificent save to keep out a goal-bound Michael Owen header, and he also denied Paul Scholes.

Eight minutes into the second half Beckham's free kick caused mayhem in the German defence and the ball found its way to Shearer at the back post. He stooped to power a header past Kahn, giving England a vital lead. It was the 29th goal of his England career and few can have given him more pleasure.

Back came Germany and it started to get really tense. Carsten Jancker and Mehmet Scholl both spurned good opportunities, before David Seaman made a magnificent point-blank save from Ulf Kirsten.

Steven Gerrard had come on for the last half-hour to make his competitive debut and looked totally at ease in this environment. It was a great shame that a subsequent injury meant he would play no further part in the tournament.

When Pierluigi Collina blew the final whistle there was celebration and relief in equal measure. England had beaten Germany in a competitive game for the first time since the 1966 World Cup Final!

Portugal had qualified whatever happened next, but England were up to second place and needed just a draw from their final group game against Romania – also in Charleroi – three days later.

Minutes before kick-off, Seaman picked up an injury and was forced to pull out of the line-up. Nigel Martyn was rapidly drafted in and made a fine save in the opening stages.

Romania were bright and dangerous early on, but their first goal had a huge slice of luck about it as Cristian Chivu's intended cross went in off the far post to leave England trailing.

The comeback had shades of St Etienne about it. First, Shearer converted a penalty for the equaliser, then Owen nipped in soon after to give England the lead, calmly beating the onrushing goalkeeper and scoring from a tight angle.

Leading 2-1 at half-time, England had one foot in the quarter-finals. But just as they had surrendered a goal to Portugal soon after going 2-0 up, so they did here just three minutes into the second half. Martyn failed to gather a cross and Dorinel Munteanu thrashed the ball back past him. Hanging on to a lead wasn't one of this team's strong points.

Amid mounting tension England inched closer to the last eight as the minutes ticked down. Romania needed to win and continued to push forward. In the final minute Viorel Moldovan got the better of Phil Neville and the Manchester United defender gave away a penalty as he tried to win the ball back. Nightmare.

Sub Ioan Ganea sent Martyn the wrong way and for the second major tournament in a row England had lost to Romania, only this time they were out.

After the final whistle and still in a state of numbness, 'Cainey' and I raced for the car. Our plan was to beat the team bus (complete with police escort) back to the training base and get some shots of the players arriving back.

We managed it – just. We were kept at a distance as we filmed the players trooping off despondently, but three men remained on the bus at the back. Despite England's EURO 2000 exit there was an important card game taking place. Keegan folded first, followed several minutes later by Owen and then the (presumably) victorious Shearer.

The next day the captain was given a special ovation by the press as he attended his farewell England news conference. It was not the way he would have wanted to bow out, but after 63 matches and 30 goals he was concentrating on his club career and international retirement – at the age of 29 – was the only way he could do that. Over the coming years Newcastle's gain would be very much England's loss.

Unsurprisingly, Keegan got a fair amount of criticism, but he expressed a desire to carry on and in September we were all in Paris to see his team face the world and European champions.

France used the friendly as a way to say thank you and goodbye to two of their all-time greats, Laurent Blanc and Didier Deschamps, who were both making their final appearances. When they were both substituted on the hour they took several minutes waving their farewells and I think the England players got a little fed up with it all.

That said, France scored soon after through Manu Petit, who beat his former Arsenal team-mate Seaman with an exquisite shot. England would not give in and fought back to grab an equaliser on 86 minutes from substitute Owen. While the French were claiming for a foul on Bixente Lizarazu, England swept up the field and Kieron Dyer delivered a beautiful cross which Owen expertly flicked in at the near post.

It was a creditable draw against international football's team of the moment, and we wondered how the side would fare as qualifying got under way for the 2002 World Cup.

It all began on a slate-grey day at Wembley, with unrelenting rain and somehow an air of foreboding as the famous old stadium staged its final England match before redevelopment and a seven-year closure.

The fact that Germany were again the opponents was another cause for concern. They came looking for revenge from Charleroi and they got it. Instead of building on the EURO 2000 victory, England seemed hesitant and they were certainly architects of their own downfall.

After 14 minutes Germany were awarded a free kick 30 yards out when Paul Scholes fouled Michael Ballack. The wall was slow to form and David Seaman was slow to respond as Dietmar Hamann caught everyone napping, his shot somehow finding its way past the distraught goalkeeper.

England had their moments but they were few and far between. The experiment of playing Gareth Southgate as a holding midfielder did not really work and at the final whistle the boos and catcalls rang out at Wembley as Keegan strode down the tunnel.

A few minutes later it emerged he had resigned. The players tried to talk him out of it, but his mind was made up.

'I just don't feel I can find that little bit extra you need at this level to find a winning formula. I just feel I have given it my best shot. I don't want to outstay my welcome,' he said.

Unbeaten in his first eight games in charge, Keegan then lost four of his last ten. His final record was seven wins, seven draws and four defeats.

Howard Wilkinson was hurriedly appointed caretaker manager because in a few days England had another qualifier in Helsinki against Finland.

Had Keegan left the team in the lurch? The timing of his resignation was far from ideal, but if he felt in his own mind he could get no more out of his group then it was the right decision.

He was a fascinating character to work with and football had by no means heard the last of Kevin Keegan.

England, meanwhile, drew 0-0 with a pretty average performance against the Finns, which made it more important than ever that a permanent successor be found. The question was who?

# 11

# The Arrival of Arsene Wenger

I FIRST interviewed Arsene Wenger on 14 January 1997 at a hotel in the north-east of England. On the same night just a few miles away Kenny Dalglish was giving his first news conference after being unveiled as the new Newcastle United manager following the resignation of Kevin Keegan.

I remember thinking at the time that I had drawn the short straw – St James' Park was where the real story was unfolding, but in fact I came to realise over the years that, actually, the opposite was true.

We were covering Arsenal's FA Cup third round replay at Sunderland and this would be one of my last visits to Roker Park before it closed at the end of the season. What an amazingly atmospheric old ground it was, and cup nights there were even more special. The Stadium of Light is a great venue but I do miss Roker Park.

This was Arsenal's third consecutive game against Sunderland. They had drawn 1-1 in the original tie at Highbury, with Michael Gray equalising John Hartson's opener for the home side.

The two teams then met in the Premier League, with Sunderland pulling off a surprise 1-0 win. Dennis Bergkamp was sent off in the opening half-hour before a Tony Adams own goal settled the match. It was one to forget from Arsenal's point of view and I was interested to find out how Wenger would approach this return to Wearside.

What I discovered was that he was a man who loved the FA Cup. The studious Frenchman impressed me from the very start, a very different character to the likes of Ferguson and Dalglish. If you asked him a straight question he would try to give you a straight answer. No other top Premier League manager was so ready to discuss all manner of subjects – he was genuinely a breath of fresh air. If you were respectful to him he would be respectful back to you, and that was fine by me.

That's not to say he couldn't be difficult too. He was by no means a soft touch and you had to come to his news conferences well prepared, but that is why I liked interviewing him so much.

The very first time he appeared before the English media at Highbury it had been a case of 'Arsene who?' More than 20 years on, how different it is now!

In that first interview Arsene made the point to me that he had been brought up watching the FA Cup Final live on French TV and that it was a competition he had a burning desire to win. He had seen his team go out of the League Cup to Liverpool on a dramatic night at Anfield back in November.

It was a match of three penalties, a red card for Steve Bould, and ultimately a 4-2 defeat. In the UEFA Cup he watched on as Borussia Monchengladbach got the better of Arsenal 6-4 on aggregate before he officially took over.

This was Arsenal's last realistic chance of silverware for the season and Wenger made sure they were pumped up for the replay. Bergkamp responded to his red card a few days earlier by scoring the first goal. Stephen Hughes also netted his only FA Cup goal for Arsenal in a fairly routine 2-0 win. Sadly for them they were to lose 1-0 at home to Leeds United in the next round.

For Wenger, that first season was very much a learning curve. He had enjoyed success in France with Monaco and also in Japan, but this was a different level and he soon realised that. It helped that he won his first Premier League game, 2-0 at former champions Blackburn – Ian Wright with both the goals.

I always remember speaking to Arsenal vice-chairman David Dein in 1997 and he had no doubts back then that the club had appointed the man who would usher in a new era of success. Hindsight can be a wonderful gift, but Dein instead predicted exactly what would happen at his club so fair play to him.

The best thing that Wenger did in those early months was to beat Tottenham in the north London derby, even though his team left it late. Arsenal led 1-0 at half-time with a Wright penalty, then Andy Sinton equalised just before the hour and with two minutes to go it was still 1-1. Goals from Adams and Bergkamp sealed a 3-1 win and the fans were chanting the new manager's name as they streamed out of Highbury.

Six wins and two draws from their final ten games propelled Arsenal up to third place but they were denied the runners-up spot and a place in the Champions League by Newcastle on goal difference. Arsene Wenger had announced his presence and this was just the start.

It was a strange Premier League season in many ways. Liverpool led the table until late March, Newcastle had had their moments too, but in the end the experience of Alex Ferguson and Manchester United proved decisive.

Yet in the autumn they suffered a meltdown that could have broken lesser teams and weaker managers. I told you about their 5-0 thrashing at Newcastle in the last chapter. The following week they lost 6-3 at Southampton, Eyal Berkovic and Egil Ostenstad scoring five goals between them. They also lost at home to Fenerbahce in the Champions League – their first home defeat in Europe in 40 years – and followed that up by losing 2-1 at Old Trafford to bogey team Chelsea. That was their first home league reverse in two years, yet the response was typical.

They then went 16 league games unbeaten, before losing at Sunderland, but won a vital league encounter in April at Anfield 3-1 with Gary Pallister of all people scoring twice.

Liverpool put together their strongest title challenge for several years and at one stage they had been five points clear before tailing off at the end. They began the last day of the season in second place, yet finished fourth.

They did manage to beat runners-up Newcastle 4-3 for the second year running and yet again it was an epic game. Steve McManaman, Patrik Berger and Robbie Fowler gave the Reds a 3-0 lead at half-time and it looked all over. With less than 20 minutes to go it was still 3-0, then Keith Gillespie scored to give the Geordies hope. Tino Asprilla pulled another one back on 87 minutes and within 60 seconds Warren Barton somehow made it 3-3.

Then the football gods deserted Newcastle and for the second time in 12 months they conceded the crucial fourth goal in added time – Fowler with his second of the night.

It was a magnificent game, but not as good – or as significant – as the one the previous season. However, I will always remember it because this was the last match at which I had a cigarette.

Ever since my son Oliver had been born, in October 1996, I knew I had to give up smoking. My wife Sara had packed in the moment she had discovered she was pregnant, but I carried on through that season and into EURO '96.

I wouldn't smoke at home and on days off would only have a couple of fags out in the garden. Once I was back at work it was a different story (20 a day no problem). There was no alternative: I just had to quit.

I bought a packet of cigarettes on the journey up to Liverpool on Monday, 10 March. The plan was to make them last all week, gradually weaning myself off the habit. That day and on the long drive home I smoked 19 (what an idiot) and I realised it would have to be now or never.

The following afternoon I walked out on to our terrace in the back garden at four o'clock with a glass of white wine in my hand and smoked my last cigarette. I won't lie, I bloody loved it! Having said that, giving up wasn't as hard as I expected. I had the best of reasons for doing it, and two decades later I am still a non-smoker.

Back to the football, and Manchester United were closing in on another title. They were ruthlessly efficient but suffered a bit after losing in the Champions League semi-final to Borussia Dortmund and Paul Lambert. European success was becoming increasingly important to the club as they continued to dominate domestically – and success wasn't too far away.

The title was won on 6 May without the players having to kick a ball. Liverpool lost 2-1 at Wimbledon and that was it. Manchester United were champions for a fourth time in five years.

It was difficult to know where the challenge to their dominance would come from, but come it did. And the man who led the charge was called Arsene Wenger.

The first time I saw Arsenal play live in the 1997/98 season was away to Leicester City at Filbert Street at the end of August. Already the team were full of goals – Ian Wright scored three in the first two games, then Dennis Bergkamp cashed in with two in the third match (a 3-1 win at Southampton).

Wenger had introduced a new, flowing continental style to Arsenal and watching them play over the years would become a pleasure for fans and neutrals alike.

Inside ten minutes Marc Overmars played a corner straight to Bergkamp. He took one touch then smashed the ball into the top corner from 20 yards out and goalkeeper Kasey Keller never even moved. Just after the hour it was 2-0, Bergkamp again, though he did get lucky with a deflection to beat Keller.

Leicester stormed back as this game turned into an absolute thriller. Emile Heskey exploited an error from David Seaman to make it 2-1, then the inspirational Matt Elliott squeezed in the equaliser in stoppage time.

Bergkamp soon restored Arsenal's lead, completing his hat-trick with a sublime goal. He chested the ball down, flicked it from his right foot to his left foot, then back again before slotting it home. This was football almost from another planet.

It was a goal worthy of winning any game – but it didn't win this one, because never-say-die Leicester had one last response. In the fifth minute of added time captain Steve Walsh sent a thumping header past Seaman for 3-3.

Wenger was hugely frustrated at losing two points so late on, but proud of the way his team had played overall. Leicester boss Martin O'Neill described Bergkamp's three goals as, 'The best hat-trick I've ever seen.' A couple of weeks later the spotlight was on Ian Wright. Visitors Bolton Wanderers had taken a surprise lead but Wright led the fightback, scoring a fine equaliser with an angled drive. He then whipped off his shirt to reveal a vest with 179 on it. Cliff Bastin was Arsenal's previous all-time record goalscorer with 178, and Wrighty thought he had the outright record.

But there was one problem – that goal was his 178th, not number 179. Happily he didn't have long to wait to set the record straight. A surging run through the middle by Bergkamp saw the ball eventually fall to Wright two yards out and with an empty goal. He couldn't miss and he didn't. It was one of the easiest goals he had ever scored, but then the celebrations could begin in earnest all over again.

Nine minutes from time he volleyed in David Platt's cross to complete his hat-trick and provide the fairytale ending to an historic day. He was such a popular, lively character with an infectious enthusiasm and we were all delighted for him.

The Wright/Bergkamp double act wasn't finished yet. In the next game Bergkamp grabbed two more in a 3-2 win at Chelsea, then they both scored in a 4-0 triumph over West Ham. The ninth game was a 2-2 draw at Everton and Wright scored.

Game number ten was a 5-0 demolition of newly promoted Barnsley. Bergkamp got two more and Wright also scored. Ten matches in and Arsenal had scored 26 goals, with Bergkamp and Wright responsible for 19 of them with the Dutchman edging it 10-9.

That goal against Barnsley was the last one Wright ever scored at Highbury. After a lightning start to the campaign, hamstring problems set in and he scored only one more in the league that season.

For a while the goals dried up for the team, and in their (unlucky) 13th match they suffered their first defeat: a 3-0 reverse at Derby County.

The next opponents were the champions and league leaders Manchester United, who arrived at Highbury off the back of two thumping home victories which had seen them score 13 goals. They thrashed Barnsley 7-0 with Andy Cole netting a hat-trick and whacked Sheffield Wednesday 6-1, when Cole scored twice and so did Teddy Sheringham.

And Sheringham scored two more in the first half of this game as United staged a great recovery from two goals down. Nicholas Anelka and Patrick Vieira had given Arsenal a commanding lead then Sheringham struck twice in eight minutes.

The second half wasn't quite as frantic but it had a dramatic ending with David Platt scoring an 83rd-minute winner to cut the gap at the top to just a point. It was Arsene Wenger's first victory over Alex Ferguson and it would not be the last that season either. United responded by winning their next six league games to stretch away again while Arsenal hit a sticky patch, with a sequence of four defeats in six games up to Christmas.

I went to the Boxing Day return game with Leicester. This time Arsenal won 2-1, with the Filbert Street hero Steve Walsh scoring an own goal which proved decisive.

In January, Wenger's side faced eight matches, five of which were cup ties. It took them two games, three and a half hours and a penalty shoot-out to see off plucky Port Vale in the third round of the FA Cup. Goals from Wright and Marc Overmars then helped them to a 2-1 win at West Ham United in the quarter-finals of the League Cup. Overmars was on target again as they won at Middlesbrough to reach round five of the FA Cup, and then he scored the opener in a 2-1 League Cup semi-final first leg win over Chelsea.

The month ended with a routine 3-0 win over Southampton, but then Wenger found himself facing a crazy sequence of EIGHT consecutive London derbies in the league and cup.

They beat Chelsea 2-0 in the Premier League but were then held 0-0 at Highbury by Crystal Palace in the FA Cup. Three days later it was Chelsea again, this time in the second leg of the League Cup semi.

It did not go well. Already losing to a Mark Hughes goal, they had Vieira sent off and conceded two more in the space of five minutes early in the second half. Bergkamp pulled a late penalty back, but it finished 4-3 on aggregate to Chelsea and they would go on to beat Middlesbrough in the final.

Typically, Wenger made sure his team bounced back. They beat Crystal Palace 1-0 in the league, then won the FA Cup replay 2-1 at Selhurst Park four days later. Palace played for over an hour with ten men and Arsenal scored twice in the opening 28 minutes through Nicolas Anelka and Bergkamp.

Next it was West Ham away in the league, where Arsenal slogged out a 0-0 draw, before facing the same opponents at home in the FA Cup quarter-finals. It was another draw (1-1 this time) and meant another replay.

The eighth and final game of the sequence was a 1-0 win at Wimbledon thanks to a goal from Christopher Wreh, which netted three more valuable points. At last Arsenal took on a team from outside London. Only it was the champions Manchester United at Old Trafford and they were nine points clear of Wenger's men, but had played three games more. Also Arsenal were on a roll, unbeaten in nine league games with six victories during that time.

Wenger would do the double over Ferguson as his team eased to a crucial 1-0 win with Overmars getting the all-important goal after 79 minutes. Yes, it was 1-0 to the Arsenal that day, but it hadn't been a gritty George Graham-type of success. This team looked comfortable passing it around and they had plenty of rock solid players too like Adams, Keown, Vieira and Petit to name but four.

Overmars was in a class of his own in that match. He shot inches wide from a tight angle, had a penalty claim turned down and hit the side-netting before deservedly scoring Arsenal's first goal at Old Trafford in the Premier League era. He nodded the ball down into his path then finished with a left-footed shot, before standing still to take the plaudits from his joyful team-mates.

Two more 1-0 wins followed before the end of the month and Arsenal went into April three points behind, but with two games in hand. Yet they had to wait for United to play twice more (a win against Blackburn and a draw with Liverpool) before they were back in action.

So the gap briefly stretched to seven points, but Arsenal had four games in hand. A 3-1 win over Newcastle was followed by a crushing 4-1 victory at Blackburn (the last team to beat them in the league, back in December) and they were back within a point of United having played two games fewer.

The leadership of the Premier League finally changed hands on 18 April. That afternoon, Arsenal stormed into an early three-goal lead against Wimbledon with Adams, Overmars and Bergkamp all scoring inside the first 20 minutes. It finished 5-0, while Manchester United were being held by Newcastle.

A win over Barnsley soon extended Arsenal's lead to four points and the end was coming into sight. In his first full season in charge Arsene Wenger was about to become the first non-British manager to win the English title. When they beat Derby County 1-0 with a Manu Petit goal on 25 April they restored their four-point lead and

Manchester United only had two games left. One more victory would be enough – and it came against Everton in style.

Admittedly Slaven Bilic gave them an early lift with a sixth-minute own goal, but this was always going to be Arsenal's day. Overmars plundered two more goals to make it 3-0, then at the end came the moment which in a sense defined Arsenal's style under Wenger. Central defender Steve Bould chipped a clever ball over the top of the Everton defence and his defensive partner Tony Adams ran through to score. That sealed an extraordinary tenth consecutive victory.

Commentator Martin Tyler was spot on as he said, 'That sums it all up…Arsenal awesome!'

Thirteen days later in the Wembley sunshine against Newcastle United goals from Overmars and Nicolas Anelka gave them the 'double Double', the second time the club had won the league and FA Cup in the same season.

This was the first FA Cup Final I had missed since 1989 as I was on holiday in Minorca before getting ready for several weeks away at the World Cup in France. It would be 2011 before I was absent from another of the showpiece occasions.

It was a fantastic achievement by Wenger – the start of the Arsenal revolution – but following it up would prove a lot harder and over the next three seasons his team had to get used to playing second fiddle. Manchester United won the title in 1999, 2000, and 2001, and each time Arsenal were runners-up.

The 1998/99 campaign was the 100th season of top-flight football in England. It began with the Double winners Arsenal comfortably beating Manchester United in the Charity Shield at Wembley. For Wenger it must have felt like normal service had resumed, as goals from Overmars, Wreh and Anelka gave them a 3-0 win.

Victory in their opening league game at Nottingham Forest on *Monday Night Football* seemed to underline that, but a run of four consecutive draws rocked them back on their heels.

At this point they faced United again, and beat them again 3-0 to move above them in the table. This time it was Adams, Anelka and Freddie Ljungberg who scored.

Nicky Butt was sent off after 51 minutes and he then repeated the feat in the Champions League against Barcelona three days later.

United had led 2-0, got pegged back to 2-2, but were 3-2 ahead thanks to a David Beckham goal when Butt got his red card. Luis Enrique, who later managed Barcelona to Champions League and La Liga glory, scored from the resulting penalty as it ended 3-3.

There was no respite for the men from Old Trafford. They saw off their great rivals Liverpool 2-0 in the next game and then had to face a Champions League group match at Bayern Munich. After going a goal down, United led 2-1 until Giovane Elber scored in the 90th minute to snatch a point. Revenge would be even sweeter (and even later) on the biggest club stage of all at the end of the season.

The return with Barcelona was another six-goal thriller. United found themselves 1-0 down, then 3-1 up before two goals from the Brazilian Rivaldo saw it finish 3-3 again. Another draw in the return game at home to Bayern and two comprehensive victories over the Danish champions Brondby (5-1 and 6-2) were enough to see Alex Ferguson's side through to the knockout stages.

Arsenal were not as successful. They had to play their home games at Wembley and won only once in three attempts. Defeats in Kiev and then at the Twin Towers against Lens sealed their fate. To compound a miserable November they also lost 5-0 at home to Chelsea in the League Cup.

In all competitions they managed just two wins and three draws from a run of ten games and were looking vulnerable.

It was at this stage that Wenger's team started to recapture the magic of the previous season as they unleashed a formidable unbeaten run. From mid-December they did not lose another Premier League game until May and were beaten in only one other match – yet those two defeats were to be the difference between repeating the double and finishing empty-handed. It's extraordinary to think that a sequence of 20 wins and five draws from 26 games would not be enough to retain either of their crowns.

Highbury was a virtual fortress all season: 15 wins and four draws in the league, with only five goals conceded at home.

Arsenal were also involved in a truly bizarre FA Cup tie. The defence of their trophy had already been incident-packed. In round three they trailed 2-0 at Preston before fighting back to win 4-2, helped by a red card for their opponents.

On 13 February in round five they took on second-tier Sheffield United. With less than 15 minutes to play the score stood at 1-1 when Blades keeper Alan Kelly deliberately put the ball into touch so that injured team-mate Lee Morris could be treated. As convention demanded, when play restarted Ray Parlour took the throw-in, intending for the ball to be returned to Sheffield United. He hadn't reckoned on the enthusiasm of debutant Nwankwo Kanu, who seized on the loose ball and charged down the line before crossing into the path of Marc Overmars. The Dutchman instinctively put the ball in the net for 2-1 as all hell broke loose.

The Arsenal players understood the howls of protest from the visitors and immediately offered a rematch, which was accepted. The original game was removed from the records so technically their run was 19 wins and five draws from 25 matches.

The rescheduled tie also finished 2-1, then Kanu grabbed an 89th-minute winner in the quarter-final with Derby, so Arsenal would line up against Manchester United in the semis at Villa Park.

United's route to the last four had also included juggling Champions League commitments, so their long unbeaten run was – if anything – even more impressive.

While Arsenal had endured a pretty miserable November, United embarked on a sequence of games which saw them win only once in nine games in all competitions before they were finally successful at home to Nottingham Forest on Boxing Day.

What followed next almost defied belief. They went 33 games unbeaten all the way to the end of the season, after displaying an incredible capacity time and again to snatch victories from the jaws of defeats (and draws).

They racked up eight wins on the bounce in the new year, before being held at home 1-1 by Arsenal. A week and a half before that game they had gone to Forest and won 8-1 with substitute Ole Gunnar Solskjaer scoring four times in the last ten minutes (so I suppose we should not have been too surprised at how their season eventually ended).

In the fourth round of the FA Cup they trailed Liverpool for 85 minutes, yet still managed a 2-1 victory with Dwight Yorke scoring in the 88th minute and Solskjaer (who else) in the 90th. In the third round against Middlesbrough (the last team to beat them that season) they had been losing at half-time before recovering to win. They needed a replay before beating Chelsea in the quarter-finals at Stamford Bridge and their showdown with Arsenal was very much seen as the battle of the big two.

This one went to a replay too, the first game a 0-0 stalemate as Arsenal hung on with ten men after Nelson Vivas got a red card.

The second match is famous for possibly the best goal ever scored in the FA Cup but it was also a game which in a sense defined both clubs' seasons, United somehow securing a vital victory, Arsenal letting glory slip between their fingers.

The first goal was superb, yet it is barely mentioned because of what followed. David Beckham curled a great shot past David Seaman from 25 yards and United were in front after 17 minutes.

Bergkamp produced an equaliser midway through the second half and a few minutes later, when David Elleray sent off Roy Keane in an FA Cup semi-final for the second time, the writing looked on the wall for United.

In stoppage time Phil Neville hauled down Ray Parlour inside the area and Bergkamp had the chance to take the holders back to Wembley. He struck the ball decently enough but Peter Schmeichel dived to his left to produce a superb save. That was Bergkamp's fourth missed penalty from his last six attempts. He never took a spot kick again.

Ten minutes from the end of extra time Patrick Vieira gave the ball away in Manchester United's half and Ryan Giggs seized on to it. He then proceeded to run for nearly 70 yards, twisting this way and that, beating four defenders in the process and crashing the ball past Seaman for a dramatically spectacular winner.

Sky's co-commentator Andy Gray was for once rendered almost speechless. He could only say, 'Words fail me, words fail me!'

At the fifth time of asking United had finally beaten Arsenal in 1998/99. Their Treble dreams still shone brightly while Wenger's 'double Double' hopes were smashed to pieces.

In the Champions League quarter-final United had been clinging on to a 2-1 aggregate lead at the San Siro against Inter Milan before Paul Scholes came up with a priceless 88th-minute goal to put the tie beyond the Italians.

In the first leg of the semi-final, Juventus led at Old Trafford through an Antonio Conte goal until the 90th minute when Ryan Giggs snatched a precious equaliser to give them a chance in the return.

And what a game that would prove to be. Filippo Inzaghi gave Juve a 2-0 lead (3-1 on aggregate) and United looked to be heading out. Keane pulled one back and inspired his team-mates that night with a huge performance. A booking meant he would be suspended from the final, as was the case for Paul Scholes, but he refused to let that affect him. Dwight Yorke equalised and then six minutes from time Andy Cole produced the winner to put United in the final for the first time in 31 years.

This two-week period the team enjoyed during April would go down in folklore. Starting with the first leg against Juventus, they then faced those two FA Cup semi-final clashes with Arsenal before returning to Premier League action and beating Sheffield Wednesday 3-0 at Old Trafford – then came that night in Turin.

Perhaps unsurprisingly, after all that excitement United drew three of their next five games to hand Arsenal the initiative in the title race.

Wenger had looked stunned and devastated when he walked down the tunnel at Villa Park after losing that semi-final, but he rallied his troops brilliantly.

In the next game Arsenal scored five goals in a 25-minute spell to overwhelm Wimbledon and they then smashed in six more at Middlesbrough on 24 April to go back to the top of the table.

On Wednesday, 5 May Arsenal went to White Hart Lane and produced a masterclass in finishing, winning the north London derby 3-1 and going three points clear at the top with just two games to play.

This looked to be the most decisive night of the season because at the same time Manchester United let a two-goal lead slip at Anfield against Liverpool, Paul Ince equalising in the 88th minute against his former club. I think many felt the balance of power had finally shifted in Arsenal's favour and that Wenger was about to win back-to-back Premier League titles.

But United dusted themselves down and won 1-0 at Middlesbrough, taking full advantage of their game in hand, so the teams were level at the top again.

Arsenal's penultimate game was at Leeds on Tuesday, 11 May. They lost 1-0 to a Jimmy Floyd Hasselbaink goal in the 86th minute and handed the momentum right back to United. Wenger would never give up but deep down he probably knew that was the moment the league slipped away from his side.

The next night United went to Blackburn, earned a 0-0 draw and crucially led the table by a point going into the last day. Their destiny was in their own hands – if they won they would be champions, whatever Arsenal did.

I was the touchline reporter at Highbury for their clash with Aston Villa, and the atmosphere was really subdued – they could still retain their title yet somehow it just never felt likely to happen that day. Many Arsenal fans felt Tottenham were unlikely to play out of their skins to beat Manchester United and thereby hand the titled to their greatest rivals.

Having said that, Les Ferdinand did put Tottenham ahead at Old Trafford to give Arsenal hope but in the space of five minutes either side of half-time goals from David Beckham and Andy Cole extinguished that hope and gave United a 2-1 lead. All they had to do was hang on.

Arsenal breathed life into the last-day drama by scoring in the 66th minute through Kanu. If Spurs then equalised Arsenal could still be champions but it never happened. Manchester United finished 2-1 winners and ended up with 79 points, Arsenal a point behind on 78.

The following weekend I was at Wembley as Manchester United took on Newcastle in the FA Cup Final. Just like the previous year Newcastle found themselves facing a team chasing the double. And just like the previous year they lost 2-0.

Teddy Sheringham (11 minutes) and Paul Scholes (53) put United in control, and when I interviewed the players on the pitch after the final whistle it was clear their mindset was two down, one to go. Yes, they were delighted to have won the FA Cup again and completed the domestic Double for the third time in six seasons, but the overriding feeling was that there was still unfinished business – namely the Champions League Final in Barcelona four days later.

The professionalism was really admirable and they would need every ounce of their unshakeable self-belief.

Six minutes into the final, United were rocked back on their heels when Mario Basler scored a deflected free kick for Bayern Munich. Now they would have to do it the hard way. The third meeting between these two clubs was another tense and tight affair and United kept on probing, but could not find a way through the German team's defence. They missed their leader Roy Keane and the midfield brilliance of Paul Scholes.

Alex Ferguson sent on Teddy Sheringham after 67 minutes, then introduced Ole Gunnar Solskjaer for Andy Cole with nine minutes to go. They still trailed in stoppage time so their giant goalkeeper Peter Schmeichel – captain in Keane's absence, and playing his final game for United – was coming up for corners.

Beckham swung another one over, Bayern failed to clear and Sheringham pounced to equalise. I was watching at home as ITV commentator Clive Tydesley immediately said, 'Name on the trophy.' Hats off to him – it certainly was.

Another Beckham corner led to another Manchester United goal from a substitute. Sheringham headed the ball down into the path of Solskjaer and the Norwegian with the knack for scoring late on volleyed in from close range for 2-1. Write that script if you dare!

No wonder a jubilant Alex Ferguson said afterwards, 'I can't believe it. Football, bloody hell!'

Arsene Wenger could only watch on in admiration. In an incredibly tight season his own team had come desperately close to retaining the Double themselves, and he was determined that Arsenal would topple United from their position as English football's champion team.

When they beat United in the Charity Shield at the start of the following season it looked a good omen. Arsenal trailed at half-time but hit back to win 2-1 with goals from Nwankwo Kanu and Ray Parlour.

Three weeks later in the Premier League at Highbury it was a different story. This time Arsenal led 1-0 at half-time, only for the champions to score twice after the interval. Both goals came from Roy Keane, the winner in the 88th minute. That set the tone as United swept their challengers aside in the league, retaining their title in utterly dominant fashion and winning it by an 18-point margin.

A week after that defeat, Arsenal were beaten at Liverpool, then in October they lost a fractious London derby against West Ham. Patrick Vieira was sent off for two bookable offences and squared up to Neil Ruddock as he left the field. The Frenchman appeared to spit at the Hammers defender before going on to clash with a police officer in the players' tunnel. He was eventually fined a record £45,000 and banned for six matches, much to Wenger's disappointment. A difficult season had just got harder.

Before Vieira actually served the suspension, Arsenal went to White Hart Lane in November but within 20 minutes they were 2-0 down. Ironically it was Vieira who pulled them back in to the game with a goal just before half-time. Then Freddie Ljungberg (53 minutes) and Martin Keown (90) were both sent off as Arsenal finished with nine men and Wenger tasted defeat against Tottenham for the first time in his three years at Arsenal.

The Champions League campaign was no happier – Barcelona and Fiorentina both won at Arsenal's temporary European home of Wembley – and they failed to get out of the group, which meant UEFA Cup football later in the season.

A spell of two wins in ten games between December and February effectively ended Arsenal's hopes in the Premier League (though they did manage a 1-1 draw at Old Trafford during that period).

On Boxing Day they had lost 3-2 to Coventry City, prompting Wenger to break up the famous Arsenal back-line. For the next game he axed Lee Dixon, Nigel Winterburn and Martin Keown. In a sense it was the end of an era.

In the FA Cup Arsenal went out 6-5 on penalties to Leicester City after two matches and three and a half hours of football failed to produce a single goal.

It had been a similar story in the League Cup. Ten days after putting five past Middlesbrough in the league game, they were held to a 2-2 draw by the same opponents and were eliminated on penalties again.

But the season was by no means over as Arsenal went on another glorious charge. Between March and May they won 12 consecutive matches, which secured second place in the table, four points ahead of Leeds. The sequence was ended by a 3-3 draw at home to Sheffield Wednesday, but even then they had fought back from 3-1 down.

Four of those victories came in the quarter-finals and semi-finals of the UEFA Cup. After disposing of Spanish side Deportivo 6-3 on aggregate in the last 16, Arsenal were paired with Werder Bremen from Germany. Thierry Henry and Freddie Ljungberg scored in a 2-0 win in the first leg at Highbury. Henry also scored in the second leg, but he was sent off and missed the first leg of the semi-final through suspension. Ray Parlour was the Arsenal hero in Bremen, scoring a hat-trick as Arsenal triumphed 4-2 and 6-2 on aggregate.

An early Bergkamp goal gave Arsenal a narrow advantage to take to northern France for the second leg of the semi against Lens. Henry gave Arsenal the lead with a vital away goal, Pascal Nourma equalised after 73 minutes, but Kanu wrapped it up in the 86th minute to send Arsenal into the UEFA Cup Final 3-1 on aggregate.

Their opponents would be the Turkish champions Galatasaray, who had dashed dreams of an all-English final by defeating Leeds United in the other semi-final. The first leg in Istanbul was totally overshadowed by crowd violence ahead of the match and two Leeds fans were stabbed to death in Taksim Square. The home side won 2-0 but that seemed totally irrelevant after what had happened.

Before the second leg Arsenal played at Elland Road in the Premier League and presented bouquets of flowers to the Leeds players. The flowers were laid at all four corners of the ground and both teams observed a minute's silence as a mark of respect for the supporters who had died.

It was billed as a potential dress rehearsal for the final, but it proved very one-sided. Arsenal won 4-0 and took a giant step towards qualifying for the Champions League at Leeds's expense.

Galatasaray played out a 2-2 draw in the second leg to advance to the final in Copenhagen on 17 May. Three days prior to meeting the Turkish side, Arsenal finished their league programme with a defeat against Newcastle after resting several players.

Sadly there was crowd trouble in the streets of the Danish capital as well, where the focus of the fighting was in City Hall Square. Four more supporters were stabbed, though none fatally. It is such a wonderful city and the Danes were very hospitable, though I suppose the violence was almost inevitable after what had happened to the Leeds fans.

Both teams had chances to score in the opening 90 minutes but it remained 0-0, which meant extra time and the Golden Goal rule. Galatasaray's Romanian playmaker Gheorghe Hagi was sent off early in extra time after clashing with Tony Adams and Arsenal should have made the extra man count. Henry was brilliantly denied by Brazilian keeper Claudio Taffarel who somehow kept out the Frenchman's close-range header. He also made a double save from Kanu.

After 120 goalless minutes the final went to penalties and for Arsenal it was a case of third time unlucky. After going out of the League Cup and FA Cup in penalty shoot-outs they suffered spot kick heartache once again.

Galatasaray went first and scored, David Seaman diving the wrong way: 1-0.

Davor Suker took Arsenal's opening penalty. He hit the inside of the post and watched it roll along the line before eventually rebounding away: still 1-0.

Hakan Sukur chipped an audacious penalty into the corner: 2-0.

Ray Parlour confidently scored for Arsenal: 2-1.

Cool as you like Umit Davala scored down the middle: 3-1.

Patrick Vieira was next up. He sent Taffarel the wrong way – and watched in horror as the ball struck the underside of the bar and bounced away: still 3-1.

Gheorghe Popescu, the team's other Romanian star, then scored in the corner to complete the demolition job: 4-1.

Galatasaray celebrated on the pitch after becoming the first Turkish team to win a European trophy. Arsenal were left to reflect on a season defined by three penalty shoot-out defeats.

\* \* \* \* \*

On the final day of the Premier League season I had gone to The Dell to watch the beginning of the end for one of football's ultimate rags-to-riches stories. Wimbledon went into that game fourth from bottom and needing to match Bradford City's result to avoid relegation.

Before the season had even started manager Joe Kinnear was forced to resign through ill health. The former Norwegian national manager Egil Olsen – the scourge of Graham Taylor's England – had been put in charge, but was sacked a couple of weeks from the end of the season after a defeat against Bradford.

I was fascinated to see if Wimbledon's famous never-say-die attitude and fighting spirit would save them. They showed all of that and more, but just did not have the quality and lost 2-0 to second-half goals from Wayne Bridge and Marian Pahars.

Worse still for them, Bradford conjured up an amazing 1-0 win over Liverpool. David Wetherall scored the all-important goal, Bradford survived, and Liverpool missed out on a place in the following season's Champions League.

So, after 14 seasons in the top flight Wimbledon were relegated – by a cruel irony it was exactly 12 years to the day since their famous FA Cup Final victory over Liverpool.

As for Manchester United, they ended the Premier League season with 11 straight wins to finish on 91 points with Arsenal a distant second on 73.

Controversially, they were unable to defend the FA Cup after the Football Association requested them to play in the inaugural FIFA World Club Cup instead. The government also got involved and the thinking at the time was that it might help England's chances of landing the 2006 FIFA World Cup – some hope!

The tournament took place in Brazil in January 2000 and United failed to make the third/fourth play-off on goal difference after a win, a draw, and a defeat.

But they had enjoyed success against South American opposition when they beat Palmeiras 1-0 to win the Intercontinental Cup in Tokyo two months earlier. Captain Roy Keane scored the goal, Ryan Giggs was named man of the match, and a little bit of history was created as they became the first English club side to win this tournament. It wasn't the one they would have necessarily wanted, but they did achieve a double of sorts.

* * * * *

That season's FA Cup was the last one with the final under the Twin Towers, because Wembley was to be redeveloped. Cardiff would stage the English domestic cup finals until 2007.

Despite United's absence, that year's competition was a memorable one for personal reasons as my team Gillingham reached the quarter-finals for the first and only time in their history. I was at Priestfield to witness two Premier League sides get knocked out in rounds four and five. In the fourth round, Andy Thomson and Barry Ashby had given the Gills a 2-0 lead before Dean Saunders pulled one back for Bradford City in the closing stages. A minute later a great goal from Jon Hodge sealed a famous 3-1 victory.

The last-16 tie was another milestone. It was featured as the first game on BBC TV's *Match of the Day* programme, and I'm pretty sure that is the only time it ever happened to Gillingham. They had trailed 1-0 at half-time to Sheffield Wednesday but swept into the sixth round with three goals in the last 20 minutes from Mark Saunders, Thomson again and a belter from Nicky Southall.

The historic quarter-final away to Chelsea was on Sunday, 20 February. Sadly I could not be there because I was on duty at Elland Road as the live tunnel reporter for Manchester United's key game against Leeds United. Andy Cole scored the only goal to give them a 1-0 win but the real story was that David Beckham had been dropped and fined a fortnight's wages (the maximum amount permitted) after missing a training session.

Sir Alex Ferguson had declined to do anything before the match, so our live interview afterwards would be the first time the media had had a chance to question him. When I asked about the Beckham story he gave me one of his famous glares before cleverly side-stepping the issue with his answer. I could tell by the look in his eyes that it was time to move on to another subject.

Now some more intrepid reporters might have dived in with a follow-up question but believe me, they would have got nowhere. All that would have happened is that they would have incurred Fergie's wrath and next time they faced him it would be even more tricky. 'Quit while you are ahead' is often a pretty decent tactic in these situations.

Shortly afterwards I was in my car and heading south while listening to commentary of Gillingham's quarter-final at Stamford Bridge. We hung on pretty well in the first half and were only 1-0 down at half-time. That became 3-0 with five minutes to go, before

Chelsea stepped up another gear and scored twice more to make it 5-0. Oh well, there's always next year.

Chelsea went to Wembley and beat Newcastle United in the semi-final and then saw off Aston Villa 1-0 in a fairly average final, Roberto Di Matteo scoring the only goal.

Gillingham also got to go to Wembley later that month. They had begun the final day of the regulation Second Division (third tier) season in the second of the two automatic promotion positions, but lost 1-0 at Wrexham and slipped into third place.

That meant a two-legged semi-final play-off against Stoke City. Going into injury time in that first game, they were losing 3-1 before Andy Hessenthaler scored a 35-yard wonder goal to give them hope.

Four days later, at a packed Priestfield, Stoke were reduced to nine men but still managed to force the tie in to extra time. Iffy Onuora (102 minutes) and Paul Smith (118) both scored late on to take the Gills back to Wembley a year after having lost to Manchester City in such unlucky circumstances.

This time Gillingham led 1-0, but then fell 2-1 behind in extra time and with seven minutes to go it looked like another heartbreaking end to the season.

Junior Lewis had other ideas, wriggling down the left flank before producing the perfect cross for veteran substitute Steve Butler to head home the equaliser. Two minutes from the end another header from another sub sent Gillingham into dreamland, Andy Thomson diving in to glance into the corner for the winner. I'm not sure if I have ever shouted so loud!

Paul Smith and Ady Pennock, who had both missed penalties in the previous season's shoot-out defeat to Manchester City, collected the trophy together and Gillingham could look forward to being in the second tier of English football for the first time in their history.

Just a few days after that Wembley triumph I was sat in Peter Taylor's car on Southend seafront as we discussed his future.

He had loved his year with Gillingham but Premier League Leicester City had come calling. He was agonising over what to do. I told him that it was a no-brainer, even though I would be really sorry to see him leave my club. The money on offer and the chance to manage in the top flight was irresistible, and I was delighted when he made such a good start at Filbert Street.

They were top of the league in October and still in the top three at Christmas, but they fell away badly towards the end of the season – losing nine of their last ten games to finish 13th.

Worse still, they suffered a damaging and embarrassing home defeat to Second Division Wycombe Wanderers in the quarter-finals of the FA Cup.

So Taylor was already under pressure before a ball was kicked the following season. I was at Filbert Street on the opening day and witnessed Leicester get pulled apart by a Kevin Nolan-inspired Bolton Wanderers. It was 4-0 at half-time and finished 5-0. The writing was on the wall and he only lasted a few weeks longer.

I got my first look at promoted Ipswich Town in 2000/01 when they drew 1-1 with Arsenal at Portman Road in September. Marcus Stewart put them ahead early in the second half before Dennis Bergkamp scored a late equaliser. Ipswich had already underlined their ability with a similar result against champions Manchester United in just their second game back in the top flight.

It became a fairly regular trip up the A12 to the county town of Suffolk. George Burley was in charge and I used to enjoy going to his news conferences, though being a canny Scot he gave very little away.

In November they knocked Arsenal out of the League Cup with James Scowcroft scoring an 89th-minute winner. They went on to reach the semi-finals before losing to Birmingham City after extra time.

In the league they ticked over nicely – very few teams got the better of them on their own pitch and a fifth-place finish was a terrific effort. It was enough to earn them a place in the following season's UEFA Cup, while Burley won the Manager of the Year award – ahead of Ferguson, Houllier, Wenger et al.

Arsenal lost on the opening day but then started to put together a decent little run which included a 1-0 win over Manchester United in October. The game was settled by a brilliant Thierry Henry volley from outside the area. Sir Alex Ferguson's team had been unbeaten until that trip to Highbury, but responded to the setback in typical fashion by winning their next eight consecutive league games.

One of those was over Taylor's Leicester, United replacing them at the top of the league, and no one was really able to sustain much of a challenge to them after that. The battle for second place was a tight one and went all the way to the end.

In February Arsene Wenger took his team to Old Trafford for the return fixture and United just blew Arsenal away. Dwight Yorke scored a hat-trick in the first 22 minutes and after 26 minutes it was 4-1, then by half-time it was 5-1. United added one more in the second half to win 6-1 and open up a 16-point lead at the top. They retained the title before the end of April and could even afford to lose their last three games yet still finish as champions by ten points.

Yet the team of the season was arguably Liverpool. They did the double over United en route to finishing third and qualifying for the Champions League for the first time since the mid-1980s, when it was the old European Cup. They also won the League Cup, the FA Cup and the UEFA Cup – giving them a remarkable treble.

A Robbie Fowler hat-trick set up an 8-0 win at Stoke in the early stages of their League Cup run but they needed extra time to beat Fulham in the quarter-finals, and lost 2-1 in the first leg of the semis at Crystal Palace.

In the return at Anfield they cruised into a 3-0 lead inside 20 minutes and went through 6-2 on aggregate.

Three days later they won a vital FA Cup tie at Leeds with goals from Nick Barmby and Emile Heskey in the 88th and 90th minutes. Earlier in the season they had lost 4-3 at Leeds in the league after leading 2-0. Australian striker Mark Viduka scored all four goals on that occasion, but in the FA Cup tie Liverpool managed to keep him quiet.

The League Cup Final, against First Division Birmingham City, was a tight affair. Fowler put Liverpool ahead with a 25-yarder but in the final minute of normal time the underdogs got a penalty which was coolly despatched by Darren Purse. Extra time failed to produce a goal, so for the first time in an English cup final we had a penalty shoot-out.

Gary McAllister sent keeper Ian Bennett the wrong way to give Liverpool the lead, then Dutchman Sander Westerveld dived to his left to keep out Martin Grainger's effort and it was definitely advantage to the Reds. Barmby scored in the top corner for 2-0, but Purse again showed nerves of steel to score and reduce the arrears to 2-1. Christian Ziege became the third of Liverpool's substitutes to score in the shoot-out, and you have to applaud Gerard Houllier for his choices!

Marcelo made it 3-2, before Bennett saved Didi Hamann's spot-kick, and then Stan Lazaridis scored to tie it up at 3-3. Fowler's audacious penalty made it 4-3, boyhood Everton fan Bryan Hughes levelled it again at 4-4, so now it was sudden death.

I don't think I have ever seen Jamie Carragher look so serious as he got ready to take his penalty, but he stuck it away calmly for 5-4, then Westerveld produced another fine save to keep out Andrew Johnson's penalty and Liverpool had their first silverware in six years.

Fowler was named man of the match. He was also the captain, so he lifted the trophy to spark some prolonged pitch celebrations.

Earlier in the day the players had watched Manchester United's demolition of Arsenal and were shaking their heads in disbelief at how easy the men from Old Trafford had made it look. When they beat United the following month (with first-half goals from Steven Gerrard and Robbie Fowler) it was a massive confidence-booster and helped set up their amazing end to the season.

Arsenal, meanwhile, continued to make progress in the FA Cup. Having disposed of Carlisle, QPR and Chelsea they then beat Blackburn 3-0 to set up a semi-final with their big rivals Tottenham at Old Trafford. It would be their third meeting in the last four in the last decade, and with one victory each this was very much seen as the decider.

The week before that semi the two teams met in the league at Highbury. Arsenal triumphed 2-0 with Robert Pires and Thierry Henry scoring in the last 20 minutes to give Arsenal a psychological advantage.

Tottenham went into the FA Cup tie with a new manager, Glenn Hoddle, and we all wondered what sort of impact the White Hart Lane legend and former England manager might have.

This time it was Tottenham who scored first, although Steffen Iversen's volley was going wide before defender Gary Doherty deflected it in with his head. After that Arsenal took charge and equalised through a fine header from Patrick Vieira. At the time, Tottenham were briefly down to ten men as captain Sol Campbell was getting treatment just off the pitch.

The second half was dominated by Arsenal, but Tottenham goalkeeper Neil Sullivan and a succession of missed chances meant that with 16 minutes to go it was still 1-1, before Pires popped up again to break Tottenham hearts. The league goal he had scored against them was a fantastic curling shot into the corner but this time he had a simple tap-in at the far post after a flowing Arsenal move.

So it would be Arsenal against Liverpool in the first FA Cup Final to be staged at the Millennium Stadium in Cardiff. Liverpool had left it late but squeezed through 2-1 against third-tier Wycombe Wanderers at Villa Park and would be returning to the scene of their League Cup success.

Before then they had to negotiate a Merseyside derby at Goodison Park and a UEFA Cup semi-final with Barcelona. They managed it largely thanks to Gary McAllister and this really would be his week. He scored a long-range free kick in the last minute to defeat Everton 3-2 and then converted a crucial penalty as Liverpool won 1-0 on aggregate against Barca.

It was a really hot and sunny day down in Cardiff, which slowed down the pace of the game – but it was still full of drama. Arsenal were furious they did not get a first-half penalty when Stephane Henchoz handled on the line to deny Thierry Henry, while Sami Hyypia would go on to make three goal-line clearances as Liverpool somehow kept Arsenal at bay.

In the last 20 minutes, Freddie Ljungburg seized on a defensive mistake and scored a cracking goal which looked as if it would be the winner. With seven minutes to go it was still 1-0 then Michael Owen pounced inside the six-yard box to fire in the equaliser. Owen had been in blistering form of late – in his three previous games he had scored one against Bradford City, two against Chelsea and three against Newcastle. That made it seven from four games and he was about to make it eight.

This was a goal worthy of winning the cup final and was quite similar to his effort against Argentina at St Etienne in the 1998 World Cup. He held off two Arsenal defenders, his pace taking him clear before he fired a great shot across David Seaman and into the corner. Arsenal looked stunned at the final whistle and must have felt they had had their pockets picked after dominating most of the game.

As I interviewed some of the Liverpool players on the pitch it was clear they were utterly jubilant. But just like the Manchester United players from two years earlier they were quick to tell me they were not finished yet as in four days they would face Alaves in the UEFA Cup Final at the Westfalenstadion in Dortmund.

Markus Babbel and Steven Gerrard put Liverpool two up in 16 minutes before Ivan Alonso pulled one back for the Spanish team. A McAllister penalty restored their advantage and gave them a 3-1 lead at the interval before this extraordinary match really burst into life.

Javi Moreno scored twice early in the second half to make it 3-3 from nowhere. Fowler must have felt he had got the winner on 73 minutes, but with just moments to go before added time Jordi Cruyff made it 4-4. In extra time Alonso looked to have scored the match-winning Golden Goal but it was ruled out for offside.

Then Magno and Antonio Karmona were then both sent off, so Alaves were down to nine when Delfi Geli headed into his own net on 117 minutes and this time that really was it. Liverpool 5-4 Alaves.

It was Liverpool's 25th cup tie as they ended the season with three trophies after winning nine of their last ten unbeaten games.

Their third-place finish in the Premier League was also a source of huge satisfaction and the belief was growing at Anfield that finally Liverpool had a team capable of challenging Manchester United for the title.

As for United, well they had won seven Premier League crowns in nine incredible seasons and equalled Liverpool's achievement from the 1980s of a hat-trick of consecutive titles.

Yet it was Arsenal – and not Liverpool – who were about to change the balance of power over the next three seasons in the English game.

# 12

# The Invincibles

ARSENE Wenger spent the summer of 2001 wondering how to get the better of Manchester United. He made one very astute (and controversial) signing: Sol Campbell. The Tottenham defender, who turned 27 in the September, was pretty much coming to the peak of his powers. He was an England regular and would go on to have an outstanding 2002 World Cup in Japan.

Veteran defenders Tony Adams and Lee Dixon were both into their last season, so Campbell's arrival came just in time. The transfer would massively heighten the tensions between Arsenal and Tottenham when the clubs met each other in the two north London derbies.

Campbell's debut for Arsenal was on the opening day at Middlesbrough. He played alongside Adams in the back four, kept a clean sheet, and Arsenal won 4-0. Three of the goals (including two from Dennis Bergkamp) came in the last three minutes. It was to be the start of a remarkably consistent run away from home in the Premier League and perhaps laid the foundations for what was to follow a couple of years later in 2004.

When the world changed with the terrorist attack on New York's World Trade Center, Arsenal were on the Spanish island of Majorca. Amazingly, UEFA sanctioned the Champions League games to go ahead that night so the Gunners found themselves in action against Mallorca. They lost 1-0 after Ashley Cole gave away an early penalty and was sent off.

I will also always remember where I was on the day of 9/11: in hospital having an invasive exploratory procedure, of which I'll say no more.

November got off to a rocky start for Arsenal with a 4-2 defeat at home to Charlton Athletic. They had led early on but fell 4-1 behind before Thierry Henry reduced the arrears. Leaving the ground afterwards, I certainly did not get the impression that the Gunners' faithful thought that this would be a very special season.

But Arsenal showed what they were made of a few days later with a 4-0 win over Manchester United in the League Cup, Sylvain Wiltord scoring a first-half hat-trick.

The next game had been in the diaries of the Tottenham fans ever since Campbell signed for their bitter rivals back on 3 July. The transfer itself had been a bit of a sensation and in many ways came out of the blue. We had been called to a news conference supposedly to unveil goalkeeper Richard Wright. Instead, Sol Campbell was there as well!

The level of abuse aimed at the Arsenal bus that day as it approached White Hart Lane with Campbell on board was something I personally had never seen before. Throughout the match he was subjected to jeering and chanting, but he played pretty well from what I recall and had it not been for Gus Poyet's last-minute equaliser he would have made a victorious return. It was another really solid performance on the road from Arsenal and this would become a theme of the season.

But there was no respite because next up it was champions Manchester United at Highbury. United led 1-0 at the interval through a Paul Scholes goal, before Arsenal surged back in the second half. Freddie Ljungberg equalised and then Henry capitalised on two late errors from his French international team-mate Fabien Barthez.

With ten minutes to go keeper Barthez hit a really poor clearance straight at Henry on the edge of the penalty area. Commentator Martin Tyler said in astonishment, 'Oh, what's he done here?'

Henry could not believe it either, but stayed cool and slotted the ball home for 2-1.

A few minutes later Henry was through one-on-one but Barthez just got to the ball first, then fumbled it, and Henry had a virtual tap-in. In the press box we were shaking our heads in disbelief but for Arsenal this was a vital three points.

It was not all plain sailing, though. In December Arsenal lost 4-0 at Blackburn in the League Cup, with Matt Jansen scoring a hat-trick. In their next game they were beaten again – this time at home by Bobby Robson's Newcastle in the Premier League. The final score was 3-1 and it was almost like the Manchester United match in reverse. Arsenal led at half-time and it was 1-1 with just a few minutes remaining before two late goals settled it.

Four days later Newcastle followed up that result with a 4-3 win at Leeds to take over at the top. The Geordies had trailed 3-1 early in the second half but fought back to win with Nobby Solano scoring in the last minute.

Just before Christmas, Arsenal went to Anfield and pulled off a key win despite having Giovanni van Bronckhorst sent off on 36 minutes. With only ten men they went 2-0 up through Henry and Ljungberg and then hung on to win 2-1.

Boxing Day produced another important result as they won 2-1 against Chelsea. Frank Lampard gave the visitors the lead, then just after half-time Campbell equalised with his first goal for the club since his summer move. Sylvain Wiltord scored the winner.

It was turning into an intriguing title race. Leeds United had set the early pace by winning five of their first seven, before their charge was checked by consecutive draws against Liverpool, Chelsea and Manchester United (Ole Gunnar Solskjaer was at it again with an 89th-minute leveller). They went 11 games unbeaten until mid-November when they lost at Sunderland.

That 4-3 defeat to Newcastle was a real choker for them and they were beaten 3-0 in the return game three weeks later, but it was a shock 2-1 loss to Cardiff City in the FA Cup which accelerated their decline. That was the start of a ten-match winless sequence which ended all hopes of silverware. They won four of their last five in the Premier League but the damage had been done. A fifth-place finish meant no Champions League place again and this would eventually have big financial implications for them.

The treble cup winners Liverpool started the season by winning two more trophies – they beat Manchester United in the Charity

Shield in Cardiff and then in Monaco they defeated Bayern Munich 3-2 to win the UEFA Super Cup (the annual match between the Champions League and UEFA Cup winners).

In October manager Gerard Houllier was taken seriously ill at the game against Leeds. He complained of 'uncomfortable chest pains' and had to have emergency heart surgery. It was to be March before he could return full-time. Assistant Phil Thomson (another big favourite of mine) took over and Liverpool continued to prosper, despite selling Robbie Fowler to Leeds.

Ironically Liverpool had taken over from Leeds at the top of the Premier League in the autumn, but then suffered a slump in form – winning just one game in nine and taking eight points out of a possible 27 as Newcastle went past them.

When Liverpool drew at Arsenal in January, Manchester United went top for the first time, but the Reds did end that poor run of form with victory at Old Trafford to complete a league double over their rivals.

As for United, it was ultimately to be their first season without a trophy since 1998, but they played their part in the title race and were involved in some hugely entertaining games. At White Hart Lane in September they were 3-0 down to Tottenham at half-time but stormed back after the interval to win 5-3. New signings Ruud van Nistelrooy and Juan Sebastian Veron were both on the scoresheet that afternoon, with David Beckham sealing the win by scoring an 87th-minute goal.

Other highlights included another 5-3 away win in London, this time at West Ham (Beckham again with the deciding goal), plus a thrilling 4-3 success at Elland Road against Leeds. They had led 4-1 but were forced to hang on at the end.

At one stage from December they won eight consecutive league games before that slip-up at home to Liverpool.

In the Champions League they reached the semi-finals before going out to Bayer Leverkusen on away goals. In the first leg at Old Trafford they led twice as it finished 2-2, then in Germany they were ahead again through a Roy Keane goal only for Oliver Neuville to equalise right on half-time. It finished 3-3 on aggregate but Leverkusen's two goals in England proved decisive. It was a particularly poignant defeat for Sir Alex Ferguson because he had set his heart on reaching the final – which was in his home town of Glasgow.

Leverkusen had also knocked Liverpool out in the quarter-finals. Sami Hyypia scored the only goal to give the home side a 1-0 win in the first leg at Anfield, then in Germany Liverpool were trailing 3-2 on the night with just six minutes to go. At that stage they were going through on the away goal rule with the aggregate scores tied at 3-3 but Lucio struck to end their dreams.

In the FA Cup, Liverpool went out to Arsenal in round four at Highbury. Dennis Bergkamp scored the only goal as Arsene Wenger's team gained revenge for that defeat in the final the previous season.

There were no late goals from Michael Owen this time but there were three red cards in the space of five minutes. Midway through the second half Martin Keown was sent off for a professional foul on Owen. Next to go was Bergkamp (Arsenal's tenth red card of the season) for a late challenge on Jamie Carragher. Then the controversy started. An object was thrown at the Liverpool defender from the crowd and he appeared to throw it back towards the fans. Referee Mike Riley dismissed him for violent conduct, so it was nine against ten for the last 15 minutes. In injury time Owen almost snatched an equaliser, but it was Arsenal who went through.

In the last 16 they faced my team Gillingham for a place in the quarter-finals. Twice Arsenal led, twice we equalised (through Marlon King on 38 minutes and Ty Gooden after 54), and that forced Arsene Wenger to send for the cavalry. Robert Pires and Thierry Henry came off the bench, Tony Adams restored the lead, and two late goals earned a slightly flattering margin of victory. Still, it was a great experience for the thousands of Gills fans at Highbury that day.

By now Arsenal were really starting to motor and after drawing 1-1 at home to Southampton on 2 February they embarked upon a sensational winning streak in the league.

The third victory of the sequence was at Newcastle, which was particularly satisfying after their home defeat to Bobby Robson's team just before Christmas, and it underlined their title credentials.

A week later they were back on Tyneside for an FA Cup quarter-final. Arsenal led through Edu, but it finished 1-1, so that meant a replay with the winners drawn to face Middlesbrough. In that second game Arsenal got off to a flyer, Pires and Bergkamp scoring in the first nine minutes. Newcastle had no answer and a third goal after half-time from Sol Campbell clinched it.

A week before the semi Campbell had to face his old team-mates again as Tottenham visited Highbury for the return league fixture. Arsenal went into the game having won seven out of seven, racking up 21 points from 21. Earlier that day Manchester United had beaten Leicester to return to the top, so there was extra pressure on Wenger's team.

Ljungberg calmed the nerves by putting Arsenal ahead, but ten minutes from time referee Mark Halsey awarded Tottenham a penalty after Gus Poyet went to ground following a challenge from goalkeeper David Seaman. Teddy Sheringham stuck away the penalty and Spurs looked to be heading for a valuable point after having been under a lot of pressure for much of the game.

On 86 minutes another big call from Halsey saw him award another penalty, this time to Arsenal as Dean Richards tangled with Henry. To add to the drama, Henry was injured and needed treatment so he could not take the penalty. Second choice Edu had already been substituted, as had Bergkamp (though he hadn't taken a penalty since the famous miss in the 1999 FA Cup semi-final).

With no one seemingly willing to take the ball, full-back Lauren stepped up to the plate. Spurs keeper Kasey Keller was bouncing up and down on the goal line to try and put him off, but the Cameroonian coolly sent him the wrong way and it was 2-1 to Arsenal.

Tottenham manager Glenn Hoddle reckoned the penalty decision was only a 50/50, but there was no doubting Arsenal deserved their victory. That made it eight wins in a row and restored their two-point lead at the top over Manchester United. Liverpool in third were two further points back.

Then it was on to Old Trafford for the FA Cup semi-final against a Middlesbrough side who had been doughty cup fighters in recent years. They certainly took the game to Arsenal, with Richard Wright making a fabulous save from Dean Windass early on. Boro missed two more good chances before Arsenal were awarded a corner. Henry swung the ball over and, under pressure from Campbell, Gianluca

Festa stuck out his right leg and deflected the ball into his own net for the only goal of the game. Lee Dixon later cleared off the line and Arsenal had to dig in but the Double had just moved a significant step closer.

Three consecutive 2-0 wins took them to the very brink of reclaiming the title. Ljungberg was in brilliant form – he grabbed both goals against Ipswich, scored the first in a tight, tense game with West Ham, and set Arsenal on their way to victory at Bolton. That made it 11 league wins in a row and a point from their next league game at Old Trafford would be enough to win the title.

Four days before that, though, Arsenal were back in Cardiff for the FA Cup Final against Chelsea. The purists weren't happy because there were still several league matches to be played – so this showpiece game was by no means the last act of the English domestic season.

Chelsea had reached the final after winning three London derbies on the way and now they faced the toughest one of all. Their fourth-round replay victory at Upton Park against West Ham was a classic cup tie. They trailed twice to Jermain Defoe goals before Barking-born John Terry broke east London hearts by snatching a last-minute winner with a powerful header from a corner.

In the quarter-final Chelsea won 4-0 at White Hart Lane, where earlier in the season Tottenham had beaten them 5-1 in the League Cup semi-final second leg. This was glorious revenge for Claudio Ranieri's side, with two goals from Eidur Gudjohnsen. Graeme Le Saux scored and got sent off in the second half.

The following week the two sides met again in the Premier League at Stamford Bridge and again Chelsea won 4-0. This time Jimmy Floyd Hasselbaink was the hero with a hat-trick.

The semi-final against local rivals Fulham at Villa Park was a much tighter affair and you had to feel a little sorry for the fans from the two south-west London clubs having to troop up to Birmingham for a 7pm kick-off on a Sunday.

John Terry was the central figure. Wearing a bandage around his head to protect an injury he almost scored with a spectacular volley, thwarted Fulham at the other end with some great defensive work, and then popped up to scramble home a deflected shot for the winner.

Twelve months on from their dramatic late defeat to Liverpool and Michael Owen, Arsenal were back in the Welsh capital to try and capture the first leg of the Double. They had had the better of an entertaining affair in the sunshine but with 70 minutes gone it was still 0-0. Sylvain Wiltord fed Ray Parlour and he strode forward before smashing a 25-yarder into the roof of the net to give Arsenal the lead.

A year previously they couldn't hang on when they had gone ahead, but this time they did. In fact they added to their lead with a stunning second goal from man-of-the moment Freddie Ljungberg. He held off a fierce challenge from Terry and somehow kept his balance before curling a wonderful shot past Carlo Cudicini into the corner from just outside the area.

Terry had been an influential figure in getting Chelsea to the final but on the morning of the game he had woken up feeling ill and was left out of the starting line-up. He did come off the bench for the second half but it was Arsenal's day and it was their players that I was interviewing live on the pitch shortly after the final whistle.

Ljungberg was named as man of the match and I managed to get to him first.

'Congratulations, Freddie!' I shouted at him over the noise of the crowd. 'What does it feel like to have won the FA Cup and completed the first leg of the Double?'

'F***ing brilliant!' was his colourful reply, before he went on to talk about the game, his goal and the possibility of winning the league title in a few days' time.

Not surprisingly, the papers were quick to pick up on what happened. Naturally we apologised, but 'Freddie's F-word joy' was one of several similar headlines I read the next day.

\* \* \* \* \*

Wednesday, 8 May at Old Trafford, Manchester. One point would be enough for Arsenal to end United's three-year reign as English champions. As it happened they got three, with a 12th consecutive league victory as the title returned to Highbury after a four-year absence.

In the 56th minute Arsenal counter-attacked and Ljungberg's fierce shot was saved by Fabien Barthez, but the ball fell to Wiltord who tucked it home for a simple goal – and that was enough to clinch the Premier League.

To win it away at the ground of the defending champions and nearest challengers spoke volumes for this Arsenal team. As the season progressed they got better and better. Thirteen wins in a row to the end of the season was outstanding. Their last Premier League defeat had been in mid-December and they finished unbeaten in 21 games (18 wins and three draws).

They fully deserved the many accolades that came their way. Thierry Henry led the Premier League's scoring charts with 24 goals, Robert Pires notched 15 assists, Freddie Ljungberg was named Premier League Player of the Season, Arsene Wenger was the Manager of the Season, and the Goal of the Season award went to Dennis Bergkamp for his turn and finish at Newcastle United.

On that same night, Liverpool beat Blackburn Rovers 4-3 to overtake Manchester United and move into second place. They led 1-0, 2-1 and 3-2, but needed an 86th-minute winner from Emile Heskey to ensure victory.

In their final game they thrashed Ipswich Town 5-0 to confirm their runners-up spot and send the East Anglians down just a year after their own top-five finish. A UEFA Cup campaign had made it harder for them, but they managed only one win from their last 17 games. Ironically Ipswich were back in the UEFA Cup the following season as winners of the Fair Play Award.

Arsenal signed off their season with that 13th consecutive win. Two goals from Henry helped them to a 4-3 victory over Everton – the team where their winning streak had started back in February.

Manchester United drew 0-0 with Charlton Athletic and for the first time in the ten seasons of the Premier League they finished outside the top two. But you knew they would respond next time – and that is just what they did.

As usual, several managers lost their jobs. This is by no means a complete list but these were all guys who had helped me a lot in that first decade of Sky Sports and I was particularly sorry to see them go. For the vast majority it was also their farewell to the Premier

League: John Gregory (Aston Villa); Jim Smith (Derby County); Walter Smith (Everton); David O'Leary (Leeds United); Peter Taylor (Leicester City); Bryan Robson (Middlesbrough); Harry Redknapp (West Ham United).

\* \* \* \* \*

If you are an Arsenal fan you would probably file the 2002/03 Premier League title race under the category 'Ones That Got Away'. In early March they led the table by eight points but in the end finished five behind Manchester United.

Perhaps the experience toughened them for the following season, but for Arsene Wenger it was still a particularly bitter pill to swallow.

Yet it began well enough. The annual curtain-raiser to the season was now officially known as the Community Shield and Arsenal lifted the trophy down in Cardiff after Gilberto Silva's goal beat Liverpool 1-0.

Nine games into the season they were clear at the top after a run of seven wins and two draws. Then they took the lead up at Goodison Park against Everton and the match was finely poised at 1-1 as stoppage time got under way.

What followed is one of those seminal moments that everyone remembers. Sixteen-year-old Wayne Rooney took the ball down over his shoulder, pivoted and smashed an instinctive shot past David Seaman from 25 yards. It made him the youngest scorer in the history of the Premier League at the time, it earned Everton three points and it stopped Arsenal in their tracks.

Wenger was also stunned. He was stunned by just how gifted Rooney appeared to be and said as much afterwards, describing the teenager as the greatest English talent under 20 he had ever seen.

The commentary of the goal at the time went along the lines of 'Remember the name!' and 'A new star is born on Merseyside.'

It took Arsenal a while to recover from the shock. They lost five of their next six matches in all competitions but eventually bounced back with a 3-0 win over Tottenham in mid-November.

Three weeks later they were back at the scene of the previous season's title triumph, only this time there was no happy ending.

Arsenal can claim (with some justification) that striker Ruud van Nistelrooy handled the ball in the build-up to the first goal and that Paul Scholes was 'borderline offside' (Andy Gray's words in commentary) as he crossed for Juan Sebastian Veron to fire United ahead, but in truth they were well beaten on the day. Scholes added a second after half-time and we left Old Trafford with the distinct feeling that United were back.

Undeterred, Arsenal went to White Hart Lane the following weekend, fought out a 1-1 draw (Robert Pires equalising from the penalty spot), and that was the start of a 12-match unbeaten run in the league that lasted until mid-March.

Liverpool began the season in storming style, clearly looking to go one better than the previous year's runners-up spot. They won nine and drew three of their opening 12 matches to move to the top. It proved 13th time unlucky as a late Gareth Southgate goal gave Middlesbrough a 1-0 win and after that Liverpool went into free-fall. They failed to win in 11 league games, taking five points out of a possible 33, and their title chances were done for.

In the League Cup they won a thriller at Villa (I've always wanted to write that), snatching a 90th-minute clincher through Danny Murphy for a 4-3 victory after letting a 3-1 lead slip. The semi-final was against Sheffield United, from the First Division, but they lost the first leg 2-1 at Bramall Lane and needed extra time before finally squeezing into the final 3-2 on aggregate. Michael Owen scored the winning goal in the 107th minute.

And on Sunday, 2 March 2003 there was an absolutely pulsating atmosphere at the Millennium Stadium in Cardiff for the final against Manchester United. I covered nearly all of the English cup finals staged in the Welsh capital, but none were as loud as this one – helped, I'm sure, by the roof being closed.

The game was pretty even, but Liverpool took their chances while United were thwarted time and again by Jerzy Dudek. The Polish goalkeeper was in inspired form and defender Stephane Henchoz cleared one off the line as well (his speciality in Cardiff cup finals). Steven Gerrard put Liverpool ahead with a long-range effort which deflected off David Beckham and Owen sealed the 2-0 win with a late goal (his speciality in Cardiff cup finals).

United would get their revenge in the league and Liverpool's season was to end in disappointment. On the final day they faced Chelsea with a Champions League place at stake and led 1-0 but lost 2-1 as Chelsea snatched fourth place and Liverpool ended in fifth.

Back to the title race and for United it was yet again a season of two halves. They lost back-to-back games in September and were beaten 3-1 in the final Manchester derby at City's Maine Road ground. Over Christmas they lost twice in the space of four days, but their Boxing Day defeat to Middlesbrough would be their last in the Premier League that season.

Fifteen wins and three draws saw them whittle away at Arsenal's lead before they eventually overhauled them. A month after losing the League Cup Final they beat Liverpool 4-0, with Ruud van Nistelrooy scoring two penalties. In their next game they went to Newcastle and won 6-2. Paul Scholes scored a hat-trick in 18 minutes and they led 6-1 with more than half an hour to play.

Four days after that, on Wednesday 16 April they travelled south to Highbury for the showdown with Arsenal. United had a three-point lead at the top but had played a game more.

Ruud van Nistelrooy gave them the lead when his electrifying pace proved too hot for Sol Campbell and Martin Keown. They still led 1-0 into the second half when Arsenal stunned them with two quickfire goals. Ashley Cole's shot looked to be going wide before it deflected off Thierry Henry and into the net for the equaliser. Then Henry scored again with a cool finish, but the TV replays showed he was offside by quite a margin.

Sixty seconds later United caught Arsenal napping and Ryan Giggs headed in to tie it up again at 2-2. Arsene Wenger looked utterly furious on the touchline at his side's lack of concentration so soon after taking a precious lead.

It felt like advantage Manchester United and so it would prove. Both teams won their next games (United defeated Blackburn 3-1 at Old Trafford, Arsenal won 2-0 at Middlesbrough).

In the following midweek United faced Real Madrid in the second leg of the Champions League quarter-finals. In an epic game they fought back to win 4-3 with two goals from substitute Beckham, but it was not quite enough and they went out 6-5 on aggregate. This was the year the final was being staged at Old Trafford – so for United it was doubly disappointing to go out as they lost the chance to appear in Europe's showpiece occasion on home turf.

Arsenal were first in action at the weekend and they moved into a 2-0 lead at Bolton Wanderers thanks to goals from Sylvain Wiltord (47 minutes) and Robert Pires (56). The relegation-threatened Wanderers then stormed back, Youri Djorkaeff made it 2-1 and with six minutes to go a Martin Keown own goal levelled the scores at 2-2. That is how it finished and for Arsenal it was very much a case of two points dropped.

Boosted by that setback for their title rivals, United won 2-0 at Tottenham and went five points clear. They had the advantage of playing first the following weekend and crushed Charlton Athletic 4-1 to lead the table by eight points.

Arsenal still had three games to go but there was no margin for error and the pressure of trying to play catch-up took its toll. Harry Kewell gave Leeds United an early lead at Highbury before Henry equalised just after the half-hour. Early in the second half Ian Harte put the visitors in front again and then it was Bergkamp to the rescue with a second equaliser on 63 minutes.

Surely Arsenal, the defending champions, would go on to win from that position? They had beaten Leeds 4-1 at Elland Road earlier in the season. The nervous tension went up as the clock ticked down – nothing less than victory would do. Eventually there was a dramatic late winner – only it came from Leeds, the Australian Mark Viduka with a wonderful effort to secure his team's safety from relegation and to end once and for all Arsenal's dreams of retaining their Double.

For so long during the season Wenger's side had looked more than capable of winning back-to-back titles, but their wonderful attacking prowess was undone by a fragility in defence and Manchester United just refused to give in, chasing them down with a ruthless efficiency.

With the title gone, Arsenal won their game in hand 6-1. They scored six goals in the first 46 minutes against Southampton, who would be their FA Cup Final opponents ten days later. Pires scored a hat-trick in 38 minutes, but Jermaine Pennant beat that by scoring his in just ten (with goals on 15, 18, and 25 minutes). On the final day of the season they won 4-0 at Sunderland to hand the home team a 15th straight league defeat.

Sunderland failed to win a single point after 11 January – their last win had been in December and they finished with just 19 points, 25 short of safety.

I was at Goodison Park on that last day to see Manchester United get presented with their eighth Premier League championship in 11 seasons. I also saw Beckham's last game and last goal in a United shirt. He spoke to me on the pitch after the game and there seemed little doubt that he knew this was the end of an era. The talk at the time was that he would sign for Barcelona, but it was their great rivals Real Madrid who secured his services and another new chapter was about to unfold for the England captain.

Saturday, 15 February was probably a crucial date in terms of Beckham's eventual move from Old Trafford. United had just lost 2-0 at home to Arsenal in the fifth round of the FA Cup and in the dressing room afterwards Sir Alex Ferguson was raging. He kicked out at a football boot and it struck Beckham just above the eye. The injury was such that he needed a couple of stitches and the normally mild-mannered Beckham had to be restrained by his team-mates as he tried to get at his manager.

So it was Arsenal who went into the quarter-finals, where they faced London rivals Chelsea – the team they had beaten in the final the previous season. John Terry gave Chelsea an early lead, Arsenal led 2-1 by half-time, but Frank Lampard forced a replay with an 86th-minute equaliser.

At Stamford Bridge, Terry again got the first goal of the game – only this time it was in the wrong net, so Arsenal led 1-0. Sylvain Wiltord increased the lead; however, any thoughts that this would be a routine victory were soon dispelled as Arsenal were reduced to ten men when Pascal Cygan was sent off after 66 minutes. Terry then scored in the right end to set up a grandstand finish, but Lauren got a third goal and the holders were through to the semi-finals.

They went back to Old Trafford where they met Sheffield United. The Yorkshire side may have been in the second tier but they had made it to the last four in both cup competitions in the same season – and that was no mean achievement.

Arsenal triumphed 1-0 to reach their third consecutive FA Cup Final – though David Seaman had to produce a world-class save to ensure his team went back to Cardiff.

I always felt that this final lacked the intensity of the two previous ones. Gordon Strachan's Southampton side fought well enough but they rarely threatened and Robert Pires clinched the trophy for Arsenal with a 38th-minute winner. The players enjoyed their lap of honour on the pitch, but deep down they knew they had let a unique chance of doing back-to-back Doubles slip from their grasp.

I mentioned earlier that Sunderland had been relegated by 25 points, yet the battle to beat the drop was still an extraordinary one. West Bromwich Albion weren't much better than Sunderland and went down with 26 points, but the third relegation place developed into a dog-fight between West Ham and Bolton which went right down to the wire.

It always amazed me that a West Ham team with the likes of Paulo Di Canio, Joe Cole, Jermain Defoe, Les Ferdinand, David James, Trevor Sinclair, Glen Johnson and John Moncur could find itself in such trouble. This was a talented squad and the phrase 'too good to go down' really did apply to them.

But by February they were in deep trouble, before they eventually found their true form. They lost just once in their final 11 games, recording six wins and four draws and picking up 22 points.

The only problem was that they managed just 20 points from their first 27 games. Their one defeat in that final run was against their relegation rivals Bolton on 19 April and it would end up costing them their Premier League status. Jay-Jay Okocha scored the only goal.

West Ham responded with three 1-0 wins, including a derby victory over high-flying Chelsea, but they went into the last day locked together on 41 points with Bolton. In any other year that number would have been more than enough.

The problem for the Hammers was that Bolton had a superior goal difference and that meant there was nothing they could do if Sam Allardyce's side won their final game, at home to Middlesbrough. West Ham were at Birmingham City and their fans were utterly despondent as news filtered through that Bolton had taken a 2-0 lead after 21 minutes through Per Frandsen and Okocha.

It was still 0-0 at half-time at St Andrew's. It was still goalless when Michael Ricketts pulled one back for Middlesbrough. Minutes later Ferdinand put West Ham ahead and if Boro could score one more goal, the Londoners could still pull off the great escape.

They couldn't. Instead, Geoff Horsfield equalised for Birmingham on 80 minutes and Stern John put them ahead after 88. There was despair for West Ham but in a rousing finish Di Canio did manage an equaliser as it ended 2-2. The Hammers were relegated on 42 points while Bolton survived with 44.

\* \* \* \* \*

There is one other memory of the 2002/03 season that I want to share. Covering Premier League football can involve a lot of charging about the country on planes, trains and automobiles, and Saturday, 3 March was no exception.

I drove from Kent to Heathrow to catch a morning flight up to Teesside Airport because I was reporting on Middlesbrough's home game against Everton and doing the post-match tunnel interviews afterwards.

My cameraman Denis Maddison picked me up from the terminal and drove us to the Riverside Stadium, where later that afternoon the match ended 1-1. Steve Watson put Everton ahead but Juninho equalised for Boro in the second half.

Now, I was on a fairly tight schedule. There were no Saturday evening flights back to London from Teesside so I had to go via Newcastle Airport. Unfortunately the post-match interviews took longer to do than expected so by the time Denis and I were leaving the ground it was already 5.50pm.

My flight was the last one back to London that night and was due to take off in just 35 minutes' time. The distance between the Riverside Stadium and Newcastle Airport is 50 miles, so while Denis put his foot down (and I won't reveal the speeds we did!) I got on to the airport to explain my plight. They were very sympathetic but pointed out that they could not delay a British Airways scheduled flight for just one person.

When we screeched up to departures there was a lady waiting to meet me to take me to the flight. The time was almost 6.35pm and as we raced through the terminal building we heard that the plane could wait no longer. It had actually pushed back and was beginning to taxi down the runway.

What happened next was pretty amazing. Another conversation on the walkie-talkie followed and suddenly I was being ushered out of a door on to the tarmac where 250 yards away the plane had now come to a halt. In the distance I could see a set of steps being manoeuvred into position. The pair of us then sprinted to the base of the steps where I said goodbye and thank you to my BA ground staff heroine. The door was opened and, puffing and panting a bit, I was ushered on board.

The first ten rows of Business Class were occupied by the players, management and officials of Chelsea, who were heading home after losing 2-1 at Newcastle United. As I slid into row 11 I heard one of the players say, 'Bloody hell, Sky Sports can even stop British Airways planes almost mid-flight!'

It was a bit of an exaggeration of course, but apparently as they had pushed back and begun to taxi, the captain had announced that there was a 'very minor technical issue, which would just take a couple of minutes to resolve'.

At which point the plane stopped until I managed to catch up with it, and once I was safely aboard we eventually took off for London. I have cut it pretty fine at airports before, but never this fine – and I am very grateful to everyone that night who enabled it to happen.

\* \* \* \* \*

In the media room at Arsenal's training ground, just near the coffee machine, is a simple picture. This is what it looks like:

W W W W D D W W W D W W W D D W D W W D W W W W
W W W W W D W D W D D D W W

It is very basic, yet incredibly effective – the playing record of the 'Invincibles' season. Twenty-six wins, 12 draws and not a single L in sight, becoming the only team to manage the feat since the first year of the Football League way back in 1889 when Preston North End completed their 22-match season unbeaten.

It is fantastic and historic achievement. And yet it could have been even better, because at times Arsenal threatened to sweep all before them. Shock defeats in the semi-finals of the League Cup and quarter-finals of the Champions League plus a narrow loss to rivals Manchester United in the last four of the FA Cup meant that they picked up just the one trophy – yet is it so fanciful to think that, with a little bit more luck, they might have achieved a clean sweep of all four?

On the other hand you could argue their unbeaten start to the season came within a whisker of ending as early as the sixth game – so it could have all been very different, but perhaps that is exactly what makes football such a fascinating sport.

Arsenal lost Sol Campbell to a red card 25 minutes into their first game of the season, but Thierry Henry and Robert Pires both scored to ensure they would get off to a winning start against Everton.

The first four games all ended in victories before they dropped two points at home to newly promoted Portsmouth in a 1-1 draw.

A few days later I was at Highbury to witness Arsenal start their Champions League group stage campaign. This was the first year of Sky Sports's live coverage and it was a tremendously exciting opportunity for a lot of us. Over the course of the next ten years I flew all over Europe reporting on the competition and it provided me with drama and memories aplenty.

At the end of August each year we would cover the draw in Monaco – this really signalled the start of the European season – and it was always an experience. Monte Carlo is an insane place, but it is worth a visit just to people-watch and admire the cars. It was also ridiculously expensive so we were thankful to be on expenses. And although we made sure we had a good time in the evenings, we also worked really hard during the day. Doing stand-up live pieces in front of the beach in a jacket and tie when the temperatures are in the high 80s is not easy.

Arsenal's first opponents were Inter Milan. The Italians moved the ball round with great confidence and counter-attacked with speed. Julio Cruz, Andy van der Mayde and Obafemi Martins all scored in the first half, and Arsenal's unbeaten start to the season was in tatters.

It finished 3-0 and afterwards I asked Arsene Wenger, 'Are you realistically now playing for second place in the group?'

His eyes blazed at me and I was surprised at the ferocity with which he snapped back a single-word answer, 'No!'

Of course Wenger would never admit his side could not achieve something until it was mathematically impossible, and I should have known that. As it happened he was proved totally right, because when we went to the San Siro Stadium for the return in November it finished Inter Milan 1 Arsenal 5. The significance was that Arsenal now had the better head-to-head record against Inter and, yes, they did go on to win the group. Arsenal scored three times in the last five minutes in that game to transform the group and I had learned another valuable lesson. Four days after that first game with Inter, Arsenal were at Old Trafford for the match that seemed to have become the most significant fixture of the Premier League season. When these two met there were always talking points and for nine consecutive seasons either one or the other finished as champions.

This latest encounter was a tight, tense and petulant affair. After 81 minutes Patrick Vieira was sent off for kicking out at (but missing) Ruud van Nistelrooy, who had fouled him. The Arsenal players seemed to blame van Nistelrooy, but the Dutchman managed to get out of the way of Vieira's retaliation and did not get involved as the Frenchman lost the plot and his temper, before finally leaving the field.

In the final minute United were awarded a penalty after Martin Keown brought down van Nistelrooy. Up he jumped to take it but he smashed the ball on to the underside of the bar, from where it rebounded to safety. Arsenal's players were ecstatic and let van Nistelrooy know in no uncertain terms.

Seconds later, as the final whistle blew, van Nistelrooy was jostled while Keown waved his arms and shouted into his face. The 'Battle of Old Trafford' had ended goalless but it still made the headlines – and Arsenal escaped with their unbeaten record still intact.

Their next three league games were all against potential title rivals – and Arsenal triumphed in all three of them. Henry scored twice in the 3-2 home win over Newcastle, Pires got the winner at Anfield as Arsenal came from behind to defeat Liverpool 2-1, then Henry grabbed the decisive goal in a 2-1 success against Chelsea.

At this stage their record was seven wins and two draws from their first nine games. After they had won the north London derby at Highbury in November it was nine wins and three draws. Darren Anderton put Spurs ahead early on but Pires eventually equalised in the 69th minute and Freddie Ljungberg got the winner ten minutes later.

Alongside the unbeaten league run, Arsenal also qualified for the knockout stages of the Champions League and the semi-finals of the League Cup, though just before Christmas Bolton again denied them a victory with a late equaliser.

As 2003 drew to a close and the Premier League reached its halfway point Arsenal had played 19, won 13, drawn six, and lost none, giving them 45 points – but they had not yet shaken off the challenges of Chelsea and Manchester United.

Despite losing 1-0 at Chelsea in late November to a Frank Lampard penalty, United ended the year on top after five consecutive victories and had 46 points from 15 wins, one draw and three defeats.

Chelsea's season had begun in deepest Slovakia on 13 August when they faced Zilina in a Champions League qualifier. It was an interesting enough trip, albeit with a couple of tortuously long coach journeys, and Chelsea did the job by winning 2-0.

In the mixed zone interview area afterwards all the talk was about the new players Chelsea had been signing. Billionaire Roman Abramovich had just bought the club and he was willing to splash the cash, investing over £100m as in came Hernan Crespo, Damien Duff, Wayne Bridge, Joe Cole and Claude Makelele. Frank Lampard told me he was relishing the challenge of trying to hold down a place in the new-look midfield. Whatever happened from here on for Chelsea it would certainly never be dull.

Four days later Chelsea opened their league campaign with an impressive 2-1 victory at Liverpool. Jimmy Floyd Hasselbaink scored the winner.

They were unbeaten in eight (with six wins) when they tasted defeat in the league for the first time, losing 2-1 at Arsenal. Their response showed just how good this Chelsea side were becoming. Five wins, five clean sheets; 35 points had been recorded from their first 14 games.

After that they tailed off a bit and went into the New Year in third place on 42 points. Like Arsenal and Manchester United, they had also reached the last 16 of the Champions League after winning their group by beating Besiktas 2-0 in Gelsenkirchen. The game was switched to Germany because of security fears following recent bombings in Istanbul.

Between 10 January and 4 February Arsenal faced Middlesbrough four times – twice in the semi-finals of the League Cup, once in the FA Cup and once in the Premier League. It finished two wins each but Arsenal's dreams of a quadruple would be over.

Henry, Pires and Ljungberg all scored in a comfortable 4-1 league win which got the series up and running. Ten days later Wenger made nine changes for the first leg of the League Cup semi-final – and paid the price as Arsenal slipped to a surprise 1-0 home defeat thanks to a goal from Juninho.

Four days after that, normal service was resumed as a much stronger team beat Boro 4-1 again, this time in the FA Cup fourth round. Ljungberg scored twice.

The fourth meeting was at the Riverside and Arsenal suffered a big blow when Keown was sent off just before half-time. Bolo Zenden increased Middlesbrough's aggregate lead to 2-0, but on 77 minutes Edu pulled one back to give Arsenal hope. Five minutes from time Jose Reyes put through his own net and the Gunners were out. Middlesbrough would go on to beat Bolton Wanderers in the final and win their first major honour after more than a century of trying.

Reyes shrugged off the anguish of that own goal to score twice as Arsenal then knocked Chelsea out of the FA Cup in the fifth round.

Six days later they went to Stamford Bridge in the Premier League and again won 2-1, after being a goal down. They had conceded within the first minute but 20 minutes later were leading after goals from Patrick Vieira and Edu.

By now the Champions League was resuming and Arsenal followed up that success at Chelsea by winning on a warm evening in northern Spain against Celta Vigo. I watched on from pitchside as players called Edu scored the first three goals. Arsenal's netted in the 18th and 58th minutes, either side of Celta Vigo's scoring in the 27th. More importantly, Pires secured a 3-2 win ten minutes from time.

They reached the last eight with a 5-2 aggregate win, but Manchester United were not quite so lucky and conceded a last-minute goal at Old Trafford in the second leg to go out to Porto on away goals. A certain Jose Mourinho famously sprinted down the touchline to join in the celebrations. Chelsea beat Stuttgart 1-0 and then drew Arsenal, so we had our very own all-English Champions League quarter-final.

Stamford Bridge hosted the first leg on Wednesday, 24 March. Eidur Gudjohnsen gave Chelsea the lead just after half-time but it did not last long as Pires soon equalised. Six minutes from time Marcel Desailly was sent off and the encounter finished with honours even.

Four days later Arsenal resumed their Premier League rivalry with Manchester United. Henry put them ahead only for Louis Saha to grab an 86th-minute equaliser; 1-1 again.

Six days on, their next game was also against United – in the semi-final of the FA Cup at Villa Park. In an absorbing contest United ended Arsenal's two-year hold on the trophy with a 1-0 win thanks to Paul Scholes's goal.

Arsenal barely had time to let that disappointment sink in because three days later they took on Chelsea in the second leg of the Champions League quarter-final. At Sky we were gutted that it was ITV's live game and I remember watching it sat next to Geoff Shreeves up on the TV gantry.

Jose Reyes gave Arsenal the lead right on half-time and the favourites looked all set to reach the semi-finals. Six minutes into the second half Frank Lampard equalised and with just three minutes to go, left-back Wayne Bridge squeezed in the winner at the far post – so it was Chelsea who progressed, and Arsenal had gone out of two major competitions in the space of a few days.

The next game was critical. Arsenal had now gone four matches without a win and I took my seat in the media area at Highbury on Good Friday, 9 April, wondering just what would unfold. All eyes were on the home side – was their season about to implode?

Five minutes in, Sami Hyypia put Liverpool ahead with a close-range header as Arsenal's worst fears looked as if they might be realised. Just after the half-hour Pires chipped a great ball over the top and Henry ran through to equalise, then just before half-time a precision finish from Michael Owen put Arsenal behind again.

The confidence was seeping out of the home team as the second half got under way and the previous couple of weeks had been incredibly tough with very little going in their favour. What they badly needed was a swift equaliser and they got it from Pires to make it 2-2, and their fans could breathe a little easier.

'Cometh the hour cometh the man' is a bit of a trite phrase, but when Arsenal needed some inspiration they found it – and the man's name was Thierry Henry. Sixty seconds after the Pires equaliser, Henry produced a moment of genius to restore the belief and give Arsenal a priceless lead. He bamboozled the Liverpool defence with a quite brilliant jinking run and finished it with a great shot into the corner. Stunning!

Twelve minutes from the end he got a slightly lucky rebound to complete his hat-trick and make it 4-2. Arsenal were back on track.

Manchester United never quite managed to find the consistency they needed in the new year. A defeat at Wolves in January was a real surprise, as was a 3-2 home loss to Middlesbrough, but the biggest blow was a 4-1 beating in the Manchester derby. Robbie Fowler and Trevor Sinclair were among the City scorers.

United never threw in the towel but a 1-0 defeat at home to Liverpool on 24 April meant that Arsenal could win the title the next day at – of all places – White Hart Lane. All they would need was a draw.

After just three minutes they took the lead with a brilliant counter-attack. Henry galloped nearly 70 yards before finding Bergkamp who set up Vieira for the first. Another slick passing move led to Pires making it 2-0 after 35 minutes. Arsenal had one hand on the trophy and co-commentator Andy Gray described it as, 'Football from another planet.'

To give Tottenham credit they kept coming at Arsenal. Jamie Redknapp reduced the arrears with a long-range effort just after the hour mark and deep into stoppage time Robbie Keane made it 2-2 from the penalty spot.

Seconds later the whistle blew and Arsenal – still unbeaten – had their third Premier League title in seven years. Kolo Toure's somersault celebration was particularly memorable. After 34 games they had won 24 and drawn ten with not a single defeat. They were four matches from immortality and each one was to prove tricky. A 0-0 draw at home to Birmingham was followed by a 1-1 draw at Portsmouth (after trailing at half-time) and a 1-0 win at Fulham, taking their record to 25 wins and 12 draws from 37 matches.

Highbury was packed to the rafters on Saturday, 15 May to see if history could be made. Opponents Leicester City obviously hadn't read the script because Paul Dickov headed them in front – against one of his old clubs – and they still led 1-0 at half-time.

Two minutes into the second half Ashley Cole was brought down and Arsenal had a penalty. Thierry Henry raced up, sent goalkeeper Ian Walker the wrong way, and it was 1-1. It was also Henry's 30th league goal of the season, the first Arsenal player to achieve that feat in more than 50 years.

Before too long Vieira made it 2-1 and Arsenal could play out the remaining minutes in relative comfort with that incredible unbeaten record not under threat. The Premier League trophy was presented amid joyous scenes and everyone there could reflect that they had witnessed something very special and utterly unique in modern day top flight English football.

For the record, they finished with 26 wins and 12 draws, 73 goals scored with 26 conceded, and 90 points. Chelsea overcame the setback of losing in the Champions League semi-finals to finish second, 11 points behind Arsenal, with Manchester United a further four points back and Liverpool a very distant fourth.

It was Chelsea's highest league finish in half a century but that wasn't enough for Claudio Ranieri to keep his job. He was sacked at the end of May and replaced three days later by Jose Mourinho.

Losing to Monaco in that Champions League semi had been a hammer blow for Ranieri's hopes of remaining in charge. Prso put the home side into a 17th-minute lead in the first leg but just five minutes later Hernan Crespo made it 1-1.

Eight minutes into the second half Akis Zikos was sent off, handing Chelsea a significant advantage. From there the least they should have been able to get was a draw but they kept going forward looking for a win and got caught out twice on the counter-attack, Fernando Morientes and Shabani Nonda giving Monaco an unexpected 3-1 lead.

Back at Stamford Bridge Chelsea soon set about repairing the damage. Jesper Gronkjaer and Frank Lampard scored to make it 3-3 on aggregate, and remember they had an away goal.

Very soon afterwards, so did Monaco. Hugo Ibarra snatched one right on half-time and then Morientes finished off the job with an equaliser in the second half as it ended 2-2, Monaco going through 5-3 on aggregate.

Manchester United won a one-sided FA Cup Final against Millwall with Cristiano Ronaldo and Ruud van Nistelrooy on the scoresheet, so at least they ended with some silverware. It would be more than a decade before they won the FA Cup again.

A couple of weeks earlier, on Sunday, 9 May, I was handed an assignment I just did not know whether I wanted or could handle. My team Gillingham went into the last day of the First Division season needing a point to stay up and I was asked to do the live in-vision inserts into Jeff Stelling's *Soccer Sunday* show.

The venue was the Britannia Stadium and opponents Stoke City were managed by Tony Pulis, who had been controversially sacked by Gillingham five years earlier. He got a terrific reception from the 4,000 travelling Gills fans, because he had been a very popular figure, but he was still at loggerheads with our chairman Paul Scally and I think everyone wondered whether he would have extra motivation to win.

My task was to try and remain neutral – which was not easy as Stoke absolutely dominated Gillingham that afternoon. Our goal led a charmed life, keeper Steve Banks was absolutely top class with a string of fine saves, and the back four of Ian Cox, Barry Ashby, Chris Hope, and John Hills all performed heroically.

The clock ticked down agonisingly slowly but Gillingham somehow survived with a 0-0 draw and lived to fight another day in the second tier. I felt exhausted at the end, but I was quite chuffed when Jeff told the TV viewers, 'You would never have known that Nick Collins is a big Gillingham fan – that's what I call professional.'

It was a nice compliment, but when it came to being professional in 2003/04 the Invincibles of Arsenal were in a league of their own.

# 13

# England – The Sven Years
## *Part One*

I HAVE seen more than half a dozen England managers unveiled, but no opening news conference quite had the aura of Sven-Goran Eriksson's arrival. The Sopwell House Hotel just outside St Albans in Hertfordshire was the venue – and it was packed.

There was a certain mystique about Sven. He was, after all, England's first overseas manager and for that reason he was accorded an extra respect. But by the same token there were elements in the media (and the game itself) who were hostile to the idea of England employing a foreign manager and sought to ridicule him if they could.

He said all the right things at that first news conference, notably that England could still qualify for the 2002 World Cup despite their stuttering start to qualifying. England, remember, had just one point from their two opening games (the 1-0 home defeat to Germany, after which Kevin Keegan had resigned, and the goalless draw in Finland, overseen by caretaker boss Howard Wilkinson).

It was only a few weeks after those games, in October 2000, that the FA announced they had their man. The only problem was that Eriksson was contracted to the Italian champions Lazio until June 2001.

Some in the media were quick to point out that Sven had agreed to join Blackburn Rovers in December 1996 from Sampdoria, then changed his mind a couple of months later and eventually signed a contract with Lazio. There was speculation the same thing might happen again – that the Swede might renege on the deal or have a change of heart (by a strange quirk of fate it was Roy Hodgson who got the Blackburn job when Sven pulled out).

Negotiations had opened with the Italian club to see if Sven could be released for two qualifiers in March, but before then England were due to play a friendly against Italy in Turin.

Peter Taylor, the former England under-21 manager, was put in charge for that fixture and he picked a young, new-look squad to see how much strength in depth England might have. He chose not to select any player aged over 30.

Most significantly he opted to hand the captain's armband to 25-year-old David Beckham and in that sense it was very much the start of a new era. After training at the Stadio delle Alpi on the eve of the game, Taylor and Beckham posed with the armband for the cameras.

It was strange being back at the ground where I had witnessed England's exit from the 1990 World Cup in that semi-final penalty shoot-out against West Germany. This was a much more low-key affair. For a start only 20,000 turned up to watch the game. The stadium looked pretty much as it did a decade earlier – only instead of a balmy summer's night this game was shrouded in mist and ended in a downpour.

Gennaro Gattuso crashed a 25-yarder in off the underside of the bar after 58 minutes to give a strong-looking Italian side a 1-0 victory. Sven watched on from the stands that night. I'm not sure what he made of England's performance, but it certainly gave him some pointers for the future.

Meanwhile in Italy Lazio were starting to struggle and criticism of Eriksson was growing. On 9 January 2001 he resigned, freeing him up to join England earlier – which is exactly what he did and that news conference at the Sopwell House Hotel followed shortly afterwards.

His first squad raised a few eyebrows because of its size – he named 31 players, including Charlton Athletic's Chris Powell and Grant McCann of Sunderland. Both would make their debuts in the game with Spain.

At Sky Sports News we covered his entire first training session at Villa Park live. This had never been done before, but it became a regular occurrence whenever a session was fully opened up to the media. There was much discussion about England's new manager. Was he a tactical genius, a Svengali-type who had masterminded league and cup doubles in three different European countries? Or was he just another foreign coach who had no direct experience of managing in England?

What did emerge from that first training session was that Sven's style was to stand back and watch on. Delegation was a key word as coaches Peter Taylor and Steve McClaren called the shots. He may not have been hands-on, but he was determined to learn fast and he wasted no opportunity to watch the England players in Premier League action whenever he could.

England gave Sven the start he would have wanted. Just before half-time Michael Owen fed Nick Barmby with a ball over the top and Barmby bravely won the race with Iker Casillas to score the first goal of the Eriksson era. Barmby had also scored the first goal England got under Glenn Hoddle four and a half years earlier.

In the second half, Emile Heskey scored from close range after Ugo Ehiogu won a vital header. Then Ehiogu, who was returning to Villa Park having left Aston Villa for Middlesbrough, got the third with another good header. Before the end Nigel Martyn plunged to his left to save Javier Moreno's penalty as England ran out 3-0 winners.

At half-time Sven had made no fewer than six substitutions and this was to be a feature of the way he approached friendlies. What he would have learned from the first 45 minutes was that England had a rock-solid central defensive pairing of Rio Ferdinand and Sol Campbell.

The real tests would follow in March when England resumed their qualifying campaign with a double-header against Finland and Albania.

Despite being at home against Finland, England wore red shirts – but that was appropriate as the game was staged in Liverpool. The Finns took the lead after Aki Riihilahti's header deflected in off Gary Neville but Sven watched on as his team fought back bravely to win.

Right on half-time a brilliant strike from Owen into the corner gave England a vital equaliser. Just five minutes into the second half it

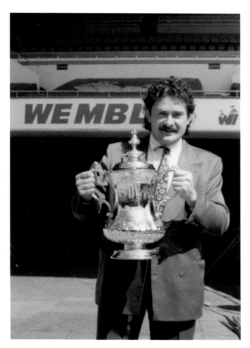

*The only way I will ever get my hands on the FA Cup. Posing with the trophy at Wembley a week before the first of the Fifty Cup Finals I covered – Manchester United v Crystal Palace, May 1990.*
Nick Collins private collection

*An iconic image from my first major tournament. Gazza's tears during the World Cup semi-final, as England lose to West Germany on penalties in Turin at Italia '90.*
Getty Images

*If you can't beat them join them. With a group of Norwegian fans in Oslo as England play a rare away game in the lead-up to EURO 96. Nick Collins private collection*

*Sky Sports' Geoff Shreeves and I on the Great Wall of China ahead of England's final EURO 96 warm-up game in Beijing. Notice how slim and youthful-looking we are! Nick Collins private collection*

*The first time I interviewed David Beckham on live TV. June 1997 in Paris after England won Le Tournoi. Getty Images*

*With Sky News colleagues Ian Woods (left) and Chris Skudder (right) as England take on Colombia in Lens at the World Cup in France, June 1998.*
*Nick Collins private collection*

*Pitchside with my best mate – cameraman David Caine – at the Stade de France in September 2000 as England prepare to face the world and European champions.*
Nick Collins private collection

*Oh what a night! Michael Owen celebrates after scoring the second of his three goals against Germany in Munich's Olympic Stadium. Owen's hat-trick set up a 5-1 win and it remains my favourite England game of the 272 I covered.* Getty Images

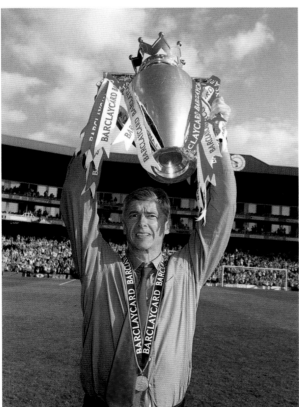

*Old Trafford October 2001 and David Beckham celebrates with Emile Heskey after scoring a sensational last-minute free kick equaliser against Greece. It was the goal which took England to the 2002 World Cup in Japan and South Korea.*
Getty Images

*Arsene Wenger with the 2004 Premier League trophy after Arsenal's 'Invincibles' completed their record-breaking unbeaten season. Of all the Premier League managers with whom I have dealt, I respect Arsene the most.*
Getty Images

*The greatest FA Cup Final goal ever? In the context of the game it has to be right up there. Steve Gerrard's 30-yarder in stoppage time to force extra time against West Ham as Liverpool go on to win on penalties in 2006, in the last FA Cup Final at Cardiff.* Getty Images

*Opening the batting for Nonington CC 2nd XI. My first innings as a 50-year-old and a triumph for substance over style.* Nick Collins private collection

*Football can be a cruel game. A distraught John Terry moments after slipping and missing the penalty that would have won Chelsea the 2008 Champions League Final...* Getty Images

*...Instead it is Manchester United who are crowned champions of Europe after a dramatic and pulsating all-English final in the rain in Moscow.* Getty Images

*Decked out in the blue and white of Gillingham my children and I prepare to set off for Wembley and the 2009 League Two play-off final. A last-minute Simeon Jackson goal gave the mighty Gills a 1-0 win over Shrewsbury (who had beaten us 7-0 in the regular season!) and promotion.* Nick Collins private collection

*Barcelona's Lionel Messi leaps high to head past Edwin van der Sar and seal victory against Manchester United in the 2009 Champions League Final in Rome. I have the perfect view from a few feet away behind the goal just to the left of van der Sar's right hand.* Getty Images

*The 'goal' that never was. Goalkeeper Manuel Neuer is beaten, the ball clearly looks over the line, but somehow the match officials fail to spot it and instead of England making it 2-2 in the 2010 World Cup last 16 clash with Germany they go on to lose 4-1.*
Getty Images

*Frank Lampard looks utterly stunned as his 'equaliser' is ruled out, despite the ball having crossed the line. Germany 4-1 England, 2010 World Cup South Africa.*
Getty Images

*Andres Iniesta scores the goal that wins the 2010 World Cup for Spain after a bruising encounter with the Netherlands. The football may not have always been great, but this remains the most enjoyable tournament I ever covered. Getty Images*

*Interviewing Gary Neville in Sofia ahead of England's 3-0 victory over Bulgaria in a EURO 2012 qualifier. Getty Images*

*I reckon I must have been sitting next to the photographer when he took this. My amazing view from right behind the goal of Didier Drogba's decisive penalty as Chelsea (finally) win the Champions League. Munich 2012. Getty Images*

*Match-winner Didier Drogba with the Champions League trophy, after Chelsea's penalty shoot-out win over Bayern Munich in their own backyard. Getty Images*

*Broadcasting from England's pre-World Cup Vale Do Lobo training camp in Portugal.*
*Getty Images*

*The 'going, going, gone' sequence of photos which appeared in* The Sun *after I took my tumble live on air outside Wembley Stadium. Several years on it still raises a laugh!*
*Nick Collins private collection*

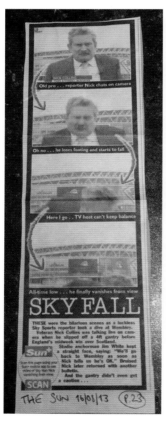

*In Switzerland at the start of England's EURO 2016 qualifying campaign.*
*Getty Images*

*Over the years Wembley has become very familiar territory and the venue for many live broadcasts. I am standing on a box (below) to make the most of the famous arch, and at least this time there is not too far to fall! Sky Images*

*On air in the Sky Sports News studios talking about Wayne Rooney becoming the England captain. Nick Collins private collection*

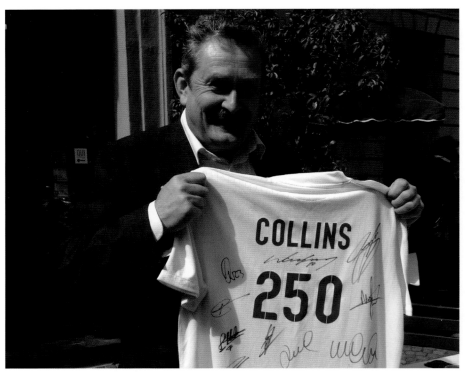

*With my Collins 250 shirt signed by the players to mark my 250th game covering England. Italy 1-1 England, Turin, 31 March 2015. Nick Collins private collection*

*8 September 2015 and Wayne Rooney becomes the first man to score 50 goals for England. A record-breaking moment for the captain as his penalty clinches a 2-0 EURO 2016 qualifying win over Switzerland at Wembley. Getty Images*

*The pre-match build-up to my 50th (and currently last) cup final. France v Portugal in Paris and the climax to EURO 2016. Getty Images*

A collection of souvenirs from that 50th final, as Portugal beat France 1-0 in extra time to win EURO 2016. *Nick Collins private collection*

*Listening to England manager Gareth Southgate thanking me for my coverage of England over the years at my final press conference for Sky Sports News. My colleagues in the media gave me a round of applause, for which I am very grateful.*
*Nick Collins private collection*

was 2-1 as Beckham finished off a sweeping move with a curling shot back across the keeper into the corner. The Anfield crowd cheered the Manchester United midfielder's goal to the rafters, scotching any notions that inter-club rivalries would damage the support England received.

That is how it stayed, Sven had his first three qualifying points and England had won their first competitive game since beating Germany at EURO 2000 nine months earlier.

The police were waiting for us when we flew into the Albanian capital Tirana a couple of days later. They insisted on providing the coach with all the journalists on board an escort to the city – because apparently there were bandits in the hills on the route. They specialised in targeting groups of western Europeans and it was a reminder that we had just arrived in one of Europe's poorest countries.

The road from our hotel to the stadium was less than a mile long and it was decent enough, but venture off it and you soon came across bumpy tracks with enormous potholes. The people were very friendly and delighted to have England in town, but every time we left our hotel by coach the police would have to jostle and push back the poorer members of society, who tried to thrust their injured or disfigured children at us and beg for money.

I won't deny that it was troubling and deeply unsettling. Your natural inclination is to want to try and help – even if it is just handing over a little bit of cash. The police would have none of it and used force to prevent any exchanges of money taking place.

On the afternoon of the qualifier the Kosovans came into town. There were a couple of large groups who raced up to the steps of the Parliament building, carrying with them huge red and black flags – the national colours of Albania. It was like some peaceful revolution was taking place. Make no mistake: they had come to cheer on Albania and these guys were some of the team's noisiest and most passionate supporters. However, they had also come to say hello and thank you to England for the help Britain had given their emerging nation over the years.

My cameraman David Caine filmed some terrific footage as they ran round the square celebrating, waving their flags and singing patriotic songs. The locals joined in hooting their car horns as they passed and a real carnival-like atmosphere built up. It was great stuff and totally unexpected and it's at times like that you realise just how lucky you are to be doing this job.

This was Sven's first away game as England manager and, although his side were firm favourites, it was a very tricky encounter. During the first half-hour Campbell had to go off injured and he was replaced by Wes Brown. Beckham's set pieces and crosses were causing Albania problems but it remained goalless at the interval.

The previous October, as England were drawing in Finland, on the same night Albania were beating Greece, so this team would be no pushovers and Sven knew his players would have to improve in the second half.

After 70 minutes it was still 0-0 and England were faced with the prospect of dropping more qualifying points, which they could ill afford. After two rounds of matches they had been bottom of Group 9 by two points – so winning in Tirana was a must.

The breakthrough eventually came from Owen, who seized on to Paul Scholes's pass and buried the ball in the net. On 85 minutes Scholes fed Andy Cole down the left and kept on running into the area where he converted the striker's cross to make it 2-0.

That should have been it, but a quickly taken throw-in and some less than diligent marking left Altin Rraklli in the clear and his angled shot beat David Seaman to make it 2-1 in the second minute of injury time. Sixty seconds later he had the ball in the net again but luckily for England the offside flag had gone up and the effort was disallowed.

In the sixth minute of added time Beckham's cross from the left found Cole and the Manchester United man finally scored his first England goal on his 13th appearance. As the England players celebrated some bottles were hurled on to the pitch and debutant Ashley Cole, who had a fine match, was struck and injured by a missile which hit him on the head. Happily he recovered, though he still looked a little shaken as he spoke afterwards, before boarding the England team bus.

So England had now won three times in a row under their new Swedish manager and they had some momentum for the final two games at the end of the season. What had been a desperate position at the bottom of the group table was starting to look a little more promising with seven points from four matches.

That said, Germany won 4-2 in Greece the same evening and still had a 100 per cent record at the halfway stage of qualifying. A runners-up place would earn England a two-legged play-off once the group games were over, so there was still plenty to play for. And as it happened the drama in this group had not even started.

On a late spring evening at Derby County's Pride Park Stadium, England took another step forward with a thrilling performance and a 4-0 win over Mexico. There were no qualifying points at stake but this was still an impressive display. Scholes started it off with a fine goal, then Robbie Fowler made it 2-0, and before half-time Beckham scored a third from a great free kick. After the break Teddy Sheringham scored an even better free kick in a game which also saw the West Ham youngsters Joe Cole and Michael Carrick make their debuts.

The friendly was a warm-up for the qualifier in Athens a week and a half later, so Sven took the team to La Manga for a warm weather training camp in the Spanish sunshine. It was a nice break for the media too at the end of another hard campaign, and there was a real sense of optimism as we boarded the flight to Greece for the final game of the season.

Four days before England played in the Greek capital, Germany finally dropped some points when they were held 2-2 in Helsinki by Finland. The Finns had led 2-0 but the Germans showed their steel by fighting back to equalise. That same night, Greece beat Albania 1-0 to underline how competitive this group was becoming.

The only change Sven made to the starting line-up from Mexico was to restore the experienced David Seaman in goal. England had their chances in the first half, and Steven Gerrard was especially convincing in midfield, but it was still 0-0 after an hour.

Then Owen, Phil Neville and Emile Heskey combined to set up Scholes for the first, the Manchester United star toe-poking home his 13th international goal.

Ashley Cole performed heroics to ensure England kept their lead and with five minutes to go they were awarded a free kick 25 yards out. Skipper Beckham produced a fantastic strike, leaving keeper Antonios Nikopolidis rooted to the spot as the ball flashed past him. It was Beckham's third goal in four games – being captain appeared to be inspiring him.

For Eriksson it was a record five wins from his first five games as England ended the season with a flourish. The only dampener on the night was that Germany had won 2-0 in Albania, so they led the table with 16 points from their six games. England were six points behind with a game in hand.

All roads, it seemed, were leading to the Olympic Stadium in Munich and the showdown between the two great rivals on Saturday, 1 September.

Three weeks after I returned from Athens my wife Sara gave birth to our third child, Louis, via a slightly alarming emergency caesarean operation, so the rest of the summer passed in a whirl. Before we knew it the new season was under way and it got off to a sensational start in Bavaria.

I covered 272 England games with BSB and BSKYB – and this was to be the proudest moment. England were quite simply sensational that night in Munich as they turned the group table on its head. Yes, I am unashamedly a big England fan and dealing with the lows as well as the highs has always been a part of the job. Some might argue there have been more lows than highs, but this was most definitely a moment to savour.

Let us be clear: England didn't just beat Germany – they absolutely destroyed them, and that was after they had given them a goal start. Owen scored 40 goals from his 89 international appearances, including that worldie against Argentina in 1998, but this was his greatest game, while Gerrard came of age as an international player – and yes, even Emile Heskey scored.

It didn't look so clever when Carsten Jancker put Germany ahead after just six minutes, yet England still threatened even in those early stages so Owen's equaliser was not such a great surprise. Beckham's free kick was not properly cleared and as the ball was knocked back in, Owen seized on it to score. It looked a very tight decision in terms of offside but the footballing gods were with England that evening and they took full advantage.

On the stroke of half-time Beckham's cross was headed back by Rio Ferdinand and Gerrard lashed a 25-yarder into the net for his first senior international goal and England had the lead.

On the touchline my cameraman David Caine, my producer Sue McCann and I looked at each other and laughed, shaking our heads in wonderment. We had covered the qualifying campaign from the beginning: from that miserable start against Germany at a wet Wembley almost a year earlier, and now England were looking as if they could take control of the group.

Never mind the players, we were flooded with a real sense of belief, and I promise you that what happened in the second half did not completely surprise us. We just truly believed from that point onwards that we would be going to the World Cup in Japan and Korea.

Sue and I had covered the original draw in Tokyo in December 1999, and when England were paired with Germany we sensed that this was going to be a special qualifying group. Japan was an amazing place – so different even from Beijing, which I had visited in 1996. Checking into the hotel that first time and being given a room on the 43rd floor which was apparently 'earthquake-proof' was a surreal experience.

Working with a local crew, instead of my mate 'Cainey', soon brought us both back down to earth. Some things may have been lost in translation, but my memory of the draw was that it was a lot harder work than it should have been.

Back to the Olympic Stadium and three minutes into the second half England extended their lead. Heskey knocked the ball down and Owen volleyed home to make it 3-1. On the touchline the three of us high-fived each other.

It wasn't finished yet by any means. Gerrard fed Owen, who ran through the defence like only he can, and he made it 4-1. Unreal. Owen celebrated his hat-trick with a somersault and if I could have done the same I would have. It really was classic Michael Owen. He just seemed to have a knack of being able to score on the big occasion.

The fifth goal underlined England's dominance as Beckham found Scholes, who in turn played in Heskey, and he made it 5-1. I know Liverpool players scored all five goals, but believe me Manchester United had a massive role in the Miracle of Munich too.

I loved some of the headlines the next day.

'Svennies From Heaven' was a particularly good one, so too was 'Svensational!'

England were three points behind with a game in hand, they had the better head-to-head record and a better goal difference (12-4, compared to 14-10). The practically unthinkable possibility of actually winning the group was now becoming a reality.

Four days later up in Newcastle, England did go top of Group 9 with a workmanlike performance against Albania. It was a bit like 'After the Lord Mayor's Show' but full credit to England for sticking to the task and getting the job done. Owen scored two minutes before half-time and Robbie Fowler scored two minutes before full-time in a 2-0 win.

So England and Germany both had 16 points from seven games, but it was advantage Sven's men. They had their destiny in their own hands as we headed to Old Trafford for that final qualifier, against Greece on Saturday, 6 October.

It did not get off to a great start for team Sky Sports News. On the night before the game my car was broken into at the Copthorne Hotel in Salford and my laptop bag was stolen. Then worse was to follow. Having eaten fish and chips at Harry Ramsden's we were unable to get a taxi back. The restaurant, I have to say, was less than sympathetic to our plight and we were ushered out of the door pointing vaguely in the direction we had to walk.

Halfway back, as we passed through one of Manchester's tougher estates, 'Cainey' and Sky News's Chris Skudder were set upon and attacked with bottles. They were walking ahead of us and we saw it all happen from a distance. They eventually got through the trouble spot and carried on towards the hotel. We still had to negotiate the problem area and were approaching it with trepidation when luckily the local police arrived.

They offered us a lift back to the hotel, which we gratefully accepted. They could not believe we had walked that route – it was notorious for muggings apparently – and nor could they believe that the restaurant staff had advised us to go that way, knowing what we faced. Apart from a couple of bruises no harm was done, but Harry Ramsden's that was not your finest hour.

On the other hand the game was to be David Beckham's finest hour (and a half). The England captain almost single-handedly dragged his team through to automatic World Cup qualification in the most dramatic circumstances imaginable.

To be honest England did not really turn up that afternoon. The Greeks had lost all three of their away qualifiers prior to that but deservedly took the lead on 36 minutes through Angelos Charisteas. Georgios Karagounis should have made it 2-0 early in the second half as England rode their luck.

Sven introduced Teddy Sheringham and ten seconds after coming on the former Manchester United favourite headed in Beckham's free kick to make it 1-1. It stayed that way for barely a minute before Demis Nikolaidis exploited some hesitant defending to put Greece back in front.

Now it was starting to get nerve-wracking. England had to match Germany's result in Gelsenkirchen against Finland, and they were drawing 0-0. Keeper Jussi Jaaskelainen was playing a blinder to keep the Germans at bay and it should not be forgotten that he was the other great hero that day.

Beckham was playing like a man possessed – he was utterly determined to lead his team to the World Cup finals – and would not be denied. Five free kicks had come close but ultimately failed, and then in the 93rd minute England were awarded another.

From 25 yards out Beckham produced a blistering effort which arrowed into the net and triggered huge celebrations on the pitch and around the ground. I don't mind admitting we lost all sense of neutrality for a moment and leapt out of our seats before rushing down to the edge of the pitch and cheering wildly. Some of the footage shows us jumping about just behind Sven, who for once shed his Scandinavian reserve and joined in the outpouring of joy.

Germany's game finished 0-0 at that moment (thank you Jussi) and as the whistle blew at Old Trafford England were off to the Far East the following summer for the 17th World Cup.

They had shown terrific resilience and self-belief to get through after such a dismal start to qualifying so you really could not begrudge them their moment of glory at Old Trafford. Maybe Sven was not the master tactician that some would have you believe, but there was no doubt the players loved playing for him and that counts for a lot.

A month later England were back in action at Old Trafford against Sweden, but I was missing from that game and instead had to watch it from my hospital bed.

Throughout 2001 I had been dogged with a stomach problem. The original diagnosis was an ulcer, but that was only part of the answer. It turned out I had picked up coeliac disease, an allergy to gluten and wheat.

It meant a radical change to my diet (no beer, pasta, pastry and worst of all no bread) and while I was getting used to it I somehow damaged my gall bladder. It swelled alarmingly and forced me into hospital at two in the morning, doubled up in pain. I spent the night in a corridor just outside a full-to-bursting A & E department at Canterbury. Mercifully the morphine made it all just about bearable.

I'm not sure how I acquired coeliac disease, but it may have been triggered by a virus I picked up at EURO 2000. In any event I was stuck in hospital as England played Sweden, which was very frustrating. Having said that Sven and some of the players sent me a get well soon card, which was nice, and Beckham was on the scoresheet again in a 1-1 draw as England brought their year to a close.

One last task in 2001 for 'Cainey' and I was to cover the World Cup draw in Busan, South Korea. The city was right on the Pacific Ocean and we enjoyed being there from the first moment. On the flight out there we found ourselves sitting one row behind American recording artist Anastacia, who would be performing 'Boom' – the official song of the 2002 World Cup.

When England were paired with old foes Argentina in their group we just knew there would be plenty of drama the following summer. The game was to be staged indoors at Sapporo, the capital of the mountainous northern Japanese island of Hokkaido. We flew there immediately after the draw to film a feature about how the pitch used to be left outside to the elements most of the time, then slid inside on giant rollers for matchdays. It was an alien, yet exciting, concept.

Playing indoors would be another fascinating experience for England, and we could not wait. The whistle-stop tour included a visit to Saitama just outside Tokyo, where we found a museum dedicated to The Beatles. On Sunday, 2 June 2002 this city would be the venue for England's opening World Cup game against Sven's countrymen Sweden, who we had not beaten since 1968. Osaka was our final port of call, which was where England's third group stage game against Nigeria would take place.

Holland's impressive Amsterdam Arena was the scene of England's opening game of 2002. It ended 1-1, which was a decent result given that Holland had beaten us 2-0 at White Hart Lane the previous August and handed Sven his first defeat.

A new-look side featured three debutants in Wayne Bridge, Michael Ricketts and Darius Vassell. Bridge looked pretty accomplished in the left-back role, Ricketts less so up front, while Vassell had a night to remember. The 21-year-old Villa striker marked his first appearance with a truly spectacular equaliser.

Trailing 1-0 at half-time, England took the game to Holland after the interval and Edwin van der Sar was by far the busier keeper. On the hour Beckham swung over a cross and Vassell connected with a flying right-foot volley which rocketed into the top corner. In that moment he probably secured himself a trip to the World Cup later that summer.

The friendly at home to Italy at the end of March was less successful. The game was played at Elland Road, Sven made 11 substitutions and England lost 2-1. That made it just one victory against Italy in nine attempts.

England's final warm-up match on home soil before leaving for the World Cup was at Anfield in mid-April against Paraguay. Facing South American opposition would be a useful exercise as England's second group game was against Argentina.

Owen was named as captain for the first time – not because the game was taking place on his home ground, but because first-choice skipper Beckham had broken a metatarsal bone in his left foot a week earlier against Deportivo La Coruna in the Champions League.

Beckham was stretchered off to hospital in some pain, and the nation began to play the waiting game of wondering whether Becks could recover in time to lead England at the tournament. The question almost became a national obsession. Even Prime Minister Tony Blair seemed to have a view on it.

Sir Alex Ferguson's verdict was 'doubtful', while others pointed out that this type of injury can take six to eight weeks from which to recover. The opening game against Sweden was just over seven weeks after the injury happened.

Owen responded in typical fashion to being given the armband – he scored a goal after just three minutes to set England on their way.

Sub Danny Murphy, Vassell (with his second in three England games), and an own goal completed the scoring in a 4-0 win, the highlight being a superb second-half performance from Joe Cole.

A week after the Paraguay victory England suffered another injury blow. Again it was a Manchester United player, again it was the left foot, and again it was a broken metatarsal bone. This time the unlucky player was right-back Gary Neville and within a few days he had ruled himself out of the World Cup – he knew he just did not have enough time to recover.

When the 23-man squad was announced in early May there were 12 players in it aged 24 or under. Joe Cole was the youngest at 20, while Martin Keown (fresh from helping Arsenal clinch the Premier League title at Old Trafford the night before) was the oldest. He was 35.

Danny Mills appeared to be the beneficiary of the Gary Neville injury, which meant no place for Gary's brother Phil nor for Jamie Carragher of Liverpool. Frank Lampard and Trevor Sinclair just missed out, Danny Murphy was named as the standby player and Andy Cole announced his international retirement after he was omitted.

England's injury problems did not end with Gary Neville. On the last day of the season Steven Gerrard limped out of Liverpool's win over Ipswich with a serious groin strain which needed surgery and six weeks of rehabilitation. Murphy was promoted to the squad and Sinclair was named as back-up.

On Friday, 17 May 'Cainey', Sue McCann and I flew out to the World Cup. We travelled via Seoul and on to the tropical volcanic island of Jeju, just off the coast of South Korea. This was where England would be based for the first few days as they prepared to face the co-hosts from Korea.

We had taken off several hours ahead of the jet carrying the England team, but they flew direct and it was a bit of a scramble getting to their hotel ahead of them. It was almost three in the morning local time as we filmed the bus sweeping through the car park up to the front entrance from where the players trooped into reception. England had arrived.

The first meeting between England and South Korea took place at Jeju's World Cup stadium in the city of Seogwipo, which would also host a group game between Brazil and China, as well as Germany's last-16 encounter with Paraguay.

Owen scrambled the ball in from close range to give England the lead at half-time but Park Ji-sung, who would later play at Manchester United for eight seasons, headed in the equaliser in a 1-1 draw. It had been a decent first half from England but they faded a bit later and Sven made eight substitutions.

At the very end of training the next day Danny Murphy fell awkwardly and was sent to hospital for an x-ray. It wasn't long before we learned the curse of the metatarsals had struck again, a broken bone meaning Murphy's World Cup was over before the tournament had even begun.

They say one man's misfortune is another man's opportunity, and so it would prove. Trevor Sinclair had flown out to the Far East as cover before returning home on the day of the Korea game. Murphy's injury meant the popular West Ham player had to turn round and come all the way back out again – earning himself the nickname among the media corps of 'Air Miles'.

Meanwhile, Beckham was still a bystander and unable to take part in either of the warm-up games. I spoke to him off camera after the final match against Cameroon in Kobe and, although he was putting on a brave face, it was clear that this would be a close-run thing. It still looked odds-against that he would feature in the World Cup opener with Sweden, which was exactly a week away.

Whenever Beckham trained all the cameras would be on him – Japan and its media just could not get enough of the England captain, but he coped with it really well and just got on with the job of getting himself fit. The first session we saw involved him working on a mini trampoline so that his injured left foot did not have to take too much impact.

Cameroon were difficult opponents and twice took the lead. Samuel Eto'o scored after just five minutes but Darius Vassell soon equalised. A great free kick from Geremi restored Cameroon's lead 12 minutes into the second half and England appeared to be heading for defeat.

To the rescue came sub Robbie Fowler, scoring with a header in the very last minute to preserve England's unbeaten record against African nations.

By now England had settled into their base on Awaji Island, which was reached via a spectacular six-lane suspension bridge. The majority of the media were based in the city of Kobe some 50 miles away, which meant a fair amount of extra travelling – but there was very little hotel accommodation on the island itself, so it couldn't be helped.

Our journey from Kobe to Saitama was my first experience of Japan's famous Shinkansen – the bullet trains which were capable of speeds of 200mph. When one first pulled into our station in Kobe we were told to be sharp on our feet because they literally stopped for just a few seconds before accelerating away again. They ran to a very strict timetable and being late was not an option for the drivers – they risked having some of their wages docked if they reached their end destination two minutes behind schedule.

With a lot of TV equipment to get on board each time, there were a couple of close calls but luckily none of our group were ever left stranded on the platform. It was a great way to travel and very comfortable, once you had got used to the speeds and the sensation of going round corners.

In Saitama we linked up with Chris Skudder and cameraman Stuart Vickery, who had been with me and Cainey in France. They had been on the trail of England's opponents Sweden and it was good to see them again.

I also met and interviewed James Bond – not the Hartlepool United reporter from almost 20 years ago, but the real thing this time. Roger Moore was helping promote the tournament and I have to say he came across as a genuinely charming, funny man. Endlessly patient, he really was very good for morale and we hoped also a good omen.

David Seaman returned to the starting line-up and so too did Beckham, after winning his race to be fit by the skin of his teeth. Owen Hargreaves was given the holding role in midfield and Vassell kept his place up front.

The Beckham 'gamble' (if indeed it was) paid off after 24 minutes when, from his corner, Sol Campbell powered in a header to put England in front with his first international goal. Ashley Cole also went close not long afterwards with a good long-range effort.

Just like against South Korea, England surrendered the lead after half-time. A poor clearance from Danny Mills was pounced on and Niclas Alexandersson levelled the scores. After that the Swedes looked the more likely team to score again, and England were hanging on a bit at the end. Beckham was less effective in the second half, but that was hardly surprising given how long he had been out injured, and was substituted after 64 minutes.

England, then, had one point from their first game, but Group F favourites Argentina already had three after beating Nigeria 1-0 in Ibaraki.

So to Sapporo and match number two where we soon bumped into a familiar face. News editor Keith James visited our live stand-up position to say hello and see how it was all going. His first World Cup watching England as a fan had been Mexico 1986, where he had witnessed Diego Maradona's infamous 'Hand of God' goal in the quarter-final against Argentina. He was desperate to see us try and gain revenge.

There was no escaping the fact that England's game with Argentina was absolutely pivotal – defeat would in all likelihood mean elimination after just two games. Sven made one change to the line-up, introducing Nicky Butt into central midfield in place of striker Vassell. It was a good move. The Manchester United player acquitted himself well and made England look a lot more solid.

Early on they needed to be as Argentina started the brighter – helped by a fourth-minute injury to Hargreaves. The Bayern Munich man eventually had to go off after 20 minutes and on came Trevor Sinclair. Originally the West Ham winger had not even been the squad's standby player, yet here he was tasting World Cup action. A great story and he didn't let anyone down.

On 24 minutes Owen took on the Argentinian defence, who retreated in panic, perhaps mindful of his goal against them at St Etienne in the last World Cup. This time his shot struck the post and rebounded to safety. How big a moment might that be, we all wondered.

Just before half-time Owen was tripped inside the area by a long-haired Mauricio Pochettino and a penalty was awarded. The future Southampton and Tottenham manager had also been involved in the challenge which had injured Hargreaves.

Beckham took the penalty and drilled it virtually down the middle. Goalkeeper Pablo Cavallero barely moved as the ball passed low to his left and England were ahead. Beckham ran to the corner flag tugging at his shirt in delight and was soon engulfed by his celebrating team-mates.

What a moment it was for Beckham – four years after being vilified for his World Cup red card against the same opponents, he was scoring what would turn out to be the winning goal. It may not have been the greatest penalty but we spent half-time excitedly talking about how well England were standing up to the challenge. Could they hang on for another 45 minutes?

Sub Teddy Sheringham came close to making it 2-0 in the second half with a spectacular volley, but in the main it was Argentina who looked the more dangerous. With 13 minutes to go Seaman made one terrific close-range save from Pochettino when we all thought he seemed certain to score.

The longer it went, the stronger the South Americans became. The final whistle could not come soon enough and the relief when it blew was palpable among players and media alike. This was a great moment and helped settle the score after Mexico '86 and France '98.

More importantly, it moved England above their old rivals in the group table. Sweden were top on goals scored after beating Nigeria 2-1 in Kobe. Both teams had four points, with Argentina on three, but Nigeria – England's final opponents – were already eliminated.

On the downside Hargreaves's injury meant he would not play again at this World Cup. He had been superb in England's warm-up games, had been one of the best players against Sweden, and was already giving Argentina problems down the left-hand side before he was hurt. Had it not been for injuries I believe he could have been a major player for England over the years.

In Osaka the equation was simple. A draw would take England into the last 16 of the World Cup, whatever the outcome of Sweden's match with Argentina.

Sven, unsurprisingly, went with most of the side that had started against Argentina, although he replaced the injured Hargreaves with Trevor Sinclair. It was hot and very humid in Osaka that afternoon, which undoubtedly affected the tempo of the game. To be honest this was one to forget. Instead of forging on with a convincing victory and topping the group, England settled for a 0-0 draw and second place.

After the final whistle the heavens opened and at the time I had never been caught in rain as heavy as this. It was a monsoon which led to flash floods within minutes and our clothes were totally saturated. There would be one game where I got even wetter – but that was still more than a decade away (Warsaw October 2012, say no more). Because of the floods it took us longer than expected to fight our way through the streets back to our live position, but at least we were reporting on England's progress into the knockout rounds.

The holders and European champions France had gone out in South Korea without even scoring a goal. We crowded around the TV in Japan to see them lose their opening game to the outsiders from Senegal and it was at that point we realised this World Cup would throw up a few surprises. Senegal finished second in their group and then beat Sweden in the last 16, so maybe we dodged a bullet by failing to beat Nigeria. Instead our opponents were the Group A winners Denmark, who had beaten France 2-0 and eliminated them from the competition.

England caught the Scandinavians cold that night at the Big Swan stadium in Niigata and stormed into the World Cup quarter-finals for the first time in 12 years with a commanding first-half performance.

They went ahead inside five minutes. Rio Ferdinand rose highest to meet Beckham's corner and Danish goalkeeper Thomas Sorensen deflected the header into his own net. Midway through the first half Butt set up Owen for his first goal of the tournament to make it 2-0. He had scored at France '98 and EURO 2000, so this was a notable hat-trick.

As the rain lashed down England pressed on and Emile Heskey's fine shot right on half-time extended the lead still further. It was Heskey's first goal since Munich and England were safely though.

The Sky Sports News team was not in such great shape. When cameraman Stuart Vickery arrived in Niigata it was evident he was not well; he was battling a serious cough and appeared to have some kind of chest virus. My cameraman 'Cainey' then got taken ill on the day we sorted out our tickets for the quarter-final against Brazil in Shizuoka. He went to hospital, was immediately put on a drip, and diagnosed with dehydration and exhaustion. The doctor wanted to keep him in for observation. No chance.

The punishing regime of early starts, a lot of travelling, and late finishes was taking its toll. Supper each night would be in our hotel's cocktail bar on the 35th floor because by the time we got back from a day's filming on Awaji Island all the restaurants in Kobe were closed. Just as well we were not vegetarians. It was swordfish or steak and that was it. Now Kobe is world famous for excellent steaks, but not the ones that were on offer to us – they were distinctly average.

'Cainey' was taken off filming duties while he recovered and Stuart was brought in to replace him. However, as I mentioned before, he was struggling too and it wasn't long before he was carted off to hospital as well.

The eight-hour time difference did not help and I remember thinking the office just did not appear to understand when we had started work, and were making demands on us that were – quite frankly – unreasonable.

Yes, we all love covering football, and are very lucky to do so – which means we will work all sorts of extra hours – but you have to get some rest too.

Then one night I woke up with searing pains in my side and I thought my gall bladder had gone again. The next morning I became the third member of our team to be admitted to hospital. Again the doctor expressed concern at my general state of well-being, but luckily it turned out my gall bladder was okay and that I had badly strained some side muscles carrying equipment.

A course of painkillers and sleeping tablets did the trick and I was able to resume duties just in time for England's quarter-final. Arriving at the ground we were greeted with the sight of Brazilian supporters dancing through the streets as if the Rio carnival was in full swing. It really was a wonderful spectacle and helped take our minds off what had happened to us in recent days. Stuart Vickery produced some great footage of the build-up to the game, even though he was still suffering.

At this stage my producer Sue McCann must have been wondering what on earth was going to happen next. I know covering the tournament took its toll on her emotionally as well, but she kept going to the very end and was a real trooper. At least she didn't wind up in hospital, but you know what they say about 'the female of the species'.

Twelve years ago I had been in the Cameroonian Embassy in west London when England last played a World Cup quarter-final. This time I was there to experience it first hand and from talking to the fans beforehand, there really did seem to be grounds to believe that the great adventure would not end here.

It was an afternoon kick-off and there's no doubt the conditions suited the Brazilians better – high humidity and stiflingly hot. Nevertheless, it was England who scored first as Owen exploited Lucio's hesitancy to remind everybody again what a world-class striker he was.

As the first half drew to a close Beckham and Scholes both missed tackles in the Brazilian half and Ronaldinho was allowed to run right at the English defence. He slipped the ball to Rivaldo and in the blink of an eye it was 1-1.

If only we could have survived to the interval, who knows how it might have unfolded?

Five minutes into the second half Brazil were awarded a free kick 35 yards out which Ronaldinho took. I still maintain he meant to cross the ball, but it wrong-footed David Seaman and flew over his head into the net for a freak goal.

Shortly afterwards Ronaldinho was harshly sent off but England could make no impact against the ten men and went out of the World Cup with a bit of a whimper. It was a crushing disappointment because you could not help but feel that whoever won this quarter-final would probably go on and win the World Cup itself. And that is exactly what happened.

The competition had been full of surprises. France and Argentina failed to get out of their groups, Japan made it to the round of 16,

Senegal got to the last eight, South Korea eliminated Italy and Spain to reach the semis and Turkey finished in third place.

Ronaldo scored two second-half goals as Brazil beat Germany 2-0 in the final in Yokohama, but by then I was back home and watching the game from my sofa. We had filmed England leaving and followed on 24 hours later – their plane had actually flown over me while I was live on air describing their departure.

It had been a memorable yet debilitating trip. I honestly believe mistakes were made at Sky, which meant it was even tougher for us than it should have been. Having said that I do genuinely believe Sky Sports News learned from the experience and as a result there was a lot more support for us at all future major tournaments. Logistics supremo Helen Kemp played a big part in making sure that happened.

After seven weeks away it was great to see the family, though my one-year-old son had forgotten who I was and hid behind his mother's legs when I opened the door. It was some time before he fully accepted me again. Don't get me wrong, I did have a truly brilliant job – but sometimes it came at a price physically as well as mentally.

The Brazil match was my 99th England game. I had hoped number 100 would be a World Cup semi-final, but instead it was a rather low-key friendly against Portugal at Villa Park in September. Alan Smith scored his first England goal on his first start and the controversial Lee Bowyer made his debut. He didn't do badly, but he never played again.

# 14

# England – The Sven Years
## *Part Two*

QUALIFYING for EURO 2004 got off to a dramatic and disturbing start. The night before the game in the Slovakian capital of Bratislava, a blood-spattered England fan staggered into the team hotel and collapsed in the foyer suffering from gunshot wounds. Happily he recovered after hospital treatment, but it was a stark reminder of the dangers that awaited those who fell foul of a particularly dangerous group of locals.

Bratislava was full of freelance 'security' men, who dressed completely in black, carried all kinds of weapons and often had a snarling dog on a short leash. In short they were like vigilantes and had come tooled up for trouble. Throw in a few thousand visiting fans and it was a toxic mix, even though the England supporters did their best to stay out of the way.

It was a bitterly cold wet night, even though it was only mid-October, and the pitch looked awful. Luckily the rain stopped for a couple of hours early in the evening, because at one stage we had been reporting the match might even be in some doubt – conditions were that bad. Slovakia might have been ranked 51st, 45 places below England, but in the first half you would never have guessed. They adapted better and had wasted several good chances before they took the lead – Middlesbrough's Szilard Nemeth squeezing his shot under David Seaman.

As half-time approached there was some crowd trouble and it soon became apparent why it was happening. Every time England's black players touched the ball they were booed, jeered and racially abused. Ashley Cole and Emile Heskey put up with a lot that night, and Emile appeared pretty shaken by it all when I spoke to him in the mixed zone afterwards.

The England supporters made very clear their thoughts on the Slovaks abusing our black players and that's why there was a problem. The police and 'security' guards eventually sorted everything out, but the racism did carry on into the second half – and the Slovakian FA received a token fine further down the line and had to play a home match behind closed doors.

Gradually England stirred themselves in the second half and drew level just after the hour with a David Beckham free kick. The momentum was with the team and eight minutes from the end Paul Scholes, on his 50th England appearance, crossed for Michael Owen to head home the winner.

Three welcome points got qualifying off to a great start but England had to survive a mini-siege in the closing stages as Slovakia piled forward and put them under enormous late pressure.

Inevitably the racist abuse dominated the media agenda and that was still the case as England prepared for the second game of their double-header a few days later against Macedonia in Southampton.

What happened in Bratislava was deeply unpleasant. The whole trip took place against a backdrop of menace and intimidation, so no wonder most of us could not wait to get out of there.

To be fair, just over a decade later I was back in Slovakia with England and the atmosphere could not have been more different. The locals were welcoming – no hint of any racism whatsoever – and the city of Bratislava looked stunning in the sunshine. As a nation they have clearly come a long way in the last ten years or so.

Macedonia was a bit of a shock to England's system. The Balkan country were not expected to be too much of a problem and yet they left St Mary's with a hard-won point.

Sol Campbell, Alan Smith and Wayne Bridge (in midfield) came in to the side, with Gareth Southgate, Emile Heskey and Nicky Butt all making way.

After ten minutes England found themselves a goal down with veteran keeper Seaman dropping a clanger. He allowed Artim Sakiri's innocuous-looking corner to pass over him and into the net. It was a misjudgement similar to the goal Ronaldinho had scored against him to knock England out of the World Cup.

Beckham soon restored parity with a clever lob, but midway through the first half England went behind again as Vanco Trajanov beat Seaman, not that he could have done a lot about it. But England's defence seemed unsettled and Macedonia wasted no opportunity throughout the game to test Seaman with a series of increasingly speculative long shots.

Steven Gerrard scored a fine goal to make it 2-2 before the interval, and we all expected England to take control after the break. It never happened and 2-2 is how it stayed.

This was England's final game of 2002 and Seaman's future was the big talking point, with many believing his international career was hanging by a thread. As the Arsenal man trudged off the pitch that night he must have been disappointed. He had been a fine servant for England over the years and fully deserved his 75 caps. Seaman would not have wanted it to end that way, but it did. Sven never picked him again as David James became the new first-choice goalkeeper.

England could look back on a year in which they had reached the quarter-finals of the World Cup and lost only twice in 13 games, but seven draws reflected that this was a team which still had to find a killer instinct.

There was no doubting the raw talent at Sven's disposal – his task now was to try and harness it more successfully. The other worry was that Turkey had leapt ahead in the qualifying group with three wins out of three and led England by five points, although they had played one game more.

If the departure from the scene of Seaman marked the changing of the guard in one sense, then there was no doubt that 2003 was also the start of a dramatic new era for England. This was the beginning of the age of Wayne Rooney.

The Boleyn Ground, Upton Park, in London's East End, was where history would be made as West Ham United hosted England against Australia on 12 February. The Aussies were really up for this one and tore into England's senior line-up in the first half. From a Stan Lazaridis free kick Tony Popic headed them in front, then Leeds United's Harry Kewell dispossessed Rio Ferdinand and doubled their lead shortly before half-time.

At this stage Sven stuck with his original plan and introduced a whole new team. Eleven substitutes came on, including Rooney in the number 23 shirt. At 17 years and 111 days he was England's youngest international, breaking a record that had stood since 1879. The teenager certainly livened things up and also played a part in Francis Jeffers's goal which put England back into the match for a while, but Brett Emerton ended any hopes of a fightback with a third goal a few minutes before the end.

It is amazing to think that Jeffers, the striker who scored on his international debut, would never play for his country again while Wayne Rooney would go on to win well over 100 caps and break the all-time national scoring record by becoming the first man to get 50 goals for England.

For his age, Rooney's physique was amazing – no wonder some called him the 'Man-Child' – but so was his footballing brain. Here was a player who seemed to know, instinctively, just what to do, when and where to make those runs. He was also as brave as a lion, though his natural aggression would have to be monitored and it did land him in some hot water over the years. That said, it was also a key part of the player he was.

Many footballing experts believed, quite rightly in my opinion, that if you removed the aggression then Rooney would lose something as a player.

There was less than seven weeks from the Australia game until England's next qualifier against Liechtenstein and during that time the media wasted no opportunity to debate the big question: should Rooney start?

Vaduz was the spectacular setting for England's third game in Group 7 against opponents ranked 151st in the world, and who once lost a World Cup qualifier 11-1 at home to Macedonia. Bordered by Austria to the east and north, and by Switzerland to the south and west, the principality of Liechtenstein is tiny. The entire country measures only 15 miles in length.

The Rheinpark Stadion in the shadow of the Alps also presented a bit of a problem. The capacity was just 3,500 and many England fans had travelled without tickets, hoping to get in on the evening. A big operation was mounted, which involved building a 'ring of steel' around the ground – in reality it was some wire fencing with checkpoints, designed to prevent anyone without tickets getting near the match.

A couple of enterprising fans managed to hide themselves in a little wooden shed inside the perimeter, before it was erected the day before the game, and emerged triumphant a few hours before kick-off. They still did not have a ticket, but quite a few supporters forced their way past the flimsy security precautions and into the ground without tickets anyway. They then swarmed into the press box and were told by the hapless stewards to sit where they liked.

Most of the media – including myself – watched the game stood up behind the goal in a specially sectioned-off area which was not meant to be used. It was a bit chaotic, but fortunately no harm was done and looking back it was all very quaint.

For a start both national anthems had the same tune, so the fans felt very much at home. England's of course is 'God Save The Queen', Liechtenstein's is called 'On The Upper Reaches Of The Young Rhine' – a catchy little title!

Liechtenstein almost did a San Marino by scoring a shock early goal but fortunately Fabio D'Elia's header flashed just wide. After a shaky start Sven's men began to improve and midway through the half Liverpool's Emile Heskey crossed for Liverpool's Michael Owen to score with a header.

Early in the second half a classic curling Beckham free kick from around 25 yards made it 2-0 and the victory was secure. With Turkey not playing, England had cut the gap back to just two points and were due to meet their group rivals in just a few days at Sunderland's Stadium of Light.

Rooney came on for the last 12 minutes in Vaduz for his first taste of competitive international football and acquitted himself well. It prompted Sven to start him against Turkey and that was to prove a key decision. England hadn't been great in Liechtenstein, but as the players pointed out afterwards, it was all about getting the points and then concentrating on the main game against Turkey.

The pre-match atmosphere up in the north-east was very tense. After the deaths of the two Leeds fans in Istanbul in 2000 there was no love lost between the two sets of supporters and this was a story which would escalate as the group progressed towards its climax in Turkey the following October.

Sven made three changes for the game with the group leaders and World Cup semi-finalists. Sol Campbell replaced Gareth Southgate, Nicky Butt came in for Kieron Dyer and Rooney took over from Heskey.

Rooney was at the heart of most of England's good moves and almost scored early on – his shot was blocked by a Turkish defender's arm, and David Beckham missed a glorious opportunity when he blazed the rebound wide. Beckham also picked up a yellow card inside the first ten minutes, which meant he was suspended from the next qualifier against Slovakia.

Turkey were strong opponents but England played with real passion and just kept on going. Even the loss of Owen to injury on 57 minutes could not stop them. Darius Vassell came on and got the all-important first goal on 75 minutes, quickly following up after Rio Ferdinand's shot was saved. The prolonged celebrations after that goal underlined just what it meant to England. This was a potentially group-defining goal.

David James then produced a world-class save with nine minutes to go to preserve the lead, showing fantastic agility to twist and stretch to tip a goal-bound header from Nihat over the bar.

In stoppage time Dyer was brought down and Beckham scored from the penalty spot to spark more joyous scenes as England moved top of Group 7 with ten points from four games. Turkey had nine from four.

The following May, England played South Africa in Durban. South Africa had lost 2-1 at Old Trafford in 1997 in the only previous meeting between the two countries, so the return game was eagerly awaited. As we flew in over the coastline, you could pick out enormous sharks in quite large numbers just out to sea. It was a spectacular sight. In Durban itself I was amazed to see city types dressed in jacket and tie come down to the beach at the end of the working day, carrying their surfboards in order to catch a few waves before sundown.

A year ago I had spent my birthday in South Korea, 12 months before that I had been in Southampton, and now here I was in South Africa. A pattern was clearly emerging but I broke the sequence the following year by going to Lord's on my birthday and giving my seven-year-old son his first taste of Test cricket.

The South African supporters started arriving at the stadium more than three hours before kick-off and flocked inside to create a marvellous atmosphere with their colourful banners and traditional songs.

England made a great start: from Beckham's free kick, Gareth Southgate headed them in front after just 36 seconds. The lead did not last too long, Benni McCarthy replying with a penalty.

The big story of the game was an injury to Beckham. He ended up going to hospital after breaking his wrist following a pretty robust challenge. Just like in Japan, Beckham could not move without getting mobbed, but luckily the injury was not too bad. He was suspended from the qualifier the following month against Slovakia anyway, but he was forced to miss the warm-up game with Serbia and Montenegro.

In the second half in Durban substitute Frank Lampard burst forward and unleashed a firm shot which rebounded to Emile Heskey for the winning goal. Six years on, the final score was again 2-1.

The friendly with Serbia took place at the Walker's Stadium in Leicester. The second half saw John Terry make his debut, while substitute Joe Cole scored the winner with a 20-yard free kick, of which Beckham would have been proud.

So to the Riverside Stadium and England's last game of the 2002/03 season. Owen was captain and he certainly led by example, scoring both goals in a 2-1 win after England had again gone behind to Slovakia. It was a very important second-half fightback because four days earlier Turkey had won in Bratislava to go back to the top of the group and England could ill afford any more slip-ups.

Owen's equaliser on 61 minutes was a penalty, which he had won himself after a superb jinking run into the area before he was fouled. Owen was Beckham's deputy when it came to spot kicks but with the Manchester United man missing, the stand-in captain stepped up and sent the keeper the wrong way for the equaliser.

Ten minutes later Steven Gerrard crossed from the left and Owen got between two taller defenders to plant a firm header into the net and give England the lead. A great night's work from Owen – and it was his 50th cap too.

Turkey also won that night, 3-2 against Macedonia, so they had 15 points from six games, while England were in second place on 13 from five.

In September just before kick-off at the Gradski Stadium in Skopje a group of Macedonian supporters behind the goal set fire to an England flag, stoking up the tension between the fans as they did so. There was only a small group of England followers at the game, and they were penned into one corner and generally given a hard time.

So it was great to see England go over at the end and celebrate a hard-fought 2-1 win right in front of them. It was also great to see Wayne Rooney score his first England goal – the first of many. He became, at the age of 17 years and 317 days, the youngest player ever to score for England, beating Michael Owen's record.

Against a backdrop of more racist chanting England fell behind in the first half and Macedonia were good value for their lead. This was another hesitant first 45 minutes, but Sven switched things round at the break and introduced Emile Heskey to provide a three-man attack.

The ploy worked and within minutes England were level, Rooney scoring his historic goal with a 20-yard shot after Heskey had teed him up. Not long afterwards Beckham was on target from the spot as England went on to claim the three points. On the same night, Turkey won in Liechtenstein so they remained top by two points, but England had a game in hand.

Four days later at Old Trafford in front of a crowd of 65,000, almost twice the entire population of Liechtenstein, England played their game in hand, won it, and moved back to the top of the group with just one match to play.

Again Liechtenstein proved stubborn opponents and were still holding England 0-0 at half-time. Seven minutes into the second half they were 2-0 down as Owen and Rooney both scored to settle the outcome.

Yet again England had improved after the break – were they just slow starters? Or was Sven saying some special words in the half-time team talk? Whatever the answer that now made it eight wins in a row, a sequence which had started in Vaduz against Liechtenstein and which had also included a 3-1 victory over Croatia at Ipswich in August. The game was notable for Frank Lampard's first England goal.

A few days after the Liechtenstein game, on 23 September, Rio Ferdinand was asked to take a random drugs test at the end of Manchester United's training session. He left without undergoing the procedure and despite contacting the club later in the day he was told the deadline had passed.

As a result Ferdinand was omitted from the England squad for the decisive final qualifier with Turkey in Istanbul. Some of the players were outraged because he had yet to be formally charged – there was even talk at one stage of a potential players' boycott of the game. Ferdinand's United team-mate Gary Neville was at the heart of the discussions that followed.

Ferdinand was subsequently charged and after a two-day hearing in December at Bolton's Reebok Stadium he received an eight-month ban from all football.

In a statement Manchester United's solicitor Maurice Watkins said, 'It is a particularly savage and unprecedented sentence which makes an appeal inevitable.'

A combination of that ban and injuries meant that after playing Croatia on 20 August 2003 Ferdinand would not appear for England again until October 2004 against Wales. In total he missed 15 internationals including the whole of EURO 2004. For his club he would be absent from January until September 2004.

Fortunately for England, John Terry was fast emerging as a more than adequate replacement. The Chelsea player started the first three games of the season and would play a crucial role in Istanbul as England went in search of the point that would guarantee them qualification for EURO 2004.

As well as Ferdinand's absence there was another factor which would make England's task that much harder. Because of the fear of crowd trouble the FA agreed with their Turkish counterparts that no tickets would be issued to England fans, so the amazing support we had seen at all the away qualifiers would now be absent for the decider.

Maybe one or two fans somehow made it past all the security – but there could not have been more than a handful who got in, and they could not afford to react at all, or they would have been ejected.

From our live point on top of a café right outside the ground we did see what appeared to be two England fans in the long queues to get inside. Just before the turnstiles they must have been spotted, because the scene turned ugly for a moment before they were led away.

The media bus got roundly booed and some Turkish supporters wanted to attack it when they saw English faces on board, but happily it was able to pass through into a secure area inside the ground.

We had to be in our position on the rooftop 12 hours before kick-off for security reasons, but as we arrived there were already queues stretching around part of the ground. Some fans really did want to get in early – it was amazing!

During the course of the afternoon I was invited to appear live on Turkish TV, where I was asked why the Sky Sports News crew were wearing stab vests. I replied that we weren't, though it was true that we had all been issued with them.

As kick-off drew closer and our preview work was done the crowds outside were still as large as ever. Somehow we would have to try and pass through them in order to get into the ground and we were not looking forward to it – we might not have been wearing stab vests, but there was no disguising the fact that we were English. The café owner sensed our dilemma and ushered us to a secret back door, which opened directly into the ground. We gratefully thanked him and headed off to the designated media area.

The national anthem was drowned out by boos, every English touch was jeered and whistled, as Turkey looked to extract the maximum from their home advantage. The match was being played across the Bosphorus in the Asian part of the city at the Sukru Saracoglu Stadium, home of Fenerbahce, and it had been given the highest priority with top referee Pierluigi Collina in charge.

In the first half he awarded England a penalty after Tugay tripped Steven Gerrard. Beckham took it, but slipped at the moment of impact and skied it way over the bar. It was his first penalty miss for England and the Turks surged round the captain to taunt him. Aston Villa defender Alpay stuck his fingers into Beckham's face and the situation started to become volatile. The tension had not calmed down before half-time because a melee broke out in the tunnel as the players left the pitch.

Order was eventually restored and in the second half England continued to remain calm under pressure. The winning run might have been about to come to an end, but the draw was the least England deserved – and they got it.

At the end the players gathered together in a huddle and celebrated in the centre of the pitch. Fair play to my cameraman Stuart Vickery who stood up in the press box and cheered when the whistle blew, much to the consternation of the Turkish media. You are supposed to be neutral, but I understood his euphoria after a couple of long and difficult days. The team came of age that night and exactly six years on from that heroic goalless draw in Rome to qualify for France '98, England had done it again.

Sven's future continued to be a talking point but he could certainly get the players to perform for him and that had to count for a lot.

Ironically, that draw was to be the start of a five-match run where England failed to win. Their next victory did not come until the following June when they beat Iceland 6-1 in the final warm-up game before heading off to EURO 2004.

England slipped to a careless 3-2 home defeat to Denmark at Old Trafford, drew 1-1 in the Algarve against Portugal in a useful preparation game for the European Championships, and then lost 1-0 in Gothenburg to Sweden. Gerrard captained England for the first time and tasted defeat in an England shirt for the first time having made more than 20 appearances.

For all his experimenting – and even UEFA seemed to get fed up with the number of substitutes he used as a maximum of six rule was introduced – Sven did know his best squad in time for the tournament. John Terry would emerge as Ferdinand's successor in central defence, with Frank Lampard taking over from Nicky Butt in midfield.

Before the tournament England had two final home friendlies in Manchester. Against Japan Sven fielded what was expected to be his first-choice line-up, but Terry injured his hamstring and would be ruled out of the opening game against the defending champions France. England led against Japan through Michael Owen but had to settle for a draw. Often these games just before the start of major tournaments can be something of a non-event, and this was no exception.

Against Iceland, though, it was a different story as England produced an all-action performance to give the nation a real morale-booster ahead of Portugal.

Lampard scored the first from 25 yards, Wayne Rooney added a second soon afterwards and then lashed in another from long distance to make it 3-0. Darius Vassell grabbed two in the second half and Wayne Bridge bagged a rare goal in a 6-1 thrashing.

Even without Rio Ferdinand, England were off to the European Championships in good heart. At Sky Sports News we were really looking forward to a month in the sunshine with all the excitement that a major tournament brings. Presenter Rob Wotton was coming out to anchor our half-hour EURO 2004 reports, complete with a temporary studio overlooking the impressive Estadio da Luz where England would begin their campaign.

The training base was the old Estadio Nacional where Celtic's Lisbon Lions had become the first British team to win the European Cup against Inter Milan back in 1967. Some of the stands had been removed, but this was still a natural amphitheatre and an historic setting – we all hoped it would help inspire England.

Ledley King came in for his first England start in place of the injured John Terry but otherwise it was the team everyone expected with David James in goal behind a back four of Gary Neville, King, Sol Campbell and Ashley Cole. In midfield it was David Beckham, Steven Gerrard, Frank Lampard and Paul Scholes while Michael Owen and Wayne Rooney were up front.

It was a gloriously warm evening in Lisbon ahead of the game, but it was not the weather which was causing the fans to get hot and bothered. The entry process was tortuous, getting through the various checkpoints was taking a lot longer than expected and some big queues were building up.

This was where we saw the benefit of digital TV cameras and they really came into their own that night. Chris Skudder and Duncan Scobell were able to move around among the fans filming and broadcasting live without having to worry about cables getting in the way. They got some great stuff which captured the frustrations of the supporters and the race against time to be inside for kick-off.

Once the game got under way it was a fascinating encounter. France looked so dangerous with Zinedine Zidane, Patrick Vieira, Robert Pires and Thierry Henry, but England had their moments too and Wayne Rooney was terrific – totally at home in a major tournament atmosphere.

It was England who struck first with Lampard burying a header from Beckham's precision free kick – the first goal France had conceded in around a dozen matches.

With just over 15 minutes remaining in the second half Rooney was pulled down for a stonewall penalty. We were watching with the fans high up behind the goal France were defending and I remember thinking, 'If this goes in it's 2-0 and we've surely won.' Instead Fabien Barthez produced a stunning save from Beckham's spot kick and they were still in the game.

With 90 minutes up on the clock England continued to lead 1-0, but then the unthinkable happened.

First Emile Heskey gave away a cheap free kick and Zidane struck a curling shot from 20 yards past David James. England looked devastated, but there was worse to come; a poor back-pass from Gerrard allowed Henry to nip in, James hauled him down, and now France had a penalty. Zidane scored again and from nowhere the holders had stolen a 2-1 victory with goals in the first and third minutes of stoppage time.

This was a cruel blow for England – they had deserved at least a draw, but they left the pitch with nothing as the French players celebrated an unlikely victory. The important thing now was to recover from this setback as quickly as possible.

Sven kept the changes to a minimum. He wanted to give that team another chance, but he did restore the fit-again John Terry to the starting line-up.

England's second game was against Switzerland in the ancient university city of Coimbra, halfway between Lisbon and Porto. The weather was again hot and sunny, the fans came out in their numbers and among them was the England band.

These guys are from Sheffield, they're big Wednesday supporters and have become a regular feature at England games over the years. My producer Keith James, as I have explained, is a fanatical Sheffield United fan. Normally Blades and Owls would give each other a wide berth, but not on this occasion. Some kind of Yorkshire bonding mechanism must have kicked in because the next thing I knew we were filming the England band playing live and on the end of the line – disguised in a hat and dark glasses – was Keith playing (or pretending to play) a trumpet.

Back at Sky they had no idea that one of their own was providing the entertainment. When they did find out, there was laughter all round – Keith had managed to fool us all.

But there was no fooling Wayne Rooney that day – the teenager became the youngest scorer at the European Championships (though the record lasted only a few days) with two goals to get England up and running.

Midway through the first half Owen picked out Rooney with a cleverly chipped cross and the youngster powered home a header from inside the six-yard box. In the second half a break left Rooney in the clear and he steered a shot off the post and the keeper into the net for 2-0. Eight minutes from time Gerrard scored at the back post after a good move involving Beckham and Gary Neville.

It was a comprehensive win for England, and with France only drawing against Croatia the group was starting to tighten up. With one game to go, France had four points from their two fixtures with England one behind. Croatia had two, from two draws, and Switzerland had the one. So we went back to Lisbon and the Estadio da Luz for the final group game against Croatia. England were unchanged but they fell behind after just five minutes to a Niko Kovac goal and they trailed for more than half an hour.

Typically Rooney played a part in the equaliser, heading the ball across goal for Paul Scholes to score his first England goal in over two years. Scholes repaid the favour just before half-time, setting up Rooney who fired in a superb shot from 25 yards to give England the lead.

Rooney then played a great one-two with Owen and galloped clear before coolly slotting the ball past the keeper for 3-1. The sensational 18-year-old had now scored four goals in the tournament and with him in this form anything was possible.

Back came Croatia, as Igor Tudor headed in from a free kick, but England would not be denied and Frank Lampard burst through to score his second goal of the tournament. The final score was 4-2 and England would meet the hosts Portugal on the same ground for a place in the semi-finals.

This time it was England who got the early goal, Owen exploiting a defensive error to spin and score with an instinctive flick after two minutes and 24 seconds. It was a great goal and Owen became the first Englishman to score in four consecutive major tournaments (France '98, EURO 2000, Japan 2002, and now EURO 2004).

Midway through the first half came, in my opinion, the most significant moment of the match and of the whole tournament. Rooney was injured in a challenge with Jorge Andrade. He broke a metatarsal bone in his foot and would play no further part. Up until then Portugal were so wary about the threat of Rooney that they were leaving spaces open for others. Once he went off they tightened up, gradually started to get on top, and it was England who were on the back foot the longer the game went.

Agonisingly, they led for 80 minutes before ex-Tottenham man Helder Postiga got between two defenders to head Portugal level. As stoppage time began Sol Campbell bundled the ball into the net after Owen had hit the bar from Beckham's free kick, but Terry was controversially judged to have fouled goalkeeper Ricardo and the effort was disallowed by referee Urs Meier. What a moment that could have been for England – instead they had to regroup for extra time.

With ten minutes remaining Rui Costa blasted home a wonderful shot off the underside of the bar and the hosts were leading 2-1, but still England refused to surrender and they came up with a goal of their own five minutes later. The knockdown was from Terry and Lampard twisted quickly to find space and score a goal that was made in Chelsea. A 2-2 draw meant the game went to penalties.

Now I had a dilemma. Should I stay and see the shoot-out from inside the ground and thereby risk missing the 'live' report I had to do at the end from our balcony overlooking the stadium? Or should I attempt a lung-busting sprint to get back to our live position before the spot-kicks began?

In the end I chose the latter, and here's why: In 1990 England lost on penalties in Turin with me in the ground; in 1996 England lost on penalties at Wembley with me in the ground; in 1998 England lost on penalties in St Etienne with me in the ground. If I wasn't actually there maybe England would win.

With seconds to spare I got back in time to slump in front of a TV and watch the drama all unfold:

First to go was Beckham for England – he ballooned the ball high over the bar, so it remained 0-0.

Deco sent David James the wrong way, 1-0 to Portugal.

Owen fired the ball straight down the middle, 1-1.

Simao also sent James the wrong way, 2-1 Portugal.

Lampard went central and scored, 2-2.

Rui Costa with the sixth penalty. He missed and it stayed level at 2-2.

Terry shot high into the middle of the goal and England had the lead 3-2, could they drive home their advantage?

Next up was 19-year-old Cristiano Ronaldo. Nerves of steel from the teenager and it was 3-3.

Owen Hargreaves shot past the keeper who barely moved, 4-3 and England were on the brink.

Maniche sent James the wrong way again and squared it at 4-4. Now it was sudden death.

Ashley Cole put England in front for the third time with a shot into the corner, 5-4.

Postiga then produced a staggering penalty given the circumstances. He waited for James to commit, then cheekily and gently rolled the ball into the net. I cursed under my breath, but it was brilliant theatre and now it was 5-5.

Penalty number 13 would prove unlucky for England. Goalkeeper Ricardo removed his gloves and dived to his left to save Darius Vassell's slightly unconvincing shot; still 5-5, but advantage Portugal.

I could barely bring myself to watch as Ricardo then stepped up and fired an unstoppable penalty past James and into the corner.

England were out of a major tournament on penalties for a fourth time and it did not get any easier to bear.

It really had felt that this could be the tournament when England's 'Golden Generation' finally came good. I promise you I did not see a better team than England at EURO 2004, and I did not see a better player there than Wayne Rooney. Had he not been injured I sincerely believe England would have beaten Portugal without the need for extra time or penalties. I am also convinced they would have seen off Holland in the semis and Greece in the final to lift the trophy and end what would have been 38 years of hurt. It's now over 50 and counting.

My theory that I was jinxing England by being in the stadium when penalties took place was also wide of the mark, and I vowed not to miss the end of another game while I was covering the national team.

I have to say that the final week of what had been a brilliant tournament to that point became a bit of an anti-climax. Once England had flown home we would trek out to Portugal's base at Alcochete to follow their progress. By this time national fervour had taken over and the players insisted on answering all the questions at the news conference in Portuguese, even though some of them could speak good English. I suppose you could not blame them, but for TV purposes it made our job much harder.

I was at the Estadio Jose Alvalade in Lisbon to see Portugal overcome the Dutch in the last four, with Ronaldo setting them on their way. Meanwhile in Porto, Greece, having dispatched France 1-0 in the quarter-finals, did the same to the Czech Republic in the semis and kept the tournament's leading scorer Milan Baros quiet in the process.

So EURO 2004 would end how it began, with Portugal losing to Greece. This time it was 1-0 (as opposed to 2-1 in the opening game), Angelos Charisteas scoring the only goal in the second half. The Greeks were limited but were very good at defending and defied odds at the start of 80/1 to win their first major tournament. Yet again I felt it could – and should – have been England.

I suppose it was almost inevitable that there would be a backlash against Sven in the media after a second quarter-final exit in a row, but the England players pledged their total confidence in him and even threatened to go on strike if their manager was dismissed, following reports of his affair with FA employee Faria Alam. The rather curious upshot of the whole story was that Sven's contract was actually extended to take in EURO 2008. Player power clearly counted, but now they would have to deliver on the pitch.

And they would have to do it without one of their best and most influential players. Paul Scholes announced in August 2004 that he was retiring from international football after seven years, 66 caps, and 14 goals. He said his family and club career had become more important, but many believed it was because in recent games he had been moved out of central midfield and played wide on the left to accommodate the burgeoning Gerrard-Lampard partnership. It was a great shame. He wasn't merely a good England player – he was almost one of the great ones, and you couldn't help but feel there must have been a way of keeping him involved centrally in a different formation.

A routine 3-0 victory over Ukraine in Newcastle was the warm-up game for England's forthcoming 2006 World Cup qualifying campaign, with Shaun Wright-Phillips scoring on his debut. The other goals came from David Beckham and Michael Owen, by now team-mates at Real Madrid.

There is usually a bump or two on the road towards qualifying and England ran into a proverbial pot hole against Austria in the opening game in Vienna. It all started well enough when they took the lead from a cleverly taken free kick. Goalkeeper Alex Manninger handled a back-pass eight yards out and was penalised. The Austrians expected Beckham to blast the set piece but instead he slid it straight to Lampard, who couldn't miss and didn't.

Later, Manninger was lucky to avoid a red card after clearly handling the ball outside the area, and then he made an outstanding one-handed save to keep the score at 1-0. It did not look as if that would matter when Steven Gerrard scored a beauty from 25 yards to double the lead on 63 minutes, but after that it started to go wrong.

A long-range free kick found its way past David James and Austria were back in it. Two minutes later the team ranked 89th in the world were level after somehow James allowed a harmless shot from Andreas Ivanschitz to slip under him. The encounter finished 2-2 and England got a pasting in the media, with the unfortunate James the main target.

James paid a high price for his mistake. He lost his place as England's first-choice goalkeeper and did not play another competitive game for his country until 2008 – four years and two days later.

The impact did not end there and the players took it upon themselves to boycott all post-match interviews after the victory in Poland a few days later, as a protest at the way James had been treated by certain sections of the media.

From Vienna we travelled five hours east by train to the Polish mining city of Katowice. It was a pretty grim-looking place and, as we pulled into the station, we saw rows of riot police lined up on the platform. The game was being played just a few miles away in Chorzow, which was the scene of England's famous defeat to Poland back in 1973. It is the only time in 19 matches that the Poles have beaten us, and it was ultimately to cost the great Sir Alf Ramsey his job.

Because of that one victory, Poland believe Chorzow is an intimidating venue – and they are not wrong. It was a difficult night for the team and in particular the fans who had flares thrown at them, while some were attacked in the streets around the stadium before and after the game.

On the pitch Paul Robinson made his competitive debut in place of the axed James while Jermain Defoe came in and scored his first England goal, taking his chance with great skill as he turned brilliantly to score. Classic Defoe. Poland equalised just after half-time but an own goal from Ashley Cole's fine cross gave England victory, three precious points, and a release from the pressure.

I know the players were upset at some of the stuff that was said and written about James, the team, and Sven himself after the Austria game. But there were plenty of us who hadn't climbed on that bandwagon, and personally I felt that it was very unfair that we were penalised as well when that post-match interview ban was announced. Shades of cutting off your nose to spite your face?

The next double-header would feature a British derby and a trip to the City of Winds (not Chicago, but Baku, the capital of Azerbaijan). First up it was Wales in Manchester. The last meeting between the two countries had been in 1984 when a Mark Hughes goal helped defeat England 1-0.

There was to be no repeat. From England's first attack Lampard's effort flew into the net off Owen's heel after just four minutes. It totally changed the direction of the shot, and these days would be classified as an Owen goal, but the record books have Lampard down as the scorer.

After that, Rooney ran the show. He was fit again after his EURO 2000 injury and despite only a couple of games for Manchester United since a big-money move from Everton, he barely looked as if he had been away.

Also back was Rio Ferdinand now that his controversial ban was finally over, and so too was Sol Campbell. It was Campbell's first England game since the European Championships and it was good to see that central defensive pairing together again for the first time since England had beaten Turkey at the Stadium of Light 18 months earlier. On that occasion they kept a clean sheet in a 2-0 win, and that was the score this time, with Beckham curling a 25-yarder right into the top corner to complete the scoring.

Then it was off to the shores of the Caspian Sea, a six-hour flight, a four-hour time difference and a step into the 'unknown'.

When the qualifying draw for the tournament was made in Frankfurt, my cameraman Stuart Vickery did a spoof piece to camera in which he said, 'No one really doubts that England will qualify from a group which also contains Austria, Poland, Wales and Northern Ireland, but the question everyone's asking is…where the f*ck is Azerbaijan?'

Spot on, Stu! And for those who still don't know: Azerbaijan is a former Soviet state which is bordered by Russia to the north, by Georgia to the north-west, by Iran to the south, by Turkey and Armenia to the west and by the world's largest lake (the Caspian Sea) to the east. Hope that clears everything up.

The day before the match was warm and sunny, but we were told it would not last – and it certainly didn't, as I'll explain in a moment.

Baku was the home city of an old (if inadvertent) friend of England football, and the Tofiq Bahramov Stadium is named after him. He was the linesman who famously gave the Geoff Hurst goal in extra time in the 1966 World Cup Final which put England 3-2 ahead against West Germany. The ball bounced down off the crossbar and the England players claimed it was over the line, but the German defenders swore blind it wasn't. It was obviously a massive talking point and the pivotal moment in England's historic victory. Still, Tofiq awarded the goal and we thank him for it to this day.

Incidentally, there is an impressive statue of him outside the stadium, which in its earlier days had been named after Stalin and Lenin – so he is in pretty exalted company.

On matchday Baku lived up to its windy reputation – and how. The conditions were absolutely atrocious with gale-force gusts and driving rain. Standing at the side of the pitch in the hours leading up to kick-off, it was hard to see how the game could go ahead – the wind was that strong!

At one stage, as I was doing a live down-the-line interview with the Sky Sports News studio in London, a heavy, metal advertising hoarding blew past me, missing narrowly. It was as if it was made of cardboard.

Mercifully, about 90 minutes before kick-off the winds eased and the game was able to take place. It was not exactly a classic, but given the state of the weather and the playing surface that was hardly surprising.

And for the fifth time in seven games as captain Michael Owen scored. David Beckham was out through suspension (but he was injured anyway) and once again the stand-in skipper made the difference, heading in Ashley Cole's cross midway through the first half. After that England could have increased their lead, but it was still job done and time for the long journey home.

After four games of the qualifying campaign England led Group 6 with ten points, but Poland were right behind on nine – and these two would battle it out all the way.

In Madrid a month later Rooney lost his cool against Spain in a friendly and had to be substituted before half-time. Yet again the racist abuse of England's black players reared its ugly head, and it was an unsatisfying evening all round. For the record Paul Robinson saved a penalty but Spain won 1-0 anyway. Ironically, beforehand both teams had lined up behind a banner proclaiming 'All United Against

Racism In Football'. If only. The qualifying campaign resumed at the end of March 2005 as England returned to Old Trafford to face another British derby – this time against Northern Ireland.

For 45 minutes goalkeeper Maik Taylor and the Irish defenders held England at bay as their 6,000 fans sang their hearts out as only they can. It was stirring stuff.

A minute after the interval that all changed when Joe Cole scored from 20 yards, then Lampard rampaged through to set up Owen for a second and Rooney's brilliance was responsible for an own goal. The scoring was completed on 61 minutes when Lampard's shot deflected in. Four goals in just over a quarter of an hour was tough on Northern Ireland, but they would show England just what they were made of later in qualifying.

The slight dampener on the day was that Poland won 8-0 against Azerbaijan to remain right on England's heels and massively improve their goal difference.

That result perhaps made the Azerbaijanis even more determined when they faced England at St James' Park a few days later. They almost stole an early lead and would have been delighted to have gone off at half-time with the scores level. There was no danger of an 8-0 thrashing, though just as they had done at the weekend England did improve in the second half with Gerrard and Beckham scoring in a 2-0 win.

Frustratingly Owen was booked, and would therefore be suspended for the next game against Wales in Cardiff in September. The free-scoring Poles could manage only one goal against Northern Ireland in Warsaw and that came in the 87th minute, but it was enough for another three points. In June they played their return game in Azerbaijan and won 3-0, so at the end of the season the top of Group 6 had Poland on 18 points from seven games with England two points back having played a game less. True, England had a game a hand and were still to meet Poland at Wembley, but they also had to face two tricky away matches against Home Nations thirsting for revenge.

By the time Poland were in action in Azerbaijan, England had already been to America, played a couple of friendlies and returned home. It was a great trip with matches against the USA in Chicago and against Colombia in New York at the Yankee Stadium.

In Chicago there was a reception for the team at the top of the 108-storey Sears Tower (it is now called the Willis Tower). At the time it was the tallest building in the western hemisphere and the views were sensational. Sven opted for an experimental line-up, giving a first cap to 20-year-old winger Kieran Richardson. He responded by scoring with a great free kick four minutes into his debut, sweeping home a second just before half-time, and then going off injured in the second half. Sol Campbell captained England for the first time while Zat Knight and Luke Young also made their debuts. Clint Dempsey pulled a goal back, but England ran out 2-1 winners.

The first thing we did when we flew into New York was to visit the site of 9/11. Almost four years on from the atrocity there were still many visible signs of the huge human tragedy which had unfolded. I found it an emotional and uplifting experience (yet also slightly depressing). Looking back I am so glad that I went that afternoon. On a happier note, I bought my first iPod on Fifth Avenue and also went up the Empire State Building.

Owen and Beckham had both been unavailable for the USA game but joined up with the rest of the squad in New York and made a big impact. Owen put England ahead on 35 minutes, after great work from Joe Cole, and added a second eight minutes later. This time Beckham and debutant Peter Crouch were involved in the build-up. Colombia immediately pulled one back, but Owen completed his hat-trick early in the second half from a cross by Beckham. He had started the game with 29 England goals and seventh on the all-time scoring list. He finished with 32 goals and had moved up to fourth – behind only Jimmy Greaves, Gary Lineker and Sir Bobby Charlton. Before the end Colombia reduced the arrears as it finished 3-2 in England's favour.

As they took their summer breaks England's players could be pretty satisfied with what they had achieved in 2004/05: eight wins and two draws from 11 matches and they were well on course to qualify for Germany the following year.

\* \* \* \* \*

Friday, 8 July 2005 (one day after the 7/7 terrorist atrocities in London) and I was driving along the M25 clockwise between junctions nine and ten. It's a route to and from work that I have taken hundreds, if not thousands, of times – only on this occasion I very nearly didn't make it.

Even though it was late morning the traffic was quite heavy so we were all doing about 60 miles per hour as we approached J10. A lorry on my inside suddenly appeared to twitch slightly and the next moment there was a car in front of me going sideways towards the crash barrier. I frantically began to slam on the brakes as the lorry, also out of control, veered across me, missing my car by just a few inches before slamming into the central reservation.

The only thing that saved me was that on this part of the M25, the crash barrier is a concrete wall. Instead of ploughing straight through the central reservation and into the oncoming traffic on the other side, the lorry hit the wall, bounced slightly and careered along down the wall, pinning the trapped car against it. That vehicle was utterly crushed and it soon turned into a fireball. A second later so did the lorry.

I watched, almost as if in a bubble that could not be pierced, as – just a few short yards away – the lorry's fuel tank ruptured on impact with the wall and then exploded into flames. After a hundred yards or so the lorry came back off the wall into the middle lanes and eventually rolled to a halt. The extra couple of seconds had made all the difference, enabling me to stop my car. I then braced, waiting for a hideous impact from the back – only it never came. Miraculously the guy behind me also managed to bring his car to a sudden halt.

The fire in the lorry was totally out of control, in fact it was spreading. Fuel had spilt across the road surface. That was also on fire, and the flames now spread to the hard shoulder where the shrubs and trees quickly caught alight too. To add to the scene of devastation the lorry's tyres began to loudly explode. A couple of helpers rushed by into the flames to see if there was anything they could do, but it all looked pretty hopeless. I was in a state of shock and just sat in the car watching the flames.

Then someone knocked on my window and yelled, 'Mate, I'd move your car if I were you-the fire is getting really close to it!'

I manoeuvred my people carrier away from a position of danger and heard the distant sound of sirens. I also saw a man on the hard shoulder about 100 yards ahead of me. All of his clothes had been burned off and he was walking very slowly in a kind of low, crouching way. Just as the first of the rescuers got to him he collapsed to the ground. I learned later that he was the driver of the car and had miraculously survived the impact and fireball before somehow climbing out of his mangled vehicle.

I learned later still that the man died in hospital that afternoon from his horrific burn injuries. His two-year-old daughter had been strapped in the back seat and, tragically, she was killed too. The lorry driver did not survive either – he was pronounced dead at the scene.

The motorway was shut for several hours as the emergency services went about their work and the crash investigation team swung into action. Those that had been a little further away from the incident were convinced that a bomb had gone off on the M25 (it was, remember, the day after 7/7), because of just how high the flames had soared.

After an hour I made my way back to the edge of the accident zone and explained to an officer that I had been driving the car nearest to the impact and offered to make a statement. He took my details and the next day the police came to my house, where they interviewed me for three hours. Nearly ten months later I appeared as the lead witness at Woking Coroner's Court to give my evidence. No prosecutions followed. How could there be? If either driver did make a mistake, he had paid for it with his life.

\* \* \* \* \*

The start of a season that ends in a World Cup is always anticipated with relish in the media – we are keen to see whether England can improve throughout, the ideal scenario then being to peak at just the right time.

Well, after England's first game of 2005/06 we were left thinking, 'Things can only get better.' It is fair to say that August in Copenhagen wasn't their finest hour. Often you can get surprising results with the first internationals of a new campaign – different countries are at different fitness levels, according to when their leagues start.

But it is fair to say none of us saw this score coming: Denmark 4 England 1, and it could have been worse. The first half wasn't great, but England did okay. After an hour it was still 0-0 and then England conceded three goals in seven minutes. The first was down to David James, who had come on at half-time for Paul Robinson. He rushed out of his area too eagerly and was left stranded, hopelessly out of position, as the ball was crossed in for a close-range finish.

I felt sorry for the big goalkeeper because he was a man under pressure and was desperate to make a good impression. He had returned after his Austria calamity on the USA tour, but had not always been very convincing. This was to be another major setback and Robinson would start the next 19 games.

To be fair to James he is one of those players who – more often than not – is prepared to stand up and be counted. He came through the mixed zone interview area afterwards and held his hands up, admitting he had made a mistake and suggesting that he had not prepared properly after learning he would be coming on at the start of the second half.

Yes, he makes mistakes (hence his 'Calamity James' nickname), but he was a great athlete and a fantastic shot stopper. I was pleased when he forced his way back into the starting line-up on a regular basis again under Fabio Capello and delighted when he eventually became England's first choice during the group stage at the 2010 World Cup. I know it didn't last, but at least I think he got the chance to prove a few of the doubters wrong.

The defensive frailties of Copenhagen were not apparent in front of nearly 71,000 fans at the Millennium Stadium in Cardiff – and that was a big relief. England dominated against Wales and wasted several good chances in the first half, but they needed a splendid save from Robinson, diving to his left, to deny the dangerous John Hartson.

Eight minutes after the interval Joe Cole scored the only goal, via a big deflection, to keep England firmly on track for qualification and we thought maybe the Denmark defeat was just a one-off.

It wasn't. Four days after Cardiff, England slipped to defeat in Belfast on a joyful night for Northern Ireland at Windsor Park. After 14 defeats and four draws in a run extending back to 1972 the Northern Irish finally recorded a victory. What's more they deserved it, for showing more appetite on the night, and refusing to give an inch.

Frustratingly, Wayne Rooney was booked (and had a bit of a spat with his captain) so he would miss the key qualifier against Austria in a month's time. This was Sven's first defeat in 22 qualifying matches and it meant his growing army of critics increased even more.

David Beckham struck the angle of post and bar with a magnificent free kick in the first half and afterwards he came and fronted up with the media, refusing to make any excuses for England's poor performance. That is one of the many great things about Beckham – he always took his responsibilities as England captain very seriously, especially in adversity.

David Healy of Leeds United scored the winner that night. Fair play to him and his team-mates, they were a credit to their country.

But where did all this leave England and their World Cup qualifying hopes? The answer was five points behind Poland, who recorded their eighth win in nine games with victory over Wales the same night, and in so doing pretty much guaranteed they would be playing in Germany the following summer – as one of the two best runners-up, if nothing else. England needed to win their final two games to be absolutely sure, but despite that defeat in Belfast it still looked odds-on that they would qualify.

One month and one day after losing to Northern Ireland, England beat Austria 1-0 and a few hours later, after Holland had beaten the Czech Republic, they booked their place at the 2006 World Cup. It meant their total of 22 points was enough to ensure going through as one of the two best second-placed teams.

It wasn't an entirely satisfactory afternoon's work. Austria dug in and made sure it would be a bit of a hard slog for England – the only goal coming via a Lampard penalty in the first half. After the break Beckham created a bit of unwanted history. Two yellow cards in the space of two minutes led to him becoming the first England player to be sent off twice in his international career.

He was also the first England captain to get a red card. The second yellow was harsh, but it provided a reminder that discipline is key at all times.

Early the following morning we were camped outside the England hotel in Manchester waiting to go live on Sky Sports News when the actor Ray Winstone popped his head out of the door. Ray is a bit of a legend and also a big England fan, so this seemed like a good opportunity to get his thoughts on the team qualifying for Germany 2006.

Nicknames are a big part of sports teams, nearly everybody at whatever level seems to have one in the dressing room, and we were no different with our team at Sky Sports News. Over the years I had become known in some quarters at Sky as 'The Guvnor', possibly because I was the chief football reporter (certainly the oldest) and a man of senior rank. It was all a bit of fun and no one took it seriously, least of all me.

My producer Keith James wandered over to Ray and said, 'Morning, guvnor, I don't suppose there's any chance you might come and do a turn for us on Sky Sports News is there?'

Ray considered the question, then ruefully shook his head and explained that he had perhaps celebrated England's qualification a little too hard the night before and was feeling a bit the worse for wear.

Then he turned towards me, pointed, and said, 'Anyway, I'm not the guvnor...HE'S the guvnor!'

I think it is fair to say that after that my nickname was well and truly established. Thanks Ray.

There was no Beckham, no Sol Campbell, and no Steven Gerrard for the match with Poland that would decide the winners of Group 6. In came Shaun Wright-Phillips, John Terry and Ledley King, while Michael Owen took over the armband.

It was a decent game too, with both teams determined to finish top dog. England scored first when Joe Cole's skilful volley was deflected in by Owen (yet again scoring when he was captain), but they couldn't hang on to their lead and Tomasz Frankowski buried a volley right on half-time for the equaliser.

It stayed that way until the final ten minutes when England came up with a spectacular winner. Cole and Owen were involved as Lampard showed superb technique to curl a volley just under the bar and into the net.

He and Owen had both scored five goals in qualifying and both had played major roles in making sure England would be going to the World Cup after winning thier group with 25 points from their ten matches, a point clear of Poland.

There would be four England games from the end of qualifying until the start of the World Cup and the first one was in neutral Switzerland, where fierce rivals Argentina provided the opposition. It was the first time the two nations had met since 2002 in Japan and it was clear the South Americans wanted revenge.

Hernan Crespo put them ahead, but Rooney – who had an excellent game – equalised before half-time in a match that was played at a really good tempo for a friendly. Walter Samuel headed Argentina back in front and it looked as if they would go on to win, until they were caught out by an Owen double in the last few minutes. Arsenal would have known how Argentina felt after what Owen did to them in the 2001 FA Cup Final.

On 87 minutes an inch-perfect Gerrard cross was met by Owen's header for the second equaliser, then in stoppage time Joe Cole chipped one in and Owen scored with his head again to give England an improbable 3-2 victory. Sven was delighted and told us afterwards that at no stage had that game seemed like a friendly.

The World Cup finals draw to determine the groups took place in Leipzig in December, and England would have been reasonably satisfied with getting Paraguay, Trinidad and old foes Sweden. It could have been a lot worse, except of course England never seem to be able to beat the Swedes.

I covered the draw in the old city, which used to be in East Germany, and then I headed west to Frankfurt to find out more about where England would open their campaign. I even managed to take in a Bundesliga game as Eintracht Frankfurt entertained Borussia Dortmund. Speaking to the fans there, it was clear that they were really looking forward to seeing David Beckham, Wayne Rooney and England the following summer.

Early in 2006 the 'Fake Sheikh' story hit the headlines. Sven was caught on tape agreeing to manage Aston Villa after the World Cup if a Middle Eastern takeover happened at the club. He was duped by a *News of the World* sting, and as a result the FA eventually made a statement to the effect that Sven would continue in his job but would leave after the World Cup and would not be staying on for EURO 2008.

On the pitch the players made it four wins in a row with another late show against South American opposition. Just like against

Argentina, England found themselves trailing to Uruguay, but hit back to win it with a last-minute goal – this time from the excellent Joe Cole. As the match ended at Anfield it began to snow, and getting out afterwards was a bit of a problem.

Once you got to the M62 motorway on the edge of the city it cleared and the journey home passed without incident. Just for a while I was expecting another slow, snowy journey and over the years I have had a few of those. It once took me nine hours to make it home from Sky via the M25 – a journey of 63 miles. On that long night I spent seven hours doing just 20 miles (it would have been quicker to walk!), but that is what can happen if the gritters are caught out by unexpected snow. Touch wood, but it does not seem to happen as often now.

At the end of April, with the World Cup squad due to be named in a week's time, England suffered a major injury blow when Wayne Rooney broke a metatarsal bone in the same foot he had injured at EURO 2004.

Immediately Sven pledged to gamble if necessary by taking Rooney in the squad even if he wasn't ready to play at the start of the tournament. His view was, 'Where do you find another Rooney?'

The medical experts were predicting he would miss at least the first game and possibly the second too, but Sven never wavered in his decision to include Rooney.

Owen won his fitness battle for the World Cup after missing several months of the season with a broken foot, but Ledley King didn't (again a broken metatarsal was the culprit).

When the squad was announced the big story was the inclusion of 17-year-old Theo Walcott, who was yet to play a first-team game for Arsenal. Another teenager, Aaron Lennon, was also included.

There were two final warm-up matches once the domestic season had finished and both were won convincingly by England. The 3-1 victory over Hungary was most notable, I suppose, for Walcott's debut as he became England's youngest player (17 years, 75 days), surpassing Rooney's record from 2003. John Terry, Steven Gerrard and sub Peter Crouch scored the goals.

Jamaica were England's final opponents before they headed for Germany and just like two years ago Sven's men flew out to the tournament having scored six goals. This one featured a hat-trick from Crouch who celebrated with his famous 'Robot' dance, which became a bit of a craze.

England were four up in 31 minutes thanks to Frank Lampard, an own goal, and two from Crouch in what was a bit of a romp at Old Trafford. At 5-0 Crouch had the chance to complete his hat-trick when he was allowed to take a penalty, but he blazed it over the bar. He got his third in the end anyway, which was great to see, and he headed off to Germany in good heart (and with the match ball). The other England goal was scored by Owen, which was encouraging given his own injury problems.

England's base in Germany was the genteel spa town of Baden-Baden, in the south-west of the country and just a few miles from the border with France. It was a delightful and peaceful place, but it gradually became the focus of more and more media attention as they followed the England wags on their nights out.

Because Germany's road network is so good we opted for a car (or rather a van) as our default means of transport and though we racked up quite a few miles following England and the tournament through to its conclusion in Berlin, it was definitely the best way to travel.

The first trip was relatively short – to sunny Frankfurt where England got off to a winning start with a third-minute own goal from Beckham's free kick. It wasn't a particularly convincing performance but the important thing was that they had three points because the other game in the group, between Sweden and Trinidad, ended in a goalless draw.

They lined up with Paul Robinson in goal; a back four of Gary Neville, Rio Ferdinand, John Terry and Ashley Cole; in midfield it was David Beckham, Steven Gerrard, Frank Lampard and Joe Cole; while up front were Michael Owen and Peter Crouch. Only Rooney was missing, but after a herculean effort he was getting ever closer to fitness.

Sky Sports News again invested a lot of money in their World Cup coverage and had constructed a purpose-built studio on the roof of a tower block overlooking the Olympic Stadium in Berlin. It was a fantastic backdrop for the daily *World Cup Reports* show, which was presented by Kelly Dalglish and David Jones. On each matchday

David would join us and present our live coverage on location. He was brilliant at it, and I think this experience definitely helped to progress his career with Sky Sports.

The setting in Nuremberg was iconic. Our live spot was by the balcony where the speeches were made at the notorious Nazi rallies in the years preceding the Second World War. They were intended to symbolise the solidarity between the German people and the Nazi party and one year the number of participants attending reached over half a million.

Jamie Carragher replaced the injured Gary Neville as England went in search of a second victory in Group B, but they were made to work very hard for it. Trinidad were far more organised than their Caribbean neighbours Jamaica had been and they also carried a threat.

After almost an hour and with the game still goalless the England fans finally got their wish as Rooney came off the bench to make his World Cup finals debut. It was great to see him back in action, though it was another substitute Aaron Lennon who was more responsible for finally providing the breakthrough. Lennon slipped in Beckham and his cross was headed home by Crouch with just seven minutes to go. It was a huge moment for England and no wonder they celebrated with feeling – it had looked as if it might be an extremely frustrating afternoon all round.

In stoppage time Gerrard smashed home a superb left-footed drive to make the game safe at 2-0, and with Sweden defeating Paraguay 1-0 it meant that England had qualified for the last 16 with a game to spare. Happy days.

A point against bogey team Sweden would be enough to win the group and avoid a potential knockout game with the hosts Germany, and that was very much the England focus as they travelled to Cologne. The match got off to the worst possible start. In the first minute Owen's right knee appeared to buckle and he went down in agony, before being stretchered off. It was cruciate ligament damage and it was a year before he played for England again. Crouch came on to replace him.

On the plus side, Rooney was passed fit enough to start while Owen Hargreaves replaced Gerrard in midfield. Gradually England recovered from the Owen shock and took the lead with one of the best goals I've seen while covering the national team.

The ball was cleared to Joe Cole some 35 yards out where he trapped it on his chest and then hit a sensational dipping, swerving volley back into the roof of the net. Unbelievable! Cole was starting to emerge as one of England's main men at this tournament.

Six minutes after half-time Sweden equalised when Marcus Allback headed in from a corner. After that, Paul Robinson made a top-class save to knock the ball on to the bar and Olof Mellberg also hit the woodwork as the Swedes pressed for a second, before England regained their composure and Gerrard came off the bench to make it 2-1 with a header from Cole's cross.

Any thoughts that a victory over Sweden was finally happening were snuffed out in injury time when England's defence failed to deal with a bouncing ball and Henrik Larsson pounced from close range to tie it up at 2-2. Still, England had finished top of their group and would now face Ecuador in Stuttgart in the last 16.

Stuttgart is where both Mercedes-Benz and Porsche have their headquarters and it was the nearest match venue to our base in Baden-Baden. There was huge English support in the city beforehand and for the first time I noticed there was a slight edge to the atmosphere. Up until now everything had seemed to pass off pretty peacefully.

Against Ecuador, Hargreaves switched to right-back and Michael Carrick played as a defensive midfielder. With no Owen, Rooney was up front on his own in a 4-1-4-1 formation.

England knew better than to underestimate Ecuador. They had opened their group with an impressive 2-0 win over Poland and followed that up by beating Costa Rica 3-0 to qualify for the knock-out stages with a game to spare.

It was a tense and cagey affair, although Frank Lampard had three great chances. His scoring record was outstanding at EURO 2004 with three goals from midfield in four games but he just could not find the net in Germany – and in a sense his frustrations mirrored England's.

But on the hour Beckham did deliver with a trademark curling 30-yard free kick up and over the wall to beat goalkeeper Cristian Mora at his near post. It was enough to see England through to the quarter-finals on a sweltering afternoon when temperatures touched 90 degrees.

Yet again it would be Luiz Felipe Scolari's Portugal in the last eight and yet again it would be a match full of drama and controversy.

The match was played in Gelsenkirchen and the England fans did the nation proud, dominating the stadium in a way that made this a very different atmosphere to the quarter-final between the two countries in Lisbon in 2004.

Gary Neville was fit again and returned at right-back so Hargreaves reverted to defensive midfield and would go on to be England's best player. He wasn't everyone's cup of tea but when it came to tournaments I always felt he found an extra gear and I was a big fan. Carrick made way.

The level of England's performances at this World Cup had come in for criticism, but against Portugal they battled magnificently in adversity and were able to hold their heads up high.

The first half probably belonged to Portugal, but England were just beginning to climb into the game when they received two major setbacks. First, Beckham was forced off by an ankle injury and the Three Lions had lost their captain, their talisman, and their most potent weapon at set pieces.

Worse followed on 62 minutes. An increasingly frustrated Rooney tangled with Armando Petit and Chelsea's Ricardo Carvalho. As he tried to get the ball he appeared to petulantly stamp on Carvalho right in front of Argentinian referee Horacio Elizondo. Portuguese players – among them his Manchester United team-mate Cristiano Ronaldo – surrounded the official, urging him to produce a red card, which he did, and Rooney was off.

Ronaldo was then captured on film winking at the bench as Rooney trudged from the field. This incensed the fans and the England players, but it also served to inspire them to greater efforts.

For the next hour, through the rest of normal time and extra time, the ten men held the 11. England had some decent chances too – a Lampard free kick had Ricardo scrambling, but substitute Aaron Lennon could not turn home the rebound. John Terry and Peter Crouch weren't far away either, but after 120 goalless minutes yet again it came down to penalties.

I stayed in my seat, alongside some of the ITV Sport guys, and inwardly prayed. My old mate from my TVS days, Simon Moore, had got me the ticket, because as non-rights holders we were finding it hard to get them through FIFA.

Here we go again, I thought, another penalty shoot-out reporting England. Could it be fifth time lucky?

Simao got it under way for Portugal and beat Paul Robinson in the corner as he dived to his right: 1-0

Lampard for England and Ricardo plunged to his left to save: still 1-0.

Hugo Viana then struck the post and it went wide (did Robinson maybe get a fingertip to it?): 1-0

Hargreaves shot into the corner, and scored: 1-1

Armando Petit across the keeper and wide (hard to see if Robbo got anything on it): still 1-1

Steve Gerrard next up for England and Ricardo dived left to save: still it was 1-1 after SIX penalties.

Helder Postiga (so good in the 2004 shoot-out) with another really cool finish: 2-1 Portugal

Jamie Carragher rushed up quickly and scored, but the referee said, 'Wait for the whistle!' and ordered a retake. Second time around and Ricardo saved to his right, becoming the first keeper in World Cup history to save three penalties in a shoot-out: 2-1

Cristiano Ronaldo with the chance to win it – and he did, no problem: 3-1 Portugal, game over. They went through to the semi-final again, England went home again.

Two years previously, IF Rooney had not been injured, England would almost certainly have won the EURO 2004 quarter-final. This time, IF Rooney had not been sent off there was every chance an increasingly strong-looking England would have gone on to victory.

We gathered around the TV sets in the media centre to watch Sven's last post-match press conference in charge. Typically, he did not think of himself, instead issuing a passionate (for him) plea not to blame Rooney too much for the red card, 'Please, don't kill him – he is the future.' How right he was.

The next day, Sven and Beckham came into the media centre in Baden-Baden to conduct their farewell media conferences. I was sad to see Sven go. He may not have been a tactical genius but he was nobody's fool either, and the players loved him. Three consecutive major tournament quarter-finals doesn't seem too bad a record in hindsight, while Manchester City, Notts County and Leicester City all employed him in the future. But on a personal level this was very much the end of the road.

The Beckham news conference was charged with emotion as he announced that he was standing down as captain. He had worn the armband with pride since that day in Turin in November 2000 when caretaker manager Peter Taylor picked him out as this generation's leader.

I loved Becks. He wasn't the greatest player, but he had such a sweet right foot and could deliver crosses, corners, and free kicks like almost no one else in the world. He was also a really decent bloke and the most grounded multi-millionaire I ever met. Dealing with him was always a pleasure. Ask me who tops my list of football's nice guys and it's David Beckham by a distance (from Frank Lampard and Steven Gerrard, in case you were wondering, with Joe Cole fourth).

What we all wondered now, with Steve McClaren taking charge, was whether Beckham even had an England future. He was tantalisingly close to 100 caps, but would he still get picked if he wasn't the captain?

After England flew home we moved on to Munich. Sadly my producer Keith James had to go home after his father was taken seriously ill, and an old friend – Alan Myers – replaced him. Alan is 'Mr Everton' in my book, with a lovely, dry sense of humour and just a touch of eccentricity.

Our live position outside the Allianz Arena was awesome (a big pat on the back to our production manager Steve Bone). We looked down on the spectacular new stadium from high up on a hill as the fans started arriving for the France v Portugal semi-final and it looked an amazing shot on camera.

The only problem was that getting back afterwards was quite an effort. After a 20-minute walk we had to run up this really steep grassy hill in the dark. Puffing frantically, I reached the top just ahead of Alan and he was so annoyed with himself for coming second that he imposed a rigorous new fitness regime on himself when he returned home. To this day I think he still keeps to it.

On to Berlin for the final: France versus Italy, and my first visit to this historic city. It had been a long drive north from Munich, but it was great to join up with all the Sky Sports News personnel who had been out in Berlin since day one, but whom we had yet to come across, like really good camera guys such as Pete Caine (brother of my best mate David) and Paul Davis.

I counted more than 50 TV news crews at the media conference ahead of the final – the interest was huge, and the only cloud on the horizon was trying to get a ticket for the match itself.

In the hours leading up to the game we pleaded with FIFA to give us access, pointing out that we had covered every single England qualifier, we were a national broadcaster, and had covered matches in every round leading to the final. It fell on deaf ears.

The last chance came about 30 minutes before kick-off when a senior FIFA official appeared on the media bridge leading into the ground with a large wad of media passes for the final. Myself and Sky News's Chris Skudder got ourselves to the front of the queue and watched aghast as they were handed out to everyone but us. I remember one photographer from Cambodia being given a pass, and he was not even that bothered about going in. As the last ticket was handed out the FIFA official turned to me and Chris and said, 'Don't you get it, Sky? You are not rights holders – we don't want you!'

He then marched off and pompously told us to go and watch the final on TV in the media centre, which is exactly what we did in the first half.

We sat there and watched Zinedine Zidane put France ahead on seven minutes from a penalty conceded by Marco Materazzi. Then we watched as Materazzi scored a header to equalise for Italy. But we did not want to watch on TV, we had spent six weeks in Germany covering every cough and splutter of this World Cup and we felt we should be inside experiencing the final first hand.

It was then that Chris said, 'I did see a small hole in one of the wire fences leading into the ground over the far side of the media compound. Do you want to give it a try?'

So we did. We had to work on the hole to make it big enough for us to fit through it, but eventually we managed it, scrambled through and started running towards the crowds near the ground. One steward did try to stop us, but we kept going until we got all the way into the press box. There was no room there at all but we just joined others sitting on the steps and no one bothered us, though we half-expected a tap on the shoulder at any time.

That is how we watched the 2006 World Cup Final. FIFA may not have invited us to their party, but we gatecrashed it anyway in the finest traditions of media blagging. The rest of the game was compelling but goalless, until it exploded to life in the 110th minute when Zidane headbutted Materazzi in the chest and was sent off in the final game of his career.

Ten-man France hung on easily enough through the rest of extra time and it was quite nice to watch a penalty shoot-out which did not involve England. David Trezeguet, the man who had scored the Golden Goal to beat Italy in the EURO 2000 Final, was the only player to miss. Fabio Gross struck the decisive penalty as Italy won 5-3 to lift the World Cup for a fourth time.

The next day, after a couple of appearances in the rooftop Sky Sports News studio, I flew home to my family and a new era for England. No Sven-Goran Eriksson and no David Beckham as captain. One thing was for sure: it would be different.

# 15

# Jose Mourinho and the Rise of Chelsea

W HEN Jose Mourinho arrived at Chelsea in June 2004 of course we knew that he had won the Champions League with Porto, but he was still mainly famous here for his emotional charge down the touchline at Old Trafford in stoppage time to celebrate Porto's dramatic equaliser in the round of 16.

That would all change very quickly. At his first Chelsea press conference he caused a bit of a sensation when he said, 'Please don't call me arrogant, because what I'm saying is true. I'm European champion – I'm not one from the bottle, I think I am a special one.'

From then on Jose was known as 'The Special One' and it certainly seemed apt as he won two Premier Leagues, two League Cups and one FA Cup in the space of three seasons. He was box office and attending his news conferences was a real highlight of any week – he had the media eating out of his hand in those early days, with his mix of no-nonsense straight talking, punctuated with wit, charm, a smile and a whole host of one-liners.

After watching Chelsea dominate a goalless draw with Tottenham at Stamford Bridge he told the media afterwards, 'As we say in Portugal they brought the bus and they left the bus in front of the goal.'

So the expression 'parking the bus' became commonplace, to denote a very defensive performance.

Jose made a great start to his time at Chelsea. He opened with a victory against Manchester United, Eidur Gudjohnsen scoring the only goal, and proceeded to win his first four league games in charge while conceding just one goal. That was scored in the first minute by Southampton's James Beattie, though in a bizarre twist he also put through his own net for the equaliser before Frank Lampard won the game with a penalty.

After eight games Jose had won six and drawn two, with still only one goal conceded. In that time he had also beaten his old team Porto in the group stage of the Champions League and in early October he steered Chelsea to a 1-0 win over Liverpool, but his team were not top of the league yet – because the champions Arsenal had made an even better start.

On 16 October Chelsea lost in the Premier League under Jose for the first time, surprisingly going down 1-0 to a Nicolas Anelka penalty at Manchester City. Eight days later would be the game that defined the early part of the season and became known as 'Pizzagate' when Arsenal took their 49-match unbeaten league run to Old Trafford.

Like Chelsea, Arsenal also opened with four straight wins – racking up 16 goals in the process, with Thierry Henry, Robert Pires and Dennis Bergkamp responsible for ten of them. They won a fifth match in a row and arrived in Manchester top of the league with 25 points from nine unbeaten fixtures.

By contrast Manchester United had started slowly. After losing 1-0 at Chelsea on the opening day they had won three and drawn five of their next eight games, and were a massive 11 points behind Arsenal when the two teams met.

For more than 70 minutes there was absolutely nothing between them – the previous year it had been billed as 'The Battle of Old Trafford', and this encounter was no less intense. Then Sol Campbell caught Wayne Rooney inside the area, Rooney made the most of it, and referee Mike Riley awarded a penalty.

Up stepped Ruud van Nistelrooy, who sent Jens Lehmann the wrong way and raced over to celebrate in the corner. He had not forgotten the taunts the Arsenal players had subjected him to the previous season and he made sure he enjoyed this moment, shouting out gleefully at the end of all the congratulations.

In stoppage time United countered and Rooney celebrated his 19th birthday by sweeping the ball in from just outside the six-yard box to seal a 2-0 win, meaning there would be no 50-match unbeaten run for Arsenal – the sequence ended tantalisingly on 49, and it took the players some time to recover. They won only one of their next six games (also losing to Manchester United in the League Cup), though that victory was 5-4 at White Hart Lane in one of the most amazing north London derbies I ever saw.

Tottenham led before Thierry Henry equalised right on half-time and that sparked a seven-goal second half. Lauren with a penalty and Patrick Vieira seemed to have put Arsenal in control at 3-1, but Jermain Defoe pulled one back only for Freddie Ljungberg to make it 4-2. Ledley King cut the gap again, Arsenal scored again through Ray Parlour, but with two minutes to go Freddie Kanoute made it 5-4 to set up a grandstand finish. Arsenal just about hung on but it really had been a case of 'you score, we score'. So much for derbies supposedly being tight, tense affairs.

Back to that Old Trafford game and the end of Arsenal's long unbeaten run – it led to some controversy behind the scenes, with soup and pizza supposedly being thrown by Arsenal players in the tunnel afterwards. 'Pizzagate' or 'The Battle of the Buffet' was how the game came to be known.

While Arsenal faltered afterwards Chelsea took full advantage, beating Blackburn, West Bromwich Albion and Fulham to go clear at the top. After that defeat to Manchester City they won six games out of seven in the league and scored four goals on five occasions. They had also won their opening four group games in the Champions League and moved smoothly through to the knockout stages, despite a 2-1 defeat at Jose's old club Porto on matchday six.

When they faced Arsenal at Highbury on Sunday, 12 December they were leading the champions by five points, with 39 from 16 games. Two weeks earlier Arsenal had also lost in the last minute at Liverpool, with Neil Mellor scoring the winner, so the Gunners could not afford to lose more ground.

Thierry Henry put his side in front early on but John Terry soon equalised with a powerful header. Henry then restored the lead with a quickly taken free kick while Petr Cech was still organising the wall. Substitute Eidur Gudjohnsen levelled it up at 2-2 soon after half-time and that was how it stayed – so Chelsea kept their five-point advantage.

After ending Arsenal's unbeaten run, Manchester United lost at Portsmouth and drew at home in the Manchester derby, so they had 18 points from 12 games. Then they clicked into gear by winning ten and drawing two of their next 12 games to reach the 50-point mark by the time they arrived at Highbury for the return with Arsenal the following February.

There were more problems in the tunnel, this time beforehand, as words were exchanged between the two teams (notably involving Patrick Vieira and Roy Keane), with referee Graham Poll having to call for calm. Arsenal led twice but Cristiano Ronaldo scored two goals and even though Mikaël Silvestre was sent off, United won 4-2 in a thrilling game. The battle for second was still very much on and United stretched their unbeaten run to 19 before consecutive defeats at Norwich and Everton stopped them in their tracks.

For Chelsea, success in the league games was being matched by a good run in the League Cup. They beat West Ham, Newcastle United and neighbours Fulham to reach the semi-finals, where they were drawn against Manchester United.

A goalless first leg at Stamford Bridge appeared to have handed the advantage to United, but at Old Trafford Chelsea found an extra gear to pull off an impressive 2-1 victory. Lampard scored a fine goal to make it 1-0, starting the move and then running 50 yards to finish it, but United felt they should have had a penalty when Quinton Fortune was brought down by Wayne Bridge. Ryan Giggs chipped in a great equaliser midway through the second half, but Chelsea won it with a freak goal five minutes from the end. Damien Duff's 50-yard free kick was intended as a cross, but somehow it found its way over goalkeeper Tim Howard and into the net.

The final against Liverpool was in Cardiff, with the roof closed at the Millennium Stadium, so a cracking atmosphere was guaranteed. Eight weeks earlier Chelsea had won 1-0 at Anfield with a late goal to maintain their push at the top of the table so they were the favourites.

But they went into this match off the back of consecutive defeats to Newcastle and Barcelona and fell behind after just 45 seconds to the quickest goal ever scored in a League Cup Final. Fernando Morientes hoisted over a cross and John Arne Riise smashed an unstoppable left-footed volley past Petr Cech. It was a sensational start to the game.

Jerzy Dudek made a couple of important saves, captain Steven Gerrard had a great chance in the second half to make it 2-0, but with 11 minutes to go it was still 1-0. A Chelsea break was stopped by a cynical foul from Dietmar Hamann, referee Stephen Bennett should have played the advantage as Chelsea had a great opportunity to counter-attack, but he pulled back play to book Hamann as Chelsea complained bitterly at the injustice.

Ironically Paulo Ferreira's subsequent free kick went in off Gerrard's head and the post for the equaliser. The own goal was tough on Liverpool, but Chelsea probably deserved to be level and soon forgot about not being allowed to play on.

There was more drama immediately after the goal when Jose walked along the touchline in front of the Liverpool fans with his finger to his lips to hush them. The crowd went mad and Jose was sent off, having to watch the rest of the final on TV inside.

Duff could have won it in normal time but didn't so extra time got under way. Halfway through it was still 1-1, then came three goals in six minutes as the cup was won and lost. Glen Johnson's long throw found its way to Didier Drogba and the club's record £24m signing flicked it in from close range to make it 2-1. Drogba pulled off his shirt and wheeled away to celebrate in front of the Chelsea fans. Not long afterwards, Lampard's free kick was not properly cleared and Mateja Kezman scrambled the ball over the line – just – before Dudek hauled it back. Chelsea were 3-1 up but within 60 seconds Antonio Nunez headed in Liverpool's second to set up a nerve-jangling finale.

The whistle was greeted with joy and relief by Chelsea. They had just won their first silverware of the Roman Abramovich era and Mourinho had also won his first cup with the club. Now they could continue their pursuit of the league title and the Champions League, knowing there was already something in the trophy cabinet.

The two defeats before the League Cup Final had both come in cup competitions. Newcastle knocked Chelsea out of the FA Cup in round five while Barcelona had taken a 2-1 first leg lead in the last

16 Champions League tie. At the Nou Camp Chelsea had led 1-0 at half-time before Drogba was sent off in the second half and Barcelona fought back to win.

The return at Stamford Bridge was a thriller as Chelsea raced into a three-goal lead inside 20 minutes, but then Ronaldinho pulled two goals back before half-time. At that stage it was 4-4 on aggregate, but Barcelona had the advantage of more away goals. With less than a quarter of an hour to go Terry powered in a header from Duff's corner to make it 4-2 on the night and 5-4 on aggregate. Goalkeeper Victor Valdes claimed he had been fouled by Ricardo Carvalho in the build-up, but the goal stood and Chelsea went through to the quarter-finals.

I was actually in Milan that night watching a Hernan Crespo goal defeat Manchester United 1-0 for a 2-0 aggregate win. I remember thinking that the Italians were very impressive and would take some stopping in that season's Champions League.

The draw for the last eight paired Chelsea with Bayern Munich, who had knocked out Arsenal 3-2 on aggregate. Two Lampard goals helped Chelsea into a 4-1 lead in the first leg before Michael Ballack scored a stoppage-time penalty to give the Germans a lifeline. In Munich Chelsea led 1-0 (Lampard) and 2-1 (Drogba) for a 6-3 aggregate advantage going into added time. Two late Bayern goals very nearly wiped the smiles off Chelsea's faces but the English side went through 6-5 on aggregate.

The outstanding quarter-final tie was Liverpool against Juventus. It was the first time the clubs had met in a competitive game since the 1985 European Cup Final when 39 supporters died in the Heysel Stadium disaster. I covered both legs as Liverpool set up an all-English semi-final with Chelsea.

Before kick-off the 'Banner of Friendship' was exchanged between the two sets of supporters and there was a minute's silence. Once the game got under way Liverpool made a terrific start with Sami Hyypia volleying in from close range after ten minutes. A quarter of an hour later Luis Garcia hit a stunning dipping volley from 20 yards and again Gianluigi Buffon had no chance.

Juventus stirred themselves with Zlatan Ibrahimovic striking the post and Alessandro Del Piero having a header ruled out for offside.

Just after the hour Fabio Cannavaro's downward header slipped through Scott Carson's fingers and it was 2-1. That is how it stayed, so it was perfectly set up for the second leg in Turin.

Another huge security operation took place and it was clear that the Juventus Ultras were determined to avenge Heysel if they could. At one stage outside the ground we spotted a group of them burning a Liverpool flag, and the match was played out against a backdrop of unrest and occasional violence. The Liverpool supporters kept a low profile beforehand, and during the game they did not react as the Ultras threw missiles and continually attacked the fencing round the section which housed the away fans.

On the pitch Liverpool battled to an heroic goalless draw. The side had been depleted by injury – captain Steven Gerrard was missing – but they defended stoutly and got a little bit of luck near the end when Cannavaro struck the post.

Speaking to the Liverpool players afterwards, they were in no doubt that this was going to be their year in the Champions League. After surviving by the skin of their teeth in the group stages thanks to Gerrard's heroics against Olympiacos, which led to Andy Gray's famous commentary, 'Take a bow, son!' it was easy to see why. Things may not have worked out particularly well in the Premier League and they would eventually finish outside the top four, but in Europe they definitely had momentum building.

Chelsea may have done the double over Liverpool in the Premier League (two 1-0 wins, with Joe Cole scoring both the goals) and beaten them in that wonderful League Cup Final, but when the Merseysiders pitched up at Stamford Bridge for the first leg of the Champions League semi-final I somehow sensed that the Londoners were going to find it tough.

For a start they were just one win away from winning their first league title in half a century. I don't care how professional you are, that must have some kind of impact. The two legs of the semi-final were just six days apart with Chelsea's visit to Bolton for the potential league-clincher right in the middle.

Liverpool went with a game plan: not to get beaten. Yet if Drogba or Lampard had taken their chances in the first half it could have been very different. That said, Petr Cech produced a top save to keep out a header from Milan Baros. A goalless draw was a bit of a disappointment when you consider this was the first ever all-English Champions League semi-final, but at the fourth time of asking Liverpool had finally managed to avoid defeat against Chelsea.

A week before that first leg Chelsea had battled out a 0-0 draw with Arsenal, then they beat Fulham 3-1 to leave themselves on the brink of the title. Arsenal had stayed in it mathematically with a 1-0 win over Tottenham but if Chelsea won at Bolton on Saturday, 30 April that was it – the league championship would return to Stamford Bridge for the first time since 1955.

Bolton certainly did not make it easy and Chelsea were forced to dig in during that first half as they came under sustained pressure. After an hour Bolton felt they should have been given a free kick as Fernando Hierro was bundled over, but referee Steve Dunn waved play on and Lampard forced his way into the penalty area, beat two defenders and buried a right-footed shot past Jussi Jaaskelainen.

Back came Bolton and Cech had to produce a stunning save to keep out a header from his own team-mate Geremi. From a Bolton corner Chelsea then counter-attacked, Lampard was in the clear, rounded the keeper and finished coolly with his left foot this time, and Chelsea were Premier League champions.

Three days later they walked out at Anfield to an absolute cacophony of noise – I've never been there when it was louder, and the Main Stand seemed to be shaking as the Liverpool fans gave their team a deafening reception. I thought Chelsea looked a little shell-shocked by the atmosphere, and within four minutes they were behind to a controversial goal.

Milan Baros knocked the ball over the onrushing Cech and was flattened, then Luis Garcia hooked a shot towards goal as William Gallas tried to clear it. Garcia celebrated, the goal was given, and Chelsea protested long and hard that the whole ball had not crossed the line. TV replays could not provide a definitive answer either. Afterwards Jose said the ball had not crossed the line and that as far as he was concerned it was a 'ghost' goal.

Six minutes of stoppage time added to the drama as Liverpool's fans whistled loudly for the game to end. In the final moments Chelsea had their best chance but Eidur Gudjohnsen flashed a shot across the goal and wide, so it was Liverpool who would go to Istanbul for the final against AC Milan, as Chelsea's dream of a Premier League, League Cup and Champions League treble was dashed.

A week later Sir Alex Ferguson ordered his Manchester United team to provide a guard of honour for Chelsea at Old Trafford as a mark of respect. Jose never forgot the gesture and that helped cement the bond between these two top managers. Chelsea won 3-1, finished the season on an unbeaten 29-match run in the league and went on to accumulate a record 95 points, 12 ahead of Arsenal and 18 clear of United in third place.

Before the 'Miracle of Istanbul', Arsenal and Manchester United fought out a bizarre and historic FA Cup Final. Arsenal became the first side to win the final without scoring. United had dominated for 120 minutes, but Arsenal held firm then nicked it on penalties. Jens Lehmann saved Paul Scholes's effort, then Patrick Vieira scored the winning penalty with his final kick as an Arsenal player.

The 2005 Champions League Final will go down as one of THE great games, but it almost passed me by. I was in Chicago with England and watched the first half in a bar downtown. When the third Milan goal went in, I left and returned to the hotel. I was suffering a bit from jet-lag and, even though it was only early afternoon, I fell fast asleep on my hotel bed.

I was woken very soon after by my phone ringing. It was Rich Smith, my producer on this England trip.

'Liverpool have just pulled a goal back!' he exclaimed, before suddenly shrieking, 'Wait, they've got another, its now 3-2! You can watch on Channel 86 on your room TV.' At which point he put the phone down, and I scrambled to find the remote control.

I may have missed Steven Gerrard's header to begin the great fightback but I did catch the replays of Vladimir Smicer's goal, and I was watching in disbelief as Dida saved Xabi Alonso's penalty. The Spanish midfielder then followed up to score from the rebound and it was 3-3. This was extraordinary stuff and the last hour of the game was equally compelling. Jerzy Dudek produced a marvellous double save near the end of extra time to keep Liverpool in it, and then came penalties.

Serginho missed the first for Milan, Dietmar Hamann scored for Liverpool: 0-1

Pirlo then had his kick saved by Dudek, Djibril Cisse was on target: 0-2

Jon Dahl Tomasson made it 1-2, then John Arne Riise missed: still 1-2

Kaka scored for Milan to tie it at 2-2, Smicer made no mistake: 2-3

Andrei Shevchenko then had his penalty saved by Dudek and that was it, against all the odds Liverpool had won after being three goals down to the favourites AC Milan. Having covered six of their games during this amazing run, I still felt I'd been a part of the story, despite missing the final. Needless to say I could not get back to sleep afterwards.

The next season Chelsea came absolutely flying out of the traps. Two Drogba goals helped them beat Arsenal 2-1 in the Community Shield, and a fortnight later he scored again as Chelsea defeated Arsenal 1-0 in the Premier League. Chelsea won their first six league games without even conceding a goal, but they didn't finish there. Three more league victories followed before Everton became the first side to take a point off Jose's champions in a 1-1 draw at Goodison Park on 23 October.

When they went to Manchester United on 6 November they had 31 points after ten wins and a draw in 11 games, but any hopes of doing an Arsenal and going all season unbeaten were ended when Darren Fletcher scored the only goal and Chelsea slipped to their first league defeat.

Two goalless draws with Liverpool in the Champions League group stage meant that four European meetings between the two clubs had produced just one goal, but the rivalry between the two would continue to grow and grow.

The year ended with Chelsea having reeled off eight more consecutive wins (including 2-0 away at Arsenal) and after 20 games they had 55 points with 18 wins and a draw. It was a phenomenal first half to the season and they were practically out of sight from their challengers. The lead grew in the spring to 18 points before they suffered a dip in form and Manchester United went on a ten-match winning streak to cut the gap back to seven.

Chelsea responded again and when the top two met each other at Stamford Bridge on 29 April, the home side needed just one point to retain their title. It was closer than the 3-0 scoreline suggests but there would be no stopping Jose Mourinho and Chelsea. William Gallas headed them in front early on, Joe Cole scored a great solo goal to make it 2-0 and Ricardo Carvalho wrapped it up with a third. Carvalho was also involved in an incident with Rooney which resulted in the England man being stretchered off with a broken metatarsal (again!), putting his World Cup chances in danger.

A week before the victory over Manchester United, Chelsea had lost 2-1 in the FA Cup semi-final to Liverpool. Again they had done the double over the Reds in the league, including a fine 4-1 success at Anfield in October, but for the second season running they lost to Liverpool for the only time in their fifth meeting. John Arne Riise and Luis Garcia both scored before Drogba pulled one back for Chelsea.

There was also disappointment in the Champions League as they went out to Barcelona in the last 16. Asier Del Horno's red card in the first half for a foul on Lionel Messi ensured it was going to be a very difficult evening, but they did lead at half-time through a Thiago Motta own goal. With less than 20 minutes to go Terry headed Messi's free kick into his own net for the equaliser and the Chelsea captain also cleared the ball off the line twice in a frantic finale. Ten minutes from the end Samuel Eto'o popped up with the winner for Barcelona, who eventually went through 3-2 after a 1-1 draw at the Nou Camp.

Manchester United finished a distant second to Chelsea, but ahead of Liverpool and Arsenal, plus they had the consolation of beating Wigan 4-0 in the League Cup Final in Cardiff.

Jose had set his heart on trying to equal Sir Alex Ferguson's achievement of three consecutive Premier League titles, but despite a third season in a row unbeaten at home in the league that dream would always remain just out of reach. No one was harder to beat than Chelsea in 2006/07, they lost just three games all season, but their title challenge ultimately faltered because they drew too many times: 11 in total.

In fact they drew their last five league matches in a row, the third of which on Sunday, 6 May 2007 handed the championship to Manchester United. It was a brave point away at Arsenal on their first visit to the new Emirates Stadium, but it was not enough. Khalid

Boulahrouz was sent off after 43 minutes and from the resulting penalty Gilberto Silva put Arsenal ahead. The ten men came back to equalise through Michael Essien's brave diving header and they pushed hard for a winner, refusing to give up their title without a fight. It stayed 1-1 and United were crowned champions for the first time since 2003.

Chelsea's next game was at home to United and Jose repaid Sir Alex the favour he had shown him in 2005 by giving the new champions a guard of honour as they came on to the pitch. The game finished a 0-0 draw, but the two teams would meet one more time before the season ended.

If the league did not quite go according to plan for Jose, the knockout competitions provided plenty of consolation – and plenty of silverware.

Jose loved the League Cup – it was the first trophy he won at Chelsea and he was seething when his team lost their grip on it in 2006 after going out early on to Charlton on penalties. He tended to field stronger teams than the other sides involved in the Champions League, and he reaped the rewards.

In round three at Blackburn Rovers Joe Cole and Salomon Kalou got Chelsea up and running with a 2-0 victory. Next they thumped Aston Villa 4-0 and followed that with a 1-0 win at Newcastle United (Didier Drogba the scorer) to earn a semi-final with League 2 side Wycombe Wanderers. Wayne Bridge gave Chelsea the lead against the underdogs at Adams Park but Jermaine Easter equalised with 13 minutes left and the fourth-tier outfit went to Stamford Bridge for the second leg with the score level at 1-1. Two goals from Andrei Shevchenko and then two more from Frank Lampard sent Chelsea into the final 5-1 on aggregate. Arsenal awaited them in Cardiff.

Meanwhile, in the Champions League, Chelsea had taken four points out of six from Barcelona in the group stage. Drogba's goal was the difference between the two teams at the Bridge, then they twice came from behind to force a really creditable 2-2 away draw – Lampard and Drogba, with a last-minute equaliser, were their scorers.

As group winners they were away in the first leg of the last 16 – to Porto, where Shevchenko scored the equaliser in a 1-1 draw. At home

Chelsea fell behind, but second-half goals from Arjen Robben and Michael Ballack saw them through to the last eight.

By this time they were also through to the quarter-finals of the FA Cup and they had won a dramatic and fiery League Cup Final. This was to be a season of 25 cup ties.

Frank Lampard scored a hat-trick to see off Macclesfield 6-1 in the third round of the FA Cup, they swept Nottingham Forest aside 3-0 in round four and then won 4-0 against Norwich in the fifth round.

The last League Cup Final at Cardiff was arguably the best. It was often played in torrential rain, it was never less than compelling, and it had some truly disturbing moments too.

Arsenal began the brighter and deserved their lead given to them by 17-year-old Theo Walcott with his first goal for the club. It did not last long: Drogba beat the offside flag (just) to blast home the equaliser. Arsene Wenger was livid at the decision and spent much of the next few minutes berating the officials. Arsenal still carried the bigger threat, even though they had chosen to rest Thierry Henry, and at half-time it was 1-1.

On 63 minutes, Terry attacked a corner and his face connected full pelt with Abou Diaby's swinging boot. It was a total accident but the impact was sickening and Terry was out cold. For a split second I must admit I feared the worst, I really did. Terry was not moving, the players were waving frantically for help, and a hush had fallen over the stadium.

Arsenal physio Gary Lewin answered the call, realising immediately that Terry had swallowed his tongue and would have choked to death but for his swift intervention. After several minutes of treatment the stricken defender was stabilised, given oxygen and strapped on to a stretcher before being taken to hospital. He recovered consciousness and amazingly returned to the ground some time after the final whistle to be with his victorious team-mates.

He was not back in time to lift the cup (that honour went to Frank Lampard), but I did witness the most poignant moment of his return, when he sought out Lewin to thank him for potentially saving his life. The two knew each other of course through England, and Terry made his gratitude very clear. Back to the game, and Lampard struck the bar as Arsenal's young team started to tire, and with just six minutes left of the 90 Robben swung over a cross from the left, which Drogba headed in with great power for the winning goal. There was still time – 12 minutes of stoppage time was played, mainly because of the Terry injury – for Andrei Shevchenko to strike the upright and for THREE players to be sent off.

A clash between John Obi Mikel and Kolo Toure started it all. Toure took exception and retaliated, prompting Lampard and Cesc Fabregas to have their own wrestling match. In the ensuing melee both managers came on to the pitch to try and restore order, and when the dust did finally settle referee Howard Webb produced red cards for Toure, Mikel and surprisingly also for Emmanuel Adebayor, though no one really seemed to know why in the latter case. It took a while to persuade Adebayor to leave the pitch, while Fabregas and Lampard both received yellows.

Jose celebrated with real vigour at the final whistle – it was his second League Cup and went nicely with his two Premier League titles.

The knockout games kept on coming. In the FA Cup sixth round Chelsea were involved in a thriller with Tottenham. Lampard scored twice, but it needed an 86th-minute equaliser from Salomon Kalou to earn them a replay after a 3-3 draw. At White Hart Lane, Chelsea snatched it 2-1 with Shaun Wright-Phillips scoring the key goal.

In the Champions League quarter-final Chelsea fell behind to Valencia at Stamford Bridge through a goal from David Silva, but again it was Drogba to the rescue with a second-half equaliser. I was at a packed Mestalla Stadium for the second leg and saw Fernando Morientes, their 2004 Champions League nemesis, put Valencia ahead. This time it was Shevchenko and Michael Essien, with a last-minute goal, who sent Chelsea into their third Champions League semi-final in four seasons.

A few days later Chelsea reached the FA Cup Final with victory over Blackburn Rovers at Old Trafford, Lampard notching his sixth goal of the competition with Michael Ballack also on target. They would face Manchester United at Wembley.

In the Premier League it had been one win each when Chelsea had met Liverpool, so another really closely fought encounter was on the cards. This time Chelsea managed to secure a lead from their first leg at home, Joe Cole (so often a scorer against Liverpool) grabbing the only goal from close range.

The second leg at Anfield was another raucous affair – the Liverpool fans seem to be able to find an extra level of noise on these big European nights, and they took great pleasure in constantly chanting, 'F*ck off Chelsea FC, you ain't got no history. Five European Cups and 18 leagues, that's what we call history!'

Halfway through the first half Daniel Agger had levelled the tie on aggregate, scoring from Steven Gerrard's clever free kick. Petr Cech and Pepe Reina both made important saves, Dirk Kuyt hit the bar and had a goal disallowed, but after 120 minutes it was 1-0 on the night and 1-1 on aggregate, so that meant penalties.

Bolo Zenden shot high into the top corner with Cech going the wrong way: 1-0

Arjen Robben's spot kick was well saved by Liverpool goalkeeper Reina: still 1-0

Xabi Alonso scored past Cech into the corner: 2-0

Frank Lampard kept Chelsea in it with his successful penalty: 2-1

Steven Gerrard sent Cech the wrong way: 3-1

Geremi – brought on as a substitute after 118 minutes specifically for penalties – saw his spot-kick saved as Reina dived to his right: 3-1 and the game was virtually up for Chelsea

Kuyt delivered the *coup de grace*, scoring into the corner to Cech's right: 4-1, a comprehensive shoot-out win, and Liverpool were off to Athens for the final. The following night, AC Milan knocked out Manchester United to set up a repeat of the 2005 classic and this time the Italians would have their revenge.

Chelsea had lost in the semi-finals for the third time in four seasons and there would be more European heartache along the way over the next few years, before the ultimate happy ending.

\* \* \* \* \*

On Saturday, 19 May 2007 the FA Cup Final returned to Wembley after an absence of seven years.

The last time I had watched football there was a few days after England had lost a World Cup qualifier to Germany in October 2000. A series of celebrity matches gradually turned the pitch into a quagmire and I interviewed among others Rod Stewart and Audley Harrison.

The redeveloped stadium looked magnificent, the media facilities were great, and the atmosphere built up as the pre-match parade of old cup heroes got under way, Prince Andrew performed the official opening and there was a fly-past from the Red Arrows. The playing surface seemed fine at the start, though it did cut up a bit, and that would be a recurring theme in the early days of 'New Wembley'.

The match itself was a bit of a let-down. Manchester United and Ryan Giggs had probably the best of the chances – but they were few and far between. Giggs had played in the previous United–Chelsea FA Cup Final back in 1994 and this was his seventh of the showpiece occasions.

Four minutes from the end of extra time, with penalties looming for a third final in a row, Drogba played a one-two with Lampard, collected the return and scored the winning goal to give Chelsea the domestic cup double. Chelsea had also won the last final at the old Wembley, so perhaps it was somehow appropriate.

Their haul of major trophies under Mourinho was five in three seasons but the bubble was about to burst.

Three wins and two draws from the first six games of the 2007/08 Premier League season was not exactly a dynamic start, but it was not too bad either. It was deemed a little sluggish by the powers-that-be at Chelsea as rumours persisted of behind-the-scenes difficulties.

There was talk of a fall-out between Jose and the owner Roman Abramovich. Only one winner was possible there and when Chelsea failed to beat the Norwegian team Rosenborg in their opening Champions League group game, the almost unthinkable happened as they parted company with the most successful manager in their history.

When Chelsea played their next league game – away to Manchester United – Avram Grant was in charge and the (first) Jose Mourinho era was over. The Blues' success continued while Jose went on to win the league title in Italy with Inter Milan and in Spain with Real Madrid. League championships in four different countries was an extraordinary achievement and Jose also lifted a second Champions League title in 2010 as Inter did the Treble.

At Stamford Bridge they continued to sing his name, in the hope that one day he would be back, and just under six years later he did return. He even delivered another Premier League crown and another League Cup, but somehow it never quite seemed as happy second time around – he often appeared to be a little world-weary – and two incidents in particular stand out.

In his first season back there was a four-way battle for the title involving Manchester City, Chelsea, Liverpool, and Arsenal. The latter two seemed quite happy talking up their prospects, but City and Chelsea were always reluctant. Jose talked of his team as being the 'little horses' in the race and not genuine contenders.

One Friday at his weekly news conference I asked Arsene Wenger why he thought this might be. His theory was that some (and no names were mentioned) might have a 'fear of failure'. Within an hour Jose had been told of the comment and hit back with the remark that Wenger was a 'specialist in failure'. It caused a furious row and the Wenger–Mourinho relationship deteriorated still further. I could not help feeling that the old Jose would have danced cleverly round an issue like that and not caused such offence.

The other episode came on the opening day of the 2015/16 season as Chelsea began the defence of their title at home to Swansea City. His public criticism of Dr Eva Carneiro, a member of his medical team, after she had gone on to the field to treat the injured Eden Hazard, seemed way over the top. The fall-out was considerable, the players seemed to be affected by it all, and the side's fortunes dipped sharply.

After a defeat away to Leicester City in December 2015 and with Chelsea hovering not far from the relegation zone, Jose Mourinho was sacked again.

# 16

# England Fail to Qualify

STEVE McClaren was appointed England manager on 4 May 2006 – but only after Portugal's Luiz Felipe Scolari had turned the job down, claiming press intrusion would make it intolerable. McClaren had been a coach under Sven-Goran Eriksson from October 2000 to November 2002 and again from just before EURO 2004 through to the 2006 World Cup, so he knew the set-up and the players. He seemed a reasonable and logical choice. The FA had announced early in 2006 that Sven would not be in charge after the World Cup, which meant his contract through to EURO 2008 was effectively ripped up following the 'Fake Sheikh' newspaper sting.

McClaren formally took over on 1 August 2006 and appointed Terry Venables as his assistant, a shrewd move designed to increase the popularity of the new regime among the public at large. He also axed David James, Sol Campbell and most notably David Beckham from his first squad, claiming he wanted to take the team in 'a different direction'.

Many England fans were horrified at the dropping of the popular former captain, especially as he was just a handful of caps away from reaching the 100 mark – something not achieved by an England player since Peter Shilton in 1988. Beckham's tearful retirement as captain in the immediate aftermath of England's 2006 World Cup exit allowed McClaren to pass the armband on to John Terry, the man who had just led Chelsea to back-to-back Premier League titles.

He was the natural leader in the group, though much less keen than Beckham had been when it came to media duties. Typically Terry got the McClaren era up and running – heading in the opening goal from close range against Greece in the first game since the 2006 World Cup. True, it was only a friendly and Greece were a pale imitation of the doughty side which had won EURO 2004, but this was still an encouraging display as England stormed into a 4-0 lead by half-time. Frank Lampard and Peter Crouch, with two, were the other scorers.

It was even easier in the next game against Andorra. EURO 2008 qualifying points were at stake and Crouch put England ahead after just four minutes, adding another in the second half. In between Steven Gerrard scored a good goal and Jermain Defoe grabbed two more in a 5-0 rout. That made it two wins out of two and nine goals from a team still missing Wayne Rooney (suspended after his red card in the World Cup quarter-final) and Michael Owen (injured long term).

Owen Hargreaves had looked particularly impressive in central midfield. In Germany during the summer he had been deployed in several positions and the Andorra game was his fifth consecutive start. Against Macedonia four days later he made it six in a row, the best sequence of his 42-cap England career.

Skopje, the capital of Macedonia, was again hot and dusty – but the city centre had seen a fair amount of redevelopment in the three years since England had last been there. It also seemed a lot more Western in outlook and the nightlife in the new complex by the river Vardar was bustling and friendly.

England did just enough in a tricky encounter, winning 1-0 with a goal in the first minute of the second half from Crouch. That was his fifth in three games and England under McClaren had six points from their first two qualifiers.

It was then that things started to go wrong – the next five matches produced just one goal, and that was in a friendly against Holland in Amsterdam, though it was Rooney's first England goal in more than a year. The next qualifier was the return with Macedonia and again England could not beat them at home. This time they couldn't even score – despite Rooney's return. Gerrard was booked so missed the away game in Zagreb just a few days later.

This would be McClaren's first defeat and it raised a lot of issues. It was most notable for the farcical own goal scored by Gary Neville, when his gentle pass back was completely missed by Paul Robinson. The goalkeeper's 'air shot' was the stuff of nightmares (and ridicule) and set the seal on a less than impressive England performance.

The tactic of playing three at the back – Neville, Rio Ferdinand and Terry – did not work, England badly missed Gerrard in midfield, and there seemed to be no plan B after going 2-0 behind. To be fair to Robinson he did produce several fine saves to keep Croatia at bay, but this was a night to forget from an English perspective.

The Maksimir Stadium was a forbidding place and Zagreb had an edgy atmosphere which made the whole trip a little intimidating. England now had seven points from four games and, while everyone else had also dropped points along the way, it was becoming clear that qualifying could not be taken for granted – even though the top two in the group were guaranteed to reach the finals in Austria and Switzerland.

England then had to wait more than five months for their next qualifier, an incredibly frustrating period for McClaren, who just wanted the chance to try and put things right. A draw with Holland and a home defeat to Spain in friendlies did not help much either, so England and their manager were coming under pressure as they prepared for a first competitive meeting with Israel, taking place in Tel Aviv.

Because of potential industrial action among air traffic controllers across Europe we flew out on the Tuesday and for the first and only time I got upgraded to first class. We had travelled via Frankfurt, so this was the height of luxury on Germany's flagship carrier. The seats, the food and the service could not be faulted, but sadly we hit the worst air turbulence I have ever encountered and this completely spoiled the experience. Oh well, maybe next time.

Tel Aviv was a vibrant beach city on the extreme south-eastern shores of the Mediterranean and, but for the security everywhere, you might have thought you were still in Europe. The arrival of the England football team later in the week was big news.

This part of the Middle East was fascinating, nowhere more so than Jerusalem – and the day after landing that is where we headed on a sightseeing/filming expedition to take in the Western ('Wailing') Wall, the Tower of David, the Yad Vashem Holocaust memorial centre, the Church of the Holy Sepulchre, and the Al-Aqsa Mosque. It was humbling and awe-inspiring in equal measure. Our two guides seemed to be a representation of the city and the region – one was Jewish, the other Palestinian. They were constantly bickering and mercilessly teasing each other, and they were also the very best of friends.

Israel had opened Group E with two wins and a draw before succumbing to an Eduardo hat-trick in a 4-3 defeat at home to the leaders Croatia. For the third qualifier in a row England failed to score and, although Jamie Carragher hit the bar with a second-half header, this was not a great performance. Some fans could even be heard chanting, 'What a load of rubbish!'

With the press box full to overflowing we had seats among the Israeli supporters and they never ceased urging on their side at a packed Ramat-Gan Stadium. England had fallen five points behind Croatia and the match reports were mostly pretty gloomy, but Israel were not a bad team – especially with West Ham's Yossi Benayoun in their ranks.

By the time we reached Barcelona, where England would face Andorra at the Olympic Stadium, it was clear that McClaren's men would have to win and win well to quieten an increasingly sceptical media as well as placate a growing number of disaffected fans.

The home of Espanyol is a world away from Barcelona's Nou Camp and this was a game with a strange atmosphere – England supporters comfortably outnumbered the locals in the 12,000 crowd and they made plain their dissatisfaction with the England team in no uncertain manner. When the teams went off at half-time with the score still 0-0 McClaren and his players were subjected to a crescendo of whistling, jeers and boos.

Four days on from Tel Aviv and it seemed England were no closer to ending their goal drought. In qualifiers it stretched to over 360 minutes, or four complete games, but then salvation came along in the shape of Steven Gerrard. First he drove in a shot from 20 yards, then added a second with a neat finish to get England up and running again. In the last minute David Nugent on his debut scored a third, touching Jermain Defoe's goal-bound shot over the line from a couple of inches out.

Despite the victory the pressure appeared to be getting to McClaren – his news conference afterwards was short and (not especially) sweet. He walked in, sat down, then said, 'Gentlemen, if you want to write whatever you want to write, you can write it – because that is all I'm going to say. Thank you.'

And with that he was off. He would not stop to talk in the mixed zone interview area either, although the players were happy enough to speak about getting back to winning ways in what had been a physical encounter against a pretty cynical team.

The next stop for England was Wembley on 1 June 2007, almost seven years after their last game there had ended with Kevin Keegan quitting. There were no shock resignations this time, though there was a sting in the tail as Brazil's Ribas Diego headed an equaliser in the dying seconds to prevent the team making a winning return home.

Up until then it had been the David Beckham show. The former captain was recalled from the international wilderness and wasted no time in showing England what they had been missing. One curling free kick whistled just inches wide, another almost set up a goal for the fit-again Michael Owen (his first England game in virtually a year), then midway through the second half Beckham's free kick picked out captain John Terry to head England in front. 'Goldenballs' was back!

He went off after 75 minutes to a standing ovation. More importantly he had convinced Steve McClaren that he still had an England future and it was no surprise when he was named in the starting line-up again five days later for the qualifier against Estonia in Tallinn.

Not quite the 'Land of the Midnight Sun', but not too far off it either, Tallinn was an engaging place with pretty much 22 hours of daylight. No wonder it was becoming such a popular stag party venue. The Estonians were very friendly, very blonde, and very Scandinavian in outlook – the former Baltic state had come a long way in the decade and a half since gaining independence. Finland was just 30 miles away from Tallinn, and it was to Helsinki we flew originally en route to Estonia. The second part of our journey was in a small twin-prop plane which afforded great views over the Gulf of Finland.

The weather was gloriously warm and sunny for England's last game of the 2006/07 season but there would be no end-of-term feel to this one. England meant business and Beckham was very much to the fore, giving the team that vital creative spark.

Joe Cole volleyed England in front, then Peter Crouch scored from a wonderful Beckham right-wing cross, and Beckham also set up Owen for the third – again with a cross from the right. Despite the problems the team had encountered they ended on a high and would go in to the following season's key qualifiers against Russia and Croatia in good heart.

McClaren had begun well with three consecutive victories, but it was just two wins from the last eight and there was still plenty of work to be done if England were to qualify for EURO 2008. With seven matches played they were fourth in their group, on 14 points. Croatia led the way on 17, Israel also had 17 but from eight matches, while Russia were third on 15 from seven.

Before England recorded their first win at the new Wembley, they suffered their first defeat there – and it was to Germany, the team who had beaten them in the last game at the old Wembley. Lampard put them ahead before another worrying error from keeper Paul Robinson gifted the Germans an equaliser. There was nothing Robinson could do about Christian Pander's spectacular winner for the visitors, but this was not the way England had hoped to prepare for the forthcoming qualifiers.

Nevertheless, the first competitive England match at the redeveloped Wembley gave the team a much-needed boost with a milestone 3-0 victory over Israel. Shaun Wright-Phillips replaced the injured Lampard and scored the first goal, Owen got another and Micah Richards notched his one and only with three lions on his chest.

Four days later England won again at Wembley and Owen scored two more goals as Russia were comprehensively beaten 3-0. McClaren's men looked to have taken a decisive step down the road towards qualifying for EURO 2008. Six goals and six points was a good week's work and confidence was restored.

That mood continued against Estonia as England served up a third consecutive 3-0 win at Wembley, with Rooney scoring his first competitive international goal since EURO 2004 – more than three years previously. Joe Cole crossed from the left, Owen stepped over the ball and Rooney scored in the corner with a slight deflection. Sol Campbell replaced the injured skipper John Terry with his first England appearance in 16 months. Onwards and upwards seemed to be the message now – victory over Russia in a few days would confirm qualification with a game to spare.

Controversially, the Russia away trip was deemed by Sky Sports News to be 'more of a news story than a sports story', so I (the chief football reporter) was left behind in favour of Dan Roan (the chief news reporter). I knew politics was at play but I was seething and took no great pleasure when that decision was later shown to be flawed. Instead of being pitchside or in the press box at the Luzhniki Stadium in Moscow I was in an edit suite at Sky, preparing a piece for the evening bulletins.

It started to go wrong for England the night before, when Terry aggravated his knee injury while training on the artificial pitch. He would subsequently be ruled out. Despite that setback England produced a spirited performance in the first half and took the lead with a cracking goal. Owen won a good header, Rooney trapped the ball on his chest then lashed an unstoppable volley into the roof of the net.

Four minutes into the second half Gerrard was totally unmarked and somehow fired wide from close range. That could have been the clincher, because at this stage England were in control and Richards also came close to extending their lead.

Russia took advantage with two goals of their own in a four-minute spell that turned the game on its head and cast huge doubts on whether England would qualify for the finals.

First Rooney pulled down Konstantin Zyryanov and a penalty was awarded. I'm not quite sure what Rooney was doing in the left-back position, and yes it was a clumsy challenge, but the original foul was clearly outside the area. None of that bothered Roman Pavlyuchenko who smashed the spot-kick into the corner beyond Paul Robinson's full-length dive. Then Robinson made a great save but the ball fell to Pavlyuchenko and the striker who would go on to play for Tottenham in the Premier League scored the winner from close range. It wasn't a bad substitution from manager Guus Hiddink, who had only brought him on just before half-time.

So what did this defeat mean for England? They were still in second place, and the top two qualified automatically, yet crucially the matter was no longer in their own hands. Russia were two points behind but with a game in hand so if they won in Israel on 17 November and followed up with a virtually guaranteed victory in Andorra there would be nothing England could do when they faced Croatia at Wembley on the 21st.

Amazingly, Russia lost in Tel Aviv to a 90th-minute goal from Omer Golan and England were back in it – they just needed one point from the Croatia game four days later. The Croats also stumbled that night, losing 2-1 in Macedonia, but Russia's defeat confirmed their qualification. The perceived wisdom was that this should help England as the visitors would have a lot less to play for – that was the theory anyway.

Injuries accounted for the absence of Terry, Ferdinand, Ashley Cole, Owen and Rooney – this was absolutely wretched luck for McClaren ahead of a game that would determine whether or not he remained as England manager. However, in many people's eyes he made the situation a lot worse by dropping Beckham and Robinson. Beckham had played in the warm-up victory in Austria, but was left on the bench for the game that would decide England's fate.

Scott Carson kept a clean sheet in Vienna but it seemed a huge gamble having a relative rookie in goal on such a big night – and so it would prove.

Eight minutes in and on a wet, slippery surface Niko Kranjcar tried his luck from fully 30 yards out. The ball bounced in front of Carson, who fumbled and somehow managed to deflect it into the roof of the net. It was a ghastly error and just the start McClaren must have been dreading.

Six minutes later Ivica Olic dribbled his way through and rounded a stunned Carson to make it 2-0. Croatia were cock-a-hoop and playing with great freedom and panache. When Russia took the lead against Andorra it was no surprise that McClaren and England were booed and jeered off at the interval.

Enter David Beckham to win his 99th cap – could he write his own script and save the day, like he had done against Greece at

Old Trafford back in 2001? Not long into the second half, another substitute, Jermain Defoe, was brought down and Lampard converted the penalty to make it 2-1. Then Beckham crossed in the 65th minute for Peter Crouch to score the equaliser. At this stage England were going to the finals after all.

As the rain continued to lash down McClaren huddled under an umbrella – a decision he would live to regret and one that saw him ruthlessly ridiculed afterwards.

Croatia kept on going for it and on 77 minutes substitute Mladen Petric fired in from 25 yards for a deserved winner. For the first time in 14 years England had failed to qualify for a major tournament and Wembley was stunned. Croatia won the group by five points from Russia and they finished six ahead of England.

McClaren disappeared down the tunnel pretty sharpish at the end. The following morning he had been summoned to attend an emergency meeting with the Football Association. He awoke to headlines proclaiming 'The Wally with the Brolly' and shortly after nine o'clock he was sacked.

Of course McClaren made mistakes – what manager doesn't? But he was also desperately unlucky with key players being injured for big games. Sometimes he did not always help himself and the decision to leave out Robinson and Beckham on such a big night was, frankly, baffling.

Having said that he was most definitely not 'The Wally with the Brolly' – maybe a coach rather than a manager, but he went up massively in my estimation when he did not cut and run after his sacking, choosing instead to conduct a farewell news conference at St Albans.

He did not duck the issues: admitting he did make mistakes, wishing his successor the best of luck, and apologising for not being able to qualify England for EURO 2008. Once he had completed his media duties he emerged from the hotel, holding his wife by the hand and headed home to the north-east no doubt a little sadder and a little wiser after his 16-month stint as England manager.

His record of nine wins from 18 matches, with four draws and five defeats, left him with a 50 per cent win ratio and quite simply that was never going to be good enough.

# 17

# Champions League Odyssey

I HAVE been lucky enough to cover six Champions League finals for Sky Sports and Sky Sports News, and what's more five of them involved English clubs – including that never-to-be-forgotten all-English clash in the rain of Moscow in 2008.

As I have explained, I was on England duty in 2005 so I missed the 'Miracle of Istanbul', but a year later I was in Paris to see if Arsene Wenger could provide a fairytale ending to what had been a magnificent Champions League campaign by his side.

When the draw was made Arsenal were grouped with FC Thun, Ajax Amsterdam and Sparta Prague. Sir Alex Ferguson reckoned it was one of the easiest groups, rather disparagingly suggesting that Arsenal had been drawn against 'a Swiss village'.

As it happened, Thun proved a very tough nut to crack. It needed a 90th-minute Dennis Bergkamp goal to clinch a 2-1 win on matchday one, though Arsenal did have to play the entire second half with ten men after Robin van Persie was sent off.

On matchday five the game was switched to Bern, because Thun's ground was not big enough, and the Swiss capital proved to be a beautiful (but freezing) place to visit. This was where I was served steak on a stone for the first time – what a brilliant way to eat – and had to buy gloves and a hat to combat the sub-zero temperatures. This time Thun had a player sent off in the first half, but Arsenal only won it very late on with a Robert Pires penalty.

That made it five wins out of five and 15 points, so qualification for the knockout stages was a breeze. It had been set up by a really impressive win at the Amsterdam Arena in the second match. Arsenal went ahead inside two minutes with a fine goal from Freddie Ljungberg, who clipped the ball over the keeper from Jose Antonio Reyes's pass. Pires extended the lead with a second-half penalty, then Arsenal resisted the Ajax fightback and hung on to win 2-1.

Back-to-back victories over Sparta Prague (2-0 away and 3-0 at home) put Arsenal in control of the group, Thierry Henry with three goals and Robin van Persie with two. The only shame was that in the final group game they were held 0-0 at Highbury by Ajax and missed out on the chance to maintain their 100 per cent group record, but they finished first and that was the important thing – the theory being it should give you a slightly easier draw in the last 16.

So much for the theory. When the draw was made in Paris, Arsenal found themselves paired with Real Madrid, but at least the second leg would be at home. Paris was chosen for the draw because it was staging the final a few months later. UEFA did the same thing with Athens the following year but scrapped that approach when Moscow was due to host the 2008 final, because I don't think they fancied a visit to the Russian capital in mid-December.

The most memorable thing about the Paris draw was that the presenter fainted on stage in the middle of a live interview. I won't embarrass the lady by naming her. Steven Gerrard, as captain of the defending champions, had brought the trophy back to UEFA for the draw ceremony – and did his best to catch the presenter as she fell. He failed, but he did gallantly help her to her feet afterwards.

Normally, all the UEFA competition draws were held in Nyon, a beguiling place on the shores of Lake Geneva. The top end of this Swiss town was very much a typical working community and nothing special, to be honest. Down at the lakeside there was a much more relaxed atmosphere. This was where you would find the tourists, among the many bars and restaurants.

Our particular favourite was an English-style pub called The Fishermen's. They had multiple TV screens and were always showing the Champions League and Europa League games ahead of the respective draws. I'm afraid I once watched Manchester City and Manchester United get knocked out in the space of a couple of minutes on neighbouring screens.

The weather in Nyon was sometimes unpredictable – at the December draws the snow could sweep in unexpectedly and cause a complete white-out, but when the sun shone it was glorious and there were spectacular views from the UEFA headquarters across Lake Geneva to France and Mont Blanc. Needless to say it provided the backdrop for many live stand-ups and pieces to camera.

One year, I think it might have been 2011, we flew into Geneva late on a Wednesday afternoon and travelled down to Nyon ready for the following Friday's Champions League last-16 draw. On the Thursday we did an interview with Giovanni Infantino. These days, 'Gianni' is the FIFA president, but back then he was UEFA secretary and happy to be interviewed in English to preview the next day's draw. He told us he was a bit concerned that many club delegates wouldn't make it to the draw because a weather front was due to sweep across Europe that night.

He was right. Southern Britain was paralysed by a massive snowfall and Heathrow Airport was at a virtual standstill, although I remember the Chelsea and Arsenal representatives (David Barnard and David Miles) did both manage to make it to Nyon – and so did Brian Marwood from Manchester City. None of them were optimistic they would get back by air. Quite a few clubs did not make it to the draw, and those that did were anxious to get away soon afterwards as even Geneva Airport was shut for a while. It re-opened, but there were many cancellations, and Arsenal's secretary David Miles hired a car and drove back through Switzerland and France overnight to make it home in time for Saturday's game.

We were not quite so lucky – our flight was one of the last to be cancelled, so by the time we had rescued our equipment we were at the very back of the queues for car hire and accommodation. Ray Ryan, Sky Sports's senior production manager, played a blinder and not only got us virtually the last rooms available in Geneva, but he paid for first-class train tickets back to Paris. The alternative was to wait until the following Monday for an available flight!

The only downside was that we had to be on the platform at 4.30am the next day, and it was well after midnight when we checked in. Still me, my cameraman Ben Bregman and producer Adam Craig made the most of what was developing into a bit of adventure. We had a late-night supper in one of the most cosmopolitan bars I have ever been in. The place was like the United Nations (maybe because of the travel chaos at the airport?) and it was great.

Sweeping through the snowy French countryside the next morning was a fabulous experience – it seemed as if nowhere had escaped, but the whiteness looked utterly beautiful. As we ate breakfast our mood was cheered even more when Ray announced that he had managed to get us some seats on the Eurostar back to London, though we had a tight turnaround – literally less than ten minutes to get across the platforms with all our TV kit.

When our train pulled into Paris we had our bags and were all set, then to our dismay we realised we were arriving at the Gare de Lyon – the Eurostar was due to pull out in a few minutes from the Gare du Nord. We grabbed a taxi, but were never going to make it in time, so were at the back of another long queue to buy tickets for London.

The only ones available were first-class. Sky Sports News was a pretty tight ship and first-class tickets were generally frowned upon, but again Ray came to our rescue and put the cost of all the travel on the Sky Sports budget.

Once aboard the Eurostar we could finally relax – or so we thought. We should have been home late Friday night, it was now 5pm French time, but it looked like we would only be 24 hours late – I was due a few days off so that was quite a relief. We had a couple of glasses of red wine to celebrate. All our cars were marooned at Heathrow, which was completely shut down, so we knew we would only be going home by tube or taxi.

As the train neared the mouth of the Channel Tunnel it slowed right down and stopped just a few yards from the entrance. This was a bit of a worry. We had been hearing while we were waiting at the Gare du Nord that the trains were struggling in the middle of the tunnel because of a lack of power. It just needed one to break down completely and we would not be getting back that night after all. I remember a year or so earlier a couple of trains being stuck for hours and horrendous stories of no air conditioning, no light and stifling temperatures underground. We certainly did not need that – so extra wine was called for while we waited.

Eventually we lurched forward into the tunnel and picked up a bit of speed, which was encouraging, but then we slowed right down to a crawl and that's the way it stayed. At times it was hard to know if we were making progress or not, then we would pass a light, and that would be a huge relief. We were still moving, no matter how slowly. The journey under the tunnel itself is meant to take less than 20 minutes but ours took almost two hours that night. We got through, however, and finally we could all start to see an end to the journey.

The others were all heading for London but I got out at Ebbsfleet International (sadly the train did not stop at Ashford, though it moved so slowly through the station I was almost tempted to try and jump out).

The snow was everywhere and there was just one taxi in the car park. It was a people-carrier and I thought it might be pre-booked, but the guy was happy enough to take me down to my little village in the east of the county.

'How much will it be?' I asked as we headed off into the snowy Kent wilderness. He replied, 'It will be whatever it will be – whatever the meter says.'

Even on the M2 motorway it was slow going, conditions were pretty treacherous and I was relieved not to be driving myself. Meanwhile the meter was doing a merry dance of its own, and by the time he dropped me off about 100 yards from my house (the road looked completely unpassable beyond the point at which he stopped) it had reached the princely sum of £182.60. I think it was a case of market forces working and I winced but paid up and gave him a tip – because at least he had brought me home.

I trudged through the snow and got to my front door 19 hours after leaving my Geneva hotel. By that stage I could barely remember who the English clubs had been drawn against (I'm pretty sure that Arsenal got Barca!).

I have one other memory of Nyon – it involved choking on a piece of steak and ending up in hospital, and having a general anaesthetic for an emergency endoscopy procedure. The evening had started pleasantly enough as we sat down at our favourite restaurant for a bite to eat the night before the quarter-final draw.

Then I managed to get a piece of steak stuck in my throat and, try as I might, I just could not free it. After a couple of hours it was becoming distinctly uncomfortable and my producer Rich Smith called in the paramedics. They took one look at me and sent me down to the local clinic in Nyon, where I was refused any treatment until I had paid out 500 Swiss francs (about £350). No such thing as the NHS here. Once I had stumped up the cash, a doctor examined me briefly and said I would have to be transferred to Lausanne. I reckon that clinic picked up about £50 a minute for the time I was there.

I was packed into the back of an ambulance and blue-lighted the 40km to Lausanne, which had a much bigger hospital. Before long I was being wheeled into the operating theatre, given a general, and woke up a little later in the recovery area. My throat felt very sore but the piece of steak was gone.

Persuading the morning shift to release me first thing was not easy, but eventually they agreed and signed the paperwork. I jumped in a taxi and headed back to Nyon, where I was met by Rich Smith and my cameraman Ben Bregman. They were surprised to see me, but I assured them I was okay and able to work. Both had been up early, preparing to carry on in my absence.

Sky Sports News, sensibly, reduced my workload that day and I got through the broadcasts with no problems. Later, when we arrived back at Heathrow, Sky had laid on a chauffeur as I was not allowed to drive for 24 hours after my general anaesthetic.

A month later Rich and Ben both received £250 after being nominated as 'Golden Balls' winners. This was an in-house incentive scheme designed to reward those who had gone above and beyond the call of duty. I did have a wry smile about actually being the guy who had climbed out of his hospital bed to do the live broadcasts – and yet had not been nominated. I concluded that the only way I could win 'Golden Balls' would be posthumously.

Anyway, back to Arsenal and 2006. Real Madrid has always been a huge name in European terms, but that season they had lost twice in their group away to Lyon and Olympiacos – so they were definitely beatable. I was at Stamford Bridge watching Chelsea lose

2-1 at home to Barcelona so I missed Arsenal's epic 1-0 victory at the Bernabeu. Thierry Henry scored the only goal just after half-time as the Londoners became the first English side to beat Real in the Spanish capital and by all accounts the win was well-deserved.

The second leg at Highbury was a really tense, tight affair with no goals and precious few chances, although both teams did hit the post and both goalkeepers made a brilliant save apiece. Afterwards the players told me they took huge confidence at the way they had defended under pressure and it was now a case of bring on whoever was left in the competition.

Liverpool had lost their grip on the trophy with a 3-0 aggregate defeat against Benfica. All told they had played 14 ties after having to come through three rounds of qualifying. In future the winners would always qualify for the group stages, no matter where they had finished in their league. Chelsea also went out at this stage after failing to get the better of Barcelona, losing 3-2 on aggregate.

For the second season running I found myself going back to Turin for a Champions League quarter-final second leg. A year ago Liverpool had hung on heroically to progress to the semi-finals at the expense of Juventus and this time Arsenal repeated the 0-0 scoreline to do the same. Crucially they had won the first leg at Highbury 2-0, with teenager Cesc Fabregas scoring the first goal and making the second for Henry. Just as significantly, Fabregas dominated former captain and hero Patrick Vieira, who was making a first return to his old club. In the dying minutes the Italians lost their discipline a bit and had Mauro Camoranesi and Jonathan Zebina sent off.

Arsenal's semi-final opponents were Villarreal, the surprise packages of that season's Champions League. The 'Yellow Submarine' as they were known had come through qualifying and had knocked Everton out to reach the group stages. They won both legs against the Merseysiders and then opened their group campaign by holding Manchester United to a 0-0 draw in a game in which Wayne Rooney was sent off. I was at the Estadio de la Ceramica that night and thought they looked very compact, very well organised and difficult to beat. Their manager was the experienced Manuel Pellegrini.

Villarreal actually finished top of Group D even though they only scored three goals in six matches, but two wins and four draws was enough to earn them first place, while United were fourth and last.

In the last 16 Villarreal inflicted more damage on British clubs, knocking out Rangers on away goals thanks to a 2-2 draw in Glasgow. The away goals rule also saw them get past Inter Milan as they followed up a 2-1 defeat at the San Siro with a 1-0 win at home to find themselves in the semi-finals on their Champions League debut.

The first leg at Highbury was dominated by Arsenal, but they were unable to create too many clear-cut chances. Henry had a goal disallowed and another effort cleared off the line while the winner came from an unlikely source – Kolo Toure scoring the only goal in the 41st minute.

The second leg was ITV's live game which gave us a few problems in terms of our access to the flash zone, where the key post-match TV interviews would be carried out. We managed to persuade UEFA to let us in 15 minutes after the final whistle, once the live rights holders had done their initial pieces.

As we arrived we were met by Arsenal's senior media officer Amanda Docherty calling to me, 'Nick, if you want to do Jens Lehmann, it'll have to be now – because he won't be going into the mixed zone!'

Amanda was doing us a massive favour because the German keeper was the man of the moment, after diving to his left to save Juan Roman Riquelme's penalty in the last minute, thereby sending Arsenal into the final. We quickly set up our camera and began filming straight away – even a few seconds' delay would have cost us the interview.

UEFA had wanted us to film any interviews in front of one of their sponsors' backdrops (and normally we would always comply), but they were still all being used, so we just had to interview Lehmann there and then, right in the middle of the flash zone.

Just as our chat was concluding I became aware of a slight disturbance behind us – it turned out that, for a few seconds, we had prevented Pellegrini from going through to the press conference. The Spanish UEFA official (you know who you are!) went absolutely ballistic and tried to get us thrown out. When that didn't happen he became deliberately obstructive and did his level best to prevent us interviewing any more Arsenal players or the manager Arsene Wenger. He failed.

Arsenal had just reached their first (and so far only) Champions League Final and they were ecstatic. For us it was all about capturing the moment – Wenger gave a brilliant interview, the players' excitement was clear to see and we were really pleased with our night's work.

The next day, said UEFA official put in a formal complaint to Sky, calling on me to be banned from the final. Luckily for me Sky's Champions League executive producer was Mark Pearman, an old friend from our Champions TV BSB days in the early 1990s. After I explained what had happened he backed me 100 per cent, and it soon became clear UEFA had no appetite to take any kind of punitive action.

Years later I spoke to Pellegrini about the incident and asked him whether he had been annoyed at being held up. He smiled and said he barely remembered it, but he certainly did not have any problems with me interviewing the man who had stopped his team getting to the Champions League Final.

The one other noteworthy incident from that night was when a fan came on to the pitch just after half-time and tried to drape a Barcelona flag around Thierry Henry. The player shrugged it off, but a few months later he signed on at the Camp Nou after ending his hugely successful career with Arsenal.

The Stade de France is a fantastic venue. It staged the 1998 World Cup Final and I had been there in 2000 when Kevin Keegan's England fought out a 1-1 draw with the world and European champions. Barcelona v Arsenal was a fitting conclusion to the 2006 Champions League competition, both teams having reached this showpiece occasion unbeaten.

The Catalans, like Arsenal, stormed their group with five wins and a draw. They just saw off Chelsea in the last 16, before beating Liverpool's conquerors Benfica, and then disposing of AC Milan 1-0 on aggregate in the semi-final.

Arsenal went to Paris on the back of an incredible ten clean sheets in a row – they had not conceded since matchday two, a phenomenal record. But what happened to the Gunners that night in the French capital was dramatic and heartbreaking in equal measure.

Twice in the opening three minutes Henry could have given Arsenal the lead, but both times goalkeeper Victor Valdes made fine saves. Lehmann was also busy early on but then he rushed out to close down Samuel Eto'o and brought the African striker down. Ludovic Giuly swept the loose ball into the net but Norwegian referee Terje Hauge had already signalled a foul, before brandishing a straight red card.

Arsenal's semi-final hero had been sent off after just 18 minutes and his team would have to somehow survive with ten men for the rest of the game. The first casualty was Robert Pires. He was substituted to allow reserve stopper Manuel Almunia to take over from Lehmann in goal.

Amazingly Arsenal took the lead in the 37th minute when Sol Campbell powered home a header, and despite huge pressure from Barcelona they were still ahead at the interval.

Could they hang on? That was the question, and early in the second half it looked as if they might even extend their lead. Freddie Ljungberg was denied by a fine save from Valdes, then Henry had a great opportunity to make it 2-0 in the 69th minute. Again Valdes made an important stop and shortly afterwards the game turned.

Barcelona substitute Henrik Larsson was the man who made the difference. The ex-Celtic striker set up Eto'o for the equaliser in the 76th minute (his sixth goal in the that season's competition), before sliding in full-back Juliano Belletti for the winner four minutes later.

Arsenal were devastated – they had battled ferociously to maintain their lead, and even with ten men had still carried a threat, but it was just not to be their night and when the final whistle blew some of the players sank to their knees in despair.

Over the next decade Barcelona would give Arsenal a lot more Champions League heartache, and so far there looks to be no end in sight to the pain. That was Wenger's third European final loss but he and his team were able to hold their heads high – they contributed hugely to an amazing occasion.

That was the first time I had witnessed an English team lose a Champions League Final, and all told I would see that happen four times – but I also saw two notable successes, starting in 2008.

Manchester United and Chelsea signalled their intent in the Champions League that year by winning their groups. United won five and drew one to finish top of Group F, ahead of Roma, Sporting FC of Lisbon, and Dynamo Kiev. Chelsea had opened Group B with a disappointing 1-1 draw at home to Rosenborg, which had ended Jose Mourinho's first spell at the club.

I was at the Mestalla Stadium in Valencia for their second Champions League game, where another poor result would have put them under pressure, but new manager Avram Grant steered them to an impressive 2-1 victory. David Villa gave the Spanish side an early lead before Joe Cole equalised and then brilliantly set up Didier Drogba for the winner, thanks to a beautifully weighted through ball with the outside of his right foot.

After that Chelsea cruised through the group, winning the return against Rosenborg in Norway 4-0 with Drogba scoring twice in the opening 20 minutes.

Liverpool and Arsenal had to come through the final qualifying round to take their place in the group stage (both won 5-0 on aggregate). Liverpool opened with a respectable draw away to Porto, then lost at home to Marseille and in Istanbul to unfancied Besiktas. The 2007 finalists were in real danger of going out but they staged a remarkable recovery to qualify in style.

Thirteen days after losing to Besiktas they beat the Turkish side 8-0 in the return at Anfield. Peter Crouch started and ended the scoring, Yossi Benayoun hit a hat-trick, Steven Gerrard grabbed one and Ryan Babel two.

Next they crushed the eventual group winners Porto 4-1 and then clinched a place in the last 16 with a thumping 4-0 success in Marseille. Sixteen goals and nine points from their last three games was some turnaround.

My Champions League campaign began in mid-August, watching Arsenal win 2-0 away against Sparta Prague with goals in the last 20 minutes from Cesc Fabregas and Alexander Hleb. Prague is a fantastic city, especially when the weather is great, and I really enjoyed my visit. I did not know it at the time but I would return in November to see Arsenal face the city's other team, Slavia Prague, when the conditions would not be quite so kind.

I saw the second leg at home against Sparta as Arsenal cruised into the group stage, and was at the Emirates to see them start with a convincing 3-0 win over Sevilla. So far so good, and they continued with a 1-0 win in Bucharest against Steaua and followed that up with a 7-0 thrashing of Slavia Prague.

I covered the return game two weeks later, when Arsenal just could not find a way past the Slavia defence. The game was played in a monsoon, my pitchside monitor soon packed in, and I got an absolute soaking with the wind and rain lashing into my face. It is fair to say that this was not my favourite 0-0 draw.

The dropped points were to prove costly because when Arsenal slipped to a 3-1 defeat in Seville (and that after they had scored first), the Spaniards took over at the top of the group. They stayed there with the Gunners qualifying in second place.

Glasgow Celtic also made it out of their group, so there were a record five British clubs in the draw for the last 16. The English teams could not face each other, while Celtic got Barcelona and went out 4-2 on aggregate.

Manchester United had to dig deep to beat the French champions Lyon and needed an 87th-minute equaliser from Carlos Tevez to avoid defeat in the first leg. Cristiano Ronaldo settled the tie with his goal just before half-time at Old Trafford.

Liverpool continued their resurgent form, beating Inter Milan home and away to go through 3-0 on aggregate, and that was also the margin by which Chelsea beat Olympiacos.

The performance of the round was to come from Arsenal. Because they did not win their group they were paired with the defending champions AC Milan, who battled to a goalless draw in London and were the firm favourites going into the second leg at the San Siro. With six minutes to go it was still 0-0 overall, then Arsenal struck twice through Cesc Fabregas and Emmanuel Adebayor to pull off a very creditable, if slightly unexpected, victory.

So all four English teams were through to the quarter-finals, and as we awaited the draw in Nyon we just knew the odds of them all avoiding each other was very slim. Sure enough two were drawn together – Arsenal and Liverpool, with the first leg at the Emirates. The winners of that tie would meet Chelsea or Fenerbahce for a place in the final – and that was the big story from the draw, a potential third Chelsea v Liverpool Champions League semi-final in four seasons.

Manchester United faced Roma again and seized the advantage with a 2-0 win in the Italian capital, before following that up with a 1-0 victory at home and they were safely though to the semi-finals.

Chelsea lost 2-1 out in Turkey to Fenerbahce, despite leading for the majority of the game. They redeemed themselves at Stamford Bridge with Michael Ballack scoring early to level the tie and then Frank Lampard sealing it with a second goal three minutes from the end, earning them a fourth Champions League semi-final in five seasons. Barcelona joined them after knocking out Schalke 04 and that just left the all-English tie.

I covered both legs as Liverpool faced a fellow Premier League side in Europe for the fourth year running. Arsenal were hoping to make home advantage pay in the first leg and took the lead midway through the first half with a header from Emmanuel Adebayor. They were good value for their lead, but it only lasted three minutes as Steven Gerrard drove into the Arsenal area to set up Dirk Kuyt for the equaliser.

On 65 minutes came the game's big talking point. Kuyt seemed to blatantly drag Alexander Hleb back by the arm as he ran into the penalty area. Arsenal's howls of protest were waved away by Dutch referee Pieter Vink, and 1-1 was how it finished. Advantage Liverpool – just.

The second leg was another one of those great European nights at Anfield that live long in the memory. It was also the third time the two clubs had met each other in six days. I was at that extra Premier League game too, another 1-1 draw, though this time Liverpool scored first through Peter Crouch, before Nicklas Bendtner earned Arsenal a point when he equalised in the second half.

As usual the Kop was in full voice as the teams came out to the UEFA anthem, but they were stunned early on when Abou Diaby squeezed the ball in from a tight angle to give Arsenal the lead right in front of them. Sami Hyypia headed Liverpool level, then Fernando Torres put Liverpool ahead for the first time on 69 minutes with a great turn and shot which ripped into the roof of the net.

Arsenal sent on Theo Walcott and with six minutes to go he raced away down the right from inside his own half and cut the ball back for Emmanuel Adebayor to make it 2-2. Full marks to Arsene Wenger for the substitution and then after that goal for telling his team to keep calm – if it stayed like this they would go through on away goals.

But Kolo Toure was not listening and rather rashly fouled Ryan Babel just a minute later. Gerrard buried the penalty in front of the adoring Kop and the celebrations began in earnest. Two minutes into stoppage time Arsenal fell victim to a Liverpool counter-attack, Babel broke clear and made it 4-2 on the night, 5-3 on aggregate. At the same time Chelsea had beaten Fenerbahce, and the home supporters streaming out of Anfield were contemplating another titanic clash with their old rivals.

One difference with this semi-final was that Liverpool would be at home in the first leg – or more to the point Chelsea would be at home for the decisive second tie. Those wearing red were convinced their team would maintain their great record against English clubs in the Champions League and there was the intriguing possibility of a final against their greatest rivals Manchester United – now that really was something to savour.

After having the better of the first half Liverpool took the lead just before half-time, with Kuyt exploiting some defensive hesitancy. How crucial might that goal be, we wondered, because all the previous encounters had been desperately tight. Chelsea got more of a foothold in the second half but Liverpool kept them at bay and also had two great chances to extend their lead.

With six minutes to go Petr Cech pulled off a stunning save to tip over Gerrard's goal-bound volley, then in stoppage time he managed to block a shot from Torres. These would be key moments because five minutes into added time Salomon Kalou sent over a cross and John Arne Riise inadvertently headed it past Pepe Reina and into the net for an own goal. His face was a study in agony as he lay on the turf afterwards. Chelsea did not care – they had a priceless away goal and now had the edge for the second leg at Stamford Bridge.

The previous seven Champions League games between the two sides had produced plenty of drama but precious few goals – just five in fact, so I suppose the law of averages suggested we should see some. What we got was as many goals in this game as in those previous seven put together.

The match had been given extra spice because 24 hours earlier a Paul Scholes goal earned Manchester United a 1-0 aggregate victory over Barcelona in the other semi, so we knew there would be an all-English final in Moscow on 21 May whatever happened. Chelsea and United were battling it out for the Premier League title with Chelsea coming into this game off the back of a 2-1 win over their rivals at Stamford Bridge just four days earlier. Ballack scored both the goals, including an 86th-minute penalty winner.

Frank Lampard was back in the Chelsea starting line-up for the first time since the death of his mother six days earlier from pneumonia. I only met Pat once but I found her to be a very gracious, hospitable and charming lady, who happily made my cameraman and I cups of tea as we waited for a young Frank to return to his parents' Essex home from training. We recorded a pre-arranged interview and Frank spoke warmly of how much of a positive influence both his mum and dad were in his career.

Chelsea were on the front foot from the start, buoyed by that last-minute own goal at Anfield and by the league victory over United. They took the lead after 33 minutes when Salomon Kalou's shot was well saved by Pepe Reina, but the rebound fell to the in-form Didier Drogba and he blasted it back past the goalkeeper before celebrating by diving spectacularly at the corner flag.

It stayed that way until the 64th minute when Torres deftly beat Cech with a first-time right-footed shot. Now everything was equal: goals (2-2) and away goals (1-1), so it was no surprise that this game would head for extra time.

Four minutes into it Michael Essien lashed the ball into the Liverpool net, but his celebrations were cut short by the official's flag – no fewer than four of his team-mates were offside, so Chelsea could hardly complain.

Soon after that, Hyypia tripped Ballack inside the area and Chelsea had a penalty. Lampard placed the ball calmly on the spot, took his time, then sent Reina the wrong way to put his side back in front.

The goal was greeted with an enormous roar from the home fans, Lampard kissed his black armband (all the players were wearing one as a mark of respect for his mother) and pointed tearfully to the heavens. It was an emotional moment, and full credit to him for being so professional.

Liverpool were rocking, and shortly afterwards Drogba made them pay with another sharp finish to make it 3-1. There looked to be no way back for the Reds but Babel let fly from 35 yards with three minutes to go and Cech somehow allowed it to slip past him. That made it 3-2 and the nerves were jangling as Liverpool poured forward, knowing that an equaliser would send them through on away goals. It never came, and after losing three semi-finals in four seasons Chelsea – at last – had made it to the final. Manager Avram Grant sank down on to his knees at the final whistle in a rare show of emotion.

In the intervening three weeks Chelsea and Manchester United squared up to each other for the Premier League title. Both followed up their Champions League wins with a victory so they would go into the season's final day level on points. United held the advantage because they had the superior goal difference by some margin (+56 to +39). They knew if they won at Wigan they would be champions and they did, goals from Cristiano Ronaldo and Ryan Giggs ensuring that they would retain their Premier League crown. At Stamford Bridge Bolton's Matt Taylor scored a last-minute equaliser so Chelsea finished two points behind in second place.

What effect might those events have on the Champions League Final? United were certainly on a high going to Moscow and looking for a double while Chelsea had to somehow pick themselves up from that last-day disappointment.

Those looking for omens reminded us that this year was the 50th anniversary of the Munich air disaster, which had claimed the lives of eight Manchester United players. In addition to the 'Busby Babes' a total of 23 passengers (including club staff members and journalists) died, with 21 people surviving. It was also exactly 40 years since United under Sir Matt Busby became the first English club to win the European Cup.

The final was being covered live by both Sky Sports and ITV, and very wisely the two companies pooled resources to charter a jet to take us all out to Moscow. We took off from Stansted on Sunday morning, with the final being played on the Wednesday. There was a good atmosphere on board and I've always enjoyed working alongside

ITV, though we were all a little apprehensive about how long it might take to clear customs with so much television equipment.

We need not have worried – the Russians pulled out all the stops that week and made us very welcome. I think they wanted the rest of Europe to see just what a good job they could do in hosting such a showpiece final. Filming in Red Square was usually a tricky exercise, requiring permission and permits, but this week it was no problem and it was fascinating to see the city gearing up for the big day.

The Luzhniki Stadium had hosted the athletics at the 1980 Olympics. This was where Scotsman Allan Wells had won gold in the 100m, where Steve Ovett beat Seb Coe in the 800m final only to see Coe gain revenge in the 1,500m, and where the incomparable Daley Thompson won the first of his two Olympic decathlon titles. It also had an artificial pitch, which had to be replaced by a grass playing surface at a cost of £160,000. UEFA allowed earlier rounds to be played on the synthetic surface but ruled that the final must be played on grass.

This was the first (and so far only) all-English final, so it was always going to be unique, and it went down in history as the first Champions League Final to be started on one day and finished on the next! Because of the time difference with western Europe and with UEFA wanting to maximise the TV audience it was agreed that the game would kick off at 22.45 local time (19.45 in the UK). Early in the second half the clock ticked past midnight and Wednesday turned into Thursday – bizarre.

In the build-up to the final the Moscow weather had been warm and sunny. On matchday it turned wet, very wet. By 2pm my shoes were totally saturated and I spent the next 14 hours squelching around in some discomfort, but it was a small price to pay for having a pitchside view of such a memorable and dramatic occasion.

United struck first: Wes Brown crossed from the right and Cristiano Ronaldo soared above the Chelsea defence to powerfully head home, Cech never even moving. Rio Ferdinand almost scored an own-goal equaliser, then Cech made an outstanding double save to deny first Carlos Tevez and then Michael Carrick.

Just before half-time Essien's speculative long shot took a couple of deflections before falling right into the path of Lampard. He tucked the ball away and again dedicated the goal to the memory of his late mother Pat.

The rain was relentless and as Wednesday became Thursday, the players were starting to struggle with the conditions. The newly relaid pitch did not help and quite a few had problems with cramp.

On 77 minutes Drogba blasted a 25-yard screamer against the post, then ten minutes later Ryan Giggs came off the bench to make his 759th appearance and break Sir Bobby Charlton's all-time club record. Sir Bobby watched on approvingly from the stands.

Before the end of the 90 Lampard turned and fired a great strike against the bar, while Giggs saw his goal-bound effort blocked by John Terry. Extra time got under way at around a quarter to one in the morning. The crowd of almost 70,000 were captivated – some of the football had been terrific and it was still impossible to call.

Four minutes from the end of extra time an ugly melee developed. Initially Chelsea were unhappy with the actions of Tevez, but it soon spread and most of the 22 were getting involved. Referee Lubos Michel restored order then sent off Drogba, who had slapped Nemanja Vidic in the face right in front of him. At the time we had no idea of how significant a moment that would prove to be. Later, it emerged that Drogba was earmarked to take Chelsea's fifth and final penalty of the shoot-out.

Neither side deserved to lose but the destiny of the 2008 Champions League was about to be decided by penalties:

Tevez was first up for United and sent Cech the wrong way: 1-0

Michael Ballack beat Edwin van der Sar with a shot into the corner: 1-1

Carrick also sent Cech the wrong way: 2-1

Juliano Belletti (Barcelona's match-winner in 2006 against Arsenal) netted: 2-2

Ronaldo stopped in his run-up, Cech dived right and saved it: still 2-2

Lampard beat van der Sar, but only just: 2-3

Owen Hargreaves scored high over Cech to the right: 3-3

Ashley Cole saw his penalty go in off van der Sar's hand: 3-4

Nani had to score to keep United in it and did, but Cech was very close: 4-4

Captain John Terry stepped forward next. He had volunteered to take the final penalty of the regulation shoot-out after Drogba's red card (and had scored one for England in EURO 2004 against Portugal).

After three semi-final defeats was this going to be his moment? As he ran up to the ball he slipped on the wet pitch at the moment of impact and sent his penalty off the post and wide. Van der Sar had dived the wrong way, Terry sat on the ground with his head in his hands. What must Drogba have been thinking at that stage? Still 4-4

Anderson beat Cech with the first penalty in sudden death: United 5-4

Salomon Kalou cooly sent van der Sar the wrong way: 5-5

Record-breaker Giggs scored to Cech's left as the keeper went the other way: 6-5

Substitute Nicolas Anelka took the 14th penalty, van der Sar dived right and guessed right, beating the ball away: 6-5 and Manchester United had won the trophy for the third time.

Terry was in tears, while many of United's players were lying down – they were mentally and physically exhausted, but they got up to provide Chelsea with a guard of honour as they went up to collect their runners-up medals. That was a classy touch.

Avram Grant threw his medal into the crowd. As second reporter to Geoff Shreeves it was my job to interview the beaten finalists, which is no easy task, especially when the margin between victory and defeat, joy and despair, was so small. Grant did not want to be interviewed, but he was always a decent guy to me and eventually agreed.

He stood on the pitch with the rain still hosing down, his face being battered by the elements, and spoke with dignity. He congratulated United, showed real sympathy for Terry, and would not be drawn about his future. Chelsea had finished runners-up in three competitions (the League Cup to Tottenham, the Premier League and Champions League to United) and three days after the final his contract was terminated with immediate effect.

United celebrated long and hard and with good reason – it had been another magnificent season. By the time they mounted the steps to collect the trophy it was two o'clock in the morning. I stood beside the pitch, soaking wet and thinking how lucky I was to witness this.

Twelve months on, in the heat of Rome, United were back in the final and aiming to become the first club in the Champions League era to retain the trophy. Yet again the English clubs dominated the competition, with three reaching the semi-finals, and Chelsea came so close to making it another all-English final.

My campaign started in Ukraine as Arsenal salvaged a slightly fortunate draw on matchday one against Dynamo Kiev, thanks to a very late equaliser from William Gallas.

I also went to Transylvania to see the little-known FC Cluj (the Romanian champions) hold Chelsea to a goalless draw, and was in Bordeaux as Chelsea fought out another draw to ensure qualification. A 3-1 defeat to Roma meant they had to settle for second place.

Arsenal also finished runners-up after being beaten in the formidable Estadio do Dragao (the Dragon Stadium) by Porto. Apart from the result, I really enjoyed the trip to Portugal's second city. The bars and restaurant down by the river were fantastic – so was the weather.

Liverpool finished top of Group D with four wins and two draws, and they then beat Real Madrid away (1-0) and home (4-0) to set up a quarter-final with – Chelsea! The Londoners had battled past Juventus 3-2 on aggregate after a 2-2 draw in Turin, where they twice had to come from behind.

Manchester United won Group E and were unbeaten with two wins and four draws. They underlined their strength and experience with a 2-0 aggregate win over Inter Milan to move smoothly through to the quarter-finals.

Arsenal's progress to the last eight was not quite so smooth. They beat Roma 1-0 at home with a Robin van Persie penalty and went to the Stadio Olimpico determined not to throw away their narrow advantage by giving away an early goal. But that is just what they did – inside ten minutes. After that both sides had their moments, but neither could find a way through and after 120 minutes we arrived at penalties.

There were over 81,000 in the ground that night – this was where the final would be staged in May – and you feared Arsenal would find it hard against such partisan support in a shoot-out. They started badly with sub Eduardo having the first penalty saved, but luckily it was not long before Mirko Vucinic struck a weak shot straight at Manuel Almunia's knees to tie it up again. I then watched on as penalty after penalty was struck home, the keepers rarely getting close. Finally, after 13 of the 15 penalties had been scored, and with Arsenal leading 7-6, Max Tonetto blazed his spot-kick over the bar and Arsene Wenger's men were through to the last eight. For the second year running all four English clubs were still in it at this stage.

The holders drew Porto in the quarter-finals but were kept to a 2-2 draw in the first leg at Old Trafford, with Mariano Gonzalez scoring an 89th-minute equaliser for the Portuguese side. United then produced a fine away performance to go through to the semi-finals. Where Arsenal had slipped up in the group, United stayed strong. They scored early through Cristiano Ronaldo and that was enough to see them through to a last-four encounter against Arsenal. The all-English games were coming thick and fast, such was the Premier League domination.

I saw Arsenal draw 1-1 at Villarreal in their quarter-final, with Emmanuel Adebayor scoring a second-half equaliser. Adebayor was also on target in the return, a comfortable 3-0 win taking Arsenal into their first Champions League semi-final for three years.

As for Liverpool against Chelsea, well where do you start? At Anfield, Fernando Torres put the home side ahead in the sixth minute but after that they were demolished. Branislav Ivanovic scored twice with headers from corners, Drogba added a third and it looked like game over.

Back at Stamford Bridge, Chelsea were expected to finish off the job without too much drama. Liverpool had other ideas and raced in to a 2-0 lead inside half an hour to tie the match up at 3-3. Normal service looked to have been restored as Drogba and Alex levelled the tie on the night at 2-2, and when Frank Lampard put Chelsea ahead it was 6-3 on aggregate. Again, Liverpool refused to be beaten – Lucas (81) and Dirk Kuyt (82) turned the game back on its head. Now one more Liverpool goal would give them a 5-3 win and victory on away goals. There was one final twist, but it was Lampard who provided it, scoring the equaliser to make it 4-4 and 7-5 on aggregate.

Twice Chelsea had knocked out Liverpool, twice Liverpool had knocked out Chelsea -- these games were becoming classics: they had now met ten times in the Champions League in five seasons. At the time of writing we are still waiting for an 11th game.

In the semi-final at Old Trafford, John O'Shea gave United a narrow win over Arsenal in a game they should have won more convincingly. At the Emirates they took their chances. Park Ji-sung and Ronaldo had them 2-0 up after 11 minutes, Ronaldo added a third in the second half and despite having Darren Fletcher sent off they cruised to a 3-1 win and reached their second consecutive final by winning 4-1 on aggregate.

Chelsea somehow clung on for a 0-0 draw in Barcelona after the home side dominated pretty much from start to finish in the first leg. At Stamford Bridge, Michael Essien put them ahead after nine minutes and when Barca's Eric Abidal was sent off midway through the second half Chelsea were firm favourites to join United in the final.

But they could not score a second goal to kill off the tie and in the 90th minute Andres Iniesta popped up with an unlikely equaliser, sending the 2006 champions through on away goals. It was utter heartbreak for Chelsea – they were convinced they would be going back to the final to avenge their penalty shoot-out defeat. Instead there was more anguish as their record stood at four semi-final defeats and one loss in the final over the previous six seasons of Champions League football.

As the defending champions and also the newly crowned Premier League winners after retaining their title, Manchester United went into the final as the slight favourites. It was still stiflingly hot in Rome when the game kicked off but United made a fast start and created a whole series of early chances – two falling to Ronaldo.

With virtually Barcelona's first attack Iniesta slipped in Samuel Eto'o, who rounded Nemanja Vidic and scored off Edwin van der Sar's body at the near post. From United's point of view it was a fairly soft goal and it transformed the final as Barcelona grew in confidence. The game had been billed as Cristiano Ronaldo versus Lionel Messi and it was the little Argentinian who became the central figure – his influence continued to grow throughout the first half, and then after the interval he supplied the killer second goal.

Midfielder Xavi crossed from the right, Messi had somehow got between Vidic and Rio Ferdinand and he soared high to plant a firm header past van der Sar. It was a classic case of 'little man big leap' and it is a moment I have captured on my study wall.

The following morning's papers had pictures of Messi jumping to score across their sports pages – and there looking on, clear as day behind the goal, is yours truly. The second reporter's position was immediately behind one of the goals and I had an exceptional view of Messi's moment. *The Sun*'s Dickie Pelham kindly gave me a copy of it, which I framed (apologies to all you Manchester United fans!).

Barcelona went on to complete the Treble that season under Pep Guardiola and two years later there would be a repeat of that final at Wembley.

In 2009/10 no English clubs got beyond the quarter-final, though Arsenal, Chelsea and United all won their group and looked set to continue the Premier League's domination. Liverpool could only finish third and went into the UEFA Cup.

I was at Stamford Bridge for the return of Jose Mourinho as he brought his impressive Inter Milan side to London defending a 2-1 lead from the first leg. The Italians were supremely well organised and duly won 1-0 to move into the quarter-finals, ending Chelsea's dreams for another year.

United beat AC Milan 3-2 away then 4-0 at home to signal their intentions – but then they came unstuck against Bayern Munich in the next round. After losing 2-1 in Germany they got off to a flyer at Old Trafford as Darron Gibson and Nani both scored in the first seven minutes and they led on aggregate 3-2. When Nani scored a second just before the interval United looked to be cruising into the semis, but a defensive lapse allowed Ivica Olic to score, so at half-time the aggregate was 4-3. Sixteen minutes from the end Arjen Robben scored with a spectacular volley from Franck Ribery's corner to tie the overall score at 4-4, and Bayern went through on away goals.

I was at the Nou Camp to witness the end of Arsenal's Champions League campaign, where they were utterly destroyed by the brilliance of Lionel Messi. After an exciting 2-2 draw in the first leg at the Emirates Barca were favourites to progress, but Nicklas Bendtner stunned the holders by giving Arsenal the lead after 19 minutes.

It did not last long – within a couple of minutes Messi lashed home an equaliser, and threatened to score almost every time he got the ball. Arsenal just could not contain him and it was no surprise when he started and finished the move which put his side ahead. He completed his hat-trick five minutes later with a clever lob over the stranded Manuel Almunia and at half-time Barcelona/Messi led 3-1. His fourth near the end was a solo goal, as he weaved past a couple of challenges and beat Almunia at the second attempt.

From my view right behind the goal I had seen close-up just how fantastic he is and in my opinion Lionel Messi is the greatest player I have ever seen and very probably the greatest of all time.

Messi and Barcelona were undone by Mourinho's Inter in the semis and the Italians then went on to beat Bayern Munich 2-0 in the final as they also completed a Treble. My involvement with the Champions League ended with Arsenal's defeat. I was excused semi-final and final duty as I was preparing for the World Cup in South Africa.

In 2011 Wembley got to host European club football's showpiece occasion for the first time since 1992 and again Barcelona looked a class apart from anyone else in the competition.

Tottenham had qualified for the first time since the early 1960s and they thoroughly enjoyed the experience, winning their group and making it to the quarter-finals. It was a great adventure and whetted the club's appetite for regular Champions League football.

Their introduction to the competition was a bit of a shock. Inside half an hour they were 3-0 down to Young Boys of Bern in the play-off round and looking like they might not even make it to the group stages. They fought back well against the Swiss side, eventually losing 3-2, and completed the recovery at White Hart Lane with a 4-0 victory in the second leg, Peter Crouch scoring a hat-trick.

Away to Werder Bremen on matchday one Spurs raced into a 2-0 lead, but were pegged back to 2-2 by the Germans – but still, they had their first Champions League point. Two weeks later they picked up their first win, scoring four goals in the second half against Dutch team FC Twente.

Then came the game that put Tottenham – and Gareth Bale – on the European map. After 35 minutes they trailed 4-0 away to the holders Inter Milan, and they were down to ten men after goalkeeper Heurelho Gomes was sent off in the eighth minute. It could have been an absolute rout but Spurs fought back bravely with Bale scoring an amazing second-half hat-trick.

For the first Bale ran 50 yards down the left flank before firing a shot across Julio Cesar and into the net. The second goal was almost identical and when Bale grabbed his third in stoppage time the defending champions were rocking. Spurs could not quite complete a sensational fightback but it completely changed the dynamic of the return game a fortnight later.

It was Tottenham who were on the front foot, playing with total belief, and deservedly beat Inter 3-1 on a great night at White Hart Lane. The atmosphere was superb, especially when chants of 'when the Spurs go marching in' echoed round the ground. Crouch and Roman Pavlyuchenko were among the scorers.

Another big home win – this time against Werder Bremen – ensured that Tottenham would qualify for the last 16. The 3-0 victory gave them ten points.

I drove to the Dutch–German border for the final group game against FC Twente. They were based in the city of Enschede, just over four hours by road from Calais. Every now and again it used to make a pleasant change from the routine of driving 100 miles west from my house to Heathrow Airport to catch a flight. I live just 25 minutes from the Channel Tunnel, so it was surprisingly convenient. Some of the clubs where I have covered Champions League games after driving there include PSV Eindhoven, AZ Alkmaar, Standard Liege and Lille. All good fun.

On this occasion it was rather snowy, but both teams defied the slippery conditions to provide a six-goal thriller. Nacer Chadli again scored against Tottenham (as he had done on matchday two in his team's 4-1 defeat) and he would eventually sign for the north Londoners. Jermain Defoe nipped in with two goals as the game finished 3-3. The big bonus for Tottenham was that Inter lost 3-0 at Werder Bremen that night, which meant Harry Redknapp's men would finish top of the group.

The draw sent them back to Italy and back to the San Siro, where this time they would face AC Milan. Crouch scored the only goal as

Tottenham gave a highly disciplined performance and came away with a valuable 1-0 win.

On the flight back next morning I was sat next to Debbie and Frank Bale, Gareth's charming parents, and they gave me a really interesting insight into what it was like being the mum and dad of a player developing into a sporting superstar. I have never elaborated on the conversation, because it was an informal chat, but it certainly helped the time pass a lot more quickly. What struck me most was how strong the family support was for Gareth.

A goalless draw in the second leg sent Tottenham into the quarter-finals, a terrific achievement, but against Real Madrid they learned the harsh realities of how good the very top teams are, and when Crouch was sent off in the 15th minute they would always be up against it. Emmanuel Adebayor scored twice, Angel Di Maria was also on target, and so too was Ronaldo. The 4-0 scoreline was a humbling experience and Ronaldo completed the formalities with the only goal of the second leg.

When Chelsea were drawn in the same group as Spartak Moscow it meant a return to the Luzhniki Stadium in Moscow, the scene of their Champions League Final heartbreak from 2008. This time there was a happy ending, plus no missed penalties, and a 2-0 win helped Chelsea towards winning the group.

Instead of a neutral crowd like in 2008 this time there were 80,000 Muscovites roaring their team on, the pitch was artificial, and temperatures plummeted to freezing. Despite all these challenges I watched Chelsea come through with few alarms. Russian Yuri Zhirkov (a former player of Spartak's rivals CSKA) whacked in a spectacular, looping, long-range volley – his first goal for the Blues – and Nicolas Anelka made it 2-0 before the break. It was a long trip but a satisfying one.

I was with Chelsea in the last 16 when they visited Copenhagen for the first leg. This time the temperature was about minus eight, and trying to concentrate when it is that cold is not easy. We watched the game from behind the goal and saw Anelka score twice to all but clinch a quarter-final place. Afterwards, in the mixed zone interview area, Frank Lampard almost walked past me because he did not recognise me under so many scarves, gloves and woolly hats.

This was the year UEFA elongated the round of the last 16, which made it possible to cover more of the knock-out matches. The downside was that it took five weeks to complete all of the games.

Having covered Spurs and Chelsea in their first legs, I switched to Arsenal for the second leg as they travelled to Barcelona defending a 2-1 lead. Could they control Lionel Messi better than a year ago, we wondered? The Argentinian chipped the ball over Manuel Almunia before rifling in his shot to give Barcelona the lead in first-half stoppage time to level the tie, but an own goal put Arsenal back in front again on aggregate.

Then came the decisive moment as Robin van Persie was sent off for a highly controversial second yellow card. He attempted a shot on goal after the whistle had been blown and received another caution, this time for time-wasting. I was right by that goal as van Persie surged towards me and I doubt there could have been more than a second between the whistle blowing and him making contact with the ball. It was ridiculously harsh and played a major part in Arsenal's exit. Don't forget there were 95,000 fans in the stadium that night, so it was no wonder van Persie claimed he did not hear the whistle.

After that Barcelona scored twice in two minutes, the second a Messi penalty, and that meant they led 4-3 on aggregate. Agonisingly, sub Nicklas Bendtner had a great chance very late on to pull a goal back. If he had scored Arsenal then would have gone through on away goals. But it was not to be and that was the start of Arsenal's difficulties in getting beyond this stage. They would go out in the last 16 seven seasons running.

The sub-plot to the all-English quarter-final between Manchester United and Chelsea was the England captaincy. Manager Fabio Capello had just re-instated John Terry at the expense of Rio Ferdinand, who was taunted by the London club's fans, but it was Rio who had the last laugh as his team won 1-0 in the first leg at Stamford Bridge. Wayne Rooney scored the decisive goal in the first half, just a few days after being charged by the FA for swearing into a camera after scoring in United's win at West Ham.

For the second leg at Old Trafford Carlo Ancelotti opted for Fernando Torres ahead of Didier Drogba and the gamble backfired. The Spanish striker failed to make an impact and it was United who extended their lead in the first half through Javier Hernandez (Chicarito – the 'Little Pea'). Drogba was brought on in the second half, Chelsea looked more dangerous, and the Ivorian gave his side hope with an equaliser to bring the aggregate score back to 2-1. Seconds later Park Ji-sung scored for United and yet again they had got the better of Chelsea in the Champions League.

Sir Alex Ferguson's side faced Schalke 04 in the semis – it was the fourth time in five seasons they had reached this stage and their greater experience told. A 2-0 win in Germany put them in control of the tie and I was at Old Trafford to witness them cruise into their third Champions League Final in four seasons.

Antonio Valencia and Darron Gibson scored in the first half to stretch United's aggregate lead to 4-0. Jose Manuel Jorado did pull one back, but two late goals from Anderson gave the home team a comfortable 6-1 aggregate win.

Their opponents at Wembley would be Barcelona, who won the 'El Clasico' semi-final against Real Madrid. Pepe's dismissal on 61 minutes turned the tie as Messi cashed in with two goals at the Bernabeu to give Barca a vital 2-0 away win. The second leg ended 1-1 and Barcelona reached their third final in six seasons.

Both teams had won this competition at Wembley before – Manchester United back in 1968 with a dramatic extra-time win over Benfica, while Barcelona triumphed there in 1992 against Sampdoria. United somehow had to try and find a way to get the better of a team who had beaten them in the Rome final two years previously, and in the first half at least they matched them.

Perhaps they were buoyed by winning a record 19th league title, overtaking Liverpool's milestone, just a couple of weeks before. A 2-1 home win over the outgoing champions Chelsea, followed by a 1-1 draw at Blackburn did the trick and Ferguson had achieved his long-term dream: to 'knock Liverpool off their perch' as England's most successful side.

This time, when Barcelona took the lead through Pedro, United had a response. Rooney played a one-two with Ryan Giggs and then drove the ball high beyond Victor Valdes for the equaliser. The English champions had a foothold but could they go on and finish the job?

The second half belonged to Barcelona and Messi – he scored the crucial second goal to restore his team's lead. No one closed the Argentinian down as he struck from 25 yards almost out of nowhere. A spectacular third goal from David Villa underlined the Catalans' superiority and they ran out 3-1 winners.

I had now been at four Champions League Finals and Barcelona had won three of them – they could rightly lay claim to being the kings of European football.

\* \* \* \* \*

Sometimes the expression 'their name is on the trophy' can be a bit of a cliché, but in 2012 you could not help thinking that massively applied to Chelsea.

Where to begin? On 4 March they sacked their manager Andre Villas-Boas after a disappointing Premier League campaign had seen them slip outside the top four. Their former player Roberto Di Matteo was appointed caretaker manager on an interim basis until the end of the season; in his third match he masterminded the heroic fightback against Napoli in the last 16 after being 3-1 down from the first leg; the extraordinary semi-final comeback in the Camp Nou against the holders Barcelona, despite only having ten men after captain John Terry was sent off; having to play the final on the home pitch of their opponents and missing FOUR players through suspension; falling behind after 83 minutes and still managing to take the game into extra time; conceding a penalty in extra time, which keeper Petr Cech then saved; trailing 3-1 in the penalty shoot-out and yet still recovering to win it.

And all that after having lost one final and four semi-finals in eight years!

There was no real hint of the drama to come as Chelsea confirmed top place in Group E with a 3-0 triumph over Valencia to move into the last 16, knowing they would have home advantage in the second leg.

I saw Arsenal's campaign open with a draw at Borussia Dortmund. It was my first visit to the Westfalenstadion (also known as Signal Iduna Park) and I was impressed. Their famous Sudtribune (South Bank) is the largest standing terrace in European football with a capacity of almost 25,000 and is known as the 'yellow wall'. Ahead of each Champions League game the area is replaced with seating, reducing the capacity – but it is still a noisy and colourful part of the ground. The Dortmund fans wear their yellow and black scarves with pride and even sing 'You'll Never Walk Alone' in English just before the teams come out. It was almost like being back at Anfield.

Robin van Persie put Arsenal ahead in the first half but the German side saved themselves just before the end with a late equaliser from Ivan Perisic, which was greeted with an enormous roar from those 'sitting' on the South Bank.

I was also in Marseille to see Aaron Ramsey come off the bench in the closing stages and snatch a last-minute winner at the Stade Velodrome to keep Arsenal in charge of the group. The return game a fortnight later was less entertaining. It ended 0-0, but Arsenal then clinched top spot with a 2-1 win over Dortmund at the Emirates on matchday five, with two goals from van Persie.

It was not a great Champions League year for Manchester as City and United both finished third and went into the Europa League.

The two English survivors both lost heavily away in the first leg of the last 16 and there was every chance the Premier League would not be represented at all in the quarter-finals.

Arsenal had crashed 4-0 in Italy to AC Milan, Zlatan Ibrahimovic completing the scoring with a penalty. We were not expecting too much from the return as we arrived at the Emirates but the Gunners staged a stirring fightback with first-half goals from Laurent Koscielny, Tomas Rosicky and a van Persie penalty. One more in the second half would have forced extra time but Arsenal could not find another way through Milan's defence and they went out 4-3 on aggregate.

Chelsea had also been in Italy for their first leg and took the lead against Napoli with a goal from Juan Mata in the 27th minute. By half-time they were trailing 2-1 as the South Americans Ezequiel Lavezzi (Argentina) and Edinson Cavani (Uruguay) both scored. Lavezzi added another in the second half and Chelsea had a mountain to climb back at Stamford Bridge.

With Di Matteo now in charge Chelsea were expected to make a powerful start but it was Walter Mazarri's visitors who dominated early on, and when Didier Drogba twisted to head Chelsea in front it was definitely against the run of play.

Just after half-time another header, this time from Terry, levelled the tie at 3-3, but a few minutes later Gokhan Inler wrestled the advantage back to Napoli with a fine volley. But 15 minutes from the end Chelsea won a penalty for handball, Frank Lampard hammered it in and the game headed into extra time.

Amidst growing excitement, defender Branislav Ivanovic arrived late in the area to finish off a fine move with a fierce shot into the roof of the net: 4-1 on the night, 5-4 on aggregate. Chelsea still had some defending to do because one more Napoli goal would have sent them through on away goals instead.

On the final whistle Di Matteo raced on to the pitch to congratulate his players. It had been an emotional night and the former Stamford Bridge midfielder and assistant manager seemed to be growing into his new role.

It was a beautiful warm late March evening in the Portuguese capital of Lisbon when Chelsea faced Benfica in the first leg of the quarter-finals. They gave a calm, measured and mature performance to ensure they did not fall behind the way they had done in Italy. There was no real surprise when Salomon Kalou scored 15 minutes from time and they hung on comfortably to win 1-0.

The second leg was a bit trickier than it should have been – especially as Lampard extended their aggregate lead to 2-0 with a 21st-minute penalty and then Benfica had Maxi Pereira sent off before half-time. The ten men battled on bravely and Javi Garcia set up a nervous finish for the home fans when he equalised in the 85th minute. One more goal would have seen Benfica go through on away goals.

There was one more goal, and it was by a Portuguese player, but it was Chelsea's Raul Meireles who scored it in the 90th minute to send his team through 3-1.

Chelsea's sixth Champions League semi-final in nine seasons was against Barcelona – the defending champions and hot favourites. The team who had twice beaten Manchester United in the final also had the advantage of playing the second leg at home. They had smashed Bayer Leverkusen 10-2 on aggregate in the last 16 (and don't forget the Germans had beaten Chelsea 2-1 in the group stages) as well as brushing aside AC Milan in the quarters.

Barcelona dominated at Stamford Bridge – Alexis Sanchez hit the crossbar early on, Ashley Cole cleared off the line from Cesc Fabregas, and Pedro struck the post in the dying seconds. Petr Cech was called into action on numerous occasions as the visitors enjoyed over 70 per cent of the possession, but it was Chelsea who scored the only goal of the first leg – and it came from Drogba in first-half stoppage time. The defence performed heroically to keep a clean sheet, but Barcelona still expected to turn it round at the Nou Camp in front of 95,000 fans.

Inside the first quarter of an hour Gary Cahill went off injured, forcing a defensive reshuffle, and it then went from bad to worse as Sergio Busquets levelled the tie on aggregate by scoring from close range at the far post. Minutes later, Terry was sent off for needlessly driving his knee into the back of Sanchez, a foul spotted by one of the referee assistants behind the goal. Lionel Messi then set up Andres Iniesta and Barcelona led the ten men of Chelsea 2-0 on the night and 2-1 on aggregate as we went into first-half stoppage time.

The Brazilian Ramires had been forced into a makeshift right-back position after Chelsea had lost their two central defenders, but he ran from deep inside his own half, exchanged passes with Lampard (and what a great return Lampard played back to him), before chipping the ball over Victor Valdes for an absolutely brilliant goal.

Chelsea were technically ahead on the away goals rule and had been hugely lifted by that as they went off at half-time, but they would still have to survive the Barcelona onslaught for another 45 minutes.

Very early in the second half Barcelona were awarded a penalty, but incredibly Messi struck the underside of the bar and the ball rebounded to safety. He also hit the post later with a deflected shot, Cech continued to perform minor miracles and the clock started ticking down.

From my position behind the goal Chelsea were attacking I was thinking, 'Could they possibly hang on for a few more minutes?'

Into stoppage time, a long clearance was hoisted out of the Chelsea defence to relieve the pressure. It dropped to Fernando Torres who strode forward, rounded Valdes's desperate lunge, and calmly rolled the ball into the net. That made it 2-2 on the night, 3-2 on aggregate and, against all the odds, Chelsea were going to the final in Munich. I suppose we should not have been so surprised by Chelsea's exploits – they had now drawn with Barcelona on their last four visits to the Nou Camp, an amazing achievement.

The next night Bayern defeated Real Madrid on penalties to qualify for the final at the superb Allianz Arena – their home ground. Chelsea would be without Terry, Ramires, Ivanovic and Raul Meireles through suspension.

They also knew, after finishing sixth in the Premier League, that their only way back into the Champions League was to win the competition.

There was a boisterous atmosphere in Munich on the afternoon of the final – the home fans were confident they would be European champions for the first time since 2001, while Chelsea's supporters lapped up the sunshine and contemplated an extraordinary cup double. Two weeks earlier they had beaten Liverpool 2-1 to win the FA Cup Final for the fourth time in six seasons, with goals from Ramires and Drogba.

Bayern dominated the first half and remained on top after the break. Chelsea just dug in, showed great resilience and defensive organisation when it really mattered, and waited for their chance. The longer the game remained scoreless, the more you felt this would play into Chelsea's hands. There was no doubt Bayern and their fans were getting anxious – impatient even – but with seven minutes to go they finally broke through. Toni Kroos crossed and Thomas Muller headed the ball down into the ground, from where it bounced up over Cech and into the net off the crossbar.

Chelsea refused to give in. With two minutes remaining Juan Mata swung over a corner and Drogba got his head to it at the near post to bring them level right in front of their jubilant fans.

In extra time Drogba blotted his copybook somewhat by tripping Franck Ribery in the area, so Bayern were awarded a penalty. Former Stamford Bridge star Arjen Robben took the spot-kick but his weak effort was easily saved by Cech going to his left. On we went, Bayern's red tide being kept at bay by Chelsea, and after 120 minutes the final whistle blew – and that meant penalties would decide the outcome of the Champions League for the first time since 2008, a night Chelsea knew only too well.

Philipp Lahm was up first for Bayern, Cech dived left and got his fingers to it, but could not keep it out: 1-0

Juan Mata for Chelsea, and his poor penalty was saved by Manuel Neuer: still 1-0

Mario Gomez aimed for the bottom right-hand corner and scored: 2-0

David Luiz next. This was a big penalty, the Brazilian took a long run-up and struck a powerful shot into the roof of the net. Chelsea off the mark: 2-1

Goalkeeper Neuer was third to go, Cech dived to his left, and the ball just crept past him into the corner: 3-1 Bayern

Captain on the night Frank Lampard went straight down the middle and scored for the second time in a Champions League Final penalty shoot-out: 3-2

Ivica Olic had the chance to extend Bayern's lead, but Cech dived left and saved it: still 3-2

Ashley Cole matched Lampard's penalty record in Champions League Final shoot-outs, and Chelsea were level at last: 3-3

Bastian Schweinsteiger hesitated in his run-up, went for placement rather than power, and just beat Cech diving full length to his left, but the ball came back off the inside of the post – and Chelsea had had another great escape: still 3-3

Drogba was the last to go. The man whose late red card in the final four years ago meant he could not take part in the Moscow shoot-out now had the chance to make amends in the most dramatic circumstances imaginable.

Behind the goal – just a few feet away from the Bayern keeper – I held my breath as Drogba placed the ball on the spot, stepped back a few paces and then began his run forward. He was calmness personified, sending Neuer the wrong way and tucking the ball into the right-hand corner right in front of me. I must confess I turned to ITV's Gabriel Clarke next to me and said, 'He's only gone and f***ing won it!' Drogba ran the length of the pitch back to the Chelsea fans and the players' celebrations began. The suspended John Terry picked up the cup with Lampard, but the biggest cheer was when the caretaker manager Roberto Di Matteo got his hands on the trophy.

Afterwards in the mixed zone interview area I got my only ever 'interview' with Chelsea owner Roman Abramovich. It went something like this:

Me, 'Congratulations, Roman, how pleased are you to finally win the Champions League?'

Roman, 'Thank you.'

And with that he was off to join in the dressing room celebrations. In truth he had barely slowed down as I threw my question at him, still I like to think of it as my attempt to interview him.

Fortunately Seb Coe was a lot more forthcoming when he came past, but it was still a long wait before the players finally emerged to do interviews.

I got back to my hotel from the ground at 4.15am, ordered a taxi to the airport and a glass of wine, went up to my room to get my luggage, came down to pay my bill, swigged back the Pinot Grigio and jumped into the cab.

I had to fly via Manchester and eventually arrived on set at Sky Sports News to do a live interview at around 3pm – by now I had been up for 33 hours, but adrenaline can be a wonderful thing and I felt wide awake. By 6pm I was back home with my family and was finally able to spend a few hours with them celebrating my 55th birthday.

In 2013 the final returned to Wembley for the second time in three seasons as part of the FA's 150th anniversary celebrations.

Chelsea's victory the previous season had denied Tottenham a Champions League place, despite them finishing fourth – so there were no Premier League teams in the play-off round. Chelsea then became the first defending champions to fail to get out of the group stages. They finished third, went into the Europa League, but then typically won that.

Manchester United finished top of their group but were narrowly beaten by Real Madrid in the knockout stage, while Manchester City had finished bottom of their group.

Arsenal's second-place finish in Group B led to them being paired with Bayern Munich. The 2012 runners-up overpowered Arsene

Wenger's team in London to win 3-1 and looked to have virtually wrapped up the tie.

Arsenal went to the Allianz Arena as complete underdogs – Wenger had even suggested it might be 'Mission Impossible' – but I watched a highly disciplined performance that almost brought about a sensational recovery. They got a great start with Olivier Giroud scoring in the third minute, then they held off Bayern for the next 82 before Laurent Koscielny levelled the tie on aggregate with a second goal. They needed one more for an improbable victory, but Bayern hung on to go through on away goals – and that was the end of the Premier League involvement in 2013.

After that I travelled with Bayern Munich, which made a change and was great fun. They fought their way past Juventus in a tight quarter-final and then destroyed Barcelona 7-0 over the two legs of their semi. It was unbelievable stuff from the German champions as Barcelona were put to the sword at the Allianz. Thomas Muller scored twice in a 4-0 win and afterwards promised me he would do an interview in English with me if Bayern won the final. Arjen Robben was the man who helped English TV out in the closing stages of that year's Champions League, as he agreed to many interviews.

Robben and Muller were on target in the second leg as Bayern won 3-0 and qualified for an all-German final against Borussia Dortmund. Jurgen Klopp's vibrant Dortmund side had won plenty of admirers in their run to the final and Klopp was undoubtedly an engaging character.

It was an intriguing game with Arjen Robben setting up Mario Mandzukic for Bayern's opening goal on the hour. A penalty from Ilkay Gundogan deservedly pulled Dortmund level, before Robben won it in the 89th minute with a composed finish from Franck Ribery's flick-on.

Afterwards Muller was as good as his word and readily agreed to an interview in English, as did Robben and goalkeeper Manuel Neuer. After the previous season's heartbreak you could not begrudge Bayern their triumph this time and overall I found them a very classy club with which to deal.

I covered Bayern Munich in two more Champions League semi-finals, in 2014 and 2015, as they lost to Real Madrid and Barcelona respectively, while my last Champions League matches with Sky were the 2016 group games between Barcelona and Manchester City. I was so impressed with the way City defeated Barcelona 3-1 at the Etihad after losing 4-0 away just a fortnight previously.

In that first encounter I saw Lionel Messi score another hat-trick – he really was just phenomenal. If Barcelona turns out to be my last Champions League trip abroad, well I'll settle for that because covering this competition for more than a decade has been an honour and a real blast.

# 18

# 'Benvenuto, Fabio'

THESE were the first words spoken to Fabio Capello at his opening news conference in December 2007 after his unveiling as England manager – the welcome was genuine, the respect for him immense, and the anticipation at what he might be able to achieve was palpable.

This was a manager who had won league titles in Italy with AC Milan, Roma and Juventus. His Milan team crushed Barcelona 4-0 in the 1994 Champions League Final. He spent two separate seasons at Real Madrid and won La Liga both times – no wonder they called him 'Don Fabio' in Spain.

As a player he had won 32 caps in Italy's midfield in the 1970s, scoring the goal in 1973 which gave Italy their first win at Wembley.

He also fell out with David Beckham in his last year at Real Madrid because of contract differences – dropping the former England captain and declaring he would never play for Real Madrid again, because he had signed a five-year deal with LA Galaxy in America.

Beckham's determination to win his place back impressed Capello and forced the Italian to change his mind. He restored him to the starting line-up, Real went on a winning run, and ended up clinching the title on the final day.

No wonder Capello told that first news conference he had had a 'contrasting' relationship with Beckham, but he was clearly prepared to consider him for his squads despite the midfielder being based on the west coast of the United States. It all made for a good story because Beckham was on 99 caps at the time. Capello was due to start work on 7 January 2008 with a four-and-a-half-year contract rumoured to be worth almost £30m. In those early weeks everyone in the media played the game of Capello spotting as he toured the clubs trying to watch as much Premier League football as possible. In the end he did not pick Beckham for the first match – a friendly with Switzerland – because he did not consider him fit enough. Capello also got a bit tetchy at all the Beckham questions aimed at him.

This was his first team, in a 4-5-1 formation: David James; Wes Brown, Rio Ferdinand, Matthew Upson, Ashley Cole; David Bentley, Jermaine Jenas, Steven Gerrard (captain), Gareth Barry, Joe Cole; Wayne Rooney.

Joe Cole crossed for Jenas to score the first goal of the Capello era, and though Switzerland equalised, substitute Shaun Wright-Phillips got the winner after being set up by Gerrard.

Owen Hargreaves, John Terry and Beckham came into the side for the game with France in Paris – so 11 and a half years after his debut the man known as 'Golden Balls' won his 100th cap, but he was not given the armband. That honour went to Rio Ferdinand as Capello rotated the captaincy in those early games while he decided on a permanent leader. I think it is fair to say he did not totally understand our national obsession over who captains the England football team.

He also brought on Michael Owen as a substitute at the start of the second half, and those 45 minutes were to be the Newcastle man's last in an England shirt. Despite 40 goals in 89 internationals and being the only Englishman to have scored at four major tournaments, Capello chose to look elsewhere when calling up strikers so Owen's England career was over before he was 30.

I always thought that was a great shame – in my opinion he was discarded too early. I know he was hit by injuries towards the end of his career but I just felt he had the knack and the ability to score goals in tight situations at international level. That was a precious commodity. He was also a good guy, and his sensational goal against Argentina at France '98 will live with me forever.

Three weeks after the France game I was among a select group of correspondents who accompanied Capello on a two-day flying visit to the land-locked mountain kingdom of Lesotho in South Africa. The trip was organised by Kick4Life to raise awareness of Aids and HIV.

It was a gruelling schedule – we flew out on Monday evening, landing in Johannesburg early on Tuesday morning. My cameraman Simon Seager and I spent all day filming, before dashing back into South Africa from Lesotho late in the evening to feed the pictures to Sky from Bloemfontein.

Crossing the border was a complicated and slightly frightening exercise – the local guards seemed highly suspicious of us and our motives, and it was some time before our passports were stamped with an exit from Lesotho and an entrance into South Africa. The whole process had to be repeated on the way back into Lesotho and by the end of it all one page of my passport was completely covered in stamps. Driving through the night, we really did appear to be in the middle of nowhere and it gave us an early insight into the size of the country.

Wednesday was more of the same, only this time we were flying back that night. Sky agreed to wait for the next batch of pictures until we arrived in London. On that second day we filmed a large football tournament for children in Maseru, the capital of Lesotho. They played barefoot with a natural exhilaration and it was great to watch. During the course of the tournament some of the youngsters were being tested for Aids and HIV, and Capello was invited in to witness one such test.

He admitted that, as a father and grandfather, he had found it very hard to watch. The atmosphere was certainly very tense inside the tent as we awaited the outcome. At last the 14-year-old boy was able to wipe away his tears after being told the test was negative. The disease has been a huge problem in Lesotho and when we were there we were told the average life expectancy for a man was just 37.

For the tournament final Capello was put in charge of one team, with former goalkeeping coach Ray Clemence looking after the other. It finished a draw, which meant a penalty shoot-out, and by a strange quirk of fate the England manager's team lost 3-1 to a side wearing maroon shirts…an exact repeat of our defeat on penalties to Portugal in the 2006 World Cup quarter-finals.

Then it was back on to a small jet for the flight to Jo'burg, followed by another 12-hour haul to Heathrow. Most of my colleagues slept for the majority of the journey and you couldn't blame them – two overnight flights in the space of 60 hours takes some getting used to.

Ahead of the trip I had gone to see my dad and was explaining about the schedule. He had been a doctor before he retired and immediately came up with some sleeping tablets, which he said would be infallible. 'Guaranteed sleep,' I think was the expression he used. I managed to get some for Simon too and looked forward to the effect they would have. My cameraman slept for seven hours on the way out and nine on the way back, saying they were the best sleeping tablets he had ever taken – with absolutely no side-effects.

I slept for 20 minutes on the way out and none on the way back – so much for 'guaranteed sleep'. Still, at least I got to catch up on a few movies, the best one I watched being *No Country For Old Men*.

\* \* \* \* \*

In May 2008, John Terry became Capello's third England captain and presided over an improved performance as he and Steven Gerrard both scored in a 2-0 win over the USA.

England's fourth captain in four games was Beckham himself as the squad travelled out to the Caribbean to face Trinidad and Tobago in Port of Spain. It was all part of the machinations of England's 2018 World Cup bid. It was a nice, relaxing way to finish off the season – but it was also the end of Sky and the BBC's contract to cover England games. We wondered what the future would hold with Setanta and ITV securing the rights.

The sun beat down, Jermain Defoe grabbed a couple of goals, and England won 3-0. It was good to see Dwight Yorke again and, as a big cricket fan, it was a real privilege for me to meet his good mate – the legendary Brian Lara.

In August, Capello announced Terry would be his permanent captain while England drew at home to the Czech Republic in their final friendly before the 2010 World Cup qualifying campaign got under way. Now the real tests would begin and we could assess Capello's true impact.

Against Andorra he gave Theo Walcott his first England start – he liked the pace of the Arsenal youngster, and believed it would help break down the resistance of the team ranked 186th in the world. It did not quite work out that way and at half-time, with the score 0-0, England again found themselves being booed off by their away following. Capello responded by sending on Joe Cole at the start of the second half. Within ten minutes he had scored twice to kill the game off – an inspired choice by the Italian and great work from Cole. He volleyed his first on 49 minutes, then latched on to Rooney's through ball to double the lead.

The next stop a few days later was Zagreb and a return to the Maksimir Stadium, where Croatia had never lost a competitive match. This was the team that had beaten England twice under Steve McClaren, costing him his job and preventing England qualifying for EURO 2008.

Walcott stayed in the team and the 19-year-old destroyed the opposition, becoming England's youngest player to score a hat-trick. Croatia just couldn't cope with him that night as he seized on a loose ball to lash in his first goal on 26 minutes. This was a far more positive performance from England, though they had to wait until the second half to increase their advantage.

By then Croatia had been reduced to ten men when Robert Kovac was rightly sent off for elbowing Joe Cole. It was a nasty challenge and Cole, with his head bloodied, was stretchered off and replaced by Jermaine Jenas. Nothing was going to halt England's momentum and it wasn't long before the impressive Rooney teed up Walcott for a second. Rooney then made it 3-0, firing home from a cross by Jenas, and he was also responsible for playing in Walcott for the teenager's hat-trick. Mario Mandzukic's goal was no more than a consolation.

Walcott went home with the match ball after two right-footed finishes and one with his left, and we did wonder whether an international star had been born that night. It is fair to say Theo has had a pretty decent England career, though it has not quite lived up to that early promise.

Meanwhile Capello could do no wrong in the eyes of the English media – this was a performance to make the nation proud and there was no doubting that England were in control of their group.

They followed it up with a 5-1 demolition of Kazakhstan at Wembley, with Rooney scoring twice, and then four days later won 3-1 in Belarus to make it played four, won four. Rooney grabbed another couple of goals on that night in Minsk, after Gerrard had started it all off with a 30-yarder in the 11th minute. It was the first time that England had won their opening four World Cup qualifiers.

The following month in Berlin a depleted England side won 2-1 against Germany in a friendly. Terry scored the winning goal as Capello completed his first year in charge with eight wins and a draw from his ten games.

Spain had rained on the parade a bit in sunny Seville in February – suffice to say the European champions were too good for Capello's England that night. Normal service was then resumed with a 4-0 friendly win over Slovakia in March, including two more goals for Rooney, which was the warm-up match for the qualifier against Ukraine.

England left it late before making it five wins from five. Peter Crouch's first-half goal was cancelled out by Andriy Shevchenko in the 74th minute but with just five minutes to go David Beckham's free kick was headed on by Gerrard for Terry to bundle the ball over the line. Relief all round as England came through another test.

The next game was to provide a test of a different kind – a seven-hour flight, a five-hour time difference and a round trip of 7,000 miles for a EUROPEAN group qualifier. Welcome to Almaty, the former capital and largest city in Kazakhstan – just 200 miles from the Chinese border.

Almaty, with its Ascension cathedral and Golden Warrior monument, was an intriguing place, more oriental than European, and the England fans who made the long trip loved it. Thousands of soldiers and police were mobilised for the game (I'm not sure why, perhaps they just wanted to see the football) and the Kazakh crowd created their own atmosphere with their constant drumming.

They were almost celebrating a shock goal in the very first minute, then they had an effort disallowed before England finally settled down. Gareth Barry scored his first competitive international goal, Emile Heskey added his first competitive goal for England in seven years, while Rooney netted with an absolutely brilliant overhead kick to make it 3-0, and a Frank Lampard penalty completed the scoring.

That made it six wins out of six as England went clear at the top of Group 6. They then kept the theme going by scoring six goals a few days later against Andorra. Rooney grabbed two more to take his hot streak to ten in seven. Substitute Jermain Defoe scored twice as England fought back to draw 2-2 against Holland in Amsterdam in the first game of the 2009/10 season and the Tottenham man was also on target in the win over Slovenia as England prepared for their final three qualifiers.

The first of those was against Croatia and what a night we had at Wembley on 09/09/09. England ran in five goals with Aaron Lennon starring early on. He was brought down for a penalty which Lampard converted, then he crossed for Gerrard to head in a second goal. After the interval Lampard made it 3-0 with another header, while Rooney's looping cross allowed Gerrard to make it 4-0, with yet another header. Goalkeeper Rob Green made two great saves, but England could not clear the ball and Eduardo finally beat him at the third time of asking. At the other end a goalkeeping howler allowed Rooney to make it 5-1 and England had qualified for the 2010 World Cup in style with eight victories out of eight and 31 goals scored.

The one setback came in Dnipropetrovsk in south eastern Ukraine. Green conceded an early penalty and became the first England goalkeeper to get a red card. His replacement, David James, dived the wrong way but the spot kick came back off the post, so England had a reprieve. Not for long as Ukraine took the lead inside the opening half hour and held on against England's ten, though Rooney came very close in the final seconds.

Dnipro, as everyone called it, had wanted to be one of the host cities for EURO 2012 and the ground was first-class. The city's big problem was a lack of hotel rooms so Donetsk was the chosen venue in this part of the country. The locals here had a tradition of attaching padlocks to all of the bridges in the city, to signify their unbreakable love for their partners. They were also partial to playing chess outside in the parks – individual games drew big crowds of onlookers – and it was clearly a national pastime.

When we arrived at the press box ahead of kick-off the seats had been double-booked, so we were all provided with chairs and a long line of English football reporters were invited to sit right by the touchline. The Ukrainians showed themselves to be good hosts on that trip and they did so again when EURO 2012 came along.

England's 100 per cent qualifying record may have gone, but a 3-0 win over Belarus at Wembley ensured they would finish comfortably top of Group 6 and they seemed to be emerging as one of the sides to watch at the World Cup in South Africa in a few months' time.

Four friendlies would take place before then, the first against Brazil in Doha – which meant a chance to catch up with an old friend, cameraman Paul Quinn, who had settled out there. Everywhere we went the Qataris were determined to push their bid for the 2022 World Cup and we smiled politely, recorded a couple of high-profile interviews, and thought to ourselves, 'They have got no chance.' A year later I was as stunned as anyone that they succeeded, but they had seemed to have no doubts.

Even with an evening kick-off conditions were still pretty hot as England, captained for the first time by Rooney, looked to try and provide a winning end to 2009. It wasn't to be as they were beaten by a good header from Nilmar with a side which showed eight changes from the final qualifier.

Doha was a place of contrasts; fabulous wealth and five-star luxury on the one hand, while the foreign workers who were bussed out of the city after a long and dusty day's work told another story.

On the morning of the match we filmed a madcap group of England fans, who we would go on to bump into all round Europe (and the world) over the next few years. They hired camels and dressed up as the Knights of St George to ride on the beach and entertain all the onlookers. Maybe it was not totally politically correct, but it was a lot of fun and made a nice little feature.

World Cup year started with two 3-1 victories over Egypt and Mexico. They were hand-picked as opposition, because England had been drawn in a group with Algeria and the USA (as well as Slovenia).

By now, Terry had been stripped of the England captaincy after allegations emerged about his private life (a reported affair with the former partner of his ex-Chelsea team-mate Wayne Bridge) and replaced by Rio Ferdinand. Terry remained a vital part of the defence and would start all of England's games at the World Cup.

Before leaving for South Africa, Capello took England altitude training in the Austrian Alps at Irdning. The regime, by all accounts, was pretty strict as the Italian laid down his demands for a highly disciplined approach at the forthcoming tournament. Their final warm-up match in the rain in Graz was against Japan. Lampard missed a penalty, England did not look terribly convincing, but they won 2-1 thanks to two own goals.

Capello had opted for a provisional 30-man squad ahead of the tournament, which included surprise call-ups for Ledley King (because of his injury record) and Jamie Carragher (because he had announced his international retirement in 2007, albeit with a proviso that he would return in certain circumstances). The game with Egypt had been his first in an England shirt for three years, but both players would make it through to the final 23, whereas midfielder Scott Parker, who had looked the best and most energetic player on view in the training sessions in Austria, did not.

It was four years since I'd covered my last major tournament so there was a great sense of anticipation leading up to the start. Leaving the family was particularly hard this time; my 11-year-old daughter Poppy got really upset and the taxi journey to Heathrow was no fun. At times like this you can't help but ask yourself asking the question, 'What have I done?' It would be six weeks before I saw the children again and just right at that moment it seemed an impossibly long time. Happily, text messages, e-mails and telephone calls all help these days to make the time away from the family pass more quickly.

I was delighted my World Cup cameraman was Chris Noonan. He had been with Stu Vickery and I at EURO 2004 and Germany 2006, so he was experienced, and he was a really decent operator – editing the pictures he shot to a high standard. He was also very good company – despite his allegiance to Coventry City – and that is important too on these long trips, especially as we were sharing a two-bed apartment at the resort of Sun City for the first four weeks.

The team that Sky Sports News assembled for that World Cup was the strongest one we ever sent to a major tournament. My producer was Gary Hughes, who I had first met at France '98 when he was working with Sky News. He is now head of football at Sky Sports. Our two presenters were Ed Chamberlain and Simon Thomas, who were based in Cape Town at our specially built studio in the shadow of Table Mountain. Thoroughly likeable, hugely professional, and endlessly enthusiastic, they deserved the success they would have later presenting *Super Sunday* and *Monday Night Football*.

David Miles, who I talked about in the opening chapter, was the senior bulletin producer – another with a seemingly effortless ability to get the job done and keep everybody happy, a real skill. Geraint Hughes came along as second England reporter and later distinguished himself, along with his producer John Curtis, with their coverage of Ghana's great run to the quarter-finals. Bryan Swanson and Gary Cotterill underlined what fine reporters they were as they covered the news and colour around the tournament, while Steve Bone, Chris Shelmerdine and Roy Goddard provided the technical expertise.

When we landed early on that first morning it was sunny but cold – this was after all the South African winter – and although the temperatures were in the 70s during the day, at night it could fall to nearly freezing. It was also dark by 5.30pm and that took a bit of getting used to, coming from an English summer.

England arrived a few hours later to a traditional welcome and settled themselves in at their base – the Royal Bafokeng Sports Complex outside Rustenburg, almost 4,000 feet above sea level. England's opening match with the United States would be here, hence that altitude training in Austria.

The next morning the media turned up in vast numbers to see England's first training session, with Gareth Barry seemingly winning his battle to be fit in time for that first game. After 20 minutes or so the cameras and reporters were asked to leave as the session then became a private one. We all dashed over to the media centre to set up for Fabio Capello's first press conference.

When he came in he looked a little shaken and went on to tell us that right at the end of the session, captain Rio Ferdinand had badly injured his knee after a collision with Emile Heskey. He went to hospital for a scan, sparking a brief media frenzy with everyone trying to get pictures, and although he sought a second opinion it was soon clear his World Cup was over before it had even started.

I felt gutted for Rio as he was so proud to be leading England into a major tournament on the African continent, and I know he would have done a fine job. The injury put a real dampener on the mood around the camp, but the show must go on and Gerrard was appointed captain with Tottenham's Michael Dawson summoned from England as cover.

Our accreditation (such as it was) from FIFA came through in the nick of time, and we only knew we would be allowed to film England's stadium training session and news conference ahead of that first game with literally a couple of hours' notice.

Our live position in Rustenburg was high up on a hill overlooking the stadium, alongside broadcasting legend Jeremy Thompson, who was working for Sky News. The local cops screeched up and checked us out a couple of times, because with England and America both involved this match was always going to have very tight security. Rumours started spreading that the air traffic control system had been jammed overhead, which was why the police were so jumpy. One of the guys looking after us called himself the 'Black Mamba' (the world's deadliest snake) and he was certainly a fearsome-looking individual. But he had good police contacts and eventually discovered that everything was okay again.

We scrambled into the stadium just before kick-off and saw England make a dream start as Heskey slid the ball into Gerrard's path and the new captain flicked it in with his right foot from about ten yards out. Less than four minutes gone and Capello's team had the lead.

That's the way it should have stayed, but five minutes before half-time Clint Dempsey tried a speculative shot from 25 yards out. It was nothing special, yet somehow Robert Green let it squirm underneath him and dribble over the line as he desperately tried to claw it back. This was a personal nightmare for Green – it should have been just a regulation save, instead England had been pegged back, and it proved the pivotal moment of the whole match. To make matters worse, Green had pipped David James in the battle to start in goal – and now his England future was looking pretty dodgy.

In the second half Heskey had a great one-on-one opportunity but shot straight at Tim Howard, and before the end Green pulled off a good save – knocking Jozy Altidore's shot on to the post and away to safety. England had tired in the second half, though they appeared to have had the stuffing knocked out of them by that Green howler.

The gamble of playing the injury-prone Ledley King in central defence did not pay off either. King came into the side for the luckless Ferdinand but was unable to come out for the second half because of a groin problem and was replaced by Carragher. The Liverpool man did okay but picked up a booking, which would cause England problems further down the line. As for King, he played no further part in the tournament.

The question for Capello was whether to keep faith with Green or restore James. In the end he went for James, and that was pretty much the end of Green's England career, though he did win one more cap – in 2012 against Norway in Oslo, the first game of the Roy Hodgson era.

Match number two was against Algeria in Cape Town, with over 64,000 fans packing into the Green Point stadium. Barry replaced James Milner, with Carragher in for the injured King. If Capello hoped his players would deliver a much-improved performance on his 64th birthday he was sadly mistaken. This was more ponderous than in the opener against the USA as the group outsiders comfortably hung on for a 0-0 draw and their first point in the World Cup (they had lost their first game to Slovenia 1-0).

At the end the fans made their feelings of frustration known to the players and as he left the pitch, Rooney was heard on camera saying, 'Nice to see your own fans booing you.' Carragher picked up his second consecutive booking so he would be banned for the final group game, forcing yet another change in central defence.

With the match between Slovenia and the USA finishing 2-2, Group C had Slovenia on top with four points, USA second with two and ahead of England only on goals scored, while Algeria were bottom with a solitary point.

Only a win against Slovenia would guarantee that England progressed to the last 16 while another draw would almost certainly see them edged out. At Port Elizabeth's Nelson Mandela Bay Stadium Capello knew he had to get his team selection right. Matthew Upson replaced the suspended Carragher, while Jermain

Defoe started up front instead of Heskey, and Milner came in for Aaron Lennon.

A couple of days earlier, former captain Terry appeared at a news conference and suggested there was some dissatisfaction within the camp at Capello's selections. He went on to talk about the mood among the players, saying they were bored and did not have a lot to do at their base, and intimated there would be a clear-the-air meeting that very night.

The evening before the Slovenia game, Gerrard and Capello poured scorn on Terry's controversial remarks, yet many felt there was no smoke without fire and it all added to the pressure on the team.

They responded positively with Defoe volleying in Milner's cross in the 22nd minute to earn victory. They should have won more convincingly and the only shame was that Landon Donovan's last-minute winner against Algeria meant the Americans won the group. That earned them a game against Ghana in England's home base of Rustenburg, while Capello's men would have to travel to Bloemfontein to face the promising young German team.

There was huge relief all round among the media group covering England – it meant we continued to be based at Sun City which had become a home from home. We were in a good routine, Chris and me, filming the training live and the news conferences, before returning to our apartment in the afternoon to edit.

We were sat there one day in the lounge with the front door slightly ajar when we got a visitor. Throughout the resort there were many baboons roaming free and we found their behaviour quite amusing. On this occasion one came straight through the door and jumped up on the kitchen sideboard where the fruit bowl was positioned. He boldly looked us both in the eye, then picked out an apple and an orange, before making his way out. We laughed and thought 'cheeky sod', but he obviously told his mates – because within seconds about eight other baboons appeared on the threshold. We just managed to slam the door shut in time, or we would have been overrun.

The layout at Sun City also provided a good circuit for going running when we did have a little time off. On the flat and jogging downhill it was fine, but when you ran uphill here you certainly knew we were at altitude. Some excellent communal spaghetti bolognese suppers and a good Indian restaurant nearby kept our spirits up, and I think it is fair to say that 'Team Sky' thoroughly enjoyed their time there.

Capello decided to keep faith with the team which started against Slovenia, so they lined up against Germany like this: David James in goal; a back four of Glen Johnson, Matthew Upson, John Terry and Ashley Cole; in midfield it was James Milner, Steven Gerrard, Frank Lampard and Gareth Barry; while up front Jermain Defoe partnered Wayne Rooney.

The Germans had lost against Serbia in one of their group games, so they were vulnerable – but they were also hugely exciting and their side was full of pace. England started brightly but Germany soon got on top when a huge punt downfield by keeper Manuel Neuer was turned past James by Miroslav Klose for 1-0. Then Lukas Podolski's left-footed shot into the corner doubled the advantage and England were in deep trouble.

Gerrard swung over a cross on 37 minutes, Neuer rushed out and didn't get there, and Upson's header made it 2-1. Seconds later came the moment that defined their World Cup experience, as far as Capello and his players were concerned. Lampard with an audacious chip which went over Neuer, hit the bar, and came down a foot over the line. Lampard raised his arms in celebration and there was jubilation on the side of the pitch from Capello as well as two goals in less than a minute had completely turned the game on its head – or so we thought.

Uruguayan referee Jorge Larrionda waved play on. He and his officials appeared to be the only people inside the Free State Stadium who had not seen the ball clearly cross the line.

It was a travesty. The fact that this incident, more than any other, finally led to goal-line technology being used was absolutely no consolation to England and Lampard. As the teams left the field David Beckham was remonstrating with the referee and I felt sorry for him. A long-term injury had robbed him of the chance to go to his fourth World Cup as a player, though he had been added to Capello's coaching staff. Now he had witnessed a blatant injustice and there was nothing he could do – it must have been so frustrating. For the record, his 115th and last England appearance had come against Belarus eight months earlier when he came off the bench for the remaining 32 minutes of that final qualifier.

Seven minutes into the second half England were awarded a free kick 35 yards out and Lampard crashed a superb shot past the beaten Neuer, only to see it come back off the crossbar. When it's not your day, it really isn't your day.

Midway through the second half they were caught out on the counter-attack twice in the space of three minutes. Germany swept away up the left and Bastian Schweinsteiger crossed for Thomas Muller to make it 3-1. Then it was Mesut Ozil's turn to exploit England's lack of pace and he picked out Muller to score again.

That is how it finished, England's heaviest defeat at the World Cup finals – and in truth it could have been more as defensively they were pulled apart on numerous occasions. And yet, if Lampard's effort had been allowed, who knows what might have happened in the second half? England could have afforded to sit back more at 2-2 and not chase the game like they did. And how would that young German team have reacted to losing a two-goal lead in less than a minute?

I guess it is all academic now, although actually England did have more possession (51 per cent) and more shots (19 to 17). Nevertheless the main statistic on that Sunday afternoon in Bloemfontein was Germany 4 England 1.

That evening a storm blew up in the city and gale force winds forced us off air from our vantage point on top of a block of flats overlooking the stadium. We said goodbye to Simon Thomas and crowded into our minibus for the seven-and-a-half-hour drive back to Sun City. As everyone else slept I kept the driver company and had time to reflect on England's performance at this World Cup. There was no escaping the fact that they had been disappointing – the nation and the fans (maybe even the players too) had somehow expected more from Fabio Capello. Now he was fighting for his job.

The next day, the Italian spoke about how he wanted the chance to put right the mistakes of this tournament by taking England to EURO 2012. He pledged to introduce young players and survived in the role by the skin of his teeth.

After England flew home, Chris Noonan, Gary Hughes and I went to Cape Town for 11 days and that was a great experience. Before we left we were allowed a day off to go on safari, but in truth it was a cold, grey afternoon and the wild animals stayed away. Luck of the draw, I suppose.

The daily *World Cup Reports* show from Cape Town was still in full swing so I appeared as a studio guest a few times and we covered Germany's quarter-final with Argentina. This looked like a mouth-watering encounter but once Muller put the Germans ahead in the third minute there really only looked like being one winner. Klose added two more in the second half and the final score was 4-0.

As we left the stadium many of us at the time believed we may well have seen the eventual champions in action. Spain, of course, had other ideas.

The next day we paid a visit to Table Mountain and what a morning that was. About 70 people crammed into the cable car while some hardy souls could be seen attempting to walk up. The views from the top were breathtaking and it remains a treasured memory, though Gary Hughes did show us that day he had no head for heights. Our erstwhile ice-cool producer was reduced to almost a quivering wreck.

Next in town were Uruguay and Holland for their semi-final. The Dutch fans poured in and turned the Waterfront area (where the trendy bars and shops were) into a sea of orange. It was a good game too. An equaliser from Diego Forlan made it 1-1 at half-time and Forlan would go on to claim the award for the tournament's best player – his five goals propelled Uruguay further than they probably expected. Wesley Sneijder and Arjen Robben scored twice in the space of two minutes to take the Dutch into the final, but Uruguay pulled a late goal back as it finished 3-2.

Soccer City and Johannesburg was the final destination of our South African adventure. All sorts of fears had been expressed beforehand about how the country would not be able to cope with staging a World Cup and that security issues would turn it into a nightmare. Nothing could have been further from the truth – the football might not have always been the greatest, but it remains my favourite major tournament.

For me it is the high point of Sky Sports News's coverage of World Cups and European Championships, though by the end we had probably heard enough vuvuzelas to last us a lifetime! Plastic horns that gave us the life-affirming sound of a continent celebrating the joy of football – or the instrument of the devil? Probably a bit of both.

On the morning of the showdown I was lucky enough to interview 80-year-old Jack Taylor, the first Englishman to referee a World Cup Final. He was living in South Africa at the time and had taken charge of the 1974 encounter between West Germany and Holland, awarding each side a penalty in the first half.

I asked him how he thought Howard Webb might get on. The Yorkshireman was about to become the second Englishman to referee the final, and Jack had a high opinion of Howard. He spoke of how much he deserved the honour.

I also talked to Danny Jordaan, the chief executive officer of the South Africa World Cup and the man who probably did more than anyone to ensure the tournament not only came to the African continent, but was also a big success. His pride was evident ahead of the final and he tipped us off that Nelson Mandela, who had been very ill, would make an appearance at the game. Indeed he did – the inspirational leader came on to the pitch in a golf buggy after the final whistle.

The final itself was memorable for the number of cards that Webb had to issue; 14 yellows and one red (for Holland's Johnny Heitinga), though I should add that it was not his fault. The Dutch were surprisingly cynical that night and Nigel de Jong was lucky he did not get a red for a chest-high challenge on Xavi.

Robben had a great chance in normal time to win it for the Dutch, but Spain (the masters of the 1-0 win) gradually wore them down and Cesc Fabregas set up Andres Iniesta for the only goal with just four minutes of extra time remaining. Spain emulated West Germany in being world and European champions at the same time and proved themselves the best team, despite losing their opening match to Switzerland. They beat Portugal, Paraguay, Germany and Holland in the knockout stages by the same scoreline: 1-0.

We flew home the next evening and could look back at a job really well done, though annoyingly I lost my voice completely on the morning after the final and could not do my very last scheduled live cross. That aside, it had been fantastic.

England's friendly in August against Hungary at Wembley would be a useful measure of how the country felt about its football team after what had happened at South Africa 2010. In the event more than 70,000 attended and generally they were supportive, despite a few jeers for the likes of Wayne Rooney (why?) and Ashley Cole.

All three goals came in the space of ten minutes in the second half and for a while Capello must have been fearing the worst. On the hour Phil Jagielka's deflection was heading in for an own goal when debutant Michael Dawson raced back and looked to have stopped the whole ball going over the line. Despite England's protests the goal was given and for the second match running the team was on the wrong end of a decision which video technology could have prevented. It was not nearly as significant as Lampard's disallowed effort in Bloemfontein, but it was no wonder the FA were big supporters of GDS – the Goal-line Decision System which was eventually introduced.

As the England players jogged back to the halfway line for the restart they would have heard the boos and whistles echoing around Wembley, but it did not intimidate them and they responded strongly – none more so than captain Gerrard. Within six minutes he had brought England level with a well-struck 20-yarder, then his deft finish on 73 minutes put them ahead. That is how it stayed and England got a good ovation as they left the field. They had passed the first test.

The opening qualifier for EURO 2012 was at home to Bulgaria, who were brushed aside by a Jermain Defoe hat-trick. It was a thoroughly well-deserved highlight for a player who always gave his all for England, no matter how many times he was left out of the starting 11 or out of the squad altogether.

Four days later in Basel came the toughest qualifier of the lot – at least on paper. Switzerland were above England in the official FIFA rankings and were therefore the top seeds in the group.

It was a very special occasion for me as well: my 200th England game, 20 years and six months after covering my first. My 150th had been in the heat of Stuttgart at the 2006 World Cup when England reached the quarter-finals with a 1-0 win over Ecuador. I was hoping for a similar outcome that night and I got it. First, though, came a pleasant surprise when Capello walked over to our live position before kick-off and presented me with a signed England shirt. On the back it had Collins 200 – a lovely gesture.

Once the game got under way it was England who immediately took charge and Rooney put them in front inside ten minutes with his first international goal for a year – a good time to end the drought. He caused Switzerland problems all evening at St Jakob's Park and the Three Lions emerged 3-1 winners with substitute Darren Bent scoring the clinching goal.

England had bounced back from their poor World Cup with three consecutive wins and six qualifying points, but the year did not end on quite such a positive note. First, unfancied Montenegro held them 0-0 at Wembley in a qualifier, then France outplayed them to win the November friendly 2-1. The best thing to emerge from these two games was that they marked the England return of the fit-again Rio Ferdinand, and he wore the captain's armband in both matches.

The opening encounter of 2011 was against Denmark in Copenhagen. Lampard was captain for the first time on that February night because Gerrard was injured. When Lampard went off, Ashley Cole took the armband, and it was later passed on to Gareth Barry. John Terry, playing his first international in six months, was overlooked each time – and Capello felt this was not right.

He was controversial, but Terry was also England's most natural leader and Capello restored the captaincy to him for the following month's qualifier in Wales. Against Denmark we also saw Jack Wilshere make his first England start (he had come on for his debut against Hungary) and he looked very impressive in midfield. Despite falling behind, England won 2-1 with goals from Bent and substitute Ashley Young.

There was a full house in Cardiff as Terry led England out for a pivotal qualifier against Gary Speed's improving Wales and Capello's men came through with flying colours. Two first-half goals from Lampard (with a penalty) and Bent put England in charge and they never relinquished their grip, consolidating their position at the top of the qualifying group.

A few days later came a very different kind of game at Wembley. Ghana, the heroes of the 2010 World Cup, paid their first visit – and brought 20,000 fans with them. It made for a unique atmosphere which even included booing Danny Welbeck when he came on for his England debut, because both his parents were born in Ghana, and the supporters clearly felt he was playing for the wrong country. Luckily, Danny took it all good-naturedly and went on to forge a fine career with England.

Another debutant that night was an old favourite of mine – former Gillingham star Matt Jarvis played his one and only international game, but he will always be a legend at Priestfield. Andy Carroll scored his first England goal that night but in an entertaining match Ghana equalised in the last minute.

The season ended with a 2-2 home draw against Switzerland but I was not involved as my mother, Adele, was gravely ill. Sadly she passed away that July, aged 81. She was not a football fan but had followed my career closely until dementia took its particularly cruel hold over her a few years earlier.

When the new season resumed England had a double-header against Bulgaria away and Wales at home. In Sofia injuries forced Capello to play debutant Chris Smalling out of position at right-back. It was a bit of a baptism of fire for the central defender, but he did okay. England kept a clean sheet and took another big stride towards the finals with a 3-0 win. Pleasingly, Rooney scored twice.

At Wembley, Wales gave England a torrid time and would have left with a point but for Robert Earnshaw's miss late on. Ashley Young scored the winner and afterwards in the mixed zone I spoke to Gary Speed for what would be the last time. He was clearly frustrated his side had not got a point, but he seemed determined to continue to push Wales up the world rankings. His sudden death a couple of months later stunned the football world – he was found hanged at his home in Cheshire. He was 42.

By this stage England were six points clear at the top of the group and would need just a draw from their final qualifier in Montenegro to make it through to EURO 2012.

There might only have been 11,500 packed in to the Podgorica City Stadium but they created an edgy and hostile atmosphere. Some supporters threw flares and missiles at Joe Hart's goal and it was an uncomfortable evening on and off the pitch – the thunder and lightning which rumbled and flashed overhead all added to the drama.

England went ahead on 11 minutes when Theo Walcott delivered a cross right on to Young's head – he simply stooped and nodded the ball into the net. Twenty minutes later it was 2-0 with Bent scoring from close range after Rooney and Young had combined.

The game took its first twist in first-half stoppage time when Montenegro pulled a goal back thanks to a deflection and the noise in the stadium went up several notches.

There was the odd anxious moment in the second half, but England were holding on comfortably enough until Rooney got himself sent off. Before the game Capello had assured the media Rooney was in the right frame of mind despite his father being arrested by police the day before. However, it didn't look like it when he kicked out at Miodrag Dzudovic as the two tussled for possession. Dzudovic made the most of the challenge, Rooney realised the folly of his over-reaction and tried to apologise, but Wolfgang Stark's red card meant he was on his way.

It also meant he would miss at least the first game of EURO 2012 through suspension. If UEFA deemed it to be violent conduct the ban could rise to three matches, ruling him out of the entire group stage – and therefore putting his participation at the finals in real jeopardy. But all of those considerations would have to wait as England faced a difficult task with only ten men.

Montenegro needed a draw to qualify for the play-offs and pushed England further and further back as the match moved towards stoppage time. I was sat next to Geoff Shreeves on the touchline and I have to say that I was not surprised when the equaliser finally came. England failed to clear a cross and Andrija Delibasic headed in at the far post to send the place into delirium. He ran round the pitch, ripped off his shirt and jumped into the crowd. The celebrations were still going on when the final whistle blew and then the fans invaded the pitch in their thousands.

It was mostly a boisterous outpouring of national pride, but a large group congregated in front of the England supporters to try and provoke them into retaliation. Those following the Three Lions that night showed commendable restraint.

Meanwhile, I was stuck on the far side of the pitch, trying to make my way past hordes of fans who were between me and the post-match interview area. It took several minutes and a few detours before I made it, by which time the heavens had opened again and we all got a fresh soaking as we tried to talk to the players. Theo Walcott was particularly patient that night and risked getting saturated as he answered our questions.

Rooney's red card was obviously the big talking point, but we also had to remember that England had qualified unbeaten with five wins and three draws so there was plenty to be positive about too.

The final two games of 2011 provided England with rare victories over two teams who had caused them plenty of difficulties over the years. To beat the reigning world and European champions Spain was a great achievement in itself, especially as they had won the last three encounters. Captain Frank Lampard scored the only goal.

Sweden were even more of a bogey team – England had failed to beat them in 12 games and 43 years, but it was 13th time lucky that night and Gareth Barry's deflected header for the winner was the national team's 2,000th goal.

It would also be Fabio Capello's last game in charge. Since the World Cup he had lost only once in 14 games and had come through 2011 unbeaten with six wins and three draws. He had led the team to a second major tournament and had already talked about wanting to learn the lessons from the failures at South Africa 2010.

In early December he had two important dates. First there was the draw for the final stages of EURO 2012, with England paired alongside France, Sweden and the co-hosts Ukraine. Then he was in Nyon to speak at Rooney's appeal hearing for the red card which threatened his chances of taking part in the tournament. UEFA agreed to cut the ban from three matches to two, so Rooney would be free to face Ukraine in Donetsk on 19 June.

A couple of weeks after Rooney's appeal hearing the Crown Prosecution Service announced that John Terry would be charged with racially abusing Anton Ferdinand, the younger brother of Rio. It followed a clash between the two of them in the QPR v Chelsea Premier League game on 23 October. Terry had issued a statement that night denying he had made a racist slur against Ferdinand, but a few days later the Metropolitan Police confirmed it had launched a formal investigation.

On 1 February Terry's trial was fixed for the week beginning 9 July, once the Euros had ended, so some of his Chelsea team-mates could appear as witnesses.

Then came the key moment of the story up until then. On 3 February Terry was stripped of the England captaincy by the FA's 14-man board, WITHOUT consulting Fabio Capello. I remember speaking with Capello's assistant Franco Baldini and, although he would not go on camera to say it, he made it clear his boss was furious that he had been left out of the process.

Capello was considering his England future and on 6 February he publicly criticised the decision to take the armband off Terry. That put him on a collision course with the FA and two days later he resigned as England manager, throwing the national team into disarray. It was four months before their opening game at EURO 2012 and three weeks before they had a friendly against Holland.

Under-21s manager Stuart Pearce was rapidly summoned to look after the game with the Dutch. He made Scott Parker captain, recalled Micah Richards and lost 3-2.

As for Capello, well he would go on to manage Russia at the 2014 World Cup – though that would be considered a failure too.

In qualifying his England record was impressive: 14 wins and three draws from 18 games – but in South Africa he won only one of four matches, drawing two and losing by a big margin to Germany.

He was a renowned disciplinarian and kept his distance from the players and, though they may not have warmed to him, they did have huge respect for him in the main.

His inability to master English also did not help his cause, though I found him to be a good guy with a nice sense of humour. He also remembered me when he became manager of Russia and agreed to an interview in the media scrum at the World Cup draw in Brazil, when it would have been far easier to walk on past. What started as 'Benvenuto, Fabio' ended – inevitably – with 'Arrivederci'.

# 19

# Roy Hodgson Takes Charge

IN an upstairs room above a pub on London's City Road I attended an England fans' forum with two of the print journalists I respect the most – Henry Winter and Ollie Holt. Back then, Henry was football correspondent of the *Daily Telegraph* before moving to *The Times*, while Ollie was chief sports writer at *The Mirror*. He is now at the *Mail on Sunday*.

It was April 2012 and we were there to discuss all things England football; how would the team get on at the upcoming European Championships and, most importantly, who would be the next England manager?

Two names stood out: Harry Redknapp and Roy Hodgson. I think it is fair to say the supporters were split over the issue, possibly slightly more favouring Redknapp – but then we were in London and he was manager of Tottenham, while Hodgson was in charge of West Bromwich Albion.

A couple of weeks later, FA chief executive David Bernstein announced that Roy would be the new boss on a four-year contract and added that he was the only candidate they had approached.

I must admit that, although I had always got on really well with Harry, I was very pleased that Roy landed the job – he was hugely experienced from an international perspective, though I appreciate that Harry was probably the 'people's choice'.

Roy gave his first news conference at Wembley on 1 May and explained that he would stay at West Bromwich until 13 May (the last day of the Premier League season) before starting with England the next day. Time was certainly of the essence: the EURO 2012 squad would be revealed on 16 May, there were warm-up games on 26 May and 2 June, and the tournament began on 8 June.

A daunting prospect maybe, but Roy certainly did not lack experience. He was a multiple title winner in Sweden and Denmark, he had been in charge of three national teams (Switzerland at the 1994 World Cup, United Arab Emirates and Finland), he'd taken Inter Milan to the 1997 UEFA Cup Final and Fulham to the 2010 Europa League Final – the same competition, renamed for the 2009/10 season – as well as also managing Blackburn Rovers, Liverpool and West Brom in the Premier League.

His first big decision was to leave the former captain Rio Ferdinand out of his squad, citing 'footballing reasons' for the omission. In the media there was much speculation that he had not wanted Rio and John Terry in the same dressing room because Terry was due to go on trial in July accused of racially abusing Rio's younger brother Anton.

That speculation grew even more when central defender Gary Cahill broke his jaw in the final warm-up game against Belgium and Roy opted for Liverpool full-back Martin Kelly as the replacement. To be fair, there were injury doubts around Rio and he had not played for England for a year. He never won another cap.

Roy's first game was away to Norway, a nation England had not beaten for 32 years. Ashley Young scored the only goal of the game to put that particular record to bed, while Alex Oxlade-Chamberlain made an accomplished debut at the age of 19. England achieved another 1-0 win over Belgium at Wembley so they went off to the Euros in fairly good heart.

Back home there was far less expectation placed on this England squad, which may have helped them. Fabio Capello's resignation, the late appointment of Hodgson and Wayne Rooney's suspension from the first two group games all played a part in a slight dampening of the usual mood of optimism.

England based themselves in the beautiful and ancient city of Krakow in southern Poland – even though all three of their group games were in Ukraine. The historic centre of Krakow was a World Heritage site and England's hotel was just off the main square.

In South Africa the players had complained they were too isolated. This time the FA opted for a city centre location to allow them to feel a part of the community in which they were staying. It meant they could walk out from their hotel (the aptly named Hotel Stary) to go for coffees or take a stroll in their free time. After an initial media frenzy it all settled down and the players were largely left alone.

It was a much smaller Sky Sports News team this time – the London Olympics was just a couple of months away and that was where the money and resources were being channelled. I was delighted to be linking up with cameraman Chris Noonan again, while Simon Vincent came along as producer and did a fine job too, despite his lack of previous experience.

Gary Cotterill and Bryan Swanson completed our reporting team – I like to think we had gone for quality rather than quantity!

England's training base was the Hutnik Municipality Stadium, a short drive from their hotel. The facilities were basic but the playing surface was good and that was the main thing. Strangely we only got to film one or two sessions here – either training was closed, or we were at the venue of the next game watching England train there instead.

The magnificent Donbass Arena in Donetsk staged England's opening game at EURO 2012 against the 2000 champions France. Flying there and back from Krakow was a 2,000-mile round trip and it wasn't much shorter when England played in Kiev, so we often arrived back at our hotel after matches between four and six in the morning. It was a tough schedule, but nobody's fault, and you just had to get used to it.

This was the England team Hodgson selected for his first competitive game: Joe Hart in goal; a back four of Glen Johnson, Joleon Lescott, John Terry and Ashley Cole; in midfield it was James Milner, Steven Gerrard (captain), Scott Parker and Alex Oxlade-Chamberlain; up front were Ashley Young and Danny Welbeck.

England showed tactical discipline and resilience, especially in the second half, and were reasonably happy with the point they got from a 1-1 draw. Gerrard's free kick was headed in by Lescott, who had escaped his marker to score his first and only England goal on the half hour.

The lead lasted less than ten minutes before Samir Nasri beat Joe Hart from 20 yards for the equaliser and after that France were probably the better team, but without Rooney this was still an encouraging performance and result.

Four days later in Kiev, Hodgson made just one change for the Sweden game, bringing in the physically imposing Andy Carroll for the teenager Oxlade-Chamberlain. There was great banter between the two sets of supporters beforehand and the Swedes were there in big numbers because all three of their group games were in Kiev. As they marched down the road to the stadium waving their blue and yellow colours the England fans on the banks above them sang, 'Your team is sh*t, but your birds are fit,' to which the Swedes replied, 'Go home to your ugly wives!'

The game itself was one of the best at EURO 2012 and provided England with their first competitive win over Sweden. The decision to pick Carroll paid off handsomely when the big striker powerfully headed England in front after 23 minutes from a cross by Gerrard. It was still 1-0 at half-time, but then careless defending allowed Sweden to score twice in the opening 15 minutes of the second half. Olof Mellberg's shot was palmed by Hart on to Johnson and over the line for a scrappy equaliser, while the second was down to rank bad marking, with Mellberg heading Sweden in front.

Hodgson responded swiftly and decisively, sending on Theo Walcott in place of Milner. Walcott was not used at the 2006 World Cup and failed to make Capello's final squad for 2010 so this would be his first taste of action at a major tournament. Within four minutes he pulled England level with a sweetly struck shot from more than 20 yards out, then in the 78th minute he burst down the right, weaved past a couple of challenges and crossed for Welbeck to back-heel in a cheeky winner. It was a great comeback from England but their defending had been slipshod at times and that would have to improve if they wanted to go really deep into the tournament.

The third game was back in Donetsk against the co-hosts Ukraine. This venue was the nearest to the Russian border and many Russian fans had made the 120-mile trip. In the match against France they had supported England, but this time it was clear their allegiance lay with Ukraine and they added to the partisan atmosphere.

Rooney was back from suspension and he replaced Carroll up front in the only change Hodgson made to his line-up. They found it difficult in the first half, with Ukraine dominating for long periods, although Rooney did miss a good chance with a header that went wide.

Early in the second half he was on target with a header, nodding in from close range to give England a valuable 1-0 lead. It was his first goal at a major tournament since 2004 and it maintained his great scoring record at the Euros – that made it five goals from five games at the finals.

If England could hang on they would face Italy (the Group C runners-up) in Kiev in the quarter-finals. They only just managed it, after surviving a big scare. This time the lack of video technology went in their favour as TV replays appeared to show that Marko Devic's shot had fractionally crossed the line before Terry scooped it clear.

Sunday, 24 June 2012 in Kiev is another one of those days that goes with Turin 1990, Wembley 1996, St Etienne 1998, Lisbon 2004 and Gelsenkirchen 2006. I'm sad to to say that I have been at them all, and it never gets any better or any easier.

England battled their way through 120 minutes against Italy and did very well to hang on for 0-0 after being second-best for long periods. Under Hodgson they had developed into a very difficult team to break down. They did have a few alarming moments, notably when Daniele De Rossi hit the post early on with Hart beaten, but they had chances as well – Rooney's late overhead kick for example.

Nevertheless, as we all got ready for penalties, I had that slightly sick feeling inside – a mixture of anticipation and dread. This is how England got knocked out of a sixth major tournament in a shoot-out:

Mario Balotelli went first for Italy and scored: 1-0

Steven Gerrard beat Gianluigi Buffon in the corner as the keeper correctly dived right: 1-1

Riccardo Montolivo's shot narrowly went wide, but Joe Hart may well have saved it anyway had it been on target: still 1-1

Wayne Rooney scored high in the corner after sending Buffon the wrong way and England had the lead: 1-2

Andrea Pirlo's key penalty was an outrageous chip into the net as Hart dived to his right: 2-2

Ashley Young sent Buffon the wrong way, but his penalty came back off the underside of the bar and bounced away: still 2-2

Antonio Nocerino converted his penalty as Hart went the wrong way: 3-2

Ashley Cole hit a fairly tame penalty, Buffon dived to his left to save and yet again England were on the brink of defeat: still 3-2

Alessandro Diamanti then finished England off – the former West Ham player sent Hart the wrong way to knock England out: 4-2.

The players looked stunned as they stood in the centre circle and watched Italy celebrating – when will it be our turn to win one of these shoot-outs again?

Roy Hodgson had not had much time to prepare, but he knocked England into pretty good shape and gave us hope that better things could lie ahead with a little more luck. Key midfielder Frank Lampard missed the tournament with a last-minute injury, while Rooney was absent from the first two matches through suspension. Ten of the players started every game, only 16 of the 23 were used and seven (Hart, Johnson, Cole, Gerrard, Terry, Lescott and Young) played all 360 minutes.

We moved on to Warsaw for the semi, where a Balotelli-inspired Italy beat Germany, and from there it was back to Kiev for the final. FIFA executive member Jim Boyce (a thoroughly good man) got Bryan Swanson and I tickets and we settled down to see if Spain could become the first team to retain their Euro title.

They were the favourites but few would have foreseen the manner and margin of their victory. The holders had been accused of being boring in the tournament – not on this night. They started well, their passing was superb and the tempo impressive.

Cesc Fabregas had a marvellous game and crossed from the right for David Silva to head Spain in front in the 14th minute. The second goal arrived just before half-time and left Italy facing a huge task. Jordi Alba's blistering run down the left was brilliantly spotted by Xavi and his fine pass allowed the left-back to shoot past Gianluigi Buffon.

When Thiago Motta went off injured, Italy were reduced to ten men because they had already used their three substitutes – and Spain ruthlessly exploited that advantage.

Substitute Fernando Torres scored in his second consecutive Euro final, then unselfishly set up his Chelsea team-mate Juan Mata in the 88th minute to make it 4-0. There was no question the best team won the tournament, but Italy were worthy finalists, while there was a feeling that if England could add some more quality to their undoubted durability then they too could have a good World Cup in two years' time.

Fifty-two days after that quarter-final defeat England faced Italy again, this time in a friendly on neutral territory in Bern. Hodgson made ten changes from the EURO 2012 encounter – Ashley Young was the only one to keep his place – and the manager would have been highly encouraged by what he saw.

He gave a debut to Jack Butland who, at 19 years and 158 days, became England's youngest goalkeeper in history – beating the record of Billy Moon which had stood since 1888.

Playing in unfamiliar white shirts and red shorts, England fell behind after 15 minutes to a goal created by the man whose penalty had knocked them out of the Euros. Diamanti's corner was headed in by Daniele De Rossi and it looked like being a difficult evening in the Swiss capital.

England were level 12 minutes later and again the goal came from a corner. This time Lampard provided the set piece and Phil Jagielka headed in his first England goal. After that Italy created chances, England had two efforts disallowed and there were just 12 minutes to go when the winning goal arrived.

England were under pressure, debutant Ryan Bertrand did superbly to clear the ball off the line, then suddenly they swept forward on the counter. Jermain Defoe wriggled his way out of one challenge then turned and fired a terrific shot into the corner from outside the area.

It was a small measure of revenge after what happened in Kiev, but more importantly it gave England a confidence boost ahead of the World Cup qualifying campaign.

I also had a new producer, who would go on to cover the next four years with me at Brazil 2014 and at the 2016 European Championships in France. It was the beginning of a great working relationship – and yet many people at Sky thought it would fail. There was a 30-year age gap for a start and at first glance we looked to be total opposites – which in a sense we were – but we also thought the same about a lot of things. For all that I may have been able to teach her, through my experience, she has taught me just as much (if not more) about the changing face of TV, the digital revolution and a whole lot of other stuff.

Gemma Davies was in her mid-20s, red-haired, and fiercely proud of her Wigan roots. She is a big supporter of both her local football and rugby league teams and I really respected her for that. I also used to have endless fun teasing her about Gillingham's play-off victory over Wigan in 2000, a game which reduced her to tears. I think it is fair to say she has got her own back over the years.

When I was made redundant Gem sent me a wonderful letter in which she said that her and her parents considered me to be her 'TV dad'. I take that as an enormous compliment.

The first qualifier was in Moldova, which meant a return to Chisinau after 16 years. The city – and the country – was a lot more prosperous, though I did have my mobile stolen while filming in one of the markets. That served me right as I took my eye off the ball.

The Zimbru Stadium had a capacity of just over 10,000, but only one entrance. As a result a big crush built up in the hour before kick-off and our live position came under a lot of pressure as supporters from both countries tried to get in. It gave Gem an early insight into what problems can unfold abroad at England matches – but she responded calmly, kept the fans at bay, and our broadcasts were able to continue.

On the pitch England destroyed the Moldovans in the first half, going ahead through a Lampard penalty after just three minutes. Lampard headed in a second goal and Defoe scored a third before the break. James Milner and Leighton Baines, with his first senior international goal, gave England a 5-0 win and it did not flatter them.

It was the perfect start to qualifying but four days later at Wembley it was a different story against Ukraine. It needed a late Lampard penalty to salvage a point after the EURO 2012 co-hosts threatened to avenge their defeat in Donetsk in the summer.

The following month England put five past San Marino at Wembley, though I think many fans probably expected us to score more. Wayne Rooney and Danny Welbeck got two goals each.

Two weeks before the game, England's new training base at St George's Park was officially opened. Set in 330 acres of the Staffordshire countryside, it has gone on to become the location for all the England football teams to prepare for matches. It is probably fair to say that its popularity has grown with each successive England manager. Roy Hodgson had some reservations, but Sam Allardyce was a big fan of SGP and Gareth Southgate is an even more committed supporter.

The other big story off the pitch was that by then John Terry had announced his international retirement. In July he had been cleared in court of the criminal charge of racially abusing Anton Ferdinand, but the Football Association still charged him with abusive behaviour. Just before that case was due to be heard, Terry issued a statement saying he was ending his 78-cap England career as the FA had made his position with the national team untenable.

It was a shame in many ways, but it was probably also inevitable. He had performed with great distinction for his country though his career was often dogged by controversy.

I did once ask him live on air whether he was a racist, but the FA would not let him reply to that question.

In the absence of Terry, it was Phil Jagielka and Joleon Lescott (who had played together in the past in Everton's back four) who provided the central defensive partnership in Poland.

The game should have been played on Tuesday 16 October but it had to be postponed for almost 24 hours because of torrential rain. I felt sorry for the majority of the 2,500 England fans who were booked on flights back on the Tuesday night and so missed the re-arranged fixture.

Many of the national papers described the whole situation as a farce and they were not wrong. The national stadium in Warsaw had been built for EURO 2012 at a cost of £400m and, crucially, it had a retractable roof. Yet the Polish officials chose not to shut the roof the night before the game – despite a very ominous weather forecast.

Once the rain started falling on the Tuesday – and it absolutely hammered it down – it was too late. The operation to close the roof takes only 15 minutes, but it cannot be done when it is raining, so we could all only stand and watch as the pitch became more and more waterlogged.

I remember doing one live broadcast about an hour before the scheduled kick-off time to give an update on the elements, and it was almost impossible. The rain was battering into my face, I could barely keep my eyes open, and I have NEVER got so wet in all my life – it was wetter even than Moscow 2008. For those watching ay home in the warmth and dry it must have seemed pretty comical (though not as funny as an incident that would take place just under a year later), but it did graphically show how bad the conditions were.

By now the fans were inside the stadium, yet a decision kept on being delayed. I think Italian referee Gianluca Rocchi was hoping for a miracle and he did not inspect the pitch until almost kick-off time (9pm local). There really was only one decision he could make and 45 minutes later it was confirmed the game had been put back to Wednesday, with a kick-off time of 5pm.

This was the first time an England game had been postponed because of the weather since November 1979, when thick fog prevented a match at Wembley against Bulgaria from going ahead. A few years earlier, a famous episode of the sitcom *Whatever Happened To The Likely Lads?* had followed the attempts of the two main characters, Bob and Terry, to avoid finding out the score of an England game until the late-night TV highlights were shown. Their efforts were all in vain, they lost their bet, and England were 'flooded out', so didn't even play!

Mercifully at around midnight it stopped raining and the roof could finally be closed, to prevent any more damage. We sneaked inside the ground early next morning to film the playing surface (strictly speaking, we should not have been there, as we were non-rights holders), and it did not look great.

It had improved by kick-off time and it was certainly playable – though it was probably a factor as to why this game was not much of a spectacle. England took the lead through Wayne Rooney's deflected header, but Poland hit back in the second half to force a draw – a result which kept England a point clear at the top of the group.

The year finished with a trip to Stockholm, where Roy Hodgson is still highly respected for all the good work he did there. England ran into a one-man army that night and his name was Zlatan Ibrahimovic. The Paris St Germain striker scored four times, including an utterly stunning 30-yard bicycle kick, as England trailed 1-0, then hit back to lead 2-1, before succumbing 4-2.

It was not the way captain Steven Gerrard would have wanted to win his 100th cap but it was still a fantastic achievement as he became the sixth England player to reach that milestone. Since his first game in 2000 I pretty much saw them all and have always been a big admirer of the Liverpool legend. He led his country at three major tournaments and took part in three World Cups (2006, 2010, 2014) and three European Championships (2000, 2004 and 2012). He may not have enjoyed any success in terms of trophies for England, but he gave his all for the cause and played with great passion.

Hodgson handed debuts to six players. Three were in the starting line-up: Steven Caulker (whose goal put England ahead), 17-year-old Raheem Sterling, and 31-year-old Leon Osman; and three came off the bench: Carl Jenkinson (who was also qualified for Finland), Wilfried Zaha (who now plays for the Ivory Coast) and Ryan Shawcross (who endured a difficult evening).

It was a year of mixed progress, not helped by Fabio Capello's resignation – England were hard to beat, well organised and tactically aware, yet they seemed to be lacking an X-factor.

Against Brazil at Wembley the following February we thought we had found it in the shape of midfielder Jack Wilshere. He produced a man-of-the-match performance as England beat the 2014 World Cup hosts for the first time in nine matches and 23 years. Rooney and Lampard scored the goals, Joe Hart saved Ronaldinho's penalty, and Ashley Cole won his 100th cap, but it was the outstanding performance by Wilshere that captured the imagination. He displayed great vision in his passing, a real eagerness to be involved, and a calm maturity in possession.

People often say that Wilshere has flattered to deceive in his England career, but I just think if he had not been so blighted by injuries he would have become a top international midfielder – maybe he still can.

That game was the first in a series of matches in 2013 which was played to celebrate the FA's 150th anniversary. Ireland, Scotland and Germany were also invited to Wembley over the course of the next few months.

England's next qualifier was at a 7,000-capacity stadium in a place called Serravalle against San Marino. It was where, for the first and only time in my 26-year career covering the national team, I saw England score EIGHT goals. Admittedly one of them was an own goal, but for the record those who found the target that night against San Marino were: Alessandro Della Valle (own goal, 12 minutes), Alex Oxlade-Chamberlain (28), Jermain Defoe (35 and 77), Ashley Young (39), Frank Lampard (42), Wayne Rooney (54), and Daniel Sturridge (70).

During the trip we were based in the nearby resort of Rimini and I actually had a room with a view of the Mediterranean Sea – another first. Fair play to the Sammarinese for hosting the England game on home territory, rather than switching it to a larger, neutral venue as they did in 1993 or as Andorra did twice in 2007 and 2008.

From there we flew to Podgorica where England were up against Montenegro, the surprise leaders of Group H. This was a different proposition altogether from the gentle run-out against San Marino, again the atmosphere was hostile and again the Montenegrins found a way to prevent England winning. Rooney took his tally to five goals in his last four qualifiers when he headed England in front inside the opening quarter of an hour. Hodgson would have been pleased with the way England controlled the first half. Before his goal Rooney had hit the post with a chip and there were other chances as well.

Equally he would have been disturbed at the manner of England's failure to increase the lead and the way they gradually capitulated in the second half. It was no surprise when Dejan Damjanovic forced the ball over the line from close range at the second (or third) attempt to make it 1-1. That was the cue for the flares to go off and England's record against Montenegro remained three draws from three encounters.

For the third consecutive time England had won the first game of their double-header, only to drop points in the second. With four matches to play England still trailed Montenegro by two points, and they would have to wait almost six months for their next qualifier.

The season ended with two more friendlies to celebrate the FA's century and a half. Yet again the Republic of Ireland frustrated England, taking the lead through Shane Long before Lampard equalised. No wonder their fans just loved singing 'You'll Never Beat The Irish' and they had a point. If you include the abandoned match of 1995 it was now six games and 28 years since England enjoyed success against them. Most importantly, though, the fixture was played in a really good atmosphere and there was no hint of the trouble which had caused the previous encounter to be halted 17 years earlier.

The very next day we flew to Rio de Janeiro for the final England game of the season. It was my first taste of South America and I liked what I saw. The Copacabana beach was stunning, as was Ipanema, and Rio seemed almost European in atmosphere – albeit in a very laid-back, relaxed way.

England had the honour of being the first team to face Brazil at the newly redeveloped Maracana Stadium and they headed home with a creditable draw. All the goals came in the second half, with Fred putting Brazil ahead before Oxlade-Chamberlain hit a superb equaliser. Rooney's deflected effort gave England a 2-1 lead but eight minutes from the end Paulinho's volley tied it up again at 2-2.

Twelve months ahead of the World Cup it was clear that the football fans in Rio were looking forward to the spectacle, but there were also plenty of rumblings of discontent and the protest movement was gathering momentum. Many felt the Brazilian government had spent too much on the tournament to the detriment of other social issues. It would become a recurring theme. However, there was no doubting what a stunning location this was going to be for a World Cup, and it whetted our appetites for the following summer.

Wednesday, 14 August 2013 was the day when England played Scotland at Wembley for the first time in 14 years. It was also an afternoon I will never forget.

Let me set the scene. Our live position was on a grassy bank just by a retail park alongside Engineers Way and around 100 yards from the stadium. By building a metal platform it was possible to get a much better shot of Wembley over my shoulder when I was doing live pieces back to the Sky Sports News studio.

I had already done one without mishap but an hour later, while I was talking about Michael Carrick's fitness, my weight shifted slightly and I felt the whole platform start to give way. A moment later I disappeared out of the shot completely and a loud clanking sound could be heard as the structure disintegrated around me. I did not actually fall that far, but I was conscious that my back would hit the ground first so I twisted at the last minute and my left shoulder took the main impact as I landed.

At that point I remember thinking two things: the first was 'ouch' and the second was 'I bet that goes viral!' I was right on both counts.

By now they had cut back to the studio where presenter Jim White was saying, 'Now that's the kind of thing which you hope never happens to you on live television, but it obviously happened to Nick there.'

Looking back at it afterwards, I thought Jim handled it just right. He wanted to play it to the maximum for laughs but he was also genuinely concerned I might have hurt myself badly, so he had to be a little careful what he said.

He went on, 'We shall obviously go back to Wembley just as soon as Nick tells us he's okay and fit to broadcast.'

Meanwhile I had picked myself up, assured everyone I was all right, and wanted to carry on. My cameraman Duncan Scobell could not help himself and started chuckling and I joined in too – because we both knew it must have looked bloody funny!

There was a slightly serious side to it, and I wanted to make sure no one would be unfairly blamed for what had happened, although I was a little concerned at the pain in my shoulder. It was several weeks and a few physio sessions later before it felt okay again.

By now a couple of minutes had passed and a group of Scottish fans came walking along, saw me, and burst into laughter. They had already seen my fall on their mobile phones and it was becoming a bit of a sensation.

Back in Kent my youngest son Louis had been watching it live at Sandwich Town Cricket Club – he thought it was hysterical and the slapstick nature of my mishap appealed to his 12-year-old sense of humour. My 17-year-old son Oliver was actually batting at the time it happened, and he told me afterwards that he knew something was up because his team-mates were walking round the boundary looking intently at their mobiles, pointing at him and then 'pissing' themselves.

My priority now was to get back on air and continue our build-up to the match. I was pleased to come through the next live broadcast unscathed, although I did look a little dishevelled. Meanwhile, more and more fans were coming over to me and it wasn't long before one yelled, 'Mind you don't fall over, mate!'

If I have heard that once, I've heard it a thousand times – and that is absolutely fine. You should never take yourself too seriously in this life and if that is what most people remember me for, then I'll happily take it. You can be well known or even infamous for all manner of bad things, so to be stopped in the street – as I sometimes am – and teased about something which is just plain funny, well that is no hardship at all.

The game itself was a good one as twice England fell behind, twice they equalised through Theo Walcott and Danny Welbeck, then Rickie Lambert came off the bench for his international debut at the age of 30 and headed the winner with his first touch. For a player who had plied his trade all round the lower leagues in his early days (we always feared him at Priestfield when he was up against the Gills), this was a great story.

When he wandered over to me afterwards in the mixed zone interview area it was no surprise that he was smiling broadly, but the expression had nothing to do with his goal. He wanted to know what had happened to me up on that platform. It was a similar story with the rest of the team – I have never found it so easy to get interviews because they all wanted to learn more about it and ask whether I was okay. Roy came over at the end to do an interview and the first thing he asked, with a big grin, was whether I still had a head for heights.

Later that night one of the biggest US TV chat shows had asked Sky for permission to run the clip, and it didn't take too long for it to start appearing on *Football's Funniest Moments* and *You've Been Framed*.

I was highly amused by the newspaper coverage over the next few days, particularly *The Sun*'s treatment of what happened. They ran a series of 'Going, Going, Gone' pictures of me toppling over, under the genius headline, 'Skyfall'.

To this day I still have a laugh about it all, although I do believe the incident has been surpassed. I forget which show it was on, but I remember watching an Australian television reporter interviewing this guy on a boat, when she turned slightly to ask him another question and fell through a gap in the rail straight into the water below. That went out on live TV and luckily she was unharmed and also a good swimmer.

When the qualifiers resumed in September, England wasted no time beating Moldova 4-0 with Welbeck scoring twice. On the same night Ukraine thrashed San Marino 9-0 and they were fast emerging as Hodgson's team's main rivals because Montenegro dropped points against Poland, having already lost their previous qualifier 4-0 at home to Ukraine.

Just over a year on from EURO 2012, Kiev was not such a friendly city when we returned with England. Some fans were injured after being ambushed in a bar a couple of nights before the game and the atmosphere was totally different from when the tournament had been taking place.

Frank Lampard led the team out as he won his 100th cap, and I must admit I stood up in the press box and applauded him. To score nearly 30 international goals from midfield at a strike rate of almost one every three games was a marvellous achievement. Like Steven Gerrard he wore the Three Lions badge with great pride and he deserves his place among England's very best players. He was an extremely bright guy; articulate, but also humble, and a pleasure to interview.

England slogged out a goalless draw and moved a point clear of Ukraine and Montenegro at the top of the group with two home games to come. Four times in a row now they had won their first match of the double-header but then only drawn the second one, which was why qualifying was still so tight.

Ukraine kept up the pressure by beating Poland in their ninth match earlier in the evening, so England knew they had to win against Montenegro to keep their World Cup hopes in their own hands. At half-time it was 0-0 and the tension inside Wembley was growing.

Hodgson had picked an attacking line-up, which included a debut for Tottenham winger Andros Townsend, and that bold strategy really paid off in the second half. Townsend set up Rooney for the all-important first goal, then the scoreline soon became 2-0, and although Montenegro pulled one back, Townsend finished them off with a stunning goal. He won possession, held off one challenge, ran straight at the defence and unleashed a fierce shot from 25 yards which swerved off the inside of the post and into the back of the net. Daniel Sturridge added a fourth goal in stoppage time and England were one win away from going to Brazil 2014.

Poland brought along massive support to Wembley for the final qualifier and pushed England all the way in an absorbing match. Again it was Rooney who got the all-important first goal, but – with Ukraine scoring eight against San Marino – Hodgson's men could not relax until Gerrard wrapped it up with a second in the 88th minute.

Rooney had been England's key player – he scored in every qualifier in which he had appeared. Six games, seven goals was an impressive record and he finished as the leading scorer in Group H.

Jubilation at the end, another unbeaten qualifying campaign, and a mood of genuine optimism among the supporters at Wembley that night.

Home defeats to Chile and Germany the following month put things in perspective and a very tough World Cup draw – with Italy, Uruguay and Costa Rica joining them in the same group – lowered the expectations still further as the year came to an end.

Before the draw, Hodgson had said he did not mind where England played as long as they didn't have to go to Manaus. The city was in the heart of the Amazon rainforest just south of the equator and playing there would involve a 4,000-mile round trip from their base in Rio.

We totally understood his reasoning, but it then became almost inevitable that England would be drawn there – and that of course is exactly what happened. Their World Cup finals campaign would begin in Manaus against Italy.

The South American media had spun Hodgson's comments and he found himself having to say that he had nothing against the city – it was just that its geographical location would make this a tougher challenge.

Despite the extra travelling involved I was hugely excited to be going there – surely one of the most exotic places where the England football team would have ever played? The draw took place just outside Salvador and we had flown there via Sao Paulo, which gave us an early insight into the vast distances which would be involved at this tournament.

Sao Paulo was also the venue for England's second match against Uruguay, while their Group D games would conclude against Costa Rica in Belo Horizonte – that of course is where England suffered the most embarrassing defeat in their history in 1950, when they lost 1-0 to the USA. We all hoped that was not a bad omen, but the more cynical among us were saying that Group D stood for Death.

A three-day trip to Nice provided an unexpected sunny interlude in February as the main draw was made for the qualifying groups ahead of EURO 2016. What struck me was how helpful Chris Coleman and the Welsh media officers were, and how confident 'Cookie' was about Wales's chances of making it to the tournament in France. History shows his confidence was not misplaced.

England's friendly in March against Denmark was Hodgson's only chance to assess potential new faces before he named his World Cup squad a couple of months later. Teenage left-back Luke Shaw made his debut and did enough to suggest he might be an option for Brazil, possibly in place of 33-year-old Ashley Cole.

Daniel Sturridge headed in the only goal of the night eight minutes from time and after those two defeats the previous autumn this victory was very welcome. A clean sheet was also pleasing, but at times England looked a little laboured and Hodgson knew there was still plenty of work to be done.

Vauxhall's headquarters in Luton was the rather unusual choice of venue for the announcement of his 23-man party and Hodgson admitted that the hardest decision had been to leave out Cole. There was no room either for Michael Carrick, but Shaw, Ross Barkley and Raheem Sterling were included to give the squad a youthful look.

With the domestic season finished Hodgson gathered his players for a short training camp in Portugal to begin the acclimatisation process. It coincided with my birthday and he very kindly gave me an England shirt signed by him and wishing me happy birthday. Thank you Roy – it was greatly appreciated.

There was one final game at Wembley for the fans to give the team a good send-off, and a comfortable 3-0 win over Peru put the players in good heart for the adventure ahead.

\* \* \* \* \*

England's base camp before the tournament was Miami, which proved a good choice. The weather in this part of southern Florida was hot and steamy, similar to the conditions England could expect for that opening game. The sun was certainly beating down when England took on Ecuador at the Sun Life Stadium in their penultimate warm-up match. It is now known as the Hard Rock Stadium and is also the home of the Miami Dolphins NFL team.

England fell behind after just eight minutes to a goal from Enner Valencia, who would go on to sign for West Ham United after the World Cup. England hit back with Rooney – playing wide on the left – equalising from close range. Rickie Lambert put them ahead, but Michael Arroyo made it 2-2 in an entertaining game.

Worryingly, Alex Oxlade-Chamberlain, who had been one of England's best players, injured his knee and would need a scan. My information was that his participation in the World Cup was already looking doubtful. Then Sterling clattered into Antonio Valencia and the Manchester United player reacted furiously by grabbing the Liverpool man – this was a year before his move to Manchester City – around the throat. Both got red cards, which meant Sterling would be out of the final game against Honduras.

Hodgson made ten changes for that match and revealed his World Cup line-up. Only Rooney started again as he needed to build up his fitness.

This was the team Hodgson chose against Honduras: Joe Hart in goal; a back four of Glen Johnson, Gary Cahill, Phil Jagielka, and Leighton Baines; in central midfield it was Steven Gerrard (captain) and Jordan Henderson; ahead of them were Adam Lallana, Wayne Rooney and Danny Welbeck, with Daniel Sturridge up top.

Midway through the first half the game was halted for 40 minutes because of a dangerous lightning storm and that seemed to affect England's momentum. They were unable to break down a durable Honduras team, who put in a few hefty tackles and were reduced to ten men with 25 minutes to go. It finished 0-0.

After the game, England left for Rio de Janeiro and we followed the next day. My cameraman in Brazil was Alex Gage, one of the best cameraman/editors in the business. I had known 'Gagey' for years because he used to work for my best friend David Caine. He was a genuinely funny guy, equally adept at dishing out the mickey-taking and getting plenty back. My producer Gem completed what would be a tight-knit trio as we followed England's fortunes for SSN.

Between games England trained at the Urca military base, with views of the Atlantic and with the spectacular Sugarloaf mountain towering above. The locals told us this was where Pele and the 1970 Brazil squad had prepared ahead of winning the World Cup in Mexico. Needless to say security was tight.

When we got to Manaus the humidity literally took your breath away. It was stiflingly hot and the city appeared to be engulfed in traffic chaos, but we eventually battled our way through to the England hotel and set up to film the team arriving. By the time they did there was a huge crowd of onlookers. World Cup fever had clearly spread all the way to the Amazon rainforest.

Afterwards, as we travelled to the stadium to film England training, we noticed our taxi driver had a small TV mounted on his dashboard and was watching Brazil's opening game against Serbia as he weaved his way through the traffic.

Manaus was a very interesting place, once you came to terms with the climatic conditions, although it helped massively that our hotel's air conditioning system was top class – so sleeping in that heat was never a problem. The opera house (known as the Amazon theatre) was an incredible sight, with a big green, yellow, and blue dome in the national colours. This is also where the Meeting of Waters takes place as the dark river Negro joins the sandy-coloured river Solimoes to form what Brazilians regard as the start of the river Amazon proper. It is an amazing spectacle.

As expected, Hodgson made only one change from the team which began against Honduras with Sterling returning after suspension in place of the unlucky Adam Lallana. Before kick-off we managed to catch some of the Uruguay v Costa Rica game and seeing the 2010 semi-finalists lose 3-1 made us realise just how competitive this group was going to be.

It was hot and sticky throughout at the Arena Amazonia as England battled Italy to a virtual standstill. Both teams faded towards the end as the heat took its toll, but this was an absorbing contest – albeit with a cruel outcome for England.

Andrea Pirlo did not touch the ball in the build-up to the first goal, but his clever dummy from a corner was pivotal in wrong-footing the defence, allowing Claudio Marchisio to drill a 25-yarder past Hart into the corner. I thought the Italian celebrations were a bit over the top – the whole squad joined in and it was some time before the game resumed. When it did England equalised almost immediately. A superb ball from Sterling found Rooney down the left and his cross was turned in by Daniel Sturridge on the half-volley at the back post.

The England goal celebrations were notable too – but in a sad way. Physio Gary Lewin badly injured his ankle after leaping up when the ball went in and had to be stretchered away to hospital. His World Cup was over.

The game continued to be tight, although Phil Jagielka had to be alert to head the ball off the line. Five minutes into the second half came another defensive lapse, Antonio Candreva got away from Leighton Baines and as the cross came in Gary Cahill was struggling for position. He was easily outjumped by the former Manchester City striker Mario Balotelli, who headed past Hart and Italy led again.

Rooney had a good chance to draw England level, and Ross Barkley, Jack Wilshere and Adam Lallana all came on, but a second equaliser would not come.

Near the end Pirlo's free kick came back off the bar, but this was still a game which England did not really deserve to lose and it would be all about how well they could recover from their first opening game defeat at a World Cup in 28 years.

Five days later in Sao Paulo their hopes were left hanging by a thread after another slightly unlucky 2-1 defeat. This time their nemesis was Luis Suarez, a player who had lit up the Premier League with Liverpool but was only just returning after being ruled out for a month following knee surgery.

Maybe the break had given him renewed energy levels because England struggled against him all night, and he headed Uruguay into the lead just before half-time after getting away from Jagielka.

Rooney looked England's most dangerous player: his free kick whistled just over and then he struck the bar with a close-range header.

With 15 minutes to go his first World Cup goal finally arrived as he tapped in Glen Johnson's inch-perfect cross. England were deservedly level, so could they hang on or even grab a winner?

The answer was neither. In the 85th minute Gerrard failed to deal with a simple long ball down the middle and allowed his club team-mate to seize on it in a flash. There only looked like being one outcome from here and Suarez stuck the ball away to give Uruguay victory.

England had never lost their first two games at a World Cup before, and no team had ever made the knockout stages after losing their opening two encounters before. England's only chance was if Italy beat Costa Rica and Uruguay and then Hodgson's men defeated Costa Rica by a wide enough margin to go through on goal difference. It was a highly unlucky scenario and it never even came close to happening.

The next day, just as our plane touched down back in Rio, we all learned the final whistle had gone in Recife. Italy had lost 1-0 to Costa Rica and England were out of the World Cup after only two games.

The feeling of anti-climax was enormous as we waited at the baggage carousel. Covering a World Cup in Brazil should be one of the highlights of your career, but it did not feel like it then, with England out so early.

The final game was in Belo Horizonte and it was there, while we were filming, that we learned our tournament was over too. Gem, Gagey and myself received three simultaneous phone calls from Sky to say that the decision had been taken to bring us home.

To this day I cannot understand the logic of it. All our flights and hotels had been paid for through to the final so Sky were never going to get any money back. We were told that the football part of the tournament was pretty much over with England going out, so the rest of the World Cup would be treated more as a news event.

Admittedly our accreditation was very limited, but we were able to cover Brazil's training sessions and news conferences, and in our view that would make a pretty damn good football story. Geraint Hughes, Bryan Swanson and Gary Cotterill would all be staying on to the conclusion of the World Cup – and that made the decision to bring us back seem particularly harsh. It was also the first time that I thought to myself that maybe my position at Sky Sports News was not as secure as I had imagined. What I did know was that my long-cherished dream of covering the World Cup Final at the iconic Maracana was crushed.

That final group fixture itself was nothing special. Hodgson made ten changes (only Gary Cahill kept his place), so that virtually everyone in the squad got a game at the World Cup. Lampard wore the captain's armband on what many people expected would be his last England appearance.

Gerrard came on in the second half for what proved to be his last international as well. His tally of 114 caps left him one behind David Beckham, but he chose not to stay on and announced his retirement a month later.

By contrast, Hodgson was quite bullish about his intention to remain, confirming that he was not going to resign. In truth there was no real appetite at the FA to replace him and he still had two years of his contract to run.

The 0-0 draw meant that Costa Rica won the group, while Uruguay beat Italy at the same time to also claim a place in the last 16. Those two results were completely overshadowed by the sensational news that – yet again – Luis Suarez had been involved in a biting controversy, this time on Georgio Chiellini. Suarez got a four-month ban and Gary Cotterill was despatched to Uruguay to follow up the story – a development which made the decision to send us home even more laughable.

Our final night in Rio was spent at a wonderful restaurant high in the hills above the city. It had been organised by our production manager Victoria Rudling, one of my oldest and closest friends at Sky. 'Tor' used to be our sound recordist years ago and covered many England matches, but her deserved promotion meant she was not on duty with the national team so often.

When I was having some intestinal problems in 2001 she told me she thought that – like her – I had coeliac disease. Months later she was proved right. It was brilliant having a fellow sufferer who was such a good organiser and who constantly provided me with gluten-free food to keep me going. I owe you a lot, Tor.

# 20

# From Perfect 10 to 0/10

A FEW weeks after the World Cup I linked up again with cameraman Alex Gage. We were down in Cardiff to cover the UEFA Super Cup Final – Real Madrid versus Sevilla, or more precisely Gareth Bale coming home.

We both still keenly felt the disappointment of our World Cup experience, at how it had ended early – though I did go in to Sky Sports News a couple of times to reflect on the semi-finals and final. I won't lie, it was great sitting on the couch watching Germany against Argentina with my two sons, but I would still far rather have been witnessing it all from inside the Maracana.

The Super Cup clash was my first visit to Cardiff City's new stadium and with 30,000 inside there was a good atmosphere generated – it was all support for the local boy who had made good and was now back in his home town. Bale was his usual humble self, and typically it was Cristiano Ronaldo who grabbed the headlines with both goals and a man-of-the-match performance as Real won 2-0.

In September a crowd of only 40,000 turned up at Wembley for England's first match after the World Cup. It was the lowest attendance at the new Wembley for an England game and for the moment the fans were voting with their feet until the national team engaged them again.

A Wayne Rooney penalty gave them victory over Norway and it also moved him up above Michael Owen into fourth place on the all-time scorer' list with 41 goals. He had also succeeded Steven Gerrard as the England captain and it looked a really good choice, with the player keen to prove he could thrive on the extra responsibility.

Just five days later in Basel, England produced an impressive all-round performance to start the process of banishing the memories of the World Cup fiasco. Switzerland were ninth in the FIFA rankings after reaching the last 16 in Brazil, while England languished down in 20th, their lowest placing in nearly two decades.

Roy Hodgson opted for a diamond midfield formation with Raheem Sterling at the tip and, intriguingly, Jack Wilshere at the base. On the left side was Fabian Delph, making his first international start, while Jordan Henderson was on the right. The system was a big success and provided England with a good platform from which to counter-attack.

Rooney led the charge for the first goal before slipping a pass to the speedy Sterling. He picked out Danny Welbeck and the Arsenal striker drilled the ball home. The move for the second, in injury time, started inside England's penalty area. Sterling raced away down the right and substitute Rickie Lambert played a neat ball on to Welbeck who finished it all off. Hodgson, watching on from the touchline, raised his arms in triumph. England were on their way.

Predictably San Marino were swept aside the following month, Rooney scoring his 42nd goal as England won 5-0 at Wembley. Then it was back to Tallinn for the first time since 2007 to face an improved Estonian team. England huffed and puffed, but eventually Rooney found the target in a 1-0 victory with a free kick from outside the area, and now it was played three, won three.

Against Slovenia at Wembley in November England conceded their first goal in qualifying and found themselves behind. Actually it was an own goal from Jordan Henderson, but the response was impressive as they equalised within two minutes and were leading 3-1 within a quarter of an hour.

The game was Rooney's 100th for his country and Sir Bobby Charlton presented him with a special golden cap to mark the milestone. Rooney began the fightback by pulling England level from the penalty spot. It was his 44th England goal, placing him alongside Jimmy Greaves in joint third place, and it was also his fourth in five matches. He certainly didn't seem to be suffering from any nerves as he chased down the record. Welbeck scored the other two to take his tally to five goals from four qualifiers.

England ended the year with a sixth consecutive victory – their failure in Brazil had been consigned to history – and this was a sweet one, away to their oldest rivals Scotland.

There was a rousing atmosphere at Celtic Park and it was England who took the lead as Wilshere's long ball forward was headed in by his Arsenal team-mate Alex Oxlade-Chamberlain. Two minutes into the second half England got a second goal with another header, this time from Rooney. Scotland did pull one back late on but Rooney struck again almost immediately to clinch victory and he celebrated his goal with a somersault in front of the England fans.

It was more than four months before they played again, but the winning run continued with a convincing 4-0 demolition of Lithuania. Rooney and Welbeck were both at it again, Welbeck with his sixth goal in five qualifiers, Rooney with his 47th England goal – yet the most memorable moment was provided by Harry Kane on his debut. The 21-year-old Tottenham sensation scored with one of his first touches a minute after coming on.

Rooney hit the bar and the woodwork as he hunted down Sir Bobby's scoring record and he might have equalled it that night with a little more luck. The other goal came from Sterling, his first for England. Halfway through qualifying it was five wins out of five and the 100 per cent record started being discussed in earnest – could they make it ten wins out of ten?

The series of victories did come to an end a few days later in Turin, but England could still take heart from a good second half performance as they fought back to gain a deserved 1-1 draw with Italy. This friendly was a significant and memorable one for me because it was my 250th England game – and I was presented with a shirt signed by Roy and the players. On the back it had Collins 250. It was a lovely gesture from the FA and I know it was my producer Gemma Davies who organised it all behind my back – so thank you, Gem!

On 22 April 2015 I drove down to Cheltenham to meet Sir Geoff Hurst and interview him at length about his World Cup memories.

It was for a documentary Sky Sports were planning to commemorate the 50th anniversary of our one and only triumph (no disrespect to our wonderful under-20 and under-17 teams who won their own World Cups in 2017) and it was to be called *The Boys of '66*.

Sir Geoff's memories were still as sharp as ever. It is a story he will never tire of telling and you can't blame him when you are the only man on the planet who has scored a hat-trick in a World Cup Final.

He was a fringe player at the start of the tournament but then for the quarter-final he replaced the team's golden boy, Jimmy Greaves, who was injured. He headed in the winner that afternoon against Argentina, retained his place for the semi and then started in the final, even though Greaves was very close to being fit again, but there were no substitutes in those days so it would have been a huge gamble to play the Spurs man. In the end Sir Alf Ramsey got his selection spot on, opted for Hurst, and history was created.

For half a century barely a day goes by without someone asking Sir Geoff whether England's crucial third goal crossed the line and he has always maintained his belief that it did – because Roger Hunt had the chance to slot home the rebound, but felt there was no need.

A few months earlier, I had spoken to Greaves near his home in Suffolk. He told me he still felt the pain of not being able to play in that final, and there is no disguising it in the TV pictures at the end which showed a man who was clearly thinking, 'If only.' He gave a tremendously passionate interview, and it was all the more poignant because not too long afterwards he suffered a major stroke.

When the documentary was aired early in January 2016 I felt his story was not given the prominence it deserved. Amid all the joy, this was the ultimate bitter-sweet experience.

Goalkeeper Gordon Banks told me about the mayhem which went on behind the scenes in the immediate aftermath of that quarter-final victory over Argentina. It had been a controversial game with their captain Antonio Rattin refusing to leave the field after being sent off. Eventually he had to be escorted away by two policemen. At the end, Sir Alf stopped the England players swapping shirts with the Argentinians because he was so incensed by their physical approach.

Feelings were still running high in the tunnel afterwards as the South Americans tried to attack their opponents. England were bundled inside the dressing room, but the drama did not end there, because a chair was thrown through a window sending a shower of glass into the room which narrowly missed the players.

In all I interviewed six of the World Cup winning team – it was a great privilege and one I will never forget.

The day after interviewing Sir Geoff, I completed a notable double by getting the chance to speak to Pele. He was in London to promote an exhibition later in the year which would celebrate his 75th birthday – some of the photographs, paintings and sculptures were on display, and they looked very impressive. Over the years I have spoken to the great man a few times. I always seem to be asking him about the England team rather than the Brazilians, but he has always been very gracious with his answers.

In early June I was in Dublin for England's first match there since the infamous riot of 1995. It wasn't a great game, but the important thing was that it passed off peacefully. The night before we had sat in our hotel bar watching Barcelona win the Champions League for the fourth time in nine years and marvelled at their amazing talent.

The season ended for England a few days later in Slovenia with the best game of the entire qualifying campaign. It provided them with a sixth straight competitive victory but only after a great tussle. An even first half suddenly went Slovenia's way just before the interval when a defensive mix-up allowed Milivoje Novakovic to score.

The second half belonged to Jack Wilshere, who scored two stunning goals – his first two for England. Adam Lallana teed up both of them but full credit to Wilshere for taking the chances. His opening goal was a fierce left-footed shot from 20 yards which sped into the roof of the net. Fifteen minutes later he repeated the feat with an even more spectacular effort that rocketed past the keeper to give England the lead.

A few minutes before the end Nejc Pecnik headed Slovenia level and the 100 per cent record looked in severe danger as the home side celebrated with gusto. Back came England and Rooney finished off a slick move with a first-time shot into the back of the net. It was his 48th England goal and pulled him level with Gary Lineker in second place and just one behind Sir Bobby Charlton.

New technology allows us to broadcast live from pretty much anywhere with the minimum of equipment and the morning after the game we reflected on England's performance aboard a tourist boat as it made its way through the picturesque heart of Ljubljana, Slovenia's beautiful capital city. For the first time in 24 years England had gone through an entire season unbeaten with six wins and two draws and they were still very much on course for the 'Perfect Ten'.

This was now becoming a firm ambition of the team and was something which England had never achieved before – ten wins out of ten in qualifiers takes some doing. What's more, Rooney had scored in five consecutive qualifiers and was on the brink of making history himself. The players could enjoy their summer holidays a lot more than they did 12 months previously.

Qualifier number seven produced win number seven as England clinched a place at EURO 2016 with three matches to spare. Rooney scored an early penalty against San Marino to equal Sir Bobby's all-time scoring record of 49, but could not add to it against the weakest team in the group. He was substituted (very much to the crowd's surprise) with still more than half an hour to go – so he would have to wait at least a few days, until the Switzerland match at Wembley, before he could try and break the record.

It was a bit of a stroll in the early-evening sunshine with Ross Barkley getting his first international goal, substitute Theo Walcott grabbing two, and Harry Kane again coming off the bench to score.

Against Switzerland the whole focus of attention was on Rooney and that record. He had one shot that went just wide, a good header that the Swiss goalkeeper Yann Sommer did well to save under the bar, but still it would not come. It was also important for the team to concentrate on maintaining that 100 per cent record, regardless of who scored.

Substitute Kane eased some of the tension inside Wembley when he latched on to Luke Shaw's cross and scored with a neat left-footed finish midway through the second half. That made it three goals from three competitive appearances for the Tottenham man – he really did seem to be settling into international football with ease.

The clock continued to tick down, meaning time was running out for Rooney and maybe he would have to wait another month for the chance to get that milestone goal. There were just a few minutes to go when the opportunity finally arrived for the happy ending that the crowd had come to see. Raheem Sterling was fouled and England were awarded a penalty.

'Um, I wonder who will take it?' said ITV's commentator Clive Tyldesley with a delicious sense of irony.

If Rooney was nervous he did not show it. He picked up the ball and strode confidently towards the penalty spot and his date with destiny. He struck a sweet shot to Sommer's right and though the keeper got the tips of his fingers to it he could not keep it out: 2-0 England and 50 for Wayne Rooney.

It was fitting that the historic goal was scored at Wembley in front of over 75,000 and Rooney celebrated with a mixture of pure joy and relief. The pressure as he closed in on such a record could have got to him – Gary Lineker had missed a penalty 23 years earlier when he had the chance to match the tally, and then failed to score in his final three games at EURO 92. By contrast Rooney galloped through the 40s and hit the magic half-century mark by scoring in seven consecutive qualifiers. I had seen 49 of his 50 goals live and afterwards when I interviewed him he told me that he was determined not to just settle for 50, but wanted to try and push on for 60 and beyond.

This was England's eighth straight win and it clinched first place in Group E with still two games to go. As it happened Rooney was injured and missed the next qualifier anyway – so it was just as well he had seized his opportunity when he did.

Estonia again proved stubborn opposition but goals from Walcott and Sterling gave England a 2-0 victory and now it was nine wins out of nine.

Vilnius was the venue for the tenth and final qualifier as England played in Lithuania for the first time. Roy Hodgson chose to rest Joe Hart, Gary Cahill and James Milner, so Phil Jagielka led the team, which showed eight changes from the Estonia game. Even with an experimental line-up England were still far too strong for their opponents. Ross Barkley put them ahead, Harry Kane's shot came back off the post, hit the keeper's head, and deflected in for an own goal, while Alex Oxlade-Chamberlain completed the scoring in the second half.

So that was it – England had their 'Perfect Ten' victories with 31 goals scored and only three conceded. This may not have been the strongest group but it was still a great achievement and had helped to completely banish the misery of Brazil 2014. They key now would be to repeat these victories against stronger opposition and in France the following summer at EURO 2016.

In November England were able to test themselves against some of Europe's best, with back-to-back friendlies against Spain away and France at Wembley.

We had a magnificent live position on the roof of a church overlooking the ground in Alicante, but for once the new technology let us down and our broadcasts had to be curtailed. England, too, came off second best that night, conceding two goals inside the last 20 minutes. Mario Gaspar scored with a flying overhead kick to break their resistance then Arsenal's Santi Cazorla added another.

It was only afterwards that we started to hear about the dreadful events happening that night in Paris. Everyone was stunned by the terrorist atrocities and we did wonder whether the following week's friendly with France could possibly go ahead.

It was a credit to both countries that it did. The Wembley arch was lit up in the red, white and blue colours of the Tricolour national flag and the teams stood together in the centre circle to pay their respects to the 129 victims.

On an emotional and poignant evening it was England who emerged as winners, although the result was secondary to the significance of the occasion. Dele Alli scored his first goal on his first start – a rasping drive from 25 yards past his Tottenham team-mate Hugo Lloris in the French goal – and Rooney made it 2-0 with a volley.

In December we travelled to Paris for the EURO 2016 finals draw and I was so impressed with the way the French capital had recovered from those shocking events on 13 November. The Parisians were back out on the streets and in the cafes, refusing to be cowed by what had happened.

For us there was even more anticipation than usual because in addition to England, Wales, Northern Ireland and the Republic of Ireland had all also qualified. Would we be drawn in the same group as one of our neighbours? Of course we would.

There was a sense of déjà vu about some of the venues as well. Just like in France '98 England would open their campaign in Marseille at the Stade Velodrome. They would also play in Lens again (where they had beaten Colombia) and they would finish off in St Etienne, the scene of that gut-wrenching penalty shoot-out defeat to Argentina.

But the big story was that England's pivotal second game would be against Wales in northern France at the refurbished Stade Bollaert-Delelis in Lens. Chris Coleman's team had finished second behind Belgium in Group B and thoroughly deserved to be the first Welsh group to qualify for the European Championships. Coleman made the very good point afterwards that his team could not concentrate too much on the England fixture to the detriment of the other two games. That said, it was a glorious prospect and we could not wait.

The first game would be against Russia and that immediately flagged up security concerns, especially as it was in Marseille where there had been so much trouble in 1998. England's final match would be against Slovakia, a team they had beaten three times out of three.

Northern Ireland came out in Group C with the world champions Germany, Poland and Ukraine. That was tough but Martin O'Neill looked positively shell-shocked when his Republic of Ireland team drew Belgium, Italy and Sweden. Nevertheless they both qualified for the last 16, which was a terrific achievement.

\* \* \* \* \*

In January 2016 I flew to New York to do a special interview with Patrick Vieira, who had just taken over as manager of the MLS side New York City. As a player he had been a fierce competitor, but the man I spoke to was charming, articulate and self-effacing. I really enjoyed speaking with him about his vision for the club and settling into life in America. He also told me how much he was looking forward to EURO 2016 and urged me to put my money on the hosts France to win it.

What made the trip a bit more special was that my cameraman was Daniel Caine, son of my big buddy David. He had moved to the United States to further his career and loved his life 'across the pond'. He was engaged to an American girl at the time and now they are married. We had a photo taken of Daniel and I in Times Square to send to Cainey, and I remember thinking just how busy it was – a typically bustling New York location.

Forty-eight hours later Times Square was deserted and all travel had been suspended after the East Coast was hit by a monster snow-storm. The taxi driver who took me to the airport two days earlier told me I was getting out just in time. How right he was.

In Berlin in March we saw England's best performance yet under Roy Hodgson as they produced a brave fightback and scored a dramatic late winner to cap an all-action display which deservedly beat the world champions.

It was a little against the run of play when Germany took the lead just before half-time, Toni Kroos with a long shot which somehow squeezed past Jack Butland at his near post. Within moments it was clear Butland had sustained a freak injury, then later it would emerge he had broken his ankle and his EURO 2016 dreams were over. It would be 2017 before he played again.

If England were feeling sorry for themselves they didn't show it and made a bright start to the second half, but then they fell further behind when Mario Gomez planted a header past substitute goalkeeper Fraser Forster.

Within minutes the complexion of the game changed. Germany thought the danger from a corner had passed as the ball appeared to be heading out of the penalty area, but Harry Kane produced a brilliant turn to wrong-foot the defence and fired in a fine shot which went past Manuel Neuer and in off the post.

Before the game the German media had been obsessed by Jamie Vardy – they loved his rags-to-riches story, coming all the way through to the England team after playing in the eighth tier. In the build-up I did several live interviews with our colleagues at Sky Deutschland and each time they wanted to hear all about Jamie Vardy. They could not believe it when he was only named among the substitutes.

A few minutes after coming off the bench Vardy produced a moment of magic which made all the German interest in him completely understandable. From Nathanial Clyne's cross he somehow back-heeled the ball into the net with an amazing flick. It was his first England goal and by now Germany looked shattered – physically and mentally.

Dele Alli was the man of the match but he was guilty of a glaring miss with just six minutes to go, blazing the ball over the bar with the goal at his mercy. At that stage I think we all thought the chance of victory had probably gone, but that it had still been a fine performance to come back from two behind.

In the first minute of stoppage time Jordan Henderson swung over a corner and Eric Dier leapt to head the ball powerfully past Neuer for the winner. It was incredible stuff, and that was Dier's first goal for England as well. This was what we had been waiting for – to see Hodgson's attacking young team playing with pace, power and tenacity.

As we left the Olympic Stadium that night you could be forgiven for thinking, 'Bring on the Euros.'

The optimism did not last long and three days later England lost at home to Holland after Vardy had given them a half-time lead. It was a reminder that the team were by no means the finished article and that the defence especially had to tighten up.

At the end of April I travelled up to Manchester to do a one-to-one sit-down interview with Wayne Rooney. The England captain spoke well about his hopes for the upcoming finals and how much he enjoyed captaining this emerging young side. This would be his third European Championships and his sixth major tournament – that kind of experience could prove invaluable.

I stayed on in the city for a couple of days and watched Leicester City move a point nearer the Premier League title with an entertaining 1-1 draw against Manchester United at Old Trafford. The 5,000/1 shot was on the verge of becoming a reality.

Just over 24 hours later I was at Stamford Bridge to watch Chelsea fight back from two goals down to deny Tottenham victory and thereby hand the crown to Leicester. The 'Battle of the Bridge', as the game became known, was possibly the most compelling match in the Premier League all season – not always for the right reasons, but you could not take your eyes off it. Spurs had a record nine players booked, there was an eye-gouging incident, and a melee on the final whistle.

But Leicester did not care – they were too busy celebrating their utterly astonishing achievement.

On 16 May Hodgson named a provisional squad of 26 for the European Championships, to take into account the fact that England had three warm-up matches first. There was no room for Theo Walcott but 18-year-old Marcus Rashford had been included, further evidence that Hodgson believed, 'If you are good enough, you are old enough.'

In the first game at the Etihad Stadium, Harry Kane opened up an early lead but Turkey equalised soon after with their first goal against us in any fixture. It had taken 11 matches and 33 years to achieve and it was very nearly enough for a draw. Seven minutes from time that man Vardy was at it again, snatching a 2-1 victory with his third goal in three outings.

The next stop was Sunderland's Stadium of Light for a friendly against Australia and the match got off to a memorable start when Rashford scored on his debut inside three minutes. Raheem Sterling's attempted shot deflected off a defender and fell to the teenager who volleyed it in with great skill. It was a highly impressive first appearance and that looked enough to win him a place in the EURO 2016 squad.

Rooney came on in the second half to extend England's lead with his 52nd goal, but Eric Dier headed into his own net to make it a slightly nervy finish. Nevertheless, England had won again and that could only help the confidence levels.

In the end Danny Drinkwater, Andros Townsend and the injured Fabian Delph were cut from the squad, so that meant Rashford would be going to France.

There was one final friendly at Wembley, against Portugal, and I wondered what kind of form guide this might prove to be ahead of the tournament. It wasn't at all as it turned out. England won 1-0 with a late goal from Chris Smalling, Portugal played with ten for more than half the match, and we learned very little about the relative strengths of the two sides.

On Sunday, 5 June I travelled to Paris on the Eurostar for my fifth European Championships and my 11th major tournament. At the Gare du Nord I caught another train out to the pretty little town of Chantilly, some 25 miles north of the French capital. This is very much horse racing country – someone once described it as like a French Ascot. The equestrian heritage has helped Chantilly become famous (along with lace and cream), and it was where England chose to stay at EURO 2016.

They had the exclusive use of the five-star Auberge du Jeu de Paume, where rooms can cost up to £500 a night. It boasted views over an ornamental lake and the Chateau de Chantilly, a former medieval fortress which was used as the villain's lair in the James Bond film *A View To A Kill*.

Their training base was nearby at the Stade des Bourgognes, home of non-league club US Chantilly. Grass seed had been imported from St George's Park and by the time England arrived the pitches looked magnificent.

Security was noticeably tight – England were guarded by armed police whenever they moved around – but Chantilly, with its population of just 11,000, still provided the players with a bit of a haven when they were off duty.

Producer Gemma Davies and I teamed up again and this time we were joined by cameraman Ben McNamara. He was the brother-in-law of Stuart Vickery, who had worked with me at several major tournaments over the years. Endlessly patient and helpful, Ben was a real pleasure to deal with – he never lost his cool, no matter how much pressure we were under.

Our live position in Marseille ahead of the first game overlooked the stadium from a balcony on the 14th floor of a block of flats. We heard about the trouble in the old port area, but were nowhere near it at any stage. Pictures of the level of violence were truly shocking and the police were perhaps understandably a little jumpy as the fans started to arrive at the ground in numbers. When a crush started to build up by one of the gates their response was to use tear gas. We could not believe how quickly the smoke spread upwards to our level – even from 14 floors away its effects could be felt.

Security was very tight at the points of entry as everyone with a ticket was searched, long queues built up and we only just squeezed into our seats before kick-off.

The big news was that Rooney would have a midfield role alongside Dier and Dele Alli. The three up front were Lallana, Kane and Sterling, while the back four was Kyle Walker, Gary Cahill, Chris Smalling and Danny Rose. Joe Hart was in goal.

It was an attacking line-up and England dominated the first half without being able to take any of the chances they were creating. Rooney was a revelation in midfield and ran the show, but the nearest he came to scoring was when his shot was pushed on to the post by keeper Igor Akinfeev.

Then with 17 minutes to go England were awarded a free kick just outside the penalty area. Kane shaped to take it, but ran over the ball allowing Spurs team-mate Dier to step forward and blast it high into the net. It was a clever move and a thoroughly deserved goal. Now all England had to do was hold on.

Surprisingly Hodgson then removed Rooney from the action, bringing on Jack Wilshere in his place to help England retain possession and keep their shape. Yet Rooney had been their best player and did not look to be tiring. The move backfired horribly in stoppage time as the team retreated and giant defender Vasili Berezutski headed the ball beyond a static Hart for the equaliser.

We raced for the exit as we had a live broadcast to do and were behind the end where Russia had just scored when it was apparent there was some kind of commotion going on inside. It was only afterwards that we learned Russian fans had stampeded towards the England supporters and tried to attack them in their seats.

It was a good performance, but a desperately disappointing result against what looked like a very average Russian team. This, definitely, was two points dropped, and still England had never won their opening game at the Euros.

Hodgson kept the same team for the match with Wales in Lens five days later, but this time they could not impose themselves in the first half. The Welsh had won their first match against Slovakia and here they looked comfortable and confident. They even took the lead just before half-time with a 30-yard free kick from Gareth Bale. It was a good strike, but the feeling around the ground was that Hart had made a bad mistake and should have kept it out.

With his job on the line Hodgson again gambled with his substitutes and this time it paid off. Vardy and Daniel Sturridge came on at the start of the second half in place of Kane and Sterling. Within minutes Vardy had scrambled in an equaliser and as England's pressure grew, Wales finally buckled in stoppage time – Sturridge showing unbelievably quick feet in a very tight space to poke the ball over the line for a dramatic winner.

England had moved to the top of the group and needing only a point from the Slovakia game to ensure a place in the last 16, and it was all thanks to their super-subs.

We expected Vardy and Sturridge to be in the starting line-up against Slovakia in St Etienne. What we hadn't anticipated was that Hodgson would make a total of six changes, leaving his captain out as well. Nathaniel Clyne replaced Kyle Walker, Ryan Bertrand came in for Danny Rose, Jack Wilshere took over from Rooney, Jordan Henderson started in place of Dele Alli, while Vardy and Sturridge got the nod over Harry Kane and Raheem Sterling.

Rooney, Kane and Alli did eventually come on in the second half, but England had lost their impetus – and they lost the leadership of Group B. Wales got off to a flier and went on to beat Russia 3-0 as they finished top. It would earn them a last-16 clash with Northern Ireland in Paris. Two days later a 94th-minute winner earned Iceland second place in Group F, and that meant they would face England in Nice.

Meanwhile, the debate was under way as to why Hodgson made so many changes – a move that seemed to have stalled England's gathering momentum. Keeping players fresh is a key part of tournament management but he then virtually reversed the tactic for the next game anyway. Walker, Rose, Rooney, Alli and Kane all returned – only Adam Lallana lost out, as Sturridge retained his place.

The day after the Slovakia match we managed to get tickets for Northern Ireland's game against the world champions Germany at the Parc des Princes in Paris. Outside the ground the atmosphere was amazing – it was total bedlam, but thoroughly enjoyable. Sometimes when you are covering England you can be in a bit of a bubble, so it is nice to step outside of it sometimes.

How this game only finished 1-0 I will never know. Mario Gomez won it for Germany with a goal in the 29th minute, but after that an inspired performance from goalkeeper Michael McGovern managed to keep the Germans at bay. It was vital that he did, because Northern Ireland finished third in their group and qualified for the knock-out stage on goal difference. It could have been a very different story but for McGovern's heroics. The Northern Irish fans were simply amazing – their support was unwavering, they never stopped singing and they created a wall of sound – it was mighty impressive.

We stopped in Paris for supper before heading back to Chantilly late in the evening. The next day we filmed at the racecourse as a meeting was taking place. It was all fairly laid-back and the crowds were pretty small, but it was interesting to experience, even though we failed to win a single euro with our bets. We were told that the prestige meeting was the Prix de Diane, the equivalent of The Oaks at Epsom, our classic for fillies. There was growing excitement in the town, because in September it would have the honour of staging the Prix de l'Arc de Triomphe, as Longchamps was being renovated.

The French Riviera was baking in 80 degree temperatures when we arrived for the Iceland match – our daytime live position was on the famous Promenade des Anglais overlooking the glorious sandy beach. On the morning of the game the entire squad took a walk along the seafront, accompanied by the inevitable media circus, but it was good to see the players looking relaxed and focussed at the same time.

As kick-off drew nearer we moved up to the Allianz Riviera stadium to a live position on top of a grassy bank which gave us a great view of the ground and the fans arriving for the game. Most sounded pretty confident and were talking in terms of a quarter-final in Paris at the Stade de France against the hosts.

An early goal was the key, I thought. If England could score quickly then they would go on to dominate an Iceland team who were ranked 34 in the world.

Ben, Gem and I took a quick selfie then settled down to watch the action and sure enough an early England goal arrived. Rooney converted the penalty in the fourth minute after Raheem Sterling had been fouled and I thought, 'Here we go.'

It wasn't long before there was another goal, but this one came from Iceland and it was a bit of a schoolboy error from an English perspective. They failed to close down one of Iceland's trademark long throws (something which England knew all about and had done some work in training to combat), allowing Ragnar Sigurdsson to equalise. Just six minutes gone and it was already 1-1.

Iceland's second was an error from Hart, the goalkeeper letting Kolbeinn Sigthorsson's shot slip through his hands. It was a bitter blow but there were still more than 70 minutes of the match left to go – ample time for England to recover the situation. Or so we thought.

The longer the game went on the more embarrassing it became. England just seemed to get worse, even simple things became difficult and by the end they looked technically inept. The players seemed shell-shocked as they left the field to some inevitable jeers. The noise echoing around the stadium was coming from the Icelandic supporters with their famous 'huh' chant – it was a fantastic sound as they acclaimed their heroes.

The fallout was only just starting. Within 20 minutes it emerged that Hodgson had resigned – after that performance from his players his position was untenable. The accepted wisdom had been that if he made the quarter-finals he would get a new contract to take England through to the World Cup in Russia in 2018. Instead the search would have to begin for his replacement.

Hodgson presided over three tournaments and two unbeaten qualifying campaigns. He had been parachuted in just before EURO 2012 and with little time to prepare he had made sure England would be a well-organised and durable team.

In time he added a layer of attacking flair and youthful pace, but still the questions remained as to how the players would perform against the top sides. Brazil 2014 gave us a few answers and they were not the ones we wanted to hear. Ten victories from ten to reach EURO 2016 was a fine achievement but winning in qualifiers just did not translate into success at tournaments. This latest humiliation was very much the last straw. At least one national newspaper awarded every player 0/10 in its match ratings, hence the title of the chapter.

The bottom line was that it was now ten years since England had won a knockout game at a major tournament, and that is a damning statistic.

The next day, Hodgson changed his mind and agreed to do a farewell news conference, despite telling the assembled journalists, 'I don't really know why I am here.' Rooney gave him his support, confirming that he wanted to carry on playing for England and continue to be captain.

With England out the spotlight switched to Wales. Their thrilling 3-1 victory in the quarter-finals against Belgium in Lille was one of the best games of the tournament. They had a first major international semi-final to contemplate and quite rightly Sky Sports News saw this as the big story.

A few hours before kick-off we were switched from covering Germany's quarter-final with Italy in Bordeaux (so we only saw the amazing 18-penalty shoot-out on TV) and headed for Brittany to hook up with Geraint Hughes and Alex Gage as the second crew following Wales. Ben and I stayed in the resort of Dinard as Wales departed for Lyon to take on Portugal. This was obviously frustrating, but we totally understood why it was necessary. We would film the Welsh team at the local airport as they took off, and then come back to get shots of their return, while Geraint and Gagey picked them up at the venue.

Being in this well-heeled and laid-back coastal resort after more than a month of covering solely England was a strange interlude. I did quite enjoy it, and it was good to do Chris Coleman's farewell news conference before the team headed home after their 2-0 defeat in the last four. Like his players he had covered himself in glory, but unlike his players he did not come out for a final night on the town.

From Brittany we moved on to Paris for the showdown between France and Portugal. The hosts were the favourites, but Portugal had Cristiano Ronaldo – so anything was possible.

Getting a ticket for the final was a bit of a challenge but it was eventually achieved after some delicate negotiations in a back alley and some sterling work by our security man Dave.

I took my seat high above the halfway line and waited for it all to unfold. The loss of Ronaldo inside the first 25 minutes looked like being a mortal blow for Portugal, but their star man defied the pain from his injury to remain on the touchline and cajole and encourage his team towards an unlikely victory.

With 12 minutes of extra time remaining Portuguese sub Eder, a former Swansea City player, beat Hugo Lloris from 25 yards to score the only goal of the final, so the team that finished third in their group – behind Iceland – became European champions for the first time.

Having done the very first live cross from France to kick off our EURO 2016 coverage at 6am on Monday, 6 June, I was determined to also do the last one from Paris five weeks later.

Once that was achieved I was ready for the Eurostar to take me home.

\* \* \* \* \*

Ten days later I was live outside Wembley with the Football Association preparing to appoint Sam Allardyce as Roy Hodgson's successor and shortly after that he was giving his first news conference at St George's Park.

Big Sam talked about being ready for the job after all his Premier League experience and you could not argue. He also said he felt he was a good fit for the job, and again I agreed.

Thanks to Adam Lallana's 95th-minute goal in Slovakia he can also boast a 100 per cent record, but it was a huge shame that he was foolish enough to be entrapped in a newspaper sting operation and be forced to relinquish his position. He lasted two months.

The next cab off the rank, as it were, was Gareth Southgate. He was given an interim role for four matches while a permanent successor to Allardyce was found. Earlier in the summer he had turned down the opportunity to hold a similar position in the immediate aftermath of EURO 2016.

He had guided England's under-21s to victory in the Toulon tournament and his stock was high. He had management experience in the Premier League and had won more than 50 England caps. Clearly Southgate was in pole position to get the job full-time if he could make a good fist of the next four games.

He was also a very intelligent, articulate guy who had an understanding of the needs of the media from his time as a pundit with ITV and of course knew many of the players in the England senior team from their time with him in the under-21s.

He had no more than a few days to prepare for his first match, but it was only against Malta – the weakest team in the group. England won comfortably enough, but it was not the landslide some were predicting as first-half goals from Dele Alli and Daniel Sturridge gave them a 2-0 result. So far so good.

A tougher assignment lay in store in Ljubljana, where Slovenia were looking to avenge their narrow defeat in 2015 to a Jack Wilshere-inspired England. For long periods England were on the back foot and they owed a big debt to Joe Hart that night. He did not have the greatest of tournaments at the Euros, but he was magnificent on this occasion as his team escaped with a 0-0 draw.

Seven points from three games was a decent tally but the next match against Scotland would be key for England and for Southgate if he was to land the job full-time. Three points, three goals and three headers made it a satisfactory night all round for England – Sturridge, Lallana and Gary Cahill were the men on target, and Southgate was on the verge of being confirmed as the permanent manager.

England's last match of 2016 was a friendly against Spain and a bit of a curate's egg. A penalty from Lallana and a diving header from Jamie Vardy put them firmly in control at 2-0, and that is how it stayed until the 89th minute when Iago Aspas pulled one back. It should just have been a case of seeing the game out, but in the sixth minute of stoppage time Isco equalised – much to Southgate's frustration. It would not affect his job prospects, but it was still annoying.

This was my 272nd England match and, as things stand, it may well be my last. As Gareth Southgate waited for news on his future I would also learn mine, and they were both very different. For one it would be confirmation of an exciting new job, for the other it would be redundancy.

I wish nothing but good luck for Gareth and the England players. Covering the fortunes of the national team at 11 major tournaments over the course of more than a quarter of a century has been the highlight of my career, and a massive privilege. My only regret is that I never saw England win a major trophy (though seeing them succeed at Le Tournoi in 1997 was a lot of fun), OR even a penalty shoot-out!

That aside, I would not have swapped a thing.

# 21

# Fifty Cup Finals

THIS last chapter is the title of my book and reflects the fact that during my time at BSKYB and BSB I covered exactly 50 cup finals – not 49 and not 51, but a nice round number. A half-century of showpiece occasions if you like. The tally is made up of the following: 25 FA Cup finals, 14 League Cup finals, six Champions League finals, three European Championship finals and two World Cup finals.

I have already written about all the World Cups, European Championships and Champions League finals – and a good few of the others, so this will bring the story up to date. By a nice touch of irony my last FA Cup Final, in 2016, was a repeat of my first one in 1990, Manchester United and Crystal Palace providing a degree of symmetry.

The 2016 final did not have the drama (or the goals) of the first one, but it was still a compelling game. Palace had reached their second FA Cup Final after putting out Premier League sides Southampton, Stoke City, Tottenham and Watford, as well as winning away at Championship club Reading in the quarter-finals.

United had needed a 93rd-minute Wayne Rooney penalty to see off League 1 Sheffield United in the third round, then came through tricky encounters at Derby County and Shrewsbury Town. In round six they won away at West Ham in a replay and defeated Everton in the Wembley semi with a goal from Antony Martial – also in the 93rd minute.

League 2 Oxford United provided the big shock of the third round, knocking out Premier League Swansea City, and three other fourth-tier teams also did really well: Exeter City and Wycombe held Liverpool and Aston Villa respectively, before losing replays, while Portsmouth upset Championship side Ipswich Town.

I was at White Hart Lane on third round weekend and saw a lively 2-2 draw between Tottenham and Leicester City, with Spurs needing an 89th-minute penalty equaliser from Harry Kane. The Londoners won the replay but in round five I watched them lose 1-0 at home to Palace with defender Martin Kelly scoring his first goal since 2011.

In the quarter-finals Everton beat Chelsea, while Arsenal's attempt to reach a third consecutive final was ended as they surprisingly lost 2-1 at home to Watford.

The two managers were the focus of most of the media attention in the build-up to the final. Alan Pardew had been in the Palace team which lost to United in 1990, while Louis van Gaal was widely expected to lose his job and be replaced by Jose Mourinho, regardless of whether he won or not.

Palace did have a couple of decisions go against them, but United had probably been the better team by the time the final entered its last 15 minutes. Jason Puncheon was gutted to have been left out of the starting line-up but he made his point when he eventually came on with a fine finish to give the underdogs the lead in the 78th minute. That prompted Pardew to start a little dance of delight on the touchline – he said afterwards he could not help himself – but his celebrations looked premature when Rooney's driving run set up Juan Mata for the equaliser with nine minutes to go.

In extra time Chris Smalling was dismissed for a second yellow card and we wondered if the momentum would shift to Palace. Instead it was United and Jesse Lingard who provided the winning moment – a fine volley to give the Red Devils the FA Cup for the 12th time. It was also their first major trophy since Sir Alex Ferguson had retired in 2013.

Afterwards, in the press conference, van Gaal was given a bit of a grilling about his future, so he was in no mood to slow down when he walked through the mixed zone interview area. As he strode past I called out to him, 'Louis, congratulations on winning the FA Cup.'

He stopped, turned round and came back, then said, 'You are the first journalist to say that to me, so thank you and I will do an interview.'

He would not expand on his future, but it was good to hear him talk about how proud he was to give the club their first major trophy of the post-Ferguson era. It was the last TV interview he did before football's worst-kept secret was finally confirmed and Mourinho returned to the Premier League.

\* \* \* \* \*

In 1992 the penalty shoot-out was introduced to the FA Cup for the first time, as a means of deciding a drawn game after a replay and extra time. Liverpool became the first team to reach the final this way after defeating Second Division Portsmouth in an absorbing semi.

The first game was at Highbury with Portsmouth's young star Darren Anderton giving them the lead just nine minutes from the end of extra time. In the other tie at Hillsborough, the first time the ground had been used for an FA Cup semi-final since the tragedy of 1989, Second Division Sunderland had already beaten Norwich City 1-0 so we were facing the prospect of a final between two teams from outside the top flight for the first time. Those thoughts were soon ended by a Ronnie Whelan equaliser in the 116th minute as Liverpool lived to fight another day.

Before the replay at Villa Park, Liverpool manager Graham Souness was admitted to hospital for a triple heart bypass operation and watched the semi-final on TV from his bed. His team dominated but could not break down a gallant Portsmouth side and after two hours of deadlock we had a penalty shoot-out.

Pompey captain Martin Kuhl missed the opening kick, John Barnes put Liverpool ahead 1-0, but Kit Symons restored parity when he scored. Ian Rush made it 2-1, then Bruce Grobbelaar saved Warren Neill's penalty and the writing was on the wall. Dean Saunders extended the lead to 3-1 and Portsmouth's misery was completed when defender John Beresford also missed. As England knew only too well from 1990, this is a truly desperate way to lose a semi-final, and you couldn't help but feel really sorry for Portsmouth.

Souness had recovered sufficiently to take his place alongside his coaching staff and watch the final from the touchline, but Ronnie Moran was the man in charge on the day.

Sunderland were the better team in the first half and their run to the final with a caretaker manager in charge was the stuff of fairytales. Malcolm Crosby had taken over after Denis Smith was sacked and masterminded a wonderful sequence of results that saw them knock out Chelsea in a thrilling quarter-final replay. I had known Crosby from my early days on the *Aldershot News* and it was great to see him again, let alone watch him walking out at Wembley ahead of his team at the FA Cup Final.

However, there was to be no happy ending for Crosby and his heroic players. Michael Thomas scored right at the end of the first half, then Ian Rush made it 2-0 midway through the second half with his fifth goal in a Wembley FA Cup Final – a record.

Fast forward 14 years and Liverpool won again, this time in the last final to be staged in Cardiff, and what a game this was – with possibly the greatest goal to be scored in the showpiece occasion.

Their route to the final nearly faltered at the first hurdle as they trailed 3-1 at Luton Town before storming back to win 5-3. Xabi Alonso famously scored a goal from inside his own half. In round four they beat Portsmouth at Fratton Park, before knocking out Manchester United to reach the quarter-finals – the first time they had beaten their big rivals in the FA Cup since 1921. Liverpool then put seven past Birmingham in a very one-sided sixth-round tie and eliminated Chelsea to make it to the Millennium Stadium.

West Ham – under Alan Pardew – defeated Norwich City, Blackburn Rovers, Bolton Wanderers (after a replay), Manchester City and Middlesbrough to reach the final for the first time in more than 25 years.

Liverpool were the favourites but were up against it from the moment Jamie Carragher inadvertently scored an own goal. Not long afterwards, Dean Ashton made it 2-0 after a mistake by Pepe Reina and it looked like a shock was on the cards. Liverpool did manage to pull a goal back before half-time through Djibril Cisse and early in the second half captain Steven Gerrard volleyed home Peter Crouch's knock-down to make it 2-2. They were not on level terms for long as

Paul Konchesky got away down the left and sent in a long, high cross which somehow sailed over Reina's head and into the net for 3-2.

At that stage you just seemed to feel West Ham's name was on the cup and as the game went into stoppage time we were gathered down by the touchline ready to go on the pitch for the post-match interviews. I was playing the 'grim reaper' role because it was my job to talk to the beaten finalists and I was working out in my mind what to say to the Liverpool players. I turned to cameraman Stuart Vickery, an old friend and a massive West Ham fan, who was just behind me, put my thumbs up and said, 'Well done, Stu, congratulations!'

As I turned to face the pitch again Gerrard unleashed an unstoppable thunderbolt from fully 35 yards which sped past Shaka Hislop and into the corner. It is a good discussion for the pub, but it was arguably the best goal ever scored in the FA Cup Final, although I accept that Tottenham and Ricky Villa might dispute the claim. Gerrard said afterwards he was so exhausted he could not run with the ball, so he just smashed it. It was a stunning goal in every sense, especially given the context, but I felt so guilty for what I had said to Stu – it was the equivalent of the commentator's curse.

It stayed 3-3 all through extra time and for the second year running we had penalties. Reina certainly made up for his slightly erratic performance during the match itself by saving spot-kicks from Bobby Zamora, Konchesky and Anton Ferdinand. Liverpool won the shoot-out 3-1 and inevitably Gerrard was also on target with his effort. Only Teddy Sheringham scored for West Ham, and he talked to me on the pitch afterwards. I think it was probably some time before Stu spoke to me again.

The last year that Sky Sports covered the FA Cup Final live was 2008, and after that ITV and Setanta took over the TV broadcasting rights. We should have known it would be an unusual competition when tiny Chasetown made it all the way to round three – the lowest-ranked club to ever do so. They lost to Cardiff City. Non-league Havant and Waterlooville actually reached round four and even led Liverpool twice at Anfield, before going down 5-2.

Meanwhile, another team from Hampshire was quietly making its way past the early stages. Harry Redknapp's Portsmouth seemed to have acquired the knack of just doing enough to get through: a

1-0 triumph at Ipswich in round three, a 2-1 victory over Plymouth in round four, and then another 1-0 away win at Preston.

That earned Pompey a daunting quarter-final at Old Trafford against the reigning Premier League champions Manchester United, who had just knocked out Arsenal 4-0. Redknapp's side really had to dig in that day as United threatened to blow them away with another dominant performance but somehow Pompey kept them out, then snatched a surprise 1-0 win with a 78th-minute Sulley Muntari penalty.

The Ghana international had to beat stand-in goalkeeper Rio Ferdinand to score after original substitute goalkeeper Tomasz Kuszczak gave away the penalty and got a red card. It was the third time a Redknapp team had knocked United out of the FA Cup, following previous successes with Bournemouth and West Ham.

Elsewhere Barnsley followed up their shock fifth-round win at Liverpool by knocking out the holders Chelsea in the quarter-finals. Cardiff had slipped almost unnoticed into the last eight (having beaten Chasetown, they went on to defeat Hereford 2-1 and Wolves 2-0) where they also produced a surprise by winning 2-0 at Premier League Middlesbrough.

This all meant that Portsmouth were the only top-flight club to make the semi-finals. The last time that had happened was exactly 100 years previously in 1908. Both semis were at Wembley, with Portsmouth squeezing out West Bromwich Albion 1-0, Nwankwo Kanu scoring in the second half. The next day an early Joe Ledley goal gave Cardiff a 1-0 victory over Barnsley as the Welsh club reached their first FA Cup Final since 1927 – when they famously beat Arsenal 1-0.

The final was a tight affair with the Premier League club just coming out on top, Kanu getting the only goal shortly before half-time to give Portsmouth the trophy and enabling Redknapp to become the first English manager to lift the FA Cup since Joe Royle's Everton upset Manchester United in the 1995 final. Pompey's last FA Cup triumph had come in 1939 when they beat Wolves 4-1, and they remained the holders until 1946 because of the outbreak of the Second World War.

\* \* \* \* \*

I have seen three teams win the FA Cup Final six times – Arsenal actually won it seven times between 1993 and 2015, but I missed their 1998 success. Chelsea's four triumphs in the space of six seasons was the most dominant period enjoyed by one club – you just felt every time you went to Wembley for the final that Chelsea would win it.

Roberto Di Matteo had scored in the 1997 and 2000 finals, and I've written about Didier Drogba securing the cup in 2007 at the new Wembley. Two years later they were back again to face Everton, though their campaign had begun with a bit of a wobble after they were held 1-1 at home by Southend United. They won the replay 4-1 at Roots Hall and made smooth progress after that. They did fall behind to Arsenal in the semi, but came back to win 2-1.

Everton knocked out their local rivals Liverpool after a replay with a late goal in extra time by Dan Gosling, but many ITV viewers missed it live because of a technical error when an advertisement was put to air. In the business many of us had a quiet chuckle about it, but there was also an element of, 'There but for the grace of God go I.' In the semi-final Everton kept their nerve to win a penalty shoot-out against Manchester United after the first three spot kicks were all missed.

The Merseysiders made a sensational start in the Wembley sunshine with Louis Saha scoring after just 25 seconds, the quickest goal ever in an FA Cup Final. Chelsea hit back when Florent Malouda's cross was headed in by Drogba, then Frank Lampard scored a spectacular winner in the second half with a rising shot from 25 yards. It was a great moment for interim boss Guus Hiddink before he returned to his full-time job as manager of Russia.

Chelsea were developing a taste for the new Wembley, and they went back there again the following year to retain the trophy and complete their first domestic Double. They had cruised through to the final with a 3-0 win over Aston Villa in the semi after a run which saw them score 16 goals and concede only one.

In a sense Portsmouth had their cup final moment in round five when they thrashed bitter rivals Southampton 4-1 away, but they also had an impressive 2-0 win over Tottenham after extra time in the other semi-final.

Wembley specialist Drogba had scored in each of his previous five visits to the stadium and he maintained that remarkable record with the winning goal from a free kick in the second half. That does not tell the full story, though, because his goal came just a few minutes after Petr Cech had saved Kevin-Prince Boateng's penalty. Drogba also hit the goal frame twice, while Lampard, John Terry and Salomon Kalou amazingly all hit it once. Lampard even missed a penalty. There was only one goal but there was plenty of excitement.

I wasn't at Wembley for Manchester City's 1-0 win over Stoke City in 2011, because I was covering Manchester United winning back their Premier League title the same day with a draw at Blackburn Rovers. I did watch the first Manchester derby to be staged at Wembley in the semi-final, when City pipped United 1-0 with a goal from Yaya Toure.

Chelsea had lost their two-year grip on the trophy in the fourth round as Leighton Baines scored a 119th-minute equaliser in the replay at Stamford Bridge, and then Everton knocked Chelsea out 4-3 on penalties to earn some revenge for 2009.

But it wasn't long before they had their hands back on the big prize. They made it three wins in four years with a 2-1 triumph over Liverpool in the 2012 final – Drogba, inevitably, scored their second goal, but Liverpool gave them a bit of a scare as Andy Carroll pulled one back and then thought he had equalised in the 81st minute. Keeper Petr Cech had done just enough to keep the ball out so Carroll's celebrations were eventually cut short.

It was cruel luck on Liverpool who had a fine run, knocking out rivals Manchester United and Everton along the way, both times with late goals. This, though, was Chelsea's year in cup competitions, as Bayern Munich also discovered in the Champions League Final.

Chelsea went all the way to the semi-final of the FA Cup the following season before losing 2-1 to Manchester City. In the fourth round City had beaten Stoke 1-0 in a repeat of the 2011 final and were overwhelming favourites to beat unfancied Wigan Athletic in the final.

Wigan had needed a replay to beat League 1 Bournemouth and only just scraped past non-league Macclesfield, but then they picked up momentum and produced impressive performances to beat Huddersfield 4-1 and Everton 3-0 at Goodison Park. In the semi they were too good for Millwall, winning 2-0, and were quietly confident when they were led out at the final by owner Dave Whelan and their popular manager Roberto Martinez.

Some people regard Wigan's 1-0 win as the biggest upset in an FA Cup Final in a quarter of a century, since Wimbledon's shock victory over Liverpool in 1988, and I can understand why. That said, it was no fluke. Winger Callum McManaman was outstanding, Wigan were not frightened to attack and as the game went into stoppage time substitute Ben Watson headed in Shaun Maloney's corner. Watson had missed much of the season through injury so it was a sweet moment for him – likewise for Whelan who had broken a leg in the 1960 final.

The aftermath was unhappy for both clubs – a few days later Wigan were relegated from the Premier League and Manchester City manager Roberto Mancini was sacked, to be replaced by Manuel Pellegrini.

Despite being in the Championship for 2013/14, Wigan staged an impressive defence of the first major trophy they had won in over 80 years, although they did need extra time and a replay to see off League 1 Milton Keynes Dons in round three. After that they proceeded to knock out three Premier League sides. Crystal Palace and Cardiff City were dispatched by the holders, then they produced a magnificent performance to win 2-1 at Manchester City in a repeat of the 2013 final. Jordi Gomez with a penalty and James Perch put Wigan 2-0 up, Samir Nasri pulled one back, but the underdogs hung on and returned to Wembley to face Arsenal in the semi-final.

The Gunners had beaten north London rivals Tottenham in the third round, and they also accounted for Liverpool in round five and Everton in the quarter-finals. The semi had extra meaning for Wigan because it was Arsenal who had sent them down the previous season with a win at the Emirates. Gomez was again on target with a penalty in the 63rd minute and another upset looked on the cards as Wigan continued their remarkable love affair with the FA Cup. Eight minutes from time Per Mertesacker scrambled in an equaliser, extra time was goalless, so a penalty shoot-out would decide the finalists.

Step forward Lukasz Fabianski. Arsenal's number two goalkeeper behind Wojciech Szczesny had been promoted just for the FA Cup ties and he saved Wigan's first two kicks, from Gary Caldwell and Jack Collison. Arsenal did not miss and it was Santi Cazorla who tucked away the decisive penalty in a 4-2 success.

I wasn't at the other semi-final, but it looked an absolute thriller, with Hull City prevailing 5-3 over League 1 Sheffield United. Steve Bruce's Premier League side reached their first FA Cup Final and were determined not to be going to Wembley just to make up the numbers.

Defenders James Chester and Curtis Davies put Hull 2-0 up in the first eight minutes, Arsenal were stunned, and Arsene Wenger's hopes of winning his first major trophy in nine years looked in tatters. In the 13th minute Kieran Gibbs headed the ball off the line, preventing Hull from going three up.

Soon after that they got a toehold in the game when Cazorla scored with a fine 20-yard free kick. That made it 2-1 and it was game on again, but Arsenal had to wait until inside the last 20 minutes for the equaliser and even then it came from a disputed corner. Laurent Koscielny turned and bundled the ball over the line and Arsenal finally began to play with their usual freedom. They could have won it in those closing stages, and in extra time Olivier Giroud struck the crossbar. The winner was well-worked: a neat back-heel from Giroud set up a first-time finish from substitute Aaron Ramsey. So after almost a decade Arsenal finally had their hands on a major trophy again and Wenger was a very relieved man.

The following season's FA Cup threw up one absolutely amazing scoreline. In the fourth round at Stamford Bridge Jose Mourinho's Premier League leaders Chelsea took a two-goal lead over League 1 Bradford City, before inexplicably collapsing and losing 4-2.

There were no surprises at my choice of game for the fourth round, although it was a decent one. I travelled down to the south coast to see Brighton take on the holders at their impressive new Amex Stadium in Falmer. Arsenal made a great start when Theo Walcott put them ahead inside 90 seconds and the crowd was quietened further as Mesut Ozil doubled the lead. In the second half Brighton stirred themselves and got a goal back, before a superb strike from Tomas Rosicky made it 3-1 and we thought that would be it, but Sam Baldock set up a tense finish with a second goal for Brighton. Arsenal, however, would not be denied.

In the sixth round Arsenal won at Old Trafford against Manchester United, with Danny Welbeck scoring the winner against his old club. That set up a semi against Championship side Reading. Like the year before against Wigan, Arsenal could not make their Premier League class count and they needed a goalkeeping error to eventually force a victory.

Aston Villa might have been struggling in the Premier League but they saw off their Midlands rivals Leicester City and West Bromwich Albion to make the last four – and then surprised Liverpool with a 2-1 win, after falling behind.

Their first FA Cup Final in 58 years should have been a joyful occasion but Villa never really showed up that day and they were lucky to only lose 4-0. Walcott got things started just before half-time, then Alexis Sanchez helped himself to a wonder goal: a dipping, swerving 25-yarder which flew into the net. Per Mertesacker and Olivier Giroud got on the scoresheet as well, as it finished up 4-0. After beating them 3-0 and 5-0 in the league, Arsenal certainly maintained their dominance over Tim Sherwood's Villa team.

The next day we were filming alongside the players as they showed off the trophy on the open-top bus parade through the streets around the Emirates and on to Islington Town Hall. It was a fabulous experience and an amazing feeling, watching all the fans hanging out of first- and second-floor windows to get a glimpse of their heroes.

New technology also helped us to bring my interviews with the players live into Sky Sports News – Aaron Ramsey, Theo Walcott and Mikel Arteta were just three of the squad who agreed to go live on SSN from the top deck of the bus. Back at the stadium we completed the formalities by interviewing Arsene Wenger at length.

\* \* \* \* \*

Over the years the League Cup Final has become a bigger and bigger event in its own right, and is no longer overshadowed quite so much by the FA Cup Final. It is also the one domestic competition that Wenger and his Arsenal team cannot seem to be able to win. They have had opportunities over the years, most notably in 2011 when they reached Wembley as the hot favourites to beat relegation-threatened Birmingham City.

Their campaign had begun at White Hart Lane against north London rivals Tottenham and the game went into extra time after a lively first 90 minutes had ended 1-1. Samir Nasri scored two quick-fire penalties to put Arsenal in charge and another goal followed as it finished 4-1.

Victories over Newcastle and Wigan put them in the semi-final against Ipswich Town from the Championship, and the East Anglians emerged from the first leg with a hard-fought 1-0 victory. In the second leg at the Emirates I watched as they hung on bravely for an hour, giving the travelling thousands a tantalising glimpse of a possible Wembley final. Niklas Bendtner, Laurent Koscielny and Cesc Fabregas then all scored in a 16-minute spell to send Arsenal though 3-1 on aggregate.

Birmingham had also beaten their great rivals on the way to Wembley. They defeated Aston Villa in a tense quarter-final at St Andrew's, with the giant Serbian Nikola Zigic grabbing an 84th-minute winner. That earned them a semi-final with West Ham, who had got through with a thumping 4-0 victory over Manchester United.

The Hammers won the first leg in east London 2-1 and when Carlton Cole put them ahead after half an hour of the second leg, it looked like being an all-London final. But credit to Birmingham for a great fightback as goals from Lee Bowyer and Roger Johnson forced the tie into extra time, then Craig Gardner came up with the winner as the Blues triumphed 4-3 on aggregate.

Arsenal were odds-on favourites to win the final but they fell behind to Zigic and came across an opposition keeper in Ben Foster who was inspired. The 2009 League Cup Final penalty shoot-out hero for Manchester United was at it again with a string of fine saves, although he could do nothing to keep out Robin van Persie's 39th-minute volley.

With extra time looming Foster pumped a long high ball down the middle which was flicked into the penalty area. Wojciech Szczesny and Laurent Koscielny both had time to clear it, both hesitated, and then got in each other's way. The ball fell to Obafemi Martins, who tucked it away to give Birmingham their first League Cup since 1963. It was a calamity for Arsenal, and they still have not won this competition since 1987.

I saw two League Cup finals between Chelsea and Tottenham, but both were very different as each side won one and lost one. In 2008 Chelsea were the holders after beating Arsenal in another all-London final the year before in Cardiff. Tottenham had crushed Arsenal 6-2 over two legs in the semi-final and with an amazing 5-1 victory at White Hart Lane in the second game so they went into the final in bullish mood.

I had been at the second leg of the other semi after being invited into the directors' box at Goodison Park by my good friend and former colleague Alan Myers. It was a novel experience, yet thoroughly enjoyable – a world away from the muck and bullets of the touchline and tunnel, or the pressures on you in the media areas. From my nice comfortable seat I watched on as Chelsea won 1-0 to complete a 3-1 aggregate win.

In the final Avram Grant's side took the lead through Didier Drogba and still led 1-0 with 20 minutes to go, but then Wayne Bridge handled inside the area and Dimitar Berbatov's penalty sent us into extra time.

The winning goal was a little strange – Petr Cech punched a free kick from Jermaine Jenas straight on to Jonathan Woodgate's head and the ball ended up just going over the goal line. After that, Spurs hung on and Chelsea would finish that season as runners-up in three competitions.

Chelsea got their revenge in 2015 as Jose Mourinho came back to claim his third League Cup. Just like in 2005 Chelsea would also go on to win the Premier League title. They took the lead just before half-time when Tottenham failed to deal with Willian's free kick and skipper John Terry's shot deflected in off Eric Dier. There was a touch of fortune about their second goal too as Costa's effort from a tight angle also took a critical deflection. It was Chelsea's day and they won 2-0.

There was also a defeat for Tottenham in the 2009 final. Having won the trophy the year before they defended it all the way to the final and through normal time and extra time at Wembley, but they came unstuck in the penalty shoot-out. Ryan Giggs put United ahead with the first spot-kick following 120 goalless minutes. Just before the shoot-out started Ben Foster borrowed goalkeeping coach Eric Steele's computer and checked on the penalty techniques of the players he was about to face. It paid dividends as he correctly worked out where Jamie O'Hara's effort would go. He dived left and saved it, which immediately handed his team the advantage, and they went on to win comfortably.

United retained the trophy the following season but only after a titanic battle with Manchester City in the semi-finals. Former Old Trafford favourite Carlos Tevez was wearing City's colours and that made him the villain of the piece in the red part of Manchester. That feeling only increased after the first leg as Tevez scored twice to help his new team come from behind to win 2-1.

With home advantage in the second leg United poured forward and made the breakthrough after half-time with a Paul Scholes goal. When Michael Carrick added a second it was 3-2 on aggregate in their favour, but Tevez intervened again, hauling City right back into it with a marvellous back-heel flick – so it was effectively Manchester United 3 Carlos Tevez 3. Extra time was looming fast when Wayne Rooney's header sent his side back to Wembley with a goal in the third minute of stoppage time.

Aston Villa won 1-0 at Ewood Park against Blackburn Rovers in the first leg of their semi-final and were hot favourites ahead of the return at Villa Park. This turned into a ten-goal classic as Rovers raced into a 2-0 lead, then found themselves 5-2 down, before recovering to 5-4. Villa had the last word and an injury-time goal from Ashley Young meant a final score on the night of 6-4, completing a 7-4 aggregate.

The big talking point of the final came early on as Gabriel Agbonlahor went through on goal and was brought down by Nemanja Vidic for a clear penalty, but crucially the Serbian avoided a red card. James Milner put Villa ahead with his spot-kick but they were still seething.

It wasn't long before the lively Michael Owen equalised, but he was forced off by injury, and it was left to substitute Rooney to come up with the winning goal – a header from Antonio Valencia's cross.

United lost their two-year hold on the trophy when they were surprisingly beaten at home by Crystal Palace in the quarter-finals. Palace were then knocked out by Cardiff City on penalties after their two-legged semi-final had finished 1-1 on aggregate.

Liverpool won at Chelsea in the quarter-finals and then overcame favourites Manchester City 3-2 in the semis. Steven Gerrard scored a penalty in each leg, but it needed a goal from Craig Bellamy to take Liverpool into the final.

We were not quite sure what to expect as Liverpool made their first Wembley appearance since losing the FA Cup Final to Manchester United in 1996, and it was the Championship underdogs Cardiff who snatched the lead through Joe Mason. They were still in front after nearly an hour and 12 months on from Arsenal's shock defeat to Birmingham we were starting to wonder whether another surprise was in store.

Liverpool stepped up the pressure and with 30 minutes to go Martin Skrtel was first to a rebound and scored from close range. No further goals meant we were in for extra time and when Liverpool finally did get their noses in front in the 108th minute through Dirk Kuyt, you sensed that was the end of Cardiff's brave resistance. Instead Ben Turner scrambled in a dramatic equaliser with two minutes to go and Liverpool were taken to penalties.

Gerrard was first to go and his kick was brilliantly saved by Tom Heaton – advantage Cardiff; Kenny Miller struck the post with his effort, so it was still 0-0; Charlie Adam went next and blasted the ball over the bar – three consecutive penalties missed and still no goals.

Don Cowie restored a measure of order by scoring to give Cardiff a 1-0 lead; Kuyt made no mistake from the spot and it was 1-1; Rudy Gestede struck the woodwork for Cardiff to wipe out their narrow advantage; Stewart Downing put Liverpool ahead for the first time, Peter Whittingham made it 2-2, before Glen Johnson restored Liverpool's lead at 3-2; the final kick of the regulation shoot-out was taken for Cardiff by Steven's cousin Anthony Gerrard, but he missed and it was Liverpool celebrating.

Kenny Dalglish won his first trophy of his second spell at the club.

The heroes of the 2013 League Cup were Bradford City from League 2. They started back on 11 August 2012 with an extra-time win at Notts County, then in round two they won at Watford with a goal in the fourth minute of injury time, and they put out Burton Albion in extra time in round three.

Then the real giant-killing started as Wigan became the first of three Premier League sides to fall victim to these amazing cup fighters. Like Wigan, Arsenal also lost on penalties after an enthralling quarter-final at Valley Parade. Thomas Vermaelen scored an 88th-minute equaliser to keep the big guns in the tie but then missed the crucial penalty in the shoot-out as his kick came back off the post. Arsenal missed three of their five shots and ironically the only two scorers from the spot were Englishmen in Jack Wilshere and Alex Oxlade-Chamberlain.

On an extraordinary night in Yorkshire, Bradford opened up a 3-1 lead over Aston Villa in the semi-final first leg, and then they followed that up by hanging on grimly at Villa Park. It looked comfortable enough when James Hanson equalised on the night but Andi Weimann's 89th-minute goal for Villa ensured a nervous ending before the Bantams' celebrations could begin.

In the other semi Swansea City won 2-0 at Chelsea in the first leg and drew 0-0 in the return, a game remembered for the infamous Eden Hazard challenge on the ball boy.

The final proved a game too far for gallant Bradford, their cause not helped by the dismissal of goalkeeper Matt Duke on the hour. By then they were 3-0 down and it finished 5-0 with Nathan Dyer and Jonathan De Guzman both scoring twice. But Bradford proved their mettle by returning to Wembley in May and winning the play-off final to gain promotion to the third tier. Congratulations were well earned by them, as they also were by my team Gillingham who won the League 2 title – their first for 50 years.

After a couple of near misses, Manchester City finally won the League Cup again in 2014 – their first success in the competition for 38 years. They liked the experience so much that they then repeated it in 2016.

Sunderland surprised Manchester United in the semi-finals and prevented an all-Manchester final with an absolutely enthralling triumph after one of the most ridiculous penalty shoot-outs ever seen – seven of the ten spot-kicks were missed.

At the Stadium of Light, Sunderland fought well and scrapped to a 2-1 victory in the first leg. Most experts did not think that would be enough at Old Trafford but again they put up a stubborn showing. The game headed into extra time after Jonny Evans cancelled out Sunderland's advantage in the 37th minute, then in the 119th minute Manchester-born David Bardsley made it 1-1 to spark huge celebrations among the travelling fans from the north-east.

Within seconds Javier Hernandez restored United's lead on the night, so the tie finished 3-3 on aggregate and penalties would decide who would face Manchester City in the final. City meanwhile had trounced West Ham 9-0 over the two legs, with Alvaro Negredo scoring five times.

The first three penalties of the shoot-out were missed, then Darren Fletcher put United ahead, but again Sunderland kept their nerve and fought back to lead 2-1. Goalkeeper Vito Mannone saved two penalties, and so did David de Gea, but in the end it was Gus Poyet's Sunderland who somehow did enough.

Fabio Borino then put Sunderland ahead in the final and they led for half the match before fading in the second half, although it took an outstanding goal from Yaya Toure to change the course of the final. He struck a thunderous shot into the roof of the net and just 60 seconds later Samir Nasri scored with the outside of his foot. A third goal in stoppage time probably flattered City, as Manuel Pellegrini won his first trophy in England.

Two years later he was back at Wembley but he knew he would be on his way out at the end of the season because Pep Guardiola was taking over at the Etihad. He remained very dignified throughout and his players were delighted he would at least leave with silverware.

Liverpool had reached the final by surviving a nerve-wracking penalty shoot-out against Stoke City, after losing at home in the second leg. City lost 2-1 at Everton in the first leg and then fell further behind to a brilliant Ross Barkley goal, but they fought their way back with a storming display and goals from Fernandinho, Kevin De Bruyne and Sergio Aguero. Everton felt the De Bruyne goal should have been disallowed after Raheem Sterling appeared to have taken the ball out before crossing for the Belgian to score.

Sterling was facing his old club and he was loudly jeered by the Liverpool fans throughout, but he ended up on the winning side and his jubilant celebrations at the end were understandable.

Fernandinho put City ahead just after half-time although Simon Mignolet should have done better, letting the shot slip under his body. He did atone with some splendid saves later on as this compelling match took a late twist. Sterling missed two glaring opportunities to extend City's lead before Philippe Coutinho equalised in the 83rd minute, stabbing home the rebound after Adam Lallana hit the post.

The build-up to the game had been dominated by Pellegrini's decision to play Willy Caballero in goal. The Argentinian had been at fault during City's 5-1 defeat to Chelsea the previous week and many fans wanted fit-again first-choice keeper Joe Hart to play in the final, even though Caballero had featured in the earlier rounds.

Pellegrini backed the man who had been with him at Malaga, and Caballero delivered an astonishing performance in the shoot-out, saving three penalties.

Emre Can put Liverpool ahead with a deft shot into the corner before Fernandinho struck the post, so it remained 1-0 Liverpool. Lucas Leiva's penalty was saved by Caballero, Jesus Navas netted to make it 1-1, then Caballero produced another great save to his left to deny Coutinho. Sergio Aguero struck to give City a 2-1 lead, and Caballero plunged to his right this time to force Lallana's shot on to the post. Yaya Toure wrapped it up with another successful penalty and City had their hands on the League Cup again.

\* \* \* \* \*

That was my 48th cup final – my journey would end with Manchester United beating Crystal Palace in the FA Cup and then Portugal overcoming France at EURO 2016.

I won't deny that I missed it when the 2017 League Cup Final came round and I wasn't there to see Manchester United just edge out Southampton. Watching on TV as Arsenal beat Chelsea in the FA Cup Final in May at Gore Court Cricket Club near Sittingbourne in

Kent was another surreal experience, but nothing lasts forever and I am truly grateful for the ones that I did see over the years.

Who knows? I may even get to attend a few more in the future, but even if I don't I will always carry around some unforgettable memories of great goals scored, of penalties saved and of dramatic moments that can almost defy description.

I was watching back at Sky editing a piece for Sky Sports News in 2012 when Manchester City scored twice in stoppage time to snatch the title away from Manchester United on the very last day of the season. Martin Tyler's epic 'Agueroooooooooooo!' commentary will live on forever, as he went on to add:

'I swear you'll never see anything like this ever again!'

But it is precisely the hope we might that keeps us going back to this great game over and over again.

And at the age of 60 I will cling to the belief that the best is yet to come.

# Appendix

## Nick's 50 cup finals

1   1990 FA Cup: Manchester United 1-0 Crystal Palace (after 3-3 draw)
2   1991 FA Cup: Tottenham Hotspur 2-1 Nottingham Forest (after extra time)
3   1992 FA Cup: Liverpool 2-0 Sunderland
4   1993 FA Cup: Arsenal 2-1 Sheffield Wednesday (after extra time & after 1-1 draw)
5   1994 FA Cup: Manchester United 4-0 Chelsea
6   1995 FA Cup: Everton 1-0 Manchester United
7   1996 FA Cup: Manchester United 1-0 Liverpool
8   1997 FA Cup: Chelsea 2-0 Middlesbrough
9   1999 FA Cup: Manchester United 2-0 Newcastle United
10  2000 FA Cup: Chelsea 1-0 Aston Villa
11  2001 League Cup: Liverpool 1-1 Birmingham City (Liverpool won 5-4 on penalties)
12  2001 FA Cup: Liverpool 2-1 Arsenal
13  2002 FA Cup: Arsenal 2-0 Chelsea
14  2003 League Cup: Liverpool 2-0 Manchester United
15  2003 FA Cup: Arsenal 1-0 Southampton
16  2004 League Cup : Middlesbrough 2-1 Bolton Wanderers
17  2004 FA Cup: Manchester United 3-0 Millwall
18  EURO 2004: Greece 1-0 Portugal
19  2005 League Cup: Chelsea 3-2 Liverpool (after extra time)
20  2005 FA Cup: Arsenal 0-0 Manchester United (Arsenal won 5-4 on penalties)
21  2006 FA Cup: Liverpool 3-3 West Ham United (Liverpool won 3-1 on penalties)

22  2006 Champions League: Barcelona 2-1 Arsenal
23  2006 World Cup: Italy 1-1 France (Italy won 5-3 on penalties)
24  2007 League Cup: Chelsea 2-1 Arsenal
25  2007 FA Cup: Chelsea 1-0 Manchester United (after extra time)
26  2008 League Cup: Tottenham Hotspur 2-1 Chelsea (after extra time)
27  2008 FA Cup: Portsmouth 1-0 Cardiff City
28  2008 Champions League: Manchester United 1-1 Chelsea (Man Utd won 6-5 on pens)
29  2009 League Cup: Manchester United 0-0 Tottenham Hotspur (Man Utd won 4-1 on pens)
30  2009 FA Cup: Chelsea 2-1 Everton
31  2009 Champions League: Barcelona 2-0 Manchester United
32  2010 League Cup: Manchester United 2-1 Aston Villa
33  2010 FA Cup: Chelsea 1-0 Portsmouth
34  2010 World Cup: Spain 1-0 Netherlands (after extra time)
35  2011 League Cup: Birmingham City 2-1 Arsenal
36  2011 Champions League: Barcelona 3-1 Manchester United
37  2012 League Cup: Liverpool 2-2 Cardiff City (Liverpool won 3-2 on penalties)
38  2012 FA Cup: Chelsea 2-1 Liverpool
39  2012 Champions League: Chelsea 1-1 Bayern Munich (Chelsea won 4-3 on penalties)
40  EURO 2012: Spain 4-0 Italy
41  2013 League Cup: Swansea City 5-0 Bradford City
42  2013 FA Cup: Wigan Athletic 1-0 Manchester City
43  2013 Champions League: Bayern Munich 2-1 Borussia Dortmund
44  2014 League Cup: Manchester City 3-1 Sunderland
45  2014 FA Cup: Arsenal 3-2 Hull City (after extra time)
46  2015 League Cup: Chelsea 2-0 Tottenham Hotspur
47  2015 FA Cup: Arsenal 4-0 Aston Villa
48  2016 League Cup: Manchester City 1-1 Liverpool (Manchester City won 3-1 on penalties)
49  2016 FA Cup: Manchester United 2-1 Crystal Palace (after extra time)
50  EURO 2016: Portugal 1-0 France (after extra time)

# LETHAL INNOCENCE

# PHILIP KEMP

# Lethal Innocence

## THE CINEMA OF ALEXANDER MACKENDRICK

### Foreword by Alec Guinness

METHUEN

First published in Great Britain 1991
by Methuen London
Michelin House, 81 Fulham Road, London SW3 6RB

Copyright © 1991 Philip Kemp

Foreword copyright © 1991 Alec Guinness

The author has asserted his moral rights

The publisher acknowledges a subsidy
from the Scottish Arts Council
towards the publication of this volume

A CIP catalogue record for this book
is available from the British Library
ISBN 0 413 64980 6

Photoset by Deltatype Ltd, Ellesmere Port, Cheshire
Printed in Great Britain
by Clays Ltd, St Ives plc

# Contents

# Illustrations

Illustrations from *Whisky Galore*, *The Man in the White Suit*, *Mandy*, *The Maggie* and *The Ladykillers* are frame enlargements taken from the films themselves. For various reasons, it proved impossible to get frame enlargements from *Sweet Smell of Success*, *Sammy Going South*, *A High Wind in Jamaica* or *Don't Make Waves*: these are illustrated by publicity stills.

Enlargements and stills from all the films except *The Ladykillers* were obtained through the British Film Institute Stills Library, and the enlargements were made by Colin Rattee of the National Film Archive at Berkhamstead. Frame enlargements from *The Ladykillers* were provided by the Weintraub laboratory at Pinewood.

Acknowledgements, and thanks for permission to reproduce illustrations, are due as follows: to John Ellis, Large Door Productions, for plate 1a; to Weintraub Entertainment Ltd for plates 1b–14b and 17–19b; to Metro-Goldwyn-Mayer Inc./United Artists Inc. for plates 15a–16b; to 20th Century Fox Co. Ltd for plates 20a–21b; to Turner Entertainment Co. (copyright © 1967 Metro-Goldwyn-Mayer Inc.) for plates 22a and 22b; to Alexander Mackendrick for plates 23a–g and to Hilary Mackendrick for plate 24.

# Foreword

Sandy Mackendrick seems to me to be a sophisticated grown-up Peter Pan – eternally youthful and prepared to tackle any Captain Hook, Mr Darling or alarming crocodile with spluttering, if somewhat pained, indignation, caustic wit, and chuckling irony. Physically he has hardly changed over the forty years I have known him; tall, handsome, pale, with a slick of straight black hair which often appears to be in his way; a light, hesitant voice, as if his ideas are constantly bubbling over each other in his head, and an accent which is half Scottish and half American. I remember him as nearly always dressed in a severe black sweater and grey flannel trousers. He is a man of great charm but of astonished outrage at the wickedness of the world and of the stupidity of men of power.

I had forgotten, when I first worked for him (in *The Man in the White Suit*) that he had been a commercial artist in an advertising agency, and I was surprised to find, pinned on a board in the studios, a sort of strip-cartoon he had sketched of all his intended shots for a scene. They were admirably and vigorously drawn, with the same clear line and precision he gave to his films. For me, an actor, I felt they were an indication of rigidity and would stand in the way of my own loose, off-the-cuff approach. I was wrong. Sandy, in fact, was marvellously good with actors – gentle, encouraging, appreciative, quick to solve their problems and seize on the best they had to offer. I cannot recall him ever expressing irritation with an actor; but his impatience with some technicians and certainly with the front office was clearly evident. For him, I feel, the enemy was always lurking behind the portals and façades of the hierarchy. In short, he is an artist, and like all artists wants his own way. Rightly.

His films were always *about* something – justice perhaps, innocence opposed to avarice or political scheming – and throughout his work, behind the irony, behind the black humour and good humour, can be found a straight warm-hearted approach to humanity. A film director I can revere and of whom I have fond memories.

Alec Guinness

# Introduction

It's customary for the first full-length study of a veteran film director to lead off by claiming that its subject is shamefully underrated, and this book will be no exception.

Admittedly, Alexander Mackendrick can hardly be described as a 'neglected director' in the sense of one whose work has been forgotten. Of the nine films he directed, at least four – *Whisky Galore*, *The Man in the White Suit*, *The Ladykillers* and *Sweet Smell of Success* – are widely known and frequently revived, and of the rest only *Don't Make Waves* could be considered obscure. Nor, during his active career, was he the object of critical indifference, let alone hostility. If anything, he was used by most reviewers with exceptional kindness. When his films were good, he was generally praised; when they weren't, critics tended to commiserate with him for having to make the best of such defective material. He never suffered the kind of onslaught that ruined Michael Powell's career, nor the almost equally damaging adulation that was lavished for a time on Carol Reed.

But while several of Mackendrick's films are well appreciated, there's been surprisingly little evaluation of his overall achievement. Few critics – with the notable exception of Charles Barr – have considered his output as a whole, and during the ten years or so after he quit directing, his reputation underwent something of a critical eclipse. In Raymond Durgnat's stimulating, sometimes wayward *A Mirror for England* (1970) Mackendrick's films come in for rather less notice than do those of, for example, Lewis Gilbert or Roy Baker. Even *The Man in the White Suit* rates only a few lines, though there aren't many movies that mirror more acutely the England of their period. And Richard Roud's 1,100-page *Cinema: A Critical Dictionary* (1980) relegates Mackendrick to four lines of an essay devoted to 'Robert Hamer and Ealing Comedy'.

If Mackendrick's Ealing work is liable to be lumped in with that of the studio in general, the post-Ealing films, less readily classified, have floated in critical limbo. *Sweet Smell*, while never lacking admirers, has been seen by some as an aberration in Mackendrick's output, an atypically savage excursion from a film-maker whose natural bent (so the theory goes) was for gentler stuff. And the films he directed in the sixties – *Sammy Going South*, *A High Wind in Jamaica* and *Don't Make Waves* – are often written off as the work of a director in decline.

Such assessments, I believe, are superficial. The contention underlying this book is that all Mackendrick's work exhibits strong thematic and stylistic links, and that *Whisky Galore* and *The Man in the White Suit* have a lot more in common with *Sweet Smell* than with their milder Ealing stablemates like *The Lavender Hill Mob*. Nor do the later films show signs of a falling-off in Mackendrick's powers. Their faults – since it can't be denied that all three of them, especially *Don't Make Waves*, are seriously flawed – stem not from any lack of directorial skill, but from the circumstances under which they were produced. *High Wind* in particular, even in the truncated version that was finally released, stands as one of Mackendrick's richest and most complex works.

This is perhaps the place to make the standard disclaimer which, in a post-auteurist era, any study of a director must include. References to 'Mackendrick's films' or 'Mackendrick's work' may seem to imply that he was the sole author of his movies. No such suggestion, of course, is intended – as Mackendrick himself, who dislikes 'the utterly unjustified cult of the director', would be the first to insist. Such phrases are shorthand, to avoid cumbersome repetition, and wherever feasible I've tried to do justice to the vital contribution made by the writers, actors, cinematographers, composers, etc., with whom Mackendrick worked.

At the same time, though, it's possible to argue, as V. F. Perkins does in *Film as Film*, that 'the director is the only member of the production team who can see (whose job it is to see) the whole film rather than particular aspects, the interrelationship of the parts rather than the parts as separate tasks'.[1] While this isn't always so, it does seem to have been true of Mackendrick, and there's a good case for treating him as the unifying creative force behind the films he directed. Fastidious in his choice of projects and exacting in his working methods, he exercised (except, as on *High Wind*, when physically prevented) a high degree of control over all aspects of the film-making process, involving himself closely in everything from the initial treatment to the mixing of the sound-track.

The distinctive visual quality of the films, the dramatic density of their cinematic language, can also on all the evidence be credited primarily to Mackendrick himself. His technique of storyboarding his scripts, sketching every set-up in vivid, eloquent strokes, created what Douglas Slocombe, cinematographer on several of his films, described as 'a strong pattern, a very strong hallmark – every image succinctly plotted to make its point'. The scripts of Mackendrick's films, as Geoff Brown has noted,[2] are never merely words awaiting illustration, but are conceived from the outset in richly visual terms.

It may be precisely because his films are constructed with such lucidity, such fluent visual and narrative flair, that it's sometimes been suggested they have little to offer beyond sheer proficiency – that there isn't, in the final analysis, very much to be said about them. But Mackendrick is a subtle and highly sophisticated film-maker who aimed (though not necessarily on a conscious level) for a 'mythic dimension' in his work – so that there's invariably far more going on than appears on the surface. And, far from there not being a lot to say, I found while writing this book so much to explore in each of the films, and in Mackendrick's work in general, that I'm uneasily conscious of aspects I've covered inadequately or not at all. It would have been easy to write a book twice as long, though perhaps at the risk of exasperating my publishers and exhausting my readers. But I hope that other writers, rather than regarding this study as in any way definitive, will be encouraged by its imperfections and omissions to dig yet deeper into the riches of Mackendrick's oeuvre.

I've chosen to follow a chronological approach, discussing each film in turn while tracing connections, echoes and premonitions within Mackendrick's output as a whole. What such a method lacks in ingenuity it more than makes up, I feel, in usefulness and accessibility. Part of the job, after all, of an initial study such as this is to map out the territory in a clear and straightforward manner; subsequent critics are then free to pick and choose, to jump forwards and backwards among the films without constantly having to stop and explain what came where.

The sequential approach also lends itself better to filling in the background. A film, perhaps even more than other creative artefacts, needs to be considered within its context, the circumstances of its production. And while this book isn't primarily a biography, a certain amount of biographical information seemed essential in order to show why Mackendrick made the films he did, how they got made (or in some cases didn't) and where each one fits in the wider trajectory of his lifespan – of which, after all, directing movies has occupied less than a quarter. It also helps to answer the question that Mackendrick's career so often provokes: what was it that led such a gifted director to abandon film-making at the height of his powers?

Peter Cowie was recently ticked off, in a review of his book on Coppola, for 'providing impossibly long, over-involved plot summaries'.[3] Anyone writing about film must sympathise with his dilemma: how to allow for those readers who aren't totally familiar with the films you're discussing, while not alienating those who are. In an attempt to overcome the problem, I've included thorough (though not, I hope, over-involved) synopses of each of the films directed by Mackendrick, but located them in the Filmography at the back of the book, where readers can consult them or not, as they prefer.

Superscript numbers in the text refer to source material, and can be safely ignored by readers indifferent to such matters. Quotes with no source reference come from my own conversations with the people concerned, who are listed in the Acknowledgements – and to all of whom I owe a huge debt of thanks.

# Acknowledgements

My prime debt of gratitude must be to Alexander Mackendrick, who gave up generous amounts of his time, answered my questions with patience and forbearance, and made available to me invaluable items of background documentation. Also to his wife Hilary, who supplemented Sandy's memory and provided her own illuminating perspective on events. Without their help, co-operation, and hospitality, this book would have been far harder to write, and far poorer in content.

I'm deeply grateful, too, to all those whose conversation, or correspondence, furnished me with so much valuable material: Lord (Michael) Birkett, Jeremy Bullmore, Denis Cannan, T. E. B. Clarke, Sidney Cole, Charles Crichton, Stephen Dalby, Monja Danischewsky, Brenda Danischewsky, Terence Davies, John Dighton, Ed Emshwiller, Harold George, Sir Alec Guinness, Bert Haanstra, John Halas, Ronald Harwood, James Hill, Jenny Holt, Jennifer Howarth, Bill Jackson, Ernest Lehman, Oscar Lewenstein, Roger MacDougall, Margaret Mackendrick, Francisco Menendez, Jeannine Minich, Oswald Morris, David Peers, Tom Pevsner, Peter Proud, Michael Relph, Douglas Slocombe, Herbie Smith, Peter Tanner, Lanham Titchener, Andrew Tsao, Ira Wallach, Chic Waterson, Joan Waterson, Jenny Wilkes and Colin Young.

I'm particularly indebted to Jonathan Balcon, for allowing me access to Sir Michael Balcon's papers; to Brian Baxter, for enabling me to watch a copy of the BBC programme *The Ealing Comedies*; to Geoff Brown, for providing me with a transcript of the original English interview with Mackendrick from *Der Produzent*; to Jerome Fletcher, for help with Spanish translation; to Ernest Lehman, for giving me a copy of *Sweet Smell of Success and other stories* and some elusive press cuttings; to Tom Pevsner, for lending me both the shooting script of *A High Wind in Jamaica* and his tape of Peter Sellers's '*Ladykillers* trailer'; to David Thompson, for providing me with videotapes and transcripts of programmes and other useful material; and to Jenny Wilkes, for lending me the tapes she recorded of Mackendrick's teaching sessions at the National Film School.

Scottish Television, in the persons of Gus Macdonald, Dermot McQuarrie and Morag Lawrie, provided me not only with a videotape of their programme *Mackendrick: The Man Who Walked Away*, but also with a full transcript of all the interviews, which included quantities of fascinating material not used in the final programme. For such courtesy, my warmest thanks.

Several ideas in Chapter 3 were sparked off by a lively masterclass on *The Man in the White Suit* at the National Film Theatre. It was run by Mamoun Hassan, and I'm grateful to him both for stimulating my thoughts and for organising a very enjoyable day.

For the help and co-operation I received in the course of research, my thanks to the staff of the British Library; of the British Newspaper Library at Colindale; of the National Library of Scotland; of the Library of Congress (Motion Picture Division) in Washington DC; to John Herron and the staff of the Weintraub archive; and above all to the staff of the British Film Institute. I also owe thanks to Rose McMurray of the Glasgow School of Art, to Stella Pence of the Telluride Film Festival and to Tana Wolf of the Belgrade Theatre, Coventry, for their kindness in providing me with the information I needed.

To Charles Barr I owe a double debt of gratitude: for the sensitivity and acuteness of his own writing on Mackendrick, which gave me the initial spur for this book; and for having kindly agreed to read the manuscript and give me the benefit of his reactions.

Several other people read parts of the text in typescript, and helped me greatly with their comments, both favourable and otherwise. I'd like to thank all of them, especially Christa Scholtz, Ernest Lehman, John Ellis, Murray Grigor, Paul Watkins, Carey Smith and Nora Kemp.

For their unfailing sympathy and enthusiasm, I'm grateful to my editors, Michael Earley, Sarah Hannigan and Ann Wilson, and to Methuen's tireless Publicity Director, Briar Silich.

The costs of producing the book, and especially of including all the illustrations, were eased by a substantial grant from the Scottish Arts Council. Their generosity is deeply appreciated.

Finally, to Theresa FitzGerald, whose encouragement and advice have been a constant support throughout the whole long project: my love, friendship and thanks.

# Chronology

1911 Marriage, on 28 April in Los Angeles, of Francis Robert Mackendrick, shipbuilding draughtsman, and Martha R. Doig.

1912 Alexander Mackendrick born Boston, Mass., 8 September, only son of Frank and Martha Mackendrick.

1918 Frank Mackendrick dies in flu epidemic in Philadelphia.

1919 Alexander Mackendrick taken back to Glasgow by grandfather, Alexander Mackendrick Sr, to be raised by his grandparents and his aunts, Janet and Margaret Mackendrick.

1919–26 Attends Hillhead High School, Glasgow.

1926–29 Enrolled at Glasgow School of Art.

1930 Joins J. Walter Thompson, London advertising agency, as layout artist; subsequently promoted to art director.

1934 Marries Eileen Ascroft, 24 March.

1935 Birth of eldest son, Kerry.

1936 Writes, with cousin Roger MacDougall, script of *Midnight Menace* (37), directed by Sinclair Hill for Grosvenor.

1940 Still at JWT, works on propaganda films for the Ministry of Information.

1943 Divorced from Eileen Ascroft. Recruited into Army Psychological Warfare Branch and sent to Algiers to work in Leaflet Section.

1943–44 With 5th Army in Italy, helping to produce *Frontpost*, weekly propaganda sheet.

1944 After capture of Rome, assigned to Film Section of PWB. Produces documentary (directed by Marcello Pagliero) on Fosse Ardeatine massacre.

1945 Returns to UK, works with Roger MacDougall at Merlin Productions, making documentaries.

1946 Joins Ealing Studios as scriptwriter and (later) as sketch artist on production design.

1947 Co-scriptwriter (with John Dighton) and storyboard designer on *Saraband for Dead Lovers*, directed by Basil Dearden.

1948 Designs storyboard for *Another Shore*, directed by Charles Crichton. Directs **Whisky Galore**. Marries Hilary Lloyd, 24 December.

1949 Co-scriptwriter and 2nd unit director on *The Blue Lamp*, directed by Dearden, and *Dance Hall*, directed by Charles Crichton.

1951 Directs **The Man in the White Suit**.

1952 Directs **Mandy**.

1953 Directs **The Maggie**.

1954 Directs **The Ladykillers**.

1955 Travels to Hollywood, where he signs contract with Hecht-Hill-Lancaster, initially to direct *The Devil's Disciple*. Gives course of lectures at the Hague and Amsterdam Film Museums (December).

1956 Directs **Sweet Smell of Success** for HHL.

1958 Starts to direct *The Devil's Disciple*, but taken off film after ten days following disagreement with producers. Member of Grand Jury to select 'Greatest Film of All Time' at Brussels World Fair (October).

1960 Starts work on *The Guns of Navarone* but leaves film after disagreement with Carl Foreman. Directs two plays: *The Grass is Greener*, by Hugh and Margaret Williams, in Coventry; and *Face of a Hero*, by Robert L. Joseph, on Broadway.

1961 Birth of son Matthew.

1962 Directs **Sammy Going South** for Michael Balcon at British Lion.

1963 Directs episode of series, *The Defenders*, for TV.

1964 Directs **A High Wind in Jamaica** for 20th Century-Fox.

1965 Birth of son John.

1966 Directs additional scenes for *Oh Dad, Poor Dad, Mamma's Hung You in the Closet and I'm Feelin' So Sad*, directed by Richard Quine for Paramount.

1967 Directs **Don't Make Waves** for MGM.

1969 Appointed Dean of Film School at newly founded California Institute of the Arts (CalArts), Los Angeles.

1971 Season of Mackendrick's films at the National Film Theatre, London.

1978 Resigns deanship. Appointed Fellow of the Institute, and continues teaching at CalArts. Retrospective of his films at the Edinburgh Film Festival.

1986 Tribute to his work at the 13th Telluride Film Festival, Colorado. Mackendrick presented with the Festival's Silver Medallion.

1990 Attends retrospective of his work at the 8th Quimper Film Festival, Brittany.

# 1 In Enemy Terrain

'Nationality is a very confusing thing. The
blood is Scots and the temperament is Scots,
but I am in fact 100 percent American.'[1]

Alexander Mackendrick

Some of the most interesting film-makers are the exiles, turning a fresh, fascinated eye on their adopted society. But even more interesting are those who contrive to be at once exiles and non-exiles, assimilated yet still retaining the outsider's quizzical, slightly incredulous gaze. This dual perspective can make for intriguingly ambiguous movies, outwardly conforming to convention while obliquely subverting it from within: Fritz Lang's films in America, Losey's in Britain, much of Billy Wilder's output, and maybe also Emeric Pressburger's contribution to his pictures with Michael Powell. One of the most subtly distanced of these clandestine exiles is Alexander Mackendrick, who from early childhood has never quite been at home anywhere. In most of the reference books, he passes for a British director (or even, now and again, 'English'). For his own part, he's always regarded himself as a Scot. But he is, and has been all his life, an American citizen.

He was born on 8 September 1912, in Boston, Massachusetts. His parents, Francis Robert Mackendrick and Martha Doig, were Glaswegians who (according to their son) had eloped to the USA to escape the disapproval of Frank Mackendrick's father, Alexander Mackendrick Sr. As elopements go, it was a thoroughly respectable affair: Frank Mackendrick travelled out on one boat, and Martha Doig followed on another. Their destination was Los Angeles, where Frank's elder brother Willie was already living, and the couple were married there on 28 April 1911.

Martha Mackendrick detested Los Angeles – 'I've always thought,' Mackendrick remarked years later, 'that my reactions to Hollywood are perhaps pre-natal'[2] – and not long before the birth of her child she persuaded her husband to move to Boston. Frank Mackendrick, who had trained as a shipbuilding draughtsman and civil engineer, found work with the engineering firm of Stone and Webster. If his marriage had caused any family ill-feeling, it was soon resolved: in 1914 the elder Alexander Mackendrick took early retirement and, together with his wife and two daughters, moved to Boston to be near his younger son.

Around 1916 Frank Mackendrick was sent by his firm to work in the shipyards of Philadelphia where, thanks to the European war, production was thriving. He took his wife and son with him, and they were still living there when he died in 1918, a victim of the great influenza epidemic that swept across Asia, Europe and America, killing more people in a few months than the war had done in four years. By macabre coincidence, Frank's brother Willie died in Los Angeles around the same time – not from influenza, but murdered. He was working as accountant for a character whom Mackendrick describes as 'a highly suspicious metaphysical guru'. A man with a grudge against the guru showed up brandishing a knife, and Willie Mackendrick, trying to disarm him, was stabbed to death.

At the age of six, Mackendrick found himself in effect orphaned. His mother, unprepared for the task of bringing up a child single-handed, handed him over to his grandparents and set out to build a career of her own as a dress designer. Mackendrick remembers her as 'a very attractive woman, a dominating red-headed lady, somewhat restless. I didn't see a lot of her; I think she had fights with my grandfather. She had a drinking problem, too, which I always forgave her – but then later on she became religious and joined the Oxford Group, which I find it much harder to forgive. That was when she reformed from her drinking habits. Frankly I preferred her when she was a tippler.' Martha Mackendrick died in America during World War II.

With both his sons dead, Alexander Mackendrick Sr had no further desire to remain in the USA. Early in 1919 he returned with his family – including his young grandson – to Glasgow, where they moved into a house in the prosperous Hillhead district. Mackendrick attended the nearby Hillhead School. Roger MacDougall, his cousin and two years his senior, recalls him not long after his arrival as 'a strange person with a baseball bat, knowing things that I couldn't understand. I saw a lot of him, but we didn't get very close, because we were so different, from different environments.'

The household in which Mackendrick grew up was cultured and artistic, ethically Calvinist though not conventionally religious. His grandmother, Margaret Elizabeth Mackendrick, was a member of the Annan family, the leading art dealers in Glasgow. Both her father, Thomas Annan, and her brother, James Craig Annan, were pioneers in the development of 19th-century photography. Before his retirement, Alexander Mackendrick Sr had managed the family business, T. & R. Annan & Sons on Sauchiehall Street. His was the dominant influence on Mackendrick's childhood; Roger MacDougall describes him as 'a typically Victorian figure, a very cultured gentleman, well-read and laid down the law'. Mackendrick's own memories are less forbidding. 'Today you'd probably look back and see him as a Calvinist, but for his time he was a real liberal. Among other things, he was an atheist. Though he was a tyrant, too, if you like; he ruled this household of women by the tactic of having terrible migraines. And when grandfather had a headache, the whole house was in a state of tension.'

Much of the task of Mackendrick's upbringing devolved upon the elder of his two aunts, Janet, who lived at home; Margaret, the younger sister, worked in London and came home only intermittently. Janet Mackendrick, according to her sister, 'was tremendously fond of Sandy and admired him, and made it possible for him to develop as he should. He was very attached to her; she was his anchor.' Even so, Margaret Mackendrick believed her nephew had a lonely and fairly unhappy childhood. 'It wasn't a very happy arrangement for him; there were no other children his own age. And I think it's bound to have a bad effect, a wounding effect, to have your mother leave you. I think fundamentally you feel injured.'

Some 40 years later, at a difficult time in his life, Mackendrick consulted a Jungian psychotherapist, Alan McGlashan. 'Alan, I think, learned a lot more about the troubles of the movie business than I learned about myself. But he called attention to something that I hadn't myself been conscious of, which was that it must have been a pretty miserable childhood. Partly evidenced by the fact that almost all of it has been wiped clean out of my memory.'

One incident that he does recall suggests that his aversion to religion developed early. Despite his grandfather's atheism, Mackendrick was initially required to attend Sunday School. 'I remember being called into my grandfather's study – a big, book-lined room just inside the front door – and challenged as to how I liked Sunday School. I told him I hated it, because it was intensely boring. He listened very carefully, nodding his head, and said, "No – that is not a sufficient reason for avoiding Sunday School." ' So the next week Mackendrick went back, and argued with the Sunday School teacher – 'because I suppose I was argumentative even then' – on rational grounds. On his return his grandfather called him in again with the same question. Mackendrick repeated the objections he had raised with the teacher. 'And he nodded his head very soon, and said, "Yes – those are sufficient reasons for not going to Sunday School." I loved him for that.'

Intellectually, if not emotionally, the household provided Mackendrick with an ideal environment, one in which his acute, sceptical intelligence could flourish. He did well at school, where his imagination was strongly taken by literature and drama. Margaret Mackendrick recalls her sister 'reading him Chaucer, because they were then doing Chaucer at school, and then he became interested in amateur theatricals. My father had a Highland cloak which was much in use in these things.' One of Mackendrick's earliest pieces of dramatic writing was prompted by a teacher who took his class through Sheridan's *School for Scandal*, concentrating especially on the Screen Scene – which, as Mackendrick later told his own students, is 'the all-time classic illustration of the principle of Dramatic Irony'. Finding the principle much to his taste, he was inspired to write a 'Screen Scene' of his own. 'Thank god the text of it is long forgotten, because it can only have been hideously inept – but I do seem to recall that, as an exercise, it was useful.'[3]

Mackendrick's greatest aptitude, though, was for drawing, for which he manifested an exceptional talent, actively encouraged by his aunt Janet. It was at her insistence that, when he turned 14 – at that time the minimum school-leaving age – he was allowed to enter art school rather than taking the safe office job advocated by his grandfather.

Mackendrick enrolled at the Glasgow School of Art from 1926 to 1929. His work there, according to Margaret Mackendrick, was very highly regarded and there were those who thought he could have made a fine portrait painter. He himself, though, with the perfectionism that would later drive his film-making colleagues to distraction, 'used to throw out everything he did – he didn't like any of it'.

The formal side of his training, the portraits and still-lifes, attracted him much less than mask-making and scenic design. 'I and a couple of other boys that I knew found ourselves hanging around the stage door of the Scottish National Players. We were stage-struck in those days, and I have been in love with the backstage, and the process of theatre, desperately in love with the greasepaint from that day on.' Mackendrick even joined the Players – a reputable troupe, precursors of the Glasgow Citizens Theatre – and took one or two walk-on parts, making 'a huge and terribly important discovery, which is that I have no talent at all as an actor'.[4] Not that it was by any means a wasted experience. 'The best way to learn how to work with actors is to have had experience of trying to act yourself – it will teach you humility if nothing else. . . . It's through appreciation of the work of the stage actor that a would-be director . . . can learn the problems of performance *from the actor's point of view*. Without such experience, and the sensitivity that comes with it, the movie director may well be "at the mercy of the actors". With fine performers this is no problem; with actors of less talent and experience it can be a huge handicap.'[5]

Leaving art school without taking a degree, Mackendrick came to London to find work. Since 1922 Margaret Mackendrick had been secretary to the managing director of J. Walter Thompson, one of the first American advertising agencies to set up in London, and it was to JWT that Mackendrick applied. Starting out on the lowest creative rung, pasting up layouts that others had devised, he soon graduated to designing advertisements in his own right. This too provided good training for a future film director. 'A layout man is given a picture, headlines, copy and captions, and a space in which to arrange these things, and what he has to do is arrange them so that there's an eye path that you follow through this limited space. This is what a director does, except that he also includes the dimension of time – he leads the eye and ear of the audience.'[6]

For the rest of his working life Mackendrick would be an expatriate Scot – just as in Scotland he had been an expatriate American – bringing something of the outsider's viewpoint, at once detached and intrigued, to whatever he did. 'I've always felt,' he told the *Scotsman* in 1962, 'that in London I'm in slightly enemy terrain.'[7] His attitude to Hollywood, when he got there, was if anything even warier.

Mackendrick stayed at JWT throughout the 1930s, developing his graphic skills and becoming one of the agency's top art directors. (Contrary to accounts in most movie reference books, he was never a screenwriter at Pinewood.) 'The training that I got in advertising was invaluable, though it's an industry that I in effect despise – not that it's any worse than the system which it represents, but that's quite bad enough. It's also got more intelligent and talented people in it than any other business I know.'

One of his fellow art directors at JWT, Harold George, remembers Mackendrick as 'a slim, delicate-looking bloke, always talking about films. Very enthusiastic and inventive; he never seemed to think, as I would, "Oh my god, where's the next idea coming from?" But the thing I could never imagine him doing in films was controlling a set and cast and a crew, and making up his mind. Because as an art director he used to have more proofs, I think, than anybody else – he was always changing his mind. It was going for perfection, I suppose. A lot of us would go to a couple of proofs, probably three; but if you hadn't got it right in *eight*, well—'

George recalls being particularly struck by the quality of Mackendrick's work on the 'Horlicks continuity ads' – the classic strip-cartoon advertisements in which sufferers from 'night starvation' achieve a good night's sleep and immediate social success, 'thanks to Horlicks'. 'Most of us just considered those ads in terms of separate, static frames. But Sandy was always trying to get movement into them, something visual that would carry over from one frame to the next. I suppose even then he was thinking in terms of cinema.'

This campaign, which was still running essentially unchanged some 40 years later, was devised, according to Mackendrick, 'by a copywriter named John Barry, in conjunction with myself. Terrible hoax, it was. Barry had managed to get doctors to agree that if you were of a nervous disposition, a hot drink, such as milk, would be very good at night – it did something to the enzymes or things like that. Well, if you mix Horlicks with it, it at least does no harm to the hot milk. And on this basis, the entire campaign was developed.

'It soon became clear that I was better at writing the terrible dialogue than the copywriters were. So I was drawing these strip cartoons and writing the balloons for them, and for things like "Mrs Goodsort of Rinso" – all, I hope, safely forgotten nowadays. I was also working on things like Ponds Cold Cream, for which we bought testimonials from titled people. We had a price

list – so much for an Honourable, so much for a Lady So-and-so, all the way
up to a Countess – we even bought some Greek princesses. I went down with
a fashion photographer and we photographed these people in their grand
manorial halls. I used privately to claim that I was working for a better new
world by exposing the corruptibility of the British aristocracy.'

Following his father's example, Mackendrick married in the face of family
disapproval. His bride was Eileen Ascroft, a journalist working on a
women's magazine. When they married, in March 1934 she was 19 and
Mackendrick 21. Their families considered them too immature, and too
poor, to get married. In retrospect, Mackendrick entirely agrees. 'We were
much too young. And she again was an only child, from a disrupted family
background – so our marriage soon broke up.' Their son, Kerry, was born in
1935. Mackendrick had friends at the *Daily Mirror* and through them
Ascroft landed a job on the paper, writing a regular column as its agony
aunt. She also fell in love with her editor, Hugh Cudlipp, whom she married
after her divorce from Mackendrick in 1943. Kerry Mackendrick remained
with his mother after his parents split up.

Around this time Mackendrick made his first venture into movies, with a
script called *War on Wednesday*. The cinema had fascinated him since his
schooldays, when he would play truant to see Fritz Lang films (*Dr Mabuse*
being a particular favourite) or Douglas Fairbanks in *The Black Pirate*. He
also loved cartooning – 'If I hadn't been a movie director, I would like to
have been a political cartoonist' – and the screenplay he now devised had as
its hero a newspaper cartoonist whose friend is killed by sinister Teutonic
villains. 'So, not knowing what they're up to, he manages to find out by the
ingenious expedient of burying in his cartoons clues which *he* doesn't know
the meaning of, to suggest to the villains that he knows more than he does;
and that's the central device of it.'

Having no idea how to lay out a movie script, Mackendrick produced in
effect an extended version of one of his Horlicks ads: a series of drawings
with dialogue captions, pasted up in sequence. He showed it to a colleague at
Thompson's, William Connor (later well-known as the *Mirror* columnist
Cassandra). 'Bill said, "Well, I don't know about the story, but the dialogue
is atrocious." I said, "That's what I thought – could you help me out with
it?", and he said, "Not on your life." ' Mackendrick accordingly turned to
his cousin, Roger MacDougall, who had also moved to London and had
taken up songwriting, playing the saxophone and writing satirical verses for
nightclub singers.

'So Roger and I rewrote my storyboard. He had an agent, a variety agent
who managed ventriloquists and acrobatic acts, and also Roger's songs. And
this man saw his chance to become a film agent – he took this damned thing,
and sold it, to everyone's total astonishment.' The script was sold to
Associated British Pictures, extensively rewritten, and filmed under the title

of *Midnight Menace*. MacDougall and Mackendrick were given Original Story credit. 'What they'd done was taken the central idea and thrown away the rest entirely. Later Roger and I wondered whether, if they'd followed our story closely, it would have made much difference, and we decided yes, it would have been even worse. It was a terrible film.'

Mackendrick exaggerates. Though no masterpiece, *Midnight Menace* buckets along cheerfully from incident to implausible incident, with dialogue snappy enough to give the impression – if rarely the substance – of wit. The final showdown (which, with pilotless bombers homing in on their target, strikingly anticipates Hitler's V-1s) is staged with a certain verve. And if the hero and heroine (Charles Farrell and Margaret Vyner) scarcely rise above their material, Fritz Kortner – Dr Schön in Pabst's *Die Büchse der Pandora* – makes a relishable villain. (Fourth-billed, playing a heavy called 'Socks', is Danny Green, whom Mackendrick later gave the best role of his career as One-Round in *The Ladykillers*.) Sinclair Hill, a veteran from the silent era, directs adequately, never quite screwing the tension up tight enough. It's tempting to wonder what Hitchcock might have made of it.

At this period, Mackendrick had no particular ambition to become a film director. 'I was just trying to earn a living; making movies was something I drifted into.'[8] While *War on Wednesday* was becoming *Midnight Menace*, he began writing film scripts of a rather different kind: seven-minute animated cinema commercials for Horlicks, to be made by George Pal. Pal, the master of stop-action puppet animation, had set up a studio at Eindhoven in the Netherlands, and Mackendrick worked there with him on the design of the films.

Between 1936 and 1938 Mackendrick scripted and storyboarded five of these commercials. Filmed in glowing thirties Technicolor, they are still a delight to watch – both for the inventive fluency of Pal's animation technique, and for their exuberant narrative drive. Various individuals – soldiers, sailors, airmen, cowboys, South Sea islanders – prove incapable, through lethargy and exhaustion, of doing whatever they should. A nightly cup of Horlicks – and triumph ensues. Within this formula, Pal and Mackendrick work ingenious variations, often spoofing established movie genres – cowboy pictures, swashbucklers, jungle adventures. Genre conventions are cheerfully mixed: the villain in *Love on the Range* sings all his lines grand-opera style, and the fight between hero and witch-doctor in *South Sea Sweethearts* gets a ringside commentary from a talking juju stick. There's even, in the pirate assault on an unwary ship in *What Ho She Bumps*, a foretaste of a similar episode in *High Wind in Jamaica*.

After the outbreak of war Mackendrick continued to work at J. Walter Thompson. As a US citizen, he was exempt from call-up – and in any case suffered from asthma, which would have ruled out active service. Apart from some air-raid warden duty in Soho, his contribution to the war effort was to make propaganda films.

During the war the Ministry of Information became the country's biggest advertiser, and Thompson's took on a good deal of MoI work. Much of it was handled by a newly formed animation studio within the agency, run by the team of Halas and Batchelor. John Halas, who had trained in Budapest under his fellow-Hungarian George Pal, arrived in London with his English wife Joy Batchelor in 1940 and set up as an autonomous unit within JWT. Several of Halas-Batchelor's earliest productions were scripted and story-boarded by Mackendrick.

John Halas attributes to Mackendrick's influence 'whatever little skill I have in thinking about story structure, character development and continuity. Sandy was a very good discipline to know; he assisted us – Joy Batchelor and myself – a great deal in teaching us how to prepare a script visually. It was very much the same approach which I experienced later with Serge Eisenstein – who was also an advocate of pre-production storyboards – relating the script to detailed story-sketches, working on the details before the crew is sent on the floor. And Sandy was a brilliant draughtsman, his character sketches were excellent, always getting down to basics, so we never had any trouble in identification.'

A series of four propaganda shorts, scripted by Mackendrick and animated by Halas-Batchelor, were made for distribution in the Middle East. Only one of these 'Abu' films – *Abu's Poisoned Well* – is extant; it features some vivid characterisation, with Hitler as a dachshund-headed cobra and Mussolini as a bloated frog. Mackendrick also helped design the first British feature-length animated film – not *Animal Farm*, as is generally believed, but an instructional film for the Admiralty called, blandly enough, *Handling Ships*. Sixty-five minutes long and made in full colour, it was started in 1943 but not finished until 1945. When it eventually appeared, *Documentary Newsletter* was impressed. 'Except for a few fancy feet at the start, every part of this film is insistently lucid. A first-rate example of training film technique.'[9] Regrettably, no prints of this forgotten epic seems to have survived.

By this stage, Mackendrick was working with Halas-Batchelor on a freelance basis, since the animation unit had been hijacked by the MoI and moved out to Hertfordshire, away from German bombs. He had also made his directorial debut, though without causing any great public stir.

Following his contribution to *Midnight Menace*, Roger MacDougall had gone on to become a regular screenwriter. In 1942 he and Mackendrick set up their own production company and made three films for the MoI – succinct little 90-second 'instructionals', to be released uncredited as items in the *Pathé Gazette* newsreel. Scripting was largely MacDougall's department, and direction Mackendrick's. No prints of the first of these shorts,

*Save Your Bacon*, have come to light, but its alternative title, *Kitchen Waste for Pigs*, probably says it all. It featured drawings by Mackendrick, as did *Contraries*, in which Lewis Carroll's Walrus and Carpenter collect paper salvage for recycling.

The third short, *Nero*, ran to live actors – only two, but an impressive cast for a 1½-minute film. Alastair Sim plays the title role, with George Cole as a schoolboy wandering round a museum. Nero's statue comes to life and boasts – in verse – of his misdeeds. Cole, distinctly unimpressed, retorts that they pale beside Hitler's. Only the burning of Rome arouses his disapproval. 'That was wasting good fuel – and that's what I call a *real* crime!' he exclaims, crowning the Emperor with his own fiddle. Throughout this bizarre trifle Sim hams outrageously, while the camera jumps from one fixed position to another. It would take the most fanatical auteurist to detect a major directorial talent in the making here.

There's more of the later Mackendrick in a short from this period that he didn't direct but only co-scripted (again with MacDougall): *Subject for Discussion*. The brief, from the Health Education Council, was to make a film about venereal disease for the general public. 'The armed forces were making scads of films on gonorrhea and so on, which they forced the poor servicemen to sit through. But the general exhibitors, quite rightly, just wouldn't accept such things. The idea of showing VD films in public cinemas was in a way a complete contradiction, for most young couples, of the purpose of going to the cinema. So our device, which I'm really rather proud of, was not to make a film about VD, but a film – which isn't very good, but could have been a lot worse – about whether VD is a fit topic for discussion.'

The film, directed by Hans Nieter and running some 15 minutes, skilfully intertwines two episodes. In one, a young boy, son of respectable middle-class parents, is losing his sight; the doctor diagnoses inherited syphilis, and tactfully confronts the father. In the other, the same doctor, invited to lead a discussion at the local ARP post, proposes VD as the topic – an idea received with distaste by the prissy Senior Warden, but supported by the other personnel, male and female. Gradually it becomes evident that the first story is being related by the doctor to overcome the Warden's objections in the second story.

Despite some stilted acting and scripting, the film is surprisingly effective. (Or perhaps not so surprisingly, given that Basil Wright was Associate Producer.) And in the scenes involving the child threatened with blindness, it verges on an intensity that anticipates *Mandy* (in which, as Mackendrick has disclosed, he had at the back of his mind congenital disease as an analogue of emotional blight). As the nature of the boy's ailment is revealed, he's being given eyedrops. The nurse hands him a cloth to hold over his eyes. He stands up and, still holding the cloth in position, walks straight up to the camera, confronting us with a pitiful image of vulnerable grief.

*Subject for Discussion* was successful enough to give rise to a sequel, *Subject Discussed*. Mackendrick, though, had no hand in it, being by then fully occupied elsewhere. In the early summer of 1943, he heard about an offbeat Anglo-American unit being formed in North Africa, which might have use for his services. 'So I went and spent about three-quarters of a day sitting waiting for this guy to show up. And when he did he was a big blond sort of character, very energetic, very fast-talking, and he said, "Mackendrick, I really don't have time, I'm just dashing off to Africa, but tell me who you are and what you've done." So I rattled through my background in advertising, photography, commercial art, propaganda, scriptwriting and so on. He cut me short and said, "Listen, you're absolutely ideal for this thing. Moreover it's very urgent. This is Monday – I want you to be in Algiers on Thursday." I said, "I can't do that," and he said, "Oh yes you can, I'll expedite it for you." And he did.'

The 'big, blond character', it transpired, was Richard Crossman, later to become a Labour Cabinet Minister, and the unit into which Mackendrick had been unceremoniously recruited was the Psychological Warfare Branch. This, according to the military historian Charles Cruickshank, 'was set up in Algiers and attached to Eisenhower's headquarters. . . . Its purpose was to handle all propaganda in the Mediterranean theatre, and it included representatives of [British and US propaganda organisations]. Neither side, British or American, was superior to the other – the function was simply to co-ordinate the propaganda directives of the two countries, and generally to ensure that a common line was followed.'[10]

The structure of the PWB was also unconventional. Mackendrick describes it as 'a four-way structure, in that a civilian, like me, would have under me military people, corporals or whatnot, and over me a major. But I also had a military equivalent, who had civilians above and below him – so there were two people to every job. Enormously cumbersome, but it meant that we were all fused together, American and British, military and civilian, interlarded all the way down in this ragbag thing.'

Mackendrick flew out to Africa 'in an old converted DC-something with a wooden broomstick stuck out the back to look like a machine gun'. He arrived in Algiers to find several people that he knew – ex-journalists and copywriters – already there. What he didn't know, since no one had told him, was what he had been recruited for. Crossman duly arrived, went down with a leg infection, and was flown straight back to London. 'So I was put on to his American side-kick, C. D. Jackson; he was a partner of Henry Luce, they'd started Time-Life together. He was the suavest American you've ever seen, immaculately dressed in this sweltering heat – instead of these silly baggy shorts the rest of us were wearing – and he called me in and said, "Do sit down. I *have* heard your name, but just what did you come out here to do?" '

Eventually, Mackendrick was assigned to the 'leaflet team', whose job was to produce propaganda sheets to undermine the enemy morale. 'We were attached to battalion HQ, so we were just behind the front line, which paradoxically is one of the safest places to be. Cities are vulnerable to bombs, and the front line is obviously extremely dangerous – but just behind it is safer than anywhere.'

Mackendrick landed in Italy in September 1943, in the wake of the 5th Army, and for the next nine months followed the war's slow progress up the peninsula. Regularly once a week, he and his colleagues would produce an issue of *Frontpost*, a single-fold, four-page leaflet to be dispatched – by plane or shell – to the German troops, inciting them to despondency and desertion. His main task was to draw maps of the Russian front, showing the defeats being suffered there by the Wehrmacht. 'Also I had to search out print-shops that had Ws, because Italian has no Ws and German is full of them. And do the layout and paste-up. After a bit I got bored with this, so I asked if I could put in some political cartoons.'

A Mackendrick cartoon first appeared in *Frontpost* of 18 November 1943, and thereafter featured in almost every issue until 1 June 1944, three days before the Allies took Rome. 'I had to be quite subtle – because how do you do caricatures when your audience is the enemy? So I tried to see things through the eyes of the ordinary German soldier – he was a noble and courageous figure, but surrounded by betrayers in the shape of his leaders.'

On 5 June 1944 Mackendrick entered Rome in the uniform of an assimilated US captain. 'I'd pulled off quite a neat one, because I was taken on as a British civilian, but then saw the chance to claim my original nationality. So I changed to American battledress, which was much more comfortable, and qualified for PX privileges, which were far better than anything you got at the NAAFI. But I was still a civilian, paid at British Army rates. It was all very complex.'

Among the problems facing the Allied administration in Rome was what to do about the Italian film industry which, based at Mussolini's grandiose Cinecittà, had grown into one of the country's largest industries. A Film Board was set up under the chairmanship of US Rear Admiral Emery W. Stone, whose attitude was brutally simple: 'The so-called Italian film was invented by the fascists, therefore it has to be suppressed. . . . Anyway, Italy is an agricultural country. What would it need a film industry for?'[11]

Fortunately, not all the Allies took such an uncompromising view. Though Cinecittà was requisitioned as a refugee camp, the Italian movie industry was allowed to survive, under Allied supervision – which apparently consisted for a while solely of Alexander Mackendrick. 'They looked around for somebody who knew something about film. And there was nobody except this strange hybrid, half-American, half-British, who had worked in an advertising agency. So for a short period, before other people were moved in above me, I was Gauleiter of all films made in Italy. My job was to find out what the Italian film-makers were doing, and tell them to stop it.'[12]

Mackendrick was allotted an office with huge columns and a marble floor – palatial, if slightly underfurnished. 'There was a chair, and a telephone on the chair. If you wanted to sit down you had to put the telephone on the floor. And there I received applications for making films, which I turned down.'[13] When this grew monotonous, he began to look for projects he might be able to approve. One such was submitted by his interpreter, the actor-director Marcello Pagliero, a Soho-born Italian. Mackendrick read the script – 'It seemed to be unexceptionable – it was about partisans being tortured by beastly fascists' – and was taken to a night-club to meet the lead actress, 'a very vivacious dark lady who sang sexy songs and kissed bald men on the top of their heads'.[14] This, it turned out, was Anna Magnani, and the film for which Mackendrick gained official approval was Rossellini's *Rome Open City*.

In fact, as he later learned, much of the film had already been shot on contraband stock. 'So although I wasn't aware of it at the time – and probably wouldn't have objected if I had been – I was the victim of a conspiracy of partisans, who had infiltrated my unit.' The unit in question was the PWB Film Production Section, since Mackendrick, in addition to his censorial role, had begun to make his own contribution to Italian film.

One of his colleagues in the PWB was Peter Proud, an art director for Hitchcock before the war, and later a director at Pinewood. A fellow-Glaswegian, he was a contemporary of Mackendrick's at Hillhead High School, though their paths hadn't crossed. The two were assigned to work on a documentary short, *I Granai del popolo*, with Mackendrick writing the script and Proud directing. 'Sandy and I had become great friends. He was a charming man. And shy – quite different from the Mackendrick that's known in the industry now. Anyway, I went off and shot this film, came back to Rome – and Sandy didn't like my stuff at all, and reshot most of it. That was my first intimation of the severer side of his nature.'

*I Granai del popolo* was a propaganda piece aimed at Italian farmers, to persuade them not to hoard their surplus grain, or dispose of it on the black market, but to sell it to government warehouses for general distribution. As such, it was typical of the PWB unit's output, much of which consisted of mildly tendentious local news items to be added to a weekly newsreel, *Notizie del mondo libero*, sent out from London. In a memo to his superiors, dated February 1945, Mackendrick lists 19 such items filmed over the previous three months, including the trial of Azzolini, former Governor of the Fascist Bank; Partisan Day celebrations in Rome; and a rally celebrating the return of the International Boy Scout Movement in Italy.

By far the most remarkable footage filmed by Mackendrick's unit concerned the aftermath of an atrocity known as the Massacre of the Fosse Ardeatine. On 23 March 1944, after Mussolini had been deposed and Rome occupied by the Germans, 33 SS men were killed by a partisan bomb in the Via Rasella, off the Piazza Barberini. On the direct orders of Hitler, reprisals were exacted. 335 hostages were rounded up: Jews, partisans, residents of the Via Rasella, petty criminals from Regina Coeli jail. All were male; the oldest was 74, the youngest 15. They were taken to the Fosse Ardeatine, a complex of caves just outside the city, and there they were shot in batches, kneeling, each with a bullet through the back of the neck, and the caves were dynamited in over their bodies.[15]

After the liberation of Rome the bodies were exhumed, and the Italians who had helped round up the victims were put on trial. The PWB unit was assigned to cover these events and compile a propaganda film for exhibition in the liberated territories of Europe. Mackendrick's team consisted of about eight men, himself included. 'You could say I was effectively the producer, because I didn't speak much Italian; Marcello Pagliero was my assistant, but he really directed it.' Others in the team included the editor Mario Serandrei and, as cameraman, Giovanni Ventimiglia, whose father had been cinematographer on Hitchcock's earliest movies.

More than once, Mackendrick was taken aback by his own reactions to what he was filming. During the exhumation, 'we sat there wearing ammonia masks, while they pulled out these decomposing bodies. Now bodies tend to rot at the neck. And at one point a workman was handling a corpse, and the head fell off and rolled away. He reached round and got hold of the *wrong head*, and was putting it back with the torso. And I found myself screaming with rage at him – then realised the terrible slapstick humour of it, and I and the unit broke into paroxysms of laughter, which went on for about five minutes. The laughter was obviously a release.'

The senior Fascist official tried for his part in the massacre was the Police Chief, Caruso, who was sentenced to death. Mackendrick filmed him being seated on a kitchen chair and shot by firing squad. 'I'd never seen that kind of formal violence before, and I remember feeling strangely unmoved – merely surprised that when a lot of lead hits you, you get thrown that far. Then I went back and ran the footage we'd shot on the moviola. And that's when I felt the after-shock – the shock of re-running the death of someone you've just seen die.'

The most dramatic event, though, occurred at Caruso's trial. A key witness was the governor of Regina Coeli prison, Caretta, by all accounts a cautious anti-fascist who had complied only under protest with Caruso's demand for hostages. While he was giving evidence, a crowd – which included relatives of the victims – broke down the outside gates, stormed in and dragged the wretched Caretta from the courtroom. Mackendrick and his unit followed. 'They dragged him out and laid him on the tram-rails for the tram to run over him. But the tram-driver refused. So they hoisted Caretta up and threw him over the parapet into the Tiber, and a couple of young men went in and beat him to death with oars. All of it covered by us, in pictures and sound. That is what *I* call documentary.'

The footage never reached London. 'It was all vaulted, labelled, dispatched, but patriotic Italians – I suspect – just lost it. Quite rightly.' The rest of the material, it seems, reached London safely, and was assembled into a short film, with a commentary by the novelist Ignazio Silone. But this too has suffered an obscure fate, with no copy listed in any archive.

At least some of the PWB footage appears to have been incorporated into a 70-minute documentary, *Giorni di Gloria*, released in Italy in 1945. This was in three parts: some partisan episodes, directed by Giuseppe de Santis; a section on the Fosse Ardeatine, credited to Pagliero, which must have been shot by Mackendrick's unit; and the trial of Caruso and lynching of Caretta. Credited director on this last section was Luchino Visconti, who wasn't a member of the PWB unit nor, Mackendrick believes, of any other film crew present at the trial. 'We were the only team that hired Italian technicians. All the others were forces units, so they weren't allowed to. What the credit probably means is that Visconti supervised the editing of the material – direction of the editor, so to speak.

'It's horrible to admit, but one of the most interesting and exciting – and even rewarding – times of my life was during the war.' Mackendrick returned to England after VE-Day with a sense of anti-climax, and no clear idea what he wanted to do. What he didn't want to do was go back into advertising. J. Walter Thompson had kept his job for him, 'and it was clear that one could have done pretty well, and indeed probably have become quite wealthy. But at that stage, and after the things I'd been doing in Italy, I knew I really couldn't go back to that.' Instead, he renewed his association with Roger MacDougall, who had joined Merlin Productions, a small outfit run by Michael Hankinson making documentaries for the MoI. Mackendrick spent several months with Merlin working on 'the tamest possible sort of things. How a combine harvester works, and cultural reviews of Kew Gardens – slightly surprising after the stuff I'd been shooting in Rome.'

A far more interesting project with John Halas never got off the ground. Around 1941 he and Mackendrick had planned a weekly two-minute animated film on a topical political subject. The concept was now revived – David Low, no less, was interested in participating – and three pilot films were made, under the title *The Pocket Cartoon*. 'They were very good ideas,' Halas recalls, 'but we could never lick the problem of production. To produce 52 two-minuters a year would have absorbed our total attention. And the distributors had no faith in it; they couldn't see where to fit it in.'

Merlin, meanwhile, had hit financial problems and was cutting staff. 'So

Roger, very typically of the Scots, came to me and said, "Listen, you're my cousin, that means if we have to cut down you're the first to go." So I quit, which was the luckiest thing that ever happened to me. With all this background, I thought it was about time I got into the movies proper.'

Mackendrick accordingly applied to Ealing Studios. He had good contacts there: MacDougall had written several scripts for the studio, including one for Basil Dearden's *The Bells Go Down*, and Peter Proud's assistant before the war had been Michael Relph, now Dearden's regular producer. On the strength of this double introduction Mackendrick was engaged as script-writer and 'sketch artist' on the current Relph-Dearden production, *Saraband for Dead Lovers*.

This was in 1946, altogether a significant year for Mackendrick. That Christmas, at the Chelsea Arts Ball, he met Hilary Lloyd, then working in the publicity department at Denham Studios. She was 21, 13 years his junior – although he looked, as he always has, far younger than his age. They were married almost exactly two years later.

Ealing, both as film-making entity and as social phenomenon, has been more extensively analysed than any other British studio, most notably by Charles Barr in his definitive study, *Ealing Studios*. In terms of continuity and consistency of output, it was perhaps the nearest the British film industry ever came to a studio after the classic Hollywood pattern. Like, say, Warners in the 1930s, Ealing had its roster of personnel – directors, writers, producers and technicians – on permanent salary; its pool of actors who reappeared in movie after movie; its recurrent thematic and social preoccupations; and, derived from all of these, a recognisable house-style of film-making.

In two important respects, though, Ealing differed from its Hollywood counterparts. It had no stars of its own (with the sole, almost accidental, exception of Alec Guinness); character actors in plenty, but no stars. And the often viciously competitive atmosphere, the constant undertone of fear fostered by the Hollywood studio heads, was almost wholly absent. In its place Ealing instilled, to a degree which sometimes seems hard to credit, a supportive and co-operative ethos among its personnel. It really was, by all accounts, what it proclaimed itself to be: The Studio with the Team Spirit.

Though this slogan was a legacy from Basil Dean, the original head of the studio, it could have been tailor-made for his successor, Michael Balcon – not least for its faintly public-school, all-together-chaps flavour. Balcon, shrewd in financial matters, had otherwise little in common with such legendary monsters as Harry Cohn or Louis B. Mayer. His role at Ealing was often likened to that of a benevolent headmaster, presiding tolerantly over (in Monja Danischewsky's celebrated phrase) 'Mr Balcon's Academy for Young Gentlemen'. Projects were agreed, and production decisions reached, at the Round Table meetings attended by all the senior personnel, where

Balcon often let himself be overruled by majority decision, with the standing joke: 'Well, if you fellows feel so strongly in favour, on my head be it.'[16]

Personally unassuming, deeply and unquestioningly patriotic, Balcon set out to produce an essentially indigenous cinema – films, in his own words, 'projecting Britain and the British character'. The studio itself, overlooking a village green on the outskirts of London, might have been expressly designed for such a task. To Danischewsky, arriving to become Director of Publicity, it had 'the air of a family business. . . . The administrative block which faced the green looked like a country cottage and was separated from the studio proper by a rose garden'[17] – to which was later added a trio of beehives.

This benign working environment inevitably entailed certain limitations, both on the films that emerged from it and on those who made them. Many of the studio's directors (Mackendrick not least) came to believe they were spoilt by their sheltered existence at Ealing, unfitted for the tougher movie-making world elsewhere. And the films themselves often verged on – and in later years increasingly succumbed to – a sentimental complacency, with potentially disruptive elements repressed or excluded. For all his democratic practices, Balcon was notoriously unwilling to admit into his pictures anything he found distasteful – such as sex, or any serious attack on British institutions.

At the time of Mackendrick's arrival, though, the Ealing mould had yet to set with its later inflexibility, and it was still possible for atypical movies to be made there. Indeed, the picture to which he was assigned, *Saraband for Dead Lovers*, was in some ways a thoroughly un-Ealing enterprise – partly because it had been wished on Balcon against his better judgement.

After taking over at Ealing in 1938 Balcon often attacked the monopolistic power of the Rank Organisation. In 1944 he performed an agile *volte-face,* concluding a pact with the enemy on highly favourable terms: Rank would provide 50 per cent of the finance, and guaranteed distribution, for all Ealing films; Rank's stable of contract artists would be available on request; and Ealing would retain full artistic control over all its productions.

Now and again, though, Rank were able to exact a *quid pro quo,* and *Saraband* was one of them. It owed its genesis to a mirage which, every few years, floats seductively before the eyes of British film-makers: the dream of breaking into the American market. At the end of the war, with weekly attendances at record levels and the British cinema flourishing as never before, Rank had decided the time was ripe for a renewed assault. This, as usual, meant big-budget, prestige productions designed to 'beat the Yanks at their own game'; hence such costly pratfalls as Gabriel Pascal's ponderous *Caesar and Cleopatra*, and a woefully inept musical, *London Town*. (To be fair, Rank weren't alone in their ambitions; Alexander Korda's candidates for transatlantic success, *Bonnie Prince Charlie* and *Anna Karenina*, flopped even more resoundingly.) *Saraband*, urged upon a sceptical Balcon with the incentive of some additional funding, was Ealing's contribution to the campaign.

A lavish costume drama, and the studio's first colour production, *Saraband* was the most expensive of all Ealing films. The story, from a romantic novel by Helen Simpson (another of whose books was adapted by Hitchcock for *Under Capricorn*), was set in late 17th-century Germany and dealt with the love affair between the Swedish adventurer Count Koenigsmark and Sophie Dorothea, wife of Prince George Louis of Hanover (later King George I of England). It was the kind of subject more usually tackled by Rank's subsidiary Gainsborough, one of whose top stars, Stewart Granger, was brought in to play Koenigsmark. However, Michael Relph, as both producer and art director, was determined 'to make a *serious* historical film, as opposed to the Gainsborough *Wicked Lady* sort of thing. So in our rather arrogant way we wanted to impose our own style on the film.'

The creation of this visual style was to be Mackendrick's job. Relph, to whom Peter Proud had enthused over Mackendrick's artistic skills, decided to put them to use by storyboarding *Saraband* – an unusual technique at that period, and possibly the first time it had been used in a British production. This, he hoped, would not only lend the film visual distinction, but help to control costs by reaching decisions on the drawing-board rather than during valuable shooting time.

Mackendrick accompanied Relph to Prague to scout locations. As always, his enthusiasm was tireless: Relph describes him 'rushing up every steeple in Prague when you could see perfectly well from the ground that it wasn't any good. But he would never accept anybody else's word.' Mackendrick, for his part, retorts that 'Michael is covering up for the fact that he doesn't like heights. One of the spires was very tall, with a tiny balcony and this terrific bird's eye view of Prague. I managed to get Michael up the stairs, but when he got outside he turned his face to the wall and wouldn't turn round. So he never saw the view.'

Mackendrick's co-writer on *Saraband* was John Dighton, one of Ealing's most experienced scriptwriters. The studio, Mackendrick believes, was 'worried that Johnny was essentially a word-monger – they felt he needed somebody to give the whole thing visual flair. And because I was weak on dialogue, and therefore protected myself by thinking in terms of spectacle, the script has all these elaborate visual sequences – like the sword fight at the end. But Johnny taught me more than I can say. Two people in my life – the other was Clifford Odets – taught me in terms of how to structure movies. Johnny was a superb craftsman. We did the old business – we had an office together, one wrote and the other paced. He would hand me something and say, "Go over that and see if you can do anything with it." And what I would do was cut down his dialogue, and introduce business and so on. Then I would work out something in visual terms, and put in terribly bad dialogue that Johnny would rewrite. And in the end, trained by him, I became not a bad dialogue writer. I owe him an immense debt for that.'

Mackendrick also gained invaluable experience from the storyboarding process. 'I had a marvellous training as a director. I stood at the elbow of Basil Dearden; and he, on a set-plan, said, "I want a shot from here," and I'd say, "Well, if you want it like that, *this* will be in the background; do you want it like this?' And he'd say, "No, bigger," or, "Farther away," or, "I want it to pan over here" – and I did this very, very rapidly in little sketches, then went away and did about a thousand drawings.'[18] When it came to the shoot, though, the technique proved less than popular, as Relph discovered: 'I thought it would help Basil. But by drawing every frame, we put him into a strait-jacket. And the actors didn't like it, so eventually it just wasn't followed.'

Granger, in particular, took the storyboard as a deliberate personal insult, though his resentment was directed not at Mackendrick but at Relph, 'a very supercilious gentleman and quite impervious to my charms. He showed his contempt for actors by having all the scenes sketched on a board with our positions marked and instructions on when we should move.'[19] Actors, Granger felt, were altogether poorly regarded at Ealing. 'The producers were God; next in order of divine importance came the writers, then the directors, then the technicians, and a long way after them came the actors. If they could have made their films with puppets they'd have been much happier.'[20] Even so, he rated *Saraband* 'one of the few [of his films] I've always been proud of'.[21]

Not without reason. *Saraband* is in many ways a better film than its drab reputation might suggest. For one thing, it's consistently good to look at; the Prague locations are atmospherically used and the interiors, all rich dark reds and browns, evoke (as Raymond Durgnat comments) 'a stifling oppressiveness'.[22] Much of this visual intensity, according to the film's cinematographer, Douglas Slocombe, can be credited to Mackendrick's drawings. 'They were absolutely magnificent – a lot of the work on *Saraband* did, fairly slavishly, copy Sandy's set-ups. And I enjoyed doing it, because it gave me a chance to use colour for the first time, and also to break almost all the Technicolor rules. One was told to light everything flat, which was anathema to me, so I treated it exactly like black-and-white and achieved dark, shadowy areas, with everything strongly cross-lit, that I really wasn't supposed to.' His recalcitrance paid off, especially in the final sword fight in which Koenigsmark meets his death, the sense of danger heightened as men lunge and feint at each other out of pools of darkness.

The film benefits from what Durgnat calls 'a quiet cynicism about the dignity of history'.[23] The Hanoverian court (source, we're reminded, of all future British royals) operates as a brutal system in which everything – innocence and idealism no less than cupidity – can be turned to account in the acquisition of power. The destruction of ingenuous Sophie Dorothea (Joan Greenwood, rather miscast) attains poignant force; the scene of her wedding-night rape by George Louis (Peter Bull at his most gross) can stand comparison with its counterpart in Stroheim's *Greed*. *Saraband* also marks the first appearance – in a fairly elementary, black-and-white form – of one of Mackendrick's key themes, the clash between innocence and experience, and the machiavellian Countess von Platen (a portrayal of controlled malevolence from Flora Robson) prefigures his gallery of ruthless manipulators from Joseph Macroon to J. J. Hunsecker.

Where *Saraband* fails is in its narrative pacing, reined in as it is by a sense of careful good taste. Relph was only too successful in purging the film of all taint of Gainsborough; a touch of the sheer vulgar gusto of *The Man in Grey* or *The Wicked Lady* might have been just what was needed. Some years later, working on a historical project of his own, *Mary Queen of Scots*, Mackendrick cited *Saraband* as a prime example of the kind of film he didn't want, full of 'talk meant to be listened to, rather than urgently acted upon. . . . What I hated about *Saraband* was a tone which I cannot blame wholly on Basil or Michael or Johnny, the Victorian relish for a grand manner. The archness and the loftiness and the swish of silk.'[24]

*Saraband* was indifferently received in Britain, even more so in America, and is widely believed – though Balcon was always cagey about box-office returns – to have been the biggest loss-maker in the studio's history. So it was fortunate that, not long before *Saraband*'s disappointing release, shooting had started on one of Ealing's all-time commercial, and critical, smash hits. Not that Balcon expected it to be anything of the sort. Nor, come to that, did anyone else concerned with it – least of all, perhaps, its director, Alexander Mackendrick.

# 2 Whisky Galore!

'Since our way of seeing things is literally our way of living, the process of communication is in fact the process of community.'[1]

Raymond Williams, *The Long Revolution*

'It looks like a home-movie; it doesn't look as if it was made by a professional at all. And it wasn't.'

Alexander Mackendrick

The Ealing film that succeeded, where *Saraband for Dead Lovers* so dismally failed, in breaking into the American market was a modest, black-and-white regional comedy whose production values were so shaky that it was very nearly released as a second feature. It also scored a hit in France, where it lent its name to a thousand *boîtes de nuit*. Yet *Whisky Galore!* would probably never have been made at all had the studio's Director of Publicity not started to feel restless.

Monja Danischewsky, born in Archangel into a Russian-Jewish family, joined Ealing in 1938, soon after Balcon had taken over the studio. A gregarious man with an irrepressible sense of humour, he had handled Ealing's publicity for ten years with ebullient flair. Among other achievements, he raised the standard of British movie advertising – hitherto drably mediocre – by persuading such artists as Henry Moore, John Piper and Edward Ardizzone to design Ealing's posters. But by 1948 he was growing tired of the job, and talked of resigning. Balcon, who hated letting anyone leave, suggested in desperation that Danischewsky might like to become a producer. He could choose any story he wanted, subject to Balcon's approval. The only condition was that the film must be made entirely on location.

The reason behind this stipulation was a piece of bungling ineptitude by the British Government. Struggling with a vast balance-of-payments deficit, and noting that Hollywood movies were taking $70 million a year out of the country, the Chancellor of the Exchequer, Hugh Dalton, had slapped a 75 per cent customs duty on all imported films. The British film industry – whom Dalton had not thought to consult – protested in dismay, but too late; the Motion Picture Association of America countered by suspending all shipments of American films to Britain. To avoid the fearful prospect of the nation's cinemas running out of movies to exhibit, the Government now coolly appealed to the patriotic spirit of British film-makers: would they, in the national interest, please step up production?

With admirable restraint, the producers responded positively. J. Arthur Rank announced an ambitious programme of 47 first-feature films to be made in 1948 and, hoping to offload a little of the burden, offered Ealing additional funding to make one or two extra pictures. Balcon was willing to oblige, but he had no space. Ealing was a tiny studio and all sound stages were committed to existing projects. Other studios were fully booked. If an extra picture was to be made, it would have to be shot on location. Hence the terms of his proposal to Danischewsky, who for his part was happy to agree. He already had a property in mind, ideally suited to a location shoot: Compton Mackenzie's recently published comic novel *Whisky Galore*.

Mackenzie had based his story on a wartime incident which has passed into Scottish legend. In the early hours of 5 February 1941, a freighter named the SS *Politician*, outward bound from Liverpool, ran aground in the channel between the Hebridean islands of Eriskay and South Uist. On board, along with pianos, bicycles and a consignment of Jamaican bank-notes, were 22,000 cases of Scotch whisky. Under prevailing conditions, with whisky stringently rationed, this was clearly a gift from the gods, and boats from every island for miles around were soon heading for the wreck. As near as anyone can estimate, some 7,000 cases were 'rescued', and 15 years later a few bottles of 'Polly' (as the *Politician*'s liquid cargo was dubbed) were still circulating in the islands, along with the occasional Jamaican ten-shilling note.[2]

At the time of the shipwreck Compton Mackenzie was commander of the Home Guard on the island of Barra and had no doubt where his duty lay. 'Word went round,' he recalled, 'that the people of Eriskay were accumulating case upon case of whisky. Kenny MacCormick suggested that he should go across with an expedition from the north end of Barra. He came back in the morning as black as a crow. . . . In a bag he was carrying about six dozen bottles of whisky.' Much to his satisfaction, Mackenzie could now once more offer his visitors a drink 'without hoping they would not help themselves too lavishly'.[3]

In his novel, the local Home Guard commander has become a pompous Englishman named Paul Waggett, whose moral outlook is a good deal less flexible. Most of the plot concerns his indignant attempts to prevent the islanders making off with the contraband liquor – attempts undermined by the Scots' vastly superior guile and tactical skill, and by the defection of Waggett's subordinate, Sergeant Odd. Though English, Odd unhesitatingly sides with the islanders, not least because he hopes to marry Peggy Macroon, daughter of the local postmaster.

*Whisky Galore*, though a self-contained story, forms a sequel to an earlier

Mackenzie novel, *Keep the Home Guard Turning*. Both are set on the islands of Great Todday and Little Todday (lightly disguised versions of South Uist and Barra), and feature the same characters. Both, too, derive much of their comedy from the rivalry between the islands, exacerbated by religion – the people of Great Todday being Presbyterian and those of Little Todday Roman Catholic. As a novel, *Whisky Galore* is an amiable, rambling affair, relying on copious local colour to make up for any lack of narrative drive, and lapsing into dire sentimentality with the introduction of Sergeant Odd's salt-of-the-earth old Cockney mum. The all-important shipwreck doesn't even occur until halfway through the book.

To pull the material together Danischewsky turned to Angus MacPhail, Ealing's scenario editor, who wrote the initial draft. From the first, the theme of the two islands and their sectarian differences was dropped – probably to placate Balcon, who found jokes about religion even more alarming than jokes about sex. In the meantime, a director had to be found. Since all the studio's directors were already engaged, Danischewsky offered the assignment to Ronald Neame, a former Ealing cinematographer who had left to launch out as a director, but received 'a flat no. I think Ronnie was worried about me, a complete amateur, having so much authority. As well he might be.'

On hearing of Neame's refusal, Mackendrick seized his opportunity. His only major assignment since *Saraband* had been to storyboard a flaccid comedy, *Another Shore*. The film's director, Charles Crichton, found the technique no less restrictive than Basil Dearden had done. 'Of course, I'm not blaming Sandy for the picture not being very good. But I don't like the precision of everything being drawn out beforehand. The unit looks, and everybody looks, and they try to do it like that. You're putting yourself in a terrible corset. He did all these beautiful drawings, but the picture just didn't work that way.' The storyboard, Mackendrick realised, would work properly only when the director had devised it himself and so could feel free to deviate from it with 'no contradiction between planning and spontaneity'. Eager to put his ideas into practice, he proposed himself to Danischewsky as director of *Whisky Galore*.

One of Balcon's most admirable traits, Mackendrick has remarked, 'is that he had great generosity towards beginners. . . . He built the studio out of comparatively unknown youngsters whom he took in and paid very little money to, but gave them a great deal of security and allowed them a great deal of freedom. . . . He was extraordinarily generous with opportunities.'[4] As early as 1924, while heading Islington studios, Balcon had given Alfred Hitchcock his first chance to direct, and at Ealing he had done the same for Dearden, Crichton, Robert Hamer and Charles Frend. He had his doubts, though, about teaming Mackendrick with Danischewsky. 'You know nothing about production, dear boy, and now you are proposing to have a director who knows nothing about direction. I agree with you that Sandy should be given the chance to direct – but let him do it for the first time under a qualified producer. You go and get yourself a chap who'll make up for your own ignorance.'[5]

Balcon's reluctance was overcome by Mackendrick's enthusiasm. As Danischewsky put it, 'it wasn't so much that Sandy was my second choice after Ronnie Neame, as that Sandy was Sandy's choice. He was wildly keen on it, which was marvellous from a producer's point of view.' (Typically, though, Balcon refused Mackendrick any increase in salary. The director of *Whisky Galore* continued to receive £35 a week, about half as much as his camera operator.) Together, Mackendrick and Danischewsky worked on further drafts of the script, tightening and refining the structure, before calling in Compton Mackenzie for final dialogue work. It was an approach to adaptation which Mackendrick found particularly fruitful. 'If you've got an original author, the thing is to take the subject entirely away from him and get it drastically rewritten by somebody else – often the director if he's a writer-director. Then, when it's in fairly good shape, throw it back to the author for the final polish on dialogue. That way, you introduce a cinematic structure, which wasn't in the original, quite early on; but when the writer sees a new story brought back to him, he feels he can move in and make it his own, in colouring the speech and the language.'

Mackenzie, after a few ritual grumbles – 'Another of my books gone west' – undertook the final draft and for the price of a box of cigars threw in a few scenes lifted from *Keep the Home Guard Turning*. (He also made a last-ditch attempt to restore the element of religious rivalry, but in vain.) Balcon, he suspected, 'was treating Danny like an indulgent uncle. It was clear to me that he was feeling very doubtful indeed about its being a successful film.'[7] Danischewsky gained much the same impression. 'When Mick saw the script, he said, "Well, I don't know, Danny, all I can see is a lot of elderly Scotsmen sitting by the fire and saying Och aye." '

Despite Balcon's misgivings, preparations went ahead for filming on the island of Barra during the summer of 1948. To allow interiors as well as exteriors to be shot there, a 'mobile studio' was set up in the village hall at Craigstone, on the west of the island. Prefabricated sets were constructed at Ealing and sent up in sections. This arrangement would allow for 'weather alternatives', interior scenes to be shot when weather conditions precluded an exterior shoot – as it turned out, a very necessary provision.[8] Also, the people of Barra could be enrolled as extras in their own environment, lending the film an authenticity hard to replicate in a London studio. As Matthew Norgate observed, 'it is often hard to say which of the small-part players are actors and which the recruited inhabitants of [Barra]. . . . The local actors were able to feel at home before the cameras, since they were at home.'[9]

This integration of professionals with amateurs was unintentionally furthered by the way the unit was housed. Mackendrick recalls that 'the man who owned the only big house on the island saw a chance to make a lot of money out of us. And Danny wouldn't stand for it, and said, "All right, we don't want it." There was one hotel which had four bedrooms, and we had to move in about a hundred people. Now for about one or two weeks in the year when the weather is bearable Barra has a tourist industry; they all set up little bed-sitting rooms. Danny bought out every room on the island, and moved the unit into them. The effect of this was that people like Joan Greenwood, who had a very good ear, were living with the Hebridean accent all the time, and being trained by natural dialogue coaches. Also, because we were using the islanders as crowd artists, you couldn't play phony. You're brought absolutely down to a level of reality because you're up against the real thing. At one point James Robertson Justice had to give a speech in Gaelic. He was a brilliant linguist, and he could have got away with it – except that all the people he was addressing were native Gaelic speakers. And he just couldn't do it. He was very apologetic for that.'

Apart from Greenwood as Peggy Macroon, nearly all the Scots roles were taken by Scottish actors. Even the Cockney Sergeant Odd was played by an Edinburgh Scot, Bruce Seton. Basil Radford, incarnation of baffled English pomposity, achieved his apotheosis as Captain Waggett. The role of Greenwood's father, the resourceful postmaster Joseph Macroon, was originally offered to Alastair Sim, who turned it down with the tart comment that he 'could not bear professional Scotsmen'. It went instead to Wylie Watson, previously best known for his performance as the hapless 'Mr Memory' in Hitchcock's *39 Steps*.

The film also gave Compton Mackenzie his screen debut, playing – at Danischewsky's suggestion – the captain of the ill-fated freighter. Mackenzie, who had always yearned to be an actor, was delighted, at least until experiencing Mackendrick's perfectionism at first hand. His performance took place at Pinewood, 'where at the end of October I said my three lines as Captain Buncher, the scene keeping me up all night until it satisfied the director'.[10]

The shooting of *Whisky Galore!* began on Barra on 27 July 1948. (The title of the film, unlike that of the novel, includes an exclamation mark which, to avoid visual irritation, is omitted from here on.) The modest resources of Ealing were stretched by having three films in simultaneous production and several members of the crew were scarcely more experienced than its leaders. Chic Waterson, making his first film as camera operator, described the shoot as 'the blind leading the blind'. Mackendrick, it seems, was still dissatisfied with the script. Herbie Smith, who was focus puller, remembers arriving on Barra, 'and the first thing was Danny tore up the script and said, "We've all got two days off, Sandy wants to rewrite it." '

The unit's problems were compounded by the weather: persistent rain, and frequent gales. As Danischewsky ruefully admitted, 'We hadn't reckoned on what the Outer Islands can produce in the way of a summer when they really try.'[11] The wreck of the SS *Cabinet Minister*, painstakingly constructed offshore, was wrecked for real before a single shot could be taken.

As shooting fell even further behind schedule Mackendrick, convinced his directorial career was over almost before it had begun, started to experience crippling asthmatic attacks. During one of them he dragged himself in the middle of the night to Barra's only telephone booth and called his fiancée, Hilary Lloyd, 'to complain that I was thinking of committing suicide. And instead of getting any sympathy, I got a terrible bawling-out. She said, "It's only a stupid bit of film!" So I went back and fell fast asleep, thinking, "An ideal wife for a movie director".'[12]

Filming was also bedevilled by disagreements between producer and director – hardly unusual, except that in this case the point at issue was the film's moral stance. While working on the script, Danischewsky 'discovered to my horror that [Mackendrick] really disapproved of the islanders taking the whisky. No real moral sanction could be found for it.' Consequently, 'as our work on the film progressed, Sandy found himself more and more in sympathy with Captain Waggett'.[13] Mackendrick puts it rather differently. 'I began suddenly to realise that the most Scottish character in *Whisky Galore* is Waggett the Englishman. He, if you like, is the only Calvinist, puritan figure, who's against looting and so on – and all the other characters aren't Scots at all, they're Irish.' He accordingly suggested that Waggett, alone of the cast, should wear a kilt, 'which of course is ersatz Scots, an invention of Prince Albert'. Danischewsky turned the idea down, feeling its subtlety would be lost on all but Scottish audiences.

In retrospect, Mackendrick feels that 'the casting of Danny and myself together, being of utterly different temperaments, was terrific' and in the long run creatively beneficial. 'Also, Danny is essentially an enchanting character who loves people, loves socialising, isn't very good at organisation. And his job, as far as I was concerned, was to get the bloody thing organised. So he was giving parties, treating people, doing something that was absolutely essential – but of course I in my short-sightedness couldn't see it – in keeping everybody happy. And the unit *was* a happy one, they really loved it.' Relations with the people of Barra remained good, the extras playing their parts with professional enthusiasm. Gordon Jackson remembered 'the old postmistress saying to Sandy at one point, "I don't think I'd be in this shot, Mr Mackendrick, I wasn't in the other angle. . . ." We corrupted them all – they were high-powered actors and actresses by the time we left.'[14]

Shooting was scheduled to take ten weeks. The unit eventually returned to Ealing five weeks over schedule, with several key exterior scenes still to be shot – hence the studio joke that the interiors were shot on Barra and the exteriors at Ealing. The budget, originally £50,000, then £85,000, finally reached £105,000. Balcon saw his worst fears justified – the more so since the material had been ineptly assembled by an unpractised editor, Joseph Sterling. Gloomily viewing the footage, Balcon proposed it should be cut to 60 minutes and released as a second feature. Since the agreement with Rank stipulated that Ealing films, unless otherwise conceded, must go out as first features, this would have been an admission of defeat, and a disgrace for Mackendrick and Danischewsky.

Disaster was averted by Charles Crichton, who protested that the material itself was fine and simply needed good editing. 'So Micky Balcon said, "All right, go into the cutting-room and see what you can do with it." So I did that, and every time I said to Sandy, "Well, I think this sequence should go like this and this and this," he said, "Well, of course, that's the way I intended it." '[15] Crichton worked on *Whisky Galore* for several weeks, uncredited and often in his own time, even shooting some additional footage with Douglas Slocombe. Meanwhile Mackendrick filmed sequences in the studio tank at Pinewood, plus the missing exteriors – including the final chase sequence, mostly shot around Bournemouth. Shooting was finally completed on 26 November, having taken 102 working days instead of the 60 originally scheduled.

Out of the shambles of this calamitous production there emerged, against all Balcon's expectations, a film now generally considered 'one of the British cinema's comedy classics'.[16] Classics are notoriously difficult to look at straight. The tendency, particularly when working from memory, is to round out unevennesses, erase failures of tone or structure and describe, through a warm haze of remembered affection, not the film that was made but an idealised reworking of it, its very defects metamorphosed into strengths.

In *The Comic Mind* Gerald Mast devotes a three-page section to *Tight Little Island* (*Whisky Galore*'s title in the USA), crediting it with 'a rich, convincing texture', a 'tight little plot (in which *everything* counts)' and 'the mixture of credibility and improbability, nature and artifice essential to a well-made comedy'.[17] Such comments might well sum up the best features of Ealing comedy in general. But as far as *Whisky Galore* is concerned, Mast seems to be describing a far more accomplished film than the one visible on the screen – the movie that Mackendrick and Danischewsky may have hoped to make, rather than the one they eventually came up with.

The vicissitudes of the film's making show up in its texture, which is often thin to the point of transparency. Several shots serve no dramatic purpose, especially a repeated view of men milling aimlessly around a village street, apparently inserted only to ease a transition between scenes. The wrecked ship is a glaringly blatant fake. Continuity is frequently shaky, with out-takes pressed into service to the exclusion of spatial logic: Farquharson's men, supposedly leaving Macroon's house, are shown once more approaching it, and Waggett's car, speeding towards Seal Bay, manages to traverse the same stretch of road three times.

These flaws, and some ragged pacing, can readily be forgiven. *Whisky Galore*, after all, never aimed for the polished gloss of a Hollywood studio comedy and much of its shaggy charm stems from the very roughness of its execution. Mackendrick himself now finds it 'painfully amateurish to look at, but with the virtues of amateurism. It has a sort of freshness that comes from innocence that one can probably never recapture.'[18] The weaknesses that mar it have less to do with production values – which are secondary in a movie of this kind – than with lapses in tone, moments when the film betrays its own standards of intelligence and dramatic integrity by falling back on a slacker, heavier convention of comedy.

Charles Barr has referred to the exhilaration conveyed by the islanders' quick-wittedness and shrewdness, 'the speed of the group's reactions'.[19] True enough, for most of the film. But sometimes – as in the scene where Macroon's daughters, their suitors and the Doctor wait anxiously at the Post Office while the islanders race to forestall seizure of the whisky – ideas develop with agonising slowness.

DOCTOR: If only I could lay my hands on that man Waggett.
PEGGY: Just for a bit of whisky to go to prison. Men!
CATRIONA: Sitting there doing nothing at all. Could you not do something to stop Waggett?
GEORGE: How can we?
CATRIONA: Soldiers! Helpless as new-born babes!
PEGGY: Aye – I can see them stopping the Germans.
DOCTOR: That stupid, stuffed-up Sassenach, playing at being a laird.
A tinpot general with his Home Guard and his roadblocks.
Roadblocks – a fat lot of use. . . . Roadblocks!

And at last, realisation dawns. The following episode, though, is even worse. George phones a fellow Home Guardist, Angus, telling him Waggett has ordered a special exercise and that he must bar passage to anyone without the password 'whisky'. Waggett is duly stopped and expostulates vainly. 'There you are, Waggett,' remarks Farquharson, 'no password – no whisky.' Angus, hearing the password, at once lets them through. To achieve this joke – a feeble enough one, in any case – the film is wrenched into an inferior mode of comedy, where humour no longer derives from character and situation, but from crude incongruity. After all, Angus has shown himself as enthusiastic as any in recovering and concealing the whisky – so why the subterfuge of a 'special exercise'? Also, the scene brings the islanders, in the person of Angus, down to Waggett's level of obtuseness and inflexibility, valuing verbal formulae (the password) over the interests of the community (stopping Waggett). Character is being distorted to fit situation, rather than situation growing – as in all good comedy – organically from character.

Such faults, it's true, are relatively brief and intermittent within the overall flow of the action. But they make *Whisky Galore* a less coherent film than its reputation might suggest, since it fails to sustain a consistent level of comedy in the way that, for example, *Man in the White Suit* does. Still, for all its imperfections, Mackendrick's first feature as director introduces several elements characteristic of his work; it is, quite recognisably – to use the slightly suspect, shorthand term – 'a Mackendrick film'.

Most evident is the theme which, first mooted in *Saraband*, is explored and reinterpreted in varying aspects throughout his work: the confrontation between Innocence and Experience, here represented by Waggett on the one hand and the islanders on the other. Mackendrick's moral universe is essentially relative and neither of these qualities ever represents an unambiguous good or evil. The balance of sympathy shifts between them from film to film and sometimes even within the space of a single film. Innocence can connote unawareness and lack of sensitivity, and is often highly dangerous – both to its possessor and to everyone else around. The experienced may be devious, corrupt and exploitative. Both sides can be ruthless in achieving their ends: the innocent because they never allow for other people's independent existence, the experienced because they despise them.

Central to all Mackendrick films is this tension between different modes of perception: how people see things or (equally important) fail to see them. The innocent in particular tend to discount whatever falls beyond the range of their preconceptions – but the experienced, too, can succumb to self-delusion. Often, what they fail to register is just how dangerous the single-mindedness of the innocent may be.

And because Mackendrick is intent on allowing his audience to read a situation and compare what we see with what the characters within it are seeing, he rarely invites us to identify with the viewpoint of any single protagonist. Point-of-view shots are scarce in his films, and on the few occasions he does use them, they fulfil a very specific dramatic function. Generally, his directorial perspective remains detached, ironically critical – as it does here, in his first feature film.

*Whisky Galore* was one of the three films released in 1949 – the other two being *Kind Hearts and Coronets* and *Passport to Pimlico* – that welded the words 'Ealing' and 'Comedy' indissolubly together. (Though the studio had produced plenty of comedies before, it had never been predominantly associated with the genre.) But despite being historically placed as the threefold fount of Ealing Comedy – with all that the term has come to imply of gentle whimsicality – the three films, as Charles Barr has pointed out, differ radically in their approach and attitude. Where they deal with similar subjects they tend to arrive at strikingly diverse conclusions.

All three engage with one of Ealing's (and Balcon's) most abiding concerns, the question of community – inclusion in it, exclusion from it, what constitutes it in the first place. In *Kind Hearts* Louis Mazzini, through accident of birth, finds himself exiled from the aristocratic clan to which he feels entitled to belong. To regain entry into his chosen circle, he coolly slaughters all the relatives who stand in his way, in the process showing himself no less callous than they – and thus ideally qualified to be a D'Ascoyne – only to wind up condemned to death by his fellow-peers, whose ranks he has taken such pains to join. Community, in Hamer's film (as elsewhere in his work), is a malign conspiracy, ruthlessness dissembled behind a facade of gentility.

*Passport* takes an altogether more benign view. The community of Miramont Place, a microcosm of society, opts out of the larger community to assert its independence – and in so doing rediscovers virtues of co-operation and self-reliance which it seemed in danger of losing. This rugged stance attracts the sympathy of the community outside (people throwing in food from passing buses) and in the end the microcosm, finding the qualities it shares with the macrocosm are more important than those which divide, is reabsorbed back within its embrace. Conflict within the community, great or small, can be resolved through compromise and good will.

The community depicted by *Whisky Galore* displays traits in common with those of both *Passport* and *Kind Hearts* – prepared to be as ruthless, in the pursuit of its interests, as Hamer's aristocracy, but also internally supportive like the people of Miramont Place. No question here, though, of compromise or integration into an external community. Todday remains fiercely independent and self-reliant, prepared to accept only those out-siders who, like the Sergeant, seek entry on the islanders' own terms. Those like Waggett, who threaten the values of the community, can expect no mercy. Sammy MacCodrum states the principle at its starkest: 'Any man who stands between us and the whisky is an enemy.'

This principle, though, allows for some interesting variants; not all enemies are equal. The people of Todday, in their determination to gain the whisky, have three opponents to contend with. The chief of them is Waggett, whose relationship with the islanders lies at the heart of the film. But if we compare the treatment meted out to him with what happens to his two allies, there's a very revealing contrast.

The Excise Officer, Farquharson, receives the wary respect due to a known and formidable adversary. If we take *Whisky Galore* as a war film (which in many ways it is), he plays the equivalent of Rommel. The subtle interplay between him and Macroon, during his abortive search of the Post Office, suggests an encounter between members of opposing armies, each appreciating the other's professionalism and tactical skill. Their verbal fencing – beautifully judged by the actors no less than by the director in its underplayed humour – conveys a tacit accord from which Waggett remains impenetrably excluded, and concludes with a parting exchange between veteran opponents:

FARQUHARSON: I'm sorry to have disturbed you, Mr Macroon. I'll call earlier next time.
MACROON: Och, I didn't mind you coming late at all, Mr Farquharson.

There's no personal animus in the islanders' attitude towards Farquharson's men – at worst the pity, tinged with mild amusement, of Macroon's comment: 'Aye, puir fellows. A dirty job, a dirty job!' The excisemen are outsiders whose activities, while they may threaten the well-being of the community, do nothing to disrupt its internal cohesion, the web of loyalty binding it together against alien incursions. The one man who fractures that solidarity – the Quisling of Todday, to extend the war-movie parallel – is the hotel-keeper, Roderick MacRurie.

In James Woodburn's portrayal, Roderick becomes a singularly ambivalent figure. Though he appears in only five scenes – and is, significantly, absent from the *rèiteach* – his part in the film is crucial. There's a note of sour satisfaction in his delivery of the key line, uttered straight into the face of the stricken Captain MacPhee: 'There is *no* whisky!' – and as he utters it, one lens of his spectacles flashes peremptorily, a visual echo of the monocle that adorned so many movie Nazis. Yet, despite his treachery, Roderick is not – or not as far as we see – subjected to the scorn and ignominy heaped on Waggett, though his betrayal surely ranks as the more heinous of the two. (Further support, it could be argued, for Mackendrick's view of Waggett as an unjustly persecuted figure.)

The contradiction, though, is only apparent, since between Roderick and the other islanders there's no innate discrepancy. He *thinks* as they do, but *acts* differently – since he, alone on the island, stands to lose by the contraband whisky. His motivation, like theirs, is candid self-interest; 'Why should I help you to ruin my business?' he demands, reasonably enough. Waggett, on the other hand, thinks and acts altruistically, out of pure principle, which in Todday terms is unforgivable.

Waggett, in other words, is *Whisky Galore*'s sole representative of Innocence. Not a very prepossessing one, either, since in him it takes the form of dismissing all views bar his own as patently misguided. Yet, partly because this very obtuseness renders him so vulnerable to the far shrewder

Scots, there's a certain pathos in his defeat. Basil Radford's performance, touchingly suggesting the lonely, frustrated man behind the bluster, evidently stemmed from a total identification with his role. Compton Mackenzie noted 'his inability to understand why Waggett was a comic figure. In his view Waggett's attitude . . . was exactly what it ought to have been.'[20]

Waggett is the first of several characters in Mackendrick's films to find not just his system of belief, but his very identity under assault. His pompous insistence on his rank ('*Captain* Waggett, if you don't mind') meeting with bland disregard, he is eventually reduced to incoherent splutterings – 'This is lunacy! It's me – I – I – I – I *am* Captain Waggett!' – only to be countered by calm Hebridean logic: 'Ah, but how do I *know* that you're Captain Waggett?' Finally even his probity, the core of his self-image, is destroyed; humiliated, broken in spirit, the wretched man is blown off the island in a gale of callous laughter.

Waggett's failure, in short, is one of empathy – the inability to think himself into a Todday frame of mind. The map we see hanging in his study neatly defines his mental geography: it shows north-west France, southern England, but not the least fragment of Scotland, let alone the Western Isles. From time to time, in his verbal collisions with the islanders, Waggett vainly tries to disseminate his 'broader picture' – as in the near-surreal logic of his exchange with Mrs Campbell:

WAGGETT: Mrs Campbell. At this very moment, our troops are
fighting in North Africa. The Germans don't stop fighting on
Sunday, so how can we?
MRS CAMPBELL: What the Germans do, Mr Waggett, is on their own
conscience, and Todday is not in North Africa, so there's no need
to bring the heathens into it. I've been told that there are
cannibals in Africa, but no one is going to persuade *my* son to eat
human flesh.
WAGGETT: No one's *asking* your son to eat human flesh!
MRS CAMPBELL (darkly): Not yet.

That the islanders never think themselves into a Waggett frame of mind is not seen as any kind of failure on their part. No reason, indeed, why it should be, given that *Whisky Galore* is a film of its time. 'Doesn't he know there's a war on?' Waggett is given to expostulating. Well, there is and there isn't. Though the action is set in 1943, the mood is unmistakably that of 1948, the era of resentful post-war austerity 'when [British] society had learned,' as David Hughes has suggested, 'that only a touch of dishonesty gave any spark to life at all'.[21]

In a film that *was* made in 1943, Carol Reed's Army recruiting-piece

*The Way Ahead*, David Niven's lieutenant harangues his skiving conscripts with arguments not unlike Waggett's – the appeal to team-spirit, to wider interests beyond the short-term advantage of the group. 'If you ever get near any real fighting . . . you'll find that you're looking to other men not to let you down. . . .' A 1943 *Whisky Galore* might well have come up with the solution that no one, in the film as made, ever thinks to propose: that the islanders should salvage the whisky, to be reshipped as their contribution to the war effort – thus achieving a patriotic compromise, and probably a fairly dire movie. In such a film, Waggett might have figured as the hero; but in 1948, audiences could be counted on to see in him, not the principled upholder of English values, but the incarnation of petty bureaucracy – the spirit of the ration-book.

In *Passport to Pimlico*, ration-books symbolise that drab, reassuring normality into which the briefly independent community relapses. *Passport* reverses the time-switch of *Whisky Galore*: though its setting is contemporary, it harks nostalgically back to the camaraderie and shared deprivation of the war years. *Whisky Galore*, by contrast, not only replays a wartime situation in a post-war mood, but compounds the irony of exploiting the dramatic conventions of a war-film – or, to be exact, a Resistance movie.

Mackendrick enjoys taking off established movie genres, though rarely at the level of overt parody. He prefers to drop hints, relying on allusive narrative techniques. In the raid sequence we see three actions intercut: the *rèiteach* in full swing, the Excise cutter scudding towards Todday, and old Hector phoning through his urgent warning. It's all designed to evoke those scenes where a Gestapo staff-car hurtles through the night towards the betrayed Resistance HQ – right down to the ensign snapping on the cutter's stern like a swastika flag on a black Mercedes. Such references offer the pleasure of recognition – but optionally, since they work perfectly well in literal terms. 'When you're trying to appeal simultaneously to popular and sophisticated audiences,' Mackendrick once remarked, 'I think it sometimes justifiable to work on different levels at the same time. . . . [to] make sense to people looking for subtleties as well as satisfying those who care only for the broad and obvious effect.'[22]

The last half-hour of the film borrows a series of war-movie episodes, never insisted upon but readily identifiable to anyone watching for them: the Gestapo house-to-house search, the duel of wits between Nazi and Resistance leader, the guerilla harassment covering the escape of Allied airmen, even the bumbling local Kommandant summoned to Headquarters to face the music. The running joke in this 'little military exercise' (as Farquharson calls it) is that Waggett himself, with his obsessive Home Guard activity, has furnished the tactics now turned against him – culminating in the barbed-wire roadblock in which, on the point of triumph, he finds his car immovably snarled, and whose construction he had ordered earlier in the movie.

The parody that acts as prologue to the film, though, is for once fairly overt. Waves breaking on a rugged coast, craggy peasant faces against the sky, the voice of a narrator (Finlay Currie, for some odd reason uncredited) setting the scene – the mode is not just documentary, but that specific British tradition of which Grierson's *Drifters* and Flaherty's *Man of Aran* are the key representatives. The sequence pays back-handed tribute both to Mackendrick's film-making apprenticeship and to a movement whose values Ealing, perhaps more than any other commercial studio, had taken on board.

Not for a moment, of course, are we meant to believe we're about to see a real documentary. Apart from anything else, the credits give the game away. A game, in fact, is just what this is, played out with our complicity, teasing us to guess how long the pretence can be kept up. Even the insertion of a sight gag ('A happy people,' says the narrator, over a shot of a weathered couple outside their cottage, 'with few and simple pleasures', as nine children, of descending age, scamper out the door) doesn't destroy the illusion, since its very point depends on slipping a sexual innuendo into the decorum of an ostensible documentary. The moment that shatters the convention, as it also shatters the community of Todday, is Roderick's fateful pronouncement: 'There is *no* whisky!'

The words, in one of Mackendrick's rare, deliberate subjective shots, are delivered straight into our faces, striking us like a personal assault. It's the film's second line of dialogue; the first, Captain MacPhee's '*Slainte mhath!*' (Good health!), has invoked the contrary principle, the health and life-blood of the island. (Specifically so since, as the narrator explains, whisky is *uisge beatha*, the water of life.) Roderick's words, hard English against soft Gaelic, constitute literally a sentence of death, threatening everything the preceding footage has built up – the sense of a small, cohesive community, at harmony with itself and its natural surroundings. To deprive it of whisky is to deprive it of life; the Captain totters home and dies, leaving his fellow-islanders 'mourning a departed spirit'.

'I only laugh at things that have some undercurrent of something deadly serious. I think to be frivolous about frivolous matters is to be boring; but to be frivolous about things that are in some way deadly serious – that's genuine comedy.'[23] *Whisky Galore* exemplifies Mackendrick's principle. The tone may be comic but, as the prologue establishes, the film broaches matters of life and death.

*Whisky Galore* is often lumped in with other Mackendrick films under the conventional assessment of 'Ealing Comedy' as something essentially trivial and harmless. Gavin Lambert argued that 'Balcon's Ealing comedies are not, like the Shaw films, comedies of ideas, but of situations. In the best of them, the situations are appealing and the invention is vivacious, but the issues are basically trivial. . . . These little victories over authority achieve nothing fundamental. Hebridean islanders get their whisky after all. . . .'[24] Such a judgement, though true of much of Ealing's output, seems as regards Mackendrick's work to betray a concentration on surface tone to the exclusion of any more searching analysis. His films *are* comedies of ideas. But his ideas (unlike Shaw's) tend to be expressed visually, or by implication, rather than being made explicit in words.

Almost invariably Mackendrick's films carry a political subtext, but it rarely obtrudes itself into the foreground. 'I believe that man is a political animal, and that anybody who doesn't have a political or indeed a moral point of view is a rather inferior human being. But I also believe that if you do anything wholeheartedly, there's no need to *introduce* politics, because it's going to show whether you want it to or not. It comes naturally; if you're involved, your attitudes will show.'[25] *Whisky Galore* could well be read as a satire on colonialism, with Waggett a mislocated Sanders of the River, exhorting the recalcitrant natives and making patronising little forays into what he sees as the quaint local lingo. 'Well, Scots wha hae!' he exclaims, rousing himself to relieve Sergeant Odd on guard duty. 'Scots wha hae what, dear?' inquires his wife (Catherine Lacey, whose quietly incredulous performance is one of the delights of the film). 'Well, it's – er, it's what they say here, darling. You know, like, er – like, um, long may your something reek.'

It's Waggett, nonetheless, who puts his finger on the real issue, in an earlier exchange with his wife. 'Would it be so terrible,' she asks, 'if the people here did get a few bottles?' Waggett is shocked. 'That's a very dangerous line of argument, Dolly – very. Once you let people take the law into their own hands, it's anarchy. Anarchy!' True, so it is. *Whisky Galore* puts forward the highly subversive doctrine that the structure of authority can be rendered powerless by consensual action of the whole community – social anarchism in its essential form.

Both *Passport to Pimlico* and *Whisky Galore* deal with anarchy. In *Passport* it's what follows after the miniature Burgundian state has declared independence. With British law suspended and controls abolished, rapacious outsiders flood in to create what Pemberton (the honest, straightforward Stanley Holloway character) calls 'a spivs' paradise'. This is the conservative view of anarchy as a ruthless free-for-all shattering the community, a Hobbesian dystopia where 'Right and Wrong, Justice and Injustice have there no place. . . . No Propriety, no Dominion, no *Mine* and *Thine* distinct; but onely that to be every mans, that he can get; and for so long, as he can keep it.'[26] To combat this alien threat the residents of Miramont Place, having thrown off external authority, are obliged to impose even more stringent controls of their own. 'The important thing,' Pemberton declares, 'is to get some law and order here.'

The people of Todday, by contrast, oppose their instinctively anarchic structure to all forms of external authority (with the notable exception of the church). They act in concert, without deferring to a leader – though Macroon, as the most resourceful, is often looked to for advice. This is anarchism from a sympathetic, left-wing viewpoint, Tolstoy's evocation of a self-regulating society where 'in the most diverse matters people . . . arrange their lives incomparably better than those who govern them arrange things for them'.[27]

So it's Waggett, wanting like Pemberton to 'get some law and order here', who in *Whisky Galore* embodies the threatening 'other', while the anarchic spirit represents indigenous solidarity against encroaching forces. And whereas Pemberton can sit down with his opponent, the civil servant Gregg, in amicable discussion, Waggett, his perceptions hopelessly at odds with those of the islanders, finds no common ground. (The contrast is underlined by the casting: Basil Radford plays both Waggett and Greg.) If, as Raymond Williams suggests, communication defines community, then those who perceive so differently as to prevent communication exclude themselves from communal acceptance.

In this light it makes dramatic sense that Mackendrick, here as elsewhere in his films, offers us no single character through whose eyes we're encouraged to view the action. The hero of *Whisky Galore* is the whole community of Todday, which the audience, through the surrogate of Sergeant Odd, is invited to enter – an invitation made explicit in the central sequence of the *rèiteach*. Again, Mackendrick makes purposive use of subjective camera. As the dance reaches its height, we find ourselves being whirled around by Peggy herself, thus becoming her partner, the Sergeant – the outsider accepted into the healed community and caught up in its rejoicing.

Like many other movies – those of Ford being the obvious example – *Whisky Galore* uses a dance as the archetypal image of social cohesion. But the *rèiteach* forms merely the central panel of a triptych of sequences which, together, show a community being revitalised and regaining its sense of purpose. The first of these – perhaps the most warmly exhilarating passage in the whole film – is the 'mouth-music' sequence which follows the salvaging of the whisky. 'I suspect all of them, Dolly – all of them!' Waggett exclaims, getting it about right once more, as we fade to two brimming glasses held by Dr Maclaren and old Hector, toasting each other and softly launching into a lilting Highland melody. By opening with Hector, whom we last saw sinking listlessly towards death, the significance is made immediately clear: this is the healing process whereby (the pun is inescapable) the spirit of the community is reanimated. From here the rhythm, both visual and musical, builds in a rising curve, first single faces, then groups of two or three and finally a whole roomful, smiling and drinking, swaying gently together, as voice after voice joins in the singing – swelling to a climax before diminishing back through a few faces to a single one: Hector again, whose beaming features fade into the dawn breaking over the island.

The whole sequence lasts less than a minute, conveying with wonderful economy the sense of regained pleasure and reaffirmed fellowship flowing back into the community. Or at least into the male half of it – the women of Todday, it seems, must wait until the *rèiteach* to partake of the process. Ernest Irving's evocative, folktune-based score attains its apotheosis with this passage – the more effective for his restraint in leaving the voices unaccompanied. Restraint also distinguishes the acting which, here as everywhere in the film, is blessedly free from broad comic mannerisms; Mackendrick, according to Gordon Jackson, impressed upon his cast that nobody was to act drunk.[28] (The sole offender in this respect is Finlay Currie's narrator, who not only slurs his words – 'When the dawn rose on that memorable morning . . .' – but introduces the hint of a hiccup.) In any case, overt inebriation would be inappropriate: the whisky, true water of life, restores capability rather than detracting from it. Refuelled, reinvigorated, the community can proceed to the rite of perpetuation.

The *rèiteach* itself is filmed with so vivid a sense of pleasure and involvement, professional actors and islanders indistinguishably mingled, that it's hard to believe we're not watching a genuine island party at which the camera just happened to be present. The scene becomes a celebration, not only of the fictional community, but of the relationship between the people of Barra and the film-makers, and perhaps should stand as a joint tribute to Mackendrick's direction and Danischewsky's gift for conviviality.

The Excise raid, though on one level interrupting the *rèiteach*, on another serves as the extension, even the climax, to it, with the islanders' newly regained vigour switched without a moment's pause into the tactics of self-defence. As Charles Barr puts it, 'the celebrations and the shrewdness flow into one another'.[29]

The whisky-hiding sequence, third panel of the triptych, outdoes even the mouth-music sequence for dramatic economy. Crichton's concise, rhythmic editing – 15 shots in less than 30 seconds – sustains the exuberant pace without ever losing visual intelligibility, conveying the practised speed of the islanders' reactions. No words are spoken, nor need to be. We see Macroon on the phone, his eyes widening as he takes in Hector's warning. Then, the moonlit exterior of the Post Office, as a silhouetted phalanx of black-hatted figures advance upon it – a solid mass of darkness flowing silently upwards from the bottom of the screen, threatening to engulf Todday in its saturnine gloom. The tension of this inexorable approach enhances the dancing agility of the sequence that follows.

First, a fast tracking shot along a table as hands grab the bottles off it. Then bottles being slipped into milk churns, water boilers, pie dishes (with a neat layer of pastry on top), clock cases, fiddle cases, cash-tills and box files;

bottles lowered into drains on a string, decanted into hot-water bottles and paraffin lamps; and finally, two bottles placed in a cot, a baby laid over the bottles, and a blanket over the baby. The baby gazes wonderingly upwards, emitting a faintly puzzled cry; and the shadow of a hat-brim falls across the Post Office door.

Enjoyable and exciting though the subsequent pursuit is, its outcome seems a foregone conclusion – as Farquharson, with his baleful air of anticipated defeat, evidently knows. We know the islanders will get away with their booty, and are simply curious to see how they manage it. The twist is that they do so by means of the whisky itself (by now endowed with near-magical powers) poured into the fuel-tank of Sammy MacCodrum's truck; and the arthritic old vehicle, rejuvenated in its turn, vanishes over the skyline in a gleam of eldritch light.

Both *Passport to Pimlico* and *Whisky Galore* end with a celebration. *Passport* offers a feast of reconciliation (curtailed by rain). *Whisky Galore* remains true to its own ruthlessness; no one thinks to extend a magnanimous hand to the wretched Waggett in his defeat. A broken and isolated figure, despised by his Excise allies, derided even by his wife, he's ignominiously laughed off the island, while the interrupted *rèiteach* is resumed, completing the ceremony of renewal.

This is the true ending, since the coda is no more than an ironic gesture, deriding the pinched morality of the prevailing censorship (with perhaps a mocking side-glance at Mackendrick's own Calvinist upbringing). So we have a brief reprise of the documentary opening, while the narrator explains that whisky became so dear, no one on Todday could afford it – and only non-whisky drinkers were happy. 'And if that isn't a moral story – what is?'

*Whisky Galore* received its premiere in June 1949, opening at two medium-sized West End venues and running for two weeks before going out on general release. With London in the grip of a heatwave, box-office returns were no more than adequate. Critical response was mostly favourable and in some cases enthusiastic. Several reviewers compared it to *Passport*, which had opened a few weeks earlier, and a few preferred Cornelius's film. One who didn't was Richard Winnington, who wrote in the *News Chronicle*: 'Even at the height of its slapstick and Gaelic junketing, *Whisky Galore* is free of the terrible affliction of self-consciousness, is gently genial with an undertinge of melancholy. It doesn't stand aside and say "Aren't we being funny?" as *Passport to Pimlico* and every other post-war British comedy consistently and ruinously does. . . . Consequently, one leaves the film, almost surprisedly, refreshed and cheered.'[30]

Mackendrick's visual flair was already being noted. The *Evening Standard*'s reviewer observed that 'While *Passport to Pimlico* had more hilarious moments, *Whisky Galore* is cinematically a better film. It relies less on verbal jokes and more on wit achieved through the camera lens.'[31] Even so, *Passport* was doing far better at the box-office and *Whisky Galore* looked unlikely to do much more than cover its costs. Audience response in Scotland, where the film opened in September, was a lot more encouraging, but the Scottish market was too small to make up for disappointing revenues in England.

*Whisky Galore*'s rise to glory began in New York. Art cinemas, showing a repertory of foreign movies (which included British) and reissued Hollywood classics, were a relatively recent development in the USA. Michael Truman, Ealing's chief editor (later to be Mackendrick's producer on *The Maggie*), had been sent over to gauge Stateside reaction to some recent and forthcoming releases on the art circuit, among them the ill-fated *Saraband*. After a highly favourable preview of *Whisky Galore* he reported back that the film 'seems to me to be the ideal type of British subject for American showing. . . . The Americans loved the treatment, the characters and the set-up.'[32] They also appreciated the clarity of the Hebridean accent, far better attuned to their ears than the throwaway English mumble.

Since the Hays Code forbade overt reference to liquor in movie titles, the film was renamed *Tight Little Island* for its American release. It opened at the Trans-Lux Theatre on 60th Street just before Christmas 1949 and at once justified Truman's optimism. 'What lifts *Tight Little Island* above its own high mark of insular drollery . . . is its mastery of the visual gag,' commented *Time*, whose reviewer was particularly taken with the whisky-hiding scenes: 'For lightness, comic movement and inventive detail, these sequences are worthy of René Clair.'[33] Audiences were equally delighted. In its first week the film took nearly $15,000, breaking box-office records at the Trans-Lux, and went on to pack movie houses all across the country.

*Whisky Galore* was also the first Ealing film to score a major hit in France. In September 1950 it was ecstatically received at the Biarritz Festival, where James Clark reported that 'the audience went wild with enthusiasm. Constant clapping, shouts and "bravos" punctuated the dialogue, and at the finish the audience demanded that the director be presented to them. He, sensible man, had slipped out the back way.'[34]

That same month the film had its Paris premiere at the Cinéma Marbeuf, under the title *Whisky à gogo*. The whisky distillers had been slow to realise the film's potential as a sales aid, but by now they had caught on. With the help of the Scottish Whisky Association, the Marbeuf's foyer was transformed into a replica of the hold of the SS *Cabinet Minister*, with crates and bottles on all sides. Compton Mackenzie, who with Mackendrick and Danischewsky attended a first-night banquet at which whisky flowed freely, hazily recalled it as 'the nearest thing to a Bacchic revel imaginable in this twentieth century'.[35] French reviewers and audiences were even more diverted than their American counterparts. The film's takings soared, sales of Scotch did likewise, and *Whisky à gogo* became the in-name for bars and night-clubs all over France. From its unpromising launch, *Whisky Galore* ended up being not just (as Danischewsky put it) 'the longest unsponsored advertisement ever to reach cinema screens the world over'[36], but the most profitable film, in relation to its costs, in the history of Ealing Studios.

It was also one of the first Ealing films that proved to have a substantial afterlife. Until then, Mackendrick observes, 'it never occurred to anyone that a film was going to have a life longer than about a year. The product was expendable – it lasted a year or so, and then it was dumped and totally forgotten.'[37] *Whisky Galore*, though, continued to attract audiences long after its initial success – and still does so, 40 years later. With his first film as a director, and rather to his surprise – 'You didn't take yourself that seriously, thank god'[38] – Mackendrick had created a lasting classic, especially in Scotland. According to John Brown (writing in 1983), *Whisky Galore* is still 'by a very large margin the most popular film ever screened in the [Scottish] islands'.[39]

For all its popularity, the film has had few successors, apart, of course, from *The Maggie*. There was a post-Ealing sequel of sorts, *Rockets Galore* (1958), produced by Danischewsky and featuring some of the previous cast; but it was sorry stuff, limply facetious and best forgotten. Perhaps *Whisky Galore*'s closest comic descendant to date is Bill Forsyth's 1983 *Local Hero*, which shares not only the West Scottish setting, but something of the earlier film's blend of irony, truculence and affectionately observed detail. Its plot also seems to derive from both *Whisky Galore* and *The Maggie* – in the latter case, according to Forsyth, purely by coincidence. 'I didn't see *The Maggie* till . . . after we had finished filming *Local Hero*. I got a bit of a fright. . . . But afterwards I felt quite touched that I had unconsciously followed the same kind of progression on from *Whisky Galore!* as Sandy Mackendrick did.'[40] Critics also picked up the affinities, as often as not by way of reproach: 'The film takes a retrograde step back into the cosy Ealing ethos of *Whisky Galore* and *The Maggie*,'[41] Tom Milne wrote in *Monthly Film Bulletin*.

Few critics, though, noticed that *Whisky Galore* had been cunningly reworked, in a very different idiom, ten years earlier. In *The Wicker Man*, directed by Robin Hardy from a script by Anthony Shaffer, the victimised outsider – a conflation of Waggett and Farquharson – becomes a puritanical Glaswegian cop, Sergeant Howie, played with grim disapproval by Edward Woodward. Summoned to the Hebridean island of Summerisle to investigate a child's disappearance, the devoutly Christian Howie is appalled by the islanders' exuberant paganism. Like Waggett, he makes no attempt to explore their beliefs, which he treats as self-evidently misguided and immoral. Again the principled outsider finds himself mocked and manipulated by the far shrewder islanders, and eventually sacrificed – literally, this being after all a horror movie – for the good of the community.

Despite some lapses in performance and in plausibility, *The Wicker Man* is in many ways a truer successor to *Whisky Galore* than Forsyth's comedy. *Local Hero*, for all its quirky wit and underlying melancholy, is essentially benevolent in its regard. The ending, with the conflicting interests of all parties harmoniously resolved, aligns it with the gentler Ealing tradition of *Passport to Pimlico*. Whereas *The Wicker Man*, like *Whisky Galore*, ends with a stark denial of reconciliation: the sergeant, trapped and burning alive in the giant effigy of the title, desperately sings a Protestant hymn, while the islanders dance around him chanting the joyous rhythm of 'Sumer Is Icumen In'. In its thematic preoccupations – perception and misperception, innocence outwitted by amoral experience – and in the gleeful blackness of its vision, *The Wicker Man* could stand in for the horror movie that Mackendrick never made.

# 3 The Man in the White Suit

'Outside Mackendrick's work, how many
British films have *intelligence* as a central
concern, valued in the characters as it is
expressed in the organisation of the film?'[1]

Charles Barr

'There's a moment towards the end of certain
kinds of comedy when they ought to get a
little nasty.'[2]

Alexander Mackendrick

The eventual triumph of *Whisky Galore* established Mackendrick as one of
Ealing's most promising directors. But during the year or more which
elapsed before the first signs of its success, Mackendrick, though not
explicitly in disgrace, was under something of a cloud. 'I'm not sure Balcon
was very happy with me – there was a slightly uncomfortable relationship
there. I remember being deeply depressed at the Round Table meetings.
Mick would go round the table – he had a very random way of dealing with
people – and he would get to me and say, "And Sandy . . . er, ye-e-es . . .
ah, what were we saying?" And I thought, "That's me done; I'm forgotten
and I'm never going to get another break." '

There was little danger that Mackendrick would be sacked. Staff were
rarely sacked from Ealing and members of 'the team' – the writers,
producers and directors who attended the Round Table conferences –
virtually never. Those that left, like Robert Hamer and Henry Cornelius,
did so of their own accord. Financially, at least, Mackendrick was secure,
which in view of his personal circumstances was just as well. He and Hilary
Lloyd were married on Christmas Eve 1948, four weeks after the completion
of *Whisky Galore*. A few months later Hilary contracted tuberculosis.
Mackendrick, who had read his Thomas Mann, was convinced that the
disease would be fatal. 'We found a hospital room for her, and I thought it
would be a long slow death of about two years. But Hilary set herself up with
a telephone and kept in touch, and people said she was the most
knowledgeable person about Ealing Studios on the end of a telephone. And
after about a year in hospital she came out of it stronger and better.'

Meanwhile Mackendrick had been assigned to scriptwriting and second-
unit work. 'Mick Balcon came back to me and said, "Erm, you know, it's

very important you should be gainfully employed and whatnot. I want you to do something – we may not have a movie for you, but. . . ." Meaning, in his stammering and flustered way, "We're demoting you." That was how I read it, anyway. So they put me on to second unit.' If he felt any resentment at the time, Mackendrick subsequently looked back on his 'demotion' as a piece of 'extraordinary good luck, that happens very rarely to directors' and an invaluable source of experience. 'You're working anonymously for another director; you don't take credit, and I think very wisely, because you're working to somebody else's conception. And you begin to see the fun about pure craft. How to make stuff that cuts well, how to make the thing move, how to get the tempo and the pacing – without any of that terrible burden of responsibility when it's an epic work of your own. So between *Whisky Galore* and *Man in the White Suit*, I learned my craft.'

Mackendrick's main assignments during this period were *Dance Hall* and *The Blue Lamp*. *Dance Hall* was directed, fairly reluctantly, by Charles Crichton. Balcon always maintained that no Ealing director 'was ever forced to make a film that he didn't want to make'.[3] Crichton agrees, but adds that Balcon would sometimes exert oblique pressure, 'especially if you had another project he knew you wanted to make. He'd hint that if you wouldn't mind just doing *this* for him first. . . . I'm not denigrating the picture; seeing it again on TV, I found it quite interesting, and I'm not ashamed of it. But there's not much of me in it.'

The plot of *Dance Hall* revolves around four young women who frequent the local Palais de Danse, one of whom, played by Natasha Parry, finds her affections torn between her insensitive husband (Donald Houston) and a dangerously exciting young man (Bonar Colleano) she meets at a dance. In the end she returns dutifully to her husband. Mackendrick received joint writing credit, along with the producer, E. V. H. Emmett, and Diana Morgan. Morgan, one of Ealing's very few female scriptwriters, found him 'very pernickety – in a perfectly nice way'[4] and tirelessly argumentative.

Mackendrick also directed second unit, covering 'all the material where the bands are playing, close-ups of trumpeters and drummers and things like that. Very good experience, and I enjoyed it thoroughly.' Crichton recalls him being 'very particular about what I wanted, and I couldn't be precise – and he tried to nail me down, the bastard! But they were very simple shots, and he took just what was wanted, that's all there was to it.'

Easily the most interesting figure in *Dance Hall* is the villain, Alec, played by Bonar Colleano. This character, one of those quick-thinking manipulators that always fascinated Mackendrick, seems so much more intensely alive than anyone else in the film that his final defeat feels like the wrong ending. It may be no coincidence that the villain is again the most vivid character in *The Blue Lamp*, where Mackendrick also had a hand in the script. The film was directed by Basil Dearden, teamed as usual with

Michael Relph as producer, and scripted by T. E. B. Clarke, Ted Willis and Jan Read, with Mackendrick credited for 'additional dialogue'.

*The Blue Lamp* is a key work in Ealing's development, laying down the pattern for the studio's serious output as did *Passport to Pimlico* for the comedies. Both films were scripted by 'Tibby' Clarke, the single most important influence on the post-war Ealing mainstream, whereas Mackendrick is often seen as the successor to Robert Hamer as chief representative of the 'other side' of Ealing – the maverick, darker, more iconoclastic aspect. Clarke himself sensed this, speaking of Mackendrick as 'quite different in many ways from the rest of us – mostly in intellectual ways. I think he was more downbeat than the average at Ealing, which was rather an upbeat studio. Sandy was a downbeat director – like Robert Hamer, in a way.' *The Blue Lamp* is the only film on which Clarke and Mackendrick worked together – the two strands, maverick and mainstream, briefly intertwined.

As Charles Barr has pointed out, *The Blue Lamp* has much in common with Clarke's comedies – and especially *Hue and Cry*, with the villain in both cases trapped by an ad hoc army of those standing at a slightly oblique angle to everyday society: schoolboys and the criminal fraternity. But the film also reflects themes and elements from Mackendrick's films, although generally playing them straight, without his distancing irony.

*The Blue Lamp* begins and ends with the same image: a London police constable on the beat, giving directions to a passer-by. The first policeman is PC George Dixon, played by Jack Warner; the second, whom we first meet as a nervous rookie under Dixon's guidance, is PC Mitchell (James Hanley). By the end of the film Dixon is dead, shot by a young delinquent, but Mitchell, now as stolid and confident a figure as his mentor, has taken over. The message is unambiguous: continuity, reassurance – *le roi est mort, vive le roi*. Mackendrick's Ealing films, too, often circle back to their starting point, as if to show that nothing has changed; but undercutting the image is an intimation of stasis and stagnancy, of a system seizing up under the dead-weight of tradition.

Like *Whisky Galore*, *The Blue Lamp* is introduced by a pseudo-documentary voice-over, providing a sociological commentary on the characters: 'The case of Diana Lewis is typical of many. . . . These restless and ill-adjusted youngsters have produced a type of delinquent which is partly responsible for the post-war increase in crime.' But where the commentary in *Whisky Galore* is played off against the images, setting up a convention only to have it undermined, *The Blue Lamp* takes its voice-over straight, assenting to the social framework it proposes ('Youths . . . who lack the code, experience and self-discipline of the professional thief. . . . The small exclusive circle which represents the underworld does not accept them') and never subverting the sententious tone. As in a real documentary, the commentator embodies the voice of authority, to be accepted without question.

The ironic mode scarcely features in *The Blue Lamp*; its dramatic tensions are linear, along the flow of the narrative, rather than cutting laterally across character or situation. At the film's climax Dixon's killer, Tom Riley (Dirk Bogarde in the best of his early roles), is hunted down by the police with the help of the London underworld. The episode recalls *M*, but with no hint of Lang's sardonically Brechtian view of crooks tracking down Peter Lorre because child-murderers are bad for business. Riley, as the commentary suggested, has transgressed a code acknowledged equally by police and criminals, and thus by general agreement placed himself beyond the communal pale. As in *Passport*, superficial disagreements are submerged in the underlying consensus: cop and villain, like Pemberton and Gregg, readily shelve their differences to work together.

Only occasionally, in the scenes between Riley and his girlfriend, Diana Lewis (Peggy Evans), can a hint of moral ambiguity, a striving towards greater psychological intensity, be sensed. It was this element, according to Michael Relph, that was Mackendrick's chief contribution to the script, to which he brought 'a rather more sophisticated viewpoint' than the other writers. One scene in particular carries an emotional and sexual charge which lifts the film briefly out of its wholesome British decorum. Riley, suspecting – or feigning to suspect – Diana of infidelity, produces a gun which he points at her belly, stroking the barrel and gaining manifest pleasure from her terrified reaction. Finally he puts the weapon aside, lies back on the bed and, with the remark 'I reckon a bit of a scare's good for your insides', pulls her down towards him. Evans's performance hints at a surreptitious excitement underlying her terror, and the *double entendre* of Bogarde's line seems, for Ealing, remarkably explicit. Mackendrick would return, with rather more subtlety, to exploring the erotic connotations of power in his first post-Ealing movie, *Sweet Smell of Success*.

There's also a hint of Mackendrick's later work in his direction of *Blue Lamp*'s second unit, whose main task was the car chase that comes towards the end of the movie. A car chase of itself invites a certain shooting technique, and it might be simplistic to attribute the contrast between the fluid, sweeping camera movements of this sequence and the contained dollying elsewhere in the film solely to Mackendrick and Dearden's respective cinematic styles. Even so, the similarities to the robbery sequence in *The Ladykillers* are often striking. A couple of characteristic Mackendrick angles are hard to miss: the menacing low-angle tracking shot of the crooks' getaway car, which will recur in *Man in the White Suit* and *Sweet Smell of Success*; and an overhead, god's-eye crane shot, anticipating the corresponding moment in *Ladykillers*, of a police car lost in a maze of tiny streets around Ladbroke Grove.

*The Blue Lamp* was released in January 1950 and *Dance Hall* five months later. By then, *Whisky Galore* was becoming an international smash hit and Mackendrick, restored to favour, was busy preparing his second film as director. Its source was a play by his cousin and former collaborator, Roger MacDougall. Since their time together at Merlin, MacDougall had achieved success as a West End playwright while continuing to write movie scripts, many of them for Ealing, though he was never on the studio's full-time staff. 'I refused to sign a contract, to be just a hack who could be commanded to do this or that. Though in fact I always did it, out of the goodness of my heart, so I might just as well have been under contract. The most I ever earned at Ealing was £60 a week, and that had to be dragged out of Mick Balcon. Not that it mattered much – most of what I wrote for them was valueless stuff anyway. Theatre's my medium; I've never enjoyed writing for film like Sandy does.'

Mackendrick had read an unperformed early play by MacDougall called 'The Flower Within the Bud'. It was a satirical comedy about the disruption caused to a mill-owning family, and to the whole textile industry, by the invention of an indestructible fabric. Mackendrick 'became interested not so much in the play as in certain characters in it.' He persuaded Balcon to take an option on it and, declining MacDougall's offer of help, wrote the first draft entirely by himself. 'I did something really rather wicked: I took Roger's hero and gave him a minor role, and pivoted the whole story around a secondary character, the one played in the film by Alec Guinness, to make a new story entirely. And Balcon liked it, and approved it. When I showed it to Roger he got very indignant, and said, "My God, you might as well have cut the hero out altogether!", and I said, "Yes, well, I did actually think of doing that." '

Having got over his initial pique, MacDougall went along with the further disruption of his play, and with the total elimination of his hero. 'Something I discovered then,' he recalls, 'is that there's a character you need in a play, but you don't need in a film, because the camera takes over from him. It's Enobarbus in *Antony and Cleopatra*, it's Horatio in *Hamlet*. The camera becomes that character who holds it all together – the viewpoint character, if you like. You don't need a person to do it for you.'

Together, the cousins worked on what was now called *The Man in the White Suit*, until MacDougall went off on tour with his play *To Dorothy, a Son* and John Dighton came in to help with the final draft of the script. The script credit for the film reads MacDougall, Dighton, Mackendrick, in that order. As MacDougall tells it, the producer, Sidney Cole, said ' "Well, Roger has a credit for original material, Sandy has a credit as director, so I'll put Johnny first as scriptwriter, because that's his only credit." But Johnny Dighton said, "Oh no, it's Roger's script, you can't put my name above his," and insisted that my name went first. That's the sort of thing that happened at Ealing.'

MacDougall's original play was never published, and received only one production – a brief run at Pitlochry in May 1954, under the same title as the film. As a result, few people have had the chance to appreciate just how skilfully Mackendrick and his collaborators reworked the piece, avoiding the least hint of the stilted, stage-bound 'filmed theatre' all too common in British cinema. 'After seeing this play,' the *Glasgow Herald*'s critic wrote of the Pitlochry production, 'one realises how much better the film treatment of it was.'[5] Purely on a reading of the text, it's hard to disagree. The play is a static and rather wordy piece, set throughout in the 'Reception Room' of the mansion of Alan Greatheart, a mill-owner, with much of the action taking place off-stage. Almost all the *dramatis personae* are drawn from the mill-owning classes or the management; Greatheart's foreman is the sole representative of the workforce, otherwise present only as a noisy off-stage mob.

The mainspring of the play's action, as of the film, is the invention by Sidney Stratton, a scientist at Greatheart's mill, of an indestructible fabric. But overlaid on this is the romance between Daphne, Greatheart's daughter, and her cousin, Geoffrey Hibberden. Hibberden is the hero whom Mackendrick excised – quite rightly, one can't help feeling. Evidently intended as a trenchant iconoclast, exposing the greed and hypocrisy of the bosses, he comes across as a pretentious ass. His notion of declaring his passion is to announce, 'I want to visit the quiet regions where self is forgotten in fulfilment, where taking is forgotten in giving, and only you can take me there.' The Daphne of the play, 'an underdeveloped, almost pre-adolescent schoolgirl of 20', is enchanted, but it's hard to imagine anyone getting away with that line to Joan Greenwood.

The script of *Man in the White Suit* retains barely half a dozen lines from the play. Taking MacDougall's central idea – that an indestructible cloth, seemingly a boon to humanity, would arouse violent hostility in bosses and workers alike – Mackendrick, the political cartoonist *manqué*, turned the story into a mordant cartoon on the state of Britain. 'It wasn't intended to be a satire only at the expense of Industry. . . . Each character in the story was intended as a caricature of a separate political attitude, covering the entire range from Communist, through official Trades Unionism, Romantic Individualism, Liberalism, Enlightened and Unenlightened Capitalism to Strong-arm Reaction. Even the central character was intended as a comic picture of Disinterested Science.'[6] *The Man in the White Suit*, like all Mackendrick's subsequent Ealing films, portrays a stagnant, post-Imperial Britain, terrified of change and clinging to a crumbling and threadbare past.

But the film can also be seen as a subversive portrait of Ealing itself, most British of studios, comfortable and well-intentioned, setting its face increasingly against any serious consideration of conflict. Such a reading is supported by the 'private' level of satire built into the film, with certain characters expressly modelled on members of the studio team – most notably the mill-owner Birnley (the Greatheart of the original play), whose flustered, paternalistic liberalism is borrowed from Michael Balcon. Not only was Birnley given several of Balcon's pet phrases, but Mackendrick told Cecil Parker, who played the role, to 'model yourself on Mick'. (Balcon, when he found out, was so delighted that Douglas Slocombe wonders 'whether Mick didn't start to emulate Cecil Parker, rather than the other way round'.)

Other caricatures included Frank, the shop steward, based on Sidney Cole, the film's producer and a staunch union man; and the bustling, bossy nurse who slaps Alec Guinness's face, 'an absolute portrait of our studio nurse', according to Mackendrick. Ernest Irving, Ealing's autocratic (and asthmatic) music director, inspired the wheezy old magnate, Sir John Kierlaw, though Slocombe believes the character also incorporates elements of Major Reg Baker, Balcon's partner and financial éminence grise. For his portrayal of Sidney Stratton, the visionary scientist, Guinness borrowed traits from a young studio technician whose innocently self-absorbed air he had noticed. Certain critics, though, have sensed something of Mackendrick himself in the role. Charles Barr suspected 'a satirical (self-) portrait of the harassed young Ealing director struggling to . . . give the world his own dazzling personal vision, in defiance of the paternalistic hand of his boss and the general inertia of the industry'[7], and Neil Sinyard noted that 'just as Sidney's inventiveness has been squashed . . . so Mackendrick's radicalism has been contained within Ealing boundaries, and the film is finally a pessimistic allegory of the artist'.[8]

From the first, Mackendrick had seen the role of Stratton as ideal for Guinness, who could bring to it both the necessary unobtrusiveness and that quality of internalised obsession which Crichton also exploited in *The Lavender Hill Mob* – a quality noted by Ken Tynan in the actor's stage portrayals of 'those iceberg characters, nine-tenths concealed, whose fascination lies not in how they look but in how their minds work. . . . Guinness can convey, by his voice and bearing, the existence of little fixed ideas, frisking about behind the deferential mask of normality.'[9]

Most Ealing films were cast from stock, drawing on a pool of players who recur in picture after picture. Some critics have seen this as a lazy, reflex habit, source of staleness and predictability – and so it can be, especially in the later Ealing movies. But in the hands of an astute director such as Hamer or Mackendrick, the casting of a figure like Miles Malleson can take on a sharper edge, the familiar persona deflected into subtle self-comment. Thus in *Kind Hearts* Malleson's hangman, spouting sententious doggerel, is as absurdly inadequate to his grim function as were the D'Ascoynes to their privileged station in society. And as the tailor in *White Suit*, paying careful attention to Stratton's measurements and none at all to his words, he's as oblivious as Birnley (or as Stratton himself, for that matter) of his whole fusty world poised to be swept into the abyss. In each case, the actor's stock waffly-old-chump serves, not just as an indulgent cameo, but to present a burlesque variation on the central theme of the film.

The casting of Cecil Parker as Birnley marks a subtle shift in the pompous authority-figure from that of *Whisky Galore*, given the differing screen personas of the actors concerned. Radford, though buffoonish, always seems sincere; duplicity is clearly beyond his mental range. Parker, while more convincingly in control – he's credible as the head of a major industrial concern, which Radford could never be – tends to ring hollow. Behind his headmasterly vowels can be sensed a windy shiftiness, a hypocritical bluster which the film effectively punctures. Later, in *The Ladykillers*, Mackendrick would mine this aspect of Parker even more pitilessly, reducing him to the quavering, shabby-genteel conman, panicking in phone-boxes and tumbling to an ignominious death from the roof.

Similar felicities of casting can be found throughout *Man in the White Suit*, but one stroke of genius deserves special note – the choice of Ernest Thesiger to play Sir John Kierlaw, the patriarch of the textile industry. In MacDougall's play, Kierlaw appears as standard-issue bloated plutocrat: he 'strides massively', smokes large cigars, affects a hearty manner to cloak his avarice. By stripping this cumbersome figure down to the frail, wizened Thesiger, the film creates a monstrous incarnation of concentrated will, indifferent to appearances and wholly unhampered by altruism. Like some science-fiction Superbrain, Kierlaw has mutated into a cerebellum of pure, malignant intelligence yoked to an atrophied body.

The shooting of *White Suit* went more smoothly than that of *Whisky Galore*, being completed almost on schedule in 59 days. Mackendrick had gained in confidence since his first movie; also, having conceived the project from the start, he was able to exert overall creative control, working from his own detailed storyboard. Not that he ever insisted on sticking rigidly to the set-ups he had sketched. 'I always plan in detail,' he once explained, 'but I never follow the plan. The plan is a rehearsal. In fact you are freer to improvise the more you plan.'[10]

*White Suit* was the first of his three films with Douglas Slocombe, whose subtly elegant cinematography complemented Mackendrick's cinematic style. Slocombe found the storyboard technique stimulating, if sometimes frustrating. 'He would do the most wonderful drawings of what he expected to see in the camera. Unfortunately no lens would have the perspectives that he could draw.'[11] Even so, the sketches conveyed Mackendrick's wishes far more fluently than his words. 'His greatest ability on the floor was his facility for drawing – for suggesting, say, a camera shooting over a parapet into the street below, and drawing it so accurately that you couldn't believe a camera hadn't already been placed there. But in the absence of a pencil, he would give you a stream of directions and descriptions that were so complicated – though presumably clear to him – that they were very much a second best. So we all knew that you had to find Sandy a pencil, quick, just to stop him talking.'

As well as designing the look of the film Mackendrick made a major contribution to the way it sounded by creating an aural 'character' for Stratton's eccentric scientific apparatus. According to his own account, though, he only embarked on this exercise to occupy himself after Sidney Cole, the producer, had thrown him out of the cutting room. 'As always I was very anxious about the editing. But the director ought to get lost for the first cut, and allow the editor a crack at the thing without the director looking over his shoulder. So I was making an absolute pain in the neck of myself, and Sid said, "Get lost, do something else. Go and play with something." And I'd got this vague idea of making a sound effect that was sort of a character, and I got hold of a jazz record, Red Nichols and his Five Pennies. Poor Mary [Haberfield, the sound editor] thought I was crazy – changed her mind later, she got an award for it. I made her make a variable area track of this record, marking all the drumbeats and things like that, and put it on a piece of graph paper about ten feet long. Everybody was saying, "Sandy's gone mad again." '[12]

Mackendrick and Haberfield reconstituted the rhythm in terms of assorted sound effects, working (according to a studio handout) 'to a score which read "Bubble, bubble, high drip, low drip, high drain, low drain". The bubbles were obtained by a glass tube blown into glycerine; the drips by pinging two different-sized pieces of brass and glass against the palm of the hand; and the drains by an air tube fed into water, with a metal tube over the bubbles, amplifying the sound.' Finally the sound supervisor, Stephen Dalby, rerecorded the whole affair, varying the pitch and tone until, to Mackendrick's delight, 'he made it sound thoroughly obscene, like breaking wind in the bath. And when we put it on to the film it sounded marvellous.'[13]

Mackendrick took similar pains over the construction of the apparatus itself. Determined to get away from the routine 'mad-scientist' devices from every horror movie since *Metropolis*, he insisted the equipment should be no mere random collection of tubes and retorts, but assembled to sound scientific principles – just as Stratton's rapid-fire scientific jargon, though sounding like gobbledegook, in fact makes good technical sense. David Peers, the assistant director, remembers Mackendrick calling in experts 'to tell us whether this retort would fit into this test-tube and so on. It was typical of Sandy that if the experts didn't agree with what he wanted he ignored their advice anyway.'[14]

For Mackendrick, fastidious attention to detail is essential to his conception of comedy. 'It's partly to convince myself that the story is utterly real, on the basis that comedy is only comic if you play it seriously, if you take the joke in fanatical earnestness. So I'm certainly guilty of *that* attitude, because it's part of *my* comic performance to be obsessively meticulous about absolutely pointless things. Because that's the joke.'

On this occasion, Mackendrick's thoroughness paid off. The apparatus works both as a memorable comic creation in its own right and as a vivid expression of Stratton's idiosyncratic energy intruding into the subdued environment of the laboratory. Repeatedly destroyed, by imperceptive lab heads or by explosion, it re-emerges on each occasion bigger and more irrepressible than before, thriving on destruction like the magic broom of the sorcerer's apprentice. Its pulsing, dynamic beat gradually imposes itself on the rhythm of the film. Or rather, of the first half of the film, since, even more markedly than *Whisky Galore*, *White Suit* falls into two sections: a thrust towards change and a blocking of that thrust.

Mackendrick announces this pattern from the start. Once again he opens with a voice-over commentary, but this time with no pretence at narrative objectivity. The voice is not that of some disembodied impartial observer, but of Birnley, hailing the restoration of 'calm and sanity' – that is, of the status quo. Radical change will be attempted but – for the time being at any rate – suppressed. Only this voice-over, with its hint of pompous authority headed for a pratfall, indicates that we're in for a comedy. The credits, with their shuttling machinery and urgent music, give us no clue; nor does the shot that follows, a grim industrial panorama recalling Dickens's prospect of Coketown: 'A town of machinery and tall chimneys, out of which interminable serpents of smoke trailed themselves for ever and ever, and never got uncoiled.'[15] As with *Whisky Galore*, the documentary-style opening establishes a way of life whose stability is threatened – the entrenched interests with which the outsider is about to tangle.

In the first half of the film, as Stratton strives to realise his vision, the aspiration to change pushes consistently forward, successively overcoming the obstacles in its path, until the suit is created in all its immaculate splendour. But now the blocking mechanisms come into play, and the movement in the remainder of the film is circular – a frantic scurrying round in a diminishing space like a rabbit in a cornfield, ending in defeat as the suit disintegrates and the achievement of the first half is cancelled out.

To reduce the film to this kind of schematic diagram, though, is to risk falling into the same easy dualism that Mackendrick satirises in showing us Sidney Stratton, all in white, confronting the black-clad figures of the textile bosses. Sidney good, bosses bad; loss of the fabric equals defeat for energy, creativity and the future. Some Ealing comedies *are* just about as simple as that, but not Mackendrick's and certainly not *Man in the White Suit*. Here, even more than in *Whisky Galore*, the interplay between innocence and experience is no straightforward clash of opposites, but a matter of ambiguities, of moral relativity. Each character is an admixture of qualities: naive in some contexts, crafty in others, as the ethical perspectives shift.

Sidney, for a start, is by no means always the simple innocent he appears. Up against Kierlaw and his colleagues he seems hopelessly naive – but earlier in the film he's a devious, underhand figure, insinuating his buccaneer experiment into the conformity of the research lab, relying on the mental limitations of his colleagues to let it pass unnoticed. Birnley, chucking over his own commercial acumen, is almost as innocent as Sidney, as incapable of seeing beyond habitual thought-patterns. And even Kierlaw, shrewdness personified, misreads Daphne, projecting on to her his own cynicism – just as she credits Sidney with idealistic motives that never entered his head.

Mackendrick recalls that before he hit upon MacDougall's play, 'Roger and I had been trying to think of a comic way to deal with the moral issue of the invention of nuclear weapons.' They failed to do so (and in any case would hardly have got far with it at Balcon's studio), but an attack on the 'so-called disinterested scientist, totally reckless and totally inconsiderate of the consequences of his actions,' still underpins the film's central ambiguity. 'Most people think of [Sidney] as an entirely idealistic and sympathetic young man. He's nothing of the sort. If you look at it closely, you'll see that he's just as selfish and self-interested as any of them. All that happens is that the industrialists choose the wrong things to bribe him with. He could easily be bought off – as is suggested by an early scene in the picture – if he was given enormous research grants; he would quite willingly have forgotten the social implications.'[16]

If, as Mackendrick suggests, we're led to side uncritically with Sidney, it's perhaps due as much to the film's narrative structure as to Guinness's performance. 'Alec and I were both convinced that [Sidney]'s as obnoxious as any of them; his behaviour to other people is really outrageous. . . . But the story's so built, you become so invested in whatever he wants to do, that audiences tend to feel he must be the person who's good, and with whom we sympathise.'[17] And Guinness plays Sidney with a shy, childlike charm which engages our sympathy as surely as it does that of most of the female characters. The diffident smile, the tousled hair, the head-scratching gesture borrowed from Stan Laurel – anyone so patently helpless, we feel, must deserve our support. It could be, perhaps, that Guinness intended to present Sidney as all the more dangerous in that his single-minded insensitivity is dissembled by boyish appeal. If so, the camouflage was a little too effective; it needed a touch more overt ruthlessness to get the point across.

Genre conditioning also plays a part; where *Whisky Galore* lifted some narrative tricks from the war-movie, *White Suit* plays off another generic formula, the Warners-style scientific bio-pic. Muni as Pasteur, Robinson as Paul Ehrlich, Tracy as Edison, Garson as Madame Curie – all inspired by their revelation of truth, all striving with heroic obstinacy against setbacks, poverty and entrenched prejudice. Since Sidney shares so many of their characteristics, not least the distracted air and sublime disregard for personal comfort ('But Professor, you must *eat*') which, in movie shorthand, have always denoted genius, we're drawn to identify with his cause.

This too may be a case of subtlety defeating itself, since Mackendrick is harnessing the conventions of the bio-pic to a film profoundly sceptical of all scientific pretension. *Man in the White Suit* presents a vision of what Mamoun Hassan has called 'Faustian science', something magical and obsessive, capable of wrecking not just a laboratory but an entire social system. Around Sidney's work there accumulate images of destruction and catastrophe, both verbal – terms like 'chain reactions', 'radioactive thorium' and 'heavy hydrogen' that recall the original nuclear sub-text – and visual. As they progress, his experiments take on the trappings of war, complete with sandbags, tin helmets and explosive plungers.

Mackendrick dramatises the destructive power of Sidney's work through its effect on the Birnley lab, first glimpsed in a subjective shot from Sidney's viewpoint – a vision (as Frankel's score confirms) of paradise, where serene white-coated figures move quietly about their work. The moment Sidney takes over, the beehive stops humming; the lab, cleared of all but him and Wilson, his assistant, is left stark and cavernous. As the explosions mount, it becomes a bombsite, with shattered windows, twisted pipes and smoke-blackened walls.

In parallel, we see the personal disintegration of Hoskins, the head of research (played by Henry Mollison, the dour Excise Officer from *Whisky Galore*). A pompous figure, he struts about the lab with an air of conscious superiority. Banished to an adjacent cubby-hole when Sidney usurps his realm, he's reduced by the explosions to an abject wreck, crouching behind a bank of sandbags and jumping when the phone rings. Science is a mythical monster; it consumes even its own children.

At this period, such a wary attitude to science was uncommon in movies, which generally viewed it as an enlightened force, bringer of health and prosperity, saviour of humankind against natural and even (as in *When Worlds Collide*) extra-terrestrial disaster. Mackendrick's film anticipates later developments, as the mid-fifties science-fiction cycle got under way and nuclear metaphors darkened its initial optimism. Indeed the blackened, pulsating pit left by Sidney's first titanic blast looks remarkably like a miniature version of those mysterious craters around which gawking bystanders would collect, to be zapped by emerging aliens.

It's even possible to see *White Suit* itself as an SF movie – as did Stuart Stock and Kenneth von Gunden, who included it among their *Twenty All-Time Great Science Fiction Films* as 'one of the most mature, enjoyable and intelligent SF films ever made'.[18] Certainly it shares the same basic narrative device as many SF films. Mackendrick himself likes to draw parallels with Gordon Douglas's 1954 monster-ant movie *Them!*: 'The formula is now an absolute tradition – my version of *Rhinoceros* worked the same way. The trick of the unbelievable thing – indestructible cloth, giant ants, people turning into rhinoceroses – is that you frustrate the audience; you stall them for so long that they've *got* to believe it. And you load the fantasy. You establish the people who believe in whatever it is as sympathetic and likeable, and you make the others – who are in fact the sane people – unsympathetic. So by having this unpleasant character who says what the audience would otherwise say – "That's nonsense!" – you make them insist on believing the unbelievable.'[19]

But if Sidney and his endeavours do appear in a more favourable light than intended, this is the film's only serious fault. After the wayward technique of *Whisky Galore*, with its fitful pacing and *faute de mieux* camerawork, *White Suit* has the incisive edge of a film whose director knows just what he wants from each scene, each shot. Nor, this time round, is character ever distorted to fit situation. At worst, there's the occasional brief lapse into movie-comedy cliché, as when Sidney is sacked from Corland's mill after his unauthorised experimenting has come to light. We see him, in close-up, bravely defying Corland – 'No, don't interrupt me – it's small minds like yours that stand in the way of progress' – before a predictable establishing shot reveals him talking to himself in the washroom.

One other questionable moment comes slightly earlier, with Sidney's very first appearance: Corland, on the point of embracing Daphne, is jostled by Sidney's trolley. Ealing's choked-off attitude to sex has often been deplored and one symptom of it was a weakness for the irritating old comic routine where two people about to kiss are interrupted by a noise, an intrusion, or whatever. Mackendrick's example at least fulfils a dramatic function. Corland is thoroughly unworthy of Daphne, and Sidney – a disruptive force from the very outset – will cause her to discover as much. Mackendrick is using the routine to reflect the relationships between his characters. But it's a pity the point wasn't put across by some less well-worn – and less repressive – device.

This apart, the humour in *White Suit* is sharp, effective, true to character and intrinsic to the development of the narrative. A good example comes just after the abortive embrace. Birnley, entering Corland's research lab, catches sight of Sidney's apparatus burbling to itself in a corner and asks what it is. In a series of gliding, lateral camera movements, each member of Corland's staff is successively drawn in, as though the device were exercising its own centripetal power, until the screen is clogged with a mass of people arguing, gesticulating and talking across each other – a perfect image of the coagulated system within whose crevices Sidney has contrived to operate.

But Mackendrick deftly uses the scene to make two additional points.

Birnley is far too amused by Corland's embarrassment to notice anything else – just as the idea of putting one over on the competition will blind him to the wider implications of the new fabric. So only Daphne observes Sidney's trolley nosing in through the door and then, as he sees the crowd round his apparatus, as quietly withdrawing. Daphne, we realise, is not only readier than anyone else to see and think about what she sees, she's also more open to what Sidney is doing.

Awareness, perception, seeing or the failure to see – in *Man in the White Suit* the central preoccupations of Mackendrick's cinema are constantly in play. The sequence in which Sidney gains admission to the Birnley lab hinges on a favourite Mackendrick device: a character duping himself through his own preconceptions. An electron microscope is being delivered to the mill, accompanied by two experts who don overalls to avoid soiling their suits. Sidney, working at Birnley's as a labourer, helps transport the instrument to the lab and, once there, stands gazing at it in delight. Next to him stands Hoskins, the head of research. His glance at Sidney expresses irritation, contempt and uncertainty; this appears to be some damned menial hanging about the lab, but then again – clothing, the primary social signifier, having been rendered ambiguous – he can't be sure. Sidney, by innocently displaying expertise about the microscope, resolves his doubts: no one so erudite could be a mere labourer. Hoskins accordingly invites him to stay on a few days 'until we get the hang of it'. No deception is necessary on Sidney's part. Hoskins, seeing only what fits his snobbish expectations, serves as his own deceiver.

Later, when Sidney's triumphal exuberance offends against protocol, Hoskins revises his view. 'A lunatic, obviously,' he remarks, pouring the miracle fluid down the sink, and extracting Sidney from one pigeon-hole in his mind to slot him neatly into another. Nor is this mental rigidity confined to the management. Bertha, a staunch unionist, though (in Vida Hope's portrayal) a far more sympathetic character than Hoskins, uses much the same defence-mechanism, producing a rapid succession of ready-made categories to which the oddity of Sidney can be assigned.

BERTHA: New, aren't you? Never worked in a mill before?
SIDNEY: Oh yes – several.
BERTHA: I know. Leave school – into the first blind-alley job that comes along . . . by the time you're 30, what are you? Flotsam floating on the floodtide of profit. There's capitalism for you!
SIDNEY: It wasn't quite like that. I got a scholarship to Cambridge.
BERTHA: But you hadn't got the Old School Tie. Oh, you can't tell *me*. Discrimination – I've seen plenty.

In *Whisky Galore*, Waggett finds himself constantly outmanoeuvred by the islanders because he can react only within rigid patterns of thought. *Man in the White Suit* portrays a whole (English?) world in which Waggettry rules, a closed system where people hear only what they want to hear and any aberration represents a threat. 'You can't tell *me*' – Bertha's phrase fits almost everybody, Sidney included. People talk past each other, never grasping what the other is saying, nor noticing that they themselves aren't being understood. When Sidney finally meets someone – Daphne – whom he *can* tell, who is alert enough to listen, he can find no better way to lead off than, 'Look – you know about the problem of polymerising amino-acid residues?'

The film's achievement lies in the lucidity with which it communicates non-communication, demonstrating with elegant clarity the mechanics of confusion and creating, through an accumulation of dynamic instances, a vision of a society gripped by inertia. The Corland scientists trotting to and fro in mounting alarm, never asking what Sidney may have done but merely how much he spent doing it; Bertha, with her pre-cast Marxist formulae; Knudsen, Birnley's butler, programmed to exclude anyone lacking an appointment; Birnley himself, ignorant of the name of his own Head of Research; Hoskins, disdainfully pouring years of work down the sink like so much cold coffee – all this would, 'if made seriously,' as Mackendrick remarked, constitute 'a horrendous attack on contemporary society. But I hope we did it with enough good humour that the undercurrents in it – which are also fairly melancholy, if you like – are not oppressive.'[20]

The pattern of mounting frustration that dominates the first third of the film culminates in a bravura sequence of visual comedy, exuberantly paced and interweaving half a dozen intricate strands of action. Yet at no time does Mackendrick fail to provide us with a clear view of whatever's happening.

What *is* happening is that Sidney, out in the rain, wants to get into Birnley's house to tell him about the success of his experiment, while Knudsen, wary of this excitable stranger, is determined to keep him out. Birnley, meanwhile, is under attack from his fellow-directors over the horrendous expenditure caused by Sidney's activities. While he tries to contact Hoskins by phone, Knudsen brings him a note from Sidney, which he waves impatiently away. Daphne, finding Sidney on the doorstep, lets him in and goes to fetch her father. Knudsen comes back and tries to eject Sidney; Birnley and Daphne come down to find them scuffling in the hall. Sidney tricks Knudsen outside and shuts him out. Sidney and Birnley hurl invective at each other while Daphne tries to mediate. Finally, Birnley readmits Knudsen, and Sidney is thrown out. All put together with a fluid precision that evokes the great days of silent comedy.

Frustration and stasis. Midway through this sequence, Birnley issues self-cancelling commands: to Hoskins, on the phone, 'Find him and send him up here,' and in the same breath, to Knudsen, 'Certainly not, tell him to go away!' When at last they meet, instead of communicating Sidney and Birnley exchange banal insults – 'You're an irresponsible young idiot!' 'And you're a pompous and ungrateful old ass!' – and the sequence ends, as it began, with Sidney shut out in the rain. We seem to have got no further forward.

At this point, though, something has to give. Apart from anything else, further frustration would become irritating to the audience; we, like Sidney, have earned a breakthrough. Communication is achieved through Daphne, the only character with the insight to decipher what Sidney is talking about and translate it into terms Birnley can understand. Brushing aside his attempt to retreat into a heavy-father role ('You need a good spanking'), she tells him exactly what Sidney has done: 'He's made a new kind of cloth. It never gets dirty, and it never wears out.' In telling him she also tells us, since Mackendrick, confident in the momentum of his comedy, has kept us waiting until this far into the movie before revealing what the White Suit means.

What it means, of course, depends – in true Mackendrick style – on who's looking at it. To Sidney it's the apotheosis of science, his dream of 'a proper laboratory with really modern equipment, and assistants of my own'. To Birnley, it means stealing a march on his competitors. To the tailor, just another measuring job. To Daphne, a boon for humankind. To the industrialists and workers, a threat to their respective livelihoods. Nobody has the complete, privileged vision. We, the audience, may think we have; but in finally making the suit disintegrate before our eyes, Mackendrick intimates that perhaps we hadn't – and that he hasn't, either.

For the moment, though, the suit seems an unqualified triumph. Having been led to empathise with Sidney in his struggles, we share his exhilaration, the spontaneous joy of his dance before the three-way mirror, even if the quadruple image might hint at an alternative angle or two on the situation. And the cloth itself, so gleaming and invulnerable (it was in fact white sharkskin, shot under ultra-violet light) also invites admiration. Clothed in it, Sidney visibly gains in stature; Mackendrick, in mock awe, views him from a low angle, like a pre-Raphaelite Arthurian tableau: the Hero Apparelled. Daphne hails him as 'a knight in shining armour'.

But their dialogue warns us that, underneath, Sidney is no more the disinterested idealist than he ever was. 'The suit – it looks as if *it*'s wearing *you*.' 'It's still a bit luminous – but it'll wear off.' Idealism is an assumed garment, an outward show; it doesn't last. As if beseeching him to live up to his image, Daphne spells out her vision. 'Don't you understand what this means? Millions of people all over the world, living lives of drudgery, fighting an endless losing battle against shabbiness and dirt – you've won that battle for them. . . . The whole world's going to bless you.' Sidney doesn't answer. They're standing side by side at the window, framed in close intimacy, gazing out across the drab industrial landscape to the distant hills. Does he hear her? Charles Barr thinks not: 'He reacts not at all but stays turned away, "deaf" to the idea.'[21] Yet the image is ambiguous; it could equally be that Sidney shares Daphne's vision, beginning for the first time to glimpse horizons beyond those of his laboratory bench.

We never find out. This is the still turning-point of the film, the furthest extent of the impetus towards change. A moment later Corland picks up a telephone and sets the vast blocking mechanisms rumbling into motion. It's appropriate that this spoiling action should be triggered by a phone call – not only to *White Suit*, with its sceptical attitude to the blessings of technology, but within Mackendrick's work as a whole, where telephones figure as unreliable, even sinister, instruments. This phenomenon, further developed in *The Maggie*, reaches a peak in *Sweet Smell of Success*, where of 16 phone calls that occur during the film, all but two serve to falsify, distort or frustrate communication.

'Get me – Sir John Kierlaw.' Corland's mid-sentence pause is portentous; formidable powers are being summoned up and, in Mephistophelean tradition, they respond without delay. Two massive black Rolls-Royces thunder north through the dusk, seen from the low-angle reverse tracking shot that always, with Mackendrick, signals the approach of something dangerous. We're in gangster-movie territory: the heavy mob are on the way and, in the back of the rearmost car, swathed in fur rugs and shadows that leave only a wrinkled hand visible, sits the Godfather.

With consummate visual aplomb, Mackendrick prepares a dramatic coup of Kierlaw's first appearance. (A few sketches surviving from the storyboard show how closely each shot adhered to Mackendrick's original concept.) Tantalisingly, he discloses only the periphery of the man – a hand, a pair of shuffling feet, the deference of his attendants, Birnley's consternation – setting up the incongruous extremes of physical frailty and moral domination. By the time we see the puny wheezing figure hunched in a high-backed chair, dwarfed by his black-clad acolytes, we can already guess what's coming. Birnley clearly hasn't the will, nor Sidney the guile, to stand against this omnipotent gnome.

Kierlaw represents – incarnates, even – Experience. Like Joseph Macroon, he can read situations and people at a glance. Yet he has a blind spot, one he shares with the equally monstrous J. J. Hunsecker of *Sweet Smell of Success*: his contempt for others. Motivated by money and power, and candid enough to admit it, he blunders when faced with anyone whose priorities lie elsewhere. This leads him to offer Sidney the wrong bribe (money rather than research facilities) and to misread Daphne's motivation; gratified to encounter, as he imagines, a cynicism to match his own, he misses the revulsion behind her words.

Satire was never Ealing's forte, as anyone who has sat through *Meet Mr*

*Lucifer* or *The Love Lottery* can testify. The studio's inherent bent towards compromise, reconciliation, seeing the other chap's point of view, tended to blunt the cutting edge of satirical purpose. In *Passport to Pimlico* or *The Lavender Hill Mob* the status quo is teased, rumpled a little, but never subjected to serious attack. Absent from such films is the touch of cruelty essential to satire, what Mackendrick called 'the snarl behind the grin' that showed through only twice in Ealing's output – in the social satire of *Kind Hearts and Coronets* and the political satire of *Man in the White Suit*.

The trio of scenes in which Kierlaw confronts first Birnley, then Sidney and finally Daphne finds the film's satiric thrust at its sharpest. Birnley never stands a chance. His flatulent liberal clichés – 'I will not stand in the way of progress. The welfare of the community must come first' – wither in the cold blast of the old man's *realpolitik*. 'Was the spinning jenny a disaster?' Birnley expostulates, 'Was the mechanical loom?' Kierlaw's response cuts straight to the economic crux: 'For those that didn't control them, yes.'

'Control' is Kierlaw's key-word. 'We need control of that discovery – complete control,' he tells Sidney. With his wasted torso, his clawlike hands and bright, hard eyes, he embodies the essence of capitalism: the sheer pleasure in acquisition and in the power it confers. And Mackendrick, repelled and delighted by the ancient monster, abets his urge to dominate by locating him at the focal point of each frame.

Sidney, by contrast, appears at his most naive. Chatting with the workers on his way to meet Kierlaw, he's oblivious to the point of idiocy of other people's reactions, brushing them off as nonchalantly as dirt from the pristine suit. To Harry's worried protest, 'But if this stuff never wears out, we'll only have one lot to make,' he responds with a cheery, 'That's right!' and, escorted by Corland's wolfish grin, is led off to the slaughter.

Penned in by the bulky black shapes of the industrialists, he regresses yet further into infancy, enthusing over Corland's cigarette-lighter-cum-fountain-pen, and trustingly accepting Birnley's flustered evasions. For a moment, he seems about to capitulate even more readily than his employer. But for all their differences, Sidney and Kierlaw have a good deal in common: one in white, one in black, but each indifferent to any viewpoint bar his own. Innocence and Experience: not contrasted opposites, but each other's negative image.

From here on, the logic of Kierlaw's position develops with inexorable clarity. Unexpectedly faced with a will to match his own, he resorts successively to bribery, violence, prostitution and, if necessary, murder. Unlike Birnley, dithering and platitudinous ('I will not resort to violence,' he splutters, reeling from an unsuccessful tussle with Sidney), Kierlaw scorns hypocrisy and not only instigates violence but, to the best of his ability, joins in. In one of the film's most lethally funny moments the old monster, as Sidney shoots past with Cranford and Corland in pursuit, lurches across the desk to take a wild swipe with his stick. And when Sidney lies felled by a bronze plaque, Kierlaw shuffles up to stare dispassionately down at the body. 'Is he – all right?' Birnley quavers. 'Yes,' says Corland. 'Pity,' Kierlaw observes drily.

Charles Barr suggests a reading of this whole sequence in terms of 'an extraordinary "family" structure':[22] Birnley as Sidney's over-indulgent father, browbeaten back into line by his brothers (Corland, Cranford) who invoke the authority of the stern old grandfather – all then uniting to crush the wayward son. The interpretation works well not only for *White Suit*, with its theme of repressive, defensive tradition, but for Mackendrick's films in general. Where families, real or surrogate, feature in his work, their function is almost invariably to choke off any impulse to growth or change.

That impulse, furthermore, often originates in, or is championed by, the female members of the family – as it does in *White Suit*. In Daphne, Kierlaw finds himself up against an alertness and cunning to equal – and in the end, outfox – his own. The scene in which she confronts the bosses, reading their motives and playing on their weaknesses with all the skill of which Sidney was incapable, is one of the finest in any Mackendrick film, displaying that delight in the dramatic play of intelligence which distinguishes him from virtually all other British directors.

The editing and framing of the action subtly mirrors its inner development. At first we see Daphne hemmed in, as was Sidney, by the dark-suited figures of the bosses. As she gains psychological ascendancy, she progressively excludes them from her space, finally taking over the screen in full close-up at the key moment when she rises to her feet, confident of achieving her aim. Throughout the scene (played with exquisitely controlled irony by Greenwood, in her best role since *Kind Hearts and Coronets*) she keeps one move ahead of her opponents, well aware of what they're driving at but deriving fierce satisfaction from forcing them to spell it out.

CRANFORD: Miss Birnley, we're trying to buy the world rights of Mr Stratton's new discovery. But he doesn't seem to trust us.
DAPHNE: *Doesn't* he? Why not?
CRANFORD: Miss Birnley, you're the daughter of an industrialist. You must realise how reckless exploitation of anything new would upset the delicate balance of trade. You understand that.
DAPHNE: I'm beginning to.
KIERLAW: Good.
DAPHNE: You want to suppress it.
KIERLAW: (nods, pleased at her perspicacity).
DAPHNE: But – if *you* aren't able to persuade him, why should I be able to?

CRANFORD: All men are susceptible, Miss Birnley. I need hardly add that you're a very attractive girl.

DAPHNE: Thank you. Well, Michael – what do *you* say?

CORLAND: It's a desperate situation, Daphne, for the, er, whole industry.

DAPHNE: Yes. Yes, I'm beginning to realise that. (She stands up.)

CRANFORD: There's no need to explain what's at stake – when I tell you that we've already offered Stratton a quarter of a million, you can see for yourself.

DAPHNE: I can indeed. But since we're on the subject of price – what do *I* get out of it?

CRANFORD: Miss Birnley!

CORLAND: Daphne!

DAPHNE: I – I haven't had much experience of this sort of thing, but I've always understood that it was comparatively well paid.

CRANFORD: Now Miss Birnley, we didn't wish to offend you—

CORLAND: Daphne, this isn't a thing to joke about—

KIERLAW (a restraining hand on Cranford's arm): I suggest – two thousand.

DAPHNE: Aren't you rating my value a little low? Wouldn't five thousand be fairer?

KIERLAW (highly appreciative): Five thousand. Agreed.

DAPHNE: Agreed. It's a pleasure to do business with you, Sir John.

In one small detail, Mackendrick's film is less audacious than MacDougall's play. In the play, Greatheart (Birnley) doesn't merely acquiesce in using his daughter as bait, but is the first to propose the idea, while the Corland figure indignantly protests. The film discreetly shunts Birnley out of the way on the pretext of a phone call (the telephone as betrayer once again), allowing him to play the outraged parent when he learns what's happening. No doubt Mackendrick and his colleagues suspected that to show a father pimping for his daughter might be more than Balcon would wear – especially a father modelled on Balcon himself.

Otherwise, the scene pulls no punches. It also reveals, perhaps better than any other, the ruthlessness that underlies Mackendrick's brand of comedy. To Charles Barr, this scene 'seems . . . to express a vision of the logic of capitalism as extreme as anything in Buñuel or Godard.'[23]

In the contempt behind Daphne's response there lies a rejection of the facile consensus which so often rounds off British movies, and Ealing movies in particular – the emphasis on finding a common language, allowing for the other fellow's attitude. (Even Bernard Miles's *Chance of a Lifetime*, which took a much less anodyne view than usual of industrial relations, and consequently got itself barred from British cinemas, ends with boss and workers united in harmonious co-operation.) But while Daphne has indeed learnt to speak other languages – her father's, Sidney's and now Kierlaw's – she uses the ability not to compromise, but to fight all the more effectively for the side she's chosen. Mackendrick's films rarely aim for reconciliation, and thereby gain in strength and cogency.

When it comes to sexuality, though, *White Suit* shares the evasions of most British movies of the period. In *Kind Hearts*, Greenwood as Sibella could be bedded by Louis, since she was the Wicked Woman to Valerie Hobson's Virtuous Widow. But in Daphne's attempted seduction of Sidney, Greenwood combines both roles: like Rita Hayworth as Gilda (that icon of ambivalent movie eroticism) she's the Virtuous Woman pretending to be wicked, and this side of her must be rejected by the innocent (virginal?) Sidney. He's justified by the plot, of course. In resisting her advances he resists the machinations of the bosses and thus makes the 'right' decision. Even so, the tactic fits neatly into the Ealing convention for dealing with (or rather, not dealing with) sex, deflecting it in the name of a higher purpose; deficiency of passion masquerading as self-denial.

The exchange is rendered even more ambiguous by the actors involved, each of whom is – perhaps unconsciously – giving out contrary signals. Sidney would supposedly like to make love to Daphne, but restrains himself because there are strings attached. Daphne is pretending she wants him to respond, but hopes he won't. However, Guinness's bemused reaction conveys no sense of desire, suppressed or otherwise; while the sensuality of Greenwood's performance suggests disappointment at his lack of response. Whether intended to or not, the scene reinforces the film's prevailing vision of communication blocked off, perceptions at cross-purposes. Daphne has misread Sidney's feelings for her just as she did the motives behind his research.

Still, she can place her cunning at his disposal, alerting him to the use of his fabric as a means of escape and gaining time by playing out her role as *femme fatale*: her tone of post-coital languor, as Birnley anxiously rattles the door-handle – 'Not *now*, father' – is toe-curlingly delicious. But after this, the film (and indeed the studio – this was Greenwood's last role for Ealing) can find no further use for her. The focus shifts to the forces stirred up by Sidney's discovery – first in collision, then in ferocious alliance. As in *Whisky Galore*, a society under threat unites against the interloper.

Some critics have taken *White Suit*'s satirical stance as nothing more subtle than 'a plague on both your houses'. Released in a year which saw Attlee's Labour Government, after two close-fought elections, replaced by the Tories under Churchill, the film can superficially be read as suggesting that between workers' party and bosses' party there's not much to choose. But Mackendrick, as might be expected, is offering nothing so trite or blandly uncommitted. His target is the system itself, class-ridden and self-perpetuating, which can ingest and remould in its own image any impulse towards change. In this film can be sensed the disillusion of those who believed in 1945 that Labour's victory could mean a new dispensation – a revolution, even – only to see it bring about what Anthony Howard described as 'the greatest restoration of traditional social values since 1660'.[24]

*The Man in the White Suit* depicts a Britain where a sterile conservatism has settled back down, like a layer of fluffy grey dust, over all classes, where the nominally progressive forces of the Left reveal themselves, when it comes to it, no less hostile to change than the moneyed interests of the Right. Instead of demanding a whole new set of rules, the workers have let themselves be inveigled into playing the bosses' game – and the film makes it obvious enough who plays it more skilfully and to greater advantage. (Without undue emphasis, Mackendrick contrasts the spacious carpets of Birnley's office with the cramped, grimy hut where Frank and Bertha work.) For all the deliberations of the works committee, power and privilege rest where they always did – in the ancient, crippled hands of Sir John Kierlaw.

In its treatment of the various factions the film is far from even-handed. The workers, though mocked for the narrow rigidity of their attitudes, are depicted much more sympathetically than the management. None of them is as unscrupulous as Kierlaw, as pompous as Birnley, as despicable as Corland – nor as deferential as the laboratory staff. There is about them an independence, and a pride, completely lacking in their layabout counterparts of *I'm All Right Jack* (a true plague-on-both-your-houses film) or in the Commie-manipulated louts of *The Angry Silence*. The first appearance of Bertha, manoeuvring a truckload of castings with practised confidence, presents an image of a capable, industrially skilled woman rare in British (or indeed American) cinema after 1945.

But Mackendrick also recognises that it's precisely because the workers *are* less nasty, less callous, than the bosses that they're always likely to lose out. Two small incidents dramatise the difference. While Birnley is dithering outside Daphne's room, Cranford, learning of Sidney's escape, comes thundering up the stairs and smashes in the door without breaking stride. Meanwhile, at Mrs Watson's house, Bertha has locked up both Sidney and the new lodger, a droop-moustached old fellow who threatened to fetch the police. The lodger, shut in the bathroom, could free himself in a moment by smashing a flimsy glass panel in the door, and at one point makes to do so. But instead – out of diffidence, or consideration for Mrs Watson – he sits down resignedly to await release. Which makes him a more likeable person than Cranford, no question of it; but a more ineffectual one, too.

Given this vision of Britain, any consensus can only be patently phony, a cynical expedient. 'My dear friends,' Cranford wheedles the workers, 'you must see that our bone of contention is non-existent. Capital and labour are hand-in-hand in this. Once again, as so often in the past, each needs the help of the other.' There's an echo here of the notorious line that ends Lang's *Metropolis*, as the warring classes are likewise implausibly reconciled: 'The mediator between the hand and the brain must be the heart.' And as if Cranford's smarmy tones weren't enough of a give-away, Corland takes a phone-call for 'Someone called *Bertha*?', unable to keep the contempt out of his voice. With this scene, Mackendrick exposes the hollowness behind the Ealing – and British – consensus mentality.

But however fragile the alliance, it's more than Sidney can do to break it. A shrewder man would play one side against the other; Sidney, blind as ever to others' motives, blurts out his intentions to Bertha and ends up locked in a basement, banister in one hand and laundry-basket lid in the other. To this ignominious level has Daphne's 'knight in shining armour' been reduced. His resolute stance is wasted on a locked door, as futile as his earlier defiant speech to a row of wash-basins. Once again a female has to supply the cunning he lacks, and this time she's a six-year-old girl.

This is the first child to play a significant part in a Mackendrick movie and Barr is surely right to see her as prefiguring much of Mackendrick's subsequent work. Not only is she played by Mandy Miller, who takes the title role in *Mandy*, but her performance – like those of all his child-actors – is direct and unselfconscious, and wholly unsentimentalised. Beside Sidney's helplessness, she appears refreshingly practical; like Daphne, she makes an instinctive moral choice, and acts on it. (She pops up again briefly during the chase sequence, just long enough to point his pursuers in the wrong direction.)

Lindsay Anderson has commented on the quality of nightmare that pervades much of Mackendrick's cinema, and the climax of *White Suit* offers a good example. Not so much in the chase itself, though Sidney's wild scramble through dark, claustrophobic alleys, conspicuous in his gleaming suit, certainly evokes the paranoid world of dreams. (Mackendrick even throws in that archetypal dream-figure, the *doppelgänger*, in the shape of a hapless baker mistaken for the scientist.) But the real nightmare sensation, in which those we thought friendly turn sudden hostile faces to us, and known dimensions slither and dissolve, comes when Sidney, skidding round a corner, receives his *coup de grâce* from the least expected quarter: from old Mrs Watson, hobbling and beshawled in the classic image of honest urban poverty. (The actress, Edie Martin, played indomitable little old ladies in countless Ealing movies.) 'Why can't you scientists leave things alone?' she demands. 'What about my bit of washing when there's no washing to do?'

Sean O'Casey, Samuel Beckett once noted, discerned 'the principle of disintegration in even the most complacent solidities'.[25] The same could be said of Mackendrick; there lurks within his films a kind of cosmic scepticism, a sardonic Uncertainty Principle poised constantly in ambush. Large, imposing structures prove frail and vulnerable: ships run aground, buildings subside and collapse. The same principle infests his characters, subverting their beliefs, gnawing at the underpinnings of their mental universes, until the whole system falls suddenly apart. Those who assume the self-evident rightness of their attitudes represent, to Mackendrick, an irresistible target for the demolition squad.

So after bribes, threats, assaults and the shock of Bertha's onslaught, all Sidney's seemingly impregnable confidence needed was this one last good shove. And as he stands dumbfounded, forced for the first time to acknowledge the needs of other people and the full implications of his experiment, Mackendrick unobtrusively redefines the cinematic space in which he's located. The narrow arches and alleyways melt away, and there opens around him a clear arena, with Sidney at the centre and the lynch-mob closing in from every side. The selfish innocence which blinkered him also protected him; without it he stands exposed and vulnerable.

The destruction of the white suit can be taken on any number of levels. In one sense, as several critics have complained, it's an evasion, a refusal to face up to the issues raised by the film; the fabric isn't stable, so there's no problem any more. It's also generic logic: this is a comedy, so the suit must be torn apart instead of Sidney. (Only a slight shift of tone and the film could be reshot, almost scene for scene, as a tragedy.) It's the disintegration of Sidney's assumptions, of the irresponsible world in which he's been operating; it's the unravelling of the myth of disinterested science – but equally it's the extinction of the ideals glimpsed by Daphne, the freeing of millions from 'lives of drudgery . . . shabbiness and dirt' – and perhaps too the rueful abandonment by Mackendrick, and others of his generation, of the brave new hopes of 1945. And, as Charles Barr suggests, it may be the farewell appearance of a quality about to be lost to Ealing, 'as if a creeping paralysis were indeed at work at that very time. The films are quite suddenly overtaken by age and weariness. . . . With the destruction of the white suit, the dimension of inventiveness that it represents vanishes from the films.'[26]

What we're left with is that most hackneyed of farcical tableaux, a man in a public place without his trousers, while the onlookers shriek with mirth. Yet it isn't funny, partly because the man-without-trousers joke depends on embarrassment, and Sidney has gone far beyond that into desolation – but also because Mackendrick subtly orchestrates our response: first the unsympathetic characters (such as Corland and Frank) laughing, then Wilson, Bertha and Daphne, all conscious of Sidney's despair. Here, as so often, the humour of Mackendrick's comedy homes in on pain.

The most effective comedy, Mackendrick has always maintained, deals with matters that would be unbearable were they not treated playfully. 'It's that hidden element of the intolerable in comedy that separates it from triviality.' While preparing *Man in the White Suit*, he narrated the plot to a

Scottish friend. 'I was trying to make it sound as entertaining as possible, and all the way through the most I could get out of him was a slight smile and a glint in the eye. But when I came to the end, when the scientist is practically lynched by both sides – at that point he gave a great Gaelic guffaw and said, "Sandy, that's very good, that's *very* good; that's not funny!" And I think that's as good a definition as any.'[27]

It's this streak of blackness (or, as he describes it, 'my perverted and malicious sense of humour')[28] within Mackendrick's comedies that, as much as their technical qualities, has kept them fresh and sharp. Beside them, even the best of their Ealing stablemates (*Kind Hearts and Coronets* always excepted) have relapsed into a slightly faded period charm. What's more debatable is how far Mackendrick's subversive purpose got through to audiences, either then or since.

Comedy, Mackendrick once remarked in an interview, 'is the only way that certain things get to be said. It lets you express things that are too dangerous, or that a certain type of audience can't accept.'[29] *White Suit*, he suggests, with its 'rather brutal theme', would never have got the go-ahead had it not been presented as a comedy. The implication is that Mackendrick was putting one over on Balcon, who preferred his comedies 'done with affection' and expressing only 'a mild protest [at] the regimentation of the times'. There's certainly little enough affection in *White Suit*, and Balcon was less than happy with its satirical edge. When Mackendrick was planning *The Ladykillers*, 'Mick had me into his office and said, "I want to tell you that I've given a promise on your behalf that there's no satire in this one." '[30]

But it could equally be argued that Balcon astutely defused his director's spiky talent by diverting it into the innocuous channel of comedy. As Ian Green points out, if 'such a supposed rupturing [of social conventions] can only be achieved within the context of comedy, the function of comedy is therefore to negate any significant . . . effect upon a society's conventions and practices'. The comic framework serves 'to avoid repress or displace the treatment of sensitive issues by, so to speak, drowning them in laughter'.[31]

This ambiguity suffuses *White Suit*'s final scene, in which Sidney departs, Chaplin-style, away down a long straight road into the sunrise. Birnley's voice-over exudes the complacency of the restored status quo: 'The crisis is over now. . . . We face the future with confidence. We have seen the last of Sidney Stratton.' Sidney meanwhile, examining his notebook, mutters, 'I see . . . I *see*!' – and, as he strides off, the jaunty apparatus-theme bubbles up on the soundtrack and a note of doubt tinges Birnley's voice. 'At least, I *hope* we've seen the last of him. . . .' Which could be taken as: the disruptive spirit of change is irrepressible and must ultimately triumph over inertia and sterility; or simply: ah, that nice Alec Guinness wasn't beaten after all, so *that's* all right. (Or indeed several other ways, such as that scientists never learn and will go on screwing up our lives no matter what.)

When the film was released in August 1951, some reviewers were put out that it should aspire to any serious meaning at all. 'The Ealing slapstick,' *Tribune*'s critic observed reproachfully, 'sometimes gets twinges of *significance*';[32] and the *Daily Express*, while appreciating the ingenuity of the plot, preferred the 'brightness, happiness and easy fun' of *The Lavender Hill Mob*.[33] In the *Observer* C. A. Lejeune quoted Bernard Shaw at length ('To laugh without sympathy is a ruinous abuse of a noble function') to justify her antipathy to the film's climax, 'a device for laughter that is more painful than funny, and sends the audience away with a sense of discomfort'.[34]

Even the more favourable critics had problems with the ending, which, thought the *Guardian*'s reviewer, 'may well leave a wry taste when the laughter is over. . . . Yet of all the many fine films which [Ealing] has produced this one is surely the bravest adventure if not the most complete success.'[35] 'It has the best comic opening of any film for years,' wrote Dilys Powell in the *Sunday Times*, adding: 'That the film manages almost without pause until a faintly disappointing end to be both funny and touching is partly due to [its] serious core: contrary to popular belief, the best comedy is about something, not about nothing.'[36] *Time and Tide* noted that 'of all the Ealing directors, Mackendrick is possibly the most individualistic' and rated *White Suit* 'the most profound of the Ealing comedies. . . . In fact one is left with the vaguely uncomfortable feeling that comedy has brushed shoulders with tragedy.'[37]

But on the whole, the film was well – and in some cases enthusiastically – received by the British press. The French liked it, too. Jean-Louis Tallenay, writing in *Cahiers du cinéma*, welcomed it as 'something new in cinema: "English comedy". . . . In every kind of comedy from Plautus to Fernandel, society is in the right, and the protagonist is funny because he doesn't conform to social norms. In "English comedy" the reverse is true: it's society that's funny, because it's at odds with itself. But this is never stated in so many words; the humour lies in seeming to agree with those who are wrong, thus making their error all the more obvious.'[38]

*White Suit* opened in New York in April 1952 to excellent notices and good box-office, though without quite equalling the success of *Whisky Galore*. The *New York Post* hailed it as 'henceforth . . . this reviewer's personal yardstick of comic perfection . . . the funniest picture he has seen in the last ten years'.[39] In the 1952 Academy Awards Mackendrick gained the only Oscar nomination of his career, cited for the screenplay together with MacDougall and Dighton.

Guinness, who at this stage in his movie career could do no wrong, was universally praised, but all the performances were liked, especially those of Greenwood and Thesiger. Everyone's favourite character, though, was the eccentric apparatus with its burbling leitmotif. An arrangement was even released on record, under the title 'The White Suit Samba'.

Mackendrick himself considers *Man in the White Suit* the best of his Ealing films. Many admirers of his work would agree. Charles Barr reckons it 'perhaps the most intelligent of British films [and] certainly one of the most complex'.[40] The public, though, have never taken it to their hearts quite so readily as *Whisky Galore* or *The Ladykillers*; it may be that for some tastes the snarl shows too clearly beneath the grin. Like certain Hamer or Cavalcanti pictures (*Went the Day Well?*, for example), *White Suit* isn't a film that fits comfortably within the Ealing canon where, as Laurence Kardish points out, ambiguity rarely figures: '[Balcon] mistrusted works that fascinated and repelled at the same time.'[41] Later, in *The Ladykillers*, Mackendrick would cover his tracks more adeptly, working both with and against the Ealing ethos in ironic counterpoint.

Still, Mackendrick's second film did his reputation nothing but good. His technical and narrative skills were unmistakable and his potential was evident. One reviewer went so far as to rate him, on the basis of just two films, on a par with Hitchcock and Kazan.[42] Mackendrick modestly demurred. But it was beginning to seem that such praise, if a little premature, wasn't by any means extravagant.

# 4 Mandy

'Melodrama is iconographically fixed by the claustrophobic atmosphere of the bourgeois home . . . reinforced stylistically by a complex handling of space in interiors.'[1]

Thomas Elsaesser, *Tales of Sound and Fury*

'Children are often better actors than adults, because they have a greater capacity for believing completely in a situation.'[2]

Alexander Mackendrick

Of the five films that Mackendrick directed at Ealing, all but one were comedies. This wasn't by deliberate choice. He had never set out to become a comedy director, and indeed by the time he quit the studio was worried about being typecast as a maker of 'cute British comedies'.[3] But for various reasons, none of his more serious, or more ambitious, projects found favour. One which would preoccupy him for most of his directorial career was *Mary Queen of Scots*, to be treated not with the usual high-flown period flummery, but in stark, anti-romantic terms. It was turned down by Balcon – on patriotic grounds, Mackendrick believes. 'The idea of being candid about the characters of royalty was more than Mick could take.' The reason isn't wholly convincing: *Saraband* had been far more offensive about the future King George I than Mackendrick planned to be about Mary. It's more likely that Balcon, in the wake of *Saraband*'s financial débâcle, had decided historical dramas were best left to more profligate studios.

The only non-comedy Mackendrick directed at Ealing wasn't a project of his own devising, but one offered to him by its producer, Leslie Norman. Norman had come across a novel about a girl born deaf and (according to Mackendrick) 'had fallen in love with it'. Or rather, with one incident in it – the moment at which the parents realise their child is deaf, 'the most moving scene in the film as far as Les was concerned'. What fascinated Mackendrick was rather the child and her struggles to communicate.

The novel was *The Day is Ours* by Hilda Lewis, a prolific author of romances, historical novels and children's books. It covers the first 27 years in the life of its deaf heroine, Tamsie (short for Thomasina), ending with the birth of her own daughter. Her mother, Christine, suffers from a guilt complex; she didn't really want Tamsie, who was a late child, and the birth was difficult (deafness being caused by a mishandled forceps). Christine also believes that Tamsie's dead grandmother has exerted posthumous vengeance by striking the child deaf.

Most of this was junked in the screenplay, which drew on only the first few chapters of the novel, borrowing little more than the names of the parents, Christine and Harry Garland, and of a sympathetic doctor, Jane Ellis – plus the theme of family opposition to the child's attending a special school. Of all Mackendrick's films, *Mandy* owes the least to its source material.

The initial draft was written by Jack Whittingham, a studio regular who scripted several Ealing films around this time. Mackendrick was dissatisfied with Whittingham's version: 'While working on it, more or less alone with Les, I saw that we had no conflict, no third-act climax.' He consulted the novelist Nigel Balchin, 'who introduced the element of transference, whereby the patient falls in love with the psychiatrist. In the case of a man helping to cure a disabled child, there's a strong tendency for the mother unconsciously to fall in love with him, and for this to be more quickly realised by the husband who sees himself displaced as a father. So it was Nigel who introduced the Jack Hawkins character, and made that key step that provided us with our story.'

Hawkins, with his air of irritable professionalism, made good casting for the awkward, prickly Dick Searle. The crucial choice, though, was the girl to play the deaf child herself. Any hint of selfconsciousness or willed pathos would be ruinous; the performance had to be utterly convincing. Yet casting a genuinely deaf child wouldn't work, as Mackendrick soon discovered. 'Deaf-mute children can be extraordinarily intelligent and perceptive; but they have this terrible desire to make you feel they've understood you when they haven't really. And this was something I knew I'd find too difficult to work with.'[4]

One of the children auditioned was Mandy Miller, the small girl in *Man in the White Suit*. 'She'd been very good in that. But it was a tiny little part, and I thought it was fairly easy to deal with child actors in short bursts. But here she had to go all the way through, and within individual scenes she had to play a great range of temperament and change of mood – and that takes real control as a performer.'[5] Mackendrick also felt that Mandy would be 'much too tough' for the role. Leslie Norman, who thought otherwise, stacked the cards a little by bringing in a talented Australian actress, Dorothy Alison (whom he'd worked with on Harry Watt's *Eureka Stockade*), to play the test scene with Mandy.

The scene chosen was the key moment at which the child, struggling to pronounce her first articulate sounds, screams in fury and frustration – and then, her tension released, succeeds in producing the sound. Mackendrick vividly recalls the response elicited by Mandy's performance. 'On the studio floor there are silences of different kinds: there are silences when people aren't talking, just whispering, but the microphone can't pick it up; or there's the moment when people are standing absolutely still; but then there's a third kind of silence when they're holding their breath. Mandy's performance was so astonishing that the unit was struck rigid, with this electrifying silence on the floor. And I was in tears. Dougie Slocombe was in tears; and afterwards both of us said, "Cancel the rest, she's *it*." '[6]

Mandy Miller was seven, the adopted daughter of a BBC producer, David Miller. She also retains vivid memories of the test, as 'a totally terrifying experience. . . . When it came to it, I couldn't scream. I opened my mouth, and out came this rather feeble noise, and Sandy very definitely wanted a full-powered scream. So *he* screamed. Now I came from a very calm and quiet, comfortable suburban background . . . so imagine suddenly being confronted with this great big gentleman, screaming. And *I* screamed. And that was it – that was obviously what he wanted to create. But the shock tactic was just amazing.'[7]

It was also, Douglas Slocombe comments, 'typical of Sandy – he'd always find just the right thing to do at the right time. There's an instinct there, and a slightly fearless quality that Sandy has – he's not afraid of making a fool of himself, whatever anybody else may think – and a complete concentration on the problem of the moment.'

Slocombe was struck, as many others have been, by Mackendrick's rapport with children. 'His technique was that he never talked down to them. He would always bring them up to his level and take for granted that they were as grown-up as he was.' For his part, Mackendrick believes he has 'learned more about working with adult actors from having worked with children. What you do when you're working with a child is that you communicate, not verbally, but really by osmosis. You get yourself so involved with the emotion of the scene that the child just picks it up from you, sensing the mood and the feeling just by contact. So the only real problem is to isolate the child and see that there is a really intense relationship between you, that you are both locked into the same make-believe.'[8]

The relationship in this case seems to have been exceptionally potent. In both the films she made with Mackendrick, but especially in *Mandy*, Miller's gravely individual personality comes across far more vividly than in her other pictures (Daniel Birt's *Background*, for example, or Wendy Toye's *Raising a Riot*). Mackendrick was amazed by her ability to 'switch on a mood without having to work herself into it. The moment a scene was finished, the mood would drop from her like a cloak being removed.'[9]

One scene in particular stayed in his memory: when Mandy, miserable as a boarder at the school, is reunited with her mother. Having rehearsed Phyllis Calvert, playing the mother, and Dorothy Alison as the teacher who escorts Mandy into the hall, 'I knelt down and talked to Mandy very quietly and said, "See, Mandy, here it is – I want you to walk down the stairs, *there* I want you to see your mother, and I want you to burst into floods of tears and run down to her." That's all I said. Well, while we were lining up the scene and Dougie was lighting it, she's holding Dot Alison's hand, and Dot – she tells me this afterwards – is going through effective memory bits or whatever. And she's interrupted by Mandy, who turns to her brightly and says, "Why am I crying?" Dot is totally thrown and asked, "Didn't Mr Mackendrick tell you?" And Mandy says, "No." So Dot, panicking, says, "Well, you know how it is – if you've been longing to see someone for a long time, but they're not here, and then suddenly you see them, you just want to burst into tears. You know what I mean, Mandy?" And Mandy says, "No."

'At that point, I called "Action". And Mandy walked down four steps, burst into floods of tears, and ran to her mother. Which tells you a lot on that score.'

The choice of Mandy Miller for the key role also determined the title of the picture. To make it simpler for Mackendrick and the other cast members to communicate with her, it was decided that Mandy should keep her own name in the film. Subsequently, the name of the character was chosen for the title, reflecting the central theme of the film as Mackendrick saw it: the child's fight to assert her own identity.

Once again, Mackendrick paid particular attention to the soundtrack, with which he hoped to communicate what it felt like to be a deaf-mute child. Working with Stephen Dalby, the sound supervisor, he devised a technique of 'subjective non-sound'. 'My first idea was to show a close-up of the child, see the world around her, and fade out the sound. Doesn't work. People think the sound system's failed. You have to do something much more complex: at the moment of fade-out, have some ongoing sound, speech or whatever, put it on a variable-speed disc and introduce the Doppler effect. So it becomes intermittent, changes pitch and drops. Then people realise the sound is being *taken away*, leaving them with silence. And even then you only have about three or four seconds' total silence, before replacing it with some sort of high-pitched ringing buzz where the sound ought to be. And all this produces the idea of absence of sound.'

Dalby, like other technicians who worked with Mackendrick, was impressed by his grasp of technical matters. 'Sandy was one director who knew exactly what he wanted when he came to the mixing session. Others had various ideas about things they wanted, but didn't really understand how they were to be done, or even if they could be done. But Sandy seemed to understand the technicalities better than anybody else – which is strange, because many of the other directors had editing experience and so on, which he didn't. But he'd obviously done his homework.'

Dalby's view bears out Michael Relph's description of Mackendrick as one of the 'few people [at Ealing] interested in the technical side'[10] – though Relph later offered a slightly acerbic gloss on his comment. 'Sandy used to work things out in a technical way, and try and impose his concept of how it should be done on the technical people. This was quite a time-wasting factor, although out of it often came something very good. He really wanted to do everybody's job for them, and was very interested in the jobs, too. I think the technicians all thought he was a little screwy, but they didn't mind too much. Usually, he eventually came round to doing what he had been told in the first place.'

Mackendrick, by his own admission, was never the easiest of directors to work with; he could be simultaneously demanding and indecisive. Douglas Slocombe recalls a notorious incident on *Mandy* when Mackendrick, having chosen a high-angle shot, had a 30-foot tower constructed – only to change his mind in favour of a low angle which needed a 10-foot pit. 'This became something of a standing joke about Sandy. But it illustrates the fact that he wasn't easily dissuaded from an original position of his own choosing – but then wouldn't flinch from changing it, and losing face if necessary, all in the interests of a better shot. Which it invariably was. Myself, I consider that to be a professional attitude, rather than a negative one; but it's obviously galling to producers, who are standing there looking at their watches and shaking their heads.' Not that such vagaries seem, in this case, to have caused any serious delays. Shooting took place between December 1951 and March 1952 and, as on *White Suit*, was completed only a day or two over schedule.

Much of the location work was shot at the school portrayed (under a pseudonym) in the film: Clyne House Residential School for the Deaf at Old Trafford. Apart from Mandy herself and a couple of other child actors – one of them the young Jane Asher – all the children were actual deaf pupils at the school. As with the presence of Barra islanders in *Whisky Galore*, this lent the scenes a sense of conviction that transmitted itself to all the actors involved. In his autobiography, Jack Hawkins described the film as 'a remarkable and moving experience', especially for 'the unrestrained affection of the children. They gave themselves wholeheartedly to anyone who could be bothered with them. Their tremendous perseverance in trying to speak fascinated me . . . with the result that three children took me over as their personal property. . . . The only problem was that when I was called away to do a scene, they wanted to come as well and I literally had to peel them off me because they would climb all over me as though I were a tree.'[11]

In some ways, it may be that the very intensity of these scenes has done the film a disservice, unbalancing it in terms of dramatic impact. Beside the sheer urgency of need emanating from the Clyne House children, a quality which also informs Mandy Miller's astounding performance, it was perhaps inevitable that the scenes of domestic conflict should seem flat by contrast: skilled, professional actors conscientiously playing out a story. As a result, *Mandy* has generally been treated as a schizoid movie, 'both inspired and trite',[12] as Richard Winnington put it: a powerful study of a handicapped child on to which has been grafted a routine marital melodrama.

Mackendrick himself partially endorses this view. The film would have body
worked better, he thinks, 'if instead of concentrating on the story of Mandy's parents, you'd met those people through the person who was trying to do something for the child, namely the Jack Hawkins character. What it needed was one more draft; and when that dawned on me, I was already two weeks into production. Also you'd have had to lose the moment when they discover the child's deafness – or played it as flashback, which would have made it expendable anyway. And I don't think I could ever have talked Les Norman out of that scene, though I considered it very seriously. But if you had lost that and started with Searle's problems, and introduced the story of the girl through his eyes, you'd have had a coherent dramatic whole.'

Nonetheless, for all its weaknesses *Mandy* is, as Charles Barr says, 'a purposeful unity – in its way, as ambitious a statement about the England of its time as its comedy predecessor'.[13] The two elements interweave: the story of Christine and Harry Garland's endangered marriage grows out of, and reflects back upon, the plight of their handicapped daughter in a complex pattern of social tensions which mirror those of a whole society.

The blanket disparagement of Ealing films as 'cosy' rests on the belief – often justified – that they present an uncritically affectionate view of England. It's not an accusation that can plausibly be levelled at Mackendrick. *Mandy* can be seen as the central panel of an informal trilogy of movies, with *The Man in the White Suit* and *The Ladykillers*, which might be described – if the term hadn't acquired overtones of portentous solemnity – as Mackendrick's Condition of England films. Taken together, they portray a stagnant, inhibited country, at once complacent and resentful, soured by snobbery and class conflict, hamstrung by deference to authority – petrified, in every sense, in the face of change.

Many Ealing films make use of the 'microcosm' device whereby one group, household or village implicitly stands for the whole country, the community as a nation. Ealing wasn't alone in this, of course, and nor was the British cinema, especially in wartime; Hollywood movies like *Since You Went Away* use exactly the same convention. But it's a device of which Ealing, with its perennial concern with community, seems to have been particularly fond. Mackendrick, as so often, takes the convention and turns it to his own ends, though so subtly that it's easy, at a superficial glance, to assume that he's simply conforming with it after the manner of, say, Basil Dearden. But on closer scrutiny it's evident that not only is Mackendrick taking a cooler, far more critical look at the national myth – he's also holding the convention itself up for quizzical examination, inviting us to consider what such ready recourse to it, in all its reductive over-simplification, implies both cinematically and socially.

These subversive tactics are most dextrously employed in *The Ladykillers*, where the whole complex of imagery centred on Mrs Wilberforce and her ramshackle little house neatly conflates Ealing with England and mocks the parochial assumptions of both. *Mandy*, too, establishes a house as its central image – and at the same time prompts the question, what kind of a country is it that can be aptly symbolised by *this* house, inhabited by *these* people?

*Mandy* is unusual among Mackendrick's films in several ways, not least in being about a family. Generally his families tend to be either absent or cancelled out. Though children feature frequently, it's as isolated figures, cut off from their parents by death (*Sammy Going South*) or distance (*High Wind in Jamaica*) – or, like Dougie in *The Maggie* or the little girl in *Man in the White Suit*, lacking any evident parentage or antecedents. Where family bonds do feature, it's as just that, something binding, chokingly possessive: Mrs Campbell's puritanical tyranny in *Whisky Galore* or Hunsecker's incestuous fixation on his sister in *Sweet Smell*. In place of his absent families, too, Mackendrick often sets up quasi-familial structures whose role is almost always repressive, such as *White Suit*'s hierarchy of bosses or the massed nannies summoned up by Mrs Wilberforce in *The Ladykillers*.

Mandy is yet another isolated child, cut off from her family by the invisible barrier of deafness. But she's also cut off *by* her family, trapped within walls of snobbish inhibition. Whenever the ties of kinship and parenthood are invoked – 'Surely, as the child's father, I must have *some* say in the matter', 'Doesn't a child's home and father mean anything to her?' – it's never supportively, to encourage her in her development, but rather to curb and confine. As in *White Suit*, the generations bear down with accumulated weight, from the grandparents through the father on to the child. It's from her family, as well as from her own muteness, that Mandy has to escape, and the film's final image shows her breaking free of both of them.

For Mackendrick, *Mandy* shows that 'there are two kinds of love: one which wants to possess the beloved and one which wants to free the beloved – even of oneself.' So the film sets up not one family, but two: a real one to play the restrictive role and a surrogate family to offer freedom. Just as Searle takes over as the father (a substitution made explicit when Harry, glancing resentfully back from the hotel foyer, sees Searle, Christine and Mandy forming a cosy group around the breakfast table), so Jane Ellis replaces Emily as a non-possessive grandmother. From this angle, the film can be seen as tracing two parallel learning processes, with Mandy discovering how to attain freedom while her family learn how to bestow it. (Or then again, perhaps they don't; the resolution is nothing if not ambiguous.)

But the film is almost as much about the mother as about the child. Christine Garland, suspended between the two families, also struggles to escape and, it's hinted in that same final sequence, doesn't quite make it. *Mandy* is also untypical of Mackendrick's films in giving a central role to a woman – not a safely asexual old lady like Mrs Wilberforce, or the prepubertal Emily of *High Wind*, but an adult, sexually active woman. And if, through limitations of script and casting, the portrayal of Christine is less than fully realised, the film still digs deeper into sexual politics than any other in Mackendrick's output.

It also presents, uniquely among Mackendrick's Ealing movies, a highly charged sexual relationship. Christine and Harry are shown as being physically attracted to a degree uncommon among Ealing's married couples; the comfortable, undemanding affection of *Blue Lamp*'s George and Mary Dixon is far closer to the norm. When, after several weeks' separation, Harry visits Christine in Manchester, they can hardly wait to get each other into bed, and Christine's feelings for Searle may owe as much to sexual deprivation as to gratitude. In the end, like the heroine of *It Always Rains on Sunday*, she accepts the constraints of domesticity, but it's an acceptance that, in Mackendrick's film as in Hamer's, carries a sense of diminution.

What *Mandy* largely lacks – not that this is inherently a fault in itself – is the child's perspective. Many films about childhood, including some of the finest – *Pather Panchali*, *Les Jeux interdits*, *Night of the Hunter* – channel most of the action through children's eyes, lending it at once distance and clarity, a wrong-end-of-the-telescope mythification. (As do both Mackendrick's later child-centred movies, *Sammy Going South* and *High Wind in Jamaica*.) For obvious reasons, *Mandy* doesn't set out to do this, any more than Penn does in *The Miracle Worker*; a film from a deaf-mute child's viewpoint could make a fascinating experiment, but one falling way outside the narrative mainstream where Mackendrick chose to operate.

Apart from scenes such as the encounter with the lorry-driver, where we share the girl's terrified incomprehension, the controlling perspective isn't hers, but Christine's. Though Mandy remains the dramatic focus of our interest, she's almost always placed within the context of her mother's reactions; indeed, it's a measure of how intimately the stories of mother and daughter are entwined that it would be hard to imagine the film working half so well – or perhaps at all – if Mandy were a boy. As Pam Cook observed, *Mandy* is a study, not only of the deaf in a world designed for the hearing, but of women in a world designed for men.[14]

In many ways, too, the film fits the pattern of the woman-centred family melodrama, even to the casting of Phyllis Calvert, who had starred in a string of such pictures for Gainsborough. But while adopting certain of the conventions – the female perspective, the emphasis on motherhood and marital ties, the conflict between 'permitted' and 'forbidden' desire – Mackendrick abstains from the emotional overdrive, the 'sound and fury' (as Thomas Elsaesser terms it) of the standard melodramatic register. If

*Mandy* can be classified as a 'woman's picture', it's not in the pejorative –
and patronising – sense of a romantic weepie, but as a film which gives
expression to a woman's concerns without trivialising or over-simplifying
them.

It's Christine's voice that introduces the film and which we hear at one or
two later points in the action. There's none of the ironic treatment accorded
to Birnley; Christine's viewpoint – rather than Harry's or Searle's or Emily's
– is apparently the one we should accept. But like Birnley, she isn't
necessarily wholly reliable, and not everything she says can be taken at face
value. After the quarrel with Harry when he slaps her, she leaves the house
and takes Mandy to the school in Manchester, while her voice tells us, 'It was
that that made up my mind. I knew what I had to do.' Yet from her
conversation with the Tabors, we know she's already decided Mandy should
attend the school and there's a hint, borne out by her letter to Harry ('I hate
having made you hit me'), that she may have provoked the quarrel as a
pretext for defying his wishes.

The ambiguity of Christine's character extends to her name, which varies
according to whom she's with. To Harry, she's 'Kit'; to her in-laws,
'Christine'; and Lily Tabor, evidently an old friend, calls her 'Chris'. When
we first meet her, she's firmly in her Kit persona – 'an ordinary housewife'
(her own description) installed in a snug little flat, looking after her
daughter, waiting for Harry to come home – and forming, precisely, part of
his 'kit': the attractive wife-and-child equipment expected of a personable
young man. The discovery of an embarrassing flaw in that kit prompts the
move to Harry's parents' house, where Kit becomes Christine – the
daughter-in-law, marginalised in the family hierarchy, sensing that Mandy is
being subtly detached from her. 'Let *me* have her,' are Emily's first words to
her, lifting the child out of her arms; words echoed by the governess, Miss
Tucker who, when Mandy comes running to Christine for comfort, whisks
her off saying: '*I'll* take her, Mrs Garland.'

Amid the cheerful bohemian clutter of the Tabors' flat, Christine relaxes
into yet another person, reclining casually with Lily on a divan while Jimmy
works at his drawing board and the children play unchecked about his feet.
This, we can guess, is her own background; in Harry's upper-middle-class
milieu with its formal decor, all 18th-century portraits and ormolu clocks,
she's never wholly at ease. Mackendrick takes advantage of a phone call to
contrast the two lifestyles, fluid horizontals set against rigid verticals –
cutting from Christine at the Tabors' to Harry framed in a heavy classical
doorway, tightly buttoned into his three-piece suit. Behind him Mandy
stands flanked by the two elderly women, Emily and Miss Tucker, staid
pillars of respectability.

As with *Man in the White Suit*, class perceptions fuel the dramatic conflict.
The Garlands, with their big old house and unobtrusive servants, typify that

sector of society which since 1945 (as Michael Frayn puts it) 'had been watching – or thought they had been watching – the gestation of a monstrous new state, in which their privileges would be forfeit, their influence dissolved and their standards irrelevant.'[15] To such people the Tory victory of 1951 had come as an inexpressible relief. Mackendrick's film (made some few weeks after the election) reflects that moment of transition. Christine, whom the script characterises as having 'trust in the Expert . . . an uncritical and optimistic belief in Progress', embodies all the left-liberal, welfare-state values that her husband's family mistrust and fear.

The year 1951, Pam Cook suggests in her essay on *Mandy*, marked a 'shift . . . in terms of changing national values, community spirit giving way to individualism and an increasing emphasis on the private domain of home and family'.[16] Harry returns from the school, having seen 'community spirit' in action, to say that 'the whole place gave me the shivers' and that Mandy must be taught 'privately, here at home with us'. Just what 'gave him the shivers' we're not told, but it was very likely the same thing that alarms his mother, a dangerous blurring of social barriers. 'It's a free school?' Emily inquires uneasily, 'but what *sort* of children are they?' – meaning of course, 'what *class* are they?' (Christine's response neatly deflects the unstated code, asserting a more vital priority: 'They're Mandy's sort – they're deaf.') To Emily, as to Harry, such indiscriminate public provision can be seen only in terms of social stigma; it means 'sending Mandy away', 'putting her in an institution'.

There's a hint of guilt behind these words, as if Mandy were a reproach to the family, to be screened from public gaze like a mad aunt in the attic. Christine's furious outburst at Harry – 'You're ashamed of Mandy, wanting to keep her out of sight' – touches a raw nerve, making him lash out. Underlying Harry's pent-up anger, his mother's possessiveness, his father's studied refusal of involvement, can be sensed a suppressed fear that they're somehow to blame for Mandy's condition. As in a way they are.

'What *Ghosts* is really about,' Michael Meyer observed in his preface to Ibsen's play, 'is the devitalizing effect of inherited convention.'[17] Much the same could be said of *Mandy*, which also shares the metaphor of congenital syphilis: explicit in Ibsen, but present as a submerged referent in Mackendrick's film, harking back to his wartime documentary, *Subject for Discussion*. As he later noted, 'One of the effects of inherited syphilis is often deafness in the child. Not that that was implied in *Mandy* as such – but it was in the background of my mind.' What Mandy (like Ibsen's Oswald Alving) can be seen as suffering from is an accumulated heritage of emotional blight – the habit of non-communication, of refusal to hear, that in her has surfaced as the *inability* to hear. Repeatedly we're shown the image of a head turned away from the camera, a person who either can't hear, or won't.

In *Subject for Discussion* the elderly Warden, objecting to a talk on VD – 'I cannot see the necessity for discussing such unpleasant topics before decent people' – is opposed by an outspoken younger woman: 'It's a matter for all of us . . . whether it's a nice subject or not.' The same dispute is played out in *Mandy*: to Christine, with her belief in communal values, Mandy's condition deserves public attention; to the Garlands, it's a private matter. The documentary ends, as befits wartime propaganda, in victory for the public over the private domain. So does *Mandy*, if more equivocally. But both pictures use remarkably similar tactics, relying on what Cook calls a 'blatant appeal to the private, personal world of the emotions'[18] to bias us in favour of the public realm. Because we want Mandy to learn to speak – how could we not? – we must also want Harry and his mother to be proved wrong; the two outcomes are inextricably linked. *Mandy* is the last Mackendrick film (save perhaps *Sammy Goes South*) in which audience sympathies are so openly enlisted; henceforward it will be harder to tell which side we're supposed to be on.

Not that *Mandy* deals, any more than Mackendrick's other films, in crude black-and-white judgements. Almost all the characters are invested with a degree of ambiguity, and the conflict between Innocence and Experience is less readily mapped here than in the comedies. Harry and Emily, though not above exerting emotional blackmail, are scarcely machiavellian; Harry often displays a naive inflexibility worthy of Captain Waggett. The only representatives of Experience in its corrupt aspect are Ackland and his secretary – shoddy, slightly pitiable figures with nothing of Kierlaw's perverted grandeur. What *Mandy* turns upon emerges rather as a variant of the dichotomy – a collision (and even in some senses a collusion) between Awareness and Unawareness.

As ever, neither quality represents an unmixed good. The aware can make connections, but can also divert them, as does Ackland, to malignant ends; and the unawareness of both Harry and Searle leaves them vulnerable to manipulation. People often reject awareness: Harry refuses to listen, his father won't get involved, Christine and Searle avoid confronting their own emotional impulses. Only one character, Jane Ellis, seems fully open, disinterestedly aware, and it's no coincidence that she's the only physically deaf adult. Lack of awareness, Mackendrick seems to suggest, is chosen, not imposed, and Jane represents an ideal at which Mandy can aim in her progress towards participation in the world around her.

This tension between awareness and unawareness is constantly symbolised in *Mandy* by images of openness and closure, cinematic space used to define emotional – and social – boundaries. All through the film, but especially in the Garland household, there occur patterns of walls, railings, closed windows, doors, of life split up into 'acceptable' and 'unacceptable' zones.

**1a.** Script conference on Barra:
Compton Mackenzie, Monja Danischewsky and Mackendrick.

**1b.** 'There is *no* whisky!'
Roderick MacRurie (James Woodburn) in *Whisky Galore*.

**2a & b.** The healing spirit: start and climax of the 'mouth-music' sequence from *Whisky Galore*.

**3a.** Drawing us into the dance:
Peggy Macroon (Joan Greenwood) at the *rèiteach* in *Whisky Galore*.

**3b.** In celebration: Joseph Macroon (Wylie Watson) and people of Barra
enjoying the *rèiteach* in *Whisky Galore*.

**4a**

**4a–7c.** The arrival
of Kierlaw
(Ernest Thesiger)
as sketched
and as shot in
*The Man in
the White Suit.*

**4b**

**4c**

5a

5b

5c

6a

6b

6c

7a

7b

7c

**8a.** In black and white: Sidney Stratton (Alec Guinness) confronts Corland
(Michael Gough), Birnley (Cecil Parker), Kierlaw and henchmen
(Howard Marion Crawford, Desmond Roberts) in *The Man in the White Suit*.

**8b.** Knight in reduced circumstances:
Sidney Stratton at bay in *The Man in the White Suit*.

From the outset Mandy's deafness is associated with physical imprisonment. As the first suspicion darkens Christine's mind, we see the child placed within the bars of her crib. Newly arrived at her grandparents', she gazes out through the barred nursery window. Shades of the prison house, in Wordsworth's metaphor, are visibly beginning to close upon the growing child. Mandy, Charles Barr suggests, 'stands for all children, for the potential locked up inside the new (English) generation'.[19]

'She spent the next five years being – sheltered,' Christine's voice-over tells us, and again the eyes are peering out, puzzled and wary, at an unattainable world – this time, through a wired-up hole in a garden wall. The geography, interior and exterior, of the Garland house is all-important, and Mackendrick evidently chose his locations with care. The house itself – another rickety exemplar of the Mackendrick Uncertainty Principle – stands shored up in what was once the middle of an imposing crescent, bombsites beside and behind it, like the end tooth in a carious jaw. Inside, the household is split into a Cartesian dichotomy: mind in one place, body in another. Emily in her sitting-room, all emotional gush; Fred, her husband, secluded in his study playing not just chess, most cerebral of games, but *postal* chess, divorced from even minimal human contact. Out the back is the garden, Mandy's sole playing-space, where she rides her tricycle in small sad circles. And around the garden, a high brick wall, breached only by the wired peephole and a narrow door.

Traditionally, the door that opens into a private garden has long stood for elusive, idealised pleasure. *Mandy* takes this potent symbol and deftly reverses it. The secret garden is a sterile and stony place, where nothing grows but a few bare twigs and a birdbath devoid of birds. But outside the gate there lies a magic land, that of everyday, unregulated life – a wasteground, where cheerfully unkempt children run and shout.

Twice Mandy ventures out into forbidden terrain, and the first time is catastrophe. Like the hunted Sidney Stratton, she finds herself in nightmare territory where cinematic space plays dangerous tricks. The waste ground suddenly contains a main road along which lorries thunder, and from one of them emerges a monster. It's rare for Mackendrick to use an extreme close-up, let alone a distorting lens, but here we get both, making us share the full impact of the child's terror and bewilderment. The enraged truck-driver, mouthing grotesquely (and voicelessly), lunges at us like a slap in the face. Our impulse is to flinch back from the screen.

Weeping and terrified, Mandy retreats from the outside world, but it's not to be shut out, for all the gates and doors. First, scruffy boys shout through the hole in the wall; getting no response, they run off yelling, 'Stingy!' Then, in the encounter with the children in the park, Mandy's failure to respond again leads to social breakdown. 'Say please,' the boy taunts, holding Mandy's ball, 'not till she says please!' Speech is the precondition of social acceptance. Like Sergeant Odd with his modicum of Gaelic, Mandy has to use words, and the right words at that. In the film's final scene she once more ventures through the garden door, speaks her own name – both asserting her identity and offering the right password – and is duly received into the circle of the community.

Throughout the film, Mackendrick parallels the physical handicap of the child with the mental handicaps of the adults. The scene where the boys shout into the garden provides a good example: as they run off, the camera cuts to a higher angle and we realise the episode has been witnessed by Harry through an upstairs window. But the window is closed. Like Mandy, he can't hear what the boys were saying and has drawn no conclusion from what he's seen. His looking out is merely an evasion, a turning away from what Christine is telling him about the school, and when he turns reluctantly to face her, it's evident he's shut out all she's been saying. 'You can't seriously suggest we should pitchfork Mandy into an – an institution . . . a barracks like that.' The child at least watches (Mandy Miller's performance marvellously conveys a lively intelligence striving to make sense of incomplete data), but her father neither looks at what he sees, nor listens to what he hears.

'There's just no contact.' Christine's words refer to herself with Mandy, but they apply far more widely. Even as she speaks, she pulls away from Harry – no contact there – and, going upstairs, overhears Miss Tucker reciting finger-speech exercises to a bored and unresponsive child. No contact, either, between Christine and Emily, nor between Emily and her husband, withdrawn into his chess-board world; no contact between Searle and his estranged, malicious wife, and certainly none between Searle and his adversary Ackland.

So it's by no means only the 'bad' characters who fail to hear or communicate. Searle, who as Lily Tabor remarks is 'rude to everybody', comes across in Hawkins's portrayal as a man who has shut off a whole area of himself – incapable of sustaining an adult relationship, he deflects his emotional commitments on to the children in his care. (And even here he seems to distance himself from any risk of personal involvement; talking about Mandy in her absence, he refers to 'the Garland child' and 'it'.) There's something clenched, even desperate, in his total dedication, as though without it he might disintegrate. His treatment of Ackland is wilfully obtuse, making no attempt at the right social noises, the tact with which the far more perceptive Jane Ellis tries to placate the solicitor's insecure self-esteem.

In establishing this background of failed communications, Mackendrick avoids the trap of facile optimism that ensnares most films about the physically handicapped – Negulesco's *Johnny Belinda*, for example, which also traces the learning process of an isolated deaf-mute. In these films the protagonist, despite setbacks and abuse, finally wins through and liberal enlightenment triumphs. *Mandy*, though following a similar storyline, almost entirely succeeds in keeping such happy-ever-after sentimentality at bay. Since non-communication is shown as the prevailing norm, those moments when contact *is* made stand out as isolated and precarious achievements.

So the exhilaration of Mandy's three breakthroughs – her first consonant, her first word and her own name – is shadowed by her distress when her father's anger, or the over-eagerness of her teacher, impedes her efforts. This sense of success being dragged, painfully and doggedly, out of failure, and threatening always to relapse back into it, is what gives the initial breakthrough its shattering emotional impact; it's Mandy's frustration at *not* being able to make the sound that impels the scream which releases her latent ability. She succeeds only through having failed.

Mackendrick preserves this underlying tension by juxtaposing scenes in which communication is furthered with others where it's blocked or foiled. Mandy's arrival at the school is intercut with the board meeting at which Searle and Ackland clash, glaring at each other from fixed positions across the table; from this stiff confrontation we shift to the fluid hubbub of the classroom, with children vigorously thumping clay, shaping it into necklaces or moustaches and sharing their delight. And the triumph of Mandy's breakthrough, all direct emotional flow, is preceded by the devious innuendo of Ackland's office as the plot against Christine and Searle is initiated.

This dialectic also affects certain key images, whose emotional polarity flips from negative to positive and back again, according to context. Early in the film, Mackendrick twice uses a shot of the back of Mandy's head to convey her deafness, her entrapment in a silent world. Later, when Christine meets Jane Ellis, the latter turns away to search for a file. Christine continues talking, asking whether the pupils could hope to 'live a normal life' – only to tail off as she registers Jane's deafness. Again, a close-up on the back of an unresponding head, but now it carries the opposite message. Since Jane can live 'a normal life', so can all children like Mandy. But the next time the image appears the head is Harry's, and its purport has switched once more: Harry, though he can hear, is deaf to what's being told him.

As so often in Mackendrick's films, we're being invited to evaluate for ourselves the images he presents us with, to consider how the same scene can vary in its meaning according to who's observing it. When Mandy, in her incomprehending fury, attacks the boy who's teasing her, his mother yells, 'She's not fit to be with other children!' From this incident Harry and Christine draw diametrically opposite conclusions, both confirmed in their respective beliefs. To Harry, it's further reason for keeping Mandy isolated; to Christine, proof that mixing with others is what her daughter most urgently needs.

Perception depends on the perceiver. Harry's first view of the school (and ours) comes as the coda to a long, dispiriting string of experts, who 'all told us, in the most reassuring way, that there was nothing to be done'. Given this, and Harry's aversion to 'institutions', it's hardly surprising that the school appears at its most horror-movie Gothic – shot from a low angle against the light, its pointed gables flanked by turrets like hands upraised in alarm. Our reaction, too, is to think, 'God, what a dismal-looking place,' and dismiss it from further consideration. Exactly the same forbidding aspect greets Christine's first visit, since she's seeing it through Harry's eyes. 'Harry saw this place,' she tells Lily Tabor, 'I don't want to go in.' But Lily persuades her, after which we never see the school's façade again. Its grim exterior has become irrelevant, in effect invisible, since what goes on inside is all that matters.

The relationship between Christine and Searle is subject to the same play of shifting perspectives – innocent, culpable or non-existent according to who's looking at it and when. To Ackland's secretary, extrapolating from her own dealings with the boss, it's clear enough – 'When a man says a girl needs helping, it's nearly always the same sort of help he means.' Her words are unconsciously echoed by Searle: 'To them, loving somebody can only mean one thing.' Yet, as he's just hinted, 'one thing' wasn't wholly absent from his mind, nor from Christine's:

CHRISTINE: But who's been saying these things? Can't I tell them—?
SEARLE: Tell them what?
CHRISTINE: That it's all nonsense.
SEARLE: Well, the trouble is, it isn't *quite* all nonsense, is it?

The echoes are unmistakable; we're in *Brief Encounter* territory. This scene, with its embarrassed understatement, its sense of erotic impulses muffled by social convention, evokes a whole English cinematic tradition of selflessly repressed passion of which Lean's film is the paradigm. Even so it's notable, in the comparable scene from the earlier picture – Alec and Laura in the boathouse, acknowledging their mutual attraction – how much *less* inhibited Lean's couple are. They face each other (literally and psychologically) and at least admit that something has happened, even while trying to suppress it: 'No, please, we must be sensible – please help me to be sensible. We mustn't behave like this.' Christine and Searle can't even go that far; they sit side by side in the car, absolved of the need to look at each other. Searle's words, 'it isn't *quite* all nonsense' – which Christine doesn't answer – are the nearest they come to an open declaration.

And even this is promptly discounted. A few moments later Christine can tell Harry, in all apparent sincerity, 'Don't you realise that Dick doesn't care about anything except the children?' Once again the boundaries are being drawn, the divisions codified. Her remark implies the same fallacious antithesis – *either* professional dedication *or* amorous self-indulgence – invoked by Fred when he asks Harry, 'I just wondered what you'd decided. . . . Has Mr Searle been making love to Christine or has he been teaching Mandy?' No reason, of course, why he shouldn't have been doing both; but not according to the socially sanctioned perspective. *This* is acceptable behaviour, *that* isn't, and the same person – so the unstated premise goes – wouldn't be capable of both.

Harry's response – 'No, I don't believe it. Kit isn't like that' – is another moment of breakthrough, signalled by the turning of his head to face Fred and Searle, and it frees the way for Mandy's emergence into the hazards and wonders of the outside world. Yet it's achieved only by setting up a further chain of restrictive assumptions like those which, up to now, have impeded her development: if Kit 'isn't like that' then Searle isn't like that either, and if he's all right morally, then he's all right as a teacher too. It's the mentality that permeated *Man in the White Suit*, slotting people into ready-made categories: scientist or madman, teacher or philanderer, this or that – but never both.

Sex roles, of course, are among the most rigid of these prescribed categories; and though it would be absurd to claim *Mandy* as a consciously feminist work *avant la lettre*, its conclusion can be read as an almost textbook example of a woman's achievement being appropriated, defused and absorbed by a patriarchal structure. As soon as Christine enters the house with Searle the process begins: Harry takes Searle into the sitting-room and closes the door, leaving Christine outside. Fred, passing Christine and Emily on his way downstairs, takes over from his wife: 'No, you stay here. This time I'll do the interfering and you do the staying out.' He too enters the sitting-room, and states the problem in bluntly patriarchal terms: 'The question of his wife's faithfulness, Harry, is one on which a man must make up his mind. He may not make it up correctly, but he must make it up.'

Matters having been resolved along satisfactorily male lines, Harry follows Christine outside to see Mandy make contact with the world. Twice Christine starts forward, as if to help or intervene; twice Harry restrains her with a hand on her arm. Finally they stand side by side, his hand still on her arm, she gazing up at him with an adoring smile, he watching Mandy with an expression of pride. The message is clear enough – Harry has reasserted his controlling influence over Mandy's progress. One door opens, another closes; Mandy's release comes only through Christine's reintegration into the role of dutiful wife. As the credits roll, Mandy's parents continue to stand watching while she plays.

So though the ending seems happy, it's by no means reassuringly so. Behind Mandy there still stands the whole repressive family and social structure into which she, like her mother, may yet be reclaimed. And behind

Searle, turning away smiling at the garden gate, there still stands Ackland, thwarted but vindictive as ever – no last-reel change of heart for him. Mandy's liberation is no more than provisional; it's had to be fought for and will need even more persistence in the future if it's to be secured.

It's in this that the film's 'purposeful unity' lies: Mandy's condition, like that of her parents and her grandparents, reflects a society locked into a system of closed mental attitudes, where any opening is liable to be achieved only at the cost of further closure, prejudices rearranged rather than overcome. But this perhaps risks making *Mandy* sound a depressing film, which it's not. Mackendrick rejects sentimentality, but not at the expense of hope. Mandy, after all, does come through.

She does it, what's more, by dint of her own achievement. While Searle and Harry quarrel downstairs, Mandy wanders into her grandfather's study. Abstracted as usual in his chess, he puts an arm round her without looking at her. But she, picking up a postcard on which a pawn move is written, starts practising her new skill, pronouncing the letters. And with this, the log-jam starts to shift. Fred is induced to turn, and look, and through him Harry does likewise. The contact has been made back across the generations and then travels down through them, reactivating the disconnected emotional current. That the channel for this contact should be the very symbol of the old man's withdrawal, his postal chess, makes the whole sequence all the more dramatically satisfying.

And from Harry, turning to face his father, we fade to a tracking shot as the camera, starting inside the garden, glides forward to the open door to gaze out across the wasteground. The movement isn't one we've seen before – Mandy's previous excursion was covered by a simple cut from inside to outside – and Mackendrick invests it with a tangible emotional charge. Though not literally a subjective shot (Mandy's already outside and Christine and Harry not yet in the garden), it feels like one, and in a way perhaps it is. What this track seems to represent is the perceptual focus of the film – the spectator's viewpoint – travelling from within to without, from enclosure to openness. For all the reservations that hedge about the ending, this movement is unmistakably affirmative. Change *has* been achieved; a relationship, however tenuous, has been initiated.

Stylistically, *Mandy* represents a development on from *Man in the White Suit*. There's a sense of Mackendrick enlarging his cinematic vocabulary, reaching outwards from a base of secure technical confidence. As always, there's no question of style for its own sake; if *Mandy* makes more extensive use of close-up than his previous movies, it's because that's what the story requires. But in several scenes he explores techniques of fast cutting and close framing, using them in the teaching sequences to trace the exhilaration of growing achievement, or in the episode in the park to build the tension that issues in Mandy's animal shriek of fury.

The impact of the latter scene, incidentally, gains from the addition of a mocking, repetitive little tune like a children's counting-rhyme. It's an imaginative touch from William Alwyn, whose score otherwise never establishes much presence, content to underline the salient emotional points. Alwyn, in Mackendrick's opinion, 'wrote awful film music, because when he saw a sentimental scene he'd say, "Oh, isn't that lovely," and write sentimental music for it. And when the music's doing the same thing as the picture, it never works because one of them's redundant. The good composer's the one who plays against the film and sees another meaning in it.'[20]

*Mandy* is also let down in places by its script, with passages of pedestrian dialogue and slipshod plotting. That the landlady should be present just when Christine embraces Searle, that Harry should pick the one evening when his wife goes out to dinner, smacks of lazy contrivance. Plot is sometimes allowed to dominate over character: Emily's abrupt change of heart ('I don't think Harry realised what he was doing') is badly under-motivated, tipping the film briefly towards the sentimentality it otherwise avoids. But the most serious weakness lies in the casting of the adult leads.

Mandy Miller's performance, outstanding though it is, is never allowed to swamp the film, and Mackendrick elicits some fine playing from his supporting cast, especially the women: Marjorie Fielding as Emily, bringing a troubled warmth to a role that could easily have lapsed into caricature; Dorothy Alison's Miss Stockton, matching Mandy's intensity with her own; the alert, compassionate Jane Ellis of Nancy Price; and Gabrielle Brune as Ackland's unnamed secretary, a lifetime of disenchantment in her glance. As Searle, Jack Hawkins gives one of the most interesting performances of his career; Mackendrick, as Charles Barr notes, 'brings out the dimension of immaturity, of not being able to apply his strength and integrity to fulfilling effect, which always underlies his solidity, but which the later [Ealing] films don't seem so sensitive to, or don't know what to do with.'[21]

Where the film loses conviction is in the central relationship between Christine and Harry. The characters, especially in their scenes together, seem to lack a dimension, and in the case of Terence Morgan's Harry the reason isn't hard to pin down. The role is badly underwritten and Harry often made to seem obtuse beyond all believing. For this, Mackendrick accepts his share of blame. 'Poor old Terence – I was guilty of feeling so unsympathetic to the role that I was probably quite unkind to him on occasion, which is unforgivable for a director. He was a very sweet guy, but I really hated the character so much that it probably shows.'

Since *Mandy* started out as Leslie Norman's project, rather than his own, Mackendrick had less say than usual on the casting. 'Terence was very much a J. Arthur Rank, middle-class figure – and so was Phyllis. Under different circumstances, I might have been happier with other actors; but one's working within the contract.' And this lack of absolute rapport between actress and director may account, to some degree at least, for what's missing from Phyllis Calvert's portrayal of Christine.

Calvert herself evidently enjoyed making the film. 'You'd have thought, "Oh, this is going to be terribly sentimental." It was the treatment by Sandy Mackendrick that made that film so real, and it wasn't at all sentimental.' She relished the opportunity for naturalistic acting after her experience of Gainsborough, where 'if you cried, you had to cry with a bland expression on your face, with glycerine tears coming slowly down your cheek. . . . [So] the first time I was allowed to cry was in *Mandy* . . . to burst into tears and crinkle my face, which I'd never been allowed to do before.'[22]

There's an appealing freshness and immediacy about her performance, and certainly *Mandy* is a far subtler film than any of her previous ones. Even so, it's striking – as Sue Aspinall points out – how much Christine Garland has in common with Calvert's role in a typical Gainsborough movie like *They Were Sisters*: 'In both . . . [she] represents an idealised view of motherhood, of endless spontaneous devotion and warmth.'[23] And on one level, that's how Christine is written. Nonetheless, the character is endowed with a potential depth and complexity that Calvert never quite manages to attain, let alone amplify. It may be that the Gainsborough years had worked their effect – those years of idealised virtue, of glycerine tears on an uncrinkled face – and that as an actress she had been groomed into a persona whose limitations, when the chance came, she could no longer transcend.

*Mandy* was released in July 1952, a year after *The Man in the White Suit*. Without exception, British reviewers enthused over Mandy Miller's performance, praising her total conviction and what Thomas Spencer in the *Daily Worker* termed her 'complete lack of precocious cuteness'.[24] Like most other reviewers, Dilys Powell in the *Sunday Times* found it 'barely possible to believe that she is acting a part and is not in fact stone-deaf'.[25] 'Either [Mandy Miller] is a genius,' declared Elspeth Grant in the *Daily Graphic*, 'or Mr Alexander Mackendrick . . . must be.'[26]

The scenes set in the school were also admired – *The Times*'s critic described them as 'lit up with an imaginative sympathy and insight . . . which turns *Mandy* from a clinical exposition into a work of art'[27] – as was Dorothy Alison's performance as the teacher. The marital conflict element, though, was found conventional, novelettish and trite. *The Times* thought it 'incredible that a film which touches the heights could descend to such depths of banality',[28] and Penelope Houston, writing in *Monthly Film Bulletin*, summed up the general verdict: 'a story which has all the arid artificiality of magazine fiction'.[29]

Not that any of this was blamed on Mackendrick, held to have done a masterly job with uneven material. Gavin Lambert, reviewing the film for *Sight and Sound*, considered that 'its best things are the most substantial he has done. . . . the rather fragmentated approach, the swift and often bold transitions . . . convey a strong sense of camera participation, unlike the more phlegmatic long takes and movement within the frame of *The Man in the White Suit*. . . . If the material here [in the family scenes] had been stronger, the result would probably have been very impressive, and as it is these scenes at least gain interest from decisive handling.'[30] In the *Daily Mail*, Fred Majdalany wrote that *Mandy* 'confirms the place of the gifted Alexander Mackendrick . . . among the top few directors locally in practice'.[31]

*Mandy* was one of three British films shown at the 1952 Venice Festival, where it was warmly received and awarded the Special Jury Prize. In March of the following year it was released in the USA, where critical response followed the British pattern. *Time* noted 'an honestly affecting quality' tempered by 'a distracting soap-opera subplot'.[32] Box-office returns, again as in Britain, were respectable but nothing special – no doubt confirming Balcon in his view that Mackendrick, though too self-willed to be coerced, should be quietly encouraged to stick to comedy.

Still, *Mandy* hadn't harmed Mackendrick's career in the least. At Ealing, no one was expected to turn out a box-office smash every time, or even most of the time, and the film had provided further evidence of his range and versatility. It also showed that he could take a relatively conventional 'social problem' subject (the sort typically assigned to Basil Dearden) and handle it with the same lucidity and narrative control he had brought to the satiric vision of *White Suit*.

For many years, *Mandy* remained one of Mackendrick's more neglected films, overshadowed in his output by the better-remembered comedies. Recently, though, its reputation has revived to the point where Pam Cook, writing in 1985, could describe it as 'a powerful masterpiece'.[33] That may be pitching it a bit high; but at least the film no longer looks so uncharacteristic of its director as it may once have seemed. For all the obvious differences, in subject matter and surface tone, from the comedies, *Mandy* is no less central to Mackendrick's work in its underlying preoccupations. Like *The Ladykillers* – another film whose subtext stands out far more clearly now than it did at the time – it works through a single special case (a deaf child, an eccentric old lady) to explore the forces and tensions within a whole society.

*Mandy*, in Cook's view, 'projects a picture of a nation on the brink of change, from which it ultimately draws back, sadly unable to rise to the challenge'.[34] To me, this seems too pessimistic a reading; it discounts the emotional thrust of the tracking shot out through the gate, of the magnitude of Mandy's final achievement, however precarious. The film does – just – come out on the affirmative side. But Cook's summary would fit Mackendrick's last two Ealing movies, both of which depict a country – first Scotland, then England – turning its face stubbornly away from change.

# 5 The Maggie

'*The Maggie* . . . represents Scotland at its
most self-lacerative.'[1]

Colin McArthur, *Scotch Reels*

'It's dealing with problems private to
Mackendrick, and of little relevance to the
rest of the world, and that's probably what's
wrong with it.'

Alexander Mackendrick

After *Mandy*, with its overt commitment to change, Mackendrick's last two
Ealing films could be seen as something of a relapse. *Mandy* represents a
gesture of defiance: an affirmation of communal values in the teeth of a
reaction back to the private domain of the family, but also a rejection of the
ethos that was coming to dominate Ealing's output. From the early fifties
onwards, the studio's films are increasingly coloured by an attachment to
tradition, often manifested, as Charles Barr points out, in a sentimental
preoccupation with 'items that are . . . little and old'.[2] And at first sight,
both *The Maggie* and *The Ladykillers* conform to the pattern: little old boat,
little old lady, little old house.

Yet in both films the victory of the traditional forces is equivocal; neither
shares the acquiescent, celebratory spirit of, for example, *The Titfield
Thunderbolt*. Mackendrick's attitude to his decrepit symbols is fiercely
ironic and the films are shot through with internal tensions which lend them a
vitality rare in late-period Ealing. In *The Ladykillers* these tensions are
contained within a framework of highly stylised black comedy. In the case of
*The Maggie* the tensions are neither contained nor resolved and the film
comes apart at the seams.

*The Maggie* is generally rated the least satisfactory of Mackendrick's
Ealing films. Mackendrick himself partly agrees. 'It *is* the least successful. I
like it, but I know why other people don't. It's the most self-indulgent of my
films, in that it's the most personal and the most private. It came at a difficult
time, because Hilary and I were having marital troubles, which is reflected in
some of the writing. All the principal characters are me, in a way.'

It's the only picture on which Mackendrick takes original story credit.
Though he believed, like most worthwhile directors, in working closely on
the screenplays of his films, he felt that 'a director should never take

screenwriter credit unless he has written, on his own, a complete draft. A director working with a writer on a script isn't functioning as a writer, he's functioning as a director.' On this principle, he only twice claimed writing credit on films he directed: on *Man in the White Suit*, where he independently wrote the first draft of the screenplay, and on *The Maggie*.

The initial inspiration for the idea dated back to the making of *Whisky Galore*. Mackendrick had become friendly with Compton Mackenzie, who told him about his experiences in trying to ship his precious library of books and records out to Barra, and about 'the near-criminal irresponsibility of the captain and crew of the disreputable vessel involved. And I was struck by the character conflict between Mackenzie, an internationally famous figure, and this crew of rascally freebooters.[3]

'It was this that led me to explore the "puffers". These ocean-going tramp steamers, I discovered, are regarded by the islanders and the Glasgow shipping industry with a mixture of hilarious contempt and some affection. . . . Quite early in developing a structure for the story, I made the decision to replace Compton Mackenzie with an American character and to establish him as an efficiency-minded executive in an airline company. There were two clear advantages: first, an American star is attractive to British film distributors; second, it obviously sharpened the dramatic conflict.'[4]

Finding himself stuck for a 'third act', Mackendrick consulted an old friend from his childhood, the journalist Alastair Borthwick. Borthwick recalled the true incident of a puffer that ran aground on the rocks and could be saved only by ditching the cargo. 'So with that I had the story, and Balcon bought it. Now the question was, who would write it?'

Mackendrick's first idea was to write his own screenplay. He decided against it – not so much from diffidence as from a belief that 'cinema is properly collaborative and, as a director, I find it much more stimulating to relinquish control at various stages in the complex process.'[5] He was considering a collaboration with Borthwick – who liked the idea, but lacked scriptwriting experience – when he was approached by William Rose, who had read the treatment and was eager to script it.

Rose, a fellow American expatriate, was born (in 1918) in Missouri, educated at Columbia, and in 1940 joined the Canadian Black Watch 'to rescue the civilisation that had produced Shakespeare and Congreve'.[6] After the war he stayed in Britain, where he spent his demob bonus training to be a screenwriter. After some routine assignments (*Once a Jolly Swagman*, *The Gift Horse*) he teamed up with an ex-Ealing director, Henry Cornelius, to make that most Ealing of non-Ealing movies, *Genevieve*. The film was hugely successful and Rose's script earned him an Oscar nomination.

Though an Anglophile, and one who relished exploring the same symbols of picturesque decrepitude that attracted T. E. B. Clarke, Rose tempers his affection with an outsider's ironic detachment – especially in the two films he made with Mackendrick. Where Clarke's delight in his rattle-trap eccentrics seems, in *Titfield Thunderbolt* or *Barnacle Bill*, to be wholly uncritical, there can be sensed in Rose's scripts an edge of exasperation at the obstinate British attachment to discomfort and inefficiency for their own sake. In *Genevieve* the hero and heroine wind up at a nightmare Brighton hotel where hot water is only available, at prior request, for about 30 minutes a day. Tired and furious, they kick up a fuss, to the amazement of the manageress (Joyce Grenfell). 'Nobody's *ever* complained before!' she gasps, while an elderly guest (the ubiquitous Edie Martin) inquires: 'Are they Americans?'

There's also, underlying Rose's humour, an intermittent note of alarm – a fear that anyone staying around these superannuated relics may end up sucked in and assimilated, trapped for ever in a mouldering past. In *The Maggie* Marshall finds his values insidiously usurped by those of the puffer's crew, and the gang in *The Ladykillers* are drawn in and ultimately destroyed by the power of Mrs Wilberforce and her rickety little house. In another Rose-scripted comedy, *The Smallest Show on Earth*, a young London couple are left an ancient, crumbling cinema in a provincial backwater. At one point the heroine has an appalled premonition of being stuck there 'for the rest of our lives' and physically turning into the doddering staff that they've inherited along with the flea-pit.

Though he and Rose clearly had a lot in common, Mackendrick was slightly taken aback by the other's enthusiasm. 'I said, "Well, I admire your work, Bill, but you know we'll have to bring in a dialogue writer." And Bill was a little huffy about that. What I didn't know was that he had married a Scots girl and lived in Scotland for years. When he turned in the script, I was astonished. I showed it to Alastair, who lives in the islands, and he couldn't fault a word. Curiously enough, the only person who objected was Paul Douglas, who didn't like some of Calvin Marshall's lines – he didn't think they were American.

'Anyway, I liked it very much indeed, possibly a little too much, because one of the things he'd done was almost eliminate one of the sub-plots, which was Marshall's relationship with his wife. In my draft, the wife appears about halfway through: there's a cutaway during a phone call and it's clear she's thinking of leaving him. And then she turns up again at the end. Now he's been trying to bribe her to stay with him; but it's just because he's thrown away the bribe, by sacrificing the cargo, that she decides to stay. So in the end she rewards him for all the humiliation he's suffered – and that's the key thing that could have made the film a popular success. Bill cut that out – but I didn't really notice, because the script was so well written.'

Mackendrick's relationship with Rose was fruitful and turbulent. Both their collaborations ended in a flaming row and temporary estrangement even before shooting had begun. Rose was notoriously short-fused – Michael Relph, who worked with him on *Davy* and *The Smallest Show on Earth*, describes him as 'really temperamental and difficult. But he was very clever, nonetheless, one of the best writers.' Since Mackendrick himself was never the most equable of directors – his wife Hilary credits him with 'a personality like a Sherman tank' – clashes were probably inevitable. In the case of *The Maggie* the rupture occurred when Mackendrick and his producer, Michael Truman, were up in Scotland about to start shooting.

'We were up there coping with some of the logistics, which were horrendous – we had to build piers and find islands and things like that. We'd cast the whole thing and were ready to go when we got a call from Bill, saying, "Can I come up and talk to you? I've got some ideas about the script." And we both said, "Bill, it's too late to have ideas, we're shooting!" But he said, "You gotta listen to me!" So he flew up and we had this session, one of the most agonising ever. He said, "First of all, at the end the boat must sink, with all hands except the boy. And in the last scene the boy turns on the American and bawls him out for having killed the others. That's your big scene at the end."

'And we sat there with our jaws dropping. I said, "Bill, I don't want to hear it, go away!" Because if we'd listened he might have convinced us and we just couldn't afford that. So he went off in a raging fury, saying, "Never, never, not if my children are starving in the street, will I work with Mackendrick again!" Now the point is that he was right. Not necessarily in that solution – though I wouldn't put it past Bill to have brought it off – but in clearly sensing that the end doesn't work.'

Location shooting for *The Maggie*, mostly on Islay and the Argyllshire coast, took place during the summer of 1953. Mackendrick contrived a projection theatre in a cowshed on Islay and summoned the editor, Peter Tanner, up from Ealing – an unusual step, as Tanner recalls. 'It wasn't the policy at Ealing to send editors away on location. But I think there was pressure from Sandy, saying he must see some cut material and talk to his editor. He was always inclined to be a little bit temperamental, especially on location, and would blow his top if he didn't get his way. But he was very good with actors and would go to great trouble to get things right.' These last two objectives didn't always coincide: a contemporary press report depicts cast-members, huddled in jerseys and raincoats, watching Mackendrick direct the local wildlife ('I want those seagulls to fly closer to the shore').[7]

In his casting Mackendrick accentuated the contrast between the American, Calvin B. Marshall, and the crew of the puffer. Opposite a Hollywood star – Paul Douglas, whose gruff, burly persona with its hint of underlying insecurity perfectly fitted the role – Mackendrick cast non-professionals with little screen experience. Only James Copeland (playing

Hamish, the mate) had ever been in a film; the boy, Tommy Kearins, was a stage hand who had never acted at all. The two other crew members – Alex Mackenzie as MacTaggart, the skipper, and Abe Barker as the engineer, McGregor – were part-time actors taking occasional walk-on roles at the Glasgow Citizens Theatre, just as Mackendrick himself had done as a student.

As in *Whisky Galore*, Mackendrick found that mixing professional and amateur actors enhanced the quality of the playing. 'If you take a polished professional like Douglas and put him in among the amateurs, it brings him right down to total belief in the character, and makes it impossible for him to use any acting tricks. And he's always subject to the fact that these amateurs are going to steal the scenes from him. He's got to work twice as hard, because what happens is that the professional provides the structure of the scene within which the amateur can flower. It's a cruel thing to do to a professional movie star, but it works wonders for the scene.'

It may not have worked wonders for the film, though. What Mackendrick had envisaged was 'a catharsis in the life of Calvin B. Marshall. I wanted him to be thoroughly nasty, a real hard, vicious executive brute, up till the point where he begins to come unstuck. And then you'd feel a warming and a softening of the character. But Paul wouldn't play nasty, because he felt insecure; he knew instinctively he was being acted off the screen by Alex Mackenzie and the wee boy, and maybe he didn't trust his director.'

The weeks of location shooting in Scotland increased Douglas's uneasiness. Tom Pevsner, second assistant on the film, had the impression that 'he was rather lost up there – both as a foreigner and in terms of the Ealing people all knowing each other. He wasn't a particularly easy character anyway and he drank heavily. Part of the time his wife [the actress Jan Lawson] was up there and then things were better; but on his own he could be very unco-operative.' It may also be that Douglas felt, not without reason, that Calvin Marshall was getting a raw deal and aimed to do what he could to redress the balance.

Whatever the cause, he plays Marshall as a straightforward, even amiable type – thus robbing the character of much of its dramatic development and deflecting the thrust of the film. Even so, it's a performance that works perfectly well on its own terms, and Charles Barr's dismissal of it as 'graceless' and 'one-note'[8] seems less than fair. Though he started in radio, only taking up screen work in his forties, Douglas was an essentially physical actor, compensating for limited facial resources with expressive body language. In *The Maggie* he acts with his shoulders and his arms. His gestures, confident and expansive when we first meet him, are gradually reduced to tense chopping movements of the hands, starting out forceful but brought up short, and the set of his shoulders sags like a sack which, once packed full and plump, has been bounced and battered till its corners droop.

Douglas's performance, despite the shift in register from what was intended, also meshes seamlessly with those of the crew. As in *Whisky Galore* – and here on a much more exposed level – Mackendrick shows himself able to integrate professional actors with amateurs so that any disparity in acting styles comes across as a difference of character, not of technique, and thus never obtrudes itself disruptively into the narrative.

This integration is crucial, since *The Maggie* is very much an ensemble film. The crew of the puffer play out their tensions among themselves – MacTaggart and McGregor have a running quarrel on the go, enjoyed by the other two as familiar entertainment – but instinctively unite against outsiders. Where *Mandy* played variations on close-ups and two-shots, the key composition of *The Maggie* is the group-shot, Marshall and the four crew members disposed at different depths within the frame, the clashes and complicities between them expressed in terms of sight-lines and cinematic space.

The film's opening titles seem to herald a cheerful and uncomplicated comedy: a model boat on charts of the Scottish Isles, recalling the toy train from the credits of *Titfield Thunderbolt*, and a bouncy accordion tune, backed by galumphing tubas and reminiscent of Larry Adler's hit theme for *Genevieve*. Midway through the credits, though, John Addison's score takes an unexpected turn, modulating into something altogether more ominous: a mournful horn motif leading – as Mackendrick's credit appears – into a descending string glissando rounded off by solemn chords in the bass. This, the score seems to imply, will be a comedy with very dark undertones – or alternatively, a fairly schizophrenic movie. Or, as it turns out, both.

The credits also hint that the main characters are to be taken on an archetypal level, billing them not by name, but as 'The American', 'The Skipper' and so on. Calvin B. Marshall in particular is clearly an emblematic figure, his name evoking both Marshall Aid, that classic exercise in self-serving benevolence, and the austere morality from which the reputedly Calvinistic Scots, here as in *Whisky Galore*, prove so singularly free. (Mackendrick's description of Waggett as that film's 'most Scottish character, the only true puritan' could equally apply to Marshall.) In political terms, *The Maggie* offers – as at least one incensed American viewer realised – 'a perfect allegory of America's fate in Europe',[9] made at a time when Britain's diminished position, both politically and economically, as a client state of the USA had become humiliatingly clear.

So if both *Whisky Galore* and *The Maggie* can be read as satires on colonialism, then where Waggett stood for the bluff forces of the Empire, hopelessly adrift amid the mists of Celtic ingenuity, Marshall represents his transatlantic successor, a good deal shrewder but scarcely less bewildered. And while Waggett, like a British District Commissioner, tries to interfere with local custom, Marshall, in the style of a visiting Commercial Attaché, simply wants the job done according to contract. Respect the USA's financial interests and you can order your affairs how you like.

But Marshall's chief fault is less that he's an outsider, of whatever nationality, than that his values contravene, and thus threaten, those of the community – which, in this case, means the crew of the *Maggie*. As so often in Mackendrick's work, the action centres on a clash of perceptions, in which people see the same circumstances and events, but draw wholly divergent conclusions from them. At its simplest, this can give rise to the misunderstandings and cross-purposes that are the natural stuff of farce. At a deeper level, Mackendrick uses these mechanisms to explore character, or to expose the tensions and frustrations underlying a whole social system: the restless change-for-change's-sake of US-style commercialism, but also the sterile self-satisfaction of the Scots.

It may be an index of the growing darkness of Mackendrick's vision – or perhaps of his increased creative confidence in expressing it – that the mediating figure, the person who can communicate with both sides, is in the course of his four Ealing comedies steadily eroded into non-existence. Both Sergeant Odd in *Whisky Galore* and Daphne in *White Suit* stand midway between the two perspectives, trying to interpret between them before declaring for one or the other. In *The Maggie* the nearest figure is Campbell, the CSS manager, who rather than mediating spends most of his time chortling over MacTaggart's audacity and Marshall's predicament. And in *The Ladykillers*, last and blackest of the four, there's no mediator at all and the conflict is resolved only by death.

The central divergence in *Whisky Galore* was ethical; in *White Suit* socio-economic; and in *The Maggie* it's temporal. Marshall, possessed by the supposedly typical American preoccupation with hustle, operates on a 'time is money' principle. Introduced as an imperious voice on the phone – 'Look, Pusey, it's been up there three whole days. Let's get this stuff moving!' – he defines himself in terms of speed and expedition, taking pride in having 'a certain reputation for being efficient, for getting the job done'. Thought, for him, translates instantly to action: from his face, incredulous on hearing that MacTaggart has evaded him, we cut straight to a plane taking off (with a sound overlap of its engine stressing the immediacy of his response). His first impulse on arriving anywhere is to locate a telephone, but as always with Mackendrick it's an instrument from which little good can come, and not one of Marshall's elaborate phoned arrangements works out.

No other Mackendrick movie, not even *Sweet Smell of Success*, is so obsessed with time as *The Maggie*. No dates or days of the week are identified, but we can easily work out that the film's action covers ten days, and what happens when. Things are repeatedly supposed to occur – though they rarely do – 'by this afternoon', 'at three o'clock tomorrow', 'in one day's sailing' or 'within half an hour'. To this rigidly scheduled dimension

MacTaggart, while evading direct confrontation, opposes his own far more fluid time-sense with which Marshall can never get to grips. (There may be a sly sideglance here at Mackendrick's own working methods, always angling for that bit more time than his producers would wear.)

The slippage between the two time-concepts is neatly demonstrated by an incident while the *Maggie* is beached in Fiona Bay. Marshall decides to walk to Loch Mora to telephone and insists MacTaggart come with him. He strides purposefully off across the sands, while the Scot ambles easily in the rear. Dissolve to Loch Mora: the Skipper, still at the same easy pace, strolls into view – then pauses and glances back as Marshall limps painfully round the corner. It's a simple enough joke – more haste less speed, tortoise and hare, and so on – but also makes a subtle point about perception. Experience, like vision, is subjective and can distort both time and distance. Marshall's ten-mile trek is MacTaggart's ten-minute stroll.

But MacTaggart's perception of time is fluid also in a more literal sense, based on tides rather than clocks – and this too he can use to his advantage. The tide that, as it turns, floats the *Maggie* off the Fiona sands is the same one that, rising to its fullness, serves to destroy the pier at Loch Mora.

This is the episode that breaks Marshall's will, leaving him too shattered to refuse MacTaggart the cargo. Mackendrick shapes the scene in an elegant crescendo, rising to a peak of frenetic activity before collapsing into despair. The mode is classic dramatic irony: *we* know what's coming – the *Maggie*, lifting on the tide, will shatter the pier and leave the cargo inaccessible on the quay – but Marshall doesn't, and we gleefully await the moment when it dawns on him. To heighten the anticipation, Mackendrick makes his camera a co-conspirator – taking in Marshall in a leisurely long-shot as he stares uneasily about him; glancing sardonically from the American to the restive Highland cattle at the end of the pier; and eventually squinnying along the jetty at ground-level to watch the planks ripple, bulge and pop up like springs from a watchcase.

The soundtrack, to which Mackendrick devoted his usual meticulous care, carries much of the scene's cumulative effect. Starting with a neat aural pun – the groan of a plank under stress twinned with a cow's lowing, which compounds the American's bemusement – Mackendrick builds up layers of sound effects in a collage of mounting hysteria. Marshall's urgent yells, the cattle mooing, the *Maggie*'s engine, the crew shouting to each other, the splintering of the pier – all this, matched by the rhythm of the cutting, climaxes as the planks cascade into the water and Marshall, stamping in fury, falls through the rotten timber.

Silence, broken only by the mournful horn motif from Addison's score. Even the puffer crew seem too awestruck to laugh. The sequence ends on a high angle of the American marooned on the shattered structure, cut off from all previously assumed certainties, his world disintegrating around him. All Mackendrick's comedies are nightmares, where people struggle vainly against amorphous, elusive forces. *The Maggie* is Calvin Marshall's nightmare, just as *Whisky Galore* was Waggett's, and he too is reduced to doubting his own identity. 'Excuse me, sir,' inquires the CSS captain, having docked at the ruined pier, 'are you Mr Marshall, sir?' 'I'm no longer absolutely sure,' comes the reply.

MacTaggart's values, for the time at least, have triumphed. Marshall, waking on board next morning, finds the boat occupied by local islanders and their livestock, all hitching a lift to Bellabegwinnie. Such wholesale usurpation can only be countered by drastic means – Marshall's bid to buy up the *Maggie*, to reclaim it for his world – which provoke even more drastic retaliation. It's noticeable, compared to *Whisky Galore*, how the tone has darkened. Waggett is cruelly humiliated, but never physically attacked. Marshall can only be stopped by a violent assault which leaves him senseless. And though the clash of wills on Todday builds to a fine level of tension, it's clear from the outset that Waggett never really stands a chance. Marshall, far more alert, and capable now and then of out-thinking MacTaggart, makes a much tougher adversary.

In effect, the Waggett-figure has in *The Maggie* been split in two, with his more buffoonish characteristics hived off on to the Englishman, Pusey. (Hubert Gregg, as Basil Wright noted, gives 'one of those small supporting performances . . . which turns out to be quite perfect and absolutely unforgettable'.)[10] Pusey, like Waggett, reverences form above substance ('He *gave* me his signature!' he protests, deeply aggrieved, 'He *signed* the inventory. . . . So naturally I chartered the boat!'), and legality above all. 'I'll not be a party to any illegal—' he splutters, even as Dougie shoves a freshly shot pheasant into his hand. His fate echoes Waggett's, too: both end up framed for someone else's crime. A man hopelessly out of tune with his environment, Pusey bangs his head on branches, falls down and twists his ankle – and even in an office, his natural habitat, manages to entangle himself in the telephone cord.

Pusey is also close kin to Hoskins, the laboratory head in *White Suit*, in his readiness to become the dupe of his own preconceptions. Encountering MacTaggart in the CSS offices, he never doubts that this shabby old reprobate is an employee of the company, and on arrival at the harbour walks straight past the *Maggie* to the far larger vessel moored alongside it. In the face of such gullibility, even MacTaggart evinces a twinge of conscience ('Seems to me yon laddie's the victim of a serious misunderstanding') – and maybe also of disappointment, like a practised haggler whose customer pays the first asking price.

Calvin Marshall, by contrast, is no pushover, being both adaptable and resourceful. Where Pusey retains his absurd costume of bowler-hat and rolled umbrella under all conditions, Marshall at least tries to assimilate.

First the greatcoat goes, then the tie; the jacket is left open; and finally he metamorphoses completely into a black crew-necked sweater and seaman's boots. (This, as it happens, was Mackendrick's favourite garb; Kenneth Tynan once described him as looking like 'a slightly pallid longshoreman'.)[11] So well does he blend in that Pusey, again fooled by appearance, fails at first to recognise him at Kiltarra.

Marshall is aware, too, that other people's minds work differently and makes creditable efforts to think his way into them. At one point, pursuing the puffer in his hired plane, he spots her making across the open sea. The *Maggie*'s crew have also sighted the plane, and guessed who's in it.

MARSHALL (in plane): Where do you figure they're headed for?
PILOT: It looks like they're putting in to Inverkerran for the night.
MARSHALL: Well, tell me: if they thought I thought they were going to Inverkerran, where d'you think they'd head for then?
PILOT: Strathcathaig, maybe.
MARSHALL: I know this sounds silly – but if they thought I'd think they were going to Strathcathaig because it looks as if they're going to Inverkerran – where would they head for then?
PILOT: My guess would be Pennymaddy.
MARSHALL: Well, if there's such a thing as a triple-bluff, I'll bet MacTaggart invented it. Okay – Pennymaddy.
MACTAGGART (on deck of puffer): Aye, he'll have guessed we were making for Inverkerran.
HAMISH: Will he not go there himself, then?
MACTAGGART: Och, no. He'll know we'll know he's seen us, so he'll be expecting us to make for Strathcathaig instead.
HAMISH: Well, then shall I set her for Pennymaddy?
MACTAGGART: No – because if it should occur to him that it's occurred to us that he'd be expecting us to make for Strathcathaig, then he'd think we'd be making for Pennymaddy.
HAMISH: Then shall I set her for Pinwhinnoich?
MACTAGGART: Och, no. We'll make for Inverkerran, just as we planned. It's the last thing he's likely to think of.

Much of the pleasure of *The Maggie* – since, for all its flaws, the film is rarely less than enjoyable – derives from this contest of ingenuities. The action is played out like a chess-game, Marshall and MacTaggart each sizing up his opponent's form, trying to out-guess moves and strategies. Nor does the Skipper have it all his own way. En route from Inverkerran, with Marshall now installed on board, MacTaggart muses speculatively:

MACTAGGART: Thirty miles to Oban. Och, many things might
   happen in thirty miles.
MCGREGOR: The engine! (Chuckles, then stops as Marshall
   approaches.)
MARSHALL: I've just been thinking about the various things that
   might happen to prevent our getting to Oban by this afternoon.
   Such as engine trouble. I think it's only fair to warn you,
   gentlemen, I *built* a better engine than that when I was eight years
   old.

A few moments later, the balance shifts again. Gazing pensively at a
clear sky, MacTaggart predicts fog: 'With the time of the year and that bit
nip in the air, and the way the wind's lying, you might call it seaman's
instinct.' The ruse is so transparent that our first reaction, like Marshall's,
is to dismiss it as humbug – but MacTaggart knows the judo trick of making
the truth look like a lie. Fade to Marshall peering wild-eyed into
impenetrable murk.

And in the end Marshall, though much brighter than Waggett, is
vulnerable to the same ploy: the cruel insult of having his own probity turned
against him. Driven near desperation, he threatens to stop payment on his
cheque. MacTaggart cheerfully refuses to believe him, 'because you're an
honourable man, Mr Marshall. I recognised you for an honourable man the
first time I saw you.'

The Ealing mainstream comedies, Charles Barr has observed, 'celebrate
the triumph of the innocent, the survival of the *un*fittest'.[12] In
Mackendrick's more callous world the innocent are liable to be defeated,
not just despite their innocence, but because of it. Marshall, far from being
the ruthless tycoon he at first appears, loses because he's incapable of
matching his opponent's unscrupulous tactics. Yet here again innocence and
experience are by no means absolute. The puffer crew, for all their cunning,
are oddly innocent figures. Their sense of self-interest is strong but short-
term; like children, they're easily distracted by immediate gratification.
Having trapped Marshall into agreeing the contract, they can't resist making
a detour to attend a party and as a result nearly lose the *Maggie*. Only Sarah
MacTaggart's stubbornness saves them.

How far this fecklessness is intended as an endearing trait, and whether
Marshall 'gets what he deserves', is debatable, since what makes *The Maggie*
an intriguing but ultimately unsatisfactory film is its inability to resolve its
own internal contradictions. Setting out to propose a simple dichotomy –
traditional values good, modern values bad – it finds itself reluctant to
endorse such a crude distinction and keeps undercutting it with reservations
and discrepancies. It's as though Mackendrick, too sceptical to take the
thesis straight, can't quite bring himself to turn it on its head and make

Calvin Marshall the hero. The result is a film that's in constant danger cf being hijacked by its own antithesis.

Not that the studio seems to have noticed. The official account of the film, as set out in the synopsis prepared for distributors and critics, assumes we shall wholeheartedly approve of MacTaggart's values and applaud their victory. Marshall, having gained 'a new outlook on life, and appreciation of the more leisurely way of living instead of the ruthlessness of business activity', finally 'takes the decision which shows that [he] has become humanised at last'.[13] This, which might be called the *Titfield* reading of *The Maggie*, takes for granted that old and rickety is superior to new and efficient, and that any established order is worthy of preservation, accepting at face value the view expressed by Fraser, the Glasgow journalist, that the puffer represents 'the old, simple, live-and-let-live human values'.

Several critics have taken *The Maggie* on these literal terms, if not always with approval. Colin McArthur, no admirer of Mackendrick's Scottish films, refers to 'a set of contrary human values invested in a range of lovable rural eccentrics and non-conformists'.[14] Yet on closer examination such a reading seems hard to sustain. Early on in the film, a defence of these 'non-conformist, contrary human values' is mounted by MacTaggart himself. Facing the mockery of the CSS officers in the pub, he rounds indignantly on them: 'Oh aye, aye – ye're very smooth wi' your gold braid, and your pensions, and your five days a week. But you're no better than hirelings, standing like wee bairns there in front of Mr Campbell's big desk. . . . Ye haven't the freedom of operations that I have. Ye haven't the dignity of your own command.'

While his comments about the CSS officers aren't far wrong – a few minutes later we witness the silent resentment of one of them, Captain Jamison, offhandedly dispatched by Campbell to summon a taxi – MacTaggart's own stance of proud independence is instantly shot from under him. Even as he speaks, Dougie dashes in to warn him harbour inspectors have boarded. Exit MacTaggart and his dignity, leaving the boy to settle for the drinks.

Of course, this is a well-loved comic routine – character expresses high-flown sentiments, only to be ignominiously shown up by events – but the process doesn't stop there. Repeatedly we're reminded of the hollowness of MacTaggart's pose. The boat, it turns out, isn't his 'own command' anyway; he can't navigate properly, despite Dougie's warnings; and when the chips are down at Loch Mora, it's the boy who thinks up the ruse that gets them out of trouble. Compared to the self-reliant Todday islanders, he cuts an unimpressive figure and his way of life shares little of their warmth and communal harmony. At times, he seems to represent hardly more than the boozy stereotype of macho Scots mythology. 'Ach, there's a man for you,' says a taxi-driver admiringly. 'Only last month in Campbeltown I seen him drunk three times in the one day.'

The portrayal of MacTaggart is also coloured by Mackendrick's sceptical attitude to hierarchy. People in authority show up badly in his films, being for the most part incompetent, dictatorial or corrupt, and *The Maggie* is no exception. The Laird is a gibbering obsessive who would rather drown than let a poacher escape. The Constable jails the wrong man. Campbell treats his employees like lackeys. Marshall tries to buy the loyalty of everybody, including his own wife. And MacTaggart, since he too represents authority in a seedy way, is exposed and undermined, forfeiting our sympathy.

It's perhaps no coincidence that one speech which might have improved our view of MacTaggart was dropped from the picture as shot. In the shooting script McGregor, nervously awaiting Dougie's return from the poaching expedition, urges the Skipper to leave the boy behind. MacTaggart refuses. 'No. It's no the thing to do. I'll not desert one of my crew.' But as the film stands, the loyalty runs all one way, from Dougie to MacTaggart, with the boy's alertness and intelligence wasted in a futile cause.

The puffer's crew presents another of Mackendrick's oppressive family structures, with two rogue grandfathers (MacTaggart and McGregor) and a reprobate uncle (Hamish) exploiting and restricting the boy, landing him with most of the work and often getting him to pay for their drinks. For them he doesn't even have a name, and not until Marshall boards the boat do we find out he's called Dougie.

If Tommy Kearins's performance has attracted less notice than Mandy Miller's in *Mandy*, it's perhaps through being set in a less satisfactory, and less emotionally compelling, movie. But it's an impressive achievement nonetheless, perfectly gauged in tone, likeable without cuteness, fresh and remarkably accomplished. As, for example, in the brief scene on the quayside at Inverkerran where Dougie first encounters Calvin Marshall. Kearins, without a word of dialogue, conveys unmistakably that he's instantly realised who Marshall is; that he's considering at least three possible courses of action (taking refuge in the puffer, feigning ignorance or dashing off to warn the others); and, quite incidentally, that the cabbage he's holding was lifted from a nearby garden. All this with no recourse to close-ups or exaggerated reactions. This is acting, and direction of acting, of a high order, the more so for its lack of ostentation.

Setting a child as the moral focus of a film can often come across as a suspect device, at once facile and implausible, but here it rings true. Though accorded no inordinate regard by the other characters, Dougie appears in many ways more clear-sighted and mature than the adults. Left alone aboard the *Maggie*, he steals into the wheelhouse and gazes about him with a look that recalls Sidney Stratton's first glimpse of the Birnley research lab. This, we gather, is the summit of his ambition and his view of MacTaggart seems sheer hero-worship. 'The Captain's the best skipper in the coastal trade,' he assures Marshall, 'everybody knows that.' Yet, as he eventually admits, he's well aware that MacTaggart's nothing of the sort, and his attitude to the old man emerges as protective, almost parental, shielding him from the mockery and contempt of the world.

Though hardly innocent in the conventional sense, helping himself with casual larceny to fountain pens or cabbages, Dougie taps into the same kind of moral clarity as Mrs Wilberforce in *The Ladykillers* (but with none of her naivety). Knowing instinctively what's right, at least by his own lights, he can induce MacTaggart to come clean about the lack of insurance and dissuade Marshall from tearing up the cheque. His exchanges with Marshall are friendly but inexorable. The American's interests, however justified, are dismissed as peripheral, since all they involve is money or amour-propre. What Dougie is defending is a way of life, a claim which – to his way of thinking – overrides all other considerations.

DOUGIE: Why won't you let the Captain take the cargo for you, Mr Marshall?

MARSHALL: Because he caused me a great deal of trouble and expense, that's why.

DOUGIE: I know he did. But why won't you let him take the cargo?

MARSHALL: Well, he made a – he double-crossed me. He disobeyed all my instructions, he didn't pay attention to anything I said. He *behaved very badly*.

DOUGIE: Mm. But why won't you let him take the cargo?

Such certitude is one facet of innocence. But the extremes of innocence and experience, as we saw in *White Suit*, can look strangely alike, and Dougie shares something of Kierlaw's single-minded ruthlessness. 'I'm sorry for what happened,' he tells Marshall after knocking him out. 'Aye, but I'd do it again! Maybe the Captain was a bit slow in getting your cargo to Kiltarra for ye. . . . But that was no reason to do what you did!'

Marshall's response to this passionate speech is stunned silence and an expression which could imply shock, fury or dawning enlightenment. Which it is we never find out, since at this point the *Maggie*'s ill-used engine shudders to a halt, cutting across a moral impasse with a physical one. Since the fault's in the connecting-rod, and Marshall's the only one who can repair it, we should perhaps infer that a connection has been made – that Marshall, forced to acknowledge interests other than his own, has realised their higher validity and can thus make the sacrifice of his cargo. 'It cost you more than the boat's worth!' protests MacTaggart. But it didn't if the *Maggie*, and the tradition that it symbolises, represents a value far greater than any mere monetary sum.

So, at any rate, runs the *Titfield* line. But by this stage the film has diverged so far from its official thesis that most of the imagery isn't so much ambiguous as pointing in the opposite direction. If it were true that, with the dumping of his cargo, Marshall had 'become humanised at last', its loss should bring some sense of liberation, the shedding of a great burden of material possessions. But instead, the surreal image of a nest of white baths floating down to the seabed conveys only an elegiac melancholy, the final foundering of any hope of saving his marriage. 'Good luck to ye!' calls Dougie on the quayside at Kiltarra, with every sign of meaning it, but Marshall's reaction is that of a man shot in the back. Nor does our parting view of him – a grim, dark figure setting out on a long uphill slope – suggest someone who's gained 'a new outlook on life'. In volunteering the sacrifice of his cargo, Marshall salvages his dignity; but otherwise his defeat is as total as Waggett's.

The most sustained attempt to clinch the film's supposed moral comes with the festivities at Bellabegwinnie. The centrepiece of *Whisky Galore* was the *rèiteach*, the joyous dance of unity that celebrated the joining of the couples and the healing of the community. *The Maggie* also leads up to a dance, this time at the 100th birthday party of Davy MacDougall, formerly mate to MacTaggart's grandfather. Marshall, like the straitlaced Mrs Campbell at the *rèiteach*, is induced to taste whisky – referred to by MacTaggart, in an echo of the earlier film, as '*uisge beatha*, the water of life' – and like Sergeant Odd he's drawn into the communal dance by a beautiful young woman. We have a speech in Gaelic, a crowd of gnarled and beaming local faces, exuberant Scots music – all the elements from *Whisky Galore* are reassembled.

Yet the party lacks the jubilant spontaneity of its predecessor, partly because of camera placement and the staging of action to the viewer. In *Whisky Galore* the camera moved *with* the dancers and the guests, becoming one of them. In *The Maggie* it moves to look *at* them, a well-meaning but detached outsider, and the feeling is of an event being created within a controlled environment. There's no sense, as there was in the earlier film, of celebration spilling irresistibly over into off-screen space.

Accordingly, the Bellabegwinnie party fails to exert the same healing power and Marshall's induction into the dance has little lasting effect. 'He learns,' Alastair Michie asserts, 'that the slower pace of Kailyard life is not so bad after all'[15] – but that's just what he doesn't learn. Waking the next day, hungover from the unaccustomed whisky, he snaps straight back into his hustle mode – 'Let's get this thing organised, let's get out of here' – and, not getting an immediate response, storms off to the nearest phone to buy up the *Maggie*. Coming back he meets the crew, and Mackendrick shoots their confrontation like a showdown on Main Street, with dialogue to match: 'All right, MacTaggart – you asked for it right from the word go, and now you've got it.' There's no reconciliation here, just stark polarity; this town ain't big enough, and someone has to go. Dougie, as usual acting decisively while the others stand aghast, chooses between two father figures and, as it were, guns down the Marshall.

It's a measure of *The Maggie*'s unevenness that this episode, tautly shot and rich in resonance, comes straight after the worst scene in the movie – perhaps the worst in any Mackendrick movie. Sitting out at the party with Sheena, the young woman who invited him to dance, Marshall is treated to a sententious parable about her two suitors: a handsome and ambitious trader and a fisherman who spends his time 'drinking or fighting or running after girls'. Marry the trader, says Marshall, 'you want a man you know can take care of you and can give you things you need'. Sheena disagrees. 'It would be exciting to be married to a man who will do big things, a man who is going so far in the world. . . . But I think it'll be the other one I'll be taking. . . . Even though he's away with his brothers so much, he'll have more time for me. He'll not be so interested in what he's trying to do, or where he's going to. . . . And when we're very old, we'll have only what we've been able to make together for ourselves – and I think perhaps that is all we'll need.' Cut to Marshall, gloomily contemplating the error of his ways.

Nowhere else in Mackendrick's work is the message thumped home so crudely. Key phrases in Sheena's speech are even underlined with distant, ethereal folk-song: these, we're to understand, are the timeless verities. To make matters worse, Fiona Clyne's accent veers disconcertingly from the Hebrides to Knightsbridge, and the episode takes place – in a film which otherwise glories in its authentic locations – on a jarringly obvious lump of studio rock. We might take it for a last-minute insertion, a desperate attempt to wrench the film back on course, were it not that the whole scene, with scarcely a word changed, is right there in the shooting script.

Such over-insistence betrays a lack of conviction on the film-makers' part. Consciously or not, they had run themselves into an impasse. On the one hand, the values supposedly being celebrated – freedom, independence, the pride of tradition, the dignity of the individual – could find no credible correlative in the film as it stands. Only on the most sentimental and fuzzy level could the puffer crew (crisply summed up by Charles Barr as 'picturesque, tenacious, but senile')[16] be seen as a worthwhile embodiment of those qualities. On the other hand, the narrative line to which Mackendrick was committed didn't leave him space to do what he would ingeniously bring off in *The Ladykillers*: turn the whole film into a subversive critique of just that kind of sentimental attitude.

Comparison with *The Ladykillers*, or come to that with *Whisky Galore*, also reveals in *The Maggie* a failure to achieve the mythic quality that could lend the story resonance beyond its immediate narrative level. It's a quality that Mackendrick believes all films should aspire to: 'When a story's a strong one, it's communicating to you in a way that's magical in the best sense of the word. It only makes sense at a mythic level, a level which is talking to you in dream language, in other words to the subconscious.'[17] Lacking such elements, *The Maggie* is reduced to an anecdote that entertains us but leaves the deeper levels untouched. Mackendrick's description of the film as 'self-indulgent' may in the end be right: in playing out conflicts within his own psyche, he hasn't left the rest of us quite enough to chew on.

But if *The Maggie* falls short of Mackendrick's best, it still has, as Charles Barr notes, 'far more life and intelligence and moral tension'[18] than anything else being made at Ealing at the time. And the ending, at least, makes its insidious point. The same old puffer steams up the same old Clyde – all that's changed is the boat's name: the *Calvin B. Marshall*. On board, Skipper and Engineman still pursue their aimless, repetitive quarrel, accompanied by Hamish's habitual accordion tune. Scotland, stuck in its old internecine ways, is ripe for takeover and it's unlikely the new owners will be fobbed off with a change of name. In returning full circle to his opening shot, Mackendrick suggests not so much survival or continuity as a wilful stagnation.

On its release, in February 1954, *The Maggie* was generally well received – rather better, in fact, than the more openly contentious *Man in the White Suit*. The majority of British reviewers, taking their cue from the studio handout, treated it as another undemanding Ealing romp. The puffer and her crew were considered 'lovable'[19] by the *Star* and 'endearing'[20] by the *Spectator*. In *Time and Tide* Fred Majdalany found 'much at which to smile and a great deal of charm. . . . The regional patois is at times hard to follow, but the film leaves a friendly taste in the mouth.'[21] Thomas Spencer in the *Daily Worker*, delighted to see international capitalism getting trounced, credited the *Maggie*'s crew with 'the sense of human dignity and enjoyment of life which the American has lost. Before the voyage is over they have taught him that money cannot buy everything in Britain and that the individual is entitled to consideration.'[22]

A few reviewers dug down to the moral ambiguity. The *Manchester Guardian*'s critic, while finding 'the enchantment irresistible', saw the film as appealing to 'those who . . . like to see the forces of modern progress confounded by romantic, reactionary dreams'.[23] Peter Wilsher, writing in the *Sunday Chronicle*, was anything but enchanted; he 'could rouse no interest in the boat's fate and was merely irritated by the folksy goings-on of the crew. My sympathies were all with Paul Douglas.'[24] To Campbell Dixon in the *Daily Telegraph* the ending of the film 'only proved that a gentle, unhappy man has been extraordinarily magnanimous to a gang of rapacious incompetents; which is not, I take it, quite what Mr Mackendrick intended'.[25]

Under the title of *High and Dry*, *The Maggie* received its New York premiere the following August. Far from taking Marshall's part, American reviewers responded with much the same cheery enjoyment as their British colleagues. 'A jolly piece of foolishness,'[26] wrote John McCarten in the *New Yorker*, echoed by the critic of the *New York Times*: 'A jolly entertainment that is as bracing as the Hebridean air.'[27] *Time* considered it 'very possibly the funniest Ealing comedy to date'.[28] It was left to one of *Time*'s readers to bring out the political subtext. In an eloquent, exasperated letter a New Yorker, Fletcher Grimm, argued that 'all Douglas wants, in return for ample pay, is to get a job done quickly and honestly. Instead, he is robbed, cheated, tricked, lied to, made a fool of, disobeyed, ignored, kicked around, drenched, almost left to drown and hit over the head. . . . That's America in Europe: taken for our money, cheated, fooled, our advice ignored, our skills wasted, our intentions sneered at – and in the end we wind up believing that it's all our fault and that there is something morally and esthetically fine about old rustbuckets.'[29] Mackendrick replied in a subsequent issue, pointing out that he and Rose were both Americans and 'saw the story very much from the viewpoint of the American. . . . The savagely unfair way in which [he] is treated, the sly insult added to injury and the ultimate indignity of being expected to feel that he is somehow "morally" in the wrong were, for us, part of the flavour of the joke.'[30]

Box-office response to the picture, in both Britain and the USA, was no better than passable – Mackendrick believes that 'it didn't actually lose money'. For all the critical enthusiasm, audiences may have felt unsettled by the film, unsure where their sympathies should lie and perhaps sensing a sour note behind the humour. Certainly *The Maggie* has never attained the popularity of Mackendrick's other early comedies, and despite regular revivals on television it remains the least known of his Ealing movies.

After one such showing, in 1979, Peter Quigley in the *Scotsman* attempted a salvage operation. Describing *The Maggie* as 'the best Scottish feature film ever made . . . the only film to deal with the Scots personality in a frank, unsentimental manner', he commended 'the uncompromising presentation of the characters', the absence of 'the colonial overtones of most film and television productions about Scotland' and 'the realistic depiction of the poverty and humanity of the ordinary people'. *The Maggie*, he concluded, was 'a model for Scottish film makers'.[31]

Quigley's view failed to gain much critical support – rather the reverse, if anything. The rise of Scots national feeling during the seventies inspired not only a revival of Scottish cinema under such film-makers as Bill Forsyth and Bill Douglas, but also a reassessment of the traditional image of Scotland as presented to the world. In particular, the movie industries of Hollywood and London were accused of peddling distorted, and even degrading, representations of the Scots. *The Maggie*, along with *Whisky Galore*, found itself singled out as a prime example. John Brown, coupling the Mackendrick films with Minnelli's *Brigadoon* and John Ford's Welsh and

Irish excursions, *How Green Was My Valley* and *The Quiet Man*, summed up the prosecution case. 'What they are held to be guilty of is that they are attempts, made from outside these countries and cultures, to embody some kind of definitive essence of them. They are not unsympathetic attempts, but the way they represent the Scots, the Welsh and the Irish . . . has long been the subject of bitter attack within these countries.'[32]

The most sustained attack was *Scotch Reels*, published in 1982. It was edited by Colin McArthur, who also contributed a long central essay entitled 'Scotland and Cinema: The Iniquity of the Fathers', in which he cited Mackendrick's Scottish comedies as specimens of Kailyard, one of the two archetypal misrepresentations of Scotland and the Scots (the other being Tartanry). Kailyard (literally, 'cabbage-patch'), whose *locus classicus* is the writings of J. M. Barrie, depicts – according to Cairns Craig's essay in *Scotch Reels* – 'a Scotland of parochial insularity, of poor, humble, puritanical folk living out dour lives lightened only by a dark and forbidding religious dogmatism. . . . Kailyard's humour is based almost entirely on convincing the reader that he/she and the author share a sophisticated sense of the world, and that the characters whose lives they look down upon are backward, parochial, narrow-minded and utterly incapable of becoming conscious of the values by which they are being found comic.'[33]

This definition might seem to have little relevance to the Scots portrayed in *Whisky Galore* or *The Maggie*. Shrewd, resourceful and anything but humble (let alone puritanical), the people of Todday and the puffer crew are also well aware how they appear to the outside world, and quite capable of turning that image to their advantage and playing the backwoods innocent when it suits them. The characters who best fit the description of parochial, narrow-minded, and with no idea how funny they look, are in fact the two Englishmen, Waggett and Pusey.

McArthur, though, takes the argument a stage or two further. Linking the Mackendrick films with a couple of other Scots comedies, *Laxdale Hall* (1952) and *Rockets Galore* (1958), he ascribes to them 'a detestation of modernity as it related to the city and to the power of capital (though the films are by no stretch of the imagination pro-socialist; they are rather pro-feudal) and particularly to the power of central government bureaucracy. Set against these ills, the films construct a set of contrary humane values invested in a range of lovable rural eccentrics and non-conformists.'[34]

What McArthur has done, with deft sleight of hand, is pick out elements from one or other of the films (and from *Laxdale Hall* in particular) and attribute them to all four. *Laxdale Hall*, a limp comedy adapted from an Eric Linklater novel, concerns Highlanders battling against Whitehall official-dom over a road tax and against predatory Glasgow poachers. Matters are resolved with the help of the Laird. 'Pro-feudal', in this case, is fair enough, but it scarcely fits the Mackendrick films where authority in any form has a pretty rough ride. The Laird in *The Maggie* is a figure of fun who gets pushed in the canal and the nearest to a feudal overlord on Todday is the despised Captain Waggett. Central government bureaucracy, in the form of the Customs men, does show up in *Whisky Galore*, but in *The Maggie* only marginally if at all (the harbour inspectors?). And so on. Altogether, Mackendrick's Scottish comedies are too idiosyncratic, and too nuanced, to lend themselves to this kind of strait-jacket approach.

McArthur goes on to extend Kailyardry into a form of wish fulfilment, whereby 'what is not achievable at the level of political struggle is attainable in the delirious Scots imagination'. Thus, 'precisely at the moment . . . when the massive penetration of American capital into Scotland was gathering pace, *The Maggie* . . . with almost wilful perversity . . . has the Scots win hands down'.[35] A similar account could be given of *Whisky Galore*, in which the historical dispossession of the Scots crofters by English (or Anglo-Scots) landlords is reversed and the English usurper driven into exile instead.

If this is Kailyardry, then Mackendrick's Scottish films may be held guilty of it. But is it? After all, the cinema of wish fulfilment, in which the little guys take on and rout the big battalions to general rejoicing, is a well-established and prolific genre in virtually every national cinema – take most of Frank Capra's output, to look no further. It can certainly be criticised on ideological grounds – making us feel that right will prevail and everything's really OK, while leaving the rich and powerful to do as they like. But does simply locating it in Scotland make it Kailyard?

By way of comparison, it may be worth looking briefly at a film which, while including an element of wish fulfilment (a Scotsman triumphs at the Melbourne Olympics), also quite unrelatedly – since that scenario could fit into a dignified and realistic framework – presents cinematic Kailyardry at its most blatant. Frank Launder and Sidney Gilliat's *Geordie* (1955) tells of a puny Scots lad who takes up body-building, grows up huge and brawny and becomes a champion hammer-thrower – a fairly dire storyline in itself. But what makes the film almost unwatchable is the archly patronising depiction of the Scottish background. *Geordie* is set in a Scotland where the distant drone of bagpipes wafts over every heather-swathed scene, a land populated by lairds, ministers, gamekeepers and bonnie wee lassies. All Scots are quaint, folksy and comically wary of anything beyond their native glen. 'I've never been further than Perth,' declares the hero when the Olympics are suggested, 'and I didna like Perth.'

Mackendrick, of course, never descends to such inanity. All the same, a hint of the same attitude does occasionally colour his films, as in the scene from *Whisky Galore* where looting has to be suspended during the Sabbath. Here the film seems, for once, to invite a sophisticated smile at the expense of the islanders. *The Maggie* is more problematic, given the difficulty of knowing quite how we're meant to take the puffer crew. But since almost any possible response, whether indulgent amusement, irritation or contempt, would seem to involve a measure of condescension, and since condescension is the essence of Kailyard, the film can't be absolved from the charge.

It might be argued, too, that Mackendrick's films, just because they *are* more subtle and better made than most, exert a more persistent influence. As John Brown observes, it's their very success that arouses particular resentment. 'The Scottish attack on *Brigadoon*, *Whisky Galore* and *The Maggie* operates at two levels. First . . . for the way the Scots are insistently portrayed as quaint and old-fashioned, comically innocent or comically cunning, and for the way the country is characterised as no more than a natural paradise of romanticised mountain, loch and glen. . . . How fortunate these peasants are, to be close to the land and the sea and the eternal verities, to be free of materialism, class conflict and other neuroses. The second level . . . takes the form of a political revulsion against the cultural/industrial institutions themselves . . . which by their very mode of operation create such images of Scotland and then impose them on the international consciousness to the exclusion of other, more authentic images.'[36]

Brown, like McArthur, over-generalises and a lot of his points apply far more to *Brigadoon* than to the Mackendrick films. 'Free of materialism' hardly sounds much like Macroon, and still less like MacTaggart. But in any case, as he goes on to point out, the argument relies on a fairly superficial reading of the films concerned, which 'are far from being simple and unambivalent works. . . . It seems to me that the representation of Scotland in these films is often misread simplistically, and that distantiating ironies are being missed when the charge of misrepresentation is raised.'[37] As so often with Mackendrick, it's easy to mistake clarity for simplicity, to miss the ambiguities swirling about beneath the lucid narrative surface.

So, as with the 'household as microcosm' device in *Mandy*, the use of an islandful of whisky-smugglers or an ancient puffer and her crew as what could, on one level, pass for national symbols, invites us on a rather different level to consider just what the recourse to such conventions implies in itself. It's this aspect that the Kailyard debate, operating as it mostly does in straight representational terms, is in danger of overlooking. Whether or not these are valid representatives of the Scottish nation, the fact that they could plausibly be proposed for the job makes a statement not only about how others see the Scots, but about how they're prepared to see themselves – just as, in *The Ladykillers*, the choice of an old lady in a dilapidated cottage to stand for England says a lot about the image, and self-image, of the English.

Throughout Mackendrick's Ealing work there can be sensed this critical perspective which, while never openly disrupting the narrative flow, sets up ironic tensions that lend even a relative failure like *The Maggie* a vitality marking it off from the bulk of the studio's output. Alastair Michie has commented on 'the damage done to the Ealing discourse by its association both with Scotland and with . . . Alexander Mackendrick.'[38] It's true that of all the Ealing films only two (barring a crass Will Hay farce, *The Ghost of St Michael's*) are set in Scotland, and that both undermine the complacent Ealing models of community and consensus. But since a similarly subversive instinct also informs *Man in the White Suit* and *Mandy*, it seems fair to attribute any damage less to Scotland than to the director himself.

Mackendrick had only one more film to make for Ealing. In it – by way of a sardonic farewell – these covert guerilla tactics would achieve their most satisfying triumph: demolishing, under the guise of conformity, all the studio's most cherished conventions.

# 6 The Ladykillers

'A dream is not merely *like* a cartoon – it *is* a cartoon.'[1]

Alan McGlashan, *Dreams and Dreamers*

'True, it's obviously a parody of Britain in its subsidence. That we were all aware of at a certain level. But it was never openly discussed, and it would have been fatal to discuss it.'

Alexander Mackendrick

By 1954 Mackendrick was starting to feel discontented. Though he was by now considered Ealing's most talented director, the system that had fostered and supported him was turning claustrophobic, restricting his creative development. Attempts to branch out into more ambitious projects, such as *A High Wind in Jamaica* or *Mary Queen of Scots*, had all been turned down. Nor was Balcon prepared to let him try his hand as a producer. 'There was one moment in my career, which I've never really forgiven Mick for, when I realised that I was really very weak on the producing side. So I went to Balcon and explained that I thought many people had profited from having been Associate Producers, and could I please be assigned such a role? And Mick, to my humiliation, started to laugh and wouldn't stop. I had to leave with the sound of his mockery in my ears. I suppose I should have learned something from that.'

Ealing itself was becoming stale and inbred, having reached the point at which, in Lindsay Anderson's phrase, 'consistency declines into sameness'.[2] It had been a surprisingly rapid process. Only six years separate the freshness of *Hue and Cry* from the self-indulgence of *Titfield Thunderbolt* – years during which Ealing seemed to lose touch with the outside world, retreating into a vision of gentle eccentricity. As the writer of both films, Tibby Clarke, later acknowledged, he and his colleagues 'had really failed to see how life was changing round about us'.[3] Mackendrick, though, was well aware that an era was coming to its end. 'Film generations seldom last longer than seven years, and . . . seven years is enough. The genre had worked its way through, we were in danger of repeating ourselves.'[4]

The studio was also in financial trouble. In 1952 the industrialist Stephen Courtauld, a director and major shareholder, was obliged to resign for health reasons and with his departure Ealing lost the backing he had secured from the National Provincial Bank. Balcon negotiated a loan from the National Film Finance Corporation, hoping to repay it out of profits; but the increasing popularity of television, boosted by the 1953 Coronation, was eroding cinema audiences, and Ealing's takings were falling. The only way to pay off the loan, Balcon came to realise, would be to sell the studio.

It would be simplistic to attribute Ealing's loss of vitality directly to the decline in its financial position; but a sense of financial insecurity may well have prompted Balcon to favour safe, tested formulas over anything audacious or unusual. At all events, little in Ealing's later output – roughly, from 1952 onwards – avoids a sense of caution, of the closing down of options.

Mackendrick's work could hardly escape being affected by this process, though with him it took on a more dynamic form: the tensions and frustrations experienced in the studio were played out within the dramatic conflicts of the films themselves. This judo skill in using the ossified weight of the Ealing tradition against itself is most evident in *The Ladykillers*, the last picture he made for the studio – and also the last of the great Ealing comedies.

The oath sworn by William Rose as he stormed off the production of *The Maggie*, 'never to work with Mackendrick again', held good for barely a year. Soon after returning from the Western Isles, Mackendrick visited the Red Lion one lunchtime and heard Rose recounting a dream that had come to him the night before. As Rose recalled it, 'I woke up one morning, at about one or two o'clock, and wakened my wife and said, "I've just dreamt a whole film." It wasn't like any dream I'd ever had; it was whole and complete, and it was original.'⁵

The dream, as Mackendrick remembers hearing it told, was about five criminals 'who lived in a little house with a little old lady and she found them out. They decided that they had to kill her, but they couldn't and so they all killed each other. That was it, and we all laughed and nobody really thought seriously about it. But another idea I was working on collapsed and this story kept haunting me. So I went back to Bill and said, "About that story you dreamt—" and he said, "I'm not going to work with you." I said, "Sure, just write the story and I'll make it." But he went to Balcon and insisted a clause be put in his contract that he was not required to talk to the director. Mick phoned me up and said, "What *is* this thing that Bill's up to?" I said, "Just sign it." Of course I'd called Bill's bluff, because after we started working together he wouldn't let me alone.'

Rose vividly recalled Balcon's reaction to the storyline. 'I told it to Mick and he watched me with those strange hooded eyes all during the telling, never took his eyes off me – just once in a while glanced at Sandy as if to say "Is it just he who has lost his mind or have you both lost your minds?" And then he leaned forward, like that [fingertips joined together], and said, "Just let me get this straight. You have six principal actors and at the end of the picture five of them are dead. And you say this is a *comedy*?" '6

It was indeed – precisely the kind to appeal to Mackendrick's 'perverted and malicious sense of humour'.7 Its gleefully homicidal plot promised a degree of blackness unplumbed in Ealing comedy since *Kind Hearts and Coronets*, and offered Mackendrick a chance to explore the nightmare element that had fleetingly surfaced in his previous films. 'The fact that it was something Bill had quite literally dreamed up really entranced me. Dreams are a marvellous source of imagery for movies.'8 The story also lent itself to another of the generic hybrids that Mackendrick loved to create: a comedy crossed with a heist movie, plus an affectionate parody of the silent Fritz Lang thrillers (*Dr Mabuse*, *Spione* and so on) he had grown up with, all deranged master-criminals, lopsided sets and sinister expressionist shadows.

Won over, despite his misgivings, by Mackendrick's enthusiasm, Balcon gave the project the go-ahead. As his producer Mackendrick chose Seth Holt, his editor on *Mandy*, who would later direct horror films of his own. Holt and Mackendrick shared similar tastes in humour and got on well – almost too well, perhaps. Some of their colleagues, according to Holt's widow Jenny, 'said Seth and Sandy should never have been allowed within a hundred miles of each other, because they led each other astray and encouraged each other in eccentricities'. Since Rose, even without encouragement, was also prone to eccentricity, the mixture was highly volatile.

Over a period of several months the three met every day for story conferences during which, as Mackendrick later recalled, 'Bill, who was a marvellous raconteur, ad-libbed the script. . . . Our role during these sessions was to a large degree passive. We would of course offer suggestions, suggest variations. But we left the initiative to the writer. This doesn't mean that we didn't have an influence; in fact, as every good story-teller will assure you, the stimulus of the audience is vitally necessary, and the performer gets a great deal of feedback as he senses the responses, the slackening of tension at some points and the heightened interest at others. Improvisation and invention are nourished by the process.'9

The masterstroke of Rose's scenario was that his gangsters should pose as a string quintet – an idea borrowed, perhaps unconsciously, from the 1938 Warners comedy-thriller, *The Amazing Dr Clitterhouse*, directed by Anatole Litvak from a script by John Huston. In this, a bunch of New York hoods run by Humphrey Bogart get together as the 'Hudson River String Quartet', complete with instruments, plus a gramophone to supply the music. (The film also features a rivalry between Bogart and Edward G. Robinson, who plays a maverick savant known as 'The Professor'.) But where Litvak's film uses the chamber-group device as a throwaway gag,

Rose develops and elaborates it, exploiting it as a source of comic imagery – ruffians and low-lifes tussling with the refinement of classical string-playing – and also to delineate character and advance the plot.

Elements like these, with their visual and dramatic potential, were seized on with delight by Mackendrick. 'By the time these story conferences were completed I was as thoroughly immersed in the whole narrative as the writer since, while he was improvising, my imagination was at work on different aspects of the movie, beginning to visualise the scenes in the terms which would later be my responsibility, seeing the action come alive in images, behaviour and sound. At the moment when Bill took his pages and pages of notes to seclude himself as he turned them into . . . the screenplay, I already had all that I needed to go off and begin work on other aspects of pre-production, planning sets with the designer, searching for locations, working on the logistics of production, including the casting.'[10]

Since the film was essentially an ensemble piece for six players, casting was the crucial factor. The role of the criminal mastermind, Professor Marcus, was originally intended for Alastair Sim, a specialist in sinister eccentrics. Balcon, though, had other ideas. 'Mick said, "No, no, we're making money with the Guinness films, we're on a run of strength there. It's got to be Guinness." So we took it to Alec, who read the script and said, "But dear boy, it's Alastair Sim you want, isn't it?" And we said, "No, no, no." But maybe in the end he did a better Alastair Sim than Alastair would have done.'

The casting of Major Courtney, the shabby-genteel conman, and of Louis, the Soho hood, proved more straightforward. The Major's hollow effusiveness marked a further stage on from *Man in the White Suit* in the unravelling of Cecil Parker's screen persona. As Louis, Herbert Lom might seem predictable casting. But though Lom had portrayed plenty of foreign-accented crooks, he had never before played comedy, and his acting style, fractionally out of key with that of his fellow criminals, emphasised his hostile status within the gang and added an edge of danger that held the film clear of *Lavender Hill Mob* whimsy. Mackendrick noted approvingly of Lom's performance that 'he acted as though he didn't know he was funny'.[11]

For the Teddy Boy, Harry, Balcon proposed Richard Attenborough, a regular choice for young-hoodlum roles since playing Pinky in John Boulting's *Brighton Rock*. Holt and Mackendrick, both ardent fans of the cult radio programme *The Goon Show*, wanted Peter Sellers, who had hitherto appeared only in obscure bit-parts. Balcon suggested Sellers should play One-Round, the impenetrably dumb ex-boxer; but Holt and Mackendrick won out and Sellers got the breakthrough his career needed. (His vocal dexterity also gained him a few secondary roles, voicing the old lady's parrots.) The part of One-Round went to the hulking Danny Green, a genuine ex-boxer with the build of a concrete mixer and a voice to match.

For the key role of the indomitable Mrs Wilberforce, Mackendrick had set his heart on the 77-year-old Katie Johnson. Johnson, a veteran player of tiny roles in countless movies, had retired two years earlier, but was happy to return for such a good part. However, Mackendrick encountered furious opposition from Holt. 'Seth turned on me and said, "Sandy, I know you, you're a ruthless bastard; you're going to kill that woman. When you want what you want, you have absolutely no consideration for anybody else. She's 77 – she'll die, and I'm not going to have her on my conscience!" I sulked like mad, and pleaded, and got nowhere. So we got another woman, who wasn't quite as old, a little bit more robust, and did all we could to whiten her hair and make her look older; and we did a test scene of her, and I think she even signed a contract. Then she went home, caught a chill, and died. Around the studio they were saying, "Listen, you think working with Sandy is tough? Here's a woman dies just at the prospect of it!" '

Without telling Holt, Mackendrick contacted the insurance company, negotiated a special deal for Johnson and took the proposition to Balcon – who agreed, subject to the medical tests. 'And she came through, strong as a horse. So Seth, having been totally outmanipulated and outmanoeuvred – and he was livid at me – agreed to go ahead with it.' But Johnson, having got wind of the discussions, came to Mackendrick, 'and she said, "You know, I've never had a part longer than a couple of pages before; this is such a good part and I so much want to do it. I have a little money saved – if there's a problem about the insurance, could I help pay it myself?" At which point I burst into tears.'

The location chosen for the film was the area of North London around Kings Cross station. This district offered everything Mackendrick needed: the rail terminus itself, venue for the robbery; a local, village-London ambience; some impressive railway topography, with tunnels, viaducts, signals and cuttings; and the majestic Gothic pile of Gilbert Scott's St Pancras, symbol of the unshakeable absolutes of Mrs Wilberforce's moral universe.

The area also included a fine clutch of tall gasometers, which Mackendrick at once saw as vantage-points for his favourite high-angle shots. To the alarm of David Peers, the unit's Production Manager, he insisted on an exploratory ascent. 'What I hadn't counted on,' Peers relates, 'was that the top of the gasometer wasn't level, it curves down towards the edge. And there were no railings round it. Sandy just marched across this thing, up to the top and down again, all round the edge. I was scared out of my bloody wits, but Sandy didn't appear to have a nerve in his body. Anyway, he was much too engrossed in seeing if we could get the angle. "Pity that building's just there," he'd say, "because we could get a wonderful shot if – I wonder – it's probably empty, maybe we could have the roof knocked off or something—" And I would solemnly have to go and see if it was possible to knock down half the building. Of course it wasn't.' In the end Mackendrick rejected the gasometers in favour of a 70-foot rostrum. With some difficulty, Peers persuaded him to settle for a telescopic extension ladder.

If Mackendrick didn't get to demolish any buildings for *Ladykillers*, he did have one constructed. Unable to find his idea of Mrs Wilberforce's house anywhere in the area, he decided to build it from scratch, and sited it at the end of a cul-de-sac, Frederica Street, which straddled a tunnel over the main line from Kings Cross. (The reverse angle from the house, with its prospect of the St Pancras clock tower, was shot in Argyle Street, about a mile south.) The house, though made of plaster, was complete inside and out, and cost nearly as much to build as a real one. Mackendrick worked closely on the design with his regular Ealing art director, Jim Morahan. 'Jim was a great art director, but not that strong in original sketch designs. He was really an architect, and a very sensitive one; and very astute in props and things like that. So I was able, thanks to my own background and training, to do sketches and hand them to Jim, who would realise them with extraordinary faithfulness.

'One of my conceits was that nothing should be quite straight, should always be a little crooked, and that this would give you a slightly funhouse quality. And when we built it, it was absolutely superb; you walked in and you had a feeling of things not quite right, a little weird – just a touch of *Caligari*. But in the film it doesn't show. Because the strange thing I learnt then about the camera is that it can't see a vertical. So you get none of that impression of unsteadiness that you had on the set. It was a huge disappointment to me.'

A further complicating factor was the sheer size of the camera. *The Ladykillers* was one of the last films to be shot in the three-strip Technicolor process, which involved the use of a massive camera built like a refrigerator. Doors and corridors had to be widened to allow for its passage, and certain tracking movements – from the sitting-room out into the hall, for example – were impossible. It says a lot for Mackendrick's skill, and for that of his cinematographer, Otto Heller, that the film retains a high degree of camera mobility – as in the sinuous gliding patterns within the house that mimic the Professor's external prowling – and that the cutting remains for the most part unobtrusive.

The score was entrusted to the composer Tristram Cary, who had written a lot of *musique concrète*. Mackendrick took the unusual step of inviting him to compose the sound effects as well and integrate them into his score. Cary took good advantage of the opportunity, working in subtle sound gags (like the staccato backfire of a distant car that accompanies Louis's first appearance) and using the eerie wails of passing trains to heighten the mood and comment on the action.

Obsessive as ever over detail, Mackendrick paid particular attention to the stolen money, proceeds of the heist. In the first place he refused to accept the usual phony mock-up banknotes, demanding something convincingly like the real thing. (Several members of the production team insist he held out for real notes, but this he firmly denies.) After negotiation with the Treasury, special dispensation was given for near-facsimiles to be used, but only on condition that the props man kept them under lock and key, and counted them after each day's shoot.

Mackendrick was also concerned that the amount stolen should be practicable. The script called for £200,000, all needing to fit into a single cello-case. Just what quantity of £1 and 10-shilling notes, he inquired, *could* a cello-case hold? (Larger denomination notes were rare at that time.) It fell to Michael Birkett, as Third Assistant, to find out. 'I took the cello-case down to my local bank, in Amersham, and said to the manager, "Look, I've got something absolutely lunatic to ask you. Would you mind filling this with bundles of banknotes, to see how many we can get in?" He said, "Of course, it's just the kind of thing we like to do for our customers." ' The case, it turned out, held £60,000 – a fairly modest haul, even in those days.

To check the mechanics of the robbery, Mackendrick consulted Scotland Yard. 'I had some contacts there from when we were making *The Blue Lamp*. And since we had to get permission to shoot on the streets, I went along to see a Chief Inspector, and said, "While you're at it, I wonder if you'd read this and see what you think about how the robbery is planned and if it would work." So this chap, a marvellous ex-army type, called me in again and looked at me very carefully and said, "Yes – Mr Mackendrick, we'd just as soon you stuck to making films." I said, "It would work, would it?" He said, "It would work all too well." I took that as a great compliment.'

Though involving himself assiduously in all aspects of the film-making process, Mackendrick was well aware the actors should be left free to evolve their own performances. 'Your role as a director is to sit there and observe and be receptive, to provide the support without intruding upon the space the actor needs to work in. It's one of the hardest things, as I find when I'm trying to teach students how to direct: to know when to listen and keep your mouth shut.'[12]

In Guinness's case, this stage could be fascinating for its own sake. 'The period in which Alec is exploring a character is a magical one for the director. He has a strange habit of working from the outside in. In the early stages he's very much a putty-nosed character, working off gimmicks, funny voices and so on. But then he gets it down and discards the inessentials, and finds the core of the character – even when he's dealing with a comic grotesque, as in *The Ladykillers*.'[13]

Guinness's first idea was to play Professor Marcus as a cripple. 'He sidled across my office as though he had a dislocated hip, which was quite gruesome but horrendously funny. So Seth and I had to say, "No, sorry, but Mick

Balcon will never stand for it.'' Alec got rather annoyed, and sulked for a little, and went and looked out of the window. And while I was talking about the script he was snipping away with a pair of scissors, and he made some paper teeth which he stuck in, then turned round and grinned at me.'[14]

The snaggling teeth, along with several other mannerisms – the lank hair, the trailing scarf, the cigarette held between second and third fingers – were borrowed, Mackendrick believes, from the critic Kenneth Tynan. 'It was an absolute personal portrait of Ken, slightly – well, more than slightly – exaggerated for gothic effect.'[15] Guinness, though, disclaims any such intention. 'I think I had in mind the Wolf in Red Riding Hood. When I first saw myself in make-up I remember saying to Sandy, "I look remarkably like an aged Ken Tynan; perhaps I'd better smoke cigarettes the way he does." But that was it. Nothing really deliberate.'[16]

In effect, Guinness had internalised his initial concept. The deformed grin became the outward sign of a brilliant, dislocated mind. While virtually everybody in *The Ladykillers* is operating at a few removes from reality, Marcus seems to be sliding steadily away from it into the sub-zero zone of total schizophrenia. Ingenious and richly detailed, 'a Ronald Searle cartoon come to life'[17] (in Garth Buckner's phrase), Guinness's performance was hailed by Dilys Powell as the finest of his comic roles to date.[18] Over three decades later, it still is.

Mackendrick suspects, though, that the concept of Marcus as teetering on the edge of insanity may have started as a macabre joke by Rose at his own expense. 'Bill was at one time very near the edge himself. He went in private terror on the subject of his own sanity.' It wasn't a subject on which he tolerated jokes from anyone else. Well before shooting started he quit the picture, leaving his final draft incomplete, after a quarrel with Seth Holt. During a script discussion, as Mackendrick recalls it, 'Seth, jokingly, told Bill that he was mad. And Bill got terribly angry, exactly as in the film, and said he'd been deeply insulted. I tried to placate him, on the lines of, "Well, you're no madder than the rest of us, we're all fairly dotty here," but Bill wouldn't accept it. And Seth wouldn't apologise. So Bill said, "I'm finished. I'm not going to write any more for you. I won't see the rough cut, and I won't even come to the premiere." And stormed off in a fury.'

Rose's script broke off at the point where One-Round is dropped into a train. The final scenes – the showdown between Marcus and Louis, and Mrs Wilberforce's confession to the police – were written by Mackendrick and Holt, working from Rose's rough outline. The only other contributor to the screenplay was Larry Stephens, a comedy writer who often collaborated on Goon Show scripts, brought in to provide a few one-liners.

*The Ladykillers* was Mackendrick's first film in colour – with which, like many directors of his generation, he was never entirely happy. 'I don't think, as a director, you're ever in control of colour. Mind you, that's not so true now, with the newer, better stocks and the larger negatives like Panavision; but I think what I wanted then probably just wasn't possible with the film stock of the period. I wanted a very crisp, strong tonal range between black and white, but fairly muted hues, all in greys and browns and greens. But what happened in Technicolor, in the three-strip process, was that in order to get a strong black, you had to intensify all the colours. The first day's rushes were brilliantly hued, like a beer ad, quite impossible. We had to stop production and repaint the set, adding grey to bring all the colours down. We had it worked out in great detail, with each of the characters colour-coded: Louis is black and verdigris, the Professor is mildew – browns and dusty shades – Harry is allowed a little brighter colour, and One-Round is just a great big grey. And then you have the absurdity of Mrs W, all high-key and pastels. But I don't think it worked.'

It may be, though, that the slightly faded prints of *Ladykillers* now in circulation have grown closer to Mackendrick's original intentions. The misty, sombre tones not only suit the film's vision of a world submerged in a dank Victorian past, but enhance its pervasive sense of dreamlike fantasy. John Ellis noted that 'the rich dark reds and browns (reminiscent of Hammer horror) show that the London of terraced streets is no longer a real location for events carrying connotations of actuality.'[19] In his final Ealing film, Mackendrick consciously cut loose from the studio's cherished basis of documentary realism. 'I knew that I was trying to work on a fable. The characters are all caricatures, fable figures; none of them is real for a moment. Indeed, one of the stylistic problems is that it's very dangerous when you let a single note of reality creep into something that's as inflated, in terms of near-fantasy, as this. You have to keep within the enclosed, fabulous world.'[20]

Balcon later described *The Ladykillers* as 'a horror comic',[21] and there certainly is a strong cartoon element to the film. Each character arrives ready-labelled in the visual equivalent of capital letters: the Little Old Lady, the Mad Professor, the Dumb Bruiser and so on. The violence, too, shares a cartoon simplicity. People are banged over the head, or pushed off a roof, and die instantly – no blood or mangled limbs to disturb the joke. (Contrast Marshall's crack on the head in *The Maggie* – that hurts, and we're meant to feel it hurts.) And, as in the cartoon world, certain characters are set up to be immune from harm. Mrs Wilberforce is as invulnerable as Tweetie Pie or the Road Runner.

Not that the characters aren't individualised; Rose's idiosyncratic writing, and the skill of the players, ensure otherwise. But they remain individual *within* their stereotypes, never transcending them – unlike, say, Waggett, or Bertha in *White Suit*. The pleasure on offer to the audience, as Ellis points out,[22] lies in recognising these types and enjoying the interplay between them, rather than in the self-recognition of many other Ealing comedies.

(For example, Mrs Pemberton's line in *Passport to Pimlico* – 'It's because we're English that we're sticking up for our right to be Burgundians' – which openly invites the laugh of national identification.) The humour of *The Ladykillers* is more detached. This is England reduced to the charm, and the cruelty, of a fairy-tale.

The opening shot of the film establishes this convention of stylised unreality. The camera peers down from a vertiginous angle on the little house, shrinking it into a toy – or rather, as the pastel-shaded figure of Mrs Wilberforce emerges from the front door, into one of those old-fashioned weather-houses from which a brightly clad woman pops out to forecast sunshine. Soon the skies will darken and her foul-weather counterpart, the black-clad man, will glide into view.

The music that accompanies Mrs W's first appearance also evokes antique miniatures: a tinkling, music-box arrangement of the old drawing-room ballad, *The Last Rose of Summer*. (Subsequently the Boccherini minuet becomes her theme, but the music-box scoring remains.) Throughout the film, Tristram Cary's score provides a series of witty leitmotifs: besides the music-box for Mrs Wilberforce, we have a purposeful fugue for the robbery, shimmering string arpeggios for the money and an ominous triple figure of descending thirds to signify murder. Cary also makes rich use of parody, especially for the 'funeral' scenes: the Major gets the Last Post, plus the coda of a four-square Anglican hymn; for Harry, there's a snatch of 12-bar blues; and Marcus's short-lived triumph is celebrated with a few bars of Elgarian *nobilmente*.

If the genteel opening seems to present Mrs Wilberforce as the innocuous old dear that the gang take her for, we're soon given hints to the contrary. The shooting script included a 'Mr Magoo' sequence, in which Mrs W, passing a building site, is narrowly missed by a huge swinging bucket which, deflected from its course, demolishes a car. Wisely, Mackendrick discarded this in favour of a subtler, simpler – and much less predictable – device. On the police-station steps, Mrs W stops to smile at a baby in its pram. Nice old lady, cute baby: we expect delighted gurgles all round. But instead the infant, recognising a walking disaster area when it sees one, lets out an urgent squawl of alarm.

The name, too, should alert us: Wilberforce. Rose rarely chooses his names at random, and a side-glance at the great 19th-century anti-slavery campaigner is surely intended. Even at her daffiest – gravely reassuring the police that flying saucers didn't, after all, visit her friend Amelia – the old lady utters a revealing phrase: 'I thought it no more than my duty to come here and explain.' In this, as in the unexpected vigour with which she bashes her water-pipes, we glimpse the steely core beneath the lavender-scented exterior.

In Mrs Wilberforce, Mackendrick presents the most absolute of all his incarnations of Innocence – and therefore the most dangerous. Barring one brief moment of weakness, she never wavers. Were the gang equally absolute in their villainy, they might stand a chance against her, but the squeamishness which affects all of them, even Louis, leaves them at a fatal disadvantage. 'In the worst of men,' Rose told Mackendrick, outlining his theme, 'there is that little touch of goodness which will destroy them.'

The same mixture of emotions – exasperation, affection, irony, reluctant admiration – that pervades Rose's scripts for *Genevieve* and *The Maggie* colours the portrayal of Mrs Wilberforce; for what she patently symbolises, besides innocence, is the past in which England is mired. Everything about her represents (in Charles Barr's words) 'a Victorian civilisation lingering on, tottering, into the postwar world'.[23] Her style of dressing evidently hasn't changed in 50 years. Her house, awash with fringes, knick-knacks and flowery wallpaper, contains not a single modern appliance: no radio, telephone or refrigerator, not even piped hot water. Her friends bear names redolent of pot-pourri and rosewater – Lettice, Constance, Hypatia – and her parrots those of bewhiskered heroes of the Empire: General Gordon, Admiral Beatty. Her London is a village street, where everybody knows each other by name, and at the police station Jack Warner, resurrected and promoted from *The Blue Lamp*, presides over a troupe of kindly local bobbies straight out of musical comedy. (Or out of previous Ealing movies: the Sergeant is played by Philip Stainton, the friendly neighbourhood copper of *Passport to Pimlico*.)

'It is hard, in the light of Mackendrick's career,' Jeffrey Richards remarks, 'to see *The Ladykillers* as anything other than an irreverent farewell to England – that England of the Conservative mid-1950s that has been characterised by Arthur Marwick as suffering from "complacency, parochialism, lack of serious, structural change".'[24] And, of course, an equally irreverent farewell to the cottage film-studio on the village green, with its roses and its beehives, and its sentimental attachment to age and eccentricity. The Englishness of Ealing, the Ealingness of England – in the imagery of *The Ladykillers* the concepts overlap and merge. The house, in which nothing hangs straight, has been knocked askew by wartime bombs; its plumbing works erratically, if at all; just behind it run steam-trains, obsolescent even then, soon to be banished to tourist Titfields in Wales or deepest Sussex. Its position, at the extremity of a dead-end street, speaks for itself; Richards entitles his chapter on the film 'Cul-de-Sac England'.

Yet if Mrs Wilberforce stands for inertia and tradition, it's questionable how far the gang can be said to represent any kind of progressive force – what Barr calls 'the dynamic of change'[25] and Richards 'those elements in 1950s society that constituted the forces of dissidence around which the youth culture was to coalesce'.[26] As with most of Mackendrick's films, the dichotomy at the heart of *The Ladykillers* is nothing if not ambivalent.

Charles Barr suggests an ingenious, partly tongue-in-cheek reading of the film as political allegory. 'The gang are the postwar Labour government. Taking over "the House", they gratify the Conservative incumbent by their civilised behaviour (that nice music) and decide to use at least the façade of respectability for their radical programme of redistributing wealth. . . . Their success is undermined by two factors, interacting: their own internecine quarrels, and the startling, paralysing charisma of the "natural" governing class, which effortlessly takes over from them again in time to exploit their gains (like the Conservatives taking over power in 1951, just as the austerity years come to an end). The gang are a social mix, like Labour's: a mix of academic (Alec Guinness), ex-officer (Cecil Parker), manual worker (Danny Green), naive youth (Peter Sellers) and hard-liner (Herbert Lom).'[27]

Barr's interpretation, elegant and enjoyable though it is, doesn't quite mesh with the imagery of the film: the gang, no less than Mrs Wilberforce, seem essentially figures from the past. (One could argue, of course, that that's precisely what was wrong with the post-war Labour government.) Marcus, with his mincing, swooping gestures and protruding teeth, is a 19th-century construct, a Dickensian Nosferatu. His confederates, One-Round and Louis in particular, hail from the never-never London under-world of the Pabst/Brecht *Dreigroschenoper*. Even Harry, representative of youth culture, seems distinctly elderly for a Teddy Boy. What they look remarkably like, in fact, is what an old lady such as Mrs Wilberforce, drawing on confused memories of books and plays and movies, might well imagine a gang of criminals to be.

From this angle, the film could be read as what it started out as – a dream. Perhaps Mrs Wilberforce, like her friend Amelia, has fallen asleep within earshot of a radio and conjured up the gang from the depths of her psyche. In which case, we could take them for an expression of repressed tendencies – to violence, to asocial behaviour – within the respectable old lady herself, an emanation from the dark underworld of Victorian morality; just as Mrs Rochester, the deranged horror in the attic, embodies the virtuous Jane Eyre's forbidden impulses. As in *Man in the White Suit*, an ostensible dichotomy reveals underlying similarities. What we're seeing is a clash, not between past and present, inertia and change, but between two versions, opposed yet interdependent, of the past. Once or twice – as when he cuts from the gang upstairs gazing awestruck at their loot to Mrs W down below surveying the laden splendours of her tea-table – Mackendrick seems to hint at some such unstated correspondence.

Certainly the materialisation of Professor Marcus suggests that someone or something must have conjured him up. Wind, torrential rain, a clap of thunder – with all the gothic appurtenances of a diabolic visitation Mackendrick heralds his appearance: first a shadow, then a reflection, then a gaunt, faceless form pacing after the unwitting old lady, circling the house (which he does anti-clockwise, or widdershins, the traditional preamble to casting spells) amid clouds of infernal vapour – before looming, the peaks of his homburg jutting like horns, through the frosted glass of the front door. And in place of the conventional hissing cat or snarling dog, three parrots that greet his presence with shrieks of 'Help!' and the morse-code signal for SOS. As the camera peers nervously down the hall, and the apparition stretches out a long goblin finger to the bell-push, the white cockatoo fluffs itself up in vivid reaction, as though – another cartoon touch – wired directly to the door-bell.

(This scene, incidentally, looks remarkably like a parody of Sidney Gilliat's *London Belongs to Me* (1948), in which Alastair Sim plays a seedy fake medium, Mr Squales. He enters as a sinister, homburg-hatted shadow cast on the front door of a London boarding-house, his hand reaching for the bell. As the landlady opens to him, he gives a deprecating grimace: 'You have a *room* to let?' The similarity to *Ladykillers* is startling, even down to the intonation of the words, though Mackendrick has no recollection of Gilliat's film. 'If I stole that intentionally, I think I'd have remembered. But one steals all the time – often without knowing it.' In any case the theft, conscious or not, is transmuted so exuberantly that no excuse is needed.)

As with Sidney Stratton versus Kierlaw, the confrontation seems at first sight a foregone conclusion. What chance has Mrs Wilberforce against this figure of demonic cunning? More innocent even than Stratton, more trapped in her own assumptions than Waggett or Marshall, she seems incapable of reading other people's intentions, and much of the film's comedy derives from her ingenuous reaction to these blatant villains. The ghoulish leer with which Marcus introduces himself would freeze the blood of a grave-robber; she accepts it as the gracious smile for which it's evidently intended. Nothing in the demeanour of his accomplices arouses her suspicion – not even Louis, glowering with mistrust, fiddle-case clutched at the approved Chicago angle.

But Mrs Wilberforce, unlike Calvin Marshall or Captain Waggett, is on her own territory. Indeed, she virtually *is* her own territory, so strong is the visual and conceptual identification between her and the house – both small, rickety, old-fashioned, and a whole lot tougher than they look. The gang may effect a little peripheral damage – knocking off a chimney-pot, inducing a brief lapse from civic virtue – but in the end it's they who crumble and fade back into the night. On his first arrival Marcus tries to straighten a picture but, as she explains, 'it's quite impossible to make it hang evenly'. It's an omen in reverse. The values of her world inexorably reimpose themselves, and Mrs W, despite all efforts to make her hang crooked, will always hang straight.

The film brings to its logical conclusion a process of stagnation and diminution that runs through all Mackendrick's Ealing work. The communities whose values are threatened, and in the end reasserted, dwindle in scale from the population of an island to a single little old lady. And while up to now the innocent figure has also been the interloper in the community, the source of disruption and change, in *The Ladykillers* innocence and the community are on the same side, pulling together. The result is an impenetrably closed system, insulated against change. Alone among all Mackendrick's innocents, Mrs Wilberforce learns nothing; her mental universe remains unassailed, her assumptions intact. We leave her, at the end of the film, no different from when we first met her. Except, of course, that she's better off by £60,000 and can buy herself – what more staidly English aspiration could be imagined? – a dozen new umbrellas.

For some critics *The Ladykillers* suffers from a failure of tone, lurching into a violence inconsistent with the lighthearted comedy – as they see it – of the earlier scenes. The irony of the film misfires, Carol Rittgers maintains, 'because errors in taste and emphasis have misdirected the audience's sympathy into a sense of desolation at the sudden barrenness of the comic scene without its pleasant rogues'.[28] Similarly, Anthony Slide feels that the film 'moves from farce to melodrama, becoming tedious and then disturbing as the gang members . . . are murdered, one after the other. Having witnessed these endearingly seedy characters chasing around trying to capture Mrs Wilberforce's errant parrot, how can one possibly wish to see them killed?'[29]

Such criticisms scarcely take account of the film's complex interplay of irony. But they also imply – on the more immediate level of dramatic structure – that Mackendrick and Rose have neglected to lay the groundwork and prepare us for the deaths of the gang. Which, demonstrably enough, isn't the case. *The Ladykillers* moves with its own inexorable, dream-like logic. Less than 15 minutes into the action, all the springs have been wound and the mechanisms set in motion. Once the gang are installed in Mrs W's house, their elimination becomes inevitable.

*The Ladykillers*, like *Man in the White Suit*, falls into two parts pivoted around a central turning-point. During the first half, despite the occasional setback, the action moves forward to achievement; in the second half, the achievement is undermined and cancelled out. Once again Mackendrick borrows an existing generic model: the classic pattern of the heist movie, as laid down by Huston's *Asphalt Jungle*. First the gang is assembled, a collection of disparate characters each with a distinct aptitude; the job – nearly always a robbery – is successfully pulled, its mechanics displayed in some detail; through internal dissension, or one fatal error, the scheme falls apart, with the gang all arrested or killed.

It's a plot that lends itself well to comic treatment, since there's something inherently funny in watching an elaborately devised structure disintegrate at the tug of a single loose thread. And in *The Lavender Hill Mob* (scripted by Tibby Clarke and directed by Charles Crichton) Ealing had already produced a heist comedy which observed the conventions of the genre while sending them up. But Crichton's film, though inventive and lively, works only by defusing any sense of danger. *The Ladykillers* restores that element. Both films are fantasies, their criminals stylised and unreal, but Mackendrick's gangsters exert the menace of true nightmare figures.

So for the latter part of *Ladykillers* to work convincingly, the first half must establish that the gang, for all their comic attributes, are potential killers – and also set them up for eventual defeat. Much of the sense of pent-up violence emanates from Louis, the disruptive outside presence in the gang, smoulderingly resentful at playing – in both senses – second fiddle. This may reflect a genuine rivalry between Guinness and Lom who, according to Tom Pevsner, the film's assistant director, 'were always desperately trying to upstage each other'. If so, Mackendrick made shrewd dramatic use of it (and may not have been above encouraging it a little). He also turned another circumstance to neat account: since Lom was currently starring in the London production of *The King and I* (having taken over from Yul Brynner), his head was shaved. Instead of fitting him with a wig, Mackendrick has Louis wear his hat indoors – a trait thoroughly in character, and a sign of his antipathy to Mrs Wilberforce's values.

The Marcus-Louis rivalry not only brings out the dangerous side of both men, but also serves to expose the fissures within the gang. No sooner are they assembled than Louis forces a vote on Marcus's plan – should it or shouldn't it include Mrs W? Mackendrick choreographs the action, placing each gang member both literally (in terms of framing and composition) and psychologically. And as the tension builds, the lighting drops in intensity and angle, creating a sense of hovering expectancy, as though a cloud of darkness were seeping from Marcus's own distorted brain. These gothic shadows are dispelled by Mrs W's entrance ('Shall I be mother?'), but only temporarily. The tension remains unresolved, and the shadows will gather again as the humour of the film darkens towards death.

The whole scene offers a fine example of the skilful workmanship that makes Mackendrick's films, at their best, so satisfying to watch – what he once sardonically referred to as 'the sordid carpentry of imparting informa-tion and laying fuses'.[30] In some five minutes of screen time (including a couple of cutaways to Mrs W downstairs) we're painlessly given all the key points and thematic elements: the robbery, and Mrs W's part in it (though just what's being stolen, and what she has to do, is withheld to whet our curiosity); the characters of the gang members and their relationships with each other; the Boccherini minuet; One-Round's lumpen sentimentality ('Sweet little old lady like her, just don't seem right'); Marcus's megalo-mania ('Only the plan is essential . . . *my* plan'); the ritual of voting, later reprised in the drawing of murderous lots; and a hint of the insanity that triggers the final showdown. Plus, midway through the scene, a crucial interruption.

At the heart of all Mackendrick's films lies the tension created by the tug of opposed perceptions. The more strongly both sides are built up, the more mileage can be gained from that tension. So Mrs Wilberforce must appear a figure of no less stature – both dramatic and mythic – than the gang. Intruding into their quarrel to offer tea (most Ealing of fluids), she lingers to reminisce. Their music reminds her of 'something that really I'd quite forgotten all about. My 21st birthday party. You see, my father had engaged a string quintet. . . . And while they were playing Boccherini, someone came in and said the old Queen had passed away. Then everyone went home. That was the end of my party. All those years ago, in Pangbourne.' It's a touching moment, anchoring her lost girlhood in the prelapsarian Edwardian myth of long golden summer evenings by the river (Queen Victoria died in January, but no matter), while undercutting any risk of sentimentality through the humour of the gang's response. ('Old Queen who?' enquires One-Round, bemused.)

And in linking Mrs Wilberforce with Queen Victoria, one coming of age as the other dies, there's an implied identification. Something of that authority, ludicrous yet formidable, has been directly transmitted. Marcus, by one of those double ironies in which Mackendrick always took delight, falls into the same trap he sets for others. The success of his plan depends on the preconceptions of the police: watching for dangerous criminals smuggling the loot aboard a train, they disregard a sweet old lady taking a trunk home in a taxi. But Marcus too fails to see beyond appearances, assuming Mrs Wilberforce to be as harmless as she looks.

Two scenes in particular reveal the intransigence, and the talent for intricate catastrophe, that lurk behind her vague, benevolent smile: the parrot chase and the assault on the barrow-boy. They're also, unfortunately, the two least satisfactory scenes in the film. Both betray Rose's weakness for set-pieces – comic fugues which, though enjoyable enough in themselves, aren't fluently integrated into the narrative and tend to leave actors mugging uneasily, sensing that the tone has shifted beneath their feet.

Of the two, the parrot scene works better, using incidental detail to explore character and foreshadow future developments: Harry's affected bravado – 'You leave it to me, Ma. I'm very good with birds' – dissolving into querulous distress, and the Major and Louis in a dry run for their later rooftop excursion. Even so, it doesn't do much to advance the plot. Nor does the barrow-boy sequence, which merely demonstrates Mrs W's knack for wholesale disaster ('All of them out of business in ten minutes,' murmurs Harry in awe) and Mackendrick's skill at staging complex action sequences. Frankie Howerd, a television-based comedian in the tradition of broad, emphatic playing, evidently had trouble adjusting to a subtler, ensemble-based style, and the whole scene briefly wrenches the film into a cruder mode of comedy.

The robbery itself, in true heist-movie tradition, is carried out with intricate precision and scarcely a word spoken. As One-Round breaks into the payroll van, Louis hands him the requisite tools right on cue, like a well-trained nurse assisting the surgeon. At strategic moments Mackendrick pulls back to a high angle, showing the vehicles manoeuvring in the narrow streets as though on a chess-board. Not so much god's-eye view, perhaps, as Marcus's mental angle on the action, exulting (and in this, standing in for the director himself) in the sheer intellectual joy of holding the whole scheme in his mind's eye.

As in *White Suit*, *Ladykillers* has a clear turning-point where everything starts to fall apart. This time, though, no outside forces have to be summoned. All the necessary elements are in place and just need to be activated. The plan has succeeded, the loot been divided, and the gang are about to leave. One-Round, lingering to say goodbye to 'Mrs Lopsided', finds himself anchored to the spot, with the strap of his cello-case caught in the door. From here on, the nightmare takes over. The house begins to exert its inexorable pull, and the whole gang – like the bourgeois dinner guests of Buñuel's *Exterminating Angel* – are sucked back in again, unable to leave. As they stand helplessly in the hall, concocting desperate stories and even more desperate kidnapping plots, the house mocks their impotence with a fine display of cloning power; pastel-clad, flower-hatted little old ladies, twittering excitedly, flood in to engulf them. The last to arrive, bearing a newspaper, is that archetypal Ealing old lady, Edie Martin, and once again it falls to her to administer the *coup de grâce*. As the hubbub briefly subsides, her voice comes through with quavering clarity: '. . . there's been a terrible robbery at Kings Cross.'

With these words, an awful transformation takes place. As realisation dawns, Mrs Wilberforce ceases to be the solicitous, tea-dispensing mother, still less the 'lopsided old grandma' of Louis's dismissive epithet. She has metamorphosed into the Nanny, that ultimate repository of domestic authority and moral certitude, and as such she establishes an immediate, paralysing ascendancy. Before her outraged glare the gang shrink in stature, Marcus peering shamefaced over the incriminating headline like a small boy caught with a catapult.

Again, there's a clear parallel with *White Suit*, as the ancient mechanism of control is wheeled into play to repress the insubordinate family members. Mrs Wilberforce, wielding like Kierlaw an authority out of all proportion to her puny physique, can call on a whole battery of auxiliary aunts to support her. In this genteel parlour where, as Charles Barr observes, 'all the imagery of age and tradition in Ealing's past films is gathered up and compressed,'[31] the threatening, anti-social impulse is marked off, one old lady per criminal, to be tamed with teacups and lace doilies. (Here too the gang seem scarcely less anachronistic than the ladies; they look like reformed East End villains press-ganged into a Salvation Army prayer-meeting.) Even their 'cover' is reduced to a patent sham: Marcus, supposed leader of a talented string quintet, accompanies the singing hunched dejectedly over a pianola. The song, another sentimental drawing-room favourite, packs an ironic sting in its final line:

> Darling, I am growing old,
> Silver threads among the gold,
> Shine upon my brow today:
> *Life is fading fast away.*

So it is – though not for the frail old ladies who are singing it.

But once the guests are gone, the gang still have spirit enough to mount a counter-attack. Ingratiatingly organising a task-force for the washing-up – such *good* boys, really – Marcus first tries economic sleight-of-hand ('So how much harm have we done anybody? One farthing's worth, Mrs Wilberforce'), then a sob-story, courtesy of the Major. In vain; Mrs Wilberforce can be confused with details, but remains unshakeable on fundamentals. Persuasion having failed, Marcus shifts his tactics and, seconded by his confederates, applies threats.

In this scene, as during the robbery, we see the gang at their best. Like the islanders in *Whisky Galore* they communicate intuitively, picking up each other's cues, playing their respective roles, hard or soft, skilfully off against each other.

MARCUS: Mrs Wilberforce, I wanted to spare you this, but I'm afraid the police are after you, too.
HARRY: That's right. You're as 'ot as the rest of us, Ma.
MRS W: As hot?
MAJOR: If they pick her up, there's no saying what they may do to her.
MRS W: Pick me up? Would you mind explaining—?
HARRY: The job was planned in her house – she carried the lolly for us.
MAJOR: True.
MRS W: Yes, I know I carried the – the lolly, but—
MARCUS: She was ignorant of the plan, of course—
MAJOR: Ignorance in the sight of the law is no excuse. Even if we swear that she didn't know what she was doing—
HARRY: They'd never believe us.

ONE-ROUND: Yeah.

HARRY: Who'd believe anything *we* said?

MRS W: Oh, but this is ridiculous. I know the Superintendent. I shall deny all knowledge—

MARCUS: She'd never stand up to it, of course.

HARRY: The grilling. The rubber hoses.

MARCUS: The rest of her life sewing mail-bags.

MRS W: Mail-bags?

HARRY: *And no one to look after the parrots.*

MRS W: Oh—

MARCUS: We won't let them get you, Mrs Wilberforce.

LOUIS: Why not? What's she ever done for us? If they get us I'll tell them she planned the whole job. I'll tell them she planned the big one – *the Eastcastle Street job*.

The scene builds like an operatic *scena*, ideas developed and decorated, tossed from one voice to another, Harry's shrewd clincher capped by Louis's frontal attack. For the moment Mrs Wilberforce has lost the initiative; excluded from their complicity and glancing bewildered from one to the next, she stands isolated on the edge of the group like an unpopular child. Even her power to invoke the forces of social constraint seems to have deserted her, to be usurped by Louis. His accusing finger, before which she quails, points not only at her but (in a swift reverse-angle cut) straight through the front door at the approaching figure of the police sergeant, summoned up from the darkness as if by the specious power of the gang's argument.

Acting concertedly like this, the gang exert mesmeric control. Mrs Wilberforce, moving as if in a trance, becomes their mouthpiece, dazedly repeating their jargon ('buttoned up . . . search warrant') and dismissing the sergeant with what, from her, verges on strong language: 'Then will you please – Buzz Off!' Their control is less than perfect, though; she fluffs her lines and Marcus, wincing and wrapping himself agitatedly in a curtain, seems less Dr Mabuse than Wizard of Oz. And in any case, the spell wears off. Back in her sitting-room, drawing strength from her household gods, Mrs Wilberforce finds her own voice again. 'No. No, I was quite wrong. . . . I know what we must do. I know I carried the lolly. But even if they do make me sew mail-bags, I would rather – rather go to the police station and give myself up.'

As she speaks, Mackendrick tracks gently in to a close-up, as he did during her Pangbourne memories. The movement – which in conventional film grammar would herald a misty flashback – links the two speeches, both at once absurd and moving; *there* we saw the source of her strength, and *this* is the product of it. And with the words 'give myself up', she glances up at the portrait of the late Captain Wilberforce, drawing moral support from his spirit. Standing stiffly at the salute, the Captain closely resembles Admiral D'Ascoyne in *Kind Hearts and Coronets*, and like the Admiral he 'remained at the salute, on the bridge' as his ship went down in the China Sea. (But only, ineffably British to the last, after ensuring the safety of the parrots.)

The Admiral, of course, was played by Alec Guinness, so the Captain perhaps represents Marcus's good daemon, that 'little touch of goodness' in the Professor which will destroy him. Yet *Kind Hearts* invites us to mock the Admiral's self-sacrifice as bone-headed patrician obstinacy. Hamer's mockery, Mackendrick seems to suggest, was in vain; the world of the D'Ascoynes is alive and well in the England of 1955, where the most fatuous behaviour may furnish a moral precedent.

Throughout *The Ladykillers*, as the tone darkens and the shadows gather in the corners, our responses are unsettled by this shifting interplay of irony, leaving us uncertain where our sympathies are supposed to lie. In the whole Ealing canon it would be hard to find a woman portrayed with more affection than Mrs Wilberforce. Her courage is admirable, and we're clearly meant to find it so. Yet, as Raymond Durgnat notes, 'the to and fro of her invincibly ignorant benevolence, and [Marcus's] seething, impotent malice which we can't but share' invest the film with 'a quality of moral paradox'.[32] Taken to this degree, innocence becomes a provocation: from the old lady's face, gazing trustingly upwards at her husband's picture, the camera slides sideways to the gang, glowering and frustrated, and on the soundtrack 'Rule Britannia' modulates into the murder motif.

Were the gang able to hold together, they might easily devise an effective murder plan. But now the fuses laid earlier in the film start to detonate: the internal tensions, the rivalry and mistrust, split them fatally apart. Marcus maliciously singles out Louis: 'It ought to be someone experienced in. . . . You've told us so often that you hate little old ladies.' Louis defensively retaliates – 'You are the one who masterminded this mess' – before instituting the fatal ceremony.

The lot-drawing scene – which reprises, in a darker mode, the sense of casting votes – is played out in total silence; no dialogue, no music, just an almost Bressonian concentration on hands and faces, shown in the extreme close-ups and subjective angles that Mackendrick always reserves for moments of key significance. The viewpoint that dominates is that of Louis, who now takes charge of events; this is what he knows, the tactics of coercion and violence. Marcus regains control only at the very end, by adopting Louis's values and becoming a killer himself.

At the point of no return, when Louis takes over, the camera noses in to extreme close-up as he spreads five matches on the back of an ashtray and cuts one across. The symbolism is unambiguous: the unity of the gang is being severed. Since killing each other is a far easier option than killing the old lady, their violence from here on is turned inwards, and the logical momentum becomes unstoppable. We know what's coming, and the fascination lies in watching it happen, as death follows death at progressively briefer intervals.

For as the match is sliced, and the process of elimination begins, we enter a darker, mythic world, which will only be dispelled with Mrs Wilberforce's reawakening in the morning light: a surreal nightworld of masonic ceremonial, sacrificial victims, processions and rituals. (In this respect *The Ladykillers* seems a forerunner of Hammer's gothic horror cycle, initiated a year later with *The Curse of Frankenstein*.) In the recurrent, Tarot-like image of two men holding a head-down corpse by the feet as they await the train that's to carry it off, we might be watching the rite of some outlandish cult, progeny of a bizarre conjunction between a train-spotters' club and the priests of Juggernaut.

In these scenes Mackendrick exploits his railside location to the full. Recurrent gusts of smoke punctuate the killings, enhancing the atmosphere of spooky grotesquerie. Each descending corpse is engulfed in a pyre of yellowish vapour that clears to reveal a string of trucks clanking fatalistically northwards, as if intended for no other freight but this. So potently unreal are these sulphurous clouds that it seems quite credible for Marcus, in his showdown with Louis, to fade in and out of them by osmosis, materialising at one point as a clump of shrubbery, Birnam Wood in miniature.

As the deaths mount up, Mrs Wilberforce gradually withdraws from the action – into her sitting room, and into sleep. Having set the process in motion, she can sit back and let it play itself out. Whether or not we think them her dreams – as One-Round is killed, there's a brief cut to her peacefully sleeping face – the gang are by now her creatures, acting under the compulsion she unwittingly exerts. She's become, as Kenneth von Gunden puts it, 'a mad joke being played upon them by hostile forces'[33] and murdering her, as Marcus realises even as he sinks into giggling dementia, would have solved nothing. Her spirit, and the social forces she embodies, are terrifyingly indestructible. 'There were only five of us. . . . But it would take 20 or 30 or 40 perhaps to deal with her, because we'll never be able to kill *her*, Louis. She'll always be with us, for ever and ever and ever, and there's nothing we can do about it.'

The reassertion of the status quo rounds off countless Ealing movies, and almost always – as in *The Blue Lamp* – it's presented as something reassuring. Even in *The Lavender Hill Mob*, where the reimposition of social norms means imprisonment and the end of the escapist dream, the hero shows no resentment: he's had his 'one superb year' and calmly submits to his fate. Marcus's words, by contrast, are a vision of desperation from which there's no escape – the same circular nightmare that encloses the labyrinth of *Dead of Night*.

And it's this sense of helpless inevitability overtaking each victim – as One-Round expires, Marcus makes a quick counting gesture with his fingers: three down, two to go – that spikes the sinister comedy of the film's climax. Each member of the gang, Marcus alone excepted, dies in a state of futile protest: the Major attempting a final pathetic spiel ('Be sensible, old man – you don't think I'd walk out on you. . . . Ha, ha, you know me better than that'); Harry appealing to One-Round's obviously non-existent 'sense of humour'; One-Round tugging frantically at a trigger that refuses to function; Louis loosing off a last vindictive shot as he topples backwards into the smoke. Only Marcus meets death unawares, granted the dignity of exiting on a highpoint of achievement.

This image of the exultant master-criminal felled, at the very moment of his triumph, by that emblem of social regulation, a railway signal, marks the final defeat of the disruptive impulse. The night is over; we're back in the familiar streets of Ealing England, under the protection of the kindly police sergeant (whose name, rather oddly, has changed from MacDonald to Harris overnight; but never mind). Nanny has won. The bad boys – whether from the unruly past or the disturbing future – have been whisked away and the good boy, who has drawn a picture of nice Mr Churchill, can be rewarded from Mrs Wilberforce's new-found wealth.

And as she trots contentedly home (her music-box tune no longer the deceptive Boccherini, but once again *The Last Rose of Summer*), we notice that the house has regained the chimney-stack that came down with the Major. A minor lapse in continuity, perhaps; or proof that it was, after all, just a dream? Or possibly Mackendrick's last sly intimation that, in this vision of what Neil Sinyard called 'elderly, paralysed, hallucinatory, hidebound England',[34] nothing in the end can really change.

Shooting on *The Ladykillers*, which took place in the summer of 1955, was slowed down both by the cumbersome three-strip Technicolor camera and by Mackendrick's tireless quest for perfection, which had become something of a standing joke. Towards the end of the shoot, Peter Sellers showed up with a tape he had assembled: a spoof trailer for the film, in which Sellers impersonated not only his fellow actors, but several members of the film crew, Mackendrick included. The tape features Danny Green trying out multiple alternative readings ('I'm staying with *Ma. I'm* staying with Ma. I'm *staying* with Ma'), fine renditions of Guinness, Parker and Lom, and – Sellers's one failure – Katie Johnson sounding more like Bluebottle from *The Goon Show*. And we're given 'a brief glimpse of the brilliant technique of Alexander Mackendrick, director'. Studio hubbub is stilled, a clapper-boy mutters, 'Scene 5, Take 73,' and Sellers emits some high-speed gibberish, to which 'Mackendrick' responds: 'Er, Peter – Peter – that's, er, that's very good. We'll do another.'

Mackendrick was known for shooting more slowly than any other Ealing director. When, at the end of each working day, the rushes of all current productions were screened, his were almost invariably the shortest. Michael Birkett recalls that after one of these sessions, 'Sandy said rather hopefully to Hal Mason, "Did you like the rushes?" And Hal said, "You know, Sandy, I'm awfully sorry, I dropped my cigarettes just then and missed them." I'm not sure Sandy ever quite forgave him for that.' But in the supportive atmosphere of Ealing, such vagaries were accepted as part of Mackendrick's creative personality. Not all his producers would prove so tolerant.

*Ladykillers* had gone over both schedule and budget, though not disastrously so. Its length was a more serious problem; the initial cut ran just short of two hours, far too long for a mere comedy. (Such lengths were reserved at Ealing for serious, prestige productions like *The Cruel Sea* or *Scott of the Antarctic*.) Several entire scenes were dropped and others truncated. Among the casualties, much to Sellers's chagrin, was a long speech from Harry, capping the Major's sob-story with one of his own about a sister who 'married a trapeze artist. Forced her into his act, he did, a hundred feet up and no net . . . and her scared of heights. . . .'

Other lost delights included Mrs W getting into the wrong taxi at Kings Cross and finding herself at cross-purposes with the driver ('Am I not right in thinking that you had a moustache?' she enquires); and a discussion between her and Professor Marcus about the previous tenant, a Mr Proudlock, who liked the rooms because he collected train numbers. (About to leave, Marcus pauses with an air of genuine bemusement: 'May I ask . . . what did Mr, er, Proudlock *do* with the engine numbers he collected?') The scene reads superbly – one can hear the actors' inflections in every phrase – and, Mackendrick recalls, 'was beautifully played'; but it was judged extraneous to the plot and had to go. Altogether some 20 minutes were cut; even so, *The Ladykillers* is the longest of all Ealing comedies except *Kind Hearts and Coronets*.

Reviews of *Ladykillers* in the British press fell broadly into two camps. On the acting, there was virtually total agreement. While Guinness, magnificently supported by the rest of the gang, had given the comic performance of his career, Katie Johnson had walked off with the picture. But for several reviewers, such as Paul Dehn in the *News Chronicle*, things went badly wrong after the revelation of the robbery: 'Then, suddenly, the mood falters . . . and before we know where we are the comedy has collapsed like a house of cards.' The direction, in Dehn's view, lacked 'gusto': Mackendrick 'seems to shrink from his unladylike task in a way which makes the audience shrink too'.[35] Virginia Graham, in the *Spectator*, felt that midway 'suddenly everything goes to pieces. The script becomes barren . . . a feasible development to the story is abandoned in favour of knockabout. The climax . . . merely seems, in its present context, in thoroughly bad taste.'[36]

Most critics, though, were enthusiastic. In the *Evening Standard* Alan

Brien called it 'undoubtedly the most stylish, inventive and funniest British comedy of the year'[37] and the *Manchester Guardian*'s critic thought it 'a thoroughly typical Ealing work – except that it is even better than most'.[38] Mackendrick, Fred Majdalany observed in *Time and Tide*, 'has juggled with violence, near-farce, Dickensian character and sentiment without for an instant seeming in danger of letting a club fall. . . . The climax . . . is one of the neatest blends of the mirthful and the macabre I can remember.'[39] Dilys Powell, in the *Sunday Times*, though finding the film 'captivating', wished for 'a shade more of the macabre; it would be a better film if it were blacker'.[40]

Not so Penelope Houston who, writing in *Sight and Sound*, relished the film's 'inconsequential tone', and 'the exuberant absurdity of its comic invention'. 'Unimpaired by any timid concessions to plausibility, *The Ladykillers* emerges as the most consistently ruthless comic fantasy produced by a British studio since *Kind Hearts and Coronets*. . . . A comic idea of splendid, savage absurdity is elaborated in an atmosphere of steadily mounting fantasy. . . . There is apparent, both in the script and in Alexander Mackendrick's spirited and inventive handling, a fine sense of the comic possibilities of the outrageous. The brakes are never applied, the fantasy runs on unchecked to a conclusion which has its own lunatic logicality.'[41]

No contemporary reviewer, though, seemed to sense any allegorical level, or to see the film as the ironic portrait of England that it now inescapably appears. Only the *Times Educational Supplement* came close, detecting a subversive element beneath 'its tight-rooted wolfsbane charm. . . . The subversiveness on which comedy thrives has here penetrated right to the springs of laughter so that, instead of smugly umpiring, the audience finds that it is no longer sure of the rules. The world is shaken up and, when it settles, one cannot be certain that the contours are exactly the same.'[42]

At the 1955 British Film Academy awards, *The Ladykillers* took Best Screenplay for William Rose, and Katie Johnson (triumphantly vindicating Mackendrick's persistence) was chosen as Best Actress. The film did well at the box-office, in Britain and also in the USA, though with the transatlantic vogue for Ealing comedy on the wane, the American critics tended to be dismissive. 'The material is simply too thin to allow for many bellylaughs,'[43] commented Hollis Alpert in the *Saturday Review*, declaring a clear preference for Danny Kaye in *The Court Jester*. Rose's screenplay was nominated for an Academy Award, but lost out to Albert Lamorisse's script for *The Red Balloon*.

Despite the BFA award, Rose kept his word and boycotted the film. Not until three years later did Mackendrick hear from him again. Rose had dropped into a showing of *Ladykillers* at his neighbourhood cinema 'just out of curiosity, really, to see if I could figure out . . . how you had managed to foul it all up so incredibly. Well, that was one of the worst afternoons I've ever had, because a, I loved it; b, I was able to see that you hadn't lost anything that was of real value whatever to me; and c, I was forced to the awful (and I mean awful) realisation that you had almost certainly improved on the stuff that I turned over to you. . . . You can imagine how embarrassing this situation was, particularly for an arrogant slob like myself.'[44]

*The Ladykillers* was Ealing's last commercial success. After it, there were only ten more films to come, none of them – barring Seth Holt's directorial debut, *Nowhere to Go* – of much interest, and all largely forgotten today. The reputation of *Ladykillers*, though, seems secure; it has become a cult classic, frequently revived and, with *Whisky Galore*, probably the most widely seen and affectionately recalled of all Mackendrick's films. It's even achieved the distinction – surely unique among British movies – of being turned into an opera: *Dáma a lupiči* (*The Lady and the Robbers*) by the Czech composer Ilja Hurník, premiered in 1967.

The five films which Mackendrick directed at Ealing represent the most distinctive and stimulating body of work of any of the studio's directors. The progress of his achievement isn't straightforwardly linear; in many ways *Man in the White Suit*, his second film, is the most accomplished and complex of the five. And from *White Suit* onwards, all his films are distinguished by a consistent flair for composition and mastery of narrative technique. Even *Whisky Galore*, for all its technical roughness, shows that from the first Mackendrick knew how to draw from his actors performances of subtlety and conviction.

These films might perhaps be best considered as a set of variations on a theme. Having established his preoccupations – the process of (mis)perception, innocence as a destructive force, the outsider versus the community – Mackendrick develops and reinterprets them in a number of modes: folk comedy (*Whisky Galore*, *The Maggie*), satire (*White Suit*), domestic melodrama (*Mandy*), black comedy (*The Ladykillers*), while at the same time experimenting with various generic formulas and parodic games. Elements are swapped around, their relationships rearranged (what happens if the innocent *isn't* an outsider?), the touch of mythic fantasy played down (*Mandy*) or heightened (*Ladykillers*). While, running through them all like a concealed motif, suggested but never explicitly spelt out, is the hint of dissent – the ironic, critical tone of the director operating 'in enemy terrain'.

Unlike Hamer, Mackendrick never confronts the Ealing ethos head-on. The films he made there trace a process of exploration, both of that ethos and of his own creative resources in exploiting and subverting it. The frustration which so often fuels the action can be seen as an expression of Mackendrick's impatience with the society, and the film-making conditions, in which he was operating. This technique of using the narrative tensions within the film to play out, and obliquely comment on, the restrictions imposed on the production process, always risks backfiring – and did so in *The Maggie*, where an undertow of sourness distorts the humour.

But at its best – as in those scenes in *White Suit*, *Mandy* and *The Ladykillers* where a whole apparatus of social convention, the repressive family in action, moves in to stifle the disruptive impulse – Mackendrick's Ealing work presents, in lucidly cinematic language, dramatic conflicts that work both on the clear narrative level and also, without becoming nudgingly symbolic, in ideological terms. In this sense at least, Mackendrick's cinema could be described as Brechtian: 'Not to *prove* but to demonstrate; not to explain but to state the thing that needs to be explained; not to tie up the ends, but to expose the contradictions.'[45] By not taking sides, by disdaining the bland, conciliatory endings that Ealing favoured, he constantly questions the studio's assumptions even while ostensibly operating within them.

Perhaps in the hope of perpetuating the subversive element, Mackendrick left Ealing a parting legacy in the shape of Kenneth Tynan. A replacement was needed for Angus MacPhail, the Script Editor, who had suffered a nervous breakdown – mainly, Mackendrick believes, 'because he was given that most intolerable of positions: total responsibility and no authority'. Tynan had recently written an appreciation of Ealing for *Films and Filming*; Balcon, much taken with the piece and knowing Mackendrick to be a friend of Tynan's, asked him whether he thought the critic would consider becoming Script Editor. No doubt thinking that Tynan's cultural and sexual iconoclasm was just what the studio needed, Mackendrick actively encouraged the idea on both sides, and Tynan took up his job in the spring of 1956. 'It was,' Mackendrick notes, 'a fair disaster.'

Tynan, as Mackendrick later observed, had no way of knowing 'the very subtle way Balcon would frustrate him'.[46] Of all the recommendations he made in his two years at Ealing, only one got made: Holt's *Nowhere to Go*, which Tynan co-scripted. Everything else was turned down, often at an advanced stage of development: Cecil Woodham-Smith's *The Reason Why* (later made as *The Charge of the Light Brigade*); Joyce Cary's *The Horse's Mouth*; an original script by Lindsay Anderson; and the project that Tynan was keen for Mackendrick to direct, William Golding's *Lord of the Flies*. It was a shrewd choice; Mackendrick would have been the ideal director to bring out the savage comedy of Golding's novel, a quality missed by the over-literal version filmed by Peter Brook. 'Ken sent me a copy of the book and said, "Why don't we make this at Ealing?" I had to write back and say, "Listen, I'd *love* to make that film; it will never be made at Ealing." And he found that out in the end.'

Even in its heyday, Ealing might have been hard pressed to accommodate

Tynan's fierce enthusiasms. But now, grown staid and timid, it was no place for him – nor, indeed, for Mackendrick. The final shot of *The Ladykillers* gazes down at the ramshackle little doll's-house, from the same remote high-angle as before, with an unmistakably valedictory air. It was time for Mackendrick to move on, and it's likely that, even had the studio not been in creative decline, he would have left anyway. His reputation was by now considerable; the skill, experience and distinctive cinematic vision that he had developed at Ealing were ripe for exercise on more ambitious subjects, in an environment whose energy could match his own.

# 7 Sweet Smell of Success

> 'Films that float outside the mainstream of a
> period can sometimes reveal the misgivings
> of that era.'[1]
>
> Nora Sayre, *Running Time*

> 'Sometimes hysteria in production problems
> can be communicated successfully as energy
> up on the screen.'
>
> Alexander Mackendrick

On 19 October 1955, a few weeks before the premiere of *The Ladykillers*, it was announced that Ealing Studios were to be sold to the BBC. Six months later, Balcon led his depleted team over to MGM at Borehamwood to live out Ealing's brief, dispiriting coda. By then, though, Mackendrick was no longer among them. He was in Hollywood working for Hecht-Hill-Lancaster, in an environment about as different from Ealing as any within the film-making world.

Following the transatlantic success of *Whisky Galore* and *The Man in the White Suit*, several bids for Mackendrick's services had come from Hollywood, most of them deftly fielded by Balcon. In any case, Mackendrick at that time had no particular desire to leave the supportive atmosphere and secure employment of Ealing for the precarious world of the American studios. But by the end of 1954 Ealing no longer seemed quite so secure. Though few people realised closure was imminent, the studio's financial problems were common knowledge and several directors, Mackendrick included, had not had their yearly contracts renewed. 'Mick told us that he wanted a gentleman's agreement. He was doing what he could to extend our contracts for a year, but he couldn't commit himself at that stage. He said, "So as far as I'm concerned I hope it'll all work out, but your contract is not renewed until I negotiate and find out what's happening." So I was not under contract.'

About this time Ronald Neame, who had been offered a script by the Hakim brothers, decided against it and sent it on to Mackendrick 'It involved Joan Collins playing a nun – and it was *terrible*. I went back to Ronnie and said, "No, thank you," and he said, "I thought that was what you'd say." ' (The film in question, *Sea Wife*, was later briefly taken on by Rossellini. It eventually appeared in 1957, credited to Bob McNaught, and amply justified

Mackendrick's misgivings.) 'Then a bit later Balcon rang me up and said, "Hey, listen, I've had an offer for your services. Now what I'd like you to do, if you don't mind, is let me do the negotiating, because I can get a much better deal for you." But what he was saying, and I knew it, was that he would pay me and take a cut off my salary from the Hakim brothers. And I was *livid*. Because I wasn't even under contract; that was why he'd had to ring me up. Otherwise he'd have done it behind my back.'

Mackendrick, who until then had never used an agent, contacted Christopher Mann, one of the leading agents in London. A few days later he received a call from Mann's secretary: Paramount had a project they wanted to discuss, could he fly out to Hollywood at once? Mackendrick, somewhat bewildered, caught a plane to Los Angeles and was met by a young man from Paramount head office, the future director Alan Pakula. Pakula took him to see Don Hartmann, the head of the studio. 'Don received me with open arms and said, "What d'you think of the project?" I said, "What project?" He said, "Oh god, didn't Chris tell you? OK – we've got a contract with Cary Grant and what he wants to do is remake *Mandy*, shot for shot, with him playing the Jack Hawkins character." '

The next day Hartmann drove Mackendrick down to Palm Springs to meet Grant. 'I had dinner alone with Cary Grant and Betsy Drake, to whom he was then married. And a butler with white gloves brought in trays with little legs underneath, and put down very good steaks in front of us, and we all watched television together. It was Noël Coward's *Blithe Spirit*. I ate this steak, looking from the butler to Gary Grant, to Betsy Drake, to the television set, thinking, "What *am* I doing here?" So I said I'd like to go away and think about it. I was stalling, trying to find out how I could get out of this gracefully, because the last thing you want to do is shoot a movie all over again.'

While playing for time, Mackendrick was taken to meet several other Hollywood producers. One of them was David Selznick, who expressed admiration for his work and offered him a seven-year contract. Mackendrick politely declined. 'Those contracts are a complete hoax. There are yearly options on *their* side, but none on yours. And there are retainers, which allow you to be farmed out. So I wanted no part of that.' A much more attractive offer came from Harold Hecht, of the independent production company Hecht-Hill-Lancaster.

Throughout the era of the great Hollywood studios, actors had repeatedly tried, rarely with much success, to fight free of the contractual tyranny of the studio bosses. In 1920 Chaplin, Pickford and Fairbanks had gained their independence by setting up United Artists; but since the coming of sound no player had achieved substantial autonomy until 1948, when Burt Lancaster and his agent, Harold Hecht, formed an independent company, Hecht-Norma. ('Norma' was Lancaster's second wife, Norma Anderson.) The first of many such outfits which helped break the hold of the major studios, Hecht-Norma – subsequently Hecht-Lancaster – established itself through a string of box-office hits, including *The Flame and the Arrow*, *Apache*, *Vera Cruz* and *Marty*. In 1953 they were joined by the screenwriter James Hill, and the company became Hecht-Hill-Lancaster.

HHL had acquired the rights to Bernard Shaw's play *The Devil's Disciple*, and this was the project Hecht wanted Mackendrick to direct. Mackendrick, a lifelong admirer of Shaw's work, accepted at once. 'So how would you treat it?' Hecht promptly demanded. Taken aback, Mackendrick asked for a few hours to think it over. Back at his hotel he took several benzedrines, and sat up all night reading the play and making notes of an outline. The next morning he returned to HHL to meet Lancaster and Hill, and discuss his initial ideas.

'Those three had a routine that they did. You'd start off talking to Harold, and then Jim would walk in. So you'd recap for Jim, and then after a bit Harold would walk out. Then, while you were talking to Jim, in would walk Burt, you'd recap again, and Jim would walk out. And so on. Finally they all walked out. After a bit I got bored, and went out into the corridor, and I saw all three of them having a little meeting at the end of the corridor.'

What the three partners were discussing – as Mackendrick only learnt later – was how to dispose of Anthony Asquith. Asquith, who had directed accomplished film versions of several British plays (including *Pygmalion*, probably the best screen adaptation of Shaw), had been HHL's first choice for *The Devil's Disciple* and was at that moment elsewhere in the building working on the script. HHL, however, had decided he was the wrong man for the job and, without having told him, were now planning to replace him with Mackendrick.

Having agreed terms with Hecht, Mackendrick was assigned a script-writer, Roland Kibbee, who had scripted *Vera Cruz*. 'A lovely man, and a worse choice for Shaw you couldn't think of. He had no sense of irony, of Shaw's style. As I talked to him, I began to realise it wasn't working.' Mackendrick went back to Hill and asked for another writer, suggesting his old mentor John Dighton. 'So they told Kibbee that I didn't want him. Which I suppose was true in a way – but they put the entire blame on me, and Kibbee never spoke to me again. Anyway, they flew Johnny over and we spent a year working on a screenplay – a very good screenplay. Shaw, I think, wrote the original play in a fortnight.'

*The Devil's Disciple*, first staged in 1897, is a tongue-in-cheek melodrama set in New Hampshire during the American War of Independence. The eponymous hero, a spirited reprobate named Dick Dudgeon, in a moment of unwonted nobility substitutes himself for the local minister, Anthony Anderson, whom the British intend to hang as a rebel. Anderson, metamorphosed from peaceable cleric into man of action, rouses the populace and rescues Dudgeon from the gallows. In the final scene Anderson decides to pursue his newfound career as a militia leader, yielding his pulpit to the reformed Devil's Disciple.

For the film, HHL hoped to cast Montgomery Clift in the title role, with Gary Cooper as Anderson. Laurence Olivier was to play General Burgoyne, the urbane British commander, while for Judith Anderson, the minister's wife who falls in love with Dudgeon, Elizabeth Taylor had been suggested. At one point, Mackendrick attended a meeting with Clift and Taylor, held at the house where Taylor and her husband, Michael Wilding, were living. 'Taylor and Clift took me into the kitchen, and said, "What the hell are you doing working with these people? They're monsters! We're not going to touch it – don't you touch it either!" So we went back in, and Taylor made impossible terms. It became quite clear she wasn't going to do it.'

With the Shaw project indefinitely shelved, Mackendrick asked to be released from his contract. Hecht vehemently refused. 'He told me, "No, you've got a contract, we're paying you! We want you to stay and make another movie for us! Listen, there's a property here we want you to work on." '

The property was Ernest Lehman's novella *Sweet Smell of Success*. A snarlingly downbeat tale set in the sleazy world of New York showbiz journalism, it had first appeared in 1950 in *Cosmopolitan* (retitled 'Tell Me About It Tomorrow!', since the editor, Herbert Mayes, objected to having the word 'smell' in a title). Lehman wrote *Sweet Smell* directly out of his own experience, possibly – judging by the sense of self-loathing that pervades it – as some form of expiation. He, like his protagonist, had worked as a press agent and had done 'some pretty awful things'[2] in the cause of furthering his clients' careers, and his own.

The narrator of the story, Sidney Wallace, is a rabidly ambitious press agent who has attached himself – as toady, gofer and all-purpose creature – to Harvey Hunsecker, chief columnist of the New York *Globe*. Hunsecker, venomous and megalomaniac, exerts terrifying power. 'The entertainment world genuflected to his sky-rocketing circulation and expanding influence with all the reverence it could muster. And he had achieved it all merely by adding new and scabrous meanings to the word *rumor*.'[3] While maintaining an attitude of lofty sententiousness – 'I am a tired man. . . . With one hand I seek the truth, and with the other I fight off the hungry wolf pack'[4] – Hunsecker uses Wallace to handle any 'distasteful business' that needs doing. Wallace, with mesmerised revulsion, realises that 'there was nothing I was not prepared to do, no new level to which I would not descend, in order to sew up Hunsecker's power for me and my clients'.[5]

Much of the force of Lehman's story derives from its intimations of twisted sexuality. Wallace, who is evidently young and attractive, addresses everyone, male and female, as 'baby' or 'sweetheart', and uses sex as a weapon, decoy or bribe. Hunsecker, by contrast, is physically repellent (Lehman describes him as 'pudgy', with a 'fat little mouth') and probably impotent, having sublimated his sexual drive into the sadistic exercise of power. His sole attachment is to his sister, Susan, for whom he feels an incestuous jealousy, reacting to potential suitors with psychotic fury.

The action of *Sweet Smell* covers some ten hours, from four in the afternoon to two in the morning, of a sweaty New York August. On Hunsecker's instructions Wallace has planted libellous stories, alleging drug-taking and Communist affiliations, about a young singer, Steve Dallas, who has been dating Susan. Shrugging off the gripings of his conscience, and of his childhood friend Irving Spahn, Steve's agent, Wallace meets Hunsecker for dinner, expecting praise and reward. Hunsecker, though, wants more – since Susan now defiantly plans to marry Steve the next day. Screwing up the boy's career is no longer enough; he has to be destroyed.

Wallace accordingly invites Steve to a night-club on the pretext of fixing him up with a booking, plants reefers on him, and tips off a venal police lieutenant. Steve is arrested and badly beaten up, and Wallace makes his way to Hunsecker's apartment to report his successful mission. Awaiting the columnist's arrival, he's vouchsafed a glimpse of the paradise for which he has traded his soul. 'As I sat there gazing at the portrait of Hunsecker on the wall, my eyes slowly closed, and I allowed the soothing music and the muted sounds of the city and the rich, sweet smell of success that permeated the room to lull my senses.'[6] His contentment is short-lived. Susan, who knows what happened to Steve, tricks Wallace into her room, rips her clothes and screams for help as Hunsecker arrives. The story ends with Wallace howling in fear as Hunsecker attacks and, perhaps, kills him. Like *Sunset Boulevard*, *Sweet Smell* can be read as first-person narration by a corpse.

The publication of the story caused outrage among Lehman's Manhattan colleagues. He had worked as assistant to Irving Hoffman, a leading New York press agent and columnist for the *Hollywood Reporter*, and Hoffman was one of those who now refused to speak to him. 'He felt that others would think that the fictional columnist was Walter Winchell and that *he* was the press agent character, because Irving Hoffman *was* very close to Winchell.'[7] Later, the two men were reconciled and in 1952 Hoffman ran a whole column in the *Reporter* praising Lehman's talents and suggesting Hollywood should snap him up. 'The fact,' Lehman adds, 'that I wrote the entire column myself is, I suppose, merely incidental.'[8]

Hollywood took the bait. Within a week of the column appearing, Lehman received a call from Paramount and was on his way to California. His first three writing credits were on *Executive Suite*, *Sabrina* and *The King and I* – two solid successes and a smash hit. By the time he sold *Sweet Smell of Success* to Hecht-Hill-Lancaster, Lehman was able to stipulate that he should not only script, but produce and direct the film as well.

Subsequently, someone had second thoughts. On his return from scouting locations, Lehman was summoned by Hecht, who 'told me that United Artists [through whom HHL were releasing] had gotten cold feet about the idea of a first-time director directing this picture, because they hadn't had such good luck with Burt Lancaster directing *The Kentuckian*.'[9] Lehman suspects, though, that he may have 'made the mistake that a first-time director sometimes makes, of directing a screen test. It gives others a chance of seeing that director in action. But dealing with those three gentlemen, you never knew where the truth lay. Jim Hill once said to me, "You know, today I pulled so many rugs out from under people that by mistake I even pulled the rug from under myself." '

With hindsight, Lehman feels that HHL's decision, however devious, may have been right. 'In my particular case they were very shrewd in disposing of me when they did. I wasn't ready to be a director. I was too close to the material; I'd lived it, it was part of my life.'

In any event, *Sweet Smell* needed a new director, and Hecht offered it to Mackendrick. At first sight, it was an anomalous choice. Nothing in Mackendrick's all-British track record suggested an affinity with such wholly indigenous material, its ethos and idiom not just American, but American of a highly specific milieu. The cut-throat cynicism of Lehman's Broadway was a far cry from Shaw's polished ironies, and even further from the conventions of Ealing comedy. It may be that Hecht had detected the mordant streak beneath the surface of Mackendrick's work, but more likely he was simply determined to get some kind of return on the company's investment.

For his part, Mackendrick was delighted. 'I'd always hankered to make a melodrama, or "film noir" as it's now called, and felt this was a chance to get out of a reputation for cute British comedies. Another [reason] was that . . . I'd had some experience of the world of tabloid journalism and was both repelled and fascinated by some of its grubbier aspects.'[10] He also relished the challenge of 'trying to capture on the screen the atmosphere of Manhattan. At the same time, I had some reservations about Ernie's screenplay. . . . It seemed to me that virtually every scene was an exchange between two characters seen sitting in a restaurant, at a bar or in a night-club. All talk.'[11]

Lehman was happy to explore ways of telling the story in more visual terms, and the two worked together on the script for several weeks. Lehman found it a stimulating experience. 'I was impressed by Sandy's inarticulate brilliance. No, "inarticulate" isn't the word; he articulated a lot, but you couldn't always work out just what he was getting at. But he was filled with energy, filled with ideas. Sandy's one of those directors who wants to hear all sides of everything. You'd come at him with an approach, and he would argue against it to force you to come up with another one. He was endlessly

**9a.** The sound of silence: Stephen Dalby, Mackendrick, Mary Haberfield and Leslie Norman working on the sound-track for *Mandy*.

**9b.** Horror-movie Gothic: the exterior of the school in *Mandy*.

**10a & b.** Inside looking out: Mandy and her father Harry (Mandy Miller and Terence Morgan) in *Mandy*.

**11a & b.** Seeking a hearing: Christine and Searle
(Phyllis Calvert, Jack Hawkins) fail to convince Harry;
Mandy finds her grandfather (Godfrey Tearle) preoccupied in *Mandy*.

**12a.** A state of collapse:
Calvin Marshall (Paul Douglas) and cattle in *The Maggie*.

**12b.** Shoot-out at Bellabegwinnie: Calvin Marshall and puffer crew
(Tommy Kearins, Alex Mackenzie, James Copeland, Abe Barker) on
collision course in *The Maggie*.

**13a.** Cul-de-sac England: Mrs Wilberforce (Katie Johnson)
and her lopsided house in *The Ladykillers*.

**13b.** Something wicked this way comes: Professor Marcus
(Alec Guinness, in silhouette) prowls around Mrs Wilberforce
in *The Ladykillers*.

**14a.** An irresistible authority: Marcus and his colleagues (Cecil Parker, Herbert Lom, Danny Green) cowed by Mrs Wilberforce in *The Ladykillers*.

**14b.** Silver threads among the gold: the gang (Peter Sellers on right) take tea with Mrs Wilberforce and friends (Edie Martin, Phoebe Hodgson, Helene Burls, Evelyn Kerry) in *The Ladykillers*.

**15a.** Boy with the ice-cream face: Sidney Falco (Tony Curtis) explains a few things to his secretary, Sally (Jeff Donnell) in *Sweet Smell of Success*.

**15b.** Hunsecker holds court: Falco, JJ Hunsecker (Burt Lancaster) and victims (Jay Adler, Autumn Russell, unnamed player) in *Sweet Smell of Success*.

**16a.** 'Match me, Sidney.' Falco, Hunsecker and waiters
in *Sweet Smell of Success*.

**16b.** Putting on the pressure: Falco talks Rita (Barbara Nichols)
into doing him a favour in *Sweet Smell of Success*.

enthusiastic. I don't think he had any idea of what would eventually happen.'

With the script virtually finished and New York location shoots being set up, Lehman fell ill with a spastic colon brought on – so he believes – by the tension of dealing with Hecht-Hill-Lancaster. On his doctor's advice he resigned from the picture, and James Hill took over as producer. Since some final polishing was needed on the script, Mackendrick was offered Paddy Chayefsky as Lehman's replacement. 'Now Paddy I was a great admirer of. But also in the building was one of my heroes, Clifford Odets.' Odets, the leading left-wing American playwright of the thirties, had gone to Hollywood in 1935 to write screenplays, thus selling out in the eyes of many of his associates. His career had foundered through a combination of political pressure and personal problems, and not since *Humoresque* in 1947 had he received a screenwriting credit. 'They said to me, "You want to work with *Clifford*?" And I said, "Yes!" "Well, all *right*!" And from then on Clifford and I got on like a house on fire.'

The script of *Sweet Smell of Success* is credited to Odets and Lehman, in that order. The plot, the situations and the characters are Lehman's, including those – such as Rita, the cigarette girl – who don't figure in the original novella; but almost all the dialogue bears the characteristic stamp of Odets. When Lehman quit the project, he left a near-complete script in which, he thought, only a few scenes needed minor rewrites, but according to Mackendrick Odets reworked almost the entire screenplay. 'Clifford came in and assured everybody that it would take him two, maybe three weeks to do the rewrite on the dialogue, because that was all we needed. It took him four months. We started shooting with no final script at all, while Clifford reconstructed the thing from stem to stern – and taught me a tremendous amount in the process.'

By the time Odets had finished, 'very little of Ernie's script was left – though the theme was still there and, with the exception of the final scenes, the plot was substantially as originally conceived. What Clifford did, in effect, was dismantle the structure of every single sequence in order to rebuild situations and relationships that were much more complex, had much greater tension and more dramatic energy. . . . What I began to recognise was that I was being given the privilege of watching the processes of a dramatic intelligence working out the "dialectics" of character interaction. . . . Clifford's instinct seemed always to devise patterns of three, four and five interacting characters. In particular he often managed to make it a pattern of five – a "quintet of voices" . . . so that, while each contributed to the composition, each followed its own melodic line.'[12]

Such an approach, though creatively fruitful, was intensely time-consuming, and time was short. There was no way the start-date could be postponed; the lead actors had other commitments and all the intricate logistics of location shooting in midtown Manhattan had been set in motion. Odets, furiously rewriting, was obliged to accompany the unit to New York. This, Mackendrick feels, exacerbated his problems. 'He was in a very neurotic state, going back to the town that had savaged him for the betrayal of going to Hollywood in the first place. He holed up in the Essex House, and there were big dramas, rather like with Bill Rose. Indeed, they were very similar in a way; both of them would get very obsessive about unimportant things in order to put off writing. With Clifford it became an issue of the curtains. First he was annoyed because I'd been given a room at the front, and he hadn't. So we swapped rooms. But then he was worried because the sunlight came in, so he had to have thick curtains. So he had this room with a marvellous view, which he blotted out with curtains so that he could sleep all day and work at night. And he wrote scenes that were terrific. The only trouble was that they were always about 50 per cent too long.

'The pages used to come to my room straight from Clifford's typewriter and I had to shoot them that day. After I'd finished shooting I'd give them to Bernie Smith, the script editor, and he'd put them into the script. So we cut the script there on the floor, with the actors, just cutting down the lines, making them more spare – what Clifford would have done himself, really, had there been time. And the marvellous thing was that he never noticed, because the lines play just fine.

'Clifford once gave me this advice: "If you're worried that my dialogue is overblown, too flowery and purple-passagey – well, *don't* worry, because the scenes are well-constructed. Play it fast, and don't pay attention to the words – just play the action, and it'll work." And he was so right. Because the scenes *are* well-constructed, and all you need do is see that the actors know precisely what their motivation is, and play it hard and fast, and get off screen fast. And then the dialogue simply explodes.'

Odets's contribution to *Sweet Smell* remains probably the finest screen-writing of his career, and certainly the most distinctive; nothing else that he wrote for the cinema can match it for tautness or intensity. (For this, credit may be due to the tight dramatic structure laid down by Lehman, both in his story and his screenplay, no less than to Mackendrick's tactful pruning.) Something of the same raw, caustic stylisation can be found in Odets's plays, but rarely elsewhere in his films – or in anyone else's, for that matter, apart perhaps from Polonsky's *Force of Evil*.

In essentials of a plot and characterisation the film sticks closely to Lehman's novella. The leading protagonists are unchanged, apart from their names: the columnist is 'JJ' Hunsecker, instead of the softer 'Harvey', and 'Sidney Wallace' becomes the more vivid 'Sidney Falco'. (The name carries obvious bird-of-prey connotations, with perhaps a sideglance at Jonson's *Volpone*, another study in social predation with a central pair, Volpone and Mosca, linked in uneasy collusion.) Steve Dallas's agent is renamed Frank

D'Angelo and becomes Falco's uncle. The action is still triggered by Hunsecker's campaign to sabotage his sister's love affair, but the focus of dramatic tension, even more than in the original, lies in the vicious, symbiotic relationship between Hunsecker and Falco.

From the first, the part of Sidney Falco had been seen as ideal for Tony Curtis. (Oddly enough, the original *Cosmopolitan* illustration of Wallace looks very like Curtis, though he was little known at that time.) Universal, however, were reluctant to loan him out, believing – rightly, as it transpired – that the role might damage his career. Curtis, tired of undemanding pretty-boy parts and desperate to prove he could act, had to fight the studio to be allowed to take it – and having won, signalled his commitment by investing in the production. Curtleigh, the company set up with his wife Janet Leigh, became co-producers of the film.

The role of Hunsecker was less readily cast. Lehman's description suggests, if anyone, Charles Laughton; for a time Orson Welles was considered. Had UA not, for box-office reasons, insisted on a 'name', Mackendrick – who had met Hunsecker's model, Walter Winchell, once or twice – would have chosen Hume Cronyn. 'Winchell looked like Cronyn. He wore a hat because he was embarrassed about being bald, and he was a little, ratlike figure, with a megalomaniac meanness and insecurity.' The idea is intriguing. A Hunsecker played by Cronyn would have dominated not through any imposing physical presence but, like Kierlaw in *White Suit*, by sheer force of malice. But it was evident that UA wanted Lancaster himself to take the role – both for his proven box-office appeal and because he and Curtis had successfully teamed in a previous HHL picture, *Trapeze*.

*Trapeze*, though, had utilised only the blandest aspects of Curtis and Lancaster – the engagingly brash youngster, the grinning acrobat. In *Sweet Smell* Mackendrick taps into far darker areas of each actor. 'One wonders,' David Thomson observed, 'if they weren't a little taken aback by what the quiet Scot had made of them. J J Hunsecker and Sidney Falco may have their roots in American tabloids and *film noir*. They are also blooms in slime, characters who forever altered our sense of the two actors and of their ability.'[13]

No film before *Sweet Smell*, and very few since, has so vividly captured the quality of New York, the peculiarly pungent mix of visual and emotional aggression that James Baldwin described as 'the sense of danger and horror barely sleeping beneath the rough, gregarious surface'.[14] For this authenticity HHL deserve a share of the credit, having granted Mackendrick the time and resources to familiarise himself with the city beforehand. 'One of the characteristic aspects of New York, particularly of the area between 42nd Street and 57th Street, is the neurotic energy of the crowded sidewalks. This was, I argued, essential to the story of characters driven by the uglier aspects of ambition and greed. Without it, the characters would seem to be even more unbelievable than they already were. I was enormously lucky to discover that the producers were instantly receptive to this idea.'[15]

Along with his cinematographer and production designer, Mackendrick flew to New York and spent several days exploring locations. 'It was on this trip that we developed the formula of starting scenes in exteriors, beginning them with short passages of dialogue on the street outside . . . before following characters into the interiors. A complex matter it was, since it meant very careful matching between material shot on night locations in New York, and studio-built sets. . . . In restrospect, I now realise that I may have been falling into a trap that is not uncommon in the profession: when a director is uneasy about some aspects of the script, he will often retreat into a concentration on technical challenges that allow him to escape from the things that are very much more important. The truth, perhaps, was that I was uncomfortable about characters and situations I didn't really believe in, so I hoped to conceal these fundamental flaws by the fancy footwork of visual effects.'[16]

Besides absorbing the local atmosphere, Mackendrick set about 'learning the image of New York' by taking multiple shots from various fixed points. Back in Hollywood, he taped the pictures into a series of panoramas which he stuck up on the wall, discovering in the process 'something that is different from the experience of living there. You think, "Great, we've got the tower and this doorway," but then you realise that you can't get them in the same frame. So gradually you take down off the wall the pictures that aren't working, and leave the ones that are. It's a simple technical problem. For instance, there's this extraordinary claustrophobic feeling you get from having skyscrapers right on top of you – but how do you show it? The only way is to get the camera low, so that if somebody walks up into camera you see the buildings above you. That's the sort of thing I discovered from living with these stills for a while, before we took the unit out there.'[17]

Mackendrick's first American film is sometimes seen as marking an unprecedented departure from his previous work. On closer consideration, this isn't so; *Sweet Smell of Success* shows a clear continuity, in terms of character, plot structure and thematic preoccupations, with the Ealing pictures. Where it *does* differ, as becomes dramatically evident right from the start, is in the feel of the film, its pace and texture.

Such a difference is hardly surprising. From working in the most British of British studios Mackendrick now found himself directing American actors and crew, in the fiercer environment of Hollywood professionalism. (This isn't to suggest that Ealing personnel weren't professional, merely that American movie-makers operated within a very different framework of assumptions.) His cinematographer was James Wong Howe, veteran master of low-key photography, and the film's subject-matter related it to a long tradition of American urban cinema, which in itself prescribed a certain overall visual approach. But perhaps the most striking change from Mackendrick's previous work is the film's unrelenting pace. His Ealing movies build cumulatively, incorporating passages of almost pastoral relaxation. *Sweet Smell* scarcely lets up for a second, creating a world (as Carol Rittgers put it) 'at once dynamic and decadent'.[18]

Much of the pulsing nervous intensity which powers the film undoubtedly derives from the conditions under which it was made, and from the mental and emotional state of its director. During most of the filming, which took place in the spring of 1957, Mackendrick remembers being scared stiff. HHL, he knew, had no compunction about firing their directors for any reason, or none at all; as a company they could be simultaneously ruthless and unsure. Colin Young, who at this time was teaching at UCLA, and often met Mackendrick socially, got the impression the partnership 'had enormously good taste in choosing directors and other talent, but would then lose faith in their own judgement during the project and keep changing their minds, trying to second-guess the talent they'd hired'.

Furthermore, the problems of having Lancaster as co-producer were nothing beside those of having him, frustrated director that he was, as lead actor. ('He chews directors alive,' Lehman had warned encouragingly.) The script was trickling out of Odets's typewriter a line at a time, barely an hour or two before it was due to be shot – a disconcerting situation for a director who believed in careful rehearsal. Storyboarding, obviously, was out of the question.

Most unnerving of all was the location. Exteriors were shot on the public streets of the noisiest, most frenetic area of New York City. (Matters weren't helped by hordes of young Curtis fans, who periodically broke through police barriers to reach their idol.) 'We started shooting in Times Square at rush hour, and we had high-powered actors and a camera-crane and police help and all the rest of it, but we didn't have any script,' Mackendrick recalls. 'We knew where we were going vaguely, but that's all. Nothing can be more likely to melt your bowels than that kind of absolute horror. At those moments the desperation you work from becomes a kind of strength – there's no moment of indecision because you've got to make a decision fast, right or wrong. The director often does the best things he does under that kind of pressure, because decisions have got to be made from the subconscious.'[19]

This mood of hysterical energy could hardly have been more apt. *Sweet Smell of Success* must be one of the most restless movies ever made; rarely does the camera stay still for more than a few seconds. Even in a scene of relative emotional tranquillity, such as Susan's acceptance of Steve's proposal, it prowls and sidles around the lovers, nervously framing and re-framing as though checking out every angle from which danger might emerge. The camera seems to be infected by the Broadway mannerisms it records, keeping on the move out of sheer self-protection. If you don't stop, they can't pin you down.

In *Sweet Smell*, by some way the darkest of Mackendrick's films, the pessimism of his vision achieves its fullest, most dynamic expression – thanks partly to his subject-matter (which can also be read as an oblique comment on the equivocal working conditions at HHL) and partly to the disenchanted *noir* tradition of which the film is one of the last and finest examples. By this point, the great cycle of Hollywood *noir* had virtually run its course, though it retained enough vitality to wind down with three late, high-baroque masterpieces: Aldrich's *Kiss Me Deadly* (1955), Welles's *Touch of Evil* (1958) and, bracketed between them, *Sweet Smell of Success*. But even within the *noir* cycle, with its gallery of rancid, self-seeking protagonists, *Sweet Smell* is exceptional – equalled perhaps only by Wilder's *Ace in the Hole* in its relish in charting the topography of rampant ambition, the ugly downside of the American Dream. It's altogether a remarkable film to have come out of the middle fifties, when the prevailing tenor of American movies, as Nora Sayre observes, was 'that ours was a splendid society, and that one ought to cooperate with it rather than criticise it'.[20]

The film's impact is intensified by Mackendrick's characteristic stance as the clear-sighted outsider – the American in Scotland, the Scot in England and now the Briton in America – turning his dispassionate gaze, at once intrigued and appalled, on the alien milieu before him. Indeed, the fluent confidence with which he adopts the *noir* idiom suggests that, had he come to the cycle earlier in its trajectory, he might have become one of its leading exponents. His lifelong admiration for Fritz Lang, father of Hollywood *noir*, stood him in good stead, but he was also exceptionally well-served by his collaborators.

The gleam of rain-washed nocturnal streets, by this stage a cliché of the *noir* style, is here revitalised by being extended to the interiors, so that everything, indoors and out, seems to glisten with a flashy lubricant sheen – apt metaphor for a world of meretricious surface appearance. In an interview, James Wong Howe explained how he achieved this effect by 'putting mushroom photoflood globes in the cocktail bars, and [using] Double-X film. And I washed the walls with oil to get the glitter.'[21] It was also, Mackendrick recalls, Howe's idea to fit Lancaster with heavy spectacles which, lit closely from a high angle, deepen his eye-sockets and lend a taut, skull-like aspect to his face. 'So throughout the entire film a light moved with Burt, just in front of him, often with Jimmy holding it himself, to produce this strange mask of a face. And that is a great cameraman at work, knowing how to create an image and hold it throughout the film.'[22]

Howe and Mackendrick, both tireless perfectionists dedicated to the primacy of the narrative, developed great mutual respect. 'It was a pleasure,' Howe remarked, 'to work with Sandy Mackendrick.'[23]

Mackendrick refers to Howe as 'quite simply, the best'[24] – though adding that 'Jimmy on occasion could be absolutely dreadful, if you didn't watch him like a hawk; he was always telling the performer to turn this way, so he could get the key light just there – and ruining your performance!'

When the relationship between director and cinematographer is working well, Mackendrick believes, the two talents blend into one. 'When an idea's good, it's hard to remember who had it first.' A case in point is *Sweet Smell*'s effectively unconventional use of lenses, as noted by an admirer of the film, the director Sydney Pollack: 'They reversed the normal shooting concept. They shot almost every master shot with long-focus lenses, from very far away, in order to pack the buildings . . . in tightly behind the people. Then they shot their close-ups with wide-angle lenses, to keep the background in focus and, again, an awareness of the buildings. These techniques create an overall effect, in which the lay moviegoer feels oppressed by the city . . . without necessarily understanding why.'[25] Howe and Mackendrick also concurred on the use of dynamic low-angle compositions, shooting the characters so that (in Stephen Schiff's phrase) 'they're always knifing up through the air, poised for the kill'.[26]

Mackendrick credits Edward Carrere, the art director, with the insight that 'all one really sees in a crowded night-club is cigarette smoke and ceilings'.[27] When the interiors were filmed, at the Goldwyn studios in Hollywood, 'sets were built two feet off the ground to accommodate smoke pots and electric cables, enabling . . . Howe to light the smoke'.[28] All this, along with Mackendrick's close framing and incisive cutting, enhances the archetypally *noir* mood of existential claustrophobia, people trapped in a framework of shadowed menace that seems less a facet of reality than an emanation of their own minds. In *Sweet Smell*, the streets through which Falco scurries seem just as closed in as the cramped interiors. Not until Scorsese's *Mean Streets*, 15 years later, has a film conveyed so intensely the scene of compulsive movement going nowhere.

The prevailing tone is immediately established in a pre-credit sequence which, like the start of *Whisky Galore*, recalls Mackendrick's grounding in documentaries: news trucks being loaded, bales hefted by dark figures outlined against the evening sky. We hear the voice of a foreman: 'All right, fellers, here they come, let's get with it! Come on, come on, we haven't got all night! Let's get going, move it outa here!' Neither his face, nor those of the other workers, are clearly visible. The atmosphere is one of anonymous febrile urgency, insistent yet routine – the mood of New York, itself as much an actor in the drama as any of the cast.

A key element, here and throughout the film, is Elmer Bernstein's tense, urban-jazzy score, on which he collaborated with Chico Hamilton (whose quintet features as Steve Dallas's backing group). The dominant theme – a raunchy six-note motif closely related to the opening of Harold Arlen's classic *Blues in the Night* ('My momma done tol' me . . .') – sets the film's edgy, dangerous rhythm, constantly resurfacing to notch up tension, and swelling to a wild crescendo as Hunsecker gazes down from his eyrie on the prone and defenceless city. The reference to Arlen's title is apt enough. Though the film's action extends the original ten-hour time-scale to some thirty-six hours (from early evening, through the next day, to the following dawn), *Sweet Smell*, like all true *noir*, is an essentially nocturnal movie. Its few daytime scenes seem drained and unreal, seen through the dilated gaze of an insomniac.

Behind the credits, the trucks roll out on to the streets of Manhattan. Displayed on their sides, too briefly to register in detail, we glimpse posters of Lancaster's eyes, baleful behind their horn-rims. One truck advances down Broadway, headlights glaring, the camera tracking backwards in its path, shooting up from ground level as though cowering before it. Sir John Kierlaw's black limousine, hurtling northwards, was viewed from just this angle, and the message is the same: something dangerous is on its way.

The Hunsecker of Lehman's novella disclaims political interests. But in the film he acquires a political angle, broadcasting patriotic bombast and voicing 'the choice and the predilections of sixty million men and women in the greatest country in the world'. This aspect of the screenplay originated not with Odets (though as a victim of HUAC, he must have relished it) but with Lehman, who by now felt safe to satirise the flag-waving of Winchell and his like. 'They never believed in their own politics; but this was part of their product, to be patriots.'

Purely in character terms the change makes sense. The Hunsecker we see on screen is a monster too grandiose to rest content as petty supremo of a showbiz gossip column. It also adds a further dimension to the film's quivering paranoia, where rumour kills and a man can be 'sentenced to death' for telling the wrong joke. Falco knows his audience; a mere drugs smear might not stick, but drugs *plus* Party membership can't fail. Neil Sinyard detected in *Sweet Smell* 'the atmospheric legacy of fifties McCarthyism, with its society of snoopers and informers'.[29] Hunsecker thrives in a world rendered pliant for him by habits of fear and deference.

Critics who reproach the film, and Hunsecker's role in particular, for being 'unrealistic' miss the point. *Sweet Smell* no more intends a naturalistic depiction of New York journalism than does *Man in the White Suit* of British industry, or *The Ladykillers* of the London underworld. In each, Mackendrick was aiming for a heightened, stylised version of reality. J J Hunsecker is a portrait of Winchell in much the same way that Charles Foster Kane is a portrait of Hearst. He can't be narrowed down to any one columnist, but stands as a fearful distillation of everything the existence of such figures implies – an expressionistic study in irresponsible power.

In this light, Hunsecker can be seen as one of Lancaster's most effective performances. Under Mackendrick's guidance he toned down his over-emphatic mannerisms (especially the toothy grin that led the screenwriter Borden Chase to nickname him 'Crockery Joe') and for the first time exploited the underside of his earlier athleticism, a slow, menacing calm suggesting reserves of dangerously repressed energy. 'Why is it,' an apprehensive senator inquires, 'that everything you say sounds like a threat?' Not only that, but everything Hunsecker does *looks* like a threat, so that his final eruption into violence comes as an admission of weakness, a circumscribing of infinite potential damage into the merely limited and actual. Until then, all his movements have been reined in and closed off, neck muscles clenched, arms rigid with the tension of a powerful man channelling his force into devious psychological outlets – just as his sexual energy has been diverted into one gnawing and unconsummated incestuous passion.

If opinions differ over Lancaster's performance, Curtis's has been universally praised. Drawing on his own streetwise Bronx background, he created (in David Thomson's words) 'one of the first portrayals of unprincipled American ambition and of the collapsible personality that goes with it'.[30] Beside Hunsecker's tensed stillness, Falco is all movement – eyes, hands, mouth executing constant nimble manoeuvrings to evade attack or stake out an advantageous position. A conscious virtuoso, relishing his own seamy ploys, he meets fresh challenges to his mendacity like an athlete pushing to the limit ('Watch me run a 50-yard dash with my legs cut off,' he tells his secretary, grabbing the phone to sweet-talk a disgruntled client), switching his boyish grin on and off with the heartless precision of the neon signs outside in Times Square. Beneath the ready charm, momentary gestures betray the aggression that drives him, often taken out on inanimate objects: a newspaper slashed viciously into the mouth of a trash-can, a tie knotted tight as though noosed around Hunsecker's neck.

In Sidney Falco, Mackendrick takes to a logical conclusion the character of the unregenerate opportunist who figures under more likeable guises in his previous films. Shorn of their folksy Celtic roguery, the tactics employed by both Macroon and MacTaggart – deceit, manipulation, covert threats and spurious charm – hardly differ from Falco's, and the moral distaste (and the fascination) that Mackendrick felt for their triumphs manifests itself most clearly in *Sweet Smell*. 'You see that grin? . . . It's part of his helpless act – he throws himself upon your mercy.' Hunsecker is describing Falco, but Calvin Marshall, raging on the quayside at Loch Mora, could have said as much of MacTaggart. The stakes are higher, and the consequences a lot more lethal, but the underlying psychological configuration is much the same.

Candour, with Falco, is a form of contempt. Since his secretary, Sally, is in no position to damage or advance him, she's insignificant enough to hear the truth. In her presence he can drop all pretences, as casually as he drops his pants without bothering to close the door between bedroom and office.

Jeff Donnell's Sally, like all the supporting roles, is sketched with fine dramatic economy. Within seconds of her first appearance we can guess, without being told, just how she came to be Falco's secretary and why despite verbal bruising and – most likely – lousy pay she stays. Her wounded look when he abuses her moves even Falco to something approaching remorse, and by way of apology he offers her his tawdry credo. 'Oh Sally, you oughta know me by now. . . . You think I'm a hero. Well, I'm no hero. I'm nice to people where it pays me to be nice. Look, I do it enough on the outside, so don't expect me to do it in my own office. . . . Hunsecker's the golden ladder to the places I want to get . . . way up high, Sal, where it's always balmy, and no one snaps his fingers and says, "Hey, shrimp, rack the ball," or "Hey, mouse! mouse! go out and buy me a pack of butts!" . . . From now on the best of everything is good enough for me.'

This, the first substantial scene in the film, sets up everything that follows. In its brief span we get Falco's character, circumstances and motivation, right from the cheap cardboard sign (SIDNEY FALCO – PUBLICITY) scotch-taped to the door, to the final exchange with Sally as he leaves: 'Take your topcoat.' 'And leave a tip in every hatcheck room in town?' We see him in action, evading two clients and trying an unsuccessful spiel on a third. And we learn the plot, in two dozen words: 'His kid sister's having a romance with some guitar player. He asked me to break it up; I thought I did but maybe I didn't.' We also gain a sample – a fairly mild one, compared with what's to come – of the richly idiosyncratic language in which *Sweet Smell of Success* is written.

*Sweet Smell*'s status as a cult movie derives above all from its dialogue. (In Barry Levinson's *Diner* (1982), one of the characters wanders around quoting it by the yard.) Everybody in the film, not just the lead players, converses in a jaggedly stylised gutter-baroque, stuffed with recondite vocabulary and gaudy images. 'Listen,' says Kello, the corrupt, sweaty cop, 'rectify me a certain thing. . . .' 'Now go make yourself a holiday!' snaps Frank D'Angelo, by way of telling Falco to get lost. And Hunsecker's secretary Mary, a pleasant unexceptional person, observes, 'You're so immersed in the theology of making a fast buck.' What she means is, 'All you're interested in is money,' but no one in *Sweet Smell* would say anything so drably straightforward.

Animal imagery and food imagery thread their way through the dialogue, both generally connoting contempt or disgust. Four times in the first few scenes Falco is likened, by himself or others, to a dog – besides the dismissive 'shrimp' and 'mouse' quoted above. A rival columnist credits Hunsecker with 'the scruples of a guinea pig and the morals of a gangster,' and Steve suggests Falco may be destined for 'dog and cat heaven' (which sounds quite an attractive place, though evidently not meant that way). Terminating their quarrel, Hunsecker demotes Steve yet further, into the insect world: 'I don't relish shooting mosquitoes with an elephant gun.'

Food imagery is similarly used to devalue people. Falco in particular is often reduced to edible terms: in a phrase which neatly sums up his transient appeal, Kello calls him 'the boy with the ice-cream face', and Hunsecker memorably remarks, 'I'd hate to take a bite out of you. You're a cookie full of arsenic.' But Hunsecker talks of himself, too, as food – 'All she has to do is put two and two together and I'm a chicken in a pot,' and 'Sidney, this syrup you're giving out with you pour over waffles, not J J Hunsecker' – as does the cigarette girl, Rita, bitterly defending her battered self-respect: 'What am I, a bowl of fruit – a tangerine that peels in a minute?' In Falco's words Steve becomes an overripe lemon, 'full of juice and vinegar, just waiting for a bigshot like you to put on the squeeze'. *Sweet Smell* portrays a world where people are objects of casual devourment, to be gulped down without even much lasting satisfaction. Most of the food referred to is what would now qualify as 'junk food' – ice cream, cookies, pretzels.

People as animals, people as junk food, people as trash in what Hunsecker describes as 'a world of old rags and bones'. *Sweet Smell* is a study of competitive degradation: the fouler your motives and the worse you treat others, the more power you accumulate. In this world Hunsecker, who can degrade more people more thoroughly than anyone else, is king, and Falco pretender to his throne, a would-be Macbeth or Godunov. We first meet Hunsecker at his table at the 21 Club, holding court among clients and sycophants, amusing himself, like the Duke in *Rigoletto*, by insulting each one in turn – Falco by no means excluded. 'Mr Falco, whom I did not invite to sit at this table tonight, is a hungry press agent, and fully up to all the tricks of his very slimy trade. Match me, Sidney,' he adds, taking out a cigarette.

The *double entendre* is wholly intentional. Matching Hunsecker, indeed becoming Hunsecker, is exactly what Falco longs to do, and Hunsecker knows it. Falco's reply – 'Not just this minute, JJ' – evinces equal self-awareness, and even greater ambiguity. A petty revolt, refusing to jump subserviently to order, it could also imply either that Falco hasn't yet, for all his slimy trade, sunk quite to Hunsecker's level – or that he doesn't feel ready, for the moment, to take on Hunsecker on his own territory. Either way, the exchange sets up the later scene (also in a restaurant) where Falco comes to realise that, given the right price, no level can be too low for him. And that price is, precisely, the chance to become Hunsecker.

In a cold, vindictive fury aroused by Steve's outburst ('Your slimy scandal and your phony patriotics – to me, Mr Hunsecker, you're a national disgrace'), Hunsecker instructs Falco to 'get Kello'. As the implication sinks in, Falco rises from the table – putting space between himself and Hunsecker, but also (the two have been sitting side by side) placing himself in the direct line of Hunsecker's gaze, the look through which the columnist's power is defined.

FALCO: JJ, it's one thing to wear your dog collar. When it turns into a noose I'd rather have my freedom.

HUNSECKER: The man in jail is always for freedom.

FALCO: Except if you'll excuse me, JJ, I'm not in jail.

HUNSECKER: You're in jail, Sidney. You're a prisoner of your own fears, your own greed and ambition. You're in jail.

FALCO: You're blind, Mr Magoo. This is the crossroads for me. I won't get Kello. Not for a lifetime pass to the polo ground. Not if you serve me Cleopatra on a plate.

HUNSECKER: Sidney, I told you—

FALCO: JJ, I swear to you on my mother's life I wouldn't do that. Not if you gave me a column would I do it for y . . .

(He stops, staring at Hunsecker in appalled realisation. Hunsecker grins.)

HUNSECKER: And who do you suppose *writes* the column while Susie and I are away for three months?

The trap snaps shut. Falco, stripped of all pretence of self-respect, must go out and confront the bloated embodiment of his corruption. For there seems to be, behind his reluctance to obey Hunsecker's order, something more than a moral objection to framing Steve Dallas. In his encounters with Kello, Falco betrays a repulsion verging on nausea: not just fear of the cop's evident sadistic lust for him, but a horrified recognition of underlying identity. If (as Richard Blackburn suggests) Falco, agile and protean, plays Ariel to Hunsecker's malign Prospero, Kello is Caliban; alternatively, Kello serves Falco as the portrait served Dorian Gray, manifesting an image of the moral decay behind his 'ice-cream face'. ('Say,' he jeers, indicating the perspiring Falco to his sidekick, 'how d'you like this face? Well, I'll be doggoned, it's melting.') If Falco's dream is to be Hunsecker, his nightmare is that he's becoming Kello.

In the course of the film, Falco meets Kello three times, each marking a stage in his descent into the abyss. The first time, under Hunsecker's protection, he can brush Kello off. Second time round, out on his own, he has to treat with the adversary. His business concluded, he scutters up an overhead walkway, trying to establish – as he did by standing up from Hunsecker's table – an illusion of detachment and moral superiority. In vain; cast out by Hunsecker and forced back down to street level, he finds himself at last delivered into Kello's brutal hands.

There is about *Sweet Smell* a certain voyeuristic fascination as we watch Sidney Falco shedding, one by one, his few remaining scruples. Surely, we feel, there must be *something* he won't do, some act from which even he must recoil in sheer revulsion? Yet at the same time we sense that there *is* no such sticking-point. The film's inexorable dramatic logic tells us as much.

At first, there's something perversely likeable about Falco's con-man resilience, as when he bounces indestructibly back after being publicly denounced by Leo Bartha. The turning-point, when we realise how far gone he is in moral decay, is the betrayal of Rita to Otis Elwell. (The scene was evidently more than the British censor could take; much of it was cut for the initial UK release.) Rita, in Barbara Nichols's touching portrayal, is the most vulnerable character in the film, more so even than Susan Hunsecker. Pathetically aware that her overblown blonde prettiness, sole asset in an unfriendly world, can last very few more years, she offers herself for old times' sake ('You still keep your key under the mat?') and from a need for warmth and comfort, only to find her offer passed on, like an IOU in a poker game, to service Falco's obligations.

The betrayal is accomplished, in visual terms, within the opening seconds of the scene. Lying barefoot on the bed, reading a magazine, Rita hears Falco's key in the lock and runs to the door as his profile appears in the glass. As he opens the door he smiles at her, and her arms lift to go around his neck – at which point Elwell steps into view from the corridor, violating the intimate space between them. With the reverse shot of Rita backing off, her expression wary and wounded, the whole situation is given to us without a word being spoken.

Indeed, the scene could even end there, were there not one more callous twist to come. Pursuing Rita into the bedroom to badger her into sleeping with Elwell, Falco starts turning on the phony indignation – 'How d'you like this? I turn myself inside out to do *you* a favour and now *I'm* the heavy' – before realising that a shrewder tactic is to plead his own interests. 'You need him for a favour, don't you? Well, so do I. I need his column tonight.' Not only is Rita, like Sally, inconsiderable enough to be given the truth, but her affection for Falco offers him leverage against her. Falco has some way yet to fall, but this scene shows him at his most intimately despicable.

As so often in Mackendrick's films, the characters in *Sweet Smell* are defined by 'how they look' – both in the obvious sense of how they appear to others and in the equally important sense of how they use their perceptions, seeing or failing to see. Hunsecker first shows up as eyes on a billboard, 'The Eyes of Broadway' that also appear at the head of his column, conduit of his corrupt influence. Presiding at his restaurant table, he uses his look rather than his hands to single out each victim – '*This* one is toting *that* one around for *you*' – switching a cold glance from Manny Davis to Linda James to Senator Walker. Remote behind their glasses his eyes, narrowed with contempt, are trained like gunsights upon their targets. 'This Dallas boy must be good for you,' he tells Susan, suggesting she bring Steve to meet him. 'This time I'll clean my glasses for a better look.' His words imply the candid stare of honesty, but the look he intends is as lethal as the basilisk's.

At the midpoint of the picture, all his schemes running to plan, Hunsecker steps out on his balcony to contemplate nocturnal Manhattan outspread below him. His expression conveys a sense of absolute possession – master, he clearly feels, of all he surveys. Yet he is, in both senses, 'overlooking' his realm: gazing out across its glittering streets, but missing a lot of what they contain. Hunsecker can see people in only one way, from above. The restricted scope of his vision renders it self-defeating, as Falco perceives: 'JJ, you've got such contempt for people it makes you stupid.'

Falco's look similarly defines his character – alert and calculating where Hunsecker's is deliberate and judgemental. To Rita's, 'Are you listening?' he replies, 'Avidly, avidly'; but the avidity is in the eyes, flickering restlessly about the crowded night-club, registering people and their movements, docketing them for possible future use. 'I got eyes, I put things together' – the line is Kello's, but (one more shared attribute) it fits Falco equally well.

Blindness, to Falco, is the ultimate peril. 'You're walking around blind, Frank, without a cane,' he warns D'Angelo. Seeing more than anyone else, he can adapt as circumstances change. But, like Hunsecker, he makes the error of contempt. Certain people are rated innocuous and therefore negligible, such as Susan Hunsecker. 'You tiptoe around on those bird legs of yours,' he tells her patronisingly, 'nervous and incompetent, with a fatality for doing wrong, picking wrong. . . . Come around some night when I'm not writing your brother's column and I'll revise that delicate outlook of life.' Almost at once, his words rebound on him. He himself has just picked badly wrong, in underestimating Susan as a free agent, and as a result his own outlook of life undergoes drastic revision. While Susan's loss of innocence brings freedom from the delusions – about Falco, her brother, and herself – in which she was trapped, Falco, who supposed himself supremely aware, finds himself snared by delusions whose existence he disregarded.

A fundamental strength of *Sweet Smell* is its uncompromising moral consistency, carried through right to the end. It must have been tempting to hedge a bet or two for the box-office – to go for the stock atonement-through-suffering finale, with Falco brought to see the error of his ways and denouncing Hunsecker and all his works. True, he threatens to expose the columnist – 'That fat cop can break my bones, but he'll never stop me from telling what I know' – but the threat is purely vindictive, and also futile; what proof does he have, and who would listen? (The line was in any case dropped in at the last minute to appease the censor.) Though both Falco and Hunsecker suffer retribution, neither is redeemed, nor is there the least suggestion they might be.

Once again, innocence has confronted experience, and the outcome replays that of *The Ladykillers*: the innocent defeats the corrupt by setting them against each other. Comparison with the earlier film, though, underlines *Sweet Smell*'s major flaw: its ineffectual depiction of innocence. Where Mrs Wilberforce attains a dramatic and mythical stature equal to that of her criminal lodgers, *Sweet Smell*'s young lovers remain pallid and bland, never engaging our interest as do their oppressors. For this the casting is largely responsible, both Susan Harrison and Marty Milner being hopelessly overmatched, in force of personality as in professional experience, by Curtis and Lancaster.

Harrison, making her screen debut, was cast by Mackendrick against the wishes of Hecht-Hill-Lancaster. 'They thought I was out of my mind. She was found by the New York casting director; she'd been in acting school, and had worked with Sandy Meisner, and she was very much a young Method actress, neurotic, strung up and quivering with tension – exactly the quality, I thought, for somebody who'd been pschologically abused and was coming apart at the seams. My main support was from Odets, who also saw her as exactly right. Tony was supportive, too; Burt and Jim and Harold went along with us, but they always thought she was a pain in the neck. They were very misogynist characters, for various reasons, that trio.' With hindsight, though, Mackendrick concedes that the partners may have been right. The role needed a stronger, more experienced player.

Marty Milner, too, comes across as less than adequate. With his clean-cut, college-boy looks and slightly pouchy features, giving him on occasion the air of a petulant chipmunk, he scarcely convinces as someone who might spend his life teasing out guitar riffs in smoky cellars. (Not that his dialogue is much help. What New York jazz musician would describe himself as 'an average Joe'?) When Susan and Steve are alone together, the emotional temperature of the film drops several degrees. But maybe no actors, however talented, could have done much with the characters, assigned as they are the drab task of representing normality in a world dominated by such fascinatingly odious monsters.

A further contrast with *The Ladykillers*, in line with *Sweet Smell*'s more sophisticated (or more cynical) attitude, is the implication that victory is attainable only at a cost: means condition ends, and the innocent can defeat the corrupt only by adopting their weapons. Mrs Wilberforce achieves her victory unwittingly, retaining her innocence unscathed. Not so Susan Hunsecker. To gain her freedom she has to resort to deception, albeit of a purely passive kind.

In the novella Susan deliberately sets out to frame Sidney for having framed Steve. The Susan of the film is less calculatingly vengeful – less, one might say, her brother's sister. Falco's prevention of her suicide attempt leads Hunsecker, arriving inopportunely, to misread the situation. However, seeing the misapprehension develop, she not only refrains from dispelling it, but fosters it with silence and significant looks – and to this extent her innocence is compromised, as Falco recognises: 'You're growing-up – cute.' Still, if innocence connotes vulnerability, to lose a little of it may be no bad thing. In the film's final shot Susan walks off into a new life which she, like Sidney Stratton, can deal with on terms of greater awareness.

As so often in Mackendrick's films, the outcome of a key scene turns on a pattern of looks and perceptions. In the showdown with Falco and her brother, Susan sees what's happening, and uses it. Falco also sees it, but can't control it, because he has led Hunsecker to perceive him as a potential usurper. And Hunsecker, trapped in the tunnel vision of his paranoia, can only read the situation one way – as the attempted rape of his sister, an assault on the most intimate sanctum of his power. Both Falco and Hunsecker are defeated because of 'how they look', one in each sense; Susan wins out because of 'how she looks' in both senses.

Perceptions, appearances, the reading or misreading of events through preconceived assumptions: for all its startling difference in surface tone, *Sweet Smell of Success* is no less characteristic of Mackendrick than the previous, more reticent Ealing work – an extension of his range, but in no way an aberration. If the Ealing pictures represent where Mackendrick was coming from, *Sweet Smell* suggests one direction in which, had things been different, his career might have developed – with, on all the evidence, formidable results.

The making of *Sweet Smell* was attended, even more than most movies, by continual tension – not only during the nerve-racking Manhattan location work, but also back in the studio. Mackendrick felt intimidated by Lancaster, while Lancaster (perhaps unconsciously recalling *The Ladykillers*) described Mackendrick as a 'mad professor' who 'worked in a world of his own'.[31] At Ealing Mackendrick had been considered an excellent director of actors, patient and supportive, but Lancaster found him remote, not much given to praise or comment. 'He just seemed so wrapped up in what he was doing . . . like a super-mechanic, moving around doing things, using us and moving us – not in any unkind or imperious way, that was just the way he seemed to work.'[32] (This distancing may well have been Mackendrick's way of dealing with the threat – as he saw it – of Lancaster's aggression.)

In particular, the crucial final scene between Falco, Hunsecker and Susan gave rise to furious disagreements on set, and to subsequent rumours of 'three different endings' having been shot. Lancaster's account (broadly supported by James Hill) is that Odets couldn't at first come up with a satisfactory ending, and that once he'd done so, Mackendrick kept changing his mind over how to shoot it.

'He'd set up shots on the soundstage for a scene that would play six minutes,' Lancaster told his biographer Robert Windeler. 'There would be thirty-five camera moves on a dolly. The whole floor was taped. We had to hit marks like crazy. The camera moved continuously – into close-ups, pulling back, shooting over here to this person. . . . We rehearsed all day, until four in the afternoon, just to get the technical part down. The head grip and the rest of the crew were sweating, knowing that if they missed one mark, the shot would be ruined. But we did it, clicked it all off. Sandy called: "Cut. Print." Then he'd stop, waiting. I'd say, "Something the matter, Sandy?" "No, it went fine, you all did it fine, only . . . let's do one more." So we went through it again. Again, fine. Cut. I was delighted. We had six minutes of film, a good day's work – and done in the most interesting style. But he still wouldn't be satisfied. He'd shake his head and say, "I don't like it, we've got to change it, change everything." Well, you put up with it because you put up with Babe Ruth even if he's drunk. We respected Sandy; he was a little kooky, but he was good.'[33]

Interviewed on a later occasion, Lancaster cast himself in a slightly less tolerant light. 'I said, "Sandy, I'm sorry, we can't do that, we'd lose a day's work. You want to take the tapes up, you better take them up at eleven in the morning." He wasn't very happy about it, but he didn't protest, so we left it. . . . As far as he was concerned, no matter what you did, no matter how good it really was, it wasn't good enough. He was always reaching for that extra dimension that was beyond anyone's grasp. But that's the way he got good things.'[34]

Mackendrick, not surprisingly, remembers things rather differently. 'What Burt doesn't mention is that that scene was shot two or three times, yet each time it was cancelled – not by me, but by Burt and Harold, in order to give it back to Clifford Odets to rewrite it. The first draft was wildly overwritten – marvellous stuff, but beyond Burt's capacity as a personality and as an actor to play – in which Hunsecker goes right round the bend and becomes absolutely paranoid. And Burt's strengths are not really in that kind of pyrotechnic performance; he's a great figure, but his skills in acting are somewhat narrow. So he stopped the performance and said, "No, no, I'm not going through with this. Get Clifford back to give it another go." '

Eventually, Odets came up with a version which satisfied Lancaster and his partners. Mackendrick, though, was unhappy with it. 'After the girl walks out, they had a scene between Burt and Tony. *That* didn't work, for a very clear reason that I kept spelling out to them: Burt's only interest is in his sister, and she's gone. So the story's over – Tony can't damage Burt, there's no action to be played. The answer was to reverse the scenes, but that they refused to do.

'At that point, I started to work with travelling camera. And this was because the editor, Alan Crosland, had come and told me that Harold Hecht had said to him, "As soon as Sandy's had his director's cut, Alan, I want you to order reprints of the entire thing, because we're going to start again and re-edit.'' This was a major shock – nothing like that had ever happened to me before. I went and challenged Harold with it as gently as I could, saying, "Listen, I admit you've got the right to do that. But I'd like to propose a deal: let me stay around at my own expense, not on the payroll, and sit in on your meetings to discuss the cutting." Harold said, "Sure, stick around if you want, but we may not listen to you. We'll do what we want with it."

'So I kept the camera moving for ulterior motives – the old rule that you can't cut while the camera's moving. I was trying to edit in the camera, so that they couldn't muck it about; so to some extent it's my fault that it was shot in such an elaborate way. But what I also did was plan it very carefully on paper in two versions. One as it was scripted: after the beating up of Tony, the girl has a showdown with her brother and walks out, and then there's a scene between Tony and Burt. But I also shot so that you could edit it with those scenes reversed.

'The trouble was that, as we started to work on it, Burt in blocking it out started to make some moves which would screw me. I had to avoid certain areas of the room during the scene with the girl, otherwise Tony would have been in frame too. To get round that I had to make excuses, saying, "Sorry, I think I've got confused with eyelines," and I'd go behind the set, trying to work out how I could change it. And Burt crept up behind me, looked over my shoulder and said, "What the fuck are you doing? You never had any trouble with eyelines before." So I confessed what I was doing, and Burt laughed and said, "All right, but you're crazy, 'cause it won't work. In a movie, you've got the last scene between the two stars. You can't bring in a two-bit actress to play the last scene with us."

'So we shot the thing, Crosland edited it the way they wanted, and we went into the viewing room. And afterwards Harold said to Burt, "It doesn't work, does it?" And I said, "Will you try it my way?" He ignored me, and said, "Call the crew for next week, and we'll get Clifford to do what he can in terms of rewrites." And I said, "*Please*, will you try it my way?" Harold said, "Sure, we'll look at it your way; but call the crew, we'll need them on Monday." So they did that; then they ran the other cut. And it was one of the most delicious moments of my life. There was a long silence. Then Harold reached for the phone, called up McWhorter, the production manager, and said, "Can we cancel for Monday?" And McWhorter said, "No, we can't – you've ordered the crew and you've got to bring them in." So they had to come in to shoot inserts and pick-up shots.'

Behind Hecht's attitude may have been the suspicion that he had a commercial disaster on his hands. On this point he was right, as Mackendrick realised at the preview. 'What you had was an audience that liked Tony Curtis, and thought he was a nice, open-faced kid on the make. And when it slowly dawned on them that he was the shit of all time, the result was physical. You could see them curling up, crossing their arms and legs, recoiling from the screen in disgust.' Lancaster's fans were no better satisfied, finding the film too static and talky; as Hill observed, they 'kept waiting to see Burt jump out of a tree'. With *Sweet Smell*, HHL suffered its first major box-office flop.

Hecht, promptly dissociating himself from failure, put the blame on Hill. 'The night of the preview, Harold said to me, "You know you've wrecked our company? We're going to lose over a million dollars on this picture." ' Lancaster, for some reason, seems to have held Ernest Lehman responsible. 'Burt threatened me at a party after the preview. He said, "You didn't have to leave – you could have made this a much better picture. I ought to beat you up." I said, "Go ahead – I could use the money." '

No one, at any rate, thought to blame Mackendrick, and the film's commercial failure scarcely harmed his reputation, being far better received by reviewers than by audiences. A few, like Robert Hatch in the *Nation*, found the whole thing way beyond credibility: 'If you could believe it, it would be a shocker; but if you could believe it, you would not be going round without an attendant. . . . The character Mr Lancaster is really playing is the mad scientist of the side-show horror movies.'[35] But most critics, though taken aback by the scabrous subject-matter and the savagery of the treatment, accorded *Sweet Smell* guarded praise. For *Time*'s reviewer the film, 'which could have been offal, is raised to considerable dramatic heights by intense acting, taut direction . . . superb camera work . . . and, above all, by its whiplash dialogue'.[36] 'A brilliantly executed slice of evil and perversion,' wrote Carol Rittgers in *Film Culture*, with 'a fascinating surface that far nobler films lack.'[37] *Saturday Review*, while finding it 'tough going' and regretting the lack of 'a poverty-haunted childhood that might explain Curtis's unscrupulous drive', praised the cinematography, the score, and Mackendrick's 'extraordinary feeling for the supercharged Times Square *milieu*'.[38] Both *Time* and the *New York Herald* included it in their ten-best lists for 1957.

British reviewers were also struck by the film's dramatic intensity. Writing in the *Evening Standard*, Philip Oakes recommended *Sweet Smell* as 'a savage and satisfying piece of picture-making', with 'the cold-blooded excitement of a stroll through the reptile house'.[39] 'Nothing like the cinema for the screaming nerve, the hand clammy with distaste,' Dilys Powell reflected in the *Sunday Times*. 'So superbly is the thing done, one's skin crawls with credulous horror. . . . And a dreadful authenticity is given by the feeling of place . . . the roaring, rushing streets, the glittering nights, the dense, sophisticated discomfort of smart bars and restaurants.'[40] Like most of her colleagues, she enthused over Curtis's performance. C. A. Lejeune of the *Observer* was almost alone in dismissing the film as 'hardy, wisecracking, slightly arty-crafty', and failing 'in the first requisite of any play, which is to bring the characters to life'.[41]

In his *International Film Annual* for 1957, William Whitebait rounded off a disenchanted survey of current British output by citing *Sweet Smell* as the kind of movie Britain ought to be making. 'Success, then, would seem to have come from abroad, those called in, and those driven away: Alexander Mackendrick in Hollywood, with his *Sweet Smell of Success*. Could no subject worthy of satire be found for him here?'[42]

Mackendrick himself is inclined to dismiss *Sweet Smell* as 'a piece of absolute hokum and melodrama',[43] and once even described it as 'my worst film'.[44] Most critics nowadays see it as his best. By 1984 Peter Waymark, writing in *The Times*, could refer to it as 'one of the finest films made in, and about, America in the 1950s',[45] and in an article in *New York* magazine in December 1985 David Denby rated it 'the most acrid, and the best' of all New York movies, capturing 'better than any film I know the atmosphere of Times Square and big-city journalism'.[46] Over the years, the picture has gained steadily in reputation, and seems to be moving from the status of cult classic to that of classic *tout court*. For David Thomson it remains 'the chief among many reasons for honoring Alexander Mackendrick – for he came to the big beast of a city and identified the way JJ and Sidney were its crucial atomic structure'.[47]

*Sweet Smell* may even be in danger of overpraise: Richard Blackburn called it 'one of the most important and underrated films ever made',[48] which verges on the extravagant. What the film unmistakably demonstrates, though, is that Mackendrick's potential range as a director was immense, far greater than might have been guessed from his previous work. After the closure of Balcon's studio, other ex-Ealing directors continued to make much the same sort of movies as before: Crichton's *Battle of the Sexes*, Dearden and Relph's *Victim* or *League of Gentlemen*. Beside these workmanlike efforts, *Sweet Smell of Success* stands out as an astonishing departure, carrying a coherent personal vision triumphantly into a completely new idiom. On the strength of *Sweet Smell*, Mackendrick seemed poised to strike out in any direction he chose, armed with the talent and experience to establish himself as a major director on an international scale.

# 8 Sammy Going South

'Coherent and complete myths are not as
frequent in movies as they sometimes seem.
What are frequent are fragments of myths,
mythological snatches at part of a problem,
hints at large, encompassing myths that
rarely seem to materialise themselves.'[1]

Michael Wood, *America in the Movies*

'There's a natural adversary position between
the director and the producer, which at its
best can be very constructive. But where
there's a fundamental disagreement in the
tone and concept of the thing, that's where a
movie comes totally unstuck.'

Alexander Mackendrick

With *Sweet Smell of Success* completed Mackendrick was free to return to London, since *The Devil's Disciple* was to be shot in England, where costs were lower. He left Hollywood with relief; quite apart from his battles with Hecht-Hill-Lancaster, he had been unhappy and lonely in Los Angeles, missing the social and professional camaraderie of Ealing.

Casting on *Devil's Disciple* was still unresolved and while Mackendrick waited for a start date, he received a call from the Dutch film-maker, Bert Haanstra. Haanstra, who had made his name with a series of lyrical, idiosyncratic documentaries – *Mirror of Holland*, *Rembrandt*, *Glass* – was planning his first feature film: a comedy about rival brass bands, to be called *Fanfare*. Both he and his scriptwriter, Jan Blokker, lacking any indigenous tradition of filmed comedy, felt in need of guidance, and Haanstra decided to consult Mackendrick, whom he'd met at the 1951 Edinburgh Film Festival.

Mackendrick readily agreed to help and Haanstra came to London to read him the script. 'When I'd finished he said, "Bert, you have a nice story – but boy, you've got a long way to go." An hour later I left with a pile of books: the development of a script from first idea, via synopsis, first script, second script, screenplay and shooting script. And the script development of *The Maggie*.'[2]

At the suggestion of Rudolf Meyer, Haanstra's producer, Mackendrick and his wife were invited to Amsterdam for a week. 'Sandy didn't make it a holiday. Practically the whole week was spent in discussing comedy in general, and *Fanfare* in particular.'[3] After a visit to the location – the village of Giethoorn, where all the streets are canals – Mackendrick made sketches for two key scenes and recorded a tape of ideas and advice. *Fanfare* was a huge success in its home market (recovering its costs within six weeks), received screenings at Cannes, Moscow, Venice and Edinburgh, and is still, according to Haanstra, 'the second most successful Dutch movie ever. But it would never have got there without that brilliant teacher, Alexander Mackendrick.'[4]

Meanwhile, the casting of *Devil's Disciple* had at last been settled. Olivier remained committed to playing Burgoyne, despite disagreements with HHL over *Separate Tables* (originally set to direct, he had resigned when Vivien Leigh was replaced by Rita Hayworth). But Montgomery Clift was now out of the question for the title role. A serious road accident had left his facial muscles badly damaged, and drugs were exacerbating his problems. Gary Cooper had turned down the role of the Rev. Anderson. Mackendrick had the impression that 'he wasn't too happy with me. I think I was too English for him.'

Once again Hecht-Hill-Lancaster went for the in-house talent. Burt Lancaster's decision to play Anderson was received with mixed feelings by Mackendrick, the experience of making *Sweet Smell* still fresh in his mind. All the same, Lancaster seemed acceptable, if not ideal, casting for the role; it was the final choice for Dick Dudgeon that aroused Mackendrick's misgivings. Here too, HHL went for a proven team. Lancaster and Kirk Douglas had struck sparks, off each other and at the box-office, in *Gunfight at the OK Corral*, so now Douglas was offered the role of the Devil's Disciple. For the financially astute Hecht, there was a further incentive: Douglas's own independent company, Bryna, would come in on the deal, spreading the capital risk.

For Mackendrick, neither actor was wrong in himself. The fault lay in the teaming of the two men, so psychologically and physically similar ('all those teeth'), which ruined the point of Shaw's play. 'The central device is that you start off with two men who are complete opposites, and each one totally miscast. The parson just isn't a parson, he's really a dangerous fighting man. And the Disciple is a born preacher. So when they change over, you get this great burst of energy. But Kirk Douglas, he's another Burt, so you lose the temperamental thing.

'There's a theory that I subscribe to, that when you're planning a film with two male stars, you have to cast them in the male and female temperaments. If the relationship between Burt and Tony Curtis works so well in *Sweet Smell*, it's because they're temperamentally so totally opposite. It worked in *Trapeze*, too. They were in a sense – I don't mean sexually, but you might call it psychosexually – the yin and yang of the human disposition.'

The rest of the cast were all British. The role of Judith Anderson, offered to Carol Baker after Taylor's refusal, finally went to Janette Scott. Harry Andrews played the punctilious Major Swindon, and the supporting cast included such veteran character actors as Basil Sidney and Mervyn Johns. The producer was originally to be James Hill, a great admirer of Shaw's work, but Hecht, mistrustful of Hill after the failure of *Sweet Smell*, arrogated the job to himself.

In July 1958 Mackendrick began shooting *The Devil's Disciple* at Elstree Studios. At the beginning of August it was announced he was quitting the picture following (according to a report in the *Daily Express*) 'a row [which] flared up over the week-end after two weeks' filming and feuding'.[5]

As usual in such cases, accounts differ over the cause of the rupture. At the time, it was ascribed to a conflict over tone, with Mackendrick objecting to Shaw's play being turned into 'a swashbuckling adventure story spiced with sex',[6] and HHL fearing the film might 'lose money by being too highbrow'.[7] Subsequently, though, Lancaster maintained that Mackendrick had been shooting too slowly. 'I explained to Sandy that because so much of our limited budget had gone towards purchasing the property, we had a 48-day shooting schedule. . . . Sandy told us not to worry, but after shooting a week he had only two days of film. So we called him in and let him go. It's ironic that his two days of film are the best in the picture. But we did what we had to do.'[8]

HHL may have been at least partly justified. Jeremy Bullmore, who worked with Mackendrick on some TV commercials not long afterwards, heard stories from the *Devil's Disciple* crew of 'Sandy keeping Laurence Olivier and Burt Lancaster in their caravans, while he got the close-up of the horse's hoof hitting the puddle so that the drops would come out exactly as he wanted them – with £10,000 a minute ticking away. Whether that's true or not, it fitted what I knew of Sandy's perfectionism to the exclusion of sanity or money or getting on with the movie.'

Mackendrick, though, denies such allegations. 'When people want to unload a director, the easy way is to claim that he doesn't know what he's doing. But often they really mean that he's trying to do something they don't want him to do.'[9] In this case, he believes, the point at issue was Lancaster's performance. To preserve, as far as possible, the contrast between the two leads, Mackendrick 'wanted at the beginning of the movie to inhibit him in every way possible from being the Burt Lancaster that we know and are fascinated by – to make him play somebody who's gauche, clumsy, shy and lacking in force, almost a Jimmy Stewart figure – so that when there's a complete switch and he lets loose this volcano of energy, it would be shocking and startling. But because nobody else was seeing it that way, Burt I'm sure felt I was trying to emasculate him.'

Mackendrick also noticed 'a certain failure to speak the same language' between the two American players and their British colleagues. 'All the English actors, including Larry Olivier, arrived word perfect for the entire part right from day one. Whereas Burt and Kirk were always wanting their parts rewritten, lines changed as they went along. That was their system of working; but the two systems were like oil and water.'[10]

Olivier himself retained oddly contradictory memories of the picture. In his autobiography, *Confessions of an Actor*, he wrote that 'I was awful in the part, as dull as ditchwater, you wouldn't think anyone could be with that pearl among parts. . . . I can't remember having such a miserable time in a job ever.'[11] Four years later, in *On Acting*, he recalled being 'particularly amused by the dry irony of Shaw's Burgoyne . . . there's no harm in an audience seeing an actor enjoying himself.'[12] Whatever his state of mind, Olivier – no doubt distracted by the breakdown of his marriage to Vivien Leigh – apparently had trouble telling his co-stars apart. This, according to Michael Munn, 'irritated Lancaster no end, and every time Olivier called him Kirk, he'd glare back and in that clipped tone of his say, "*Burt!*" '[13]

Other cast members also experienced problems. 'I couldn't say it was the happiest film of my life,' Janette Scott told an interviewer a few years later. 'The trouble was that Kirk Douglas and Burt Lancaster are very much frustrated directors themselves. . . . Sandy is very shy and very quiet. Like the tiger . . . you never know when he'll pounce.' She found Mackendrick as a director 'marvellous, terribly hard – he had me in tears a couple of times. But ever since I've been dying to work with him again. . . The moment you get to know why he works the way he does, you understand him completely.'[14]

Harold Hecht, it seems, had begun planning to replace Mackendrick even before the final row. Three days after shooting had begun, the director Philip Leacock, then working for HHL in Hollywood, received a call from Hecht inviting him to take over the picture. Leacock, a personal friend of Mackendrick, turned the offer down flat. Hecht then approached another British director, Guy Hamilton, who refused until he 'was assured that as from Tuesday the film would be without a director. So I accepted.'[15]

James Hill, deploring his partner's decision, still maintains Mackendrick should have stood his ground. 'Part of Sandy's greatness is the fact that he's going to indulge himself, to get away with as much as he can to make it as good as he can make it. . . . By the time I got over there the damage had been done, they had another director. But to this day I can't understand why Sandy let them fire him. I know that if he had stood up to Hecht, he would have kept that job. So I can only feel that for whatever reason he had somehow decided he wanted to walk away.'[16] Mackendrick dismisses this argument, concurring with Leacock's comment that 'if the producer and the major star decide they don't want you in there directing, then there's not a lot you can do'.[17]

*The Devil's Disciple* was released a year later, to lacklustre notices and poor box-office on both sides of the Atlantic. For most reviewers, the film fell between two stools: too wordy to be a good swashbuckler, too brash to be good Shaw, it suffered, felt the *Guardian*'s critic, from 'the sort of vestigial respectfulness which damages a play without creating an honest-to-goodness film'.[18] Its sole virtue – and sole Shavian performance – was, by general consensus, Olivier's Burgoyne, stylish, urbane, and effortlessly walking off with the picture. Since Mackendrick had directed all Olivier's scenes, the reviews may have afforded him some wry amusement. Nonetheless his dismissal came as a severe blow to his confidence, and one from which his career as a director – hitherto set on a strongly rising curve – never wholly recovered.

In the meantime, to earn some money, he returned to his old trade of advertising. Hilary Mackendrick had set up her own company to make television commercials, and through her he found himself working not only for his former agency, J. Walter Thompson, but on the Horlicks account for which, a quarter-century earlier, he had created strip-cartoon press ads. In 1958 and 1959 he directed eight 45-second commercials, tightly structured mini-dramas in each of which an individual under stress is enabled to cope by getting a good night's sleep – thanks, of course, to Horlicks.

Mackendrick's producer, and co-scriptwriter, was Jeremy Bullmore, later chairman of JWT. He found Mackendrick 'an amazing man; if I know anything about how to assess the technical side of a film, I learnt it from him. It was the first time I realised that you didn't write film, you thought it – and wrote it down afterwards. It was Sandy who made me see that you could communicate without a word of dialogue – just visually, or with sounds. And I think we're both minimalists at heart, so we could agree that the movement of an eye or a finger would be quite enough to convey what we wanted, without any broad effects.

'He didn't argue his ideas particularly persuasively. But if you said to yourself, "He's got a picture in his head, and these words are his attempt to describe it" – then the words *did* make sense. I think a lot of Sandy's difficulties were, first that he couldn't understand why people couldn't see he was self-evidently right, because he's not diffident; and second, that he never used words on their own, they were always in conjunction with pictures. And the words were shared, but the pictures weren't, because they were up there in his head. Which of course is why he made such very good movies, but I think it may have contributed to his problems in working with people.

'Also, he was very contemptuous of anyone who tried to keep within the budget. He'd say, "We need another half-day on this," and there just wasn't money for it. So you'd say, "No, what we've got is good enough," and he'd come back with, "What you're paying me, Mackendrick, for is to tell you that's *not* good enough, and we *do* need another half-day." You can't win those purist arguments. All you can do is say no as tactfully as you can, and hope he won't hate you forever.'

In undertaking to direct television commercials, Mackendrick may have started a trend. Hitherto, established movie directors regarded TV advertising as disdainfully as artists in 'legitimate theatre' had once regarded the upstart movie business. But once a director as respected as Mackendrick had shown the way, others – such as Joseph Losey and Karel Reisz – soon followed. Within a few years it was considered perfectly normal, and in no way demeaning, for a director to take on a TV commercial or two between films.

Meanwhile, Mackendrick was exploring movie projects. *High Toby*, which he and William Rose had discussed some years earlier, concerned an 18th-century highwayman based on the historical figure of Jack Sheppard. Rose now suggested they should revive the idea and wrote a treatment which, Mackendrick recalls, 'appealed to me a great deal, in that it was highly technical. He went into a lot of things that were rather like a Western – how you use horses to establish an alibi, and all the mechanics of the robberies, stuff like that. And he had the concept – which influenced me a great deal on *Mary Queen of Scots* – of getting right away from the studio-bound, lace-on-the-cuff approach, making it very earthy, with the kind of attention to squalid period realities that give real colour to the text.' The villain would have been the notorious 'thief-taker', Jonathan Wild, hero of Fielding's satirical novel. 'But at that time I just didn't have any producers that I could get interested – it was the usual problem, it wasn't the sort of thing I'd done before.'

Another project in which Mackendrick became involved around this time – attracted by his lifelong love of jazz – was an adaptation of *Paris Blues*, Harold Flender's novel about black American jazz musicians in Paris. For black actors to star in a film set in a predominantly white context would have been, at that period, a highly unconventional approach. The film did eventually get made, though not by Mackendrick. Martin Ritt directed, with a black couple (Sidney Poitier and Diahann Carroll) playing subplot to the white leads, Paul Newman and Joanne Woodward.

Among the producers whom Mackendrick contacted was Carl Foreman, actively rebuilding his career after a decade on the blacklist. Foreman turned down both *High Toby* and *Paris Blues*, but invited Mackendrick to direct his forthcoming production of *The Guns of Navarone*, based on Alastair MacLean's best-selling novel. Budgeted at £2½ million, with an international star cast, this was to be the most expensive British movie yet made, and Foreman hoped to emulate the box-office success of *Bridge on the River Kwai* (which he had co-scripted anonymously).

MacLean's novel deals with a fictitious wartime expedition, by a small force of commandos and Greek Resistance fighters, to destroy two massive guns installed by the Germans on an Aegean island. Foreman's script, which sticks quite closely to the plot of the book, is (like most of his screenwriting) competent but verbose, full of banal philosophising about the dilemmas of war, the nature of heroism, and so forth. This fairly inert material, Mackendrick hoped, might be moulded into something more complex and visually interesting, while not losing the straightforward narrative drive.

'I wanted to introduce some qualities that – how shall I put this without sounding too pretentious? – would have brought out the mythic value of the story, but without ever being self-conscious about it. I think it could have worked, as great adventure stories often do, both on a very cartoon level, with plenty of swashbuckle, but also as a fable. And partly because of the visual element of the guns, I wanted to relate it to the Greek myth of the Minotaur, with Irene Papas playing the Ariadne role – the small band of heroes setting out to overcome the fabulous monster. Nobody would have noticed it, I hope, but there would have been these echoes, these overtones of the Aegean mythology, without ever conflicting with the adventure story that it was.'

Mackendrick's approach was never put to the test. After a few days shooting 'second unit stuff, with the Greek navy', he was taken off the film. The official reason was 'a serious back ailment',[19] which may have had some basis in truth – he had been suffering for some time from a slipped disc. A few months later, Foreman spoke of his director having 'had a break-down'.[20] Mackendrick, though reticent about the whole episode, believes that his ideas about the script 'took off like a lead balloon', and that he ran up against 'these personal ambitions – Carl wanted to direct that film himself, but the distributors [Columbia] wouldn't let him'.

Ossie Morris, cinematographer on the picture, disagrees. 'I don't think Carl had any ambitions to take over. He was a very nervous person, very insecure, and with a picture of that size you have to drive it along, you need a director that can shout around a bit. The last thing Carl wanted was any form of disruption, but pressures were brought to bear on him – from Columbia, I should imagine.' Morris spent about six weeks scouting locations with Mackendrick on the mainland and on Rhodes. 'Sandy's a deep-thinking, intellectual director, and he just wanted everything to be right. We climbed over rocks and mountains, and up cliffs; we marked places all over the island. He was working very hard, he never stopped. But we didn't actually turn much film in the camera. He wanted tracking shots in the most inaccessible places, so we had to get dollies up there on mules. But Sandy knew what he wanted, and the logistics weren't going to stop him. In the end, I don't think that went down too well with the powers that be, back in California.'

At all events, Mackendrick was dropped; J. Lee Thompson was flown in to replace him; and the film scored a huge commercial success, besides winning an Oscar for Special Effects. Whatever Foreman's opinion of Mackendrick's ideas, some trace of them may have survived in the film's prologue, spoken by James Robertson Justice over shots of seascapes and classical ruins. 'Greece and the islands of the Aegean have given birth to many myths and legends. . . . These once-proud stones, these ruined and shattered temples, bear witness . . . to the demi-gods and heroes who inspired those legends on this sea and these islands. But though the stage is the same, ours is a legend of our own times. . . .' Not much of this mythic quality, though, can be detected in the movie that follows.

Many people within the industry considered Mackendrick had been unfairly treated. Even so, that he had been dismissed from two pictures in succession, and hadn't had a commercial hit for over five years, inevitably dented both his reputation and his self-esteem. Feeling that a break from movie-making might boost his morale – and perhaps with a view to exploring an alternative career – Mackendrick made a brief excursion into theatre, the first since his student days with the Scottish National Players.

The initial impulse came from the writer Robert L. Joseph, who had adapted for television a novel, *Face of a Hero*, by Pierre Boulle (author of *Bridge on the River Kwai*). This adaptation, starring Jack Lemmon and directed by John Frankenheimer, had been shown in 1959 in the CBS *Playhouse 90* series, and favourably received. Lemmon, eager to prove himself as a stage actor, encouraged Joseph to adapt the piece for theatre, and Joseph, who knew Mackendrick, showed him a draft of the stage treatment, 'just saying would I read it and what did I think of it as a play. And I made the mistake of suggesting how to make it work better. So pretty soon I was a consultant to the story-doctoring of his play, and before I knew it I was suddenly offered the chance to direct it. I'd never directed for the stage. But it was a Broadway production, so whatever the dangers I jumped at it.'

While Joseph's play was being set up, Mackendrick took on a repertory production at the Belgrade Theatre in Coventry, 'just to get my hand in'. The play was *The Grass is Greener* by Hugh and Margaret Williams, a romantic comedy which had been a hit in the West End, and was later filmed, without much sparkle, by Stanley Donen. Mackendrick's production played for three weeks in August 1960, to respectable notices from the local press. 'The play runs the risk of being static,' observed the *Coventry Standard*, 'but all credit to Alexander Mackendrick's direction for success-fully avoiding this danger.'[21]

The following month, *Face of a Hero* opened for its out-of-town run in Philadelphia. The cast was a fine one: besides Lemmon, it included George Grizzard, Betsy Blair, Albert Dekker, Sandy Dennis, Martin Gabel and Ed Asner. Their material was rather less impressive. Lemmon recalls the play as one 'which the audience couldn't understand, I couldn't understand. In fact, none of the cast could understand.'[22] Rehearsals were unhappy, not least because Joseph insisted at the last minute on replacing the leading lady, Patricia Cutts, with Betsy Blair. When this didn't help he tried to replace Mackendrick, calling in the veteran stage director Harold Clurman. Clurman, a friend of Mackendrick's, refused but stayed around to offer help and advice.

Clurman, Mackendrick recalled, saw 'what we were all trying to ignore – that the piece was not only unplayable – but that the original concept was impossible to dramatise. So a salvage job was already doomed. All one could do was simplify and clarify.'[23] The Faulknerish plot concerned a District Attorney (Lemmon) in the Deep South, who prosecutes a rich young racist for a murder of which the DA knows him to be innocent. All of which, Alan Pryce-Jones noted in *Theatre Arts*, 'is well enough acted . . . but it remains totally unconnected with real life'. The dialogue, he added, was 'so dense that for minutes at a stretch the audience is left without so much as a sense of direction'.[24]

Compared to most other reviews, Pryce-Jones's remarks were mild. After the Broadway opening at the Eugene O'Neill Theater, Howard Taubman wrote in the *New York Times*: 'Egg splatters the *Face of a Hero*. . . . Some was flung by intent; a great deal more landed inadvertently, thanks to the ineptitude of the playwright. . . . How so many people of good repute got into this misadventure is one of those Broadway mysteries. Alexander Mackendrick, who has notable films to his credit, is responsible for the direction, such as it is.'[25] The play ran just a month at the O'Neill, closing after 36 performances.

Despite this débâcle, Mackendrick found Lemmon 'an absolute sweetheart' to work with, and thought the whole episode 'a terrific experience. I'd have loved to do more in theatre – if I had been younger, and hadn't had a family to support.' (Hilary Mackendrick was at this time expecting their first child, Matthew, born the following year.) 'It's very difficult to survive, unless you're a big success, as a theatre director in Britain – and on Broadway, I should think, only if you've been in it from the beginning, and I was an outsider.'

Instead, he went back to developing movie projects, in particular *Mary Queen of Scots*, on which he had now gained a collaborator. The Scottish writer James Kennaway, whose first novel, *Tunes of Glory*, brought him to public notice, had taken up screenwriting at the suggestion of Michael Relph. Through Relph he met Mackendrick, who became a close friend and (in the words of Kennaway's biographer, Trevor Royle) a 'magisterial figure . . . both mentor and father-figure'[26] to the younger man, who 'looked on Mackendrick as being the one genius he knew in the movie world'.[27]

Kennaway, whose iconoclastic view of Scotland's favourite tragic heroine coincided with that of Mackendrick, threw himself into the project with enthusiasm. The film they envisaged was to be tough, grimy and determinedly anti-romantic, a study in *realpolitik* in a dung-strewn Edinburgh, 'a Mexican border town with bandits', with Holyrood 'more like a slum than a palace'. Mary would figure as one of Mackendrick's self-destructive innocents, a fastidious, French-accented outsider as hopelessly outwitted as Captain Waggett by the ruthless Scots around her. ('Up to her armpits in nasty wee Scotsmen,'[28] as Mackendrick put it, reversing the image of Professor Marcus's gang marooned in a sea of little old ladies.) Against her bright, doomed elegance would stand the grim dourness of John Knox, and the machiavellian Secretary of State, Maitland of Lethington.

In his letters to Kennaway, Mackendrick emphasised his aversion to the speechy grandiosity of conventional costume drama. The dialogue 'could be poetry of a sort . . . but like the primitive and savagely economical words of the Border Ballads'. Above all, it should be 'a film where character is told *firstly* in action – and reaction – and not in description or comment. Why am I so bigoted on this point? *Because of the bloody period* – because I believe . . . that the vulgar commercial producers are *absolutely* right in believing that historicals are boring because they do not have just this quality of *action* . . . associated with westerns and cops-and-robbers.'[29]

Over several months the two men exchanged draft treatments and individual scenes, Mackendrick always urging terseness and concision. 'There's still *too much bloody TALK*! What I feel it really needs is . . . sweating out the fat and flabbiness, the inessentials. Making fewer words work harder.'[30]

Leslie Caron was considered for Mary, also Jeanne Moreau. But it was the character of Maitland that most fascinated Mackendrick: 'a lying, cheating . . . brilliantly devious and ingenious bastard – who has *edge*, and a frightening cold passion – but no feeling. Brain – *in action* and in a furious hurry of desperate aggression. It's a mistake, I feel sure, to give him any elegancies at all – his egotism and his hubris would be those of the proletarian fascist, not the would-be gentleman.'[31]

This downbeat view of history was hardly calculated to attract potential backers, for whom period movies meant colour, spectacle and the broad romantic sweep. With funding elusive, and several problems of dramatic structure unresolved, the project was set aside when Mackendrick was offered another assignment – by Michael Balcon, who had turned down *Mary Queen of Scots* ten years earlier.

After the final disintegration of Ealing in 1958, Balcon had become chairman of a newly formed consortium, Bryanston Films. Several of his former colleagues – Michael Relph, Basil Dearden, Charles Crichton – also joined the organisation which produced, for the most part, pictures of a palely post-Ealing kind. Many of them were released as supporting features, and none (apart from the Woodfall films, of which more later) could remotely have been described as the 'original and unusual subjects of international importance'[32] Balcon had promised when he first became chairman. It may have been frustration that led him to undertake a more ambitious project – his only production for Bryanston and, in the event, his last in a producing career stretching back to 1921.

W. H. Canaway's novel, *Sammy Going South*, was published in 1961, and praised by some reviewers as 'a little masterpiece'.[33] It tells of a ten-year-old English boy, Sammy Hartland, whose parents are killed in the 1956 bombing of Port Said. Knowing only that he has an aunt in Durban, which is somewhere south, Sammy sets out to walk the length of Africa. En route his path crosses those of various individuals who help or hinder him: a Syrian trader, who is blinded in an accident and dies of snakebite; an American tourist, Winnie van Imhoff; an Italian journalist, Tebaldo Predappio; and Abu Lubaba, a Sudanese pilgrim. Lost in the Ugandan bush, he meets an eccentric old ivory-poacher, Cocky Wainwright, and spends some time in his camp before Wainwright's partner, Lem, flies him to South Africa. Sammy completes his journey by train; evading the attentions of a bounty-hunter (his disappearance is headline news, and rewards are being offered), he arrives safely at his aunt's hotel.

There is about *Sammy Going South* a calm, almost casual, sense of horror which prevents it slipping into mere Boys' Own adventure. Surveying Canaway's novels as a whole (he wrote more than a dozen, although *Sammy* remains the best known), Isabel Quigley observed that 'in each case the hero has to face, not just physical dangers . . . but the dangers inherent in himself, in his own outlook, spirit and limitations. . . . Even when Canaway writes about children, an uncosy sense of adult evil lies about them, and at his quietest there is a sense of violence . . . violence of feeling, reaction and spirit. His characters are not likeable, on the whole, and this includes his child characters.'[34] Sammy is presented with matter-of-fact acceptance of his callousness and occasional cruelty, a convincing portrayal that rejects both censure and sentimentality.

Understated as it is, this darker side of the story may have escaped Balcon's notice. Discussing the project, Mackendrick realised Balcon envisaged simply 'a marvellous adventure story with these terrific locations', in which courage would triumph heartwarmingly over adversity. Mackendrick, however, was immediately taken by the story's psychological potential, seeing in it 'the inward odyssey of a deeply disturbed child, who destroys everybody he comes up against. It's that same theme that I'm often accused of favouring, the destructive power of innocence.' The film, he felt, could be made to work on more than one level: as a picaresque adventure to satisfy Balcon (and with luck the box-office), but also exploring the subtler undertones for those that cared to see them.

Mackendrick wasn't Balcon's first choice as director. Originally, aiming as ever to promote new talent, he had offered the assignment to Freddie Francis, a fine cinematographer just starting out as a director. Along with the scriptwriter, Denis Cannan, Francis was sent on a location-hunting trip to East Africa. But Seven Arts, the Hollywood outfit with whom Bryanston had set up a co-production deal, objected to an inexperienced director handling a major production, and Balcon brought in Mackendrick instead. Cannan thought it 'odd that Mick didn't offer it to Sandy in the first place, given that he'd made *Mandy*. But they had a rather abrasive relationship, those two. Once, when Sandy was thumping the table about a matter of principle, I remember Mick Balcon saying, "Sandy, you may rest assured that we will spare neither time nor – time to give you what you want!" '

The film's credited producer – executive producer under Balcon, in effect – was Hal Mason, former head of production at Ealing. Cannan recalls a meeting with Mason, Mackendrick and Balcon, 'when Hal suddenly threw down his script, and said he thought the whole thing was a mistake, and if he were in charge he'd take his money out and not put a penny behind it. And then he walked out of the room. And Mick said, "I apologise for that. Now let's see, where were we?" Struck me as rather odd, as this was the man who was his executive producer.'

Cannan himself, a distinguished playwright, had little previous experience of screenwriting. 'I've always been disastrous writing for the movies – I've never understood why they have to go through this awful rewriting process, whereas most of the greatest plays have been written straight off by one person in less than five weeks. But Sandy was lovely to work with on a story, because he would instantly think visually. As soon as you started discussing a scene, his finger would be itching, he'd have it all down: he'd get the tower here, and Mahmoud in the foreground, and the boy there, all drawn out, fast and beautifully. Which is after all as it should be, because what's a director's job but to turn the word into a visual image?'

Mackendrick found Cannan equally congenial to work with. 'The first draft that Denis had written was missing that dimension that interested me – the character evolution of the disturbed child. But when I started to talk about it he responded instantly, and so the second draft that I worked on with him was full of studies of the neurotic and psychotic behaviour of an abused child. That was something we didn't even discuss with Mick, because he wouldn't have had the faintest idea what we were on about – he'd have felt really uncomfortable about it. So the curing of the child's dangerous neurosis should have run parallel to the adventure story – and in the end it was that dimension you substantially lost, although some of it's still there.'

In its plot, the film of *Sammy Going South* deviates very little from Canaway's novel. A few incidents, such as Sammy's encounter with the bounty-hunter, are dropped, but the rest occur in the same order, and carry much the same weight, as in the book. Of the novel's main characters, none undergoes substantial alteration. The Italian journalist, Predappio, becomes Dracondopoulos, a Greek tourist guide. Winnie van Imhoff is rechristened Gloria, and acquires some travelling companions. Aunt Jane's role is diminished. She figures fairly prominently in the book, taking active steps to find Sammy; it's she, rather than van Imhoff, who commissions Predappio to trace the boy. In the film she appears only once, briefly, before the final reunion.

In counterbalance, the role of Cocky Wainwright is considerably expanded – partly, of course, to accommodate the film's only major star. But the change in emphasis also fits Mackendrick's intentions. Aunt Jane's activities are peripheral; but Sammy's stay in the bush camp, his relationship with the old man, are central to the healing process, and need more scope than the two dozen pages allotted them in the novel. Cocky, to fit the casting of Edward G. Robinson, becomes American and – at Cannan's insistence – a diamond-smuggler instead of an ivory-poacher. 'I said, you can't possibly make a sympathetic character of an ivory-poacher, we'll have to change it. And just as well I did, otherwise I'm not sure you could even show it now.'

Most of the action of the film takes place outdoors, and Balcon intended to shoot all exteriors on location in Africa. In an interview with *Sight and Sound* he totted up the effect of this decision on his budget: £20,000 on air fares, cast and crew entitled to two and a half times the UK rate of pay.[35] (Mackendrick received a fee of £17,500.) Logistical problems were compounded by politics. East African locations could be readily arranged; Egypt was another matter. Not only was the Suez crisis a taboo subject, but no crew working for a Jewish producer would ever be allowed in. And while desert was desert, and almost anywhere could look like Port Said (in the end, Mombasa did), the great statue of Memnon at Luxor, where Mrs van Imhoff finds the exhausted Sammy, would be difficult to fake convincingly.

Mackendrick came up with an ingenious solution. 'I suggested to Hal Mason that they send me off as an independent, to make a fake documentary about Monuments of Egypt. So I would go to Luxor and shoot material that we could incorporate in the film.' Mason agreed, and called in a documentary film-maker, John Tunstall, who had good contacts with the Egyptian government. In February 1962 Mackendrick flew out with a small crew, plus Tunstall and his wife. 'And it worked a treat, because – this was all very wicked – we chose to go in Ramadan, when everything closes down in Egypt. We were supposed to be met by an official from the Ministry of Information, but by purest chance he was late, or didn't show up. We made no great effort to search for him, but flew on to Luxor and got on with it. We dressed Tunstall's wife up as Mrs van Imhoff, and we found a little Arab boy and put Sammy's costume on him, and by the time the official turned up, we'd shot all the stuff that I needed.

'So we continued shooting for a little while, and then I sloped off, taking with me these huge cans of 35mm Technicolor film. I didn't go back through Cairo, I flew on to Kenya, where the customs would be easier to get through. And all I needed was to pay a big fat bribe to take out of the country these huge cans I was claiming as home movies.' The association with Tunstall would later lead to a High Court action, affording the British press great sport. But for the time being the subterfuge went exactly as planned, and Mackendrick continued on to join Hal Mason on location.

This, as it turned out, was about the last thing that did go according to plan. Any large-scale location shoot, as Mason observed, 'can be relied upon to provide all kinds of unknown factors to knock the schedule sideways',[36] but *Sammy* seems to be have been exceptionally plagued. Two crew members were bitten by snakes; the unit doctor was injured in a car crash; vehicles bogged down in inaccessible places; Mackendrick suffered a recurrence of his back complaint; and a white hunter, much to Mackendrick's amusement, fell out of a tree and broke a leg.

Matters were also slowed by Mackendrick's passion for detail. At one point, dissatisfied with costumes provided for the African extras, he took Mason on a tour of the nearby streets. 'Whenever he saw an African dressed in the authentic kind of dirty old clothes he wanted . . . he got an interpreter to stop [him]. The proposition was simple: the African would give Mackendrick the clothes he was wearing. . . . Mackendrick would . . . buy him a complete new set of replacements – plus ten shillings for his trouble.'[37] For a brief longshot in which a boatload of passengers disembark, watched by 200 Africans, he 'spent half an hour giving [each passenger] a story to act out as they disembarked. He told them the reasons they were on the boat and gave them business to do on the quayside. If he'd had time he'd have done the same for the 200 Africans.'[38]

But all this was relatively minor stuff. On 18 June, on location in the Tanganyikan bush, real disaster struck: the 68-year-old Edward G. Robinson suffered a heart attack. He was flown to Nairobi, and a few days later to London. The insurers proposed to abandon the film, or to reshoot the footage with another actor, but Jane Robinson, fearing that either move might kill her husband, dissuaded them. Robinson's doctors, though, insisted his remaining scenes be shot in England.

Meanwhile, Mackendrick and his team continued filming as best they could. 'We found we had a props man who was exactly the same build as Eddie, so we could shoot long shots, or over-shoulder shots – that is, on the back of his head and playing on to the boy. And we continued to shoot with the little boy; I gave the cues and read Eddie's part to Fergus McClelland, who played back to them. Later, when we got back to Britain, we were in the other situation: because of the boy having to go to school we didn't have much time with him. So I on my knees played the boy's role to Eddie. When the film came out, I rejoiced in a review by one of the critics who said that the only interesting thing about it was the sensitive interplay between the little boy and the old man.'[39]

For all the ingenuity of these devices, Mackendrick believes the uncertainty affected the remaining location work. 'Everyone's morale, and mine unfortunately to some degree with it, dropped tremendously, and it was very difficult to keep up enthusiasm and stamina. So there are many scenes that I think are poor work from my own point of view, because of the awful depression of having to work not knowing if the film was going to be finished.'

Eventually, Mackendrick and his unit were summoned home. Robinson's heart attack had caused additional costs, and the remaining 'African' exteriors were to be shot in England. The scenes with Zia Mohyeddin as the Syrian were filmed partly on the studio floor, partly in gravel pits near Staines, with painted hardboard mountains for a backdrop. 'The problems of trying to fake the desert,' Mackendrick recalls, 'were so horrendous that I didn't really get the intense quality I wanted.'

Even more damaging to the film as Mackendrick conceived it were the cuts he was asked to make. Not having let Balcon in on his thinking, he could hardly now explain why certain seemingly dispensable episodes were crucial to the underlying thematic development. (It could also be that Balcon, a less naive man than he often appeared, was taking the opportunity to prune material whose implications he found distasteful.) The discrepancy between their views showed most acutely in their attitude to the opening scenes. To Balcon, the simple linear progress of Sammy's journey was what mattered, and the sooner he could be started on it the better. For Mackendrick, it was vital to establish the severe mental injury inflicted on the boy, to justify the long arduous trek of the healing process.

Three scenes in particular, all dropped from the opening section, might have done much to counter the deficiencies from which the film suffers. The behaviour of Mahmoud, Sammy's Egyptian friend who turns viciously on a boy still shattered by the sight of his mother's corpse, sets a disquieting note of xenophobia which is never wholly dispelled. The missing factor here is Mahmoud's father Hassan, concierge of the building where Sammy lives, and fatally injured in the bombing. In the shooting script, Mahmoud has just seen his father dying from a British bomb, and takes out his grief – understandably, at least – on the nearest Britisher to hand.

Immediately after Mahmoud's attack, Sammy (again, in the script) takes shelter in the office where his father worked, now deserted and wrecked, with BRITISH GO HOME scrawled on the wall and dirt smeared on the Queen's portrait. Some reviewers found the film's premise implausible, since there would surely be friends or neighbours to take the boy in, but this scene would have established that he believes himself abandoned by his entire nation.

The third of the missing scenes was perhaps the film's most serious loss. In the novel, Sammy finds himself on the coast somewhere near Suez. The shore is alive with crabs. Sammy devises a game; in Canaway's words: 'He was a bomber, and the crabs . . . were people. He bombed them with stones, littering the beach with cracked shells oozing yellow body substance amongst aimlessly twitching legs and claws. He made roaring sounds, and ran from time to time with his arms out . . . and all the while his long shadow stretched over the little battlefield towards the sea.'[40]

As Mackendrick envisaged it, this would have been 'very ugly, indeed unbearable. Without it the film became slow . . . and certain things are left unclear.'[41] In the script, having cornered a crab against a rock, Sammy stands over it and smashes it with a stone, shouting, 'I'm God! That's what God did to—' and bursts into angry tears. Mackendrick saw it as 'the key scene, which shows you what a little killer-monster he's become. You can gather what I felt when that went.'

The loss of these scenes, and the disaffected atmosphere following Robinson's heart attack, may explain why much of *Sammy* feels curiously impersonal, lacking that sense of an acute, probing intelligence that generally marks Mackendrick's work. It may also be that a linear, episodic narrative was never ideal for Mackendrick, whose films work best within a cohesive social unit – a house, an island, a boat – where characters can act and react on each other, tightening the interplays of relationships. Though the film takes place on a far broader stage than his previous movies – widescreen, two-hour duration and a whole continent for backdrop – the breadth leads to diffusion rather than to a richer, more comprehensive vision.

Even so, the opening scenes of *Sammy* exert as powerful an impact as anything in Mackendrick's output, suffused as they are with the emotional intensity that the plight of an isolated child always arouses in him. The first image – captioned 'Port Said, November 1956' – is of a loudspeaker emitting frenzied Arabic. No subtitles, no translation, no word of explanation; we find ourselves plunged, as Sammy soon will be, into an incomprehensible, angry and dangerous environment.

By way of contrast, Sammy is introduced within a deceptively safe and enclosed world. Balconies, corridors and doorways shut off sections of the screen, defining the contained, essentially domestic space from which he will be violently exiled, and which he spends the rest of the film trying to regain. For this world holds within it the symbols of its own imminent annihilation, and Sammy is playing with them – a helicopter-toy whose rotor swoops down like the bombers about to attack the town, and the compass-whistle which will lead him out into the wilderness.

As if sharing the child's sheltered life, Mackendrick keeps his camera tracking near ground level, held close in on Sammy. Adults are perceived (as in a Tom and Jerry cartoon) as off-screen voices or from the knees down, irrelevant intrusions into his self-sufficient territory. Only once do we see his mother's face, in a brief close-up – and from the subjective angle that, for Mackendrick, signals key emotional significance – as she says, 'We'll see.' His parents' conversation, like the announcer on the radio (both giving us vital expository information), comes to Sammy as a soothing background drone, reassuring but irrelevant. In this brief scene Mackendrick establishes the warm, protective relationship surrounding the boy, making the loss of it all the more desolating.

From this pre-cataclysm perspective, the convoys rumbling through the streets are exciting rather than threatening, just bigger toys, a spectacle laid on for Sammy's amusement. Similarly, the maze of alleyways into which he descends serves as an extension of the apartment, an enclosed territory through which he moves with practised ease until, reaching the harbour, he emerges for the first time into an open, undefended space which – as for Mandy and for Sidney Stratton – spells unpredictability and danger.

And at this point Mackendrick unleashes the full expanse of the Cinema-Scope screen, emphasising the suddenly redefined space around Sammy – the broad quayside under a clear blue sky from which the warplanes come scything down in their lethal beauty. It almost seems as if the planes are conjured up by Sammy himself; as he puts the whistle to his lips, their scream bursts on the soundtrack in horrifying response. At the heart of Sammy's trauma, it's hinted, lies the irrational guilt of believing – since he left the flat against his mother's prohibition – that he himself somehow caused his parents' death. (Hence, perhaps, his slaughter of the crabs, with the cry of 'I'm God!')

By the time Sammy picks himself up and scurries terrified for home, his parents are dying, and his childhood Eden lies in ruins. He doesn't know it yet, of course, and nor do we, but already the world has changed. The familiar alleys have become alien terrain, choked with rubble and barred by gates; the behaviour of soldiers is no longer exciting, but obscure and threatening. This is the landscape of nightmare, where familiar people turn hostile faces to us and known structures shift and disintegrate. Sammy's home, when he reaches it, has also been sucked into this entropic world, its solid walls a mass of dust and rubble, to which officials bar him access.

Panic-stricken, he yells for his mother and – as in those ghost stories (*The Monkey's Paw*, for example) where you get *exactly* what you ask, in the most horrible way – his mother comes to him: dead, shrouded in a blanket, only one dangling blood-red slipper revealing her identity. As her body is brought down, Mackendrick moves in on Sammy's screaming face in ever-tighter framings, ending on a close-up of his eyes widening at the instant of realisation. (In *The Birds*, made that same year, Hitchcock too uses this camera movement to convey shock, approaching a corpse's gouged eye-sockets by jerks rather than with a smooth track or zoom. But while Hitchcock focuses our attention on the shocking object, Mackendrick is concerned with the person undergoing the shock.) As he registers his mother's death, Sammy lapses into a numbed silence more eloquent than any scream. The body is loaded on a truck, and as the tailboard is raised, shutting off his face from our view (and shutting him off from his mother for ever), its hinges emit an anguished shriek of protest.

There follows Mahmoud's attack, which takes place in one of those same narrow alleys where Sammy, ten minutes earlier, felt so much at home. Abandoned by his parents, betrayed by his friends, the very streets turned enemy territory, he has had the structure of his known universe knocked from under him even more decisively than it was for Waggett or Calvin Marshall. Huddled that night on the stairs outside his shattered home, barbed wire forbidding him entry, he weeps hopelessly, taking from his pocket small familiar objects to comfort himself. One of them, the compass, prompts a solution to his predicament. As he turns it, the needle points south, and Tristram Cary's score picks up the title theme, evoking infinite warm distances.

The wilderness into which Sammy is thrust is as much that of his mind as of the African continent. 'The terrain,' as Jim Kitses put it, describing Anthony Mann's Westerns of the fifties, 'is so coloured by the action that it finally seems an inner landscape, the unnatural world of a disturbed mind.'[42] Sammy's odyssey becomes a trek through his own seared psyche, as he gradually comes to terms with the past – from the harshness of the Egyptian desert, through the gentler riverscape of the Nile, to the generous abundance of the East African bush where the healing process is accomplished.

This process is paralleled, in terms of costume, by Sammy's progressive assimilation to the environments through which he passes. Setting out into the desert, an outlandish figure in his European garb, he soon adopts, at the Syrian's prompting, the *galabieh* (Arab headdress) suited to the area, and merges with his surroundings effectively enough to pass for Egyptian. Twice – by van Imhoff and again by Dracondopoulos – he's restored to 'correct' European dress, and each time reverts, via improvisation and general scruffiness, to local colouring. By the time he reaches Durban, the instinct has reversed itself. Far from merging back into civilisation, his first act on arriving at his aunt's hotel is to regain the 'wild' attire which now feels natural, and stand leopardskin-clad in an urban sitting-room, chattering of diamond-smuggling.

In leaving us with this image of Sammy, Mackendrick suggests that even when 'cooped up in Durban with school and a little blazer with a crest on the pocket' (as Cocky predicts), something of this liberating wildness will remain with him. The contrast between formal interiors and dangerous exterior freedom (which also confronted Mandy) underlies the film, as in the abrupt cut from Sammy slumped, delirious and exhausted, at the foot of Memnon's statue to the upholstered comforts of the Luxor hotel. Sammy's initial view of this, the first room he's entered since his home was destroyed, is one of smothering enclosure: a great circular tent of blue gauze, swagged down from the ceiling as if in a harem – a perfect metaphor, at once enveloping and insubstantial, of Gloria van Imhoff's concern for him.

Outside, Sammy is free to find himself, to take his own risks. Even when shackled by the Syrian, he can still continue in his chosen direction; whereas those who confine and re-Europeanise him, in hotels or doctors' surgeries, try to divert him from his course. 'A compass not work in a car,' Dracondopoulos lies, when Sammy notices the jeep is heading east. The boy's wishes, his words imply, are irrelevant in an adult, European world. He miscalculates badly; they're out in the bush, in Sammy's territory, and having immobilised the vehicle the boy heads unerringly south, while the Greek stumbles in circles, hopelessly lost. Not until Sammy is accepted as a person on his own terms are the opposites reconciled, in Cocky's hut – a house of sorts, but one without doors.

The film can also be seen as Sammy's quest to replace the parents he lost, to recreate his family and his home. Almost all the action is framed between the demolition of two houses, and after each one Sammy lies in the ruins and cries himself to sleep. But in the interval between the two destructions, not only has the boy become more resilient, he has re-established his own identity within a new family, gaining the confidence to recognise Cocky's apparent rejection of him as a ruse. So the second loss is less grievous than the first, and its effect less lasting.

The key moment in this process comes when, waking in sudden panic in Cocky's truck to see unknown black faces around him, Sammy is soothed back to sleep by the Africans' song. The lullaby marks his readoption into the familial relationship that was ripped away from him by the bombs. By saving the life of his father-figure, he atones for the earlier 'killing' of his parents, even acquiring a child of his own (the bush-baby). In the dialogue with Cocky, his status within the community is confirmed: 'Can I stay here for ever?' 'You stay here. You stay here as long as you want to.' For the first time since his parents' death, Sammy is somewhere as of right.

En route to his surrogate family Sammy encounters, and escapes, various alternative parent-figures, whose offers of help mask selfish or mercenary motives: the Syrian, Gloria van Imhoff, Dracondopoulos. The least unsympathetic of them, van Imhoff, annexes him merely out of a self-indulgent weakness for hard-luck cases. 'Travelling with Gloria, it's like rolling a snowball,' grumbles her companion Bob. 'The party gets bigger all the time.' Far less silly and lachrymose, in Constance Cummings's warm portrayal, than her equivalent in the novel, she incurs nothing worse than disappointment.

The Syrian, though, suffers blinding and a slow, agonising death. Of all the victims of innocence in Mackendrick's films, none meets with a nastier fate – not Professor Marcus's gang, nor even the pirates in *High Wind*. Cannan and Mackendrick make a point of Sammy's complicity in the accident. In the novel, the Syrian spontaneously decides to bake bread, and gathers flat stones for his fire, one of which explodes in his face. But in the film the bread-baking is prompted by Sammy's petulant outburst – 'Rice! I hate rice! It's always rice!' – and it's he who collects the fatal stones. Nor does the Syrian die of snakebite, as in the original, but of his wounds – killed, directly if unwittingly, through the boy's doing.

To Sammy, this death compounds that of his parents, deepening the trauma of undischarged guilt – as is suggested by the hovering vultures that, as he trudges away from the Syrian's body, swoop avidly down like the warplanes over Port Said. (Later, just before meeting Cocky, he flinches at the sight of vultures feasting on a dead elephant.) Already, he has been publicly branded guilty, shackled like a felon by the blinded Syrian: 'Now you don't leave me, and I don't leave you. . . . Like a policeman taking a thief to prison.' An apt simile, since after the man's death Sammy makes off with his wallet and his donkeys.

Blindness, traditionally, bestows clairvoyance. The Syrian's words come true; even after death, he does indeed not leave Sammy, but haunts him in the guise of the wallet. Stuffed with grimy notes and pictures of women, it becomes one of those mythic objects acquired by dubious means which, like the Niebelungs' Ring, both aid and imperil their new owner. Impervious to Gloria's attempts at New World sanitisation ('We'll change that dirty money for new notes . . . all put into a nice, new, clean wallet'), it arouses Bob's suspicions, but also pays for the river journey. Only within the healing circle of his new family, and encouraged by Cocky's confession of complicity in his wife's death, can Sammy shed his incubus. 'He put the wrong sort of stone in the fire. It exploded and blew out his eyes. Then I went off with the donkeys – and I took his money. . . . It's funny – I thought I'd forgotten all about that. . . . But I hadn't. It was in my head all the time.' (Here as elsewhere, Cannan's script explains rather too much.)

Dracondopoulos appears as a comic counterpart to the Syrian, buffoonish where the other was sinister. Both see Sammy as a potential source of profit, and are given to laying claim to spurious expertise – the Syrian's, 'I know all about it,' echoed by the Greek's, 'Come, I know all about you.' But unlike the pedlar, who even when blinded retains an instinctive dexterity, Dracondopoulos (like Pusey in *The Maggie*) is ludicrously unadapted to his environment – bumping into people, banging his head on low roofs, struggling to co-ordinate maps, clothes and baggage, and constantly gulping pills against stomach ailments: 'Is a *dirty* country. I'm not well myself.' Nor does he establish any comparable hold over Sammy's conscience. Having stranded the wretched man in the bush and left him possibly to die, the boy shows no trace of remorse, and dismisses him from his mind.

This callousness on Sammy's part may be in character, but it's disturbing that the film seems to invite us to share his attitude. Dracondopoulos's outburst in the District Commissioner's office leaves something of the same queasy aftertaste as Shylock's 'My daughter! O my ducats! O my daughter!' – neither laughter nor sympathy seems a valid response. 'I have no client. She went back to America. I can collect $300 from the bank . . . $100 less than what I spent. . . . I come all the way from Luxor. I get dysentery. I nearly die for this—' ending in a torrent of furious Greek epithets as he storms out of the room. The indignity of this exit, staged away from camera, reduces him to a stock figure – incomprehensible foreigner, raving off into distance – and leaves the last word with the DC, pipe-smoking in the foreground: 'Emotional chaps, these, er – whatever he is.' True, the smugly incurious Englishman is also being mocked; but not for the last time, *Sammy Going South* is marred by an unpalatable hint of racial condescension.

Until Sammy meets Cocky Wainwright, only one person on his journey shows him disinterested kindness, and is treated by the film with corresponding respect. This is the Sudanese *haji*, Abu Lubaba (played with immense dignity by Orlando Martins, and the sole African character, in this picture set wholly in Africa, to be granted anything like a substantial role). To him, Sammy responds with instinctive trust, handing over the talismanic wallet and preferring his company, with the steerage passengers on the lighter, to that of the whites on the steamer. Mackendrick points up the contrast, cutting from the ragged boy drinking in the spectacle of the river-life with absorbed curiosity, to well-dressed whites getting it all at one remove through their cameras.

With the adaptability of the young, Sammy participates in the life around him – bowing and muttering with the pilgrims in their prayers, letting his head be searched for lice. But though this is an organic community, it's not one within which he can find lasting shelter; it remains exterior to him, an intriguing but transient game. Promised the chance of finding Aunt Jane, he's off without a moment's thought and has to be reminded to toss an offhand 'Thanks' to Abu Lubaba – a father-figure rejected as decisively, if not as drastically, as Dracondopoulos or the Syrian. In this case, though, the incompatibility is perhaps as much religious as racial. Salvation in Mackendrick's films never comes from external forces, whether religion, law or social authorities.

The community into which Sammy does eventually fit is one which, like that of Todday, derives its vitality from lawbreaking, the law being patently wrong-headed. 'Now you and I,' Cocky explains, 'believe that the fruits of the earth should be free for all men, don't we? Well, there's some, er, officials take a different view.' But if diamond-smuggling is its raison d'être and source of income, the activity which defines the community seems to be shooting, and Sammy, like any youngster in a Western, is initiated into manhood with a gun, a successful killing his ultimate rite of passage. ('It was her or you,' says Cocky, in another echo from the Old West.) Tarzan-like in his leopard-skin trophy, the young champion is ready to usurp the ageing monarch. It's the realisation that he's getting too old to fire the elephant gun, as much as the desire to decoy the police from Sammy's escape, that prompts Cocky to give himself up.

If the equation of gunplay with maturity seems incongruous in a Mackendrick movie, so too does the largely unquestioning attitude to racial politics. In some ways, *Sammy* is closer to the Ealing mainstream than any of the films Mackendrick made there – not the comedy mainstream, but that of Harry Watt's liberal-paternalist African sagas *Where No Vultures Fly* and *West of Zanzibar*, in which benevolent whites safeguard the best interests of noble, childlike Africans. Pre-Suez, such a nostalgic dispensation might just about pass muster; six years after Suez, in a movie which takes that post-imperialist blunder as its starting-point, one would expect a similar situation to be treated, at the least, with a touch of irony. But Cocky Wainwright, for all his genial outlawry, calls the shots in much the old Sanders-of-the-River style, and by much the same right – that of occupation. 'This is the land that God forgot, and only old Cocky remembered.' He and a few hundred Africans who happened to be living there, most likely.

The lack of irony, here as elsewhere in the film, corresponds in visual terms to the scarcity (except in the opening scenes) of those fluid, complex compositions characteristic of Mackendrick's previous work. Visually as well as dramatically, *Sammy* operates at a relatively low level of density – partly, perhaps, because it was his first film in CinemaScope, a ratio with which he never felt happy. 'I hated widescreen. The basic anamorphic lens used in those days was an adaptation of something like a 50mm, which flattens the image – so you can't get any depth, any visual perspective.'

Not that the film betrays any sense of inexperience in handling the wider span. Indeed, Basil Wright credited Mackendrick with 'a great affinity for the wide screen. His compositions for this often recalcitrant area are always right and often strikingly beautiful.'[43] In *Sammy*, as always, Mackendrick creates images of fluent and unobtrusive elegance; his cinematographer was Erwin Hillier, a veteran craftsman with extensive experience both of widescreen and of filming in Africa. But though the film remains consistently good to look at, it does on occasion (as during the Nile sequence) veer dangerously towards the blandness of travelogue. A similar emollience afflicts Tristram Cary's music. After the spiky, inventive wit of his score for *The Ladykillers*, his sweeping strings and wordless female voices seem conventional, and even at times sentimental.

All these problems of tone are compounded by the physical appearance of

Sammy himself. The performance Mackendrick drew from Fergus McClelland is impressive in many ways – alert, tenacious, resolutely uningratiating, and conveying with exceptional subtlety the boy's growing independence of spirit. But never for one moment does he look like a half-starved, disease-ridden waif.

The original casting wasn't at fault. At the time Mackendrick picked McClelland for the role, he was 'a lean, hard little boy, tough as old nails, a really strong character. He had the hunted look of an abused child, which in some ways he was. He came from a disturbed home; his parents were getting divorced, and there were problems. So he was perfect casting. But when he went out to Africa, he started having the time of his life. The unit adored him, and to my dismay started to feed him – he put on weight, and there was no way I could stop it. So instead of this hunted, abused child who's supposed to be starving and neurotic, you had a sturdy, stocky, well-fed little character. A good actor – but the physique betrayed itself.'

The quality of McClelland's performance can be judged from the opening scenes where, undistracted by outward incongruity – since at this stage a well-nourished Sammy is apposite enough – we receive the full shock of the boy's anguish. But thereafter, as the trek progresses and Sammy remains outwardly unchanged, credibility ebbs away. We get the grim determination, but little of the hardship, the deprivation and suffering. It's this shortfall in visual credence at the centre of the film, as much as any weakness in the script, that diminishes its power, robbing it of the impact that could have placed it alongside *Los Olvidados* or *Les Jeux interdits*. A film that should unnerve and disquiet ends up, for the most part, undemandingly affirmative.

Sporadically, there are glimpses of the mood of uncompromising 'strangeness and cruelty' Mackendrick had wanted. One such unsettling moment occurs when the Syrian, gazing thoughtfully at Sammy by their camp-fire, leans forward and, in a brief pederastic impulse, holds an end of the headdress up across the boy's face like a yashmak. Or after the blinding, when the trader, moaning horribly, gropes for liquor, pours it over the smashed ruin of his eyes, screams in agony and passes out. And later, alone in the bush at nightfall and scared by the noises around him, Sammy wedges himself high in a tree and responds to the squawks and howls by shouting a ribald rhyme at the top of his lungs – one small animal giving voice among many, as Mackendrick pulls back to a startlingly lovely and desolate long-shot. But such moments are too few and separate to forge connections across the expanses of less intensely charged narrative.

The emotional focus of the film lies in the relationship between Sammy and Cocky Wainwright – a relationship which Mackendrick's most acute and sympathetic critic, Charles Barr, describes as 'perhaps the high point of all his work',[44] climax of the varied and complex use of child-figures in

Mackendrick's films. For once, it seems difficult to go along with Barr's assessment. Purely on the level of narrative development, admittedly, the interplay between the two comes off well. Robinson, who enjoyed working with Mackendrick ('A fine director, extremely intelligent. Just a bit of temperament now and then,'[45] he remarked after the film was finished), gives a likeable and relaxed performance, laconic enough to avoid senti-mentality. The growing trust between him and the boy is marked by subtle details of word and gesture: Cocky's reaction, a half-sketched embrace, after the leopard-shooting incident, and Sammy's adoption not only of the old man's idiom ('Jumping Jehosaphat, don't you think I've got eyes in my head?') but – a nicely underplayed touch of mimicry by McClelland – a hint of his walk.

Their rapport is all the more convincing for being based on mutual need, Cocky being in search of a son as Sammy is of a father. Like Searle in *Mandy*, Cocky can be seen as a man suffering from emotional unfulfilment: still blaming himself for his wife's death, unable since then to sustain an adult relationship, and subsisting on glorified memories. 'Yeah, you sailed round the Horn,' sneers Lem, Thersitean jester at Cocky's court, 'on a stinking Greek ship full of bird crap.' This debunking leaves Sammy unmoved, since he too appreciates the joys of fantasy. 'We had lots of servants – they all wore baggy trousers made of silk,' he tells Dracondopoulos. 'One of them was a eunuch. . . . Well, he was a sort of ex-eunuch.'

But compared to other key Mackendrick child/adult relationships – between Mandy and her family, Dougie and Calvin Marshall, Emily and Chavez – that between Sammy and Cocky is uncomplex, lacking in tension and ambiguity. In other films the adults are shaken and radically altered, sometimes fatally, by their collision with the devastating force of innocence. Cocky is merely confirmed in his outlook, finding in Sammy a young echo of himself whom he can mould and adopt. True, he gets himself arrested to let Sammy escape, but deliberately, as part of his own plans. At no point are his assumptions undermined, or even called into question.

Nor are the values he represents, though running counter to the law, much different from those of the world he rejects. In its racial hierarchy and reliance on weaponry, as in its political structure, Cocky's 'tribal' com-munity reproduces, in a more easy-going idiom, the forms of conventional society. Essentially, he runs a benign dictatorship. When Lem questions his decision to let Sammy stay, on the grounds (wholly justified, as it transpires) that it endangers their joint enterprise, Cocky never gives his partner's view a moment's consideration, but simply offers to buy him out. And, having done so, takes the opportunity to humiliate him by boasting of the fortune he (Cocky) has stashed away in a private bank account. Robinson carries off the scene with truculent charm, but as a piece of sheer capitalist bullying it beats anything Calvin Marshall ever attempted.

This, in the end, is where *Sammy Going South* most crucially fails: the central opposition between 'civilisation' and 'wildness', whose polarity should sustain the film, is inadequately defined. Cocky's community, for all its therapeutic effect, is never sufficiently 'other' – merely a freewheeling replica of the society from which Sammy was ejected, and to which he finally returns. So his reintegration into adult, urban life merely feels like a comfortable happy ending, with little sense of poignancy or loss – unlike the corresponding scene in *High Wind in Jamaica*. *Sammy*, in many ways, sketches in themes that Mackendrick's next film, despite its mutilated state, more satisfyingly develops.

Much to Balcon's gratification, *Sammy Going South* was chosen for the Royal Film Performance of 1963. This in itself was enough to guarantee it a rough ride from British critics. Philip Oakes, in the *Sunday Telegraph*, found it 'long, decent and dull – the prime attributes . . . of any Royal Performance film',[46] and the *Observer* dismissed it as 'a right nothing of a picture', fit for 'the annual Royal Film Horseshow'.[47] *The Times*, even more damningly, described it as 'a nice little film', adding that 'all [Mackendrick's] films, with the exception of his Hollywood adventure, have remained inescapably nice little films; accomplished, attractive, impersonal'.[48]

Other reviewers, more sympathetic – or less condescending – expressed disappointment: after a six-year interval, something more challenging was to be expected from Mackendrick, a further advance on the acrid brilliance of *Sweet Smell of Success*. Instead, *Sammy* looked like a retrograde step, 'a gross misuse of [Mackendrick's] sharp talents',[49] as Patrick Gibbs put it in the *Daily Telegraph*. Robinson's performance, for several critics, was the only good thing in the film. Over McClelland, opinions diverged. 'As vivid and unaffected a child actor as the screen has brought us,' *The Times* enthused. Others, like John Coleman in the *New Statesman*, found him dull, '[going] through the motions plausibly but without spark'.[50]

Reviews in the specialist film journals were less disparaging. '*Sammy* is often a serious film posing as a simple one,' wrote John Cutts in *Films and Filming*, praising Mackendrick's rejection of 'synthetic sentimentality'. 'Wee Sammy is no more than a little brute who uses everyone who crosses his path . . . not a romanticised figure, all cute tricks and grave wisdom, but a sharp little cookie who deserves our respect. . . . Whilst not wholly pleasing, *Sammy* bears enough evidence that Mackendrick is still the best of British directors.'[51]

Similarly, Ian Cameron in *Movie*, while acknowledging that *Sammy* fell short of Mackendrick's finest work, thought it 'a very honourable film', commending 'his refusal to pretend that Sammy is unusually lovable'. The final reunion at the hotel 'invites disaster, but Mackendrick's grip of his subject . . . makes it succeed admirably. The meeting is handled with an almost Hawksian economy of statement. . . . As a reminder of the standards which British cinema could set itself in presenting a story that is not particularly unusual, [*Sammy*] is invaluable.'[52]

Such comments could scarcely save the film from failure at the box-office. It did no better in the USA, where it was cut to 88 minutes and withheld from release for nearly two years, finally appearing under the unprepossessing title *A Boy Ten Feet Tall*. Such drastic pruning, though, may have improved the shape and pacing of the story, since in this version the film gained a rare rave review – in *Time* magazine, whose reviewer derived from it 'more enchantment per reel than most movies of twice its ambition'.[53]

The vicissitudes of the making of *Sammy* were to have long-term consequences – some trivial, others more serious. In November 1965, in the High Court of Justice, there opened the case of Tunstall v Michael Balcon Productions Ltd. John Tunstall, the freelance film-maker called in to help with Mackendrick's Egyptian subterfuge, sued Balcon for breach of contract, claiming he had been forced to incur an additional £5,600 of expenses. Part of this sum, according to Tunstall's QC, had been needed to pacify an irate sheikh after Mackendrick had insisted on photographing Arab women, and a further part to pay off customs officials when Mackendrick was caught trying to smuggle film stock. Such stories were seized on with glee by the press. 'Film men clashed with Sheikh over women,' chortled the *Daily Express*.[54]

Mackendrick, suffering from a heavy cold, spent two days in the witness box giving evidence. The case lasted 14 days, after which the judge, Mr Justice Mocatta, gave judgement in favour of Balcon, awarding costs against the plaintiff. To support his case, Tunstall had produced footage of the crew making repeated visits to the same location. Mackendrick, with the rest of the court, watched this film: 'And I thought, we only went there once – then I suddenly saw something and said, "Edge numbers!" and the judge, who was sitting beside me playing dumb, turned on me and said, "Keep quiet!" – because he'd seen it too. So when we checked the numbers along the edge of the film, there was the evidence that it had been re-edited. And that was the thing that destroyed Tunstall's case.'

By the time Balcon won his court case, he was no longer chairman of Bryanston Films, since Bryanston no longer existed. The consortium had folded earlier that year, a débâcle for which *Sammy Going South* was largely, if indirectly, responsible.

The liveliest pictures released under the Bryanston logo were those made by Woodfall Films, a company set up by Tony Richardson and John Osborne, and employing members of the Free Cinema movement, which evolved into the 'British New Wave'. Their first production was the film version of *Look Back in Anger*, a *succès d'estime* that failed at the box office and was hated by its backers, Warner Bros. Woodfall then concluded a deal with Bryanston, through whom they released their next four pictures: *The*

*Entertainer*, *Saturday Night and Sunday Morning*, *A Taste of Honey* and *The Loneliness of the Long-Distance Runner*. The first of these out-flopped its predecessor, but the others did well. *Saturday Night* cleared £½ million profit on a budget of £100,000.

*Tom Jones*, scripted by Osborne from Fielding's novel for Richardson to direct, was intended as Woodfall's 'holiday film', a break from sullen northern gloom. But as a costume drama, and the company's first venture into colour, it needed a larger budget – something in the order of £350,000, a blockbuster by Bryanston's standards. The project came up early in 1962, with shooting about to start on *Sammy*. Several members of the consortium (including Balcon, always uneasy with the political and sexual outspokenness of Woodfall's output) balked at committing themselves to two simultaneous major projections. Eventually it was agreed Bryanston should put up 70 per cent of an estimated £300,000.

Richardson, irked by these restrictions, was looking for the rest of the finance when United Artists offered to put up 100 per cent of his original budget. *Tom Jones* was made without Bryanston's involvement, and took between $30 and $40 million worldwide. In his autobiography Balcon ruefully noted, 'If I had had the courage to pawn everything I possessed and risk it on *Tom Jones* it would have been a wise decision. . . . No doubt *Tom Jones* is engraved on my heart.'[55]

The success of UA's investment alerted the other Hollywood companies who, sensing a bonanza, began flinging dollars at any promising British project. Bryanston, already hard hit by *Sammy*'s poor showing at the box-office, couldn't compete. In January 1965 it ceased production, and sold its assets (some 30 movies, *Sammy* included) to a television company, Associated Rediffusion. Balcon went off to spend an unhappy two years as chairman of the distribution network, British Lion, but by now the kind of modest, staunchly indigenous British cinema he had always stood for had almost ceased to exist.

Meanwhile, in the aftermath of *Tom Jones* a new style of British cinema – consciously (or self-consciously) international, fuelled by American money and the myth of Swinging London – took off into its sixties boom. By March 1966 the National Film Finance Corporation could report that 'London is fast becoming, if it is not already, the greatest film-making centre in the world',[56] with by far the greater part of this activity bankrolled from the USA. It couldn't last; and when the crash came a few years later, one of its casualties – ironically enough, given his inadvertent role in starting the whole trend – would be Mackendrick's own directorial career.

# 9 A High Wind in Jamaica

'Paganism, woman and the Ocean, these
three desires and these three great fears of
man, are mingled in this strange legend and
come to a tempestuous and terrible end.'[1]

A. S. Byatt, *Possession*

'It's too good a book to have been attempted
as a film, so it was bound to be second-rate.'

Alexander Mackendrick

There are few film-makers whose careers are not littered with might-have-beens, the unrealised projects to which they often devoted more time and trouble than to those that got made. It's tempting to speculate not only what such 'lost movies' as Welles's *Don Quixote* or Losey's *A la recherche du temps perdu* would have been like, but how differently the careers of those directors might have evolved had their abortive projects come to fruition. For his part, Mackendrick is inclined to discourage such speculation. 'It's sheer sentimentality. A high percentage of what you do is things that don't work, and they're best forgotten.' Which, from the film-maker's point of view, may well be true. But the unmade films can often cast a revealing light on a director's work as a whole, bringing out hidden facets, suggesting how themes and preoccupations might have been developed, transformed or diverted to unexpected ends.

While working with Denis Cannan on the script of *Sammy Going South*, Mackendrick mentioned an idea for a comedy called *The Man Who Wasn't There*. Like the Soviet satire *Lieutenant Kizhe*, it would centre on a non-existent person, invented as a joke, who starts to take on a disconcerting life of his own. Cannan was intrigued and, with *Sammy* finished, the two started to collaborate on a treatment.

The idea had originally come from Monja Danischewsky, producer on *Whisky Galore*. Mackendrick worked on it over several years: 'It went through endless drafts, and we never really got the story licked. It was a long way from Monja's original idea by the time we finished with it.' (According to Danischewsky's wife Brenda, 'Sandy over-complicated it and over-psychologised it, as usual.') In the version he developed with Cannan, the story concerns a young couple, childhood friends, whose relationship is close but platonic. The man, for whom Mackendrick mentally cast Jack Lemmon, is a ghost writer, helping celebrities with their memoirs.

'The two of them, as a joke, invent a mysterious explorer who's always away in some other part of the world. At which point a third person, a much more devious figure – Denis based him on Binkie Beaumont, the theatrical impresario – sees there's money to be made from this fictitious character. And the joke becomes an extended hoax, and then a serious swindle. A house is bought and furnished in this character's name and the girl poses as his wife. And before long, everybody claims to be an intimate friend of the celebrity who doesn't exist. The only person who's left out is the hero, who realises he's been displaced by this invention who's in fact himself as he'd like to be.

'So, in a moment of drink and obstreperousness, he makes a wild pass at his childhood friend. And they fall in love. Now the trick of the film is that the whole story is narrated, in voice-over, by the non-existent character – sort of *Sunset Boulevard* device. And at this point he gets very angry – "*My best friend, and my wife—!*" – and sets out to destroy them. He burns down the house and they're both accused of his murder. They confess to the hoax, but of course no one believes them.'

The film, it seems, would have worked a fresh twist on Mackendrick's perennial dichotomy – innocence and experience not antagonists but accomplices, creating between them something beyond their control, a Frankenstein monster of the imagination. Or perhaps the Beaumont-figure was to be utterly Mephistophelean, urging the naive young couple on until their harmless joke becomes the agent of their destruction. Either way, *The Man Who Wasn't There* sounds like a new departure, enriching Mackendrick's dark comedy with a swirling frisson of the supernatural.

The idea may have been too off-beat for its own good; nobody was prepared to back it, and Mackendrick found himself once again with no work in prospect. Fearing that his reputed indifference to money and time was harming his career, he decided to demonstrate publicly that he could shoot fast and stick to budget. 'I went to my agents, Peter Shaw and Christopher Mann, and said, "I want to direct for American television – a regular series episode." The standard pattern if you were doing one of these episodes was that you rehearsed and shot in five days. It's a 50-minute piece, so you've got to shoot ten minutes of screen time a day.'

The chosen assignment was an episode of *The Defenders*, Reginald Rose's prestigious CBS series about a father-and-son legal firm, starring E. G. Marshall and Robert Reed, which ran between 1961 and 1965. Apart from a few commercials, it remains Mackendrick's only television work, though not from any lack of enthusiasm. 'It gave me tremendous confidence. We did very rapid total rewrites the weekend before, then shot ten minutes a day and came in bang on schedule. Dumb thing as it was, it's journalism, so it goes with a gusto and an energy – and it proved to me that those people who said I can't shoot fast were full of crap.'

Around this time, Mackendrick worked on a project for Woodfall Films, collaborating with John Osborne on a potential follow-up to *Tom Jones*, an adaptation of Defoe's *Moll Flanders*. 'John and I were not very compatible, at least in one way. John could get more drama into a monologue than anybody else I knew. He wrote monologues, but not interaction between people. It's probably quite legitimate for his kind of theatre, but I'm not sure it's so good for movies.'

Perhaps for this reason, *Moll Flanders* got nowhere. But while talking to Oscar Lewenstein, who was on the board of Woodfall, Mackendrick mentioned his admiration for the comedian Tony Hancock, then appearing at the London Palladium. 'And Oscar said, "Do you think you could make a film for us with Hancock?" This was something I'd already thought about, so I said, "Yes – I'd like him to play Bérenger in *Rhinoceros*." '

Eugène Ionesco's play, his greatest international success, was staged in London in 1960 in a production by Orson Welles, with Laurence Olivier in the lead. A political allegory, it was inspired by memories of pre-war Romania, when one by one Ionesco's friends were joining the fascist Iron Guard. In a French provincial town, a rhinoceros is sighted charging down the main street; then another; then several. The hero, Bérenger, realises the inhabitants are changing into rhinos – and are eager to do so. Defiantly, he proclaims his faith in humanity, but even his best friend, Jean, and his girlfriend, Daisy, succumb to rhinoceritis. Bérenger is the only human left. Finally he capitulates, only to discover that he alone can't rhinocerise, even if he wants to.

Mackendrick believed Hancock would be perfect for Bérenger. 'He was *so* right. He had this hunted look of a person who *knew* that everybody was turning into a rhinoceros.' Working with the playwright Clive Exton, Mackendrick prepared a script which differed considerably from Ionesco's original. 'I wanted to make it, unlike the play, literally surrealist. The climactic scene is between Bérenger and Jean, set in Harrods' basement. Bérenger's been going there to shop, just lifting things off the shelves – and there he meets Jean, who's now a rhinoceros, and there's a shootout. He has to kill this rhinoceros who was his best friend, and then he sits down and weeps over the body. And it's a very moving scene, I promise you. But the ending's upbeat, in a way. He's back home, lying in bed listening to the rhinoceroses all around, and he hears running human feet. He gets up and yells, "Who's there?" Nothing. So he gets huge posters which he pastes up everywhere, like Luther: All Human Beings Assemble Trafalgar Square, Sunday. And that's the end of the film.'

In *The Theatre of the Absurd*, Martin Esslin characterises Ionesco's work as 'laced with a bitter, farcically tragic humour . . . a far harsher convention of the theatre than one based on mere pleasantness.'[2] It's a description that would fit Mackendrick's comedies, and the film of *Rhinoceros* might well have formed a companion-piece to *Man in the White Suit*, its vision of the loner in a viciously conformist world pushed even further into caricature. Of all Mackendrick's unrealised projects, *Rhinoceros* is the one of which – despite his strictures on sentimentality – he speaks with the most affection, and an unmistakable note of regret. 'I'd still make it like a shot, if there was any chance of doing it,' he remarked in 1988.

Lewenstein, who still feels Hancock 'would have been absolutely brilliant casting for Bérenger', was equally keen on the idea. Hancock's agent, his brother Roger, was also enthusiastic; together, he and Mackendrick flew to New York to invite Zero Mostel to play Jean. Nicholas Roeg, brought in as cinematographer, shot some test scenes in Harrods' basement with a rubber rhinoceros. The main stumbling-block was Hancock himself; insecure and indecisive, at once flattered and terrified at the thought of filling Olivier's shoes, he repeatedly backed off from committing himself.

As negotiations dragged on, doubts began to surface. The insurers, worried about Hancock's drinking, insisted on a clause stipulating that any claims 'arising through the Artiste having met with an accident or suffering from an illness attributable directly or indirectly to alcoholism . . . will be subject to a deduction in excess of $10,000'.[3] For different reasons, Lewenstein was becoming uneasy about Mackendrick. 'There wasn't a feeling of going in the same direction all the time. Sandy's a very complicated fellow, and I don't think I understood him very well. He always seemed to see things upside-down from other people – which may be a good way of looking at *Rhinoceros*, of course, but difficult for his colleagues.'

Finally Hancock pulled out, having decided the part wasn't right for him, and the project collapsed. Mackendrick had worked on it, unpaid, for the best part of a year. By way of compensation, Lewenstein gave him the film rights to Ionesco's play.

Out of all the long-term projects Mackendrick nurtured during his directorial career, only one eventually reached the screen. This was *A High Wind in Jamaica*, whose genesis as a movie dated back to a chance meeting around 1950 in Ealing's unofficial annexe, the Red Lion. One lunchtime, Mackendrick found himself 'alone in the bar with a rather extraordinary gentleman who was very tall, very erect and handsome, with grey hair and a grey forked beard that gave him a slightly diabolical look. He was drinking a dark brown liquid which turned out to be neat Worcester Sauce. I was a little astonished at this, and he explained that it's very good for a hangover.'[4]

This, it turned out, was the Welsh novelist Richard Hughes, brought in to co-script Charles Frend's feeble comedy, *A Run for Your Money*. Mackendrick, though, knew him as the author of *A High Wind in Jamaica*, a book he greatly admired and promptly re-read. He then went to Balcon and told him that 'this, above all, was the film that I wanted to make'.

*A High Wind in Jamaica*, Hughes's first novel, was published in 1929 and soon attained the status of a modern classic. It begins in Jamaica in the mid-19th century. On a small ramshackle estate live an English family, the Thorntons: father, mother and five young children. A hurricane destroys the house and the parents decide to send the children to school in England. They're put aboard a sailing barque along with two Creole children, Margaret and Harry Fernandez; off Cuba it's attacked by pirates, who loot the ship. By accident the children end up aboard the pirate schooner and the barque's captain, thinking them murdered, makes off. The pirates return to their home port, hoping to leave the children there; but the eldest boy, John, is accidentally killed and the schooner puts to sea again with the others still on board.

The children's unthinking behaviour demoralises the crew, but an affection develops between the ten-year-old Emily Thornton and Jonsen, the pirate captain, and when she's wounded he nurses her back to health. During her illness the pirates take a Dutch ship whose captain is stabbed to death by Emily in delirious horror. Eventually Jonsen unloads the children on to a passing steamer, but Emily reveals the truth, and the schooner is captured. At the trial in London Emily, questioned about the Dutchman's death, blurts out incoherent words which are enough to have the pirates hanged.

The distinction of *High Wind in Jamaica* – besides its limpid prose, which has all the effortless clarity of sustained hallucination – lies in its wholly unsentimental treatment of the children. Hughes depicts them as in no way exceptional, neither angels nor devils, but an alien species, their mental processes opaque to even the most sympathetic adult. 'Their minds are not just more ignorant and stupider than ours, but differ in kind of thinking (are *mad*, in fact).'[5] The pirates, denounced as bloodthirsty monsters, are a well-meaning and relatively innocuous bunch, defenceless against the children's casual amorality – which destroys them.

Soon after the novel's publication, the film rights were brought by Fox for a few hundred pounds, and over the years various writers tried to fashion a screenplay from it. None succeeded; but under Hollywood's eccentric accounting system, each attempt increased the value of the property. At Mackendrick's urging, Balcon made inquiries about the rights, 'and when he got the answer he was so indignant that he wouldn't talk to me for a fortnight'.[6] Mackendrick accordingly decided that his only recourse was to steal the story.

'So I rewrote it, and instead of pirates I had Sicilian bandits – it was set at the time of the Giuliano troubles – who captured an English family, and the family were much more frightening than the bandits. It was a treatment which I then gave to Nigel Balchin to write. Nigel, terribly lazy, wrote a first-draft screenplay that was so bad Mick turned it down and refused to pay his fee. And his agents, A. D. Peters, looked at the small print and found that meant Nigel owned the rights of the script. I was livid, because he was stealing my property – neatly ignoring, of course, the fact that I'd stolen it myself in the first place.'[7]

Concluding that *High Wind*, in whatever form, would never get made at Ealing, Mackendrick reluctantly put the idea aside. But he still longed to film it, and some years later mentioned it to James Mason, and to the producer Jerry Wald, who had set up an independent unit within the Fox studio. Wald showed interest, but not until 1962 did Mackendrick receive a cable from T. E. B. Clarke, then working for Wald in Hollywood. Wald had decided to make *High Wind*, with Clarke scripting, Mason playing the captain and his 13-year-old daughter Portland Mason as Emily. Would Mackendrick consider directing? Mackendrick, knowing that both Wald and Mason were receptive to his ideas, was overjoyed. 'I wired back instantly, "Soonest, yes, yes, yes!" And there was a long silence – because Jerry Wald had then had a heart attack and died.'

Frustrated, Mackendrick again set out to steal the story, this time relocating it in 1913 Mexico, during the Zapatista rising. Collaborating with the novelist Hugh Wheeler (who later worked with Stephen Sondheim on *A Little Night Music* and *Sweeney Todd*) – and borrowing elements from a contemporary journal, Edith O'Shaughnessy's *A Diplomat's Wife in Mexico* – Mackendrick fashioned a screenplay called *Viva Miss Brown!* 'It was an absolute steal of the Sicilian one I'd written, including some stuff I pinched from Nigel Balchin's version.'[8] Miss Brown is a prim young Bostonian governess, travelling by train from Mexico City to Vera Cruz with her charges. Thrown off the train, she runs into Zapatistas and is gradually metamorphosed into a gun-toting bandit chief. In replacing Emily with an adult leading lady, Mackendrick feels that 'already I'd started the changes and restructuring that would make the story more palatable'.

Mackendrick's agents offered *Viva Miss Brown!* to Elmo Williams, head of 20th Century-Fox in Europe. 'Elmo said, "It's a very interesting script; we'd probably do it, but for the fact that we're already making something vaguely similar." And I knew what was coming. I said, "What is it?" and he said, "Oh, you wouldn't have heard of it, it's called *High Wind in Jamaica*. Peter Ustinov's going to direct and star in it." So that was that.'

Ustinov, however, fresh from making *Billy Budd*, decided that if working with boats was tough, boats-plus-children was inviting disaster. He pulled out, and Chris Mann called Mackendrick. 'He said, "Listen, I can get the job for you – on one condition: that you won't act up and turn down the script, you'll just make it as written. You're hard up, you need the money." So I said, "Yes, OK." Then I read the script.'

After Wald's death, the *High Wind* rights reverted to Darryl F. Zanuck, who had succeeded Spyros Skouras as head of Fox after the *Cleopatra* débâcle. Zanuck evidently knew little of Hughes's novel. Mackendrick saw a telegram from him 'which said, "This a great family subject, the sort of thing Disney is doing so well," and went on like this until the last line, which was, "Somebody should read the book to find out how close we are to the original." ' A new script, with a happy ending, was written by Nunnally Johnson, and the eight-year-old Karen Dotrice, well-received in Disney's *The Three Lives of Thomasina*, was chosen as Emily. Since Ustinov had quit as both director and star, someone new was needed to play the captain (who was now a curate in disguise), and Fox were considering Terry-Thomas.

This was the version to which Mackendrick had committed himself. 'So from then on I started to screw the producers. First of all I got at Anthony Quinn.' Quinn was in line for the mate, but Mackendrick persuaded Fox he would be better as the captain. Together, he and Elmo Williams flew to Paris to meet Quinn. 'And Tony pleaded jetlag, and said, "Can we talk this evening? And I'll riffle through the script again – it's very interesting, but I'd like to clarify my ideas about it." This signalled to me loud and clear, knowing actors, that he hadn't read a word of it. So right there, in Elmo's presence, I said, "By the way, you might like to skim through this, too," and handed him a copy of Hughes's book.

'Now I can't prove this, but I'll lay my bottom dollar on it – that he opened the Nunnally Johnson script, saw it was shit, then read the novel from start to finish. Because that evening at dinner, Quinn avoided my eye and looked entirely at Elmo. He said he thought it was very interesting, but what he'd like us to do was see a film that he thought had some relevance to this story. And the film he showed us the next day was *Sundays and Cybele*.'

Serge Bourguignon's *Cybèle ou les dimanches de Ville d'Avray* (1962), a fashionable film of its time now largely forgotten, concerns a sentimental friendship between an amnesiac pilot and a 12-year-old orphan girl. 'And what Quinn had cottoned on to immediately was the sexual current between the adolescent girl and the pirate. So between us, we managed to talk Elmo away from the Johnson script.' Quinn, fresh from his personal triumph in *Zorba the Greek*, wielded considerable influence, and with his backing Mackendrick persuaded Fox to pay off Karen Dotrice and to bring in a new scriptwriter.

The new writer was Ronald Harwood, then in his twenties with no film-writing experience. 'I was intimidated, of course, because Sandy was such a famous director, but he was extremely kind to me. And I was very lucky to have that kind of director, scrupulously professional, to guide my early steps. He taught me how to think visually, which is absolutely essential in writing a screenplay. Also, he taught me the whole way you plot the construction –putting each scene on a card, so you can change them around, edit the structure just like a film. I still use that to this day.

'I found him a difficult personality – I wasn't at ease, I was constantly alert, which I think is a good thing. He'd say things like, "Is that the best we can do?" It would throw you into a slight panic, because you thought you'd already come up with the definitive answer. Sometimes in the end he'd go back to your very first idea – but he'd like to move it about a bit, find another way of thinking about things entirely. The studio were in a terrible hurry, and we wrote it in six weeks, which I couldn't do now – but when you're young you can do anything.'

At the last minute Fox demanded a major change: Lila Kedrova had just won an Oscar for *Zorba*, and a substantial role had to be written in for her at 48 hours' notice. Even so, Mackendrick was pleased with the new version: 'We went right back to the novel, and turned out something that was about 80 per cent faithful to it, which I thought was pretty good. Meanwhile Elmo went ahead with building the boats and all the rest of it, and sent the script off to Zanuck. And Zanuck cancelled the picture.

'But then they discovered they'd spent so much money on it, it would be cheaper to go ahead and make the damn thing. So they brought in a Hollywood scriptwriter, Stanley Mann. Stanley was extremely honest, he said, "I know what you're up against, but you've gotta play the money, do what Zanuck wants – you've gotta build up the Lila Kedrova part, strengthen the relationship between the captain and the mate, make it a buddies film. Forget your book." And he turned out a script which Zanuck accepted.'

Fox's PR department tried to set up a televised discussion between Mackendrick and Richard Hughes. Mackendrick vehemently refused. 'The last person I wanted to meet just then was Dickon Hughes, since I was deeply conscious of the betrayal of his novel on which I was engaged. But, piecemeal, I continued my subversion – working as far back to the novel as I was allowed to go.' In a final bid to redress the balance, Mackendrick called in yet another writer: his collaborator on *Sammy*, Denis Cannan.

Cannan attended a meeting at the Fox offices in Soho Square. 'There was an atmosphere you could cut with a knife. Sandy was there, and all these Fox executives, and they asked what I thought of the script. I said I felt they'd lost Emily, and lost something of the Englishness. And they said, "Well, go away and write it, then." So I did, but by the time I'd finished Sandy was off on location, so I'm not sure how much of my stuff they ever used.'

In the summer of 1964, some 15 years after conceiving the project, Mackendrick flew to the Caribbean to begin filming *A High Wind in Jamaica*. It was his first costume picture; he had a script with which he was far from happy, a studio head (Zanuck) suspicious of the whole enterprise, and a budget that had been slashed to the bone. He had to deal with two ships, half-a-dozen children, complex locations and a notoriously self-willed lead actor in a position of power. On top of everything, the wranglings over the script had put the schedule back several weeks, and the hurricane season was imminent.

On the credit side, he was working with old associates from his Ealing days: Douglas Slocombe as cinematographer, Chic Waterson as camera operator and Tom Pevsner as assistant director (though billed for subsidy reasons as Associate Producer). In casting the children Mackendrick, to the studio's bemusement, had followed his regular approach and chosen non-professionals. For the crucial role of Emily he found a ten-year-old, Deborah Baxter, with a fresh, mobile face and just the right quality of incipient sexuality.

Over the casting of the principal adult roles, though, Mackendrick had little control. Quinn, of course, was a fixture: 'I was absolutely in hock to him, because he'd salvaged the project from the Terry-Thomas period. And he's not easy to work with, a very egocentric actor who looks out for himself. I think he overplayed, but there was nothing I could do about it.' As the mate, Fox had cast James Coburn – an imaginative choice, his lithe, laconic style at once setting off and undercutting Quinn's lumbering pathos. Neither he, nor Kedrova as the madame of the Tampico brothel, were by any means miscast; but their screen personas, Mackendrick feared, lent themselves to the broadening and simplifying process begun with Stanley Mann's rewrite.

Given that most of the film was shot on location, and that most of the locations were on board ship, the production was relatively free of disasters. There were a few near misses; at one point a real hurricane blew up and the ship nearly foundered on a reef. Mackendrick also recalls 'one really horrifying moment when the longboat – and it *is* a long boat, about 12 feet long – that's lashed to one side of this heaving deck came loose and came crashing across the wet deck where the children were squealing and running around. One was witnessing what could have been a massacre of crew or children or whatever. Slocombe tells me, and I'm appalled to think that it's probably true, that he caught sight of me at this moment watching with olympian calm.'[9]

Such incidents, though, were nothing unusual on location shoots, and did no great harm. Far more destructive of morale was the continual harassment by studio executives. What Chic Waterson describes as 'a string of hatchet men' descended on the shoot, each one intent on shaving a few more dollars off the already inadequate budget. The ships, a major item of expenditure, offered a prime target for cost-cutting. Douglas Slocombe recalls that the sailing barque representing Marpole's ship, the *Clorinda*, 'had to be partially rebuilt, and they didn't have the money to finish the top two layers of sails. So the suggestion was that, as we were in Cinemascope, we should do all our longshots with this ship at the top of the screen – so you wouldn't have to see the topsails.'

With this kind of haggling going on – plainly conveying that the front office had little confidence in the production and were concerned only to cut their losses – it was unlikely the shoot would be a happy one. Nor was it. From the start, Mackendrick found himself at loggerheads with his art director, John Hoesli, a Fox appointee who, he suspected, 'was still trying to make it a Disney picture'. Seeking a run-down fishing village to represent Tampico, Mackendrick had found 'an absolutely marvellous decrepit barn-like old house, cross-beamed with all the plaster falling off, and chose the location for that. And while we were back in London, this damned art director moved in and plastered the whole thing. So the first row was, "Take everything you've put on, and take it off again!" That put us at daggers drawn from the beginning.'

Unhappy about the concessions he had already had to make, Mackendrick became even more exacting over details. Tom Pevsner recalls that the set dresser, Peter James, 'stomped off to the office and said he was leaving, and would only remain on condition that he never had to speak to the director again. I think Sandy was driving him mad, searching endlessly for the perfect article to put on the set without ever being able to tell him what it was.' Even the normally equable Slocombe lost his temper over the lighting of the figurehead, threw a light-meter at Mackendrick ('I think I missed him') and walked off in a huff.

James Coburn, though, was impressed by Mackendrick's patience and untiring energy. 'It was wonderful to watch him – he was producing the thing, he was directing it, he helped with building the sets, moving things, he was doing more than anybody could possibly ask, because he wanted this thing to be really good. He felt responsible to it. *I* didn't have that kind of energy, and I was probably 20 years younger than he was. . . . And he didn't lose his patience with anybody; but he's not a guy, I understand, who's very patient with a lot of people. Maybe this was his last patience experiment.[10]

'It was 80 or 90 degrees with total humidity, and it would be raining in five minutes. In that five minutes he would never once slow down, never lose that intention of what it was he was going for. . . . He gave us an atmosphere to work in, a freedom to find out what the relationship was between the two pirates, Tony and me, and all the others around us. Sandy worked for that, it wasn't just a shot or the camera angle, show-off stuff – he didn't have any time for that. . . . I think he taught me the value of film, the honour of making film – of dealing with a magical instrument, the realisation of certain visions, the solidifying of dreams. . . . It's not something that's given to you, you have to earn it. And he earned it.'[11]

In describing Mackendrick acting as his own producer, Coburn scarcely exaggerates. The credited producer, John Croydon, was the production manager; as an Englishman, he had been nominally promoted to qualify the film for Eady money. But he never came out to Jamaica, and producing functions were split – none too amicably – between Mackendrick himself and Elmo Williams, with Zanuck a remote, hostile presence. Williams, as Mackendrick remarks, 'was in an intolerable position, caught between

Zanuck and myself, both giving him a hard time'. He was also, according to Pevsner, 'a frustrated director, very keen to be active on the creative side. There was a moment of crisis during the production when there were strong moves afoot to get rid of Sandy, and if that had happened Elmo would certainly have been keen to take over himself.'

Which, in effect, he eventually did. With the shoot over, and *High Wind* in post-production, Mackendrick was taken off the movie. 'Elmo, rather scared, came to me and said, "I know this doesn't happen, but I'm under instructions from Zanuck to remove you from any further connection with the editing and post-production." And at that stage I had to give up, because they have the right to do that. There were a couple of other films that were also being made by Fox, and Elmo, who had been an editor, got so neurotic that he had three offices in Soho Square set up as cutting rooms. So he could dodge from one office to another, and relieve his anxieties over what Zanuck was putting him through by watching the slaughtering of three films.'

Stephen Dalby, sound supervisor on Mackendrick's Ealing films, was now at Twickenham Studios and was called in to work on the mixing of *High Wind*. 'It was a rather complex picture soundwise, with all the background tracks. And I had no contact with Sandy; we just had the sound editor, Matt McCarthy, and this Fox executive, Elmo Williams, who came down every so often to hear what we'd done. So the mixing took ages, because we'd be held up waiting for this gentleman to appear. And that way – especially without the director – you lose the feel of it, the continuity. For me, it's not the way to mix a picture.'

To Mackendrick's disgust, Williams also insisted on adding a sung ballad to the soundtrack. As editor on *High Noon* (for which he won an Oscar), he claimed credit for the idea of the theme ballad 'Do Not Forsake Me, Oh My Darlin' ' – a key element, he believed, in the film's success. Hoping to repeat the trick, he got Larry Adler, whom he had commissioned to write the score, to provide a suitably romantic number with words by Christopher Logue. Mackendrick, who had wanted to use Tristram Cary again, detested not only the ballad ('It really makes me throw up') but Adler's whole score. Not that Adler himself thinks very highly of it: 'I didn't think it was one of my better efforts. That's because I wasn't inspired by the picture itself – and had I had any integrity at all, I'd have turned the whole thing down. But I'm a miserable coward – you throw a hunk of money at me, and I say oh goody.'[12]

Despite Adler's comments – and Mackendrick's – the music is attractively and delicately scored, largely avoiding the wash of lavish orchestration the subject might easily have inspired. Often in the shipboard scenes Adler limits himself to solo guitar, whose plangent tones suit the mood of sunlit melancholy. Even the ballad – in any case one of the less obnoxious of its type – occurs only over the opening and closing credits, making it relatively unobtrusive. But it's doubtful if any score, no matter how brilliant, could by this stage have pleased Mackendrick, such was his bitterness over the mutilation inflicted on his film.

*A High Wind in Jamaica* was registered for copyright at a length of 135 minutes, which probably corresponds to Mackendrick's own cut. When it was released, the film ran 103 minutes, a loss of just under 25 per cent of the movie. Since none of the missing footage has so far resurfaced, conjectural reconstruction has to rely on the memories of those involved, plus the evidence of the shooting script. On this slightly shaky basis, the chief differences between the 'complete film' and the release version can be summarised as follows:

1.  Most of the scenes concentrating on the children, to the exclusion of the pirates, have been dropped – in Mackendrick's opinion, 'some of the best stuff I ever shot'.

2.  Occasional voice-overs by Emily, either representing a letter to her mother, or just musing on events, are omitted.

3.  The relationship between Chavez, Zac and Rosa has lost most of its motivation. In the full version, Rosa owns the ship, and 50 per cent of all booty; Chavez and Zac conspire to conceal the £900 from her; Rosa finds out by questioning Emily and sends her lover, the Guardia captain, to retrieve the money; back at sea, Chavez and Zac talk of selling the ship and making off with the proceeds.

4.  All the events following the loss of the anchor – evading the British cutter, the 'funeral at sea', the game with Chavez's hat, the sequence with the figurehead – have been moved from after the Tampico episode to before it. (This explains the absence of John from these scenes, since they were shot as happening after his death.)

Any evaluation of *High Wind* has to deal with the film as released, since – barring a reappearance of the original version – that's all we have. Few Hollywood films, after all, end up *exactly* as their directors left them. Even so, given that of all Mackendrick's movies *High Wind* was the most seriously distorted by studio interference, and that these distortions were, for the most part, beyond his control, it seems fair to allow where relevant for the ghosts of missing scenes and thwarted creative intentions. Like a broken statue, *A High Wind in Jamaica* requires a dual critical perspective – taking into account both what's there, and what was meant to be.

What *is* there, despite the cuts, is a vigour and a narrative zest surpassed in Mackendrick's output only by *Sweet Smell* (and which suggests that, for all his aversion to Hollywood, he instinctively responded to the professional energy of American movie-making). *High Wind*, as Andrew Sarris noted, 'revel[s] in the emotional gusto of tall stories'.[13] As always with

Mackendrick, there's a lot going on beneath the surface; but purely on the level of colourful story-telling the film (like the novel) is never less than entertaining.

In pictorial terms, too, *High Wind* needs no excuses. It says a lot for Mackendrick's skill, and that of his collaborators, that despite the studio's penny-pinching the film never looks under-budgeted. On the contrary, it's the most visually opulent of his pictures, thanks not least to the rick dark tones of Slocombe's cinematography. Ever since *Saraband*, Slocombe had developed his unorthodox approach to colour photography, rejecting the bland primary look advocated by the colour labs in favour of bold cross-lighting and strong tonal contrast. It was a technique ideally suited to *High Wind*, conveying – for example in the scenes set in the ship's hold, filmed in the studio in London – a tangible sense of all-enveloping tropical warmth. Light throughout the film is at once intense and deflected: filtered through leaves, sails and shrouds, refracted off water or deck-planks, funnelled into hatches and portholes. With its mood of subtly shadowed clarity, Slocombe's lighting recreates in filmic terms the hallucinatory quality of Hughes's prose.

It's hardly surprising that *High Wind* should contain a high proportion of beautiful shots; dark sails against ragged tropical sunsets are a gift to any film-maker. But often the beauty is tinged with a mythic strangeness – for example when the pirate ship, reft of its anchor, is secured in its hiding-place by ropes tethered to rocks and trees, with palm-fronds lashed to its mastheads. There's no arbitrary mystification: we see the lines being attached, and we know why they're needed. Yet Mackendrick builds a quietly eerie mood, boats moving soundlessly through the twilight directed by whistled signals, until the ship, almost invisible against the darkness of the island but for long white ropes snaking away in the moonlight, suggests something out of the Arabian Nights – as though, like a captive balloon, the vessel might at any moment float up into the sky.

This pervasive sense of strangeness is enhanced by the use of language. Throughout the action, Spanish-speakers address each other in Spanish, instead of the phoney-accented English normal in Hollywood movies of the time. Ronald Harwood recalls 'a big argument over that with Elmo Williams. He wanted it all in Hollywood Hispanic, "Eh, Señor, 'ow you doing?" and all that. But it was a joint decision that Sandy and I made early, and we stuck to it.' They won their argument by the simple device of making the mate (Coburn) ignorant of Spanish, so that he could act as the audience's stand-in. For his benefit, important dialogue would always be translated.

Not only does this lend authenticity, it emphasises the gulf between children and pirates. To the children, the pirate crew represent an alien spectacle – enthralling but almost totally incomprehensible. Here again the film effectively recreates a key element of the novel: 'Remember that to them this was a pantomime: no word spoken to explain, and so the eyes exercised a peculiar clearness.'[14]

These qualities have generally passed unnoticed by those who find the film inadequate as a version of the original. It's commonly argued that good books make bad movies, and vice versa; in Stanley Kauffmann's words, 'the farther down the scale from greatness to competence that our original novel lies, the more likely it is to be successfully adapted for the screen; for it is less likely to be dependent on its original form for its effect'.[15] This principle is often applied to *High Wind*, not least by Mackendrick himself: 'It was a mistake. Second-rate books you can make films of, but true masterpieces surely can never really be transferred to the screen – and *High Wind in Jamaica* is a masterpiece.'[16]

Those who agree with Mackendrick tend to cite failures in tone and emphasis, rather than any distortions of the plot. Indeed, for all its troubled genesis, the film takes remarkably few liberties with Hughes's narrative. None of the main characters is lost and only one, Rosa, added – and even she derives from the formidable wife of the Chief Magistrate who queens it over the pirates' home port (shifted, for some reason, from Santa Lucia in Cuba to Tampico in Mexico). The captain and the mate are remodelled to fit the stars: Jonsen and Otto, Danish and Austrian respectively, become the Mexican Chavez and the American Zac (whose costume suggests a deserter from the Union Army). But such details do little damage to the story.

Only one character is seriously diminished in the film – the 15-year-old Creole girl, Margaret Fernandez. In the novel she acts as a 'shadow figure' to Emily, overtly presenting the sexuality which in the younger girl remains implicit, and ends up brutalised, pregnant and mentally unhinged. While traces of this remain in the film, the role has become so sketchy it's often hard to determine her motivation, or even exactly what happens to her. It seems she simply becomes Alberto's mistress – though it's hinted he shares her with the rest of the crew.

But otherwise, given the compression needed to turn even a relatively short novel into a feature-length film, *High Wind* loses little of crucial importance from the plot. The major cuts come from the beginning and end of the story. Hughes's opening chapter evokes the children's wild idyll on Jamaica; Mackendrick launches straight in with the hurricane. The ending is even more drastically telescoped. In the book, the Dutchman's death occurs about halfway through, followed some time later by the transfer of the children to an English steamer, their passage to England, reunion with their parents, and so on. The film sweeps us from the killing, through the (offscreen) capture of the pirate ship, into Mathias's chambers in just 50 seconds.

From a literary standpoint, this may seem abrupt. But in cinematic terms – in terms of action and reaction – it works. Hughes's opening chapter is superbly achieved, warm tactile prose shot through with a slow ripple of disquiet. Mackendrick concentrates this background into the hurricane sequence. What the children have become is shown by their reactions – to the hurricane, to their parents, to the voodoo ceremony. And in the denouement, Mackendrick cuts straight to the jugular. Once Chavez has grown attached to Emily, and Emily has killed, the trap is set. All that matters is the lethal clincher of the trial, and the film pitches us into it without delay.

The only cut in the release version that seriously damages the plot is of something that was never in the book: the whole Chavez-Zac-Rosa cash nexus, whose absence unbalances the Tampico episode. Several scenes in the brothel are invested with an unresolved emotional charge which makes no sense unless we know what's behind them: that Rosa is the pirates' paymistress; that her suspicions about booty are confirmed by what Emily tells her; and that her refusal to take the children isn't merely self-protection, but punishment of Chavez and Zac for trying to cheat her.

These excisions not only mar the Tampico scenes – many of which seem ill-proportioned, disfigured by awkward cutting – they also undermine some subtle 'laying of fuses' elsewhere in the film. Mackendrick carefully establishes that Emily witnesses the dealings with Marpole, which she can then reveal to Rosa. And this unwitting betrayal foreshadows – or would, if it were still there – her outburst at the trial. (There's a hint of sadness in Chavez's affection for her, as though sensing that, having betrayed him once, she'll do so again.) We also lose – oddly, if the idea was to favour the star roles – an aspect of the characters of Chavez and Zac, who hoped with the money to quit piracy and buy, respectively, a rancho and 'a little cantina with maybe a couple of girls'.

Still, these cuts can hardly be said to damage Hughes's story, whose elements largely survive intact. The balance between the elements, though, has shifted, and with it the dramatic emphasis. To Mackendrick, this was the film's greatest shortcoming. 'I was quite convinced of the way it should be shot: big close-up material on the children, with the adults seen at the edge of the screen and in the background. So you live in the child's world, while latching on through the visual irony to all the things that they don't understand. But Mann switched the emphasis to the buddy movie of Coburn and Quinn, and Elmo quite ruthlessly cut out the scenes with the children. So in the end it was a betrayal of Hughes's book.'

As so often, Mackendrick is unduly harsh on his own work. If the film loses something of the novel's ironic tone and complexity, it replaces them with a distinctive tone and complexity of its own. Where the novel is coolly anthropological in its detachment, the film, engaging more closely with the emotional flux of events, creates a sense of poignancy and loss. Also, in exploring details only glanced on in the book, Mackendrick brings out –

visually and metaphorically rather than verbally – dimensions of the story that Hughes perhaps never envisaged. And rightly so, any good adaptation being (in Neil Sinyard's words) a matter of 'interpretation more than reproduction . . . a critical gloss on the novels and a freshly imagined cinematic experience'.[17]

Which isn't to say Mackendrick's comments are wholly unjustified, especially as regards the portrayal of the children. It may be that Williams's cuts are chiefly responsible, or that Mackendrick himself, having not one but six or seven children to deal with (plus ships, recalcitrant colleagues, and so forth), failed to elicit the concentrated, intimate results he needed. But though Deborah Baxter as Emily gives a fresh, convincing and – especially in the trial scene – moving portrayal, she never matches the intensity of Mandy Miller, or even of Fergus McClelland.

None of the other children – and it's probably here that the cut scenes are most acutely missed – ever makes much of a dramatic impact. Not that their performances (with one possible exception) are bad, and as with all Mackendrick's children they're refreshingly uncute. But they tend to offer isolated quirks of personality – Rachel's moral absolutism, Laura's self-absorption – rather than sustained characterisation. Least successful is John, as played by Martin Amis. The future novelist gives a sullen and detached performance, as if he'd rather be somewhere else entirely. Tom Pevsner got the impression that 'his mother or someone was keen for him to be an actor; I'm not sure who it was, but it certainly wasn't him.'

'One can,' Richard Hughes observes, 'by an effort of will and imagination, think like a child.'[18] It was something of this order that Mackendrick hoped to bring off – that through *his* will and imagination, he would enable us, his audience, to think like children. But though the film lets us see through the children's eyes – or at any rate through Emily's – it never quite goes that crucial stage further and lets us inhabit their thoughts. And in that, perhaps, it betrays its source, and falls short of its potential.

Even so, to describe *High Wind* as 'a buddy movie' is a gross exaggeration. Though the roles of Coburn and Quinn have been expanded, the relationship between captain and mate figures scarcely more largely in the film than in the novel. The relationship that *has* been given more prominence is that between Emily and Chavez, which becomes the central thread of the narrative. *High Wind*, in its screen version, isn't a buddy movie, nor even a pirate movie, so much as a love story.

Love, in Mackendrick's work, generally appears as a weakness, the source of dangerous errors of judgement. In *Sweet Smell*, Hunsecker can be harmed only through his obsession with his sister. Mandy's father, Harry Garland, blinded by jealousy, comes close to destroying his marriage and ruining his daughter's future. Carlo Cofield in *Don't Make Waves* constructs a whole precarious existence for himself in his attempt to impress Malibu, the nubile sky-diver. (We could even add One-Round, whose lunkheaded attachment to Mrs Wilberforce in *The Ladykillers* triggers the gang's downfall.) And Chavez, most disastrously infatuated of all, brings himself and his crew to the gallows through his devotion to Emily.

All these fools for love are male; women in Mackendrick's films are almost invariably more level-headed than the men. Yet the destructive power of love, like that of innocence, is essentially unconscious. None of the women intend, or are even for the most part aware of, the devastating effect they're having.

So *High Wind*, unlike *Lord of the Flies*, isn't a parable of Original Sin. There's no particular malice in Emily's behaviour, nor seductive intent, and the reviewer who called her 'a pint-sized Circe attuned to evils as old as the human heart'[19] was way off the mark. Like the other children, she acts with the unwitting ruthlessness of a force of nature, no more setting out to destroy Chavez than the hurricane set out to destroy the Thorntons' house.

This identification is hinted in the very first shot of the film. Rather than establishing Emily in close-up, then pulling back to show her caught in the storm, Mackendrick opens with a sustained long-shot of the tiny bedraggled figure merged with the churning elements, her cries of 'Tabby!' echoed by the shrieks of the wind. Distressed for her cat, not for herself, she takes the hurricane in her stride – as do her siblings, enjoying the spectacle while their parents panic. 'It's all right, there's nothing to be afraid of!' cries Mrs Thornton, scrabbling through her prayer-book, a rising note of hysteria belying her words.

*High Wind*, in Brian Baxter's estimation, is 'not only . . . one of the most deeply observant portraits of children in cinema, it also makes brilliant use of the children to illuminate the characters of the adults confronted with them'.[20] At its best the film, like the novel, works from two angles at once, showing us adults through the eyes of children, children through the eyes of adults, and the mutual incomprehension of both. But in these opening scenes Mackendrick is setting up other dichotomies – between instinct and culture, order and chaos, masculine and feminine – whose tension defines and structures the action. In *High Wind in Jamaica*, the clash of conflicting perceptions which runs through all Mackendrick's work attains its most intricate expression.

In this, the film succeeds where *Sammy Going South* failed. Sammy finds shelter in a community which – maverick but conventional in structure – simply replicates the society from which he's been ejected. *High Wind*, by contrast, endorses the validity of alternative modes of being. The film can be seen in terms of a particular way of life – white, adult, rational and colonialist – coming under stress, breaking down, and finally reasserting itself at the expense of those who flout its values. (From this angle, *High Wind* can be read as a post-imperialist film, which *Sammy* conspicuously wasn't.) Not

**17.** On safari: Mackendrick directing
*Sammy Going South* in East Africa.

**18a.** A sheltered existence: Sammy (Fergus McClelland)
before the bombing in *Sammy Going South*.

**18b.** Homeless again: Sammy in the ruins of
Cocky Wainwright's hut in *Sammy Going South*.

**19a & b.** Victims of innocence: the Syrian (Zia Moyheddin)
with Sammy; Spyros Dracondopoulos (Paul Stassino,
with African extra) in *Sammy Going South*.

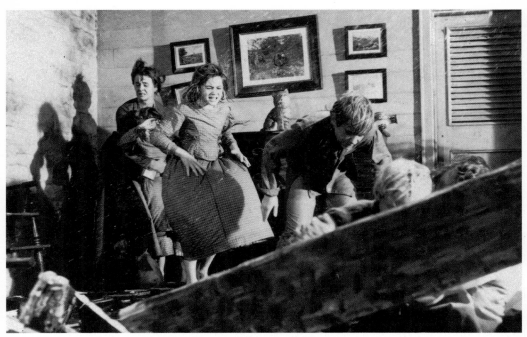

**20a.** Down the rabbit-hole: Emily Thornton (Deborah Baxter) and her family take refuge in the cellar in *A High Wind in Jamaica*.

**20b**. Moment of truth: Chavez (Anthony Quinn) grapples with Emily on the deck in *A High Wind in Jamaica*.

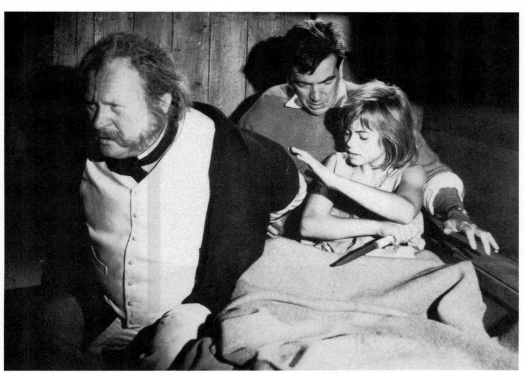

**21a & b.** Making the point: Mackendrick rehearses Deborah Baxter for . . .
the stabbing of the Dutch Captain (Gert Frobe)
in *A High Wind in Jamaica*.

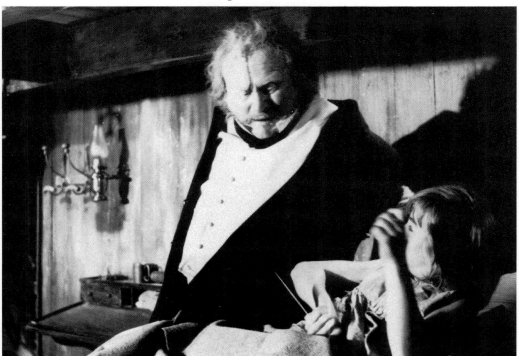

**22a.** 'Interesting fringe benefits.'
Diane Prescott (Joanna Barnes) makes Carlo Cofield
(Tony Curtis) a proposition in *Don't Make Waves.*

**22b.** Fall-guy: Carlo Cofield loses
another battle with the elements
in *Don't Make Waves.*

**23a**

**23a–g.**
The Battle of Carberry Hill:
Mackendrick's pre-production
sketches for an episode in
*Mary Queen of Scots.*

**23b**

**23c**

**23d**

**23e**

**23f**

**23g**

**24.** Alexander Mackendrick, 1990.

that the alternatives – the children, the pirates, the black Jamaicans, the raffish lowlifes of Tampico – are at all romanticised. Mackendrick's irony exposes their weakness, but also suggests how the dominant culture needs such outsiders to reinforce its own authority. 'Well,' Chavez remarks at the trial, 'they had to hang *some*body.'

Like *Sammy*, *High Wind* begins with the collapse of a house that brings down with it a whole nexus of assumptions. As the storm rises, the Thorntons retreat into their living-room on the wooden ground-floor, while the black servants and plantation hands take more prudent refuge in the stone cellar. The hurricane makes short work of this racial segregation, shattering the upper storeys and bringing down a beam which smashes through to the cellar. The children, ushered down the resultant hole by their parents, descend (like Alice down the rabbit-hole) not so much to an underworld as an otherworld – a dark cluttered intimate space, realm of the instincts and the emotions, where the decorous Victorian values of the living-room are distorted and overturned.

And it's in this turbulent parody-world that most of the rest of the film takes place. Just as the cellar prefigures the hold of the pirate ship, so the things that happen in it – breaking down carefully constructed barriers, throwing distinctions into question – foreshadow the events that follow. And if *The Ladykillers* represented Mrs Wilberforce's dream, we can take *High Wind in Jamaica* as the madeira-induced nightmare of Emily Thornton, falling drunkenly asleep in the cellar with voodoo rhythms echoing through her head.

To her parents, what happens in the cellar is a nightmare in itself, as they see their children, the heirs of superior European culture, happily 'going native', eager to join in the chanting and the sacrifice. Disturbingly well-informed, the young Thorntons patiently explain matters to their outraged father. 'They're casting a spell.' 'A magic spell.' 'Against duppies,' adds Rachel, throwing her hair over her face; 'duppies have their heads on back to front.'

Order – European order – has to be restored. Christianity and alcohol, proven remedies in the face of recalcitrant natives, are duly trotted out. Religion has some limited effect – Mamie, the housekeeper, switches fluently from her obeah chant to invoking the Lord Jesus – though Mr Thornton's madeira proves more persuasive. But just as calm is being established, Emily sees Tabby outside and opens the window. The cat streaks in, followed by half a dozen wild cats and the hurricane, overturning the lamp and plunging the cellar into darkness. The forces of chaos have been admitted.

In Mackendrick's previous films the disruptive elements – Waggett, Sidney Stratton, the *Ladykillers* gang – were outsiders against whom the community could unite, expelling or destroying them. The Thorntons –

themselves outsiders, besieged by an alien culture and climate – are faced with a far more appalling prospect: the disruptive principle, as in a horror movie, has possessed their own offspring. 'It's this place, Frederick!' laments Mrs Thornton. 'It's turned them into savages!' Distinctions of class and race, the whole raison d'être of colonialism, are under threat; and since, as she sees it, the children absorb by osmosis the spirit of their surroundings, they must be consigned to 'a decent school in England'.

She isn't entirely wrong. The children's ability to adapt to any society, while ignoring all its essential proprieties – their innocence, in other words – is exactly what makes them so dangerous. Even as she mentions 'a decent school' we cut to the image of the barque *Clorinda*, whose master, Captain Marpole, assures her that 'a ship is the finest nursery in the world'. True enough, since a ship will serve the children both as a school and as an extension of their home life – an environment in which their education, and their 'savagery', can develop far beyond anything their parents envisaged. No sooner aboard the *Clorinda* than the young Thorntons have taken it over, scampering in every direction, while Emily shins up the rigging after the ship's monkey. 'Emily! Will you come *down* from there!' bawls Mr Thornton from the departing rowboat, in a last vain attempt to impose order.

Once aboard the pirate ship, the process of usurpation gathers pace. The children establish their own space in the hold, a warm dark cavern crammed with the detritus of Victorian civilisation – a penny-farthing bicycle, a dressmaker's dummy, several grandfather clocks – as though amid the salvaged remnants of their home. From here, having repelled the pirates' half-hearted intrusion (the abortive rape scene), they issue forth to assert their claim – climbing, swinging and sliding everywhere, annexing the whole ship as their adventure playground, even invading Chavez's cabin and trying on his clothes. Mackendrick often conveys their ubiquitous influence by shooting from near deck level (a device, as Basil Wright noted, that he shares with Ozu)[21] to suggest that their outlook, whether they're physically present or not, is insidiously pervading events.

Eventually the crew, driven to desperation, confine their tormentors to the longboat. But even this the children can turn to advantage, redefining their cramped space as the only valid one, transforming the rest of the deck into 'sea' and exiling the pirates from their own territory. 'You're drowning! You're drowning!' they shout gleefully at the horrified crew, who leap for safety.

The pirates' fatal weakness – which the children, with casual cruelty, instinctively home in on – isn't so much their superstition as their kindliness. Like the criminals in *The Ladykillers*, it's their 'touch of goodness' that destroys them, since they're not merely innocent but anachronisms, doomed to extinction in a world of steamships and telegraphs, degenerate heirs of a once pitiless race. Even the children are aware that their captors fall short of the authentic myth. 'If I was a *real* pirate,' says Edward, with a trace of contempt in his voice, 'I wouldn't have girls on board.'

Quinn's performance as Chavez has found few admirers, even among those who like the film. Mackendrick, Basil Wright maintained, 'would have succeeded totally [in capturing the quality of the novel] had it not been for the egregious casting of Anthony Quinn. . . . Every time Quinn launches out into a piece of "larger than life" acting or puts on his special "pirate's guffaw", the frail, dangerous truth of Emily and the other children is flawed or cracked.'[22] Mackendrick agrees. 'I think Quinn was playing towards the Disney thing. I didn't like the comic hat he insisted on wearing, but there was no way of talking him out of that.'

Quinn is notoriously given to overacting, and no doubt James Mason could have brought to the role (as he did to a similar part in *Lolita*) more subtlety, a more inward pain. Even so, and *pace* Mackendrick's views, it's arguable that Quinn's portrayal of Chavez has been misinterpreted and underestimated. All the elements – the guffaw, the absurd hat, the half-hearted swashbuckling and the attempts to run 'a serious boat' – make perfect sense if we accept that Quinn isn't playing a pirate, but someone *trying to be a pirate*: a Mexican peasant, born nowhere near the sea, doing his best to live up to what he thinks a pirate ought to be.

Chavez, as Quinn plays him, is a pirate chief in much the way that Don Quixote was a knight errant: impersonating, on a theoretical basis, the behaviour of an obsolete species. Even the guffaw has a nervous, sidelong edge – 'Is this it? Am I doing it right?' – and every so often the camera catches him mooching about the ship, patently at a loss: what does a pirate captain *do* when there's no pirating to be done? Like so many of Mackendrick's characters, Chavez feels not just his authority being undermined ('Nobody listens,' he mutters gloomily) but his very identity – hence the comic-opera hat and his disproportionate fury when the children toss it around the deck.

James Coburn's playing of the mate neatly complements Quinn's performance – Zac is a lot brighter than Chavez, but less imaginative, concerned not with how things should be, but simply whether or not they work. The scene in Marpole's cabin epitomises their relationship. Chavez, finding a locked strongbox, decides to shoot off the lock, buccaneer-style. His pistol misses fire; he squints at it, blows down the barrel, tries again. Another misfire. Zac, checking the ledger, casually draws a knife and one-handedly prises open the lock. His expression, and his whole attitude to Chavez, conveys tolerant affection; in the film as in the novel, the homosexual bond between the two is understated but clear. This is a comfortable, self-sufficient relationship, about to be badly disrupted.

'The history of pirates,' Mackendrick notes, 'is rather fascinating. They were masculine communities who feared the influence of women, the influence, if you like, of female love.'[23] It's this distracting, unpredictable feminine principle – male anxieties projected on to the dangerous 'other' – that the children, and Emily in particular, represent. Even before he discovers them on board, Chavez senses something awry, grunting uneasily in response to Zac's reassuring, 'Everything's fine. What's wrong?' 'I don't know—' he mutters, just as Alberto appears from below, dragging Margaret behind him.

If the pirates find Margaret less disconcerting than Emily, it's perhaps because, being a crucial few years older, she can be taken – literally – on a straightforward sexual level. Emily, though, is doubly 'other', at once woman and child, unfathomable on both counts. (On top of this, there's the racial aspect: Margaret, like most of the crew, is Hispanic, where the Englishness, both linguistic and racial, of the Thorntons sets them at a further remove.) 'Why doesn't Margaret stay with us any more?' Edward asks. 'She thinks she's too grown up,' Emily replies disdainfully; but her tone betrays a hint of uneasiness, a surmise that she too may be 'growing up' in ways that disturb her.

The progress of this awareness, with both Emily and Chavez reluctantly sensing the implications of their feelings, forms the central thread of the film, and Mackendrick traces it with sensitivity. There's a dawning premonition in their very first encounter, as Chavez hauls himself up over the bow of the *Clorinda* to meet Emily's astonished gaze. Confused and taken aback, he drops his eyes – glances back, as if incredulous – then once more looks away in embarrassment. Zac, coming up after him, looks straight through the girl; to him, children are an irrelevance. The rest of the crew, struck by the incongruity, merely laugh.

After the looting of the *Clorinda*, the pirates celebrate their prize, dancing to a drum rhythm that echoes the voodoo chant in the cellar. The disguised 'women' gyrate seductively, wiggling and flaunting – femaleness parodied and defused – while Chavez charges at them, imitating a bull. But this display of rampant masculinity is also spurious; catching Emily's eye, he again looks shamefaced, as though caught out in unworthy conduct, before ordering the children to be taken below. Trying to recover his self-possession, he butts Margaret in the bottom as she passes.

Later that night, fortified by drink and egged on by the crew, Chavez descends into the hold in a final attempt to live up to his lusty image. We're back in the unruly underworld of the instincts, but now child and adult behaviour patterns seem reversed, with the pirates reeling and giggling, and the children grave, watchful and faintly disapproving. ('You're drunk, aren't you?' accuses Rachel, echoing her verdict on the dead monkey.) Once again, it's Emily's gaze that disconcerts Chavez; he absently pats her head, upon which (with blatantly Freudian symbolism) she bites his thumb. Her action, though, gives him his escape route. Since anger becomes a pirate no less than lust, he can conceal his diffidence under a show of rage, turning on his sniggering crew and driving them back on deck.

Having failed as a rapist, Chavez is equally unsuccessful in convincing himself that his feelings towards Emily are simply paternal. At one point, having noticed Laura playing with her collection of dolls, he starts constructing a present for Emily – a touchingly naive little figure made of chicken feathers and a potato. Bringing it to her, he overhears her dispassionate verdict on him and his kind – 'Grown-ups never *do* tell you anything. You have to guess' – and, realising that contact between them will need a lot more sophistication than he thought, moodily tosses his love-gift away.

In one sense, though, fatherly feelings might have been quite appropriate. It's possible to detect within *High Wind* resonances of the more psychologically charged children's classics such as *Alice* and *Treasure Island* – but above all of *Peter Pan*, with its lost band of children and nursery turned secret den turned pirate ship. Most stage productions of Barrie's play have one actor playing Mr Darling and Captain Hook; and Chavez – especially if we take the story as Emily's fantasy – doubles Mr Thornton as incestuous father-figure. (Even more so, had James and Portland Mason been cast in the roles.)

Not that the sexual attraction between Emily and Chavez is ever openly acknowledged, still less acted upon. But there's a key moment when they're obliged to realise that such an attraction exists. Chavez, infuriated by the children's game with his hat, pursues them and captures Edward. Before he can take punitive action, Emily flings herself on him; releasing Edward, he grapples with her on the deck, rolling on top of her. Shooting the encounter close in at deck level, Mackendrick includes us in the intimacy of the inadvertent embrace – and conveys, through facial reactions alone, that Chavez is getting an erection, and that Emily knows it. At once she breaks free and attacks the captain (who makes no attempt to stop her), pummelling his back and screaming, 'You're a wicked pirate! You're going to be hanged and go to hell!'

This is prescient, since Chavez's attraction to Emily is exactly what gets him hanged. But Emily is also masking one unwelcome truth – her sexuality – with another, having till now maintained the fiction that Chavez and his men are 'pilots'. Overwhelmed by her moral confusion she escapes up the mast, while Chavez descends to his cabin, where he finds Margaret waiting – perhaps hoping to deflect his aroused desire away from Emily? – and brusquely ejects her. Zac, entering as she leaves, misreads the situation and tries to distract him with talk of Tampico. Without success; as Chavez slumps brooding on his bunk, a quick cut to Emily, wrapped pensively around the cross-piece of the mast, reveals the mutual drift of their thoughts.

Though the affair between them can never be consummated, it develops after Emily's wounding into a gentle intimacy. If her injury looks like symbolic rape (her thigh pierced by the marlin-spike dislodged by Alberto, who has already deflowered Margaret), its aftermath becomes a wedding: Chavez carries her like a bride over the threshold of his cabin, beds her down in his bunk and tends her like a solicitous lover. The mutiny, which leaves Chavez chained and locked in the cabin, brings them still closer, reduced to the level of helpless children seeking comfort in storytelling. 'Tell me about you,' Emily pleads, sensing his anguish at Zac's betrayal, 'when you were a little boy at sea.' But Chavez's memories are harsh and barren – 'When I was a little boy there was no water. Only hills and rocks' – while Emily's own past haunts her with thoughts of death and 'bad dreams – awful dreams'. And one of these dreams soon transforms itself into horrifying reality: a duppy, with its backwards face, come to claim her as its victim.

The critical consensus that dismisses *High Wind* as an inadequate rendering of Hughes's book ignores one factor in particular: that while the novel undeniably contains fine things that are lacking in the film, the reverse is equally true. Several of the film's most telling scenes – the voodoo ceremony in the cellar, the losing of the anchor – don't feature in the book at all, or are built up from incidental details. Above all there's the creation, from a passing reference to 'duppies', of a whole rich complex of supernatural imagery rooted in the film's interplay of duality and otherness, the darkness of the shadow side.

In the image of the duppy, the ghost with its head on backwards, Mackendrick's ambivalent view of innocence finds its most vivid expression. In Jamaican folk-lore, duppies are the spirits of deceased friends (though no less malignant for that), and once again Mackendrick captures the sense of nightmare reversal, the skull beneath the skin, as what seemed harmless and familiar transforms itself into something alien and threatening. Significantly, it's Rachel and Laura, the two youngest and (in theory) most innocent of the children, who are keenest on playing duppies. But the film's masterstroke is to link this mythical image with Mackendrick's own conception of the figure-head, with its swivelling, detachable head – serene, idealised female features on one side, worm-eaten death's-head the other.

Movie directors often take credit for their collaborators' ideas. In this case, though, it's legitimate to describe the figurehead as Mackendrick's 'own conception'. 'That was all Sandy,' Ronald Harwood recalls, 'his invention right from the start. No one else contributed to that.' Even its construction was Mackendrick's work. 'That was another huge row between myself and the art director. I tried to get him to make it, and he refused – so with the help of a plasterer I modelled that head myself.'

Mackendrick subtly prepares his visual coup, weaving around it a web of omens and premonitions. As Edward and Harry loll in the netting under the bowsprit, and Edward makes his remark about not having girls on board, the head swivels slightly on the torso, as if to stare at him – loose, but maybe also possessed. Meanwhile one of the crew is unwillingly diving for the anchor. 'He's afraid,' says Chavez, 'he says the kids bring bad luck.' Even the sceptical Zac is affected: 'Yeah, well, he may be right there. You know, these kids *are* dangerous. They scare *me*.'

Back on board, Chavez finds the 'burial at sea' in progress, loses his hat and his temper, and has his conjunction with Emily. A terrified yell from the boat's crew: the head has swivelled round, presenting a rotting aspect resembling a skull. To the crew – and, though he tries to master his fear, to Chavez – the implications are appalling. Since a ship's figurehead serves as a talisman to avert the perils of the sea, the 'bad luck' Chavez speaks of has infected the very source of good fortune. The vessel itself has turned hostile, and the figure embodies the treacherous female principle: a gentle countenance one moment, the duppy's grin of death the next.

Chavez's attempt to right the head makes things worse. It slips from his grasp and falls, to bob about in the sea like a drowning woman – or like the severed head of an executed criminal. Zac retrieves it and tosses it on deck, where Rachel picks it up and reprises her duppy act, parading about with the head reversed. As before, this public display of otherness appals her adult audience. Her behaviour confirms all the crew's forebodings, identifying the children with everything malign and untoward.

But though the children can invoke the duppy, symbol of the dark and instinctual, they can't command it, and when it manifests, it turns not against the pirates, but against Emily herself. To her delirious vision, the wretched Dutch captain – bound, grunting, shuffling backwards and peering desperately over his shoulder – is transformed into a duppy, gibbering at her with its reversed face and brandishing a knife. In killing him, she's killing the savagery that's possessed her and her siblings; from now on, they're metamorphosed into well brought-up Victorian children, sitting politely in Mathias's chambers or playing decorous games in a park.

But at the same time her attack is also directed against Chavez, or at least against the darker, sexual aspects of him. Her frenzied movements, stabbing at the Dutchman's back, replicate – except that now she has a knife – those she made in pounding Chavez with her fists. Nor is the act only symbolic – she *does* kill Chavez, since for this murder he, and his crew, will hang. (The Dutch ship, the *Thelma* in the novel, is now the *Brunhilde*, after the woman who brought about her lover's death.) And perhaps she's also killing her real father for having deserted her; the Dutchman's dying words (spoken in Dutch) are: 'But I have a wife and children.'

Over his words, almost drowning them out, comes the off-screen voice of a British officer calling on the pirates to surrender – followed a few seconds later (and fractionally preceding the cut to his chambers) by that of Mathias.

These two voices intrude upon the image of Emily, Chavez and the murdered Dutchman in the tones of the dominant culture, rigid, male and judgemental, reasserting itself. Until this juncture the conflict has been between children and pirates, two modes of innocence. Now the forces of experience take over, turning both groups into victims.

Mathias (a smoothly insinuating cameo from Dennis Price) makes a twin figure to Captain Marpole. Both seem a little too good to be true – the bluff sea-dog, the urbane barrister – and are treated by the children with well-founded suspicion, since both prove thoroughly unprincipled. Marpole will sacrifice his passengers' lives to keep his gold; Mathias will sacrifice truth and justice for a spectacular verdict. 'Without [the children's] help,' he tells Thornton, 'we may fail to get a conviction,' and to him, only one kind of conviction counts. 'Since 1837,' he tells the court, 'piracy has ceased to be a hanging offence unless accompanied by murder. . . . Now if you decide that one of these men – *any* one of these men – is responsible for the death of the boy or the Dutch captain, you are bound to convict them all.'

The irony of *A High Wind in Jamaica* – in the film as in the novel – is that the pirates, this riffraff and scum of the earth, are morally superior to those who condemn and kill them. Chavez, for all his insecurity and bluster, is a better captain (in seamanship, in regard for his passengers and crew) than the pompous, craven Marpole; and none of the crew is as bloodthirsty as the courtroom mob shouting, 'Hang them all!' or the cabbie who tells Thornton, 'They deserved to hang.' Like the workers in *Man in the White Suit*, they're much less nasty than their opponents, and therefore are fated to lose out. 'I don't want to die innocent!' Zac protests. Chavez laughs wryly: 'Zac, you must be guilty of – of something?' We might conclude that what they're all guilty of is, precisely, innocence.

Mackendrick stages the court sequence to show Emily as a tool in the hands of the lawyer and of the legal process he represents. With Mathias's words to Thornton – 'I feel we'll have to produce at least one [of the children]. . . . Emily' – we cut to her bewildered face as a door opens in front of her. A confused welter of voices, that of Mathias coming to dominate, as the camera tracks with her as she moves forward. Dark shapes of people, only partially glimpsed, pass in front of her, giving a nervous effect like quick cutting; disembodied hands touch her, guiding her. Not until she's in the witness box does Mackendrick cut away, following the line of her gaze. What she's looking at is the pirates in the dock, the focus of her interest; but they're also the target, on which Mathias will train her like a loaded gun.

The trial is played out in a pattern of looks, with emotional links and tensions expressed in eyes meeting across the courtroom. Emily's gaze repeatedly returns to Chavez, beseeching support, understanding or forgiveness; she even appeals to him verbally ('You *said* I had a dream'), but never looks towards her father. Thornton's eyes flick between Chavez and his daughter; Mathias's from Emily to the jury as his questioning grows more insistent, blocking her appeal to Chavez – 'But Emily, you're not having a dream now' – and driving her inexorably towards the point he's set on proving.

> MATHIAS: There was blood at the foot of the stairs. Was that your blood? Or was it the blood of Captain Vandervoort? There was blood on Chavez's hands!
> EMILY: He – had a knife.
> MATHIAS: Who had a knife? Emily – *was Captain Chavez in the cabin?*
> EMILY: He – I – don't remember. We were – it was awful!
> MATHIAS: So you saw Captain Chavez?
> EMILY: He – he made an – awful noise – and then he died! He died!

Thornton's outburst – 'Stop it! I will not permit my daughter to be subjected to this!' – is richly ambiguous (especially if we take into account a brief scene in the shooting script where, from Emily's ravings in a nightmare, he infers the truth about the Dutchman's death). His solicitude could equally be fear of what more she might say – to exculpate Chavez, incriminate herself or perhaps even reveal what he suspects about her feeling for the pirate. The glare he directs at Chavez, half triumph, half guilty complicity, suggests not so much vengeance for his son's death as exultation over the defeat of a sexual rival.

This ambiguity carries over into the final scene, in which Thornton joins his wife and children by the Round Pond in Kensington Gardens. The setting, in contrast to the turmoil of the film's opening, presents nature at its most demure: well-groomed grass and shrubs, a safe, shallow expanse of water, and in the backround a classical portico, emblem of civilised enlightenment. Emily, hair beautifully brushed, racket and shuttlecock in hand, stands among her siblings; they, and the other children around them, are neatly attired, playing charmingly under benevolent parental eyes. It's a picture-book image, respectable and reassuring, exuding Victorian complacency.

The smugness, though, is undercut by the demeanour of the three principals. Thornton, black-clad and 'walking with the measured tread of a pallbearer',[24] as Philip French put it, nods grimly at his wife as he sits down. The executions, we gather, have been carried out, but there's no satisfaction in his face, and the look Mrs Thornton directs at Emily is troubled and faintly apprehensive.

Emily herself is turned away, staring out over the pond at a toy boat that looks very like the pirate schooner. For the final shot of *Queen Christina*,

Mamoulian told Garbo to make her face 'a blank sheet of paper'[25] where the audience could inscribe what emotions they wished; and (for all the vast discrepancy in acting skills) there's something of the same uncompromising blankness in Baxter's gaze, far more expressive than any carefully registered reaction. The impression is of a deliberate forgetting, a repression of memories too disturbing to bear. Where the ending of *Mandy* left us with an image of liberating possibilities opening up in one child's life and in the society around her, *High Wind* shows us those possibilities being shut off and denied. Mackendrick's last major film closes with an aching sense of loss.

Having trimmed it to what they considered an acceptable length, Fox gave *High Wind* a half-hearted release, with minimal publicity, in May 1965. Mackendrick's disappointment over the final version was shared by the majority of reviewers, many of whom compared it to the book. In the *Spectator*, Isabel Quigley found that 'the film rather gruesomely resembles [the novel] in a way that is always just wrong. . . . In spite of murder and violence, all is sweetness and light: there is no fear, no shock, no horror.' The movie, she concluded, 'is perfectly acceptable *on its own level* – but not on the book's'.[26]

Most other critics agreed, feeling that Hughes's story had been softened and 'Disneyfied', and often comparing the film unfavourably with Peter Brook's *Lord of the Flies*. Apart from a brief but appreciative notice from Dilys Powell in the *Sunday Times*,[27] it was left to Philip French, in one of his earliest reviews in the *Observer*, to come out strongly in favour, commending the film's 'delicate and rapid shifts of mood', its 'subtlety and understatement' and its 'visual inventiveness in capturing and extending Hughes's dark poetry'. The novelist could 'think himself lucky that [*High Wind*] has fallen into the hands of Alexander Mackendrick, one of our finest and least prolific directors', who had sustained the spirit of the book and turned it into 'a film of distinction'.[28]

Such praise could do little to rescue the film from box-office disaster. It also performed poorly in the States, where most reviewers treated it as 'a family picture' – though one or two detected darker undertones. ('Only discerning palates,' *Time*'s critic suggested, 'will pucker at the aftertaste.')[29] Only in France did *High Wind* meet with much critical acclaim, being hailed by Jean-André Fieschi in *Cahiers du cinéma* as 'a surprise, and a kind of miracle. . . . The intuition which governed the exceptional choice of actors, the unaffected authority with which they're directed, the confident control of a narrative which, as it develops, grows increasingly less predictable: all this evinces a mastery which the beauty of the original story certainly brings out but couldn't, on its own, have engendered.' Rating the film on a par with *Pather Panchali* and Renoir's *The River* in its evocation of the mysteries of childhood, Fieschi added that 'what *Lord of the Flies* heavily expounded in terms of crude caricature, *A High Wind in Jamaica* gradually reveals, with intelligence and restraint, a little at a time'.[30]

Michel Ciment, writing in *Positif*, was no less impressed, describing it as 'a film of looks and gestures . . . a calm and incisive film where atmosphere is more important than words, where the director has a sense of action and of how to organise a sequence. . . . Mackendrick has captured childhood in all its ambiguity: neither innocent nor guilty, no more stamped with original purity than victim of social deviation.' *High Wind* represented a paradox, 'a film as anachronistic as its own pirates, a film of perfect classicism . . . but one that displays, within those narrow bounds, an astonishing vitality'.[31]

Unlike *Sweet Smell*, whose reputation and cult following have grown over the years, *High Wind* still awaits rehabilitation. For most critics, it ranks only as the least unsatisfactory of Mackendrick's later films, further evidence of the creative decline that blighted his career during the sixties. David Thomson summed up the consensus: 'His work became more conventional and impersonal. . . . Of his three most recent films only *High Wind in Jamaica* seems to belong to him and that is somehow choked off, as if Mackendrick could no longer face its meaning.'[32]

Even so, the film has its admirers; opinions differ more widely over it than over any other Mackendrick movie. Gilbert Adair coupled it with *Sweet Smell* as 'arguably his finest [films]';[33] for Joel Finler, it was 'Mackendrick's blackest movie';[34] and Brian Baxter, introducing a Mackendrick retrospective at the National Film Theatre in 1971, unequivocally rated it not only his finest work, but 'one of the best movies about children ever made', in which 'only the over-sunny, wide-screen photography and marginal enlargement of the star roles stop it from attaining the Buñuel class as a masterpiece of irony and pessimism'.[35]

It also found an unexpected partisan in the writer-director John Milius, who discovered Mackendrick's work in film school and – despite the ideological gulf between them – has stayed an enthusiastic admirer ever since. To Milius, *High Wind* is 'a very subtle film', full of 'a sense of thrilled vitality . . . a celebration of rebellious freedom in a way, and not an obvious one. I can live in that film, you know.' In *The Wind and the Lion*, his best film to date, Milius 'openly tried to steal as much of the flavour of [*High Wind*] as I could',[36] and even went so far as to cast Deborah Baxter (in her only other screen role so far) as Teddy Roosevelt's daughter, by way of homage.

Mackendrick's own opinion of *High Wind* remains low. 'I blame myself entirely – it was a mistake, right from the beginning. The only redeeming feature as far as I was concerned was that, in his gracious manner, old Hughes was quite kindly about it.' None of the films Mackendrick had made since leaving Ealing had been a notably happy experience; but the vitiation – as he saw it – of his most cherished project caused him particular despondency. Increasingly, he was finding the satisfactions of movie-directing outweighed by the frustrations.

# 10 Don't Make Waves

'It suits some . . . critics to build elaborate interpretations of films that may have been made by men aghast at the silliness of their material and the obtuseness of their colleagues.'[1]

David Thomson, *America in the Dark*

'It is a film of such silliness that it is a humiliation even to have to talk about it.'

Alexander Mackendrick

It was as a comedy director that Mackendrick had made his name. Since leaving Ealing, though, all his attempts to return to the genre – *The Devil's Disciple*, *Rhinoceros*, *The Man Who Wasn't There* – had proved abortive. Not until 12 years after *The Ladykillers* did another comedy appear bearing his name; and when it did, many people felt disappointed. Mackendrick himself would have shared their reaction, had not his expectations of the film, even before he began shooting, already sunk about as low as they could get.

By the mid-sixties, Mackendrick found himself nearly broke. He had invested a lot of his own time and money in the various unrealised projects. Of the films he had directed since Ealing, two had been critical failures, and all three had lost money. Within the industry he was becoming known not just an exacting and perfectionist director, but – far less forgivably – as one who failed to deliver at the box-office. He also had a young family to support: Matthew, born in 1961, had been followed by a second son, John, in 1965. It may have been this financial pressure that led Mackendrick, normally a canny and sceptical man, to fall for an elementary trick pulled by the producer Martin Ransohoff.

Ransohoff was the head of Filmways, an independent production company set up to make television material, which had moved into feature films in the early sixties. Michael Birkett, for a time the company's European representative, describes him as 'an old-fashioned mogul, who likes things shot fast and cheap and a big success, and he wants the million to turn into twenty'. Not that Ransohoff favoured trashy exploitation material. He had, as Birkett adds, 'a lot of tolerance for talent', and produced such interestingly off-beat ventures as *The Americanization of Emily*, *The Cincinnati Kid*, *Castle Keep* and *10 Rillington Place*.

Ransohoff offered Mackendrick a project which, he claimed, could make an ideal comedy vehicle for Tony Curtis. 'That whole operation,' as Mackendrick relates it, 'was Hollywood at its worst. I had an agent at that time – he's dead now – who was a buddy of Ransohoff's. The pair of them went to Tony and told him, "Sandy has this subject he's dying to make, and he got on very well with you – so he wants to know if you would do it, because it's something that's very dear to his heart." And then they came to me and said, "Tony Curtis has this subject that's very dear to his heart," and so on. We later found out both of us thought the material was absolute rubbish.'

The property that Ransohoff had lined up was a script adapted, at some distance, from a 1959 novel by Ira Wallach, *Muscle Beach*. A laconic, wisecracking work poised stylistically somewhere between Peter de Vries and Joseph Heller, the book recounts, in the first person, the exploits of a smooth-tongued salesman named Carlo Cofield. After wartime military service Cofield returns to his native New York, but soon finds himself sickened by the city's mental and physical squalor. He accordingly parlays himself into a job with a swimming-pool company in Los Angeles.

There he meets the songwriter Prescott Tom and his sister Toby. Tom's career is in trouble; Carlo suggests he should install a second swimming-pool, a ploy which proves effective. He also learns about Toby's disagreeable lover, Chris Danzig. Toby takes Carlo to Muscle Beach where he becomes infatuated with Jocie Kilbrough, a young woman of stupendous beauty. But she already has a boyfriend, Harry Fennerman, a body-builder.

Harry, who fears sex may debilitate his muscles, puts great faith in Madame Lavinia, a local astrologer. Carlo bribes her to tell Harry to lay off sex for two years. Jocie, as intended, takes up with Carlo – and promptly moves in, planning to get married and have six kids. Carlo is dismayed to find everything about her bores him except her body. Refusing to stoop to cruelty or abuse, he sets out to appear ridiculous in her eyes by practising body-building. The ruse works; Jocie goes back to Harry, who has decided muscles aren't everything. Toby meanwhile has ditched Danzig, and she and Carlo settle down together.

The book's title, perhaps intentionally, echoes that of Joseph Strick's slyly satirical 1948 documentary on Californian beach mores. Wallach's novel, though, isn't essentially a satire. While poking fun at the nuttier aspects of West Coast lifestyle, it depicts Southern California as a far more enjoyable place to live than New York. His Angelenos, far from recalling the monomaniac grotesques of *Day of the Locust* or *The Loved One*, are a generally likeable bunch, the nearest to a villain on offer being Danzig, the Chicago businessman. Satire feeds off scorn or disgust; the prevailing attitude in *Muscle Beach* is tolerant amusement. The novel ends with the mock-Voltairean adage, 'Children, let us cultivate our swimming-pools.'[2]

Having acquired the film rights, Ransohoff invited Wallach, who had written screenplays before, to provide a script. It was an experience the novelist recalls without relish – though he absolves Mackendrick, whom he found 'co-operative and pleasant to work with', from any blame. 'The first screenplay I wrote was good. The producers, however, asked for changes. Their suggestions confirmed my conviction that a good writer knows more about what constitutes a good script than almost any producer. I submitted a revised script, only to be told that the producers wanted further changes – for the worse. Again I obliged, because I was under contract, and when I submitted the third version, it was sufficiently bad to suit their taste. By that time, I had washed my hands of the whole affair. I took the money and ran.'[3]

After Wallach's departure, Ransohoff and his co-producer, John Calley, called in another writer, George Kirgo, whom Mackendrick found impossible to get on with. The screenplay was a mess, but Curtis had other commitments and time was running short. The producers resolved to start shooting, patching up the script as they went along. Ten years earlier, Mackendrick had embarked on *Sweet Smell of Success* under similar circumstances – but with some confidence in the quality of his material and the skill of his colleagues. Not so with the present venture. He decided to cut his losses, and asked to be taken off the picture. 'Upon which my agent, for reasons of his own, said, "If you do that, it's not just a matter of you never working in Hollywood again. They're committed to the contracts, so they'll sue you out of existence. You have to go through with it." So I gritted my teeth, and went into something that I knew from the beginning was going to be a disaster.'

Faced with a script virtually devoid of verbal or dramatic distinction, Mackendrick started to search for elements with some degree of visual potential. 'Because we had no story at all, I suggested to them that they steal – and it *is* a frank steal – from *The Gold Rush* the idea of the house that tips over. It was the idea of taking the couples that are mismatched and putting them in a house that you turn upside-down and roll down the hillside. And they let me go away and do a storyboard, a visual impression of how this might be achieved.'

Like most Filmways productions, *Don't Make Waves* (as the picture was now called) was to be released through MGM. Metro, though in decline from its former glory, still boasted the finest technical department in the world, and its resources were placed at Mackendrick's disposal. 'There were two little old craftsmen who had been with MGM since the year dot, and were responsible for all the travelling matte and special effects and miniature trickwork right back to the original *Ben-Hur*. They were delighted to have somebody interested in that aspect of the thing, so we worked very happily together on the mechanics of the house that was on rockers and built upside-down, and the exterior and interior models, and travelling mattes and so on. All very typical of what happens to a director when he's got absolutely no confidence in the material – you take it out in technical invention.'

Although Mackendrick now denies even having heard of Wallach's novel, it may be that his idea of the glissading house was sparked off – either directly, or via one of Wallach's versions of the script – by a passing image from the book's opening pages. 'Water has made the clay hills treacherous. . . . Along the Pacific Coast Highway, three tract houses, built with more faith than wisdom on soggy platforms cut into a mountain, slid silently towards the ocean, barely disturbing the inhabitants, who were well-to-do Zen Buddhists devoted to the Goren system of contract bridge.'[4] A good deal of *Muscle Beach* survives in *Don't Make Waves* in terms of character and incident; what's missing is the novel's tone of quizzical irony, for which the film never succeeds in substituting a consistent mood of its own.

It would be absurd to claim *Don't Make Waves* as any kind of creative success. It is, undeniably, the least accomplished of Mackendrick's films, and makes an unsatisfying conclusion to his directorial career. Even so, it can be seen to embody, in blurred and incoherent form, several of his characteristic themes, and isn't by any means as negligible as has been made out – especially by Mackendrick himself.

As with *High Wind in Jamaica*, *Don't Make Waves* presents the problem of assessing a film from which several chunks have gone missing – though here it may not be that they were excised, but that no one got round to supplying them in the first place. Scenes end in abrupt jump-cuts where fades would seem called for, and continuity is erratic – at one point Curtis smokes a cigar half a minute before it's offered him. Roles have been truncated: one featured actress (Mary Grace Canfield, playing a seamstress) appears in a single scene, for all of 15 seconds, with no dialogue and nothing to do. According to the studio synopsis, Curtis's character is an Ivy League professor, dismissed 'after being caught in a police raid on a student party'.[5] Nothing of this appears, or is mentioned, in the film as released, and almost certainly none of it was shot.

The film's dishevelled condition may be also due, not just to what was left out, but to what was put in. At a late stage, according to Mackendrick, the co-producer John Calley ('a sinister and charming character') called in Terry Southern to provide uncredited additional dialogue. Calley and Southern, who were personal friends, 'sat up all night smoking – well, smoking – and writing funny, outrageous lines of dialogue. All the funniest stuff in the film, such as it was, was ad-libbed by Calley and Southern.'

Not surprisingly, *Don't Make Waves* suffers badly from conceptual discontinuity; neither the characters, nor the overall tone of the film, are ever held in sustained focus. (The plot, perhaps more by luck than judgement, is reasonably coherent.) It seems to have been intended, if that

isn't too strong a word, as a satire on the Californian way of life – a target
Mackendrick believes to be 'in itself so fictitious, so surreal, that there's no
scope for satire'. All the same, several scenes work quite well on this level,
and would work even better were it not that the movie, through loss of nerve
or failure of intention, keeps lurching into less demanding styles of comedy,
vacillating between romantic bedroom farce in the Rock Hudson-Doris Day
mode, or a late entry in the teen-market 'beach comedy' cycle that spawned
such ephemera as *Gidget*, *Beach Party* and *How to Stuff a Wild Bikini*.

Inevitably, this fuzziness of purpose undermines the depiction of the
characters. Worst affected is Cofield himself, who seems to switch personas
from one scene to the next – through no fault of Curtis, who like most of the
cast strives honourably to make the best of his material. The Cofield of the
novel is an engaging hustler, verbally and psychologically adroit, and given
to disorienting sneak attacks on the underside of his victims' sensibilities.
Even so, he does maintain certain principles, not least a distaste for cruelty
in any form. 'In my own defense,' he remarks, not wholly disingenuously,
'let me say that although I have lied, cheated, resorted to insidious dodges,
bribed astrologers, and oversold swimming pools, I have always been a
gentleman in everything I did.'[6]

This character could have provided an ideal role for Curtis, suggesting as
it does a more amiable version of Sidney Falco. But at some point it was
decided to make him into a fall-guy, the accident-prone butt of fate, given to
tumbling into swimming pools and banging his head on low ceilings. This too
might have worked, though offering less scope for Curtis's talents. Some of
the farcical scenes are ingenious and funny, as when Carlo, trying to make
love to Malibu, is repeatedly hampered by her discarded sky-diving gear,
ending up with her helmet jammed on his kneecap – a burlesque of the
desired penetration. Where the film goes wrong is in running both roles in
tandem; at one moment Carlo comes on as the practised manipulator,
protean and confident, the next he's a buffoon. The two halves of the
character never coalesce – as though the Jekyll-and-Hyde-potion device had
been cut from *The Nutty Professor*, leaving the Jerry Lewis alter egos
unexplained.

The character's function is further weakened by the loss of the 'Ivy League
professor' element. Satire, as Mackendrick observes, needs the outsider
figure, through whose alien regard the audience can perceive the
absurdities. 'The film would only have worked if you'd pivoted it on the
introduction of some deadpan square, a European or East Coast figure, to
throw the insanities into relief. Without that outside set of values,
everything is eccentric, so everything is trivial.' Lacking the material to build
on, Curtis never manages to establish himself as any kind of convincing
'outsider', and the satire is deprived of its anchor point.

Even so, *Don't Make Waves* does intermittently succeed in exposing an acquisitive and materialistic society, where people – especially women – are reduced to the status of commodities, adjuncts to a lifestyle based on the accumulation of consumer goods. Laura Califatti, Prescott's mistress, sums herself up as 'a tax-deductible item', and Diane Prescott, offering Carlo the running of her company, includes her own sexual favours under the heading of 'interesting fringe benefits'. 'I know what you doing,' the jealous Laura tells Carlo, 'new house, new car, now you want to try new girlfriend.' Carlo looks pained; what else does she expect?

This theme is brought out in one of the film's most effective scenes. Returning to Laura's apartment after having landed his job with Seaspray, Carlo leafs through a copy of *Esquire*, homing in on the advertisements, while she makes coffee.

LAURA:  Now that you have a job, what will you do? What do you want?

CARLO:  Some cream. You know what I want? A box of 25 Monte Cristo panatellas. I want a king-size vibrator bed. I want a 35 mm Hasselblad – a Rolls-Royce convertible . . . I want driving gloves made from the underside of antelope ears. A bold men's cologne for the man who does something for women – a cashmere double-breasted jacket that's going to get me there first.

LAURA:  Get where?

CARLO:  Doesn't matter. I want to be where the action is. I want to live a life of understated elegance.

LAURA *(picking up another magazine)*:  A hi-fi set with 300 component parts and, er, vicuna underwear—

CARLO:  A Yamaha Big Bear scrambler—

LAURA:  And 12 credit cards – and a window seat in the first class of Cosmic Airlines, and, er—

CARLO *(contemplating double-page spread of naked woman)*:  Mmmm.

LAURA:  I don't think you'll have any trouble.

'I want to be where the action is.' There's an unmistakable echo here of Sidney Falco aspiring to get 'way up high . . . where it's always balmy', where he could have 'the best of everything'. *Don't Make Waves* intermittently comes across as a lighter, less acrid counterpart to *Sweet Smell of Success*, with Carlo and Rod Prescott replaying Falco and Hunsecker, the pupil again aspiring to supplant the master. 'What is it you want?' asks Prescott, scenting blackmail, to which Carlo replies, 'Everything you've got.' He nearly gets it, too – at one point Prescott's job, his wife and his mistress all seem within Carlo's grasp. 'I'll admit I've got a couple of numbers to learn,' he observes, settling in behind Prescott's desk, 'but with you as a teacher, I mean, how can I miss?'

Scenes like these seem like fragments of the film that *Don't Make Waves* set out to be – and might have been, had Mackendrick been given more control and a comedy writer of the ability of Dighton or Rose: the comedy of one of his dangerous outsiders, stranded amid the conspicuous consumerism of California, elated and appalled to find he can beat the locals at their own game.

Such a satire would have caught the spirit of the times. The hollowness within the Californian utopia became an increasingly popular theme in the movies of the sixties. A similar mood of fascinated distaste pervades the literature of the period – Gavin Lambert's *The Slide Area*, or Alison Lurie's *The Nowhere City* – prompted perhaps, as the demographic balance of the USA shifted south and westwards towards the 'sunbelt' states, by the realisation that Southern California might represent the shape of the future, the American dream at its peak of material fulfilment. A more fully achieved *Don't Make Waves* would have ranked with such West Coast comedies of disillusion as *The Graduate* (which shares its metaphoric use of swimming pools) and Richard Lester's underrated *Petulia*.

Now and again, *Don't Make Waves* comes close to implementing this satirical thrust. The ruins of a swimming pool dangling 300 feet above a coastal highway – could there be any more graphic encapsulation of what Reyner Banham called 'the heartbreak that ends the Angeleno dream'?[7] But, taken as a whole, the film seems more like a freeway interchange system stalled for lack of funds: thematic routes can be seen launching themselves off in promising directions, connections standing ready to be made, only to end abruptly in mid-air abyss as the momentum of plot construction fails them.

Indeed, for a film seriously flawed on almost every level, *Don't Make Waves* has a good many interesting things going on in it, several recalling, and even developing, elements from Mackendrick's earlier work. The uncertainty principle, the motif of falling and collapse that haunts his films, appears here at its most universal. In this society everything and everybody is on the slide – not just psychologically, as in *Sweet Smell*, but physically as well. Carlo himself, in his fall-guy persona, is under assault from all four elements – set on fire, nearly drowned (twice), blown out of a plane, and shoved down a cliff by a wave of mud. Laura's artistic pretensions are as insecure as her easel which, subsiding from under her canvas, prompts her to send the painting skimming down into the ocean. Possessions entail the literal downfall of their owners. In the opening reel, Carlo's car is rolled down a hillside, and him with it; in the final reel his house follows suit, with all six principal characters tumbled about inside it like dice in a shaker.

In this jerry-built world, the self is just another precarious construct.

Carlo, having been 'wiped out in 30 seconds' by Laura, dons Rod's clothes and takes on the role of a salesman, which he defines as 'nothing more than a collection of personality defects'. Laura, failed movie actress, has converted herself into an all-purpose ethnic provider (by implication, sexually as well as gastronomically): 'I can do everything, I don' know, Chinese, Japanese, um, Italian, French – what do you like?' Most people operate from behind façades. Rod Prescott, the masterful, affluent boss-figure, dwindles on closer acquaintance into a mere employee of his wife's company. Madame Lavinia, votary of spiritual forces, turns out to be a man, and materialistic with it. Even Malibu, the bronzed superwoman, transforms to Carlo's chagrin into a domestic bubblehead, sitting in bed with hair in curlers, gorging crisps and gazing vacantly at TV programmes in a language she can't understand.

In this case at least, Carlo's deception is self-induced; Malibu never claims to be much other than a superb body. She and Harry are the most innocent of all Mackendrick's innocents, almost to the point of idiocy, incapable of guile or malice on their own account, and blind to such qualities in others. Naively preoccupied with their own appearances, they unquestioningly accept appearance as reality. And in the end their innocence – like that of Mrs Wilberforce – emerges as strength, shaming the manipulative characters around them. 'Why is it so simple for some people?' asks Diane Prescott, watching the reunited couple blissfully massaging each other's shoulders. 'Because they're simple-minded, that's why,' her husband retorts, a note of envy tempering his disdain.

Malibu and Harry's territory is the beach, whose culture represents (in Reyner Banham's words) 'a symbolic reaction to the values of the consumer society, a place where a man needs to own only what he stands up in'.[8] Home for them is a battered beach-bus, inside which Harry manoeuvres with perfect comfort, while the much shorter Carlo keeps colliding with the roof. Against this is Rod's money-made world of the swimming pool, closed and artificial where the ocean is natural and limitless, controlled where the ocean is unpredictable. Or theoretically so; Carlo, attuned to neither environment, nearly drowns in his pool as he did in the sea. Eventually nature takes its revenge on this protected enclave, draining the pool before dropping it down the hillside, while Carlo – in one of the film's best gags – vainly invokes the forces of social order, calling the fire brigade and police to complain that his pool is cracked.

To the beach-dwellers, nature is a benign force. After Malibu has left him, we see Harry driving away, tears streaming down his face. In the next shot, the skies have opened; all creation weeps in sympathy, and the deluge will reunite the lovers. Malibu too, in contrast to Carlo, works in harmony with the elements. For her, falling is not a mishap but a skill; jumping from a plane or bounding on a trampoline, she performs with grace and sureness.

Her instinctual gifts show to advantage in the upside-down house where she adapts unconcernedly, swinging lithely about while the others scramble and grope. At one point, feeling hungry, she opens the refrigerator, which has landed flat on its back. Unexpectedly, it lights up; then, with a crackle and a sputter, all the other lights come on again, giving the surreal impression that she has intuitively restored the current. Her reunion with Harry, soon afterwards, extends the metaphor: they, and the other two couples, can start making all the right connections.

*Don't Make Waves* shares a central theme with *Smiles of a Summer Night*: the necessity of establishing, and accepting, one's own identity and that of others. (Bergman's film, though of course immeasurably more subtle, also ends with the recombining of mismatched pairs.) In the upended house, the materialist values of the Coast are turned on their heads, enabling each couple to shake free of illusions and see themselves clearly. 'You are just as stupid as I am,' Laura tells Carlo, '*I* don't like to look at who *I* am.' Acknowledging that Rod will continue to screw around, Diane offers him a controlling share of the company plus the liberty to 'carry on with those miscellaneous expenses which your crumbling ego seems to need'. Communication having been severally achieved, the house can now tumble further, decanting them finally on to the seashore, in the beach-territory of candour and physical immediacy.

Once again, Mackendrick expresses psychological upheaval in terms of redefined cinematic space. When we first see inside Carlo's house, its open-plan architecture offers no scope for intimacy – he and Laura have to conduct their quarrel with a bemused interior decorator dodging between them, staggering under the weight of a potted shrub. Upturned and devastated, the house subdivides itself into several small, snug refuges, allowing each couple their own space for negotiating terms. The episode parallels that in Jacques Tati's *Playtime*, where the disintegration of a stiffly formal restaurant permits the emergence within it of a small, human-sized area in which a bistro can spontaneously evolve.

Earlier in the film, Carlo has undergone the reverse spatial process, finding himself – like Sammy, or like Sidney Stratton at the climax of *Man in the White Suit* – suddenly left vulnerable in an open arena. Awakened by Rod's unscheduled arrival, Carlo is bundled out of Laura's apartment to hide on the patio, only to discover (as Mackendrick reveals with a quiet leftward pan) there's in fact nowhere he *can* hide. Absurdly huddled in the junction of two huge plate-glass windows, he stands exposed to Rod's first casual glance. And from there he's expelled even further into the wilderness, down on to a windswept beach ('You'll recognise it,' Rod observes spitefully, 'it's covered with sand') with only a blanket for shelter.

This view of the beach as bleak terrain of exile is almost immediately cancelled – in a brisk and startling transition – by an eruption of activity as

Carlo wakes to the spectacle of Muscle Beach. Harking back once more to his documentary roots, Mackendrick treats us to an exhilarating montage of energy: surfboarders, sunbathers, weightlifters, gymnasts, windsurfers, jousters on mopeds, seine fishermen, and even – in one fetchingly offbeat image – a surfboarding alsatian. Carlo, responding to this new and seemingly benign environment, strips off his ruined trousers and goes swimming, gets clouted over the head by Malibu's surfboard and is carted back to Laura's apartment – exiled again, since in the interim he's glimpsed paradise.

In countless movies the hero, knocked unconscious, revives to see the heroine's lovely face leaning over him, eyes wide with concern. *Don't Make Waves* works its own ribald twist on the convention: Carlo, coming blearily round, focuses on a vision of Malibu's superb bottom as she drags him up the beach. A moment later, as she bends down to give the kiss of life, the equally impressive frontal view follows. (The key emotional impact of these sights is conveyed by Mackendrick's use of subjective camera, purposeful as always.) From here on, fuelled by twin obsessions, Carlo will oscillate between two incompatible worlds, trying to merge them into one overriding achievement: material success *and* Malibu.

The attempt is foredoomed, as the film's theme song (a forgettable ballad by The Byrds) has hinted: 'And when the toys that you dreamed of have finally come, They all will break and you're back where you started from.' Like the goblin gold that crumbles in mortal hands, the achievements of the beach world are devalued in that of the swimming pool, and vice versa. The sharp practices so effective in selling pools also serve to outwit Harry – but the victory leaves a sour taste. Malibu, away from her beach, diminishes into a mindless bore. Even before his house starts to slide, Carlo's carefully constructed hybrid of the good life is coming apart; the graft has failed to take, the compound (shades of the White Suit) isn't stable.

By the end, Carlo has realised where he belongs: on the border between the two worlds, along with the other borderline character, Laura. He also accepts transience as a way of life; to embark on their relationship is 'probably the most self-destructive thing I could possibly do'. The final shot, in which they break away from the crowd gathered around the house to run along the seashore, stripping off and splashing in the waves, might suggest they've chosen to join Harry and Malibu in prelapsarian simplicity, swapping sides from experience to innocence. Other Mackendrick films end with innocence (Sammy, Sidney Stratton, Susan Hunsecker) gaining something of the insight of experience; *Don't Make Waves* offers the only example of characters reverting the other way. As a resolution, though, the scene hardly convinces, and still less as deliberate irony; to subject it to analysis may be conferring more dignity than it deserves on a contrived 'happy ending' in the most perfunctory Hollywood tradition.

In any case, relevance rarely counts for much in this screenplay. The humour tends to seem extraneous to the plot, tacked on by way of afterthought, as for example Lingonberry's account of his unfinished bomb shelter: 'I started digging it during the Eisenhower administration, then I stopped digging it during the Kennedy administration – and now I'm wondering if it's big enough.'

One or two jokes, though, do tie in more securely to character, like the running gag at the expense of Carlo's physique. Malibu, worried about Harry's reluctance to make love: 'Mr Cofield – do you find me attractive? I mean, if you were a man – would you be attracted to me?' (The scene gains from the fact that Malibu is ingenuously stripping off at the time, and from Curtis's impeccably timed triple-take.) And in response to Harry's concern over the effect of sex on the male musculature, Carlo rolls up his trouser leg, remarking, 'Well, I can only show you the price that *I* have to pay.'

The film also features two elements fashionable in Hollywood comedies of the period: an animated cartoon intro, running under the titles, and cameo appearances from guest stars. Both, as so often, seem to suggest a certain misgiving on the part of the film-makers, a nervous nudging of the audience as if to say, 'Hey, guys! This movie is *funny!*' The animated titles (uncredited, but in standard mid-60s UPA-style) depict Carlo's orange Volkswagen travelling across the USA from a snowbound New England, and probably represent all that remains of the Ivy League opening. Still, in having the car stand in for its owner, the sequence does set up the idea of vehicles as extensions of people's characters: Harry and Malibu's hippie beach-bus, Carlo's aspirational Rolls (succeeding his radical-chic, Euro-cultured Beetle) and Laura's showy, temperamental Lincoln convertible.

The cameos, too, become slightly more than incidental diversions by using each guest's persona to illustrate sharp practice in action. The gullible movie star whom Carlo talks into installing Seaspray's swishest pool is Jim Backus, James Dean's ineffectual father in *Rebel Without a Cause*, and voice of the myopic Mr Magoo. Carlo in his turn is conned into buying a Slide Area house by the slick-tongued Sam Lingonberry, played by the satirical comedian Mort Sahl. And Zack Rosenkrantz, the cynical manipulator who operates as Madame Lavinia, is portrayed by Edgar Bergen, erstwhile radio ventriloquist, creator and speaker of Charlie McCarthy.

This last scene – in which Carlo, a cut-rate Faustus, goes to do a deal with the devil – gives us a brief, intriguing idea of what a Mackendrick horror movie might have looked like. (*The Ladykillers*, of course, skirts a corner of the same territory.) Carlo, nervously approaching high, wrought-iron gates at night, is bidden entry by a disembodied voice; the gates creak rustily open and, as he ventures up the shadowed path, a sound midway between bark and croak erupts from the undergrowth, suggesting some outlandish dog-frog escaped from the island of Dr Moreau. Inside, the camera tracks at oblique angles up a winding staircase into a room strewn with bizarre objects (including a ship's figurehead left over from *High Wind*) where Rosenkrantz, urbanely sinister in silk dressing-gown, is enjoying a midnight breakfast.

Bergen's performance, fastidiously buttering toast while specifying in elaborate detail the astrological swimming pool he requires as quid pro quo for misleading Harry, is gauged at just the right level. As, indeed, are almost all the performances in *Don't Make Waves*. Despite the limitations of the material, there's rarely any overplaying. Robert Webber's Rod Prescott, frigidly contemptuous beneath the most cursory layer of charm, hints at what might have been, given better scripting, a memorably rebarbative portrayal.

Nonetheless, there can be detected in his performance (as in several others, especially Claudia Cardinale's) the desperation of an actor trapped in what he suspects is a compromised film teetering out of control. Mackendrick himself, openly unhappy from the start, became increasingly so as shooting progressed. At one point James Hill and James Kennaway (who were trying to set up a movie with MGM for Mackendrick to direct) visited him on set. As Hill tells it, 'I asked him, "What's it like working with Marty Ransohoff?" And Sandy went [throat-slitting gesture]: "Ransohoff? Yeucch!" I looked round, and there's Ransohoff, standing right behind him. So Jimmy and I said, "OK, Sandy – see you later." '

Joanna Barnes was cast as Diane Prescott by the producers without even having met Mackendrick. 'He's a man of immense delicacy of taste, of wonderful sympathy with his material, of great selectivity. If you look at those early comedies of his, they were light, they were airborne – and I don't think you can just do this sort of comedy by committee. People overrode him, and in the end it did end up being the product of a number of people, largely the producers. . . . I think he must have had what is indelicately known in the burlesque trade as "the flop sweats". We all had it to some extent – we knew that it was a downhill slide from day one. But we were all doing our best. When you're on a sinking ship, you bale like crazy – and that's what we were doing.'[9]

Intentionally or not, Mackendrick's introduction of the subsiding-house climax proved all too apposite; as with *Sweet Smell of Success*, *Don't Make Waves* can be seen as an allegory of the fraught circumstances under which the picture was made. Having been conned, like Cofield, into taking on a ramshackle structure founded on shifting ground, Mackendrick found himself and his cast embarked on an unstoppable slide into disaster. The film opened, in May 1967, to the worst reviews of his career – not so much hostile, on the whole, as dismissive. American critics generally wrote the picture off as trivial, though conceding the odd diverting moment. Their British colleagues followed suit, adding a note of puzzlement – understandably, since 12 minutes had been chopped out of the British release print with little regard for narrative logic.

Even so, it was hardly the kind of setback that seriously damages a director's reputation. Had it not turned out to be his last film, *Don't Make Waves* would probably seem no more relevant to the overall trajectory of Mackendrick's career than, say, *Jamaica Inn* to Hitchcock's. Almost all reviewers treated him sympathetically, absolving him of blame for the faults, and crediting him with what virtues they could find. Tom Nairn, in the *New Statesman*, was typical. 'Mackendrick has a remarkably visual sense of humour, and the really comic moments of the film are his. . . . Flashes like these recall the best of Mackendrick's other comedy successes, and cause one to regret what *Don't Make Waves* actually becomes. In fact, it is an unequal battle between the director's talent and two painful obstacles: a limping script . . . and the unspeakably inept person of the female lead, Claudia Cardinale . . . [who] identifies humour with Italian noise and expostulation. . . . Both she and Mackendrick have been victims of MGM's machinations.'[10]

One of the rare favourable reviews came from Andrew Sarris who, writing in the *Village Voice*, called *Don't Make Waves* 'one of the more underrated comedies of the season'. Suggesting that the humour may have been too subtle for most critics, he commended Mackendrick's direction as 'longer on quiet chuckles than noisy belly laughs', and Curtis for 'his most perceptive performance since *Sweet Smell of Success*'. He went along with Nairn's verdict on Cardinale, though: she 'should never act in English until she can read lines as skilfully as Sophia Loren. . . . Claudia's troubles are compounded by the fact that she is out-vavavoomed by Sharon Tate in the biggest Hollywood cheesecake robbery since Betty Grable displaced Alice Faye in *Tin Pan Alley*.'[11]

Virtually the only person to have a good word for Cardinale was Mackendrick himself. 'I never really got to know her – one couldn't, under the circumstances – but I think she gives a very funny performance. Though I can take no credit for anything she does, because the whole thing was such a mess.'

*Don't Make Waves* remains the least known of all Mackendrick's films, seldom revived and rarely referred to – although Basil Wright, generous and open-minded as always, put in a good word for it in *The Long View*. This neglect seems unlikely to cause its director much regret. 'It's best forgotten. But it taught me something I should have known in the first place, that comedy is a flower that does not transplant. I think I proved the hard way that the kind of humour I had developed in Britain I, at least, cannot do in America.'

The conclusion is questionable, to say the least; if *Don't Make Waves* proved anything, it was simply that Mackendrick – like almost any director, however talented – couldn't win out against a duff script and devious producers. At all events, the experience was enough to put him off Hollywood for good. The project Hill and Kennaway had been working on – a version of Kennaway's novel *The Bells of Shoreditch*, with Rex Harrison to play the lead – was getting nowhere, and Mackendrick resolved to return to London. His only other Hollywood work at this period was a brief assignment ('That was again a piece of blackmail, but I've forgotten why I had to do it') for the producer Ray Stark, who had a film in deep trouble.

A rough rule of thumb on movie titles: any film whose title exceeds six words is probably a turkey, and the more words over six, the worse it will be. Like most rules, it admits exceptions – *I Am a Fugitive from a Chain Gang* comes to mind – but not many, and *Oh Dad, Poor Dad, Mama's Hung You in the Closet and I'm Feelin' So Sad* is emphatically not one of them. A black comedy based on a play by Arthur Kopit, it was filmed in 1965 for Stark's Seven Arts company, with Richard Quine directing a fine cast which included Rosalind Russell and Barbara Harris. On completion, the film was put into preview; audience response started at derisive and worked downwards. Stark pulled the picture from release schedule and sat on it for a year or so before attempting a salvage operation.

In the hope of clarifying the self-consciously zany narrative, a prologue and several inserts were added in which Jonathan Winters, playing Russell's late husband, comments on the action from a celestial cloud. It was these episodes that Stark asked Mackendrick to direct. 'It was dreadful, because I couldn't cope with Jonathan Winters. He's a very funny man, but he was uncomfortable with me, and I was uncomfortable with him. So it was just a chore, a day's work.' It was also a lost cause. *Oh Dad* was released in 1967 to atrocious notices and worse box-office, and Mackendrick's contributions could do little to redeem it. By comparison, *Don't Make Waves* looks like a masterpiece of sophisticated comedy.

Back in London, Mackendrick set out to reactivate two of his unrealised projects. Jay Kanter, recently appointed head of Universal's London operation, had announced a bold and imaginative slate of films. Offered *Mary Queen of Scots*, he responded with enthusiasm to Mackendrick's iconoclastic approach. And despite the tepid box-office response to *Don't Make Waves*, the idea of a revised version of *Rhinoceros* attracted the interest of Martin Ransohoff.

It might seem remarkable, given his recent experiences, that Mackendrick would consider working for Filmways again. This time, though, the circumstances were rather different. Since he himself owned the rights to Ionesco's play, he could keep the script firmly within his control. Also, Ransohoff would be involved only at one remove. The effective producer was Michael Birkett, Filmways' European representative and former assistant on *The Ladykillers*, with whom Mackendrick got on well.

For Ransohoff, the attraction lay in the casting. Peter Sellers, whose film career had taken off thanks to *The Ladykillers*, was interested in playing Bérenger, with Peter Ustinov as his friend Jean. The two Peters had never appeared together – and, as things turned out, never did; they could, as Mackendrick says, have made a great team. Ustinov, Birkett recalls, was particularly keen on his role from the start. 'Sandy said, "You'll play the last one to turn into a rhinoceros," and Peter said, "Yes, I know the play – oh, right—" and then immediately, without any pause, he started breathing heavily through his nose and rubbing his shoulder up against the doorpost. I really think Sandy was convinced he was going to change there and then.'

At Sellers's suggestion, the action was to be set in Hamburg, culminating in a gigantic rhino rally amid brutalist architecture; rhinoceritis as fascism. Mackendrick had his misgivings about this. Ionesco's play satirises social conformism in any form; to narrow it down to one specific political target diminishes its power. But for the time being he went along with the idea to keep Sellers happy. John Bird had been brought in to write the script – in Birkett's view, not an ideal choice. 'John's a dear and slightly daffy creature, and daffy writers aren't what Sandy needs. He needs a down-to-earth writer who knows exactly where the plot's going, then he can fantasise all around it. So I was desperately trying to make some sense of the whole thing, and it was getting bigger and bigger. John Calley, Marty's sidekick, had come over, an exceedingly brilliant and witty man, and he had the most marvellous notions about it. It was he who encouraged us to plan it on a huge scale.'

The new version of *Rhinoceros* treated Ionesco's play even more freely than the Hancock/Exton version. Later, for his students at CalArts, Mackendrick storyboarded an excerpt in which a minor traffic incident escalates into mass hysteria and viciously comic mayhem. The sequence, from near the start of the film, establishes a sense of violence shimmering like a haze over the city streets, where every individual except the hapless hero (here called Willi) seethes with barely contained rage. Rhinoceritis, it seems, would have symbolised not so much fascism as the expression of a psychic violence brimming over into mass dementia. Had it been made, it appears that *Rhinoceros* Mk II would have exploited the full savagery of Mackendrick's comic vision to devastating effect.

A test was shot to see if multiple rhinos could be convincingly loosed into a cityscape. Birkett spent an enjoyable day with Mackendrick at London Zoo, 'with a bemused camera crew and these two lunatics in the rhino pen'. The results went to the laboratory for matte work, 'and sure enough, there was Horse Guards Parade with rhinoceroses roaming all over it. So we said, "Well, that proves you can have rhinos wherever you want." MGM were a bit nonplussed by all this, but they said, "Well, OK, Marty, sure – Sellers and Ustinov, OK." '

At this juncture, history repeated itself. Sellers, like Hancock five years earlier, decided the whole thing was wrong for him and backed out. According to Birkett it was Sellers's agent, David Begelman (later to achieve notoriety in the great Columbia embezzlement scandal),[12] who talked him out of it. 'He'd read up about Ionesco, and he said, "This is a fringe-theatre nutters' piece. You shouldn't be in this sort of thing, you're a big mainstream star actor." ' Neither Birkett nor Mackendrick could reconvince Sellers – Mackendrick, indeed, was unable to get near him, Begelman having thrown up a protective screen around his client. And without Sellers, as far as Ransohoff and MGM were concerned, the deal was off. Mackendrick, to his indignation, found himself blamed for the débâcle. 'Ransohoff held me responsible for not having delivered the two stars – which was monstrous, because that was no part of my job – and refused to go ahead with the production.'

Universal, at least, seemed firmly committed to *Mary Queen of Scots*. Jay Kanter, cultured and soft-spoken, was a movie boss of a very different stamp from Ransohoff, and Universal were known as an exceptionally straight-dealing studio. John Heyman, who produced Peter Watkins's *Privilege* for them, described them as 'clean to work for, unbelievably honest, offering no arguments of a mean or frustrating nature to the people they signed'.[13] Their British production programme included films directed by Truffaut, Losey, Chaplin, Reisz, Peter Hall, Jack Gold and Albert Finney, on an ambitious range of subjects. It's one of the more dismal ironies of cinema history that such a programme should have turned out, as Alexander Walker noted, 'a failure of unanticipated and unparalleled proportions'.[14]

For the time being, though, Universal offered Mackendrick his most congenial working environment since Ealing. Interviewed in May 1968, he outlined, with evident gusto, his vision of the picture he had been waiting to make for nearly twenty years, a film that would 'cut the lace off the dialogue . . . a gangster story which smells of cow-dung'.[15]

*Mary Queen of Scots*, as Mackendrick described it, would have explored another of those collisions of fatally incomprehending perceptions that recur throughout his work. 'Sixteenth-century Scotland was frontier territory populated by cut-throats, gangsters and cattle thieves. And she was a highly sophisticated French lady up to her neck in you know what. She had been Queen of France, but now she was in Boot Hill.' There would be no grand-opera confrontations with Elizabeth, no noble death on an English scaffold. The action was restricted to 14 months, from the murder of Rizzio, through her forced marriage to Bothwell, to 'the moment when – with the Edinburgh mob shouting "Burn the hoor" in the streets – she's marched back a prisoner – aged 24, is it?'[16]

Mackendrick's account, and the drawings and storyboards that survive, vividly convey the mood of brooding claustrophobia he was aiming for: Highland clansmen crouched like wild animals, dirks at the ready; surly crowds in narrow streets and cramped, dungy courtyards; Rizzio meeting his death in a dark poky room, 'eight men in there slashing about by candlelight. It's almost farce.'[17] The script Mackendrick had prepared with James Kennaway was once more redrafted, with Gore Vidal contributing some additional dialogue. Sets were being constructed, and casting was under way: Vanessa Redgrave had been considered for the title role, but Mackendrick hoped for a French actress, possibly Catherine Deneuve.

At which point, with everything set to go, the chickens hatched earlier in the decade, when Bryanston missed out on *Tom Jones*, began winging back to roost. The profits cleared by United Artists on Woodfall's period romp had enticed the rest of Hollywood across the Atlantic. For a few ecstatic years, while censorship eased, local production costs stayed low, and the fantasy of Swinging London spread Beatles LPs and Union-Jack knickers across the globe, it seemed that few films made in Britain on American money could fail to please. In 1967 and 1968, Hollywood was providing some 90 per cent of the finance behind the British film industry; but the investment was starting to turn sour. Public taste, and in particular American taste, was tiring of Britishness. All at once it became possible for movies to be young, with-it *and* American: *Bonnie and Clyde* proved as much, to be followed by *The Graduate* and *Easy Rider*.

Suddenly films that, a year or two earlier, could have confidently cashed in at the box-office on their British appeal were falling flat - and a disproportionate number of them were Universal productions. Of the dozen Universal UK releases from 1967 to 1969, not one was a hit, nor even a modest success. Regretfully, but without recriminations, the head office called a halt. Kanter resigned, the London operation was closed down and six projects in active preparation were abandoned. One of them was *Mary Queen of Scots*. A few weeks later, in December 1968, James Kennaway, who had contributed almost as much to the project as Mackendrick himself, died of a heart attack at the wheel of his car. He was 40 years old.

In 1972, Universal released the film *Mary Queen of Scots*. Vanessa Redgrave played the title role, and was nominated for an Academy Award. But the picture had nothing to do with Mackendrick, nor with Kennaway. Scripted by John Hale, directed by Charles Jarrott, it was about as remote from Mackendrick's conception as could be imagined: romantic, conventional and devoid of visual distinction. Nonetheless, it did tolerably well at the box-office, thus putting paid, at least for the immediate future, to any thought of a remake. And by then, in any case, Mackendrick was no longer directing films.

Throughout 1969, one Hollywood studio after another followed Universal's lead in cutting UK investment, and the British film industry imploded like a punctured beach ball. Most film-makers of any talent or ambition found themselves obliged to pursue their projects overseas, and later that year Mackendrick, suppressing his distaste for Hollywood, was in Los Angeles preparing a subject for Universal, 'a thriller of some sort about heart transplants – something of no consequence whatever'. One day he was unexpectedly invited to a meeting about the establishment of a new academic foundation in Southern California. As the discussion proceeded, Mackendrick realised he was being offered the post of Dean of the film school. 'I thought they must be kidding, but they weren't. So I jumped at the chance.'

# 11 Conclusions

'I have never claimed to be happy – but what
I will say is that I wake up every morning
now in a way that I never did in the movie
business, with an eager mixture of
exasperation and curiosity.'[1]

Alexander Mackendrick

Around 1975, John Halas visited Mackendrick in California and watched him teaching a film class. 'He behaved not unlike a super-conductor, a Toscanini. He was rushing from one place to another to show his students how to angle the camera, how to set it up and what to look out for in a shot, everything right down to the last detail. So in fact it was nothing else but what he used to do on the studio floor, but now his actors were the students.'

Mackendrick maintains that he never quit making films – since training future film-makers is an integral part of the movie-making process – but simply stopped directing them. Nor was it a sudden decision. For some years he had been coming to realise that the life of a freelance director – in which clinching the deal is often more important, and always more time-consuming, than making the movie – was one for which he had little taste and less aptitude. 'To spend, say, 50 per cent of your time trying to get the job, and 50 per cent of your time doing the job – that's a fair break. If you spend 95 per cent of your time trying to get the job, and only 5 per cent doing it, you're in the wrong business.

'The industry really divides into two sorts of people – the people who make deals, and the people who make films. At a certain level you don't get to make the films unless you're also a deal maker; and when I reached that level, I began to wonder whether I was in the right industry. It sounds very sympathetic to say that you're no good at the money side, but that's just sheer self-indulgence, because money-making is what the business is about. The deal is the real product, and the movie is a sort of incidental by-product of the deal. . . . So I had a disheartening time in many ways as a freelance director on the open market; I was never really suited for that.'[2]

Mackendrick also believes he was spoilt by his experience of working within large organisations, insulated from the hard-edged, money-making decisions – not just at Ealing, but earlier at J. Walter Thompson, and also in the Army. 'I've always been happiest in these big organisations, where I'm free to make mischief from within – where I get all the centralised support, but I've got enough skill to exploit it for my own benefit. I should probably have joined the BBC, or something like that.' Instead, he joined the California Institute of the Arts as the first Dean of its film school.

CalArts (as it's generally known) was founded posthumously by Walt Disney, one of the grandiose projects to which he devoted his later years. It represented, according to Richard Schickel, 'on a grand scale, [Disney's] old dream of an artist's utopia reconstituted . . . a place where all the arts might mingle and stimulate one another, as he had once hoped they might in his movies.' However, 'he had rejected the idea of putting his name on the place on the ground that students and potential faculty members might be put off by its nonscholarly associations'.[3]

The new institute, endowed by a massive bequest from Disney's estate, opened in 1970 in temporary quarters in Burbank. A year later it moved to its permanent campus on a commanding hilltop site at Valencia, some 30 miles north of Los Angeles, on what used to be part of the studio ranch. The concept behind CalArts was that it should not be in any narrow sense vocational, but creatively interdisciplinary: painting, sculpture, music, film, animation, dance and theatre should interact and cross-fertilise, with students encouraged to move outside their chosen fields and both study, and practise, all the other arts.

This free-form approach, coinciding with the radical ferment of the period, created an ethos wholly at odds with that of the morally and politically conservative Disney Organisation. One student wittily summed up the contradictions within the Institute by dubbing it 'the Mickey Mauhaus'. Even by Californian standards, teaching methods were informal. One of Mackendrick's first students, F. X. Feeney (who became film critic of the *Los Angeles Weekly*) recalls that 'there were no grades; there were classes, but they had no clocks anywhere in the building. You showed up if you wanted to, if the vibes were right.'[4] More than once the Disney trustees came close to cutting off funding – especially after a well-publicised incident when a staff member stripped naked at a faculty meeting to make a point about open administration.

'Looking back,' Patricia Goldstone wrote in *American Film* in 1979, 'it can be said that CalArts suffered, as did the sixties in general, from unreal expectations. It was sprawling and overly ambitious and probably demanded too much of the young people who entered its doors expecting something easy, like a job, at the end of the rainbow. But as an experiment, it was a noble one.'[5] Gradually – if only to avoid alienating its main source of income – the Institute adopted a more conventional style of teaching. Even so it remains, in the opinion of Charles Champlain, Arts Editor of the *Los Angeles Times*, 'the most open-minded, avant-garde school of higher education in the West, and almost any place in the country'.[6]

The post of Dean of the film school was first offered to Rossellini, but negotiations foundered over his desire to spend half the year in Italy. Instead the job went to Mackendrick, who held it until 1978 when, at the age of 65, he stepped down as Dean with the comment: 'The fiefdoms of strong figures in film study are one of its greatest failings. It's time for someone else's vision now.'[7] He stayed on, though, as a Fellow of the Institute, and continued to teach as actively as ever.

During his time as Dean, Mackendrick built up the film school's reputation as one of the finest in the country, and his own as one of the great teachers of film. Seeing a clear continuity with his previous work ('I wasn't in the least scared of learning how to teach, because I think that's what a director is doing mostly'),[8] he brought to his teaching the qualities that distinguished him as a film-maker: the perfectionism, the attention to detail, the acute visual sense and the belief in narrative structure as the core of movie-making. From the first, his approach was resolutely practical, treating film as a craft to be learned, rather than a vehicle for the expression of a personal vision. Feeney noticed that 'it was only Sandy Mackendrick, of any of the teachers there, who was very loath to call anybody an artist. He said, "If I ever use the word artist, it's with a small a. I have always seen myself as a craftsman." He thought that was a word of honor.' Also, though he seemed 'the shyest and most diffident person in that arrogant circle . . . he was the one who held truest to his guns. Over the five years that I was there, he was the only one not to make outlandish promises about a revolutionary school.'[9]

'There's a lot to be said,' Mackendrick wrote in an introductory hand-out for his students, 'for the view that directing . . . can be learned, but cannot be taught. Few professional directors I know ever took classes in the subject. Most textbooks on the subject are, in my opinion, poor. It's not stuff you can learn from a book. How is the knack of film directing acquired? Three ways, I suggest: *First*, by going to see films, watching them over and over again till you see how it's done. . . . *Second*, by working for an experienced director in some capacity where you are close enough to watch the (often subconscious) thought processes. . . . *Thirdly*, by writing. By planning on your own, then re-writing over and over and over. . . .

'Having established that it's impossible, I will attempt to "teach" some "rules" for beginning directors. This really means, I'll tell you how I have developed a method that suits me. If I bully you into trying my way, it is not because it's the only way. Or the best way. Certainly it will, in the end, probably not be your way. I suggest, however, that you make a real effort to follow my formula – *as an exercise*. Not to "express yourself" – not yet; you can do that as much as you like – later. Put aside your hunger for instant gratification and creativity – at least for long enough to understand some basic formulas which you are perfectly entitled to discard later. (Anybody who wants out please say so now.)'[10]

Quite a few did. To most CalArts students this down-to-earth, hard-graft approach came as a shock, and each year several dropped out in favour of easier options. The toughness of Mackendrick's teaching methods, according to his colleague Bill Jackson, is deliberate policy: 'He makes it extremely difficult for the student, and creates this tremendous challenge, and the better students grit their teeth and dig in there. They bring their work to Sandy, and he savages them, and sends them back again and again – and if they can take it, their work becomes so much better. I don't know of anyone who teaches with the effectiveness that he does – because what students often don't understand is how much work it takes to create something of real quality. And he actually works harder than they do – it's an incredible giving.'

The basis of Mackendrick's teaching (which deserves a whole book to itself) rests, like his own film-making, on the primacy of narrative. Most aspirant film students, he believes, approach their subject backwards-on, with grand Wellesian notions of scripting, directing, editing and starring in their own unique cinematic vision – screenwriting being merely 'a means to becoming directors of their own stories'.[11] Instead, he insists they first learn how stories are told – not just in the cinema, but in terms of basic dramatic principles going back to Aristotle – before being allowed anywhere near the director's chair.

Likewise with the assimilation of cinematic technique. Initially, Mackendrick taught a course on Film Grammar to his first year students, following it with Dramatic Construction in the second year. This, he came to believe, was the wrong way about: 'Film Grammar exercises and demonstrations work well when they evolve out of some of the ideas debated in Dramatic Construction. (For instance, screen sizes and eyelines as a means to express the dramatic point of view.) [They're] less interesting when they are presented in a very general way: they seem to be better grasped as solutions to specific narrative problems.'[12]

And while master-minding a whole project from initial concept to post-production may be 'almost certainly a very exciting (if costly) experience, it is also one in which the student never has a chance to learn what works and what doesn't'.[13] Instead, the sequence of experience should be reversed, with students learning their craft rather as directors used to at Ealing (or, come to that, in Hollywood) by working on *other people's* material: editing their footage, adapting their ideas into screenplays, helping to produce or direct their scripts – while handing their own treatments to someone else to work on as writer or director. In this way, the student can stand back from the creative material, seeing its strengths and weaknesses – just as Mackendrick himself had learned his craft by working as writer and second unit director on other people's pictures.

Such an approach also trains students to submerge their egos and work as part of a team. 'If you're talking about making movies, then you have to learn the hard way, to be a cog in the machine,' Mackendrick observes. 'That's a very painful experience for most students.'[14] Jack Valero, another graduate of the film school, describes Mackendrick as 'the first cold water we were hit with. He prepared us to face the film business world, told us a little bit about the kind of grim realities we'd be facing. . . . We saw a lot of people get weeded out, and . . . at times it seemed he was being extremely hard on us, but I guess that was the way he showed his affection towards particular people who he saw potential in.'[15]

It would have been easy for Mackendrick, particularly in the climate of the early seventies, to present himself as a misunderstood artist, victim of the insensitive Hollywood system like Orson Welles or Nicholas Ray. Instead, he offers his own career as a cautionary tale, insisting that the decision to quit film directing for teaching wasn't something he regrets in the least. Some two years after he had joined CalArts, he had occasion to drive to Beverley Hills: 'As I manoeuvred into a parking space I suddenly realised that my stomach was in a knot, and I wondered why it was. Then I realised that I was parked outside my ex-agent's place. And at that point I started to relax, because of the utter relief that I wasn't in that business any more. And that's when I knew that I had made the right decision.'[16]

Only once did he seriously consider quitting CalArts. In 1972 the British Film Institute was seeking a new director. At the suggestion of Colin Young, then heading the National Film School at Beaconsfield, Mackendrick applied for the job and, according to Young, made it to the final shortlist of two. Had he been appointed, it would have been the first time in its existence that the BFI had chosen a director with experience of mainstream film-making. But once again the Governors played safe and picked an academic: Keith Lucas, who taught film at the Royal College of Art but had never worked in the movie industry. Young believes that 'Sandy would really have shaken the place up, and that could be what worried them. But they rejected him on the grounds that he wasn't an administrator, and couldn't organise a piss-up in a brewery. I think history's proved them wrong, if you look at what he did at CalArts, creating something from nothing against all the odds.'

Not until some years later, after resigning the deanship, did Mackendrick take up Young's other suggestion: that he should come and teach a course at the NFS. He taught only one semester, in the summer of 1979, but by all accounts it was hugely successful. Among his students were Terence Davies and Jennifer Howarth, later respectively director and producer of *Distant Voices, Still Lives* – and another future director, Jenny Wilkes, for whom 'those few weeks were worth the whole three years [at the school]. There was nobody in his league; I didn't learn anything from anybody else that came near the stuff Sandy was teaching.' In 1982 her graduation film, *Mother's Wedding*, won an Oscar for Best Student Fiction Film. 'I could invite one honoured guest, so I asked Sandy. And in my speech I said I'd learnt everything from Alexander Mackendrick, and there he was sitting in the audience. But nobody in Hollywood knew anything about him; they had no idea of the treasure they had living there in Westwood.'

Mackendrick found his semester at Beaconsfield as stimulating as did his students. 'Maybe the teacher learned more than those he taught,'[17] he told Colin Young afterwards. Further visits, though, were ruled out by his state of health. The asthma from which he had long suffered had developed into emphysema, making air travel difficult and trips to Britain, thanks to the climate, especially hazardous.

Apart from this, though, Mackendrick refuses to let illness hamper him. At the age of 78 he continues to teach regularly at CalArts, takes an active role in international seminars, and could, in theory, even resume directing films. John Huston, after all, was older and in far worse health when he made *The Dead*. But Mackendrick's resolution remains unshakeable: his exit from the movie industry is apparently final.

It's also, on a personal level, undoubtedly justified. It would be unreasonable to deplore his decision, at age 57, to regenerate his career by quitting a profession in which he felt increasingly frustrated for one which affords him such evident satisfaction. Even so, considering the movies that he made and, had things gone differently, might still be making, it's hard not to agree with Douglas Slocombe in seeing Mackendrick's departure as 'an enormous loss to the film industry, and to us all'.

In his *Critical History of British Cinema* Roy Armes observes that 'it is virtually impossible – despite the wealth of talent and occasional achievements of outstanding quality – to find a British film-making career that has the fullness of that of, say, Jean Renoir or Howard Hawks'.[18] And Gavin Lambert, comparing the British cinema with the French, noted the lack of 'a kind of momentum, a kind of general impetus'.[19] At first sight, Mackendrick might seem to furnish an apt example. Certainly in terms of sheer output – nine films spread across 18 years – he falls far short not only of Renoir and Hawks, but of his British contemporaries such as Powell and Reed.

But 'fullness', it could be argued, isn't just a matter of quantity. It also implies a richness and density of texture (both visual and conceptual), a continuity of creative impulse that can cut across genre, lend a personal dynamic to routine or even mediocre movies, and form a distinctive body of work with its own internal connections and consistencies. And it's in this sense that Mackendrick's work, for all the sparsity of his output, possesses a quality for which fullness isn't such an inappropriate term.

All the same, it can't be denied that probably the strongest single impression created by Mackendrick's directorial career is one of frustration, of great potential left unfulfilled – which may partly account for the critical neglect of his work. There are more obvious attractions in studying a film-maker like Hitchcock, whose early promise can be seen burgeoning into achievement – or such romantically *maudit* figures as Welles or Stroheim, where we can point to one or two towering masterpieces as earnest of what might have been. Rather more, in Mackendrick's case, has to be allowed for, in a career where so much seemed always about to happen but never did.

The paradox of Mackendrick's career is that he was both made, and ruined, by Ealing Studios. Were it not for Ealing, it's possible he would never have directed films at all; film-making, after all, was merely something he 'drifted into'. And almost certainly no other studio would have been so generous either with the initial opportunity, or with the continuing support that he needed to build his career. Yet this uniquely sympathetic atmosphere left him, along with many of his colleagues, disastrously unfitted for the realities of film-making anywhere else. Even Michael Relph, who in his workmanlike partnership with Basil Dearden was better prepared than most, feels that 'we were really feather-bedded. It was Shangri-La. And I don't think we realised how lucky we were until we had to face the outside world.'

Mackendrick too came to recall Ealing as a lost Eden. 'Thereafter I never found a place in which I was so fully supported, in terms of being allowed to make the projects that I wanted to make. . . . And so the difficulties that I had in Hollywood, apart from other things, were that I had in fact been given an indulgence and support which perhaps made me not fully able to cope with the tougher and more independent – although very much more lucrative – world of California.'[20]

Ealing also blighted – and, to some extent, continues to blight – Mackendrick's critical reputation. Despite Barr's definitive study, there's still a tendency for the term 'Ealing' to be applied as indiscriminately as 'Hollywood' used to be (before *Cahiers du cinéma* taught us all better): to brand the studio's entire Balcon-era production with some such epithet as 'cosy' or 'whimsical'. As a result, it's difficult for any director who started out in this supposedly toytown world ever to be taken entirely seriously. In Mackendrick's case, a couple more films as snarlingly un-Ealing as *Sweet Smell* would have done the trick. But since that remained unique in his output, it could be dismissed as a chance aberration – as it was by the critic who wrote that 'his films, except for his Hollywood adventure, have remained inescapably nice little films: accomplished, attractive, impersonal'.[21]

That was written in 1963, but similar attitudes persist. As recently as 1985, Anthony Slide could assert that 'Mackendrick's work is always interesting and sound, but that is about all one can say of it. His films are no better or worse than those from any of the other Ealing directors.'[22] Such a judgment could be written off as boneheadedly imperceptive, were it not just an extreme example of the undervaluing to which Mackendrick's work has been consistently subject. Even a critic as acute as Raymond Durgnat questioned whether his films 'bear the obvious imprint of a particular directorial personality'.[23] It might be added that Mackendrick himself, who despises self-promotion and habitually disparages his own films, hasn't done much to improve things. But his work itself also abets the process through the sheer transparency of its style – what Barr describes as 'the essential, underestimated quality of lucidity'.[24]

Much of the accomplishment of Mackendrick's cinema lies in what he *doesn't* do, which can therefore easily be overlooked. He never overwhelms us with the beauty of his composition, or invites us to marvel at the ingenuity of his technique. His style of film-making doesn't call attention to itself, being intended simply to further the narrative. Which isn't to say that it's in the least subfusc or anonymous. 'His style, like all styles, has its procedures, its rhetoric, its mannerisms, but, compared with the work of most noted stylists, it seems to efface itself, to turn the screen into a window.'[25] The passage comes from Durgnat's book on Franju, but the description fits Mackendrick remarkably well.

'Mackendrick's skill,' Ian Cameron once wrote, 'is [that] he knows how to put a sequence together. One might think that this is the easiest part of film-making, but in fact it is the most difficult. Think how many British directors can construct a sequence so that it presents the action and the meaning or motivation which the director sees behind it, with clarity and economy. This skill is shared by perhaps half a dozen British directors, and one to be treasured.'[26] Mackendrick's compositions discreetly guide the eye. Even in scenes of swift, complex action – such as the pirate attack on Marpole's ship in *High Wind* – we're never confused over where to look. (Not by any means always the case, as comparison with similar scenes in most other swash-bucklers will show.)

Nor are his compositions inflexible or austere. On the contrary, he composes fluidly and in depth; at any point there's likely to be a good deal of covert interplay going on within a scene, and repeated viewings reveal details and nuances which may have escaped us first time round. But the narrative essentials come across immediately. Never, while watching one of his films, will we find ourselves left wondering what's happening, or why we're being shown a particular event. Mackendrick is often subtle, but never obscure.

A touch of obscurity, though, could be just what his reputation needed. His very lucidity may have done him a disservice, with clarity taken for simplicity or lack of depth. There may be something more immediately enticing, to a critic's eye, in directors like Powell or Roeg, whose story line is often of such patent eccentricity, whose imagery so evidently packed with hermetic tropes, as to signal at once that things are going on beneath the surface, inviting excavation. By comparison Mackendrick's pictures, which can be enjoyed on the most straightforward narrative level, might seem to have less to offer. To a superficial glance, their limpid flow conceals the cross-currents swirling beneath.

In content as in style, Mackendrick is a reticent director, in the sense that his personality, his attitudes and beliefs, don't obtrude inescapably into his films as do those of, say, Ford or Bergman or Tarkovsky. Remove the credits, and an attentive viewer could watch – for example – *Sweet Smell of Success* and *Mandy* without registering that they were directed by the same person. But on closer examination the connections emerge clearly enough, integral to both style and subject. In all Mackendrick's films we find the same visual and mental acuity, the mordant humour laced with melancholy, and the astringent, sardonic vision that takes nothing for granted, and nothing on trust.

'I would rate the appeal to intelligence and human emotions higher than that to the pleasures of the sensual eye and ear.'[27] The remark may seem anomalous, coming from a director whose films are so intensely visual. Mackendrick's *mise-en-scène* is invariably elegant, and there's scarcely an awkward or inept composition anywhere in his work. But the pictorial values are never for their own sake, always at the service of the drama – and of the ideas which, themselves, emerge organically from the story rather than being imposed upon it. Only very rarely in a Mackendrick movie (the dire scene with Sheena in *The Maggie* being the prime example) are we jarred by any sense of an insistent message. John Russell Taylor wrote of Fritz Lang that 'he makes films with ideas rather than films of ideas. . . . In the end it is his power to embody his ideas visually which accounts for the lasting effect of his films.'[28] Very much the same could be said of Mackendrick.

Indeed, far from lacking complexity, his films often include scenes – the disintegration of the white suit, the concluding sequence of *Mandy*, Emily's killing of the Dutch captain – which carry such a metaphoric density of meaning, and are operating on so many levels at once, that analysis can seem almost intrusive. Beside the immediacy of the images, verbal attempts to tease out and pin down all the layers of significance feel hopelessly cumbersome. Insights conveyed on the screen with swift dexterity may end up, on the page, sounding portentous and heavy-handed.

Even so, there's great satisfaction to be gained from exploring films that engage us, intellectually and emotionally, in such intricate and lively dialogue. The viewer of a Mackendrick film, as Charles Barr observes, 'has to comprehend . . . a continuous interplay of motives and perceptions, and the process – because of the amount that is left unsaid and unsignposted – is an active one, akin to that which faces the characters themselves. The director . . . plays gently with our ability to perceive, to infer, to make connections and ultimately judgments.'[29]

This process of perception – of which the dichotomy between innocence and experience is one crucial aspect – lies at the heart of Mackendrick's work. In defining his characters in terms of 'how they look' (both what they look like to others and how they themselves see, or don't see, what's around them) he's also concerned with how his films 'look' – and thus how we, his audience, look at them. Hence his shrewd camera placement and discriminating use of film grammar: extreme close-ups and point-of-view shots featuring only sparingly, and always for a specific dramatic purpose. Rather than emphasise selectively within a set-up, Mackendrick prefers whenever possible to hold back and let us take in the situation as a whole, allowing us to form our own view instead of imposing his, or that of any given character.

The same relativism extends from the visual to the moral perspective of his films. There are no privileged characters whose outlook we're called on to endorse; those with whom we tend to identify, such as Christine Garland or Sammy, are still portrayed with an edge of ironic reserve. Nor does Mackendrick fob us off with facile denouements. His films, with the exception of *Don't Make Waves*, reject consensus and reconciliation, or such easy devices as repentant villains seeing the error of their ways. Conflicts are less likely to be resolved than to be cut off short by defeat or death. Even seemingly happy endings, like those of *Mandy* and *Sweet Smell*, are tentative. Mackendrick's films are myths, not fairy-tales, and no one lives happily ever after.

Certainty, in any form, is suspect in Mackendrick's sceptical world, a delusion always liable to be undermined. The uncertainty principle that saps his characters' beliefs, topples houses and runs ships aground also infests the social hierarchy. Religion is irrelevant (not a single clergyman appears in any Mackendrick film), and officialdom corrupt or ineffectual. If the law intervenes, it's either to abet the criminals or arrest the wrong person. The resolution of his films isn't to be looked for from external forces: there's no Seventh Cavalry on the way, no god emerging from the machine.

All of which might sound fairly dispiriting. What saves Mackendrick's films from lapsing into the sour misanthropy that mars those of such directors as Clouzot is the energy, the sheer joy in narrative drive, with which they're made. There are also certain qualities that Mackendrick shares with Buñuel: a fierce, gleeful delight in the blackness of his vision, as well as a sly satisfaction in the process of subversion, in slipping dark disquieting ambiguities into the clearcut world of Ealing comedy or Hollywood swashbuckle.

Subversion, not revolution. Mackendrick never set out to be a trail-blazer, and his technique, though fresh and idiosyncratic, isn't innovatory in any startling sense. Technical challenges stimulated him, and he loved devising ways to surmount them – but always within the parameters of conventional narrative style. His virtue are those of classic mainstream cinema: pace, clarity, dramatic coherence and the ability to convey ideas in terms of action and visual imagery. In this, he's true to his professional roots, since Ealing as a studio hardly encouraged formal experiment, and neither as director or teacher has he shown interest in overtly avant-garde techniques.

And within the field of classic cinema, Mackendrick's temperament points him towards certain types of film – not in terms of genre, since there's no reason to think he couldn't have tackled generic material of any kind, but in terms of dramatic shape. Just as he himself feels happiest working in the confines of an organisation, so his directorial gifts operate most effectively within contained limits: a narrow physical compass (a boat, an island, the streets around Times Square) and a plot that observes a compact dramatic unity, often spiralling back towards its starting-point. Given the wrong context, or an incompatible narrative flow, his unobtrusive style can become flat and impersonal, as in parts of *Sammy Goes South*. Linear, episodic stories never suited him. He's at his best in a situation of psychological claustrophobia, where he can develop a sense of emotions turning on themselves in a tight incestuous circle.

Yet within this enclosed situation there's usually one unintegrated figure to set it off (in both senses): the outsider, bemused or appalled, often in the person of an isolated child. And even without reference to Mackendrick's personal history – the orphaned childhood, the divided cultural identity – we might be inclined to see this figure, the embodiment of the external viewpoint, as standing in for the director. For though there's no hint of condescension (to his characters or to the audience), Mackendrick sometimes gives the impression of standing slightly aside from the action, or even poised above it at that same god's-eye angle that, in *The Ladykillers*, gazes down on Mrs Wilberforce's cottage – fascinated but fractionally apart.

This isn't a question of working methods – Mackendrick, we know from his colleagues, was always fully involved in the film-making process, hyperactive and curious about everything – but of psychological stance. Nor does it imply any lack of impact or dramatic grip. On the contrary, it's this dual vision, the split perspective of the half-assimilated outsider, that makes Mackendrick's work so intriguing – since it's the ambivalence of his regard that sets up the moral tensions within his films, preventing their conflicts from becoming schematised or simplistic. And it's also the source of an underlying loneliness, a melancholy that lends his work emotional depth, and at times (as in the final scene of *High Wind*) sharpens into a poignant sense of exile and elegiac loss.

Nonetheless, it's revealing to compare Mackendrick's films with those of a director like Renoir, who even when he's not acting in them seems to be right in the middle of his movies, digging in up to his elbows. Beside such total engagement, Mackendrick's ironic standpoint can feel like a withdrawal, a subtle distancing from his material. This sense of detachment, of observing rather than participating, may explain how he could disengage himself relatively painlessly from directing, where others whose careers hit problems – Welles, Ray, Fuller, Peckinpah and indeed Renoir himself – all in their different ways hung in there, contriving or not contriving to make movies, but never able simply to walk away and do something else. And it may also explain why Mackendrick's films, for all their fine qualities, in the last analysis fall just short of greatness.

'Greatness', of course, is a suspect term, and any attempt to define it – no matter how hedged about with critical method – usually comes down to an elaborate rationalisation of gut feelings. It may make better sense to abandon all pretence at objectivity in favour of poetic metaphor. In *Wuthering Heights*, Cathy talks of dreams that have 'gone through and through me, like wine through water, and altered the colour of my mind'.[30] This, perhaps, offers as good a yardstick as any for the greatest films (and for the greatest poems, paintings, compositions or whatever): that they lastingly 'alter the colour of our minds'. On this criterion, none of Mackendrick's films ranks among the very greatest – although *Sweet Smell of Success* may come close.

But if Mackendrick never quite succeeded in producing the cinematic masterpieces of which, on all the evidence, he was capable, he still created a body of work that, for its subtlety and individuality, its visual and conceptual energy, its darkness and its humour, bears comparison with that of any other director. David Shipman once provocatively suggested that 'American films, when they seem to change with the passing of years, become either better or worse, while on re-examination British films, if they change at all, only become worse'.[31] If that's true, then Mackendrick's work offers a signal exception. At their best (which is most of the time), his films display a vitality, a freshness and a complexity that makes them a pleasure to watch, and increasingly rewarding on each subsequent viewing. Whatever his own ironic reservations on the subject, Mackendrick's achievement as a film-maker looks set to endure.

# Source Notes

Frequently-quoted sources are given short references, e.g. Barr, *Ealing Studios*, p. 142. Full publication details can be found in the Bibliography.

'Op cit' refers to sources quoted within the same chapter.

## Introduction

1. V. F. Perkins, *Film as Film: Understanding and Judging Movies* (Penguin, Harmondsworth 1972), p. 183.
2. Brown (ed), *Der Produzent*, p. 135.
3. Lawrence Alster in the *Listener*, 16.2.89.

## 1 In Enemy Terrain

1. Interview for *The Man Who Walked Away* (Scottish TV, 21.8.86).
2. Ibid.
3. CalArts handout, *Dramatic Irony*, 1.12.81.
4. Interview for *The Man Who Walked Away* (Scottish TV, 21.8.86).
5. CalArts handout, *How Not To Learn To Direct Movies*, undated.
6. Interview for *The Man Who Walked Away* (Scottish TV, 21.8.86).
7. Interviewed by Conrad Wilson in the *Scotsman*, 29.10.62.
8. Interview for *The Man Who Walked Away* (Scottish TV, 21.8.86).
9. *Documentary Newsletter*, Jan 1946, p. 8.
10. Charles Cruickshank, *The Fourth Arm: Psychological Warfare 1939–1945* (Davis-Poynter, London 1977), pp. 38–9.
11. Quoted in Mira Liehm, *Passion and Defiance: Film in Italy from 1942 to the Present* (University of California Press, Berkeley 1984), p. 61.
12. Interview for *The Man Who Walked Away* (Scottish TV, 21.8.86).
13. Ibid.
14. Ibid.
15. For a full account of these events, see Robert Katz, *Death in Rome* (Cape, London 1967). Katz's book was the basis for a film, *Rappresaglia/Massacre in Rome* (1973), directed by George Pan Cosmatos and starring Richard Burton and Marcello Mastroianni.
16. Geoff Brown and Laurence Kardish, *Michael Balcon: The Pursuit of British Cinema* (Museum of Modern Art, New York 1984), p. 7.
17. Danischewsky, *White Russian – Red Face*, p. 127.
18. Interview for *Omnibus: Ealing* (BBC TV, 2.5.86).
19. Stewart Granger, *Sparks Fly Upward* (Granada, London 1981), p. 113.
20. Ibid, pp. 110–11.
21. Ibid, p. 113.
22. Durgnat, *A Mirror for England*, p. 179.
23. Ibid.

24. Letter to James Kennaway, undated (probably 1961).


## 2 Whisky Galore!

1. Raymond Williams, *The Long Revolution* (Chatto and Windus, London 1961), p. 38.
2. For a detailed account of the whole affair, see Arthur Swinson's *Scotch on the Rocks* (Peter Davies, London 1963).
3. Mackenzie, *My Life and Times, Octave Eight*, p. 121.
4. Interviewed by Helmut Wietz in Brown (ed), *Der Produzent*, pp. 156–7.
5. Danischewsky, *White Russian – Red Face*, p. 161.
6. Mackenzie, *My Life and Times, Octave Nine*, p. 181.
7. Ibid, p. 182.
8. The technical background to the shoot is described by Baynham Honri in *The Cine-Technician*, Sept/Oct 1950, pp. 146–56.
9. Roger Manvell (ed), *The Cinema 1950* (Penguin, Hardmondsworth 1950), p. 85.
10. Mackenzie, *My Life and Times, Octave Nine*, p. 183.
11. Danischewsky, op cit, p. 156.
12. Interview for *The Man Who Walked Away* (Scottish TV, 21.8.86).
13. Danischewsky, op cit, p. 162.
14. Interview for *The Man Who Walked Away* (Scottish TV, 21.8.86).
15. Ibid.
16. Jerry Vermilyea, *The Great British Films* (Citadel Press, Secaucus NJ 1978), p. 130.
17. Gerald Mast, *The Comic Mind: Comedy and the Movies* (Bobbs-Merrill, Indianapolis & New York, 1973), pp. 329–31.
18. Interview for *The Man Who Walked Away* (Scottish TV, 21.8.86).
19. Barr, *Ealing Studios*, p. 114.
20. Mackenzie, *My Life and Times, Octave Nine*, p. 184.
21. Sissons and French (eds), *The Age of Austerity*, p. 71.
22. *Film Teacher*, Spring 1953, pp. 9–10.
23. Interview for *Omnibus: Ealing* (BBC TV, 2.5.86).
24. 'Notes on the British Cinema' in *Quarterly of Film, Radio and Television*, Fall 56, p. 10.
25. Interview for *The Man Who Walked Away* (Scottish TV, 21.8.86).
26. Thomas Hobbes, *Leviathan*, pt 1 ch 13.
27. Leo Tolstoy, tr Aylmer Maude, *The Slavery of Our Times* (C. W. Daniel, London 1918), p. 97.
28. Interview for *The Man Who Walked Away* (Scottish TV, 21.8.86).
29. Barr, *Screen*, Summer 1974, p. 139.
30. *News Chronicle*, 18.6.49.
31. *Evening Standard*, 16.6.49.
32. 'Cutting British Films for the United States' in *Film Industry*, 17.11.49, p. 8.
33. *Time*, 23.1.50.
34. James Clark, *Report for the Boston Film Society*, undated.
35. Mackenzie, *My Life and Times, Octave Nine*, p. 244.
36. Danischewsky, op cit, p. 156.
37. Interview for *The Man Who Walked Away* (Scottish TV, 21.8.86).
38. Ibid.
39. 'Land Beyond Brigadoon' in *Sight and Sound*, Winter 1983/84, p. 41.

40. Interview in *Sight and Sound*, Summer 1983, p. 159.
41. *Monthly Film Bulletin*, April 1983, pp. 87–8.


## 3 The Man in the White Suit

1. Barr, *Screen*, Summer 1974, p. 139.
2. *New York Times*, 6.1.85.
3. Interviewed by John Ellis in Brown (ed), *Der Produzent*, p. 30.
4. Interview for *The Man Who Walked Away* (Scottish TV, 21.8.86).
5. *Glasgow Herald*, 10.5.54.
6. *Film Teacher*, Spring 1953, p. 10.
7. Barr, *Ealing Studios*, p. 145.
8. Boris Ford (ed), *The Cambridge Guide to the Arts in Britain, vol 9: Since the Second World War* (Cambridge University Press, Cambridge 1988), p. 244.
9. Kenneth Tynan, *Alec Guinness* (Rockliff, London 1953), p. 93.
10. Interviewed by Helmut Wietz in Brown (ed), *Der Produzent*, p. 161.
11. Interview for *Omnibus: Ealing* (BBC TV, 2.5.86).
12. Tape of Mackendrick teaching at the National Film School, May/June 1979.
13. Ibid.
14. *Scene*, 9.3.63, p. 22.
15. Charles Dickens, *Hard Times*, ch 5.
16. Interview for *The Man Who Walked Away* (Scottish TV, 21.8.86).
17. Interview for *Omnibus: Ealing* (BBC TV, 2.5.86).
18. Stuart H. Stock and Kenneth von Gunden, *Twenty All-Time Great Science Fiction Films* (Arlington House, New York 1982), p. 50.
19. Tape of Mackendrick teaching at the National Film School, May/June 1979.
20. Interview for *Omnibus: Ealing* (BBC TV, 2.5.86).
21. Barr, *Screen*, Summer 1974, p. 142.
22. Barr, *Ealing Studios*, p. 140.
23. Ibid, p. 142.
24. Sissons and French (eds), *The Age of Austerity*, p. 19.
25. Samuel Beckett, *Disjecta* (John Calder, London 1983), p. 82.
26. Barr, *Ealing Studios*, p. 145.
27. Interview for *The Ealing Comedies* (BBC TV, 8.9.70).
28. Interview for *Omnibus: Ealing* (BBC TV, 2.5.86).
29. *Positif*, Feb 1968, p. 41.
30. Interview for *Omnibus: Ealing* (BBC TV, 2.5.86).
31. James Curran and Vincent Porter (eds), *British Cinema History* (Weidenfeld & Nicolson, London 1983), pp. 296–7.
32. *Tribune*, 26.8.51.
33. *Daily Express*, 10.8.51.
34. *Observer*, 12.8.51.
35. *Manchester Guardian*, 11.8.51.
36. *Sunday Times*, 12.8.51.
37. *Time and Tide*, 18.8.51.
38. *Cahiers du cinéma*, March 1952, p. 62.
39. *New York Post*, 1.4.52.
40. Barr, *Screen*, Summer 1974, p. 140.
41. Geoff Brown and Laurence Kardish, *Michael Balcon: The Pursuit of British Cinema* (Museum of Modern Art, New York 1984), p. 45.
42. Ewart Hodgson in *News of the World*, 12.8.51.

## 4 Mandy

1. Christine Gledhill (ed), *Home Is Where the Heart Is: Studies in Melodrama and the Woman's Film* (BFI Publishing, London 1987), p. 62.
2. *Film Teacher*, Spring 1953, p. 12.
3. CalArts handout on *Sweet Smell of Success*, undated.
4. Interview for *The Man Who Walked Away* (Scottish TV, 21.8.86).
5. Ibid.
6. Ibid.
7. Ibid.
8. Ibid.
9. Studio publicity handout, undated.
10. Interviewed by Charles Barr et al in Brown (ed), *Der Produzent*, p. 213.
11. Jack Hawkins, *Anything for a Quiet Life* (Elm Tree Books, London 1973), p. 97.
12. *News Chronicle*, 2.8.52.
13. Barr, *Ealing Studios*, p. 152.
14. Pam Cook, 'Mandy: Daughter of Transition' in Barr (ed), *All Our Yesterdays*, pp. 355–61.
15. Sissons and French (eds), *The Age of Austerity*, p. 307.
16. Cook, op cit, p. 355.
17. Henrik Ibsen, tr and intro Michael Meyer, *Ghosts* (Hart-Davis, London 1962), p. 18.
18. Cook, op. cit, p. 357.
19. Barr, *Ealing Studios*, p. 152.
20. Tape of Mackendrick teaching at the National Film School, May/June 1979.
21. Barr, *Ealing Studios*, p. 156.
22. Interview for *Fifties Features* (Channel 4 TV, 21.9.86).
23. Sue Aspinall, 'Women, Realism and Reality in British Films, 1943–53', in Curran and Porter (eds), *British Cinema History*, p. 290.
24. *Daily Worker*, 2.8.52.
25. *Sunday Times*, 3.8.52.
26. *Daily Graphic*, 1.8.52.
27. *The Times*, 4.8.52.
28. Ibid.
29. *Monthly Film Bulletin*, Aug 1952, p. 123.
30. *Sight and Sound*, Oct–Dec 1952, p. 78.
31. *Daily Mail*, 1.8.52.
32. *Time*, 9.3.53.
33. Cook, op cit, p. 356.
34. Ibid, p. 358.

## 5 The Maggie

1. McArthur (ed), *Scotch Reels*, p. 47.
2. Barr, *Ealing Studios*, p. 158.
3. CalArts handout, *The Puffer*, undated.
4. Ibid.
5. Ibid.
6. *The Times*, 14.2.87.
7. *Daily Express*, 29.6.53.
8. Barr, *Ealing Studios*, p. 169.

9. Letter from Fletcher Grimm in *Time*, 27.9.54.
10. Basil Wright, *The Long View* (Secker & Warburg, London 1974), p. 328.
11. 'Ealing's Way of Life' by Kenneth Tynan, *Films and Filming*, Dec 1955, p. 10.
12. Barr, *Ealing Studios*, p. 117.
13. Studio publicity leaflet, undated.
14. McArthur (ed), op cit, p. 47.
15. Alastair Michie, 'Scotland: Strategies of Centralisation', in Barr (ed), *All Our Yesterdays*, p. 261.
16. Barr, *Ealing Studios*, p. 169.
17. Tape of Mackendrick teaching at the National Film School, May/June 1979.
18. Barr, *Ealing Studios*, p. 166.
19. *Star*, 26.2.54.
20. *Spectator*, 28.2.54.
21. *Time and Tide*, 6.3.54.
22. *Daily Worker*, 27.2.54.
23. *Manchester Guardian*, 27.2.54.
24. *Sunday Chronicle*, 28.2.54.
25. *Daily Telegraph*, 27.2.54.
26. *New Yorker*, 11.9.54.
27. *New York Times*, 31.8.54.
28. *Time*, 13.9.54.
29. Letter in *Time*, 27.9.54.
30. Letter in *Time*, 25.10.54.
31. *Scotsman*, 29.10.79.
32. John Brown, 'Land Beyond Brigadoon' in *Sight and Sound*, Winter 1983/84, p. 41.
33. McArthur (ed), *Scotch Reels*, p. 7.
34. Ibid, p. 47.
35. Ibid, pp. 47–8.
36. Brown, op cit, p. 41.
37. Ibid, pp. 41–2.
38. Michie, op cit, p. 260.

## 6 The Ladykillers

1. Alan McGlashan, *Dreams and Dreamers* (Newman Neame, London 1964), p. 12.
2. Lindsay Anderson, *Making a Film* (Allen and Unwin, London 1952), p. 14.
3. Interview for *Omnibus: Ealing* (BBC TV, 2.5.86).
4. Interviewed by Helmut Wietz in Brown (ed), *Der Produzent*, pp. 169–70.
5. Interview for *Omnibus: Ealing* (BBC TV, 2.5.86).
6. Ibid.
7. Ibid.
8. Ibid.
9. CalArts handout, *Bill Rose's 'Ladykillers' Notes*, undated.
10. Ibid.
11. *New York Times*, 6.1.85.
12. Interview for *The Man Who Walked Away* (Scottish TV, 21.8.86).
13. Ibid.
14. Ibid.
15. Ibid.

16. Letter to the author, 26.9.86.
17. Garth Buckner, 'The Development of Comedie Noire', *Film Journal*, June 1958, p. 28.
18. *Sunday Times*, 11.12.55.
19. John Ellis, 'Made in Ealing', *Screen*, Spring 1975, p. 89.
20. Interview for *Omnibus: Ealing* (BBC TV, 2.5.86).
21. Campbell Dixon (ed), *International Film Annual No 1* (John Calder, London 1957), p. 63.
22. Ellis, op cit, p. 90.
23. Barr, *Ealing Studios*, p. 171.
24. Richards and Aldgate, *Best of British*, p. 109.
25. Barr, *Ealing Studios*, p. 173.
26. Richards, op cit, p. 111.
27. Barr, *Ealing Studios* pp. 171–2.
28. *Film Culture* vol 2 no 2, 1956, p. 29.
29. Anthony Slide, *Fifty Classic British Films 1932–1983* (Dover, New York 1985), p. 88.
30. Letter to James Kennaway, undated (probably 1961).
31. Barr, *Ealing Studios*, p. 173.
32. Durgnat, *A Mirror for England*, p. 38.
33. Kenneth Von Gunden, *Alec Guinness: The Films* (McFarland, Jefferson N Carolina 1987), p. 88.
34. Neil Sinyard, *Filming Literature* (Croom Helm, London 1986), p. 59.
35. *News Chronicle*, 9.12.55.
36. *Spectator*, 9.12.55.
37. *Evening Standard*, 8.12.55.
38. *Manchester Guardian*, 10.12.55.
39. *Time and Tide*, 17.12.55.
40. *Sunday Times*, 11.12.55.
41. *Sight and Sound*, Winter 1955/56, p. 148.
42. *Times Educational Supplement*, 13.1.56.
43. *Saturday Review*, 4.2.56.
44. Letter to Mackendrick, 20.10.58.
45. Not Brecht's own words, but a concise summary of his doctrine from Simon Callow, *Charles Laughton* (Methuen, London 1987), p. 169.
46. Quoted in Kathleen Tynan, *The Life of Kenneth Tynan* (Methuen, London 1988), p. 140.

# 7 Sweet Smell of Success

1. Nora Sayre, *Running Time: Films of the Cold War* (Dial Press, New York 1982), p. 182.
2. Quoted by Richard Blackburn in 'Bullies of Broadway', *American Film*, Dec 1983, p. 17.
3. *Cosmopolitan*, Apr 1950, p. 170.
4. Ibid, p. 176.
5. Ibid, p. 170.
6. Ibid, p. 182.
7. John Brady, *The Craft of the Screenwriter: Interviews with Six Celebrated Screenwriters* (Simon & Schuster, New York 1981), p. 193.
8. Ibid.

9. Ibid, p. 206.
10. CalArts handout, *Sweet Smell of Success: Some Personal Background*, undated.
11. Ibid.
12. CalArts handout, *Notes on 'Sweet Smell of Success'*, undated.
13. Programme note for 13th Telluride Film Festival, August 1986.
14. James Baldwin, *Another Country* (Dial Press, New York 1962), p. 222.
15. CalArts handout, *Notes on 'Sweet Smell of Success'*, undated.
16. Ibid.
17. Interview for *The Man Who Walked Away* (Scottish TV, 21.8.86).
18. *Film Culture*, Oct 1957, p. 16.
19. Joseph McBride (ed), *Filmmakers on Filmmaking, Vol 2* (J P Tarcher Inc, Los Angeles 1983), p. 215.
20. Nora Sayre, *Running Time: Films of the Cold War* (Dial Press, New York 1982), p. 99.
21. *Sight and Sound*, Autumn 1967, p. 196.
22. Interview for *The Man Who Walked Away* (Scottish TV, 21.8.86).
23. Charles Higham, *Hollywood Cameramen* (Thames & Hudson, London 1970), p. 93.
24. Todd Rainsberger, *James Wong Howe: Cinematographer* (A. S. Barnes, New York 1981), p. 66.
25. William Bluem and Jason E. Squire, *The Movie Business* (Hastings House, New York 1972), p. 168.
26. *Boston Phoenix*, 5.6.79, section 3 p. 4.
27. Blackburn, op cit, p. 18.
28. Ibid.
29. Neil Sinyard, *The Films of Richard Lester* (Croom Helm, London 1985), p. 65.
30. David Thomson, *A Biographical Dictionary of the Cinema*, revised edition (Secker & Warburg 1980), p. 125.
31. Interview for *The Man Who Walked Away* (Scottish TV, 21.8.86).
32. Ibid.
33. Robert Windeler, *Burt Lancaster* (W. H. Allen, London 1984), pp. 98–9.
34. Interview for *The Man Who Walked Away* (Scottish TV, 21.8.86).
35. *Nation*, 20.7.57.
36. *Time*, 24.6.57.
37. *Film Culture*, Oct 1957, p. 16.
38. *Saturday Review*, 6.7.57.
39. *Evening Standard*, 11.7.57.
40. *Sunday Times*, 14.7.57.
41. *Observer*, 14.7.57.
42. William Whitebait, *International Film Annual No 2*, (John Calder, London 1958), p. 16.
43. Tape of Mackendrick teaching at the National Film School, May/June 1979.
44. *Scotsman*, 29.10.62.
45. *The Times*, 25.2.84.
46. *New York*, 23.12.85, p. 71.
47. Programme note for 13th Telluride Film Festival, August 1986.
48. Blackburn, op cit, p. 17.

## 8 Sammy Going South

1. Michael Wood, *America in the Movies* (Basic Books, New York 1975), p. 21.

2. Letter to the author, 28.3.89.
3. Ibid.
4. Ibid.
5. *Daily Express*, 4.8.58.
6. Ibid.
7. *Daily Sketch*, 4.8.58.
8. Robert Windeler, *Burt Lancaster* (W. H. Allen, London 1984), pp. 105–6.
9. Interview for *The Man Who Walked Away* (Scottish TV, 21.8.86).
10. Ibid.
11. Laurence Olivier, *Confessions of an Actor* (Weidenfeld & Nicolson, London 1982), p. 187.
12. Laurence Olivier, *On Acting* (Weidenfeld & Nicolson, London 1986), p. 218.
13. Michael Munn, *Kirk Douglas* (Robson Books, London 1985), p. 75.
14. *Scene*, 9.3.63, p. 25.
15. *Daily Express*, 4.8.58.
16. Interview for *The Man Who Walked Away* (Scottish TV, 21.8.86).
17. Ibid.
18. *Guardian*, 5.9.59.
19. *Daily Express*, 8.3.60.
20. *Daily Mail*, 23.9.60.
21. *Coventry Standard*, 5.8.60.
22. Michael Freedland, *Jack Lemmon* (Weidenfeld & Nicolson, London 1985), p. 72.
23. Letter to James Kennaway, undated (probably 1961).
24. *Theatre Arts*, Dec 1960.
25. *New York Times*, 21.10.60.
26. Trevor Royle, *James & Jim: A Biography of James Kennaway* (Mainstream Publishing, Edinburgh 1963), pp. 133–4.
27. Ibid, pp. 142–3.
28. Interview for *The Man Who Walked Away* (Scottish TV, 21.8.86).
29. Letter to James Kennaway, undated (probably 1961).
30. Ibid.
31. Ibid.
32. *Films and Filming*, June 1959, p. 28.
33. Peter Green in *Daily Telegraph*, 19.5.61.
34. James Vinson (ed), *Contemporary Novelists* (St James Press, London 1972), p. 233.
35. *Sight and Sound*, Winter 1962/63, p. 15.
36. Royal Film Performance Programme, 18.3.63.
37. *Scene*, 9.3.63, p. 20.
38. Ibid, p. 22.
39. Interview for *The Man Who Walked Away* (Scottish TV, 21.8.86).
40. W. H. Canaway, *Sammy Going South* (Hutchinson, London 1961), p. 27.
41. *Positif*, Feb 1968, p. 44.
42. Jim Kitses, *Horizons West* (Thames & Hudson, London 1969), p. 72.
43. Basil Wright, *The Long View* (Secker & Warburg, London 1974), p. 328.
44. Barr, *Screen*, Summer 1974, p. 145.
45. *Scene*, 6.4.63, p. 10.
46. *Sunday Telegraph*, 24.3.63.
47. *Observer*, 24.3.63.
48. *The Times*, 19.3.63.

49. *Daily Telegraph*, 19.3.63.
50. *New Statesman*, 22.3.63.
51. *Films and Filming*, May 1963, p. 28.
52. *Movie*, May 1963, pp. 29–30.
53. *Time*, 26.3.65.
54. *Daily Express*, 30.11.65.
55. Michael Balcon, *Michael Balcon Presents. . . . A Lifetime of Films* (Hutchinson, London 1969), p. 198.
56. Quoted in Alexander Walker, *Hollywood, England* (Michael Joseph, London 1974), p. 287.

## 9 A High Wind in Jamaica

1. A. S. Byatt, *Possession* (Chatto & Windus, London 1990), p. 349.
2. Martin Esslin, *The Theatre of the Absurd*, 3rd edition (Pelican, Harmondsworth 1980), p. 179.
3. Quoted in Freddie Hancock and David Nathan, *Hancock* (William Kimber, London 1969), p. 145.
4. Interview for *The Man Who Walked Away* (Scottish TV, 21.8.86).
5. Richard Hughes, *A High Wind in Jamaica* (Chatto and Windus, London 1929), p. 158.
6. Interview for *New Comment* (BBC Radio 3, 26.5.65).
7. Tape of Mackendrick teaching at the National Film School, May/June 1979.
8. Ibid.
9. Interview for *The Man Who Walked Away* (Scottish TV, 21.8.86).
10. Ibid.
11. Ibid.
12. Ibid.
13. Andrew Sarris, *The American Cinema: Directors and Directions 1929–1968* (E. P. Dutton, New York 1968), p. 133.
14. Hughes, op cit, p. 103.
15. *New Republic*, 29.8.60.
16. Interview for *The Man Who Walked Away* (Scottish TV, 21.8.86).
17. Neil Sinyard, *Filming Literature* (Croom Helm, London 1986), pp. 117–18.
18. Hughes, op cit, p. 158.
19. *Time*, 2.7.65.
20. Brian Baxter, National Film Theatre programme note, 31.3.71.
21. Basil Wright, *The Long View* (Secker & Warburg, London 1974), p. 328.
22. Ibid, p. 326.
23. Interview for *New Comment* (BBC Radio 3, 26.5.65).
24. *Observer*, 23.5.65.
25. Tom Milne, *Rouben Mamoulian* (Thames & Hudson, London 1969), p. 74.
26. *Spectator*, 28.5.65.
27. *Sunday Times*, 23.5.65.
28. *Observer*, 23.5.65.
29. *Time*, 2.7.65.
30. *Cahiers du cinéma*, Sept 1965, p. 56.
31. *Positif*, Dec 1965/Jan 1966, pp. 90–2.
32. David Thomson, *A Biographical Dictionary of the Cinema*, revised edition (Secker & Warburg 1980), p. 369.
33. Gilbert Adair and Nick Roddick, *A Night at the Pictures: Ten Decades of British*

*Film* (Columbus Books, Bromley 1985), p. 59.
34. Joel Finler, *The Movie Directors Story* (Octopus, London 1985), p. 123.
35. National Film Theatre programme, Feb/March 1971, p. 25.
36. Interview for *The Man Who Walked Away* (Scottish TV, 21.8.86).

## 10 Don't Make Waves

1. David Thomson, *America in the Dark: The Impact of Hollywood Films on American Culture* (William Morrow, New York 1977), p. 89.
2. Wallach, *Muscle Beach*, p. 236.
3. Letter to the author, 21.6.88.
4. Wallach, op cit, p. 4.
5. Studio publicity leaflet, undated.
6. Wallach, op cit, p. 223.
7. Reyner Banham, *Los Angeles: The Architecture of Four Ecologies* (Allen Lane, London 1971), p. 54.
8. Ibid, pp. 38–9.
9. Interview for *The Man Who Walked Away* (Scottish TV, 21.8.86).
10. *New Statesman*, 18.8.67.
11. *Village Voice*, 29.6.67.
12. For a full account of the Begelman affair, see David McClintick, *Indecent Exposure* (Columbus, London 1983).
13. Quoted in Alexander Walker, *Hollywood, England* (Michael Joseph, London 1974), p. 358.
14. Walker, op cit, p. 343.
15. *The Times*, 7.5.68.
16. Ibid.
17. Ibid.

## 11 Conclusions

1. Interview for *The Man Who Walked Away* (Scottish TV, 21.8.86).
2. Ibid.
3. Richard Schickel, *The Disney Version*, revised edition (Pavilion Books, London 1986), p. 359.
4. Interview for *The Man Who Walked Away* (Scottish TV, 21.8.86).
5. Patricia Goldstone, 'The Mackendrick Legacy', in *American Film*, March 1979, p. 69.
6. Interview for *The Man Who Walked Away* (Scottish TV, 2.8.86).
7. Quoted in Goldstone, op cit, p. 68.
8. Interview for *The Man Who Walked Away* (Scottish TV, 21.8.86).
9. Ibid.
10. CalArts handout, *Directing Features*, undated.
11. CalArts handout, *How Not To Learn To Direct Movies*, undated.
12. Letter to Colin Young, 24.7.79.
13. CalArts handout, *How Not To Learn To Direct Movies*, undated.
14. Interview for *The Man Who Walked Away* (Scottish TV, 21.8.86).
15. Ibid.
16. Ibid.
17. Letter to Colin Young, 24.7.79.

18. Roy Armes, *A Critical History of the British Cinema* (Oxford University Press, New York 1978), p. 335.
19. *Screen*, Summer 1972, p. 63.
20. Interviewed by Helmut Wietz in Brown (ed), *Der Produzent*, p. 170.
21. *The Times*, 19.3.63.
22. Anthony Slide, *Fifty Classic British Films 1932–1983* (Dover, New York 1985), p. 88.
23. Durgnat, *A Mirror for England*, p. 217.
24. Barr, *Screen*, Summer 1974, p. 134.
25. Raymond Durgnat, *Franju* (Studio Vista, London 1967), p. 9.
26. *Movie*, May 1963, p. 29.
27. CalArts handout, *Translating Aristotle*, undated.
28. *Sight and Sound*, Winter 1961/62, p. 46.
29. Barr, *Ealing Studios*, p. 115.
30. Emily Brontë, *Wuthering Heights*, ch 9.
31. David Shipman, *The Story of Cinema, Vol 2* (Hodder & Stoughton, London 1983), p. 558.

# Annotated Bibliography

## Books

ALDGATE, Anthony: see RICHARDS.

ANDERSON, Lindsay: *Making a Film* (Allen & Unwin, London 1952). Assiduously detailed account of filming of Thorold Dickinson's *Secret People* at Ealing. Valuable for insights into the studio's working methods.

ANDREW, Geoff: *The Film Handbook* (Longman, Harlow 1989). Mainstream guide covering some 200 movie directors. Appreciative entry on Mackendrick pp. 181–2.

ARMES, Roy: *A Critical History of British Cinema* (OUP, London & New York 1978). Concise, authoritative general survey with excellent bibliography. Section on Mackendrick pp. 193–7.

BALCON, Michael: *Michael Balcon Presents . . . A Lifetime of Films* (Hutchinson, London 1969). Autobiography of Mackendrick's boss at Ealing, polite and non-committal, offering few revelations. Chapter on the Ealing comedies (pp. 156–68) includes passing references to Mackendrick.

BALCON, Michael (intro): *Saraband for Dead Lovers: The Film and its Production at Ealing Studios* (Convoy Publications, London 1948). Lavish 106-page hardback put out as publicity material for the film. Includes some of Mackendrick's sketches for camera set-ups.

BARR, Charles: *Ealing Studios* (Cameron & Tayleur/David & Charles, London 1977). Acute, influential study of the Balcon years at Ealing. Detailed accounts of Mackendrick's five Ealing movies.

BARR, Charles (ed): *All Our Yesterdays: 90 Years of British Cinema* (BFI Publishing, London 1986). Includes chapter on *Mandy* by Pam COOK (pp. 355–61); also chapter on the presentation of Scotland in the movies by Alastair MICHIE (pp. 252–71), touching on *Whisky Galore* and *The Maggie*.

BRADY, John; *The Craft of the Screenwriter: Interviews with Six Celebrated Screenwriters* (Simon & Schuster, New York 1981). Interview with Ernest Lehman (pp. 177–247) includes discussion of *Sweet Smell of Success*.

BROWN, Geoff (ed): *Der Produzent: Michael Balcon und der englische Film* (Volker Spiess, Berlin 1981). Useful anthology on Balcon's career, including interview (pp. 156–71) with Mackendrick by Helmut WIETZ. Regrettably, available only in German.

BROWN, Geoff and KARDISH, Laurence: *Michael Balcon: The Pursuit of British Cinema* (Museum of Modern Art, New York 1984). Two long essays on Balcon's career, plus extensive chronology, filmography, etc, produced to accompany 1984 *British Film* retrospective at MOMA

BUTLER, Ivan: *Cinema in Britain: an Illustrated Survey* (Tantivy Press, London

1973). Selective pictorial survey covering period 1895–1971. Entries on all five of Mackendrick's Ealing movies.

CANAWAY, W. H.: *Sammy Going South* (Hutchinson, London 1961). Novel, basis of Mackendrick's 1963 film.

CLARKE, T. E. B.: *This Is Where I Came In* (Michael Joseph, London 1974). Autobiography of Ealing's foremost screenwriter. Lively anecdotes of life at Ealing; Mackendrick mentioned in passing.

CLIFTON, N. Roy: *The Figure in Film* (Associated University Presses, East Brunswick NJ 1983). Ingenious study of 'figures of rhetoric' in filmic terms, illustrated by copious examples, including several from *Mandy*, *The Maggie* and *The Ladykillers*.

COOK, Pam: see BARR.

CORLISS, Richard: *Talking Pictures: Screenwriters in the American Cinema 1927–1973* (Overlook Press, Woodstock, NY 1974). Chapter on Ernest Lehman includes account of *Sweet Smell of Success* (pp. 189–91).

CROSS, Robin: *The Big Book of British Films* (Charles Herridge, Bideford 1984). A perceptive and detailed account of the period 1939–1970. Mackendrick's Ealing films are discussed on pp. 91–5, 98–9.

CURRAN, James and PORTER, Vincent (eds): *British Cinema History* (Weidenfeld & Nicolson, London 1983). Variable collection of essays, with excellent bibliography but no index. Mackendrick's work features in 'The Context of Creativity: Ealing Studios and Hammer Films' by Vincent PORTER (pp. 179–207) and 'Ealing: In the Comedy Frame' by Ian GREEN (pp. 294–302).

DANISCHEWSKY, Monja: *White Russian – Red Face* (Gollancz, London 1966). Highly entertaining autobiography by Mackendrick's producer on *Whisky Galore*. Vivid account (pp. 154–67) of the filming and of their disagreements.

DURGNAT, Raymond: *A Mirror for England: British Movies from Austerity to Affluence* (Faber & Faber, London 1970). Idiosyncratic survey of British cinema 1945–1968, full of illuminating insights.

EASTMAN, Max: *The Enjoyment of Laughter* (Simon & Schuster, New York 1936). Theoretical study of the psychology of humour, cited by Mackendrick as 'the only good book I've read on the subject'.

FINLER, Joel W.: *The Movie Directors Story* (Octopus, London 1985). Succinct accounts of careers of 140 directors who worked in English-language cinema. Entry on Mackendrick p. 123.

FORD, Boris (ed): *The Cambridge Guide to the Arts in Britain, Vol 9: Since the Second World War* (Cambridge University Press, Cambridge 1988). Chapter on Film by Neil SINYARD includes section on 'Ealing and Alexander Mackendrick' (pp. 242–5).

FRENCH, Philip: see SISSONS.

GIFFORD, Denis: *British Animated Films, 1895–1985: A Filmography* (McFarland & Co., Jefferson, N Carolina 1987). First reference work on the subject; includes details of several advertising and propaganda films of Mackendrick's early career.

GREEN, Ian: see CURRAN.

HARDY, Forsyth: *Scotland in Film* (Edinburgh University Press, Edinburgh 1990). Historical survey of films made, or set, in Scotland. Friendly accounts of *Whisky Galore* (pp. 69–72) and *The Maggie* (pp. 89–90).

HUGHES, Richard: *A High Wind in Jamaica* (Chatto & Windus, London 1929). Novel, basis of Mackendrick's 1965 film.

KARDISH, Laurence; see BROWN.

LEFEVRE, Raymond and LACOURBE, Roland: *30 Ans de cinéma britannique*

(Editions Cinéma 76, Paris 1976). Affectionate, wide-ranging guide to British cinema, concentrating on period 1940–75.

LEHMAN, Ernest: *Sweet Smell of Success and other stories* (New American Library, New York 1957). Short story collection; title story the basis of Mackendrick's 1957 film.

LEWIS, Hilda: *The Day is Ours* (Jarrolds, London 1947). Novel, source of Mackendrick's 1952 film *Mandy*.

MCARTHUR, Colin (ed): *Scotch Reels: Scotland in Cinema and Television* (BFI, London 1982). Essays, mainly polemical, on screen representation of Scotland and the Scots. *Whisky Galore* and *The Maggie* come under vigorous attack.

MACKENZIE, Compton: *Keep the Home Guard Turning* (Chatto & Windus, London 1943). Novel, source of two or three additional scenes for the film of *Whisky Galore*.

MACKENZIE, Compton: *Whisky Galore* (Chatto & Windus, London 1947). Novel, basis of Mackendrick's 1949 film.

MACKENZIE, Compton: *My Life and Times* (Chatto & Windus, London). Autobiography in ten 'octaves'. Octave 8, *1939–1946* (1969) includes author's recollection of wreck of SS *Politician* (p. 121). Octave 9, *1946–1953* (1970) features account of author's participation in making *Whisky Galore* (pp. 180–5).

MALKIEWICZ, Kris: *Film Lighting: Talks with Hollywood's Cinematographers and Gaffers* (Prentice Hall, New York 1986). Opening chapter includes several illuminating quotes from Mackendrick on his attitude to cinematography.

MANVELL, Roger (ed): *The Cinema 1950* (Penguin, Harmondsworth 1950). Anthology of essays, successor to *Penguin Film Review*. Article by Matthew NORGATE on *Whisky Galore* (pp. 82–6.)

MICHIE, Alastair: see BARR.

NORGATE, Matthew: see MANVELL.

PERRY, George: *Forever Ealing: a Celebration of the Great British Film Studio* (Pavilion/Michael Joseph, London 1981). Concentrates mainly on Balcon era. Lavishly illustrated, short on critical insights.

PORTER, Vincent: see CURRAN.

RAINSBERGER, Todd: *James Wong Howe: Cinematographer* (A. S. Barnes and Co., New York/Tantivy, London 1981). Detailed consideration of *Sweet Smell of Success* (pp. 223–8) plus other references to Howe's working relationship with Mackendrick.

RICHARDS, Jeffrey and ALDGATE, Anthony: *Best of British: Cinema and Society 1930–1960* (Basil Blackwell, Oxford 1983). Ten British feature films considered in their social context; chapter on *The Ladykillers* (pp. 99–114) also refers briefly to Mackendrick's other Ealing comedies.

SINYARD, Neil: see FORD.

SISSONS, Michael and FRENCH, Philip (eds): *Age of Austerity* (Hodder & Stoughton, London 1963). Classic collection of essays on social and political aspects of post-1945 Britain, providing useful background to Mackendrick's time at Ealing.

SLIDE, Anthony: *Fifty Classic British Films 1932–1983: a Pictorial Record* (Dover Publications, New York 1985). Stills, brief cast-list and credits, synopsis and commentary for each film chosen. Unenthusiastic entry on *The Ladykillers* (pp. 88–9).

STOCK, Stuart H. and VON GUNDEN, Kenneth: *Twenty All-Time Great Science Fiction Films* (Arlington House, New York 1982). Includes chapter on *The Man in the White Suit* (pp. 49–58) as 'a classic example of the science fiction film that isn't considered science fiction'.

THOMSON, David: *A Biographical Dictionary of the Cinema* (Secker & Warburg, London 1975, rev 1980). Refreshingly opinionated reference book. Entry on Mackendrick pp. 368–9.

VERMILYE, Jerry: *The Great British Films* (Citadel Press, Secaucus, NJ 1978). Casual run-though of 75 movies, including *Whisky Galore*, *The Man in the White Suit* and *The Ladykillers*.

VON GUNDEN, Kenneth: *Alec Guinness: The Films* (McFarland & Co., Jefferson, N. Carolina 1987). A considered account of Guinness's screen career. Chapters on *The Man in the White Suit* (pp. 50–5) and *The Ladykillers* (pp. 86–91).

VON GUNDEN, Kenneth: see STOCK.

WAKEMAN, John (ed): *World Film Directors*, vol 2 (H. W. Wilson Co., New York 1988). Detailed and judicious reference work. Entry on Mackendrick (pp. 627–30) provides useful account of his career.

WALKER, Alexander: *Hollywood, England* (Michael Joseph, London 1974). Lucid account of the British film industry in the 1960s, particularly strong on economic and production detail. Chapter on *Tom Jones* (pp. 133–52) fills in background to making of *Sammy Going South*.

WALLACH, Ira: *Muscle Beach* (Little, Brown, Boston 1959). Novel, basis of Mackendrick's 1967 film *Don't Make Waves*.

WHITE, James Dillon: *The Maggie* (Heinemann, London 1954). Novelisation of William Rose's script for the film.

WIETZ, Helmut: see BROWN.

WRIGHT, Basil: *The Long View* (Secker & Warburg, London 1974). Thoughtful, wide-ranging survey of world cinema. Brief but perceptive section on Mackendrick's films, pp. 323–8.

## Periodicals

*American Film* vol 4, no 5 (March 1979), pp. 68–9: 'The Mackendrick Legacy' by Patricia GOLDSTONE. Survey of Mackendrick's deanship of CalArts.

*American Film* vol 9, no 3 (December 1983), pp. 17–18: 'Bullies of Broadway' by Richard BLACKBURN. Account of filming of *Sweet Smell of Success*.

*Boston Phoenix* (5 June 1979), section 3 pp. 4, 12: 'The sweet smell of the '50s' by Stephen SCHIFF. Appreciation of *Sweet Smell of Success*.

*British Journal of Photography* vol 123, no 15 (9 April 1976), pp. 310–15: 'The Golden Ages of Ealing Studios', part 3, by Baynham HONRI. The Balcon era at Ealing from a technical standpoint.

*Cinestudio* no 79 (November 1969), pp. 25–9: 'Obra Olvidada: Dos peliculas "malditas" de Alexander Mackendrick' by Adolfo BELLIDO. Discussion (in Spanish) of *Sammy Going South* and *A High Wind in Jamaica*.

*The Cine-Technician* (September–October 1950), pp. 146–56: 'Mobile Studio Units for Feature Films' by Baynham HONRI. Detailed technical description of shooting *Whisky Galore* on Barra.

*Cosmopolitan* vol 128, no 4 (April 1950), pp. 32, 170–184: 'Tell me about it Tomorrow!' by Ernest LEHMAN. Original publication of novella later retitled *Sweet Smell of Success*, basis of Mackendrick's 1957 film.

*Dialogue on Film* vol 2, no 1 (1972), pp. 3–23: transcript of meeting of Advisory Committee on Film Training and Film Studies, chaired by Charlton Heston. Those taking part include Mackendrick, Alfred Hitchcock, George Stevens and Robert Wise.

*Le Figaro* (19 April 1990), p. 37: 'Le cinéma pur scotch whisky'. Interview with Mackendrick at Quimper Film Festival by Gilbert GUEZ.

*Film* vol 1, no 3 (February 1981), pp. 40–3, and vol 1, no 4 (March 1981), pp. 30–5: 'Balcon's Britain' by Dennis John HALL. Two-part film-by-film survey of Ealing's output.

*Film Dope* no 37 (June 1987), pp. 35–6: 'Alexander Mackendrick'. Entry giving brief biographical details, and listing credits – mostly accurate. Also extract from 1953 *Film Teacher* interview (see below).

*Film Journal* no 10 (June 1958), pp. 3–35: 'The Development of Comedie Noire' by Garth BUCKNER. Includes discussion of *The Ladykillers*.

*Film Teacher* (Spring 1953), pp. 8–12: 'As I See It'. Interview with Mackendrick by Derek J. DAVIES.

*Films and Filming* vol 2, no 2 (November 1955), p. 4, and vol 2, no 3 (December 1955), p. 10: 'Ealing: The Studio in Suburbia' by Kenneth TYNAN. Retrospective account of Balcon's tenure at Ealing.

*Films and Filming* (June 1957), pp. 8–9, 30: 'Mackendrick Finds the Sweet Smell of Success' by John CUTTS. Summary of Mackendrick's career shortly after his departure from Ealing.

*Films and Filming* (January 1963), p. 7. Brief unsigned piece on Mackendrick shooting *Sammy Going South*.

*Films in Review* vol 26, no 2 (February 1975), pp. 101–7: 'The Ealing Story' by Roy PICKARD. Short account of the studio's output.

*Image et Son* no 143 bis (Summer 1961), pp. 29–30: 'L'Homme au complet blanc' by Guy GAUTHIER. Notes on *The Man in the White Suit*.

*The Listener* (23 September 1954), pp. 482–3, 489: 'A Film Director and His Public' by Alexander MACKENDRICK. Transcript of talk given on BBC Home Service, 15 September 1954.

*National Film Theatre Programme* (February/March 1971), pp. 25–7: notes on season of Mackendrick's films, with introduction by Brian BAXTER.

*New York Times* (6 January 1985), pp. 17, 20: 'This American Mastered British Humor' by Nora SAYRE. Article on Mackendrick's Ealing comedies, linked to retrospective showings at MOMA.

*Positif* no 92 (February 1968), pp. 40–5: 'Entretien avec Mackendrick'. Interview by Bernard COHN.

*Quarterly of Film, Radio and Television* vol XI, no 1 (Fall 1956), pp. 1–13: 'Notes on the British Cinema' by Gavin LAMBERT. Brief critical survey, touching on Mackendrick's Ealing work in passing.

*Quimper Festival Programme* (6–17 April 1990), pp. 46–63: 'Hommage à Alexander Mackendrick'. Includes biofilmography, plot summaries and article by Jean-Pierre BERTHOMÉ: 'Alexander Mackendrick – Spectrographie d'un météore'.

*Scen och Salong* vol 43, no 8 (August 1958), pp. 29–32: 'A. Mackendrick: Mannen med Massor av Succé (A Man with Success Galore)' by Gösta OHLSSON. First of two articles (in Swedish) surveying Mackendrick's career and output to date.

*Scen och Salong* vol 43, no 9 (September 1958), pp. 4–7: 'A. Mackendrick – en mästeres signatur (the signature of a master)' by Gösta OHLSSON. Continuation and conclusion of previous article.

*Scene* no 20 (9 March 1963), pp. 20–5: 'The Devil's Disciple'. Unsigned, anecdotal piece on filming of *Sammy Going South* and on Mackendrick's reputation in the industry.

*Screen* vol 15, no 1 (Spring 1974), pp. 87–121, and vol 15, no 2 (Summer 1974), pp. 129–63: 'Projecting Britain and the British Character: Ealing Studios' by Charles

BARR. Two articles, parts of them later reworked into Barr's *Ealing Studios*, qv. Second article deals with Mackendrick's work at length.

*Screen* vol 16, no 1 (Spring 1975), pp. 78–127: 'Made in Ealing' by John ELLIS. Consideration of Ealing's output as influenced by technical, economic and social conditions of the period.

*Screen International* no 776 (29 September 1990), p. 16: 'A conversation with Alexander Mackendrick' by Theresa FITZGERALD. Interview with Mackendrick at the Quimper Film Festival.

*Sight and Sound* (April 1951), pp. 462–3: 'A Day in the Life of a Film'. Brief, unsigned article on filming of *The Man in the White Suit*, with photographs by Daniel Farson.

*Sight and Sound* (October–December 1951), pp. 57: 'In the Script'. Excerpts from shooting scripts of four recent British releases, including *The Man in the White Suit*.

*Sight and Sound* (Summer 1977), pp. 164–7: 'Ealing, your Ealing' by Geoff BROWN. Article reviewing Charles Barr's *Ealing Studios* and enlarging on some of its themes.

*Sight and Sound* (Winter 1983/84), pp. 40–6; 'Land Beyond Brigadoon' by John BROWN. Considers image of Scotland as purveyed by the cinema, with specific reference to *Whisky Galore* and *The Maggie*.

*Sight and Sound* (Winter 1988/89), pp. 48–52: 'Mackendrickland' by Philip KEMP. Survey of Mackendrick's directorial career, tracing thematic and stylistic patterns.

*Sight and Sound* (Summer 1990), p. 149: 'Saving Grace: Mackendrick at Quimper' by Philip KEMP. Short report on Mackendrick's attendance at a retrospective of his films at the Quimper Festival.

## Radio and TV (*in chronological order*)

'A Film Director and his Public.' Radio talk by Mackendrick, BBC Home Service, 9.55–10.15pm, 15 September 1954. Text published in the *Listener*, 23 September 1954.

'Location Kings Cross.' TV programme on the filming of *The Ladykillers*, introduced by Mackendrick. BBC, 7.30–8pm, 5 January 1956. (Producer: Alan Sleath.)

'New Comment.' Radio interview with Mackendrick by Paul Mayersberg, on filming of *High Wind in Jamaica*. BBC Radio 3, 8.15–8.30pm, 26 May 1965. (Producer: Philip French.)

'The Ealing Comedies or, Kind Hearts and Overdrafts.' TV programme, including interviews with Mackendrick, Michael Balcon, Joan Greenwood, Alec Guinness, etc. BBC1, 9.10–10.25pm, 8 September 1970. (Producer/Director: Harry Hastings.)

'Scope: Alexander Mackendrick.' Interview with Mackendrick on his career in films and on teaching at CalArts, by W. Gordon Smith. BBC1 (Scotland) TV, 10.50–11.20pm, 17 March 1975. (Producer/Director: W. Gordon Smith.)

'Omnibus.' TV programme on Ealing, including interviews with Mackendrick, Balcon, William Rose, Douglas Slocombe, etc. BBC1, 9.30–10.30pm, 2 May 1986. (Producer: Roland Keating.)

'Mackendrick: The Man Who Walked Away.' TV survey of Mackendrick's career, including interviews with Burt Lancaster, James Coburn, Charles Crichton, etc., and Mackendrick himself. Scottish TV, 10.35–11.30pm, 21 August 1986. (Producer: Russell Galbraith; Director: Dermot McQuarrie.)

'Fifties Features: The Women Behind the Pictures – The Way We Lived.' First of three TV programmes on women in post-war British film industry. Includes interviews Television, broadcast on Channel 4, 5.15–6.00pm, 21 September 1986. (Producer: Victoria Wegg-Prosser; Directors: Esther Ronay, Jo Ann Kaplan.)

'Britannia – the Film: Ealing Can Make It!' Fifth programme in eight-part radio series considering British cinema as a reflection of contemporary society and attitudes. Includes quotes from Mackendrick, Balcon, Alec Guinness. BBC Radio 4, 10.30–11.00am, 29 July 1989. (Director: John Powell.)

## Unpublished Sources

BALCON ARCHIVES: Large, mostly unclassified, collection of miscellaneous documents relating to whole career of Sir Michael Balcon, held partly by the British Film Institute and partly by Jonathan Balcon.

MACDOUGALL, Roger: 'The Man in the White Suit.' Three-act play, basis for Mackendrick's 1951 film; originally entitled 'The Flower Within the Bud.' British Library's Department of Manuscripts (No. 6568).

MACKENDRICK, Alexander: Letters to James Kennaway. Collection of letters, all undated, but probably written around 1961, relating particularly to the script, of the unrealised *Mary Queen of Scots* project. Included, along with drafts of the script, in the Kennaway papers held by the National Library of Scotland (Acc. 5696, Box 3, Folder 1).

MACKENDRICK, Alexander: CalArts teaching material. Huge collection of photocopied 'handouts', some running to 50 pages or more, prepared for Mackendrick's students at the California Institute of the Arts and stored there in his files.

NFS TAPES: Tape recordings of classes held by Mackendrick at the National Film School at Beaconsfield, summer 1979. Tapes recorded, and owned, by Jenny Wilkes.

OUTTAKES: Transcripts of interviews filmed for BBC Scotland programme 'Scope' and for STV programme 'The Man Who Walked Away' (see above under *Radio and TV*), including much material not used in the final broadcasts.

SHOOTING SCRIPTS: Scripts for all Mackendrick's Ealing films, plus *Sammy Going South*, held by the British Film Institute library. Also shooting script of *A High Wind in Jamaica*, in the private collection of Tom Pevsner. All differ, in some cases considerably, from the films as shot.

# Filmography

## 1 Non-feature film work

*On Parade* (GB/Netherlands 1936)
Gasparcolor, 7 mins

*Production Company*: J. Walter Thompson
  for Horlicks
*Director/Animator*: George Pal
*Script/Storyboard*: Alexander Mackendrick
*Camera*: Frank Hendrix
*Music*: Debroy Somers
*Narrator*: Malcolm MacEachern

*Sky Pirates* (GB/Netherlands 1937)
Technicolor, 6½ mins

*Production Company*: J. Walter Thompson
  for Horlicks
*Director/Animation*: George Pal
*Script/Storyboard*: Alexander Mackendrick
*Camera*: Frank Hendrix
*Music*: Debroy Somers

*Love on the Range* (GB/Netherlands
  1937)
Technicolor, 6½ mins

*Production Company*: J. Walter Thompson
  for Horlicks
*Director/Animation*: George Pal
*Script/Storyboard*: Alexander Mackendrick
*Camera*: Frank Hendrix
*Music*: Debroy Somers

*What Ho She Bumps* (GB/Netherlands
  1937)
Technicolor, 7½ mins

*Production Company*: J. Walter Thompson
  for Horlicks
*Director/Animation*: George Pal
*Script/Storyboard*: Alexander Mackendrick
*Camera*: Frank Hendrix
*Music*: Debroy Somers

*South Sea Sweethearts* (GB/
  Netherlands 1938)
Technicolor, 6½ mins

*Production Company*: J. Walter Thompson
  for Horlicks
*Director/Animation*: George Pal
*Script/Storyboard*: Alexander Mackendrick
*Camera*: Frank Hendrix
*Music*: Debroy Somers

*Carnival in the Clothes Cupboard* (GB
  1940) 5 mins

*Production Company*: J. Walter Thompson
  for Lux
*Directors/Animation*: John Halas, Joy
  Batchelor
*Script/Storyboard*: Alexander Mackendrick
*Music*: Francis Chagrin

*Fable of the Fabrics* (GB 1940)
5 mins

*Production Company*: J. Walter Thompson
  for Lux
*Directors/Animation*: John Halas, Joy
  Batchelor
*Script/Storyboard*: Alexander Mackendrick
*Music*: Francis Chagrin

*Train Trouble* (GB 1940)
8 mins

*Production Company*: J. Walter Thompson
  for Kelloggs
*Directors/Animation*: John Halas, Joy
  Batchelor
*Script/Storyboard*: Alexander Mackendrick
*Music*: Francis Chagrin

*Save Your Bacon* (aka: *Kitchen Waste
  For Pigs*) (GB 1942)
1½ mins

*Production Company*: MacDougall and
  Mackendrick for Ministry of Information
  and Ministry of Food
*Director/Drawings*: Alexander Mackendrick

*Script*: Roger MacDougall

*Contraries* (GB 1943)
1½ mins

*Production Company*: MacDougall and
  Mackendrick for Ministry of Information
*Director/Drawings*: Alexander Mackendrick
*Script*: Roger MacDougall

*Nero* (GB 1943)
1½ mins

*Production Company*: MacDougall and
  Mackendrick for Ministry of Information
  and Ministry of Fuel and Power
*Director*: Alexander Mackendrick
*Script*: Roger MacDougall

Alastair Sim, George Cole

Abu series: *Abu's Dungeon*; *Abu's
Poisoned Well*; *Abu's Harvest*; *Abu
Builds a Dam* (GB 1943)
9 mins each

*Production Company*: Halas-Batchelor for
  Ministry of Information
*Producers*: John Halas, Joy Batchelor
*Directors/Animation*: John Halas, Joy
  Batchelor
*Script*: Alexander Mackendrick, Nuri
*Music*: Matyas Seiber

*Subject for Discussion* (GB 1944)
15 mins (1302 ft)

*Production Company*: Seven League for
  Council for Health Education
*Producer*: Basil Wright
*Director*: Hans Nieter
*Script*: Roger MacDougall, Alexander
  Mackendrick
*Cinematographer*: W. Suschitzky
*Music*: E. H. Meyer
*Sound*: H. G. Halstead

*Handling Ships* (GB 1944/5)
Technicolor, 65 mins

*Production Company*: Halas-Batchelor for
  the Admiralty
*Producers*: John Halas, Joy Batchelor
*Directors*: John Halas, Robert E. Privett
*Script*: Alan Crick
*Design/Animation*: John Halas, Rosalie
  Crook, Christine Jollow, et al
*Design Consultant*: Alexander Mackendrick
*Camera*: Percy Wright
*Music*: Ernest H. Meyer

*I Granai del Popolo* (Italy 1944)
?15 mins

*Production Company*: Psychological
  Warfare Branch
*Producer*: Alexander Mackendrick
*Director*: Alexander Mackendrick, Peter
  Proud
*Script*: Alexander Mackendrick
*Camera*: Giovanni Ventimiglia

*Giorni di Gloria*: (Italy 1945)
(Fosse Ardeatini episode) 22 mins

*Production Company*: Psychological
  Warfare Branch
*Producer*: Alexander Mackendrick
*Director*: Marcello Pagliero
*Script*: Mario Serandrei, Ignazio Silone
*Camera*: Giovanni Ventimiglia

Charley series: *New Town*; *Your Very
Good Health*; *Charley's March of
Time*; *Robinson Charley*; *Charley's
Black Magic*; *Farmer Charley*;
*Charley Junior's Schooldays* (GB
1948/49)
Technicolor, 9–10 mins each

*Production Company*: Halas-Batchelor for
  Central Office of Information
*Producers*: John Halas, Joy Batchelor
*Directors/Script*: John Halas, Joy Batchelor
*Music*: Matyas Seiber
*Camera*: Percy Wright
*Consultant*: Alexander Mackendrick

## 2 Feature film work other than directorial

*Midnight Menace* (US: *Bombs over
London*) (GB 1937)
78 mins (7042 ft)

*Production Company*: Grosvenor Sound
  Films
*Released by*: ABFD
*Producer*: Harcourt Templeman
*Director*: Sinclair Hill
*Screenplay*: G. H. Moresby-White
*Dialogue*: D. B. Wyndham-Lewis
*From story by*: Roger MacDougall,
  Alexander Mackendrick
*Cinematographer*: Cyril Bristow
*Editor*: Michael Hankinson

Charles Farrell, Fritz Kortner, Margaret Vyner, Danny Green, Wallace Evenett, Monte de Lyle, Dino Galvani, Arthur Finn, Lawrence Hanray.

*Saraband for Dead Lovers* (US: *Saraband*) (GB 1948)
Technicolor, 96 mins (8627 ft)

*Production Company*: Ealing Studios
*Producer*: Michael Balcon
*Associate Producer*: Michael Relph
*Director*: Basil Dearden
*Screenplay*: John Dighton, Alexander Mackendrick
*From the novel by*: Helen Simpson
*Cinematographer*: Douglas Slocombe
*Editor*: Michael Truman
*Music*: Alan Rawsthorne
*Art Director*: Michael Relph, Jim Morahan, William Kellner
*Storyboard Designer (unc)*: Alexander Mackendrick

Stewart Granger, Joan Greenwood, Flora Robson, Francoise Rosay, Frederick Valk, Peter Bull, Anthony Quayle, Michael Gough, Megs Jenkins, Jill Balcon.

*Another Shore* (GB 1948)
77 mins (6956 ft)

*Production Company*: Ealing Studios
*Producer*: Michael Balcon
*Associate Producer*: Ivor Montagu
*Director*: Charles Crichton
*Screenplay*: Walter Meade
*From the novel by*: Kenneth Reddin
*Cinematographer*: Douglas Slocombe
*Editor*: Bernard Gribble
*Music*: Georges Auric
*Art Director*: Malcolm Baker-Smith
*Storyboard Designer (unc)*: Alexander Mackendrick

Robert Beatty, Moira Lister, Stanley Holloway, Michael Medwin, Maureen Delaney, Dermot Kelly, Wilfred Brambell, Irene Worth.

*The Blue Lamp* (GB 1950)
84 mins (7547 ft)

*Production Company*: Ealing Studios
*Producer*: Michael Relph
*Director*: Basil Dearden
*Screenplay*: T. E. B. Clarke
*From story by*: Ted Willis, Jan Read
*Additional Dialogue*: Alexander Mackendrick

*Cinematographer*: Gordon Dines
*Editor*: Peter Tanner
*Music*: Ernest Irving
*Art Director*: Tom Morahan
*2nd unit director (unc)*: Alexander Mackendrick

Jack Warner, James Hanley, Robert Flemyng, Bernard Lee, Dirk Bogarde, Patric Noonan, Peggy Evans, Frederick Piper, Betty Ann Davies, Dora Bryan, Norman Shelley, Gladys Henson, Bruce Seton.

*Dance Hall* (GB 1950)
80 mins (7244 ft)

*Production Company*: Ealing Studios
*Producer*: Michael Balcon
*Associate Producer*: E. V. H. Emmett
*Director*: Charles Crichton
*Screenplay*: E. V. H. Emmett, Diana Morgan, Alexander Mackendrick
*Cinematographer*: Douglas Slocombe
*Editor*: Seth Holt
*Music*: Geraldo and other orchestras
*Musical Director*: Ernest Irving
*Art Director*: Norman Arnold
*2nd unit director (unc)*: Alexander Mackendrick

Natasha Parry, Jane Hylton, Diana Dors, Petula Clark, Donald Houston, Bonar Colleano, Douglas Barr, Fred Johnson, Gladys Henson, Dandy Nichols, Sydney Tafler, James Carney, Kay Kendall.

*Fanfare* (Netherlands 1958)
93 mins (8370 ft)

*Production Company*: Sapphire
*Producer*: Rudolf Meyer
*Director*: Bert Haanstra
*Screenplay*: Bert Haanstra, Jan Blokker
*Script Assistance*: Alexander Mackendrick
*Cinematographer*: Edouard van der Enden
*Editor*: Edouard van der Enden
*Music*: Jan Mul

Bernhard Droog, Andrea Domburg, Hans Kaart, Ineke Brinkman, Johan Valk, Wim van den Heuvel, Henk van Buuren, Herbert Joeks.

# 3 Feature films directed by Alexander Mackendrick

*Whisky Galore!* (US: *Tight Little Island*) (GB 1949)

*Production Company*: Ealing Studios
*Producer*: Michael Balcon
*Associate Producer*: Monja Danischewsky
*Director*: Alexander Mackendrick
*Screenplay*: Compton Mackenzie, Angus
  MacPhail
*From the novel by*: Compton Mackenzie
*Cinematographer*: Gerald Gibbs
*Editor*: Joseph Sterling
*Music*: Ernest Irving
*Music Director*: Ernest Irving with the
  Philharmonia Orchestra
*Art Director*: Jim Morahan
*Sound Supervisor*: Stephen Dalby
*Production Supervisor*: Hal Mason
*Assistant Director*: Harry Kratz
*Camera Operator*: Chick Waterson
*Sound Recordist*: Leonard B. Bulkley
*Special Effects*: Geoffrey Dickinson, Sydney
  Pearson
*Continuity*: Marjorie Owens
*Unit Production Manager*: L. C. Rudkin

The English: Basil Radford (Captain Paul
  Waggett), Catherine Lacey (Mrs
  Waggett), Bruce Seaton (Sergeant Odd);
  The Islanders: Joan Greenwood (Peggy
  Macroon), Wylie Watson (Joseph
  Macroon), Gabrielle Blunt (Catriona
  Macroon), Gordon Jackson (George
  Campbell), Jean Cadell (Mrs Campbell),
  James Robertson Justice (Dr Maclaren),
  Morland Graham (The Biffer), John
  Gregson (Sammy MacCodrum), James
  Woodburn (Roderick MacRurie), James
  Anderson (Old Hector), Jameson Clark
  (Constable Macrae), Duncan Macrae
  (Angus MacCormac), Mary MacNeil
  (Mrs MacCormac), Norman MacOwan
  (Captain MacPhee), Alastair Hunter
  (Captain MacKechnie); The Others:
  Henry Mollison (Mr Farquharson), Frank
  Webster (First Mate), Compton
  Mackenzie (Captain Buncher); Finlay
  Currie (narrator, uncredited on most
  prints).

*Running time*: 82 mins (7457 ft)
*Premiere*: London, 16 June 1949

## Plot Synopsis

The Narrator introduces the remote
Hebridean island of Todday, whose people
live frugal but contented lives. But in 1943 a
great disaster overwhelms them: the island
runs dry of whisky. Capt. MacPhee, an old
seafarer, is so stricken by this that he takes
to his bed and dies.

The survivors are plunged in gloom –
none more so than Joseph Macroon, the
postmaster. To add to his worries, his
daughter Catriona has agreed to marry
George Campbell, the schoolmaster. At the
Post Office, Catriona teases her sister Peggy
about the imminent return of her English
admirer, Sgt Odd.

On board the *Island Queen* Sgt Odd, back
from Africa after two years, chats with the
skipper, Capt. MacKechnie. In his absence,
he learns, the Todday Home Guard have
grown disaffected under their commander,
Paul Waggett, the island's resident
Englishman. At his house, Waggett urges
PC Macrae to order MacKechnie to carry
some wrongly assigned ammunition back to
the mainland.

On the quayside Sgt Odd greets Joseph
and the other islanders, but their only
concern is whether the ferry has brought
any whisky – which it has not. MacKechnie
adamantly refuses to carry the ammunition.
Reluctantly, Waggett agrees to store it
temporarily at the Post Office.

Mrs Campbell, George's domineering
mother, berates him for daring to
contemplate marrying Catriona. Under
Waggett's command, the Home Guard
listlessly set up a roadblock, thus delaying
Dr Maclaren, who pours scorn on the whole
exercise.

On the beach, Sgt Odd proposes to
Peggy. She accepts him, but only after he
switches to faltering Gaelic. At the Post
Office, George is upbraided by Catriona for
not standing up to his mother.

A foggy night. Dr Maclaren visits Hector,
an elderly patient who, without whisky,
lacks the will to live. Offshore, a ship hoots
in the fog. At the Harbour Office Capt.
MacKechnie wonders if the *Island Queen*
will be able to sail.

Out at sea, the SS *Cabinet Minister* inches
through the fog, and hits a rock. Those
listening at the Harbour Office hear its
hooter stop. Two islanders, The Biffer and
Sammy MacCodrum, decide to see if help is
needed. Rowing out, they encounter the
crew in a lifeboat, and learn that the
wrecked ship carries 50,000 cases of whisky.

Word spreads rapidly. At the Harbour
Office, Joseph persuades MacKechnie to
sail, taking the *Cabinet Minister*'s crew with
him. As the islanders make for their boats,
the clock strikes 12. Realisation dawns – the
Sabbath has begun. Sadly they turn away,
leaving Sgt Odd dumbfounded.

Through the long day men gather on the
clifftop, gazing mournfully at the wreck.
Waggett meantime decides his duty is to
prevent looting. He tries to contact George

Campbell, his second-in-command; but
George is banished to his bedroom, and
Waggett seen off, by the formidable Mrs
Campbell.

At the Post Office, Sgt Odd tries to elicit
Joseph's parental consent. Waggett comes
to tell Odd to help him guard the wreck. He
leaves again; Joseph muses that a wedding
needs a *rèiteach* (betrothal party), and a
*rèiteach* cannot be held without whisky. . . .

Midnight strikes. A flotilla of boats set
out. Sgt Odd, on guard on the cliff, lets
himself be overpowered. Sammy summons
George, who leaves via his bedroom
window. At the wreck, the islanders pile
their boats with cases of whisky. Biffer,
trapped by falling cases as the wreck lists, is
rescued by George. As they row away, the
ship sinks. Onshore, the bulk of the liquor is
stored in a cave at Seal Bay.

Waggett, arriving to relieve Sgt Odd,
finds him tied up and helpless. He phones
his commanding officer, gets scant support,
then calls PC Macrae to insist on a thorough
search. Meanwhile, the islanders toast their
good fortune. Joy has returned to Todday.

George is driven home by Dr Maclaren
and Catriona. Fortified by whisky, he routs
his outraged mother. Macrae, making
perfunctory inquiries, calls on old Hector,
finding him much restored. The innkeeper,
Roderick MacRurie, resentful over his lost
trade, suggests Waggett should explore Seal
Bay. Waggett finds Sammy snoring on the
sands, and traces his footsteps back to the
cave.

At the Post Office Catriona, stashing
away bottles, stores a few in the
ammunition box. Waggett phones his CO to
arrange a visit, but explains the ruse to his
wife – he intends to call on the Excise.
Waggett's absence, Peggy suggests, makes a
perfect occasion for the double *rèiteach*.

The *rèiteach* is celebrated at the Post
Office with drinking, dancing and pipe
music. Even Mrs Campbell unbends and
joins in the merriment. Meanwhile, a
Revenue cutter speeds towards Todday; on
board with Waggett are Farquharson, the
Excise Officer, and his men. Hector, seeing
it from his window, phones through a
warning.

Whisky and people vanish like magic;
Joseph receives the excise men in his night
clothes. A house-to-house search yields
nothing. Farquharson and Waggett make
for Seal Bay in Waggett's car. The islanders
pile into Sammy's truck, hoping to get there
first.

While Waggett is delayed by various
ruses, the islanders load the truck with
whisky. As it leaves, Waggett and
Farquharson arrive, and give chase. They
have almost caught up when the car is
trapped in a hastily devised roadblock, and
the truck vanishes into the night.

Back at Waggett's house, Farquharson
receives a phone call: Waggett's
ammunition boxes, reaching the mainland,
have been found to contain contraband
whisky. Mrs Waggett breaks into helpless
laughter, which is taken up by the whole of
Todday as Waggett embarks for the
mainland, and the *rèiteach* resumes.

## *The Man in the White Suit* (GB 1951)

*Production Company*: Ealing Studios
*Producer*: Michael Balcon
*Associate Producer*: Sidney Cole
*Director*: Alexander Mackendrick
*Screenplay*: Roger MacDougall, John
  Dighton, Alexander Mackendrick
*From the play by*: Roger MacDougall
*Cinematographer*: Douglas Slocombe
*Additional Photography*: Lionel Banes
*Editor*: Bernard Gribble
*Music*: Benjamin Frankel
*Conducted by*: Ernest Irving with the
  Philharmonia Orchestra
*Art Director*: Jim Morahan
*Costume Designer*: Anthony Mendleson
*Sound Supervisor*: Stephen Dalby
*Production Supervisor*: Hal Mason
*Assistant Director*: David Peers
*Camera Operator*: Jeff Seaholme
*Sound Recordist*: Arthur Bradburn
*Special Processes*: Geoffrey Dickinson
*Special Effects*: Sydney Pearson
*Make-up*: Ernest Taylor, Harry Frampton
*Hair Styles*: Barbara Barnard
*Continuity*: Felicia Manheim
*Scientific Advisor*: Geoffrey Myers
*Unit Production Manager*: L. C. Rudkin

Alec Guinness (Sidney Stratton), Joan
  Greenwood (Daphne Birnley), Cecil
  Parker (Alan Birnley), Michael Gough
  (Michael Corland), Ernest Thesiger (Sir
  John Kierlaw), Howard Marion Crawford
  (Cranford), Henry Mollison (Hoskins),
  Vida Hope (Bertha), Patric Doonan
  (Frank), Duncan Lamont (Harry),
  Harold Goodwin (Wilkins), Colin
  Gordon (Hill), Joan Harben (Miss
  Johnson), Arthur Howard (Roberts),
  Roddy Hughes (Green), Stuart Latham
  (Harrison), Miles Malleson (The Tailor),
  Edie Martin (Mrs Watson), Mandy Miller
  (Gladdie), Charlotte Mitchell (Mill Girl),

Olaf Olsen (Knudsen), Desmond Roberts (Mannering), Ewan Roberts (Fotheringay), John Rudling (Wilson), Charles Saynor (Pete), Russell Waters (Davidson), Brian Worth (King), George Benson (The Lodger), Frank Atkinson (The Baker), Charles Cullum (1st Company Director), F. B. J. Sharp (2nd Company Director), Scott Harold (Express Reporter), Jack Howarth (Corland Mill Receptionist), Jack McNaughton (Taxi Driver), Judith Furse (Nurse Gamage), Billy Russell (Nightwatchman).

*Running time*: 85 mins (7673 ft)
*Premiere*: London, 27 July 1951

## Plot Synopsis

In voice-over, mill-owner Alan Birnley recalls the 'recent crisis' in the textile industry, which began during his visit to the mill owned by Michael Corland, his prospective son-in-law.

Corland shows Birnley round, hoping to impress him; but the going is sticky, as he confides to Birnley's daughter Daphne when she arrives. Their embrace is interrupted by a trolley pushed by lab assistant Sidney Stratton. In the research lab, Birnley notices a bizarre, bubbling apparatus which no one seems able to explain. The embarrassed Corland, leaving his staff to solve the mystery, takes Birnley and Daphne to lunch.

An invoice for £4,000, unearthed in the Accounts Dept, is conveyed up through the hierarchy to Corland, who chokes on his lunch. Various lab personnel are summoned to his presence, and lastly Sidney, who is sacked. Eloquently, he denounces Corland's small-mindedness – by himself in the men's washroom.

At the Employment Exchange, Sidney takes a labouring job at Birnley's – where, clumsily manoeuvring a trolley, he is helped by his fellow-worker Bertha, a staunch union member. Later, having helped carry an electron microscope up to the research lab, he impresses Hoskins, the head of research, with his expertise. Taking him for a senior technician, Hoskins asks if Sidney could stay on a few days to help them.

At his lodgings, Sidney explains to Bertha and his landlady, Mrs Watson, that he won't get paid in his new job, and persuades Bertha not to cause a fuss. She offers him her savings; he thanks her offhandedly.

Daphne fails to persuade her father to

finance Corland. Storming out, she recognises Sidney in the corridor, tracks him to the lab – and sees the bubbling apparatus. Delighted, she heads off to taunt Birnley with the news. Sidney, managing to forestall her, excitedly expounds his theories. That evening at home, she starts studying abstruse scientific articles.

Alone in the lab one lunch hour Sidney completes his experiment. It works, producing a luminous white fluid. Rushing off to see Birnley, he is stopped by Hoskins, who treats him as a hysteric and pours the fluid down the sink.

Sidney, trying to reach Birnley at home, is shut out by the butler, Knudsen; inside, Birnley's fellow-directors express outrage over the unwarranted expenditure. Daphne lets Sidney in and fetches Birnley; they return to find him tussling with Knudsen in the hall. Sidney insults Birnley and is thrown out. Daphne, furious, tells her father that Sidney has invented an indestructible fabric that repels dirt.

Sidney, to Hoskins's chagrin, is given the run of Birnley's lab. With an assistant, Wilson, he tries to replicate his experiment, which causes a gigantic explosion. So do the next two attempts; expenditure soars, the wretched Hoskins becomes a nervous wreck. Bertha tells Frank, the shop steward, that Sidney deserves danger money; Frank is unsympathetic.

Finally, the experiment is successful. The fibre is produced, woven into brilliant white cloth, and Sidney is fitted for a suit, cut out with oxy-acetylene torches. He proudly displays himself to Daphne, who hails him as a 'knight in shining armour', benefactor of humankind.

Rumours reach Corland, who contacts Sir John Kierlaw, godfather of the industry. Kierlaw, with his henchmen Cranford and Mannering, arrives from London to confront the euphoric Birnley with the implications of his plans. Sidney, meeting Bertha and Frank, cheerfully explains his invention; they too start to register how it could affect the industry.

The industrialists present Sidney with a new contract; about to sign, he realises they mean to suppress his discovery. They offer him £¼ million; he refuses and tries to leave. An undignified scuffle ends with Sidney knocked unconscious.

Bertha and Frank, looking for Sidney at his lodgings, learn he's moved to Birnley's house. While he sits imprisoned in Daphne's room, the bosses, beset by rumours of falling markets, squabble fractiously. When

Daphne comes to demand why Sidney is locked in, they suggest she might help induce his co-operation. Contemptuously, she forces them to put a financial value on her services.

Daphne makes a pass at Sidney, offering to go with him if he accepts the money. Though tempted, he turns her down; she eagerly helps him escape by lowering him from the window on a thread of his fabric. Planning to reveal all to the Manchester press, Sidney reaches the station, but lacks the fare. He dashes back to his lodgings, where Bertha, learning his intentions, locks him in.

At Birnley's house the workers announce that Sidney is now with them; but he, with the help of a sympathetic small girl, has contrived to escape. Hearing this, workers and bosses, acknowledging their common purpose, rush off in pursuit.

Cut off at the station, Sidney flees through the streets, a conspicuous quarry in his luminous white suit. Meanwhile Wilson, working late at the lab, finds the fabric is breaking down – an unstable compound. The hunted Sidney encounters old Mrs Watson, and begs a blanket from her pile of laundry. Instead, she berates him: 'What's to become of my bit of washing?' As he stands dumbfounded, the lynch-mob closes in; but when they grasp his suit, it disintegrates. Amid their hysterical laughter Sidney stands forlorn in his underpants.

Birnley, watching Sidney leave the mill, expresses in voice-over his relief that the whole matter is over. But Sidney, glancing through his notebook, murmurs, 'I *see*!' – and strides off, renewed confidence in his bearing.

## Mandy (US: *The Crash of Silence*) (GB 1952)

*Production Company*: Ealing Studios
*Producer*: Leslie Norman (A Michael Balcon Production)
*Director*: Alexander Mackendrick
*Screenplay*: Nigel Balchin, Jack Whittingham
*From the novel* The Day is Ours *by*: Hilda Lewis
*Cinematographer*: Douglas Slocombe
*Editor*: Seth Holt
*Music*: William Alwyn
*Conducted by*: Ernest Irving with the Philharmonia Orchestra
*Art Director*: Jim Morahan
*Costume Designer*: Anthony Mendleson

*Sound Supervisor*: Stephen Dalby
*Production Supervisor*: Hal Mason
*Assistant Director*: Norman Priggen
*Camera Operator*: Jeff Seaholme
*Sound Recordist*: Arthur Bradburn
*Make-up*: Harry Frampton
*Hair Styles*: Barbara Barnard
*Continuity*: Jean Graham
*Advisor on Tuition of the Deaf*: Ethel C. Goldsack
*Unit Production Managers*: Leonard C. Rudkin, Harry Kratz

Phyllis Calvert (Christine), Jack Hawkins (Searle), Terence Morgan (Harry), Mandy Miller (Mandy), Godfrey Tearle (Mr Garland), Marjorie Fielding (Mrs Garland), Nancy Price (Jane Ellis), Edward Chapman (Ackland), Patricia Plunkett (Miss Crocker), Eleanor Summerfield (Lily Tabor), Colin Gordon (Woollard Junior), Dorothy Alison (Miss Stockton), Julian Amyes (Jimmy Tabor), Gabrielle Brune (The Secretary), John Cazabon (Davey), Gwen Bacon (Mrs Paul), W. E. Holloway (Woollard Senior), Phyllis Morris (Miss Tucker), Gabrielle Blunt, (Miss Larner), Jean Shepherd (Mrs Jackson), Jane Asher (Nina), Marlene Maddox (Leonie), Michael Mallinson, Doreen Taylor, Doreen Gallagher, Michael Davis, Colin Wilkinson, Joan Peters (Pupils at Clyne House).

*Running time*: 93 mins (8393 ft)
*Premiere*: London, 31 July 1952

## Plot Synopsis

In voice-over, Christine Garland introduces her two-year-old daughter, Mandy, whom we see being bathed, and playing. To her friend Lily Tabor, visiting with her small son, Christine expresses worry that Mandy hasn't started talking. Christine's husband Harry arrives home; Lily leaves to return to Manchester.

Christine voices her fear: can Mandy hear at all? Harry deprecates the idea. But a test shows that Mandy is stone-deaf. Specialists confirm that nothing can be done; Mandy will always be deaf, and probably dumb. Harry, having seen and disliked a special school, proposes a private teacher. Since there's no room in their flat, they decide to take up his parents' offer of accommodation.

All three move in with Harry's parents: Fred, preoccupied with his postal-chess games, and Emily, who is delighted. Five years pass; Mandy is still sheltered from the outside world.

The family dog strays out on the road. Mandy, trying to retrieve it, is nearly hit by a truck, whose driver berates her. Weeping, she rushes indoors, where Christine tries to comfort her. The governess, Miss Tucker, takes Mandy off for a sign-language lesson, leaving Christine feeling helpless.

Lily takes Christine to see the Manchester school Harry disliked, and to meet the headmaster, Dick Searle. An awkward, ungracious man, Searle nonetheless impresses her in his dedication to the children. Her last doubts are resolved by the school's founder, Jane Ellis, who she only realises to be deaf after some minutes' conversation. Searle interviews a new teacher, Miss Crocker, about whom he has doubts.

At the Tabors' flat, Christine phones Harry about the school. He and Emily are unenthusiastic. To the Tabors, Christine admits she's already asked Searle to take Mandy on.

Mandy tricycles round the tiny garden. Local kids call through a gap in the wall; getting no reply, they run off shouting abuse. Christine argues with Harry and Emily, who are opposed to the school.

In the park, Mandy wanders off with her ball while Christine and Harry argue. A brother and sister take the ball, forcing Mandy to play 'piggy-in-the-middle'. In frustration, Mandy attacks the boy and is dragged off him by his mother, who shouts that Mandy is mad. Back at the house, Christine flares up, accusing Harry of selfishness. He slaps her; she leaves home with Mandy.

Christine brings Mandy to the school. Searle is in a board meeting. Ackland, the school solicitor and member of the governing trust, queries proposed expenditure. He and Searle, old antagonists, quarrel. Mandy's teacher, Miss Stockton, takes her into the class; initially shy, she becomes drawn into the activity. Christine quietly leaves.

Harry consults Woollards, his solicitors, who suggest putting pressure on the school via Ackland.

Mandy wakes weeping in the night. Miss Crocker, losing patience, is rebuked by Jane Ellis, while Searle comforts Mandy. But she won't eat, or respond in class, or play with the other children. Searle, feeling he's failed, asks Christine to collect her. As he drives them into town, Christine suggests she takes a room nearby, and Mandy becomes a day pupil.

Ackland shows Searle the letter from Woollards. Searle, intent on the children, dismisses him curtly. Christine returns Mandy to her class.

Ackland's secretary suggests Christine and Searle may be having an affair; Ackland sets an employee, Davey, to snoop.

A breakthrough. With Miss Stockton's help, Mandy pronounces her first consonant, and proudly demonstrates it to Christine. Seeing this, Miss Crocker tells Searle she wants to stay on.

Harry reads Emily a letter from Christine; Emily suggests he should go and see her. Christine and Mandy receive his telegram, and meet him at the station. At a hotel Harry and Christine enjoy a passionate reunion.

At breakfast, Harry proposes finding another school in London; Christine insists Mandy should stay where she is. Searle arrives; Harry leaves resentfully. Back home, he tells Emily Christine is obsessed with 'the witch-doctor'.

Searle offers to coach Mandy in the evenings. Arriving at Christine's lodgings, he passes Davey talking to the landlady. Under his coaching, Mandy makes rapid progress. Davey reports to Ackland who recalls a malicious letter written to the Board by Searle's estranged wife.

During one evening session, Mandy articulates her first word: 'Mummy'. Delighted, Christine impulsively kisses Searle – a scene witnessed by the landlady, who tells Davey. Returning to the school, Searle is warned by Jane Ellis that Ackland has asked about Mrs Searle's letter. She suggests further tuition should take place at the school.

Phoning Ackland, Woollards learn from his secretary what's happening. They contact Harry, who dashes home, packs a case and heads north, leaving his parents troubled.

Ackland reproaches his secretary for indiscretion. Harry arrives, hears what's going on, and storms off to see Christine – who is out for a celebratory dinner with Searle, leaving Mandy with a babysitter. Furious, he awaits Christine's return.

After dinner, Searle tells Christine of the malicious rumours. At the lodgings they find Harry, who demands proof of Mandy's progress. Searle leaves; Harry announces he's taking Mandy back to London. Christine tries to get Mandy to speak, but fails. Harry accuses her of kissing Searle, and departs with Mandy, leaving her weeping.

Early next morning Harry and Mandy arrive home; later, Christine turns up with Searle, who tells Harry that Ackland is using him. Mandy, wandering into Fred's room, starts reading aloud. Interrupting the confrontation, Fred induces Harry to admit he believes Christine innocent. Meanwhile, Mandy has strayed out on the wasteland. As Christine and Harry watch, she approaches the other kids, speaks her own name, and joins in their game.

## The Maggie (US: *High and Dry*) (GB 1954)

*Production Company*: Ealing Studios
*Producer*: Michael Truman (A Michael Balcon Production)
*Director*: Alexander Mackendrick
*Screenplay*: William Rose
*Original story*: Alexander Mackendrick
*Cinematographer*: Gordon Dines
*Editor*: Peter Tanner
*Music*: John Addison
*Conducted by*: Dock Mathieson with the Philharmonia Orchestra
*Art Director*: Jim Morahan
*Costumes*: Anthony Mendleson
*Sound Supervisor*: Stephen Dalby
*Production Supervisor*: Hal Mason
*Assistant Director*: Frank Gollings
*Camera Operators*: Chic Waterson, Hugh Wilson
*Sound Recordist*: Leo Wilkins
*Special Processes*: Geoffrey Dickinson
*Special Effects*: Sydney Pearson
*Make-up*: Alex Garfath
*Continuity*: Barbara Cole
*Unit Production Manager*: L. C. Rudkin

Paul Douglas (Calvin B. Marshall), Alex Mackenzie (The Skipper), James Copeland (The Mate), Abe Barker (The Engineer), Tommy Kearins (The Wee Boy), Hubert Gregg (Pusey), Geoffrey Keen (Campbell), Dorothy Alison (Miss Peters), Andrew Keir (The Reporter), Meg Buchanan (Sarah), Mark Dignam (The Laird), Jameson Clark (Dirty Dan), Moultrie Kelsall (CSS Skipper), Fiona Clyne (Sheena), Sheila Shand Gibbs (Barmaid), Betty Henderson (Campbell's Secretary), Russell Waters, Duncan Macintyre (Hailing Officers), Roddy McMillan (Inverkerran Driver), Jack Macguire (Highland Innkeeper), John Rae (The Constable), Jack Stewart, Eric Woodburn (Skippers), Douglas Robin, R. B. Wharrie (Inspectors), David Cameron (Hired Car Driver), Catherine Fletcher (Postmistress), William Crichton (Harbour Master), Andrew Downie (Aircraft Pilot), Herbert C. Cameron (Gillie), Gilbert Stevenson (Davy MacDougall).

*Running time*: 92 mins (8330 ft)
*Premiere*: London, 25 February 1954

## Plot Synopsis

An ancient puffer-boat, the *Maggie*, steams up the Clyde, observed by two harbour officials who recall troubles involving her skipper, MacTaggart. As she docks the Engineman, McGregor, berates MacTaggart with his folly in arriving so openly. They come ashore with Hamish, the mate, leaving the Wee Boy, Dougie, on board. Two inspectors turn up looking for MacTaggart; Dougie vainly tries to mislead them.

In the pub, MacTaggart defends himself against the mockery of some CSS (Clyde Shipping Services) officers. Dougie rushes in with news of the inspectors' arrival. To renewed laughter the crew depart, leaving Dougie to settle up. The boy attacks a CSS man who disparages MacTaggart, and is thrown out by the landlord.

On board, the inspectors announce that unless the *Maggie* has £300 worth of repairs, she'll lose her loading licence. The crew are sunk in gloom.

At the CSS offices, the crew come to offer the Manager, Campbell, a part-share in the *Maggie* (in fact owned by MacTaggart's sister Sarah). Campbell is too busy to listen; but MacTaggart overhears an Englishman, Pusey, trying unsuccessfully to charter a boat on behalf of his boss, the American Calvin B. Marshall, European boss of World International Airlines. Campbell having left, MacTaggart offers Pusey his services.

At the quayside Pusey, having taken for MacTaggart's a far larger boat lying alongside, charters the *Maggie* to carry a cargo of domestic equipment to the island of Kiltarra, where Marshall has bought a house as a surprise for his wife. MacTaggart asks £300 for the trip, and takes a £50 cash advance.

The cargo is loaded. After a festive evening at the pub, the crew sail at low tide, dismissing Dougie's warnings. The *Maggie* runs aground on an underwater subway tunnel.

From London, Pusey phones Campbell to check everything's OK. Campbell, convulsed with laughter, enlightens him. The horrified Pusey breaks the news to his boss.

While MacTaggart, watched by an appreciative crowd, waits for the tide to turn, Marshall flies north with his secretary and Pusey. Arriving in Glasgow, he finds a facetious report in the local paper.

The *Maggie*, freed by the tide, steams away. At his hotel Marshall contacts Campbell, who comes over to explain matters. Along with him come Fraser, a local reporter, and an irate Sarah MacTaggart.

At Greenock the *Maggie*, hailed with a message from Marshall, turns tail and heads out again. Marshall hires a plane to track the boat's course, then a car to intercept it in the Crinan Canal, where Hamish and Dougie are doing some casual poaching.

Catching up with the *Maggie*, Marshall orders MacTaggart to return to Ardrishaig with the cargo, leaving Pusey aboard to ensure it. He departs. Learning what Hamish and Dougie are doing, Pusey, outraged, goes to find them. The local Laird, hearing shots, combs the woods, while his factor fetches the police.

Pusey encounters Dougie; both are chased by the Laird, whom Pusey inadvertently pushes in the canal. Pusey is arrested, while the crew escape on the *Maggie*.

In Glasgow, Marshall invites Fraser to his hotel for a talk. Campbell rings: no sign of the *Maggie* at Ardrishaig. Pusey phones from the police station, to Marshall's fury and Fraser's delight. Back in his cell, Pusey awaits his hearing before the local sheriff – the Laird.

Marshall charters another plane, and eventually tracks down the *Maggie* at Inverkerran. Phoning Campbell, he arranges to rendezvous with a CSS ship at Oban, and himself boards the *Maggie*.

En route, fog descends; MacTaggart beaches the *Maggie* in Fiona Bay. While the tide's out Marshall, taking MacTaggart with him, walks to Loch Mora and again phones Campbell, while MacTaggart and the publican discuss a forthcoming 100th-birthday party in Bellabegwinnie.

Marshall and MacTaggart return to the *Maggie* and sail to Loch Mora, where Marshall's cargo is unloaded on the quayside, pending collection by a CSS ship from the dilapidated pier. At Dougie's suggestion, MacTaggart leaves the boat jutting under the pier. The tide rises; the pier is demolished, leaving Marshall

distraught and the cargo inaccessible to the CSS ship. Forced to charter the *Maggie*, Marshall pays over the rest of the £300.

Once more at sea, Marshall finds the *Maggie* is carrying passengers – party guests for Bellabegwinnie, where the boat apparently needs to take on coal. There Marshall phones his wife, who has discovered his plans; she hangs up on him. Back at the *Maggie*, he finds all the crew except Dougie absent at the party. Seeking out MacTaggart, Marshall threatens to stop his cheque, but the skipper refuses to believe him. Retreating glumly to his cabin, Marshall is lured back by the music and invited into the party; there he's drawn into the dancing by a young woman, Sheena.

Later, sitting outside, Sheena tells Marshall how she must choose between an ambitious storekeeper and a simple fisherman – and intends to marry the latter.

Waking late and hungover, Marshall finds the *Maggie* still moored and half the crew missing. Rejecting MacTaggart's excuses, he storms off to phone Pusey – returning to announce he's bought the *Maggie*, will sail her to Kiltarra, then sell her for scrap. The crew are dumbfounded – but Dougie follows Marshall to the boat, where he knocks him unconscious.

Pusey calls back: Sarah won't sell. Overjoyed, the crew set sail. When Marshall revives the *Maggie* is nearing Kiltarra. He sends for the boy, who angrily defies him. Abruptly, the boat's engine stops. The *Maggie* drifts towards a reef.

While McGregor rants bitterly against MacTaggart, Marshall struggles to repair the engine. He succeeds – just as the *Maggie* runs aground. MacTaggart prepares to abandon ship. Marshall can safely trans-ship his cargo, but the *Maggie* will break up on the rocks. Marshall orders him to save the boat by jettisoning the cargo – even though MacTaggart admits he never insured the goods.

Pusey, on the quayside at Kiltarra, is staggered to find the cargo gone. MacTaggart tentatively offers Marshall his cheque back; he's about to take it when Dougie vehemently protests. Relinquishing the money, Marshall walks off to meet his wife.

The harbour officials are surprised to see, steaming up the Clyde, a puffer named the *Calvin B. Marshall*. On board, MacTaggart and McGregor squabble furiously.

*The Ladykillers* (GB 1955)
Technicolor

*Production Company*: Ealing Studios
*Producer*: Michael Balcon
*Associate Producer*: Seth Holt
*Director*: Alexander Mackendrick
*Screenplay*: William Rose
*Cinematographer*: Otto Heller
*Editor*: Jack Harris
*Music*: Tristram Cary
*Conducted by*: Dock Mathieson with the
  Sinfonia of London
*Art Director*: Jim Morahan
*Costume Designer*: Anthony Mendleson
*Sound Supervisor*: Stephen Dalby
*Production Supervisor*: Hal Mason
*Assistant Director*: Tom Pevsner
*Camera Operator*: Chic Waterson
*Sound Editor*: Gordon Stone
*Sound Recordist*: Leo Wilkins
*Special Effects*: Sydney Pearson
*Make-up*: Alex Garfath
*Hair Styles*: Daphne Martin
*Scenic Artist*: W. Simpson Robinson
*Continuity*: Felicia Manheim
*Technicolor Colour Consultant*: Joan Bridge
*Unit Production Manager*: David Peers

Alec Guinness (Professor Marcus), Cecil
  Parker (Major Courtney), Herbert Lom
  (Louis), Peter Sellers (Harry), Danny
  Green (One-Round), Katie Johnson (Mrs
  Wilberforce), Jack Warner (Police
  Superintendent), Frankie Howerd
  (Barrow Boy), Philip Stainton (Police
  Sergeant), Fred Griffiths (The Junkman),
  Kenneth Connor (Cab Driver), Sam
  Kydd (2nd Cab Driver), Phoebe Hodgson
  (Old Lady), Helene Burls (Hypatia),
  Edie Martin (Lettice), Evelyn Kerry
  (Amelia), Neil Wilson (Policeman),
  Ewan Roberts (Constable in Police
  Station), Michael Corcoran (Burglar),
  Harold Goodwin (Left Luggage Clerk),
  Jack Melford (Scotland Yard Man),
  Robert Moore (Constable), John Rudling
  (Nervous Man), Madge Brindley (Large
  Lady), Lucy Griffiths (Miss Pringle),
  Leonard Sharp (Pavement Artist).

*Running time*: 96 mins (8750 ft)
*Premiere*: London, 8 December 1955

## Plot Synopsis

Mrs Wilberforce, an elderly widow living
near Kings Cross, visits the police station to
explain that her friend Amelia's recent
sighting of a spaceship had been merely a
dream. The Superintendent thanks her
politely for the information.

A storm builds up. At the newsagent's,
no response to Mrs W's 'Rooms to Let'
advertisement. As she leaves, a sinister
figure follows her home and prowls round
outside, unnoticed by her, but alarming her
parrots. The prowler rings the doorbell:
Professor Marcus, come to see the rooms.
He announces he will move in the next day.
He has formed an amateur string quintet;
his friends will be coming to practise. Mrs
W is delighted.

The next evening. Marcus's friends arrive:
the urbane Major Courtney; the hulking
'One-Round' Lawson; Harry Robinson, a
Teddy Boy; and the saturnine gangster,
Louis Harvey. Marcus puts on a record of
Boccherini, while the quintet discuss his
plan, a payroll robbery involving Mrs W's
unwitting help. Louis opposes the idea;
Harry and One-Round have misgivings. Mrs
W, charmed by the music, comes to offer
tea. When she leaves, the argument
resumes. Marcus takes a vote, and wins
when Louis angers One-Round. Louis
describes the plan as 'dreamt up in the
booby-hatch'; Mrs W, returning with the
teapot, averts disaster.

At Kings Cross, Marcus times the arrival
of a payroll van. Meanwhile, the others
endure Mrs W's interruptions. She requests
help with a parrot; Harry volunteers, but
gets his finger bitten. One-Round, trying to
help, demolishes a chair. The parrot escapes
to the roof, pursued by Louis and the
Major. Marcus, returning, effortlessly
recaptures the bird.

Packed into a black saloon, the gang wait
tensely. At 1.00 precisely they take off in
several vehicles, blocking the payroll van in
a street near Kings Cross. The guards are
overpowered; the police pursue Louis's car
while the money, stashed in a trunk, is
taken by taxi to the station. Harry, dressed
as a porter, deposits it with arrival luggage.
While the police check departing
consignments, Mrs W arrives by cab to pick
up a trunk 'arriving from Cambridge'.

In a phone box, Marcus takes a call from
the Major at Kings Cross, watching the
trunk loaded into Mrs W's taxi. She departs
– but returns, alarming the gang, to retrieve
her umbrella. On her way home Mrs W,
seeing a barrow-boy shooing off a scrap-
dealer's greedy horse, intervenes to protect
the animal. The barrow-boy, enraged, turns
on the cab driver. Their scuffle alarms the
horse; it rears, spills the scrap, overturns the
barrow and bolts. As the police arrive, the

barrow-boy attacks the cab, while the scrap dealer appears yelling for his horse. The gang, watching in dismay, drive slowly off.

At the house the Major waits anxiously. The trunk sits on the police station steps, observed by the gang from a distance. The Superintendent, trying to restore calm, details a constable to take Mrs W home. Seeing a police car arrive, the Major flees in panic. Two policemen bring in the trunk. The Major encounters the others who, once the police have left, return to the house, carry the trunk upstairs and gloat over its contents. Downstairs, Mrs W prepares a tea-party.

With the loot in their instrument-cases, the gang take leave of Mrs W, who regrets they can't stay for her friends. One-Round, lingering behind, gets his cello-case caught in the door. The rest watch impatiently as he rings the doorbell, then tugs. The case flies open, scattering banknotes, as Mrs W opens the door.

Erupting from the car, the gang scoop up the money and pile back in, leaving Mrs W bemused. But realising they must allay her suspicions, they return to concoct explanations. Mrs W's friends – four more little old ladies – arrive, overjoyed to find the 'musicians' still there. One carries a newspaper reporting the robbery; Mrs W realises the truth. Deeply shocked, she tells the gang they must stay. Harry, returning from moving the car, finds Marcus accompanying the ladies on the pianola, while the others gloomily drink tea.

Afterwards, Marcus tries to talk Mrs W round – first by explaining that insurance will cover the robbery, then by eliciting a sob-story from the Major. When this fails, the gang try threats: she too is implicated in the robbery, and faces jail.

A police sergeant calls to reassure Mrs W about the earlier rumpus. The gang induce her to send him away. But she still insists the money be returned, and decides that, after all, they must confess.

Upstairs, the gang debate how to eliminate her. Louis devises lots to choose the killer. It falls to the Major; the others go down, sending Mrs W up. While they wait nervously the Major, ostensibly fetching the police, escapes through the window – but One-Round, loitering in the back doorway, blocks his route.

Bursting in, the others find the Major (and the money) gone. A drifting banknote betrays his presence on the roof. The Major drops the cello-case full of money, which Mrs W confiscates, locking it in a chest.

Louis climbs up after the Major, who falls to his death.

One-Round, vetoing further attempts on Mrs W, is decoyed out of the way; the lot falls to Harry. While Marcus and One-Round wheel the Major away, Harry creeps into the sitting-room. Finding Mrs W asleep, he unlocks the chest and makes off with the money.

The Major is dropped into a passing goods-train. One-Round, suspicious, bursts into the house, finding Mrs W seemingly strangled. He pursues Harry and kills him. As he turns on the others Mrs W appears, indignant that the money is gone.

One-Round retrieves the cello-case – and Harry's gun. Returning the money to Mrs W, he insists on staying with her. Louis and Marcus wheel Harry away; Mrs W, still expecting the Major's return with the police, drifts back to sleep.

Marcus and Louis, awaiting the next train, debate who should kill One-Round, and who Mrs W. As they drop Harry, One-Round appears behind them with the gun. But the safety-catch is on; Louis moves in with his knife.

While they await yet another train, Marcus talks wildly; Louis accuses him of being crazy. Marcus turns nasty, vanishing in the smoke.

Louis drops One-Round, draws the gun and, seeking the elusive Marcus, climbs down a ladder beside the tunnel. Marcus, hiding underneath, loosens the ladder, dropping Louis into a train. As he stands triumphant, a signal above him crashes down on his head.

The next morning. At the police station, Mrs W tells her story. The Sergeant tolerantly suggests she keeps the money. Bestowing £1 on a pavement artist, she makes her way home.

## Sweet Smell of Success (USA 1957)

*Production Company*: Hecht-Hill-Lancaster (A Norma-Curtleigh Production, released through United Artists)
*Producer*: James Hill
*Executive Producer*: Harold Hecht
*Director*: Alexander Mackendrick
*Screenplay*: Clifford Odets, Ernest Lehman
*From the novella by*: Ernest Lehman
*Music*: Elmer Bernstein
*Conducted by*: Elmer Bernstein
*Songs by*: Chico Hamilton, Fred Katz
*Cinematographer*: James Wong Howe
*Editor*: Alan Crosland Jr

*Art Director*: Edward Carrere
*Set Design* Edward Boyle
*Costumes*: Mary Grant
*Sound*: Jack Solomon
*Production Manager*: Richard McWhorter
*Assistant Director*: Richard Maybery
*Special Effects*: Robert Carlisle
*Make-up*: Robert Schiffer
*Music Editor*: Lloyd Young

Burt Lancaster (J. J. Hunsecker), Tony Curtis (Sidney Falco), Susan Harrison (Susan Hunsecker), Marty Milner (Steve Dallas), Sam Levene (Frank D'Angelo), Barbara Nichols (Rita), Jeff Donnell (Sally), Joseph Leon (Robard), Edith Atwater (Mary), Emile Meyer (Harry Kello), Joe Frisco (Herbie Temple), David White (Otis Elwell), Lawrence Dobkin (Leo Bartha), Lurene Tuttle (Mrs Bartha), Queenie Smith (Mildred Tam), Autumn Russell (Linda), Jay Adler (Manny Davis), Lewis Charles (Al Evans), The Chico Hamilton Quintet (Themselves).

*Running time*: 96 mins (8750 ft) (103 mins at press showing)
*Premiere*: New York, 27 June 1957

## Plot Synopsis

Early evening in Times Square. Sydney Falco, ambitious press agent, buys a paper and finds in it nothing to please him. Back in his shabby office-cum-apartment, he ducks a phone call from an irate client and rebuffs the sympathy of his secretary, Sally. While changing, he explains to her that his exclusion from J. J. Hunsecker's all-powerful column is a punishment; he failed to break up the affair between Hunsecker's sister Susan and a young jazz guitarist, Steve Dallas.

At the Elysian Rooms, where Dallas's quintet is playing, Falco finds his uncle Frank D'Angelo, Steve's manager, who assures him that the affair between Steve and Susan is over. Falco's scepticism is confirmed when the club's cigarette girl, Rita, whispers that Susan is out back waiting for Steve.

Outside, Susan tells Steve that she accepts his proposal – though she has yet to inform her brother. Falco interrupts them, acting friendly, but Steve treats him with angry contempt. Back in the club, Rita begs Falco for help – she rejected a pass from a columnist, Leo Bartha, and now faces the sack. Falco makes a date with her for later and leaves to see Susan home.

In the taxi, Susan tells Falco of her marriage plans. He feigns approval, drops her at her apartment and heads for the 21 Club, where Hunsecker is dining and holding court. At his table are a senator, an aspiring singer and her agent; Hunsecker patronises the former and insults the other two, before leaving with Falco. Outside, they encounter Lieutenant Kello, a corrupt cop in Hunsecker's pocket. On hearing of Susan's engagement, Hunsecker demands immediate action from Falco to ruin Steve's career.

At Toots Shor's club Falco finds Leo Bartha and his wife, and, using Rita's story, tries to put the screws on Bartha to print a smear item about Steve. Bartha calls his bluff by confessing to his wife. Falco switches targets to another columnist, the lecherous Otis Elwell; bribing him with the promise of an easy lay. Back at Falco's office, Rita is waiting for him. Falco arrives with Elwell, browbeats the reluctant Rita into co-operating, and leaves them together. He phones Hunsecker to report success.

The next day, Falco sweet-talks Hunsecker's secretary, Mary, into letting him sneak a look at the column proofs, and finds an item about an obscure comedian, Herbie Temple. Tracking down Temple at the theatre, Falco boasts of his pull with Hunsecker, impressing Temple by pretending to phone in the paragraph he just read.

Steve and Frank D'Angelo are waiting for Falco at his office. Steve accuses Falco of planting the smear; Falco denies it, and phones Hunsecker to ask him to get Steve reinstated. In Hunsecker's apartment, Susan also asks her brother to help; he agrees to meet Steve before giving his TV broadcast that evening. At the TV studio, Falco outlines his plan to Hunsecker. When Steve arrives with Susan and D'Angelo, Falco needles him into abusing Hunsecker, who makes Susan promise to break off the relationship.

Over dinner, Hunsecker tells Falco to have Steve destroyed, using Kello as the instrument. Falco refuses, but can't resist the ultimate bait: a spell as guest-editor of Hunsecker's column. At Jack Robard's club, where the quintet are playing, he plants reefers in Steve's pocket and tips off the waiting Kello. As Steve leaves the club, Kello moves in for the kill.

Drunkenly celebrating with other press agents, Falco receives a phone message to come to Hunsecker's apartment. Susan, who has heard what happened to Steve, is waiting; she denounces Falco, then tries to throw herself from the balcony. He prevents her, dragging her back into her room just as her brother arrives. Believing Falco was trying to rape Susan, Hunsecker beats him up, then phones Kello. Susan, having realised Hunsecker's part in the plot, walks out on him for good. Down on the street, Falco is brutally beaten by Kello and taken into custody. Susan walks off into the dawn to join Steve.

*Sammy Goes South* (US: *A Boy Ten Feet Tall*) (GB 1963)
Eastman Colour, CinemaScope

*Production Company*: Bryanston Seven Arts (A British Lion Release)
*Producer*: Hal Mason (A Michael Balcon Production)
*Director*: Alexander Mackendrick
*Screenplay*: Denis Cannan
*From the novel by*: W. H. Canaway
*Cinematographer*: Erwin Hillier
*Editor*: Jack Harris
*2nd Unit Photography*: Norman Warwick
*Music*: Tristram Cary
*Played by*: Sinfonia of London
*Art Director*: Edward Tester
*Set Designer*: Scott Slimon
*Costumes*: Ernest Farrer
*Sound Editor*: Leslie Hodgson
*Assistant Director*: Peter Price
*Camera Operator*: Robert Kindred
*Camera Assistant*: George Pink
*Assistant Editor*: Mary Kessel
*Sound Recordist*: H. L. Bird
*Make-up*: Philip Leakey
*Hairdresser*: Henry Montsash
*Continuity*: Joan Kirk
*Casting Director*: Robert Lennard
*Assistant Casting Director*: Judith Jourd
*Stills Photographer*: Laurie Turner
*Production Manager*: Philip Shipway

Edward G. Robinson (Cocky Wainwright), Fergus McClelland (Sammy), Constance Cummings (Gloria van Imhoff), Harry H. Corbett (Lem), Paul Stassino (Spyros Dracondopoulos), Zia Mohyeddin (The Syrian), Orlando Martins (Abu Lubaba), John Turner (Heneker), Zena Walker (Aunt Jane), Jack Gwillim (District Commissioner), Patricia Donahue (Cathie), Jared Allen (Bob), Guy Deghy (Doctor), Steven Scott (Egyptian Policeman, Luxor), Frederick Schiller (Head Porter, Luxor Hotel), Swaleh,

Tajiri, Faith Brown (Members of Cocky's Camp).

*Running time*: 128 mins (11,603 ft)
*Premiere*: London, 18 March 1963

## Plot Synopsis

Port Said, November 1956. Ten-year-old Sammy Hartland wanders restlessly about the apartment while his parents discuss sending him to his Aunt Jane who owns a hotel in Durban. The radio emits news of the Suez crisis. Outside, troop convoys rumble past. From the balcony, Sammy calls down to his friend Mahmoud in the street, but gets no response. He descends and makes his way to the harbour. From nowhere, two warplanes swoop down; everyone scatters in panic as bombs crash.

Scurrying home through chaos and rubble, Sammy finds a crowd around his apartment block, which is half-destroyed. Officials hold him back; as he screams for his mother, her body is brought down on a stretcher. An official asks if anyone knows the boy; Mahmoud steps forward, and leads Sammy to a quiet alley – where he starts beating him, calling him 'English pig'. Sammy escapes and hides. That night he crouches whimpering on the stairs outside the ruined apartment, clutching his treasured whistle-cum-compass. He turns the compass till the needle points south.

A desert road. A bus stops; Sammy is ejected, having no more money. He treks into the wild, beds down among rocks, and wakes to find a Syrian trader watching him. Questioning him, the Syrian sees the chance of a reward from Aunt Jane, and offers to guide him through the mountains to the Sudan. Mistrustfully, Sammy accepts.

High in the mountains. Tired of rice, Sammy demands bread. The Syrian agrees, telling him to find flat stones for the fire. One of them explodes, blinding the man. Moaning in agony, he gropes for Sammy, and shackles the boy to him.

Sammy awakes to find the Syrian dead. He frees himself, takes the man's wallet and donkeys, and plods onward. Reaching a huge statue, he curls up at its feet, delirious. Luxor, December 1956. Gloria van Imhoff, an American tourist, finds Sammy and takes him to her hotel. Despite the misgivings of her travelling companions, Bob and Cathie, who suspect the wallet was stolen, she resolves to take Sammy to Port Said with her. At the station Sammy evades Spyros Dracondopoulos, Gloria's tourist guide, grabs the wallet and jumps on a train heading south.

The White Nile, January 1957. With the help of a pilgrim, Abu Lubaba, Sammy boards a river boat and travels up the Nile, living in steerage and watching the life of the river.

The Sudan, February 1957. As the boat docks, a Sudanese spots Sammy and fetches Dracondopoulos, who's searching for the boy. Sammy flees, but the guide catches him, gives him a bath and new clothes, and takes him to an Italian doctor, who injects him and pulls two teeth. Dracondopoulos borrows a jeep to take the boy to Mrs van Imhoff, but Sammy, sore and resentful, notices they are no longer going south. When Dracondopoulos stops to relieve his uneasy bowels, the boy immobilises the jeep and vanishes into the bush.

Determinedly, Sammy trudges southwards. At night he sleeps in trees to avoid wild animals. Hearing jungle cries around him, he chants ribald verses in response.

Dracondopoulos, rescued from his jeep, tells the British authorities about Sammy. Heneker, the game warden, notices that Sammy is near the territory of Cocky Wainwright, a notorious diamond smuggler – a perfect excuse for extra resources to track down both at once. Dracondopoulos receives word from Mrs van Imhoff: she has lost interest. Sick, furious and out of pocket, he departs.

In the Ugandan bush Sammy encounters Cocky who, amazed at his story, takes the boy back to camp. There Sammy finds a substitute family, and starts to recover from his experiences. Affection grows between him and the old man, who gives him a pet bush-baby, and teaches him to shoot. Out hunting, Sammy saves Cocky from a leopard, and receives the skin as a trophy. Cocky's partner Lem arrives in his plane and objects to Sammy's presence, insisting it will attract the authorities, but Cocky refuses to send the boy away.

Heneker locates the camp. Cocky sends Sammy off with Lem; to make him go, he pretends he only wanted the reward offered for the boy's recovery. Cocky is captured; Lem takes off, but Sammy stays behind, hidden, and sees the camp demolished. That night he lies weeping in the ruins of Cocky's hut. Next morning Lem returns to find Sammy and the packet of diamonds Cocky left behind. They fly to Mozambique, where Sammy can catch a train for Durban.

In jail, Cocky makes a will leaving everything to Sammy. When Aunt Jane arrives he tells her not to find Sammy: the boy must complete his journey unaided. She should return to Durban and await his arrival.

Durban, March 1957. Arriving at his aunt's hotel in a taxi, Sammy finds her waiting for him, along with his leopardskin. He tells her he plans to become a diamond-smuggler when he grows up.

## A High Wind in Jamaica (GB 1965)
DeLuxe Color, CinemaScope

*Production Company*: 20th Century-Fox
*Producer*: John Croydon
*Associative Producers*: Clifford Parkes, Tom Pevsner
*Director*: Alexander Mackendrick
*Screenplay*: Stanley Mann, Ronald Harwood, Denis Cannan
*From the novel by*: Richard Hughes
*Cinematographer*: Douglas Slocombe
*Editor*: Derek York
*2nd Unit Cinematography*: Cecil Cooney
*Music*: Larry Adler
*Conducted by*: Philip Martell
*Lyrics by*: Christopher Logue
*Sung by*: Mike LeRoy
*Supervising Art Director*: John Howell
*Art Director*: John Hoesli
*Wardrobe*: John McCorry
*Sound Editor*: Matt McCarthy
*Sound Recordists*: H. L. Bird, Stephen Dalby
*Assistant Director*: Jim Brennan
*Director of Nautical Operations*: Fred Zendar
*Camera Operator*: Chic Waterson
*Boom Operator*: Derek Kavanagh
*Special Effects*: Bowie Films
*Make-up*: Bill Lodge, Freddie Williamson
*Hairdressing*: Daphne Martin
*Continuity*: Helen Whitson
*Location Manager*: Bryan Coates
*Casting Director*: Stuart Lyons
*Production Secretary*: Barbara Allen

Anthony Quinn (Chavez), James Coburn (Zac), Dennis Price (Mathias), Lila Kedrova (Rosa), Nigel Davenport (Mr Thornton), Isabel Dean (Mrs Thornton), Kenneth J. Warren (Captain Marpole), Benito Carruthers (Alberto), Gert Frobe (Dutch Captain), Brian Phelan (Curtis), Trader Faulkner (The Dancer), Charles Laurence (The Tallyman), Charles Hyatt (Little One), Dan Jackson (The Big One), Viviane Ventura (Margaret

Fernandez), Kenji Takaki (Cook), Deborah Baxter (Emily Thornton), Roberta Tovey (Rachel), Martin Amis (John), Jeffrey Chandler (Edward), Karen Flack (Laura), Henry Beltran (Harry Fernandez), Phillip Madoc (Guardia Civile).

*Running time*: 103 mins (9257 ft) (Original version 135 mins)
*Premiere*: Los Angeles, 25 May 1965

## Plot Synopsis

Jamaica, 1870. Through the rising hurricane runs ten-year-old Emily Thornton, calling for her cat, Tabby. At the house the blacks are taking shelter in the cellar, and her parents are hustling her four siblings indoors. Ignoring their calls, she runs on and, seeing Tabby up a tree, climbs up with her father after her. All three fall to the ground. Cat escapes, Thornton drags Emily back to the house.

Inside, Mrs Thornton hysterically reassures the children. As Thornton and Emily arrive, the house starts to break up. Thornton pushes his family down into the cellar (grabbing some madeira en route) where a voodoo ceremony is in progress. To distract the celebrants, Thornton passes round bottles; the children drink too. Old Sam, seeing the donkey outside, goes to save it. Tabby appears at the window; Emily opens it; wild cats pour in, overturning the lamp. Everyone sinks into drunken slumber.

The next morning. Wreckage everywhere; house demolished. Sam's wife Mamie, finding his body, grieves volubly. The children play noisily in a nearby puddle. Mrs Thornton, shocked by their callousness, insists they be sent to school in England.

Montego Bay. The barque *Clorinda*, commanded by Captain Marpole, prepares to sail. The Thorntons row out with their five children: Emily, John (12), Edward (8), Rachel (6) and Laura (4). On board, Mrs Fernandez is seeing off Margaret (15) and Harry (7), with their nurse. The Thornton children board – their parents are prevented by Marpole, anxious to sail – and are captivated by the ship. Parents, waving tearfully, are almost forgotten.

A day or two later. The children are fascinated by seamen preparing to amputate the ship's monkey's gangrened tail. Monkey, plied with rum, escapes up the rigging and falls to his death. Look-out sights ship billowing smoke; female figures approach in a rowboat. Once aboard, they prove to be armed men. Their leader, Alberto, overpowers the *Clorinda*'s mate, Curtis; from another boat Chavez, the pirate captain, and Zac, his mate, board the ship. The *Clorinda*'s crew surrender and are locked away.

Chavez descends to the cabin, to Marpole's drunken outrage. A strongbox proves empty, but Zac finds payment entered in the log. Watched by Emily, Chavez hauls Marpole on deck, shuts the children in the galley and (having made them all crouch low) has a volley fired into it. Marpole remains stubborn. Angrily, Chavez frees the children, ties Marpole to the mast, and lights a fire under him. Marpole reveals hiding-place of money.

Chavez and Zac find £900 in the cabin. The pirate crew swing the barque's cargo over to their schooner. The children join in, are swung over and explore the schooner's hold. Elated, the pirates shut the hold without noticing them and sail off. The *Clorinda*'s crew break out, free Marpole and find the children gone.

Alberto emerges from his cabin with Margaret in tow. Chavez is furious – even more so when the other children appear. They're bedded down in the hold, while the pirates celebrate their prize. Later the pirates descend into the hold, egging the reluctant Chavez on to rape. The children are puzzled, but only Margaret is really scared. When Emily bites Chavez's hand, he explodes with anger against the crew, driving them all up on deck.

A windy day. The deck, tilted and wet, makes a perfect slide for the children. Chavez bawls them out; they retreat to his cabin and play with his cocked hat. Chavez enters and growls at them, but wins their respect by eating a spoonful of cayenne. Emily apologises for biting him.

Emily and Harry debate whether they're being taken to England. Chavez shows Edward how to tie knots, and starts making a toy for Emily, but thinks better of it. A British cutter is sighted, and the pirates prepare to flee. Edward accidentally releases the anchor; Alberto, trying to stop it, snaps the chain. The schooner hides inside a reef, secured with ropes. Darkness falls; the cutter passes without seeing them.

The next day Chavez dives to locate the anchor. On board, one of Laura's 'dolls', a marlinspike, nearly skewers the cook. Edward and Harry lie in a net under the figurehead. Chavez finds Emily, Rachel and Laura playing burial-at-sea; he drops his hat, which the children toss from one to the next. Chasing them, he grapples with Emily, who denounces him as 'a wicked pirate'.

The boat-crew, returning with the anchor, yell in terror: the figurehead's head is reversed. Chavez, trying to right it, drops it; it floats, to the crew's alarm. Zac dives in and tosses the head on deck, where Rachel picks it up. The crew back away. Chavez, furious, sends the children below. In his cabin he finds Margaret, and orders her out as Zac enters.

Tampico. While Chavez and Zac auction the booty, Alberto tidies the children. Evading him, Emily dashes off to post a letter, and is spotted by Rosa, madame of the brothel, who sends a servant to fetch her. While Rosa questions Emily, Chavez and Zac arrive with the other children. John strays upstairs, leans out to watch a cockfight, and falls to his death. Rosa, alarmed, packs pirates and children back on board.

Chavez can't bring himself to tell the children about John's death. Emily comes to ask if Edward can have John's blanket.

The children, put in the long-boat to be out of the way, play a game – the deck is sea, so the crew are drowning. The crew aren't amused. As the children are hustled below, Laura's marlinspike falls, transfixing Emily's leg. Chavez carries her to his cabin and tends the wound. Zac tells him the crew want the children marooned.

Chavez and the cook nurse the delirious Emily. A Dutch paddle-steamer is sighted; the crew prepare to take her, but despite Zac's urging, Chavez insists they should only put the children aboard. The crew mutiny. Zac knocks Chavez out to save him being killed, and has him locked in his cabin. Emily wakes in pain; Chavez soothes her while we hear the steamer being taken.

Shouts of panic; the British cutter has returned. Zac tells the crew to dump the Dutch sailors on the schooner and escape on the steamer. He releases Chavez, asking him to resume command, but Chavez refuses. The Dutch captain, bound, stumbles into Chavez's cabin; finding Emily there, he tries to give her a knife to free him. Delirious and terrified, she stabs him. Chavez returns to find him dying. The British commander orders the pirates to surrender.

London. In his chambers the lawyer, Mathias, questions the children. Getting nowhere, he lets them go, but tells Thornton he will call Emily as a witness. In court, Mathias questions Emily closely about the death of the Dutchman. Under pressure, she screams incoherent words – enough to incriminate Chavez and ensure that the pirates will hang.

Thornton joins his wife in Kensington Gardens, where the children are playing. A boat like the pirate schooner sails on the pond. Emily watches it, her expression unfathomable.

## Don't Make Waves (USA 1967)
Metrocolor, Panavision

*Production Company*: Filmways-Renard (Presented by Metro-Goldwyn-Mayer)
*Producers*: John Calley, Martin Ransohoff
*Associate Producer*: Julian Bercovici
*Director*: Alexander Mackendrick
*Screenplay*: Ira Wallach, George Kirgo
*Adaptation*: Maurice Richlin
*Additional Dialogue (unc)*: Terry Southern
*From the novel* Muscle Beach *by*: Ira Wallach
*Cinematographer*: Philip H. Lathrop
*Editors*: Rita Roland, Thomas Stanford
*Music*: Vic Mizzy
*Song* Don't Make Waves *by*: Jim McGuinn, Chris Hillman
*Performed by*: The Byrds
*Art Directors*: George W. Davis, Edward Carfagno
*Set Designers*: Henry Grace, Charles S. Thompson
*Costumes*: Donfeld
*Recording Supervisor*: Franklin Milton
*Assistant Directors*: Carl Beringer, Erich von Stroheim Jr
*Make-up*: William Tuttle
*Hair Styles*: Sydney Guilaroff
*Technical Advisor*: Eduardo Tirella
*Sky Diving Sequence*: Leigh Hunt
*Unit Production Manager*: Edward Woehler

Tony Curtis (Carlo Cofield), Claudia Cardinale (Laura Califatti), Robert Webber (Rod Prescott), Joanna Barnes (Diane Prescott), Sharon Tate (Malibu), David Draper (Harry Hollard), Mort Sahl (Sam Lingonberry), Dub Taylor (Electrician), Jim Backus (himself), Henny Backus (herself), Ann Elder (Millie Gunder), Chester Yorton (Ted Gunder), Reg Lewis (Monster), Marc London (Fred Barker), Douglas Henderson (Henderson), Sarah Selby (Ethyl), Mary Grace Canfield (Seamstress), Julie Payne (Helen), Holly Haze (Myrna), Edgar Bergen (Madame Lavinia), Paul Barselow (Pilot), George Tyne, David Fresco, Gil Green

(Newspapermen), Eduardo Tirella (Decorator).

*Running time*: 97 mins (8825 ft)
*Premiere*: New York, 16 May 1967

## Plot Synopsis

Under the credits, an animated-cartoon orange Volkswagen Beetle crosses the USA from east to west. As it reaches California, we switch to live-action. Ascending a hill, the Beetle parks at the top by a wall overlooking the ocean. Carlo Cofield gets out, sits on the wall to eat his lunch. Just below him an artist, Laura Califatti, is having trouble with her easel. She finally hurls her canvas into the sea, and storms back to her white convertible. Driving off, she nudges the Beetle, which starts to run back down the hill.

Pursued by Carlo, the car goes over the edge. It lands upside-down, just missing Laura's car and a beach-bus coming the other way. Four youngsters (Harry, Monster, and Millie and Ted Gunder) pile out of the bus. Laura, raging, drops a match; the Beetle goes up in flames. Carlo, trying to rescue his jacket, gets his trousers on fire; Monster douses him with water. Soaking, trouserless, he rounds in fury on Laura. At first disconcerted, she then bursts out laughing and offers him a lift to her apartment.

At her beachside apartment, over dinner, Laura explains that her acting career has been a disaster, but that she now has a 'patron'. Carlo is allowed to sleep on the couch. In the middle of the night the patron, Rod Prescott, shows up. Laura hastily bundles Carlo out on the patio, but Rod discovers him. Professing to believe their flustered excuses, he sends Carlo off to sleep on the beach.

Carlo awakes to the flamboyant activity of Muscle Beach. Going in swimming, he's knocked out by a surfboard, and revived by its rider, the staggeringly beautiful Malibu. Laura arrives, and has Carlo carried to her apartment. Rod phones, having left his briefcase, and tells Laura his insurance won't cover Carlo. Overhearing this, Carlo appropriates Rod's clothes and rifles his briefcase. Rod works for Seaspray Swimming Pools; finding the address of a prospect, Carlo gets Laura to drive him there.

The prospect is Jim Backus and his wife; Carlo talks them into buying a premium pool. Driving downtown, Laura explains

Rod can't marry her, as his wife has polio. At Rod's office Carlo meets Diane Prescott, in perfect health. Rod scents blackmail, but Carlo simply wants a job – which he gets when Rod learns of the Backus sale.

At the beach, Carlo watches Malibu, a skydiver by profession, work out on the trampoline. From Millie Gunder he learns about body-building, also that Malibu is Harry's girlfriend. Monster, Harry's trainer, and devotee of astrologer Madame Lavinia, suggests sex is bad for body-builders.

Laura's apartment. Rod leaves; Carlo enters, announcing he plans to move in, platonically. Leafing through *Esquire*, he indulges his material dreams.

Laura summons Carlo from the office to a hillside house above the beach, owned by Sam Lingonberry. But instead of selling Sam a pool, Carlo winds up buying the house, with a Rolls thrown in. Back at the beach, he watches Harry working out and Malibu massaging him.

Laura helps Carlo move in; Harry, Malibu and their friends arrive to shift furniture. Carlo suggests Malibu might skydive into his new pool, and sows further doubt in Harry's mind about sex, promising a private reading with Madame Lavinia. Diane Prescott arrives; she knows about Laura, plans to divorce Rod and sack him from Seaspray, which she owns. She suggests Carlo might take over. Laura, jealous, accuses Carlo of designs on Malibu, and storms off.

At night, Carlo calls at Madame Lavinia's gothic mansion. Madame (real name Zack Rosenkrantz) agrees to co-operate in return for a bargain-rate pool. Meeting Laura, Harry sadly tells her Madame Lavinia has prescribed chastity.

Carlo asks Rod for a special deal on Madame's pool. Rod vetoes it, and also the skydiving plan; but Carlo resolves to go ahead anyway. At the beach, Malibu fears Harry no longer finds her attractive.

The opening ceremony at Carlo's pool. Above in a plane, as Malibu prepares to dive, Carlo starts a speech over the PA system, but slips and falls out. Malibu jumps after him and catches him; they land together in the pool as Rod arrives, furious. Carlo, dragged out half-drowned, is accidentally knocked back in by Rod. Reviving to find Malibu tending him, he declares his love. Harry, come to collect Malibu, drives off alone in tears.

Malibu sits in bed, hair in curlers, eating crisps and watching Spanish TV without understanding it. Beside her, Carlo tries to sleep.

Torrential rain. Carlo arrives home to find his pool cracked and empty. While he phones for help, Rod arrives, having received divorce papers. Diane arrives, followed by Malibu, and finally by Laura, who finds the front door jammed. As she comes past the pool, it slides off down the hillside; the others, trying to get out the back, pull her to safety and retreat inside as the house tips sideways.

Night falls; all exits are blocked. Laura, who has also received divorce papers, discovers Diane's identity. The house slides down the hillside and stops, suspended, upside-down. Rescue services collect below. Footsteps on the floor overhead; Harry appears, having learnt the truth from Madame Lavinia. He wants Malibu back, and hopes to marry her.

Variously, the three couples pair off: Harry back with Malibu, Diane reconciled with Rod, Carlo and Laura acknowledging mutual attraction. At dawn the house slides again, arriving right-side up on the beach. Everyone staggers out into a crowd of reporters. Carlo and Laura break away and run along the water's edge together.

# 4 Other directorial work

*The Devil's Disciple* (GB 1959)
83 mins (7497 ft)

*Production Company*:
Hecht-Hill-Lancaster/Brynaprod
*Released by*: United Artists
*Producer*: Harold Hecht
*Director*: Guy Hamilton, (unc) Alexander Mackendrick
*Screenplay*: John Dighton, Roland Kibbee, (unc) Alexander Mackendrick
*From the play by*: George Bernard Shaw
*Cinematographer*: Jack Hildyard
*Editor*: Alan Osbiston
*Music*: Richard Rodney Bennett
*Art Director*: Terence Verity, Edward Carrere
*Sound*: Leslie Hammond

Burt Lancaster, Kirk Douglas, Laurence Olivier, Eva Le Gallienne, Janette Scott, Harry Andrews, Basil Sidney, George Rose, Neil McCallum, David Horne, Mervyn Johns.

*The Guns of Navarone* (GB 1961)
Technicolor, CinemaScope, 157 min (14,130 ft)

*Production Company*: Open Road, for Columbia
*Executive Producer*: Carl Foreman
*Producer*: Cecil F. Ford
*Director*: J. Lee Thompson, (unc) Alexander Mackendrick
*Screenplay*: Carl Foreman
*From the novel by*: Alistair Maclean
*Cinematographer*: Oswald Morris
*Editor*: Alan Osbiston
*Music*: Dimitri Tiomkin
*Production Designer*: Geoffrey Drake
*Sound*: Chris Greenham

Gregory Peck, David Niven, Anthony Quinn, Stanley Baker, Anthony Quayle, James Darren, Irene Papas, Gia Scala, James Robertson Justice, Richard Harris.

*Oh Dad, Poor Dad, Mama's Hung You in the Closet and I'm Feelin' So Sad* (USA 1965/67)
Technicolor, 86 mins (7768 ft)

*Production Company*: Richard Quine Productions for Seven Arts and Ray Stark
*Distribution*: Paramount
*Producers*: Ray Stark, Stanley Rubin
*Director*: Richard Quine
*Additional sequences directed by*: Alexander Mackendrick
*Screenplay*: Ian Bernard
*From the play by*: Arthur Kopit
*Cinematographer*: Geoffrey Unsworth, Charles Lawton Jr
*Editor*: Warren Low
*Music*: Neal Hefti
*Art Director*: Phil Jeffries
*Sound*: Josh Westmoreland

Rosalind Russell, Robert Morse, Barbara Harris, Hugh Griffith, Jonathan Winters, Lionel Jeffries, Cyril Delavanti, Hiram Sherman, George Kirby, Janis Hansen.

# 5 Television work

*The Defenders* (third series) – Episode 90: 'The Hidden Fury'
CBS TV, 9–10pm, 28 March 1964

*Production Company*: CBS
*Producer*: Herbert Brodkin
*Director*: Alexander Mackendrick

*Script Supervisor*: Reginald Rose

E. G. Marshall, Robert Reed, Susan Oliver, Joseph Anthony.

## 6 Theatre work

### *The Grass is Greener*

*Authors*: Hugh and Margaret Williams
*Director*: Alexander Mackendrick
*Assistant Director*: Anthony Carrick
*Decor*: Colin Winslow

Richard Wordsworth, John Saunders, Patricia Marmont, Michael Malnick, Patricia Heneghan.
Belgrade Theatre, Coventry, 1–20 August 1960

### *Face of a Hero*

*Author*: Robert L. Joseph
*From novel by*: Pierre Boule
*Directed by*: Alexander Mackendrick

Jack Lemmon, George Grizzard, Betsy Blair, Albert Dekker, Sandy Dennis, Martin Gabel, James Donald, Frank Conroy, Russell Collins, Edward Asner.
Walnut Theater, Philadelphia, 14 September–1 October 1960.
Transferred to Eugene O'Neill Theater, 230 W 49th St, New York, opened 20 October 1960. Closed 19 November 1960.

# Index

*All titles refer to feature films unless otherwise indicated.*